D#335322

COLOSSIANS

VOLUME 34 B

THE ANCHOR BIBLE is a fresh approach to the world's greatest classic. Its object is to make the Bible accessible to the modern reader, its method is to arrive at the meaning of biblical literature through exact translation and extended exposition, and to reconstruct the ancient setting of the biblical story, as well as the circumstances of its transcription and the characteristics of its transcribers.

THE ANCHOR BIBLE is a project of international and interfaith scope. Protestant, Catholic, and Jewish scholars from many countries contribute individual volumes. The project is not sponsored by any ecclesiastical organization and is not intended to reflect any particular theological doctrine. Prepared under our joint supervision, THE ANCHOR BIBLE is an effort to make available all the significant historical and linguistic knowledge which bears on the interpretation of the biblical record.

THE ANCHOR BIBLE is aimed at the general reader with no special formal training in biblical studies; yet, it is written with the most exacting standards of scholarship, reflecting the highest technical accomplishment.

This project marks the beginning of a new era of cooperation among scholars in biblical research, thus forming a common body of knowledge to be shared by all.

William Foxwell Albright
David Noel Freedman
GENERAL EDITORS

THE ANCHOR BIBLE

COLOSSIANS

♦

A New Translation
with
Introduction and Commentary

MARKUS BARTH
AND HELMUT BLANKE
TRANSLATED BY ASTRID B. BECK

THE ANCHOR BIBLE

Doubleday

New York London Toronto Sydney Auckland

THE ANCHOR BIBLE
PUBLISHED BY DOUBLEDAY
a division of Bantam Doubleday Dell Publishing Group, Inc.,
1540 Broadway, New York, New York 10036

THE ANCHOR BIBLE, DOUBLEDAY, and the portrayal
of an anchor with the letters AB are trademarks of
Doubleday, a division of Bantam Doubleday Dell Publishing
Group, Inc.

Library of Congress Cataloging-in-Publication Data

Bible. N.T. Colossians. English. Beck. 1994.
    Colossians: a new translation with introduction and commentary /
Markus Barth and Helmut Blanke; translated by Astrid B. Beck.
        p.   cm. — (The Anchor Bible; 34B)
    Includes bibliographical references and index.
    1. Bible. N.T. Colossians—Commentaries.   I. Barth, Markus.
II. Blanke, Helmut.   III. Beck, Astrid B.   IV. Title.   V. Series:
Bible. English. Anchor Bible. 1964: v. 34B.
    BS192.2.A1   1964.G3   vol. 34A
    [BS2713]
    220.7'7 s—dc20
    [227' .7077]   93-35736
                                                              CIP

ISBN 0-385-11068-5

Copyright © 1994 by Doubleday, a division of Bantam Doubleday
Dell Publishing Group, Inc.

All Rights Reserved
Printed in the United States of America
November 1994

First Edition

10 9 8 7 6 5 4 3 2 1

CONTENTS

♦

Contents

Contents

PREFACE

♦

Translating is difficult work, especially translating German. Mark Twain wrote an essay a little more than a century ago on "The Awful German Language," which is a masterpiece of exaggerated humor, but he gets to the crux of the matter. (The essay is reprinted in *Mark Twain at His Best* [Garden City, N.Y.: Doubleday, 1986]). A more recent translator, Curt Rosenthal, wrote a brief preface to his translation of Georg Simmel's *Sociology of Religion,* in which he refers to his own frustrations within the larger context of the "difficulties and exasperations accruing in the translation of a German scholar (as these are) vividly described by the translators of the writings of Max Weber. In discussing the style of German professors they comment: 'They use parentheses, qualifying clauses, inversions and complex sentences. . . . At their best, they erect a grammatical edifice, in which mental balconies and watchtowers, as well as bridges and recesses, decorate the main structure' " (New York: Philosophical Library, Inc., 1959, p.v). I feel a bond with this group of translators, as our craft joins us in our struggles and labors, in our common goal to disentangle the interwoven strands of convoluted sentences and phrases set together in varied patterns of thought with textured modifying clauses. Our task is to transfer these weavings into readable, comprehensible English. I have struggled, and I am sure I have failed in this endeavor many times. For this, I offer my humble apologies to the reader of this commentary.

Let me return to the beginning of this project, and to Markus Barth, the initial author of this commentary, who is an extraordinary human being. He was born in Switzerland in 1915 to one of the world's foremost theologians, Karl Barth. His university education was at Berne (1934–35), Basel (1935–37), Berlin (1937–38), and Edinburgh (1938–39). From 1940 to 1953, he was a parish minister of the Evangelical Reformed Church in Bubendorf, Baselland, Switzerland. His doctoral degree in theology (1947) is from the University of Göttingen, Germany. He received a faculty appointment at the Theological Seminary of the University of Dubuque, Iowa, in 1953, was appointed Associate Professor of New Testament at the University of Chicago in 1956, and Professor at Pittsburgh Seminary in 1963. In 1973, he returned to his native Switzerland and to the University of Basel. He has always spoken enthusiastically of his experiences in the United States and has returned numerous times for speaking engagements. His five children spent their formative years here, and his library contains a huge number of books in English, in all disciplines, which he has incorporated into his work. Note, for example, his reference to Robert Frost's poem "Mending Wall" in his discussion of Paul's concept of the destruction of a document in Ephesians 2:14 and Colossians 2:14 (*Ephesians*, p. 263).

It was during his years at Pittsburgh Seminary, when he and David Noel Freedman were colleagues there, that he began his work on the Anchor Bible Critical Commentaries on *Ephesians*, *Colossians*, and *Philemon*. *Ephesians* was published in 1974 (two volumes). His work on *Colossians* progressed, but more slowly when his health began to decline. I was brought into the picture in 1985, in an effort to improve the situation. The plan was for him to work with Helmut Blanke, his student at the University of Basel, who would continue the writing in German, while I would translate it. Markus Barth had already written the introduction in English, but it needed extensive revision, since he was no longer as fluent in English as he had been in earlier years. I worked on the language and style of the introduction. Markus Barth and Helmut Blanke collaborated on the commentary, and sent it to me for translation. After the German text of the commentary was completed, Markus's health became so frail that he was no longer able to be of much help on *Colossians*. He became seriously ill in 1991 and required further heart surgery. In September last year, we received news of the death of Rose Marie, his wife of many years, who had always buoyed his flagging spirit. In this period, Markus has not been able to correspond or work on the text. His last letter to me is dated April 1992 and concerns *Philemon*. Helmut Blanke, meanwhile, finished his doctorate and accepted a pastoral position in northern Germany.

It has been a struggle to finish this commentary. David Noel Freedman has carefully edited the text with "his proverbial thoroughness and efficiency," to cite Jerry Quinn in *Letter to Titus* (p. xiii). I wish to express an enormous debt of gratitude to him, which I also extend for the three of us.

Despite all the difficulties, I am grateful for the opportunity that this project has afforded me. It has been a tremendous learning experience, a sort of trial by fire. I have also come to know Markus Barth, and I regard him with deep respect and great admiration. He has drawn on his extensive expertise in both Testaments of the Bible, as well as on his lifelong experiences, in the preparation and elucidation of this commentary, which has occupied his creative energy for perhaps the last twenty-five years. This is especially evident in the Comments. In translating, I could hear Markus speak as he often did when we were working together, either at his chalet, which was perched precariously on the side of the Weisshorn Alp at La Sage, the twin of the Matterhorn, or here in Ann Arbor, where he gave a mini-course on "The Lord's Supper." His interests are diverse, and his perception of the world is keen. He relates well to people. To his surprise, this erudite man was extremely popular with our Michigan students, who are not attuned to theological issues, but who attended his mini-course in droves; we had to close the course enrollment, finally, at 335 students. I recall especially his kindness when, after long hours of work, he would suddenly announce that I had worked hard enough for the day and deserved to go on a hike. He would accompany me partway, and then send me on with his best wishes, knowing that I love the Alpine haunts, for they remind me of my childhood days.

Since Markus has not been able to communicate in recent times, the completion of this commentary has fallen to me. I thank the Doubleday religion editors, Tom Cahill and Mike Iannazzi, for their great patience, understanding, and hard work. I also thank my children for their encouragement and endurance, especially my grandson and weekend charge, Michael, who learned at a very young age what a "manuscript" is all about.

Astrid Billes Beck
Ann Arbor, Michigan
April 1994

Note: The references in this Commentary are based on the Greek Septuagint text (LXX). Where the chapter enumeration in the LXX differs from the Hebrew and/or English chapters, the differing chapter number is cited in parentheses following the Greek chapter number.

Principal Abbreviations

♦

AB	The Anchor Bible, New York, N.Y.: Doubleday
AB 34/34A	M. Barth: *Ephesians*
AbRNat	ʾ*Abot R. Nat.* ʾ*Abot de Rabbi Nathan*
AGSU	Arbeiten zur Geschichte desSpätjudentums und Urchristentums, Leiden
AnBibl	Analecta Biblica, Rome
ASNU	Acta seminarii neotestamentici Upsaliensis, Stockholm, etc.
AT	Altes Testament (OT)
ATD	Das Alte Testament Deutsch
AThANT	Abhandlungen zur Theologie des Alten und Neuen Testaments, Zürich, etc.
ATR	*Anglican Theological Review*, Evanstan, IL
AUSS	Andrews University Seminary Studies, Berrien Springs, Mich.
BauerLex	W. Bauer: *Griechisch-Deutsches Wörterbuch*
BBB	Bonner biblische Beiträge, Bonn
BDF	F. Blas, A. Debrunner, and R. W. Funk: *A Greek Grammar of the New Testament and Other Early Christian Literature*, Chicago 1961
BDR	Blass, F.; Debrunner, A.: *Grammatik des neutestamentlichen Griechisch*
BEvTh	Beiträge zur evangelischen Theologie, München
BGU	Ägyptische Urkunden aus den Königlichen Museen zu Berlin: Griechische Urkunden I–VIII (1895–1933)
BHT	Beiträge zur historischen Theologie
BHTh	Beiträge zur historischen Theologie, Tübingen
Bibl	Biblica. Commentarii periodici ad rem biblicam scientifice investigandam, Rome
BibLeb	*Bibel und Leben*
BiTod	Bible Today, Collegeville, Minn.
BJRL	*Bulletin of the John Rylands University Library of Manchester*
BR	Biblical Research. Papers of the Chicago Society of Biblical Research, Amsterdam
BS	Bibliotheca sacra. A theological quarterly, Dallas, Tex.
BSac	*Bibliotheca Sacra*

BTN	Bibliotheca theologica Norvegica, Oslo
BU	Biblische Untersuchungen, Regensburg
BZ	Biblische Zeitschrift, Paderborn
BZAW	Beihefte zur Zeitschrift für die alttestamentliche Wissenschaft, Berlin, etc.
BZNW	Beihefte zur Zeitschrift für die neutestamentliche Wissenschaft, Berlin, etc.
CBQ	Catholic Biblical Quarterly, Washington, D.C.
CGTC	Cambridge Greek Testament Commentaries, Cambridge: University Press
CNT	Coniectanea neotestamentica, Uppsala
CR	Corpus reformatorum, Brunsuiga: Schwetschke 1895 (repr. New York/London: Johnson; Frankfurt: Minerva 1964)
CSEL	Corpus scriptorum ecclesiasticorum latinorum
CTQ	Concordia Theological Quarterly, Fort Wayne, Ind.
Dib.-Gr.	Dibelius-Greeven: *An die Kolosser, Epheser, an Philemon*
DR	Downside Review. A Quarterly of Catholic Thought and of Monastic History, Bath
EE	Mitton: *The Epistle to the Ephesians*
EKK	Evangelisch-katholischer Kommentar zum Neuen Testament, Zürich/Einsiedeln/Köln: Benziger; Neukirchen: Neukirchener Verlag
Epigr. Gr.	*Epigrammata Graeca ex lapidibus collecta*, ed. G. Kaibel, Berlin, 1878
Er	Eranos. Acta philologica Suecana, Uppsala etc.
Erg. Bd.	Ergänzungsband (Supplementary Volume)
ES	F. Zeilinger: *Der Erstgeborene der Schöpfung*
ESpg	F. Zeilinger: *Der Erstgeborene der Schöpfung*
ET	Expository Times, Edinburgh
EVB	E. Käsemann: *Exegetische Versuche und Besinnungen*
EvQ	Evangelical Quarterly, London
EvTH	Evangelische Theologie, München
EzNT	A. Schlatter: *Erläuterungen zum Neuen Testament*, Stuttgart: Calwer
FBK	W. G. Kümmel (P. Feine and J. Behm, prev. authors.): *Introduction to the New Testament*
FoB	Forschung zur Bibel, Würzburg: Echter
FRLANT	Forschungen zur Religion und Literatur des Alten und Neuen Testaments, Göttingen
FTS	Frankfurter theologische Studien, Frankfurt
GK	*Gesenius' Hebräische Grammatik*, Leipzig, 1909. E. Kautzsch, ed. of repr. edition, Hildesheim, 1962
GNANT	Die Bibel im heutigen Deutsch. Die Gute Nachricht des

	Alten und Neuen Testaments, Stuttgart: Deutsche Bibelgesellschaft, 1982
GNT	Grundrisse zum Neuen Testament
GSC	Geneva Series Commentary
GuL	Geist und Leben. Zeitschrift für Askese und Mystik, Würzburg
HAW	Handbuch der Altertumswissenschaft
HBNT	Handbuch zum Neuen Testament
HC	Hand-Commentar zum Neuen Testament, Freiburg i.B.: Mohr
HNT	Handbuch zum Neuen Testament, Tübingen: Mohr
HThK	Herders theologischer Kommentar zum Neuen Testament, Freiburg i.B.: Herder
HTR	*Harvard Theological Review*
IBS	Irish Biblical Studies, London
ICC	International Critical Commentary, Edinburgh: Clark
IJT	Indian Journal of Theology, Serampore
ILS	*Inscriptiones Latinae selectae*, ed. H. Dessau, 3 vols. in 5 pts, Berlin, 1892–1916, repr.
Interp.	Interpretation. A Journal of Bible and Theology, Richmond, Virg.
JAAR	*Journal of the American Academy of Religion*
JAC	Jahrbuch für Antike und Christentum, Münster: Aschendorff
JAC Erg	Jahrbuch für Antike und Christentum, Ergänzung (Supplement)
JB	The Jerusalem Bible, Garden City, N.Y.: Doubleday, 1966
JBL	Journal of Biblical Literature, Philadelphia
JETS	Journal of the Evangelical Theological Society, Wheaton, Ill.
JNES	*Journal of Near Eastern Studies*, Chicago
JNTS	*Journal of New Testament Studies*
JSHRZ	*Jüdische Schriften aus hellenistisch-römischer Zeit*, ed. W. Kümmel, Gütersloh: Mohn, 1973ff.
JSNT	Journal of the Study of the New Testament
JThS	Journal of Theological Studies, Oxford, etc.
JTS	*Journal of Theological Studies*, Oxford
JTSA	Journal of Theology for Southern Africa, Braamfontein, Transvaal
Jub.	Jubilees (Pseudepigrapha)
KEH	Kurzgefaßtes exegetisches Handbuch, Leipzig: Weidmann
KEK	Kritisch-exegetischer Kommentar über das Neue Testament, begr. von H. A. W. Meyer, Göttingen: Vandenhoeck & Ruprecht

Key	E. J. Goodspeed: *Index Patristicus sive Clavis Justini Martyris Patrum Apostolicarum*, 1963
KJ	Holy Bible. The King James, or Authorized Version of 1611
KNT	Kommentar zum Neuen Testament, Leipzig: Deichert
KolB	J. Lähnemann: *Der Kolosserbrief*
KuD	Kerygma und Dogma, Göttingen
lat syr	Latin Syciac
LB'84	Die Bibel. Nach der Übersetzung Martin Luthers. Bibeltext in der revidierten Fassung von 1984, Stuttgart: Deutsche Bibelgesellschaft, 1985
LF	Liturgiegeschichtliche Forschungen, Münster
LouvSt	Louvain Studies. Semiannual publ. of the faculty of theology of the university of Louvain, Louvain
LSLex	H. G. Liddell; R. Scott: *A Greek-English Lexicon*
LXX	Septuaginta, ed. A. Rahlfs, Stuttgart: Deutsche Bibelgesellschaft, 1935
MeyerK	H. A. W. Meyer: *Kritisch-exegetischer Kommentar über das Neue Testament*
mins	minuscules
MMLex	J. H. Moulton; G. Milligan: *The Vocabulary of the Greek Testament*
MThS	Münchener theologische Studien, München
MThS.H	Münchener theologische Studien, Historische Abteilung
NCC	New Century Bible Commentary, Grand Rapids, Mich.: Eerdmans; London: Morgan & Scott
NEB	The New English Bible, Oxford: University Press; Cambridge: University Press 1970
.NF	Neue Folge (new sequence)
NIC	New International Commentary on the New Testament, Grand Rapids, Mich.: Eerdmans
NT	Novum testamentum. An international quarterly for New Testament and related studies, Leiden
NTA	Neutestamentliche Abhandlungen, Münster
NTD	Das Neue Testament Deutsch, Göttingen: Vandenhoeck & Ruprecht
NTF	Neutestamentliche Forschung, Gütersloh
NTS	New Testament Studies. An international journal publ. under the auspices of studiorum novi testamenti societas, Cambridge
NT.S	Novum testamentum, Supplement, Leiden
NTTEV	Good News for Modern Man: The New Testament in Today's English Version, New York: American Bible Society, 1960
OGIS	Orientis Graeci Inscriptiones Selectae, Bd. I+II, ed. W. Dittenberger, Leipzig, 1903–1905

Pauly-W.	*Paulys Real-Encyclopädie der classischen Alterthumswissen-schaft*
PG	*Patrologia graeca*, ed. J.-P. Migne, Paris: Migne
Ph	Philologus. Zeitschrift für das klassische Altertum, Wiesbaden, etc.
PHZ	F.-J. Steinmetz: *Protologische Heilszuversicht*
PKE	E. Percy: *Die Probleme der Kolosser- und Epheserbriefe*
PL	*Patrologia latina*, ed. J.-P. Migne, Paris: Migne
Preisigke Lex	Preisigke, F.; Kießling, E.: *Wörterbuch der griechischen Papyrusurkunden*
Proph.	Prophezei. Schweizerisches Bibelwerk für die Gemeinde, Zürich: Zwingli Verlag
QH	*Hôdāyôt (Thanksgiving Hymns)* from Qumran Cave
QM	*Milḥāmāh. (War Scroll)* from Qumran Cave
QSb	Appendix B *(Blessings)* to *Manual of Rule of the Community* at Qumran
RAC	Reallexikon für Antike und Christentum, Stuttgart
RB	Revue biblique, Paris
RefR(H)	Reformed Review. Western Theological Seminary, Holland, Mich.
RevExp	*Review and Expositor*, Louisville, Ky.
RevQ	*Revue de Qumran*, Paris
RExp	Review and Expositor. Faculty of Southern Baptist Theological Seminary, Louisville, Ky.
Rez	Rezension (review)
RGG	Die Religon in Geschichte und Gegenwart, 3. Aufl., Tübingen
RHPhR	Revue d'histoire et de philosophie religieuses, Strasbourg
RHR	*Revue de l'histoire des religions*, Paris
RivB	*Rivista biblica*, Bologna
RNT	Regensburger Neues Testament, Regensburg: Pustet
RQ	Römische Quartalsschrift für christliche Altertumskunde und für Kirchengeschichte, Freiburg i.B.
RSR	*Recherches de science religieuse*, Paris
RSV	The Revised Standard Version, 1946, 1952
RVV	Religionsgeschichtliche Versuche und Vorarbeiten, Gießen, etc.
SBL.MS	Society of Biblical Literature Monograph Series, Missoula, Mont.
SBM	Stuttgarter biblische Monographien, Stuttgart
SBS	Stuttgarter Bibelstudien, Stuttgart
SBT	Studies in Biblical Theology, London
SegB	Segond Bible, rev. ed. Geneva: Maison de la Bible 1964

SF	Studia Friburgensia, Fribourg
SHAW	Sitzungsberichte der Heidelberger Akademie der Wissenschaften
SHVL	Skrifter utgivna av k. humanistika vetenskapssamfundet i Lund. Acta r. societatis humaniorum litterarum Lundensis, Lund
SJT	*Scottish Journal of Theology*, Edinburgh
SIG	*Sylloge Inscriptionum Graecarum*, ed. W. Dittenberger, 3. Aufl., Leipzig, 1915–1924
SNT	Studien zum Neuen Testament
SNTS.MS	Studiorum novi testamenti societas monograph series, Cambridge
SO	Symbolae Osloenses. Societas Graeco-Latina, Oslo
SpgM	H. Hegermann: *Der Schöpfungsmittler im hellenistischen Judentum und Urchristentum*
StANT	Studien zum Alten und Neuen Testament, München
St.-B.	H. Strack; P. Billerbeck: *Kommentar zum Neuen Testament. Aus Talmud und Midrasch*, Bd. I–VI, München: Beck
StNT	Studien zum Neuen Testament, Gütersloh
StTh	Studia theologica. Scandinavian Journal of Theology, Lund
StUNT	Studien zur Umwelt des Neuen Testaments, Göttingen
TEH.NF	Theologische Existenz heute. Neue Folge, München
THAT	E. Jenni, Westermann, C., eds.: *Theologisches Handwörterbuch zum Alten Testament*
ThB	Theologische Bücherei. Neudrucke und Berichte aus dem 20. Jahrhundert, München
ThBl	Theologische Blätter, Leipzig
ThLZ	Theologische Literaturzeitung, Leipzig
ThQ	Theologische Quartalsschrift, Tübingen
ThST	*Theologische Studien*, ed. K. Barth u.a., Zürich
ThStKr	Theologische Studien und Kritiken. Zeitschrift für das gesamte Gebiet der Theologie, Hamburg
ThTo	Theology Today, Princeton
ThViat	Theologia viatorum. Jahrbuch der kirchlichen Hochschule Berlin
ThWNT	*Theologisches Wörterbuch zum Neuen Testament*
ThZ	Theologische Zeitschrift, Basel
TQ	*Theologische Quartalschrift*
TRE	Theologische Realenzyklopädie, Berlin, 1977ff.
TThSt	Trierer theologische Studien, Trier
TU	Texte und Untersuchungen zur Geschichte der altchristlichen Literatur, Berlin

TWNT	*Theologisches Wörterbuch zum Neuen Testament*: 8 vols.; G. Kittel and G. Friedrich, eds. (*ThWNT*)
UNT	Untersuchungen zum Neuen Testament, Leipzig
VD	Verbum domini. Commentarii de re biblica, Rome
vgcl	Vulgate, Clementine edition (Rome, 1592)
vgmss	Vulgate manuscripts
VT	Vetus testamentum. Quarterly publ. by international organisation of Old Testament scholars, Leiden
VT.S	Vetus testamentum, Supplement
WA	Martin Luther; Werke. Kritische Gesamtausgabe, Weimar, 1883ff.
WBC	Word Biblical Commentary, Waco, Tex.: Word Books
WdF	Wege der Forschung, Darmstadt: Wiss. Buchgesellschaft
WMANT	Wissenschaftliche Monographien zum Alten und Neuen Testament, Neukirchen
WPKG	Wissenschaft und Praxis in Kirche und Gesellschaft, Göttingen
WThJ	Westminster Theological Journal, Philadelphia
WuD	Wort und Dienst. Jahrbuch der theologischen Schule Bethel, Bielefeld
WUNT	Wissenschaftliche Untersuchungen zum Neuen Testament, Tübingen
ZAW	*Zeitschrift für die alttestamentliche Wissenschaft*, Berlin
ZB	Zürischer Bibel, Zürich: Zwingli Verlag, 1935
ZBK	Zürischer Bibelkommentare, Zürich: Theologischer Verlag
ZEE	Zeitschrift für evangelische Ethik, Gütersloh
ZKTh	Zeitschrift für katholische Theologie, Wien
ZNW	Zeitschrift für die neutestamentliche Wissenschaft und die Kunde der älteren Kirche, Berlin
z.St.	*ad locum citatum (loc cit)*
ZSTh	Zeitschrift für systematische Theologie, Berlin
ZThK	Zeitschrift für Theologie und Kirche, Tübingen
ZWiss Theol	*Zeitschrift für wissenschaftliche Theologie*

NOTE: For works cited by author's name only throughout the volume, see the Bibliography at the back of the volume.

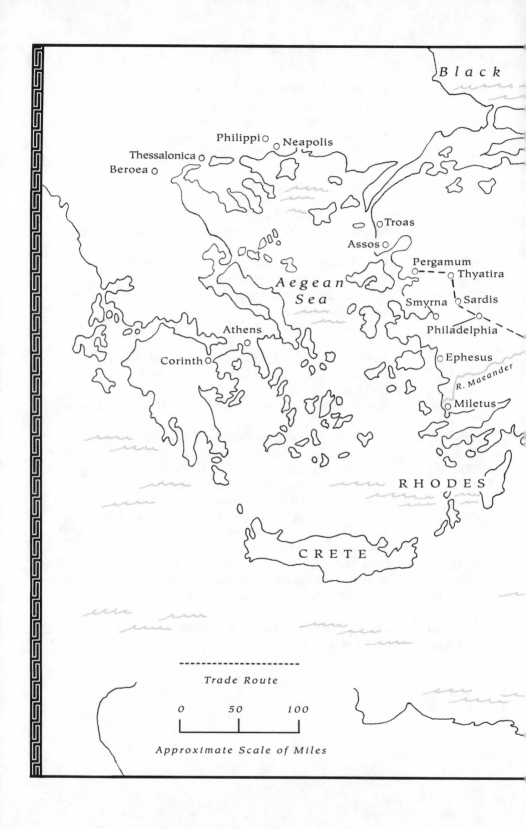

Black

Philippi○ ○Neapolis
Thessalonica ○
Beroea ○

Troas ○
Assos ○

Pergamum ○
Thyatira ○
Aegean
Sea
Smyrna ○ Sardis ○
Philadelphia ○

Athens
Ephesus ○
Corinth ○
R. Maeander

Miletus ○

RHODES

CRETE

- - - - - - - - - - - - - - - -
Trade Route

0   50   100

Approximate Scale of Miles

Sea

COLOSSAE AND
ITS SURROUNDING
REGIONS

o Antioch (Pisidia)
o Iconium
o Hierapolis
o Laodicea
o Lystra
o Derbe
o Tarsus
Colossae
o Perga
o Antioch (Syria)
Attalia
o Patara

CYPRUS

Paphos o

Mediterranean Sea

Caesarea o

Jerusalem o

TRANSLATION OF COLOSSIANS, CHAPTERS 1–4

The Epistolary Address (1:1–2)

1 From Paul, who by the will of God is apostle of the Messiah Jesus, and from Timothy, our brother. 2 To the saints at Colossae, who are true brothers and who confess the Messiah as Lord. Grace to you and peace from God our Father.

Thanksgiving (1:3–8)

3 We thank God the Father of our Lord Jesus (Christ) always for you in our prayer. 4 Because we have heard of your faithfulness to the Messiah Jesus, that is the love that you have for all the saints, 5 because of the hope that is securely stored up for you in heaven. Of this you have heard previously through the word of truth, (namely) the gospel. 6 This came to you and became at home with you as it also continuously brings forth fruit and grows in the whole world, as also among you, since the day when you heard and knew the grace of God as truth. 7 As you (certainly) learned it from Epaphras, our beloved fellow servant. He is a faithful servant of the Messiah in our place; 8 and he has also reported to us of your love, which is a gift of the Spirit.

The Intercession (1:9–14)

9 Therefore we also do not cease, since the (first) day when we heard (the good news about you), to pray for you. We ask that God may fill you with the knowledge of his will, by the gift of all spiritual wisdom and all spiritual understanding, 10 so that you will live a life worthy of the Lord, pleasing in all things. He who lives thus brings forth fruit and grows in every good work, through the knowledge of God! 11 He lets himself be made powerful with all power, according to his glorious strength, for all endurance and patience with joy! 12 He thanks the Father, who has qualified you to take part in the inheritance of the saints, (which is) in the light. 13 He has delivered us from the dominion of darkness and transferred us into the kingdom of his beloved Son. 14 In him freedom belongs to us, forgiveness of sins.

The Hymn (1:15–20)

15a He is the image of God, who is not seen.
  b   First-born over all creation.
16a For in Him all things were created,
  b   in the heavens and upon earth,
  c   what is seen, and what is not seen

1

d	be they thrones or dominions,
e	be they principalities or powers;
f	all things were created through Him and to Him.

* * *

17a	And it is He who reigns over all things,
b	and all things exist in Him.
18a	And it is He who is the head—
b	of the body: of the church.

* * *

c	He is ruler
d	first-born, raised from the dead,
e	so that among all things He should be the first;
19	For it was the will of God to let in Him dwell all the fullness,
20a	and to reconcile through Him with Him all things
b	by creating peace through His blood of the cross,
c	through Him, be it that, which is on earth, be it that, which is in the heavens.

The Conclusion of the Prayer of Thanksgiving and Intercession (1:21–23)

21 You also, who formerly were excluded and enemies, with a mind that evokes evil works, 22 but now he has reconciled (you) in the flesh of his body through the death, in order to place you holy, blameless and irreproachable before him. 23 If only you (continue to) remain faithful, firmly grounded, and do not let yourselves be moved away from the hope, that you know through the gospel that you have heard (and) that is proclaimed in all of creation under heaven. I, Paul, have become its servant.

Paul, Servant of the Colossians (1:24–2:5)

24 Thus I rejoice in my sufferings, which I suffer for you. Indeed, I repay for His body (i.e. the church), what is still lacking of Christ's afflictions in my flesh. 25 Because I have become servant of the church according to the will of God who gave me my commission, with the purpose to fulfill specifically for you his word; 26 (i.e.) the secret, which has been hidden since far-distant ages. Now, however, it has been revealed to his saints! 27 To them God wanted to make known what are the glorious riches of this secret among the gentiles: this is the Messiah among you, the glorious hope. 28 Him we proclaim, by

admonishing each person and teaching each person in all wisdom, because we want to present each person perfect in Christ. 29 And for this I struggle and strive, because his power works mightily in me. 2:1 For I want you to know what a struggle I have for you and for the (brothers) in Laodicea, even for all those who (also) do not know me personally. 2 So that all your hearts will be comforted, held together in love, in order to gain all the abounding fullness of understanding, namely the knowledge of the secret of God, that is the Messiah. 3 In him all the treasures of wisdom and knowledge are stored, (specifically) hidden. 4 All this I say, so that no one may delude you with specious arguments. 5 For even if I am absent in body, I am still with you in spirit, as someone who rejoices and who sees your orderly discipline and the constancy of your faith in the Messiah.

The Messiah and "The Deceitful Religion" (2:6–15)

6 As you have now received the Messiah Jesus, the Lord, (so) lead your lives in obedience to him: 7 it is suitable for you to be firmly rooted and to be built up in him, namely to be made firm in faith, as you have been taught; but above all, overflow with thanksgiving! 8 Beware that no one may appear, who would carry you away as prey, by "philosophy," and (namely) by empty deception accomplished by the betrayal of people according to the elements of the world and not according to the Messiah. 9 For in him resides all the fullness of the deity in corporal form. 10 And you have (also) been fulfilled in him who is the head of every rule and power. 11 In him you are also circumcised with a circumcision not performed by human hands, because the human body was cast off in the circumcision of the Messiah. 12 With him (also) you have been buried in baptism. In him you have also been resurrected through the powerful working of the faith of God, who resurrected him from the dead. 13 You also who were dead in your sins namely because of the uncircumcision of your flesh, (even) you he made alive with him by having forgiven us all our sins. 14 Thus he has also canceled a bill of indictment against us that indicted us with legal charges. He specifically removed this by nailing it to the cross. 15 By disarming the powers and forces, he has publicly exposed them as they truly are. In him he has revealed them.

The Opponents (2:16–23)

16 Therefore do not let anyone judge you concerning food and drink or that which concerns feast day or new moon or sabbath, 17 things that are only shadows of what is to come, because the body belongs to the Messiah! 18 Let not those condemn you, who find pleasure in self-abasement and worship of angels, who are (only) concerned with justifying what they have envisioned; who are puffed up by their sensuous orientation without basis, 19 and who do not hold fast to the head, from which the entire body, as it is provided and

joined together with ligaments and sinews, grows in the manner as God ordains it. 20 When you (thus) have died with Christ to the elements of the world, what regulations will (then) be made for you, as though you were still living under the dominion of the world. 21 Do not handle! Do not taste! Do not touch! 22 All that leads to corruption if it is used according to the commands and teachings of human beings. 23 These—even though they have an appearance of wisdom, through willing piety and humility and severe treatment of the body, not however through deference toward someone—these lead (only) to gratification of the flesh.

The Old and the New Self (3:1–17)

3:1 Since you have thus now arisen with the Messiah, seek that which is on high, where the Messiah is, sitting at the right hand of God. 2 Orient yourselves also toward that which is on high, not toward that which is on earth. 3 For you have died, and your life is hidden with the Messiah in God. 4 When the Messiah, your life, is revealed, then you will also be revealed with him in glory.

5 Now put to death the members that are on the earth: fornication, impurity, passion, evil desire, and always wanting to have more, which is idolatry. 6 Through these the wrath of God comes upon the sons of disobedience. 7 You also walked in these (vices) formerly, when you lived in them. 8 But now you also have cast off all this: wrath, anger, malice, slander, abusive language from your mouth. 9 Do not lie to one another. It is self-evident for you that you have taken off the old self with its practices 10 and have put on the new (self) which is constantly renewed in knowledge according to the image of him who has created him. 11 Where we no longer have Greek and Jew, circumcised and uncircumcised, barbarian, Scythian, slave, free person—rather all things and in all (things is) the Messiah. 12 Now put on, as the chosen ones of God, as holy and beloved ones: a heart full of compassion, kindness, humility, meekness, patience. 13 It is fitting for you to bear one another and to forgive one another if someone has a complaint against someone else. As the Lord has also forgiven you, so also you (forgive one another). 14 Beyond all (this), put on love, that is the band of completeness. 15 And let the peace of the Messiah rule in your hearts, for which you also are called in one body. And become thankful: 16 Let the word of the Messiah dwell among you in its richness. For you it is (then only) reasonable to teach each other in all wisdom, and to exhort with psalms, hymns, and songs produced by the spirit, (and) to sing to God from the heart (standing) in grace. 17 And concerning everything, whatever you do in word or deed, (do) everything in the name of the Lord Jesus. Thank God, the Father, through him.

The Haustafel (3:18–4:1)

18 Wives, be subject to your husbands, as it is fitting in the Lord. 19 Husbands, love your wives and be not harsh with them. 20 Children, be

obedient to your parents in all things, for that is well-pleasing in the Lord. 21 Fathers, do not embitter your children, so that they will not lose courage. 22 Slaves, obey your earthly masters in all things, not with eye-service, as someone who wishes to please human beings, but rather fear the Lord with a sincere heart. 23 Whatever you do, do it from the heart for the Lord and not for human beings. 24 For you know that you will receive the reward, the inheritance, from the Lord. (Thus) serve the Lord the Messiah! 25 Because the unrighteous will receive whatever he has done wrong—without regard of person. 4:1 Masters, give your slaves whatever is right and fair. For you know that you also have a master in heaven.

Concluding Petitions and Exhortations (4:2–6)

2 Be steadfast in prayer: be watchful therein with thanksgiving. 3 Pray also for us, that God may open a door for our word, to proclaim the secret, the Messiah. Because of this (secret) I am also bound, 4 so that I may reveal it, as it is determined for me, to proclaim (it). 5 In wisdom conduct your lives toward those who are on the outside; redeem that which is offered now. 6 Let your word be determined by grace at all times, seasoned with salt; then you will know how you are to answer every one.

The Conclusion of the Epistle (4:7–18)

7 Tychicus will tell you all the things that concern me; (he is) the beloved brother and steadfast minister and fellow servant in the Lord. 8 I have sent him to you precisely so that you may know how it is with us, and that he may strengthen your hearts. 9 With (him I have sent) Onesimus, the steadfast and beloved brother, who is from your midst. They will tell you everything (that has taken place) here. 10 Aristarchus, my fellow prisoner, greets you, and Marcus, cousin of Barnabas, concerning whom you have received instructions: when he comes to you, receive him; 11 and Jesus, who is called Justus, who are of the circumcision. These alone have become co-workers for the kingdom of God. They have become a comfort to me. 12 Epaphras greets you, the servant of the Messiah Jesus, who is from your midst. He always fights for you with prayers so that you may stand complete and fulfilled in the whole will of God. 13 For I testify for him that he has (endured) great hardship for your well-being and for those in Laodicea and in Hierapolis. 14 Luke, the beloved physician, greets you and Demas. 15 Give (my) greetings to the brothers in Laodicea, and to Nympha and to the community in her house. 16 And when the letter has been read among you, arrange to have it read also in the community of the Laodiceans, and you yourselves also read the letter from Laodicea. 17 And say to Archippus, "Be mindful of your ministry, which you have received in the Lord, that you fulfill it." 18 The greeting, with my hand, of Paul. Remember my chains. Grace (be) with you.

INTRODUCTION
by Markus Barth

◆

I. THE CITY OF COLOSSAE

Occasional remarks in ancient Greek, Roman, and Christian literature, a few ruins, inscriptions, and coins, later reports of travelers and conclusions of scholars of modern times—these are the sources of information available for the description of the site and history, the population and the daily life of Colossae and the cities in its neighborhood.[1]

The name "Colossae," sometimes spelled Colassae, is probably not con-

---

1. Herodotus *historiae* VII 30:1; Xenophon *anabasis* I 2:6; Strabo *geographica* XII 8:13, 16; cf. X 1:9; XIII 4:14; Pliny *historia naturalis* V 145; cf. 105; XXI 51; Tacitus *annales* XIV 27; *Sibylline Oracles* (Leipzig: Hinrichs, 1902) III 471; IV 107–8; V 290–91; XIV 85–86. Sources among early Christian documents, are only Colossians (not, e.g., Revelation), and much later, Eusebius *chronicon* I 21, ed. A. Schoene (Berlin: Weidmann, 1884), pp. 155, 212: GSC 20 (Leipzig: Hinrichs, 1911), p. 215; GSC 24, 1913, p. 183, and Augustine's Portuguese contemporary Orosius *historia adversus paganos* VII 7:12. A few inscriptions dating from Constantinian times are reproduced and described in W. H. Buckler and W. M. Calder, ed., *Monumenta Asia Minoris Antiqua*, vol. VI (Manchester: University Press, 1939), XI, 15–18, Plates 8–16; and (concerning Hierapolis) vol. IV (1933), Plates 276A–C, 315. The site of Colossae was discovered and identified by W. J. Hamilton in 1835; see his *Researches in Asia Minor, Pontus, and Armenia* I (London: Murray, 1842), pp. 507–13. Among other pertinent works are W. M. Ramsay, *The Cities and Bishoprics of Phrygia* I (Oxford: Clarendon, 1895), pp. 208–16; D. Magies, *Roman Rule in Asia Minor* (Princeton: University Press, 1950) I 126–27; II 985–86; *British Museum Catalogue of Greek Coins*, vol. Phrygia (London: British Museum, 1906), pp. 154–57; J. B. Lightfoot, *St. Paul's Epistles to the Colossians and to Philemon* (London: Macmillan, 1875; in the following quoted as *Colossians*), pp. 1–72; S. E. Johnson, "Laodicea and its Neighbors," BA 13 (1950), no. 1, pp. 1–18; Bo Reicke, "The Historical Setting of Colossians," RevExp 20 (Louisville, 1973), pp. 429–38.

The second century (after Christ) writer Apuleius [*metamorphoses* XI 5(269)] states that in Phrygia the first-born of mankind were living. In the New Testament, only in the two letters addressed to Phrygian cities (Colossae and Laodicea) do the formulae occur, "[Christ is] the first-born of all creation," "the beginning, the first-born from the dead" (Rev 3:14; Col 1:15, 18; but cf. Rom 8:29).

nected with Coloss (Colossus). The city was situated 125 miles east of the Aegean Sea and 90 miles north of the Mediterranean coast in the central highlands of Asia Minor, ca. 800 feet above sea level. It was exposed to grim winters, lovely springs, and hot summers. Its central section, including a theater of modest size and an acropolis of less than majestic dimensions, lay south of the river Lycus. This tributary of the Maeander rushes into and through a gorge near ancient Colossae. The Lycus Valley is dominated on its northeastern side by the mountain Salbacus, and in the southwest by the snow-capped Cadmos. Precipices, partly covered with gleaming white travertine, form walls on both sides of the valley.

The products of the fertile land on both sides of the river included primarily figs, olives, and sheep, some of the latter raven-black in color. The processing, weaving, and dying of wool ("Colossian" was the trade name of a world famous purple-red) were among the sources of income for artisans and tradesmen. The city benefited from its location on the southern great trade-route that ran parallel to a northern highway, both of which led from the Euphrates and Syria through the "inner" or "upper" parts of Asia Minor toward the cities at the Aegean Sea. At Colossae, minor roads leading north and south over easily accessible passes crossed the main thoroughfare. To the Persian invaders, Xerxes and Cyrus the Younger in the early and late fifth century B.C.E., Colossae must have been one of the populated, prosperous, and famous cities of the kingdom of Phrygia.

The Phrygians had originally come from Thracia and spread over several parts of Asia Minor, until an invasion of Gallians (later called the Galatians) stopped them from eastward expansion. According to Homer's *Iliad* (II 862–63, III 184–85), the ancient Phrygians were a vigorous and heroic people, who supported the Trojans. However, with the arrival of the Persians, their political independence came to an end. Eventually, a Phrygian name was considered proper for a slave.

The history of Colossae was affected by others besides Phrygians and Persians. The development of trade and travel through Phrygia resulted in a mixed population in the cities on or near the trade routes. Eventually, after the conquest of the whole of Asia Minor by Alexander the Great in 330 B.C.E., Greeks settled in the region. The defeat of the Seleucid Antiochus III by the Romans in 190 B.C.E. and the deeding of Asia Minor to the Romans through Attalus of Pergamum in 132 B.C.E. brought Romans into former Phrygia. Col 3:11 may indicate that even "Scythians," in late antiquity a threat to civilized people equivalent to the menace of the Vandals and Huns in the Middle Ages, and other "barbarians" were living in Colossae. The presence of Jews who were also part of the population of the territory will be discussed in the next section. In 49 C.E., after a good deal of wavering, Rome decided definitely to join the southwestern region of Phrygia, including Colossae, to the province called "Asia," rather than to "Galatia."

Between Persian and New Testament times, the size and importance of

Colossae declined. The city was overshadowed by two neighbors in the south-western corner of Phrygia. Ten miles from Colossae in a (north)westerly direction and six miles apart from one another stood, enthroned on plateaus, the industrial, banking, and administrative metropolis Laodicea and the health resort Hierapolis, both with several magnificent theaters and gymnasia. Hierapolis was the birthplace of the philosopher Epictetus. About 80 miles to the northeast flourished the great trading center Apamea, called *Kibōtos,* the "(treasure- or tax-?) chest." Apamea was the cradle of the Jewish philosopher Aristoboulus. Colossae could not make comparable claims, although Col 2:8 mentions a "philosophy" promoted among its inhabitants. When in the second decade of the first century after Christ Strabo wrote his *geographia,* Colossae was at best a town *(polisma).* Still, it is likely that it continued to have a share in the prosperity of its neighbors. The testimony of tombstones found in Hierapolis is confirmed by the boasting of the Christian congregation at Laodicea mentioned in Rev 3:17, "I am rich. . . ." Business life was running smoothly[2]—except at times of recession, drought, epidemics, or other catastrophes.

In 61 or 62 C.E., perhaps at or near the time of the apostle Paul's death, one of the many earthquakes which ravaged the area destroyed Laodicea and Hierapolis. Although about 60 years after the event Tacitus, and with him the *Sibylline Oracles,* mention the destruction (and prompt rebuilding, without the aid of imperial grants) only of Laodicea,[3] the less significant Colossae may have suffered the same fate. Several New Testament writings deal with situations in Asia Minor in the second half of the first century; but in the epistles to the Colossians and to Philemon references to the destruction of Colossae are not found. However, in the time of Emperor Constantine, Eusebius, on the basis of sources as yet unknown, counts Colossae among the victims. Coins minted

---

2. Allusions to the business mentality of the Colossians (and their neighbors) may be contained in the choice of vocabulary and themes in the epistle addressed to them. However, the terms and topics "hope deposited in the heavens" (Col 1:5), "gave us a title," "share of the saints' allotment" (1:12), "wiping out the bond" (2:14), and the discussion of the master-slave relation in 3:22–4:1 were not so extraordinary as to demonstrate that the Christians in Colossae more than those in, e.g., Corinth and Rome, were absorbed in their mercantile occupations and concerns. K. Wengst, "Versöhnung und Befreiung," EvTh 36 (1976), pp. 14–26, especially pp. 15–27, presupposes that a kind of sophisticated bourgeois mentality—a compromise made with all existing powers in order to make the best of them and to have a share in them— threatened to engulf the Christians at Colossae. Though an anticipation of modern "Christian-Democratic" party ideology cannot be totally excluded, the evidence available in the epistle to the Colossians is too sparse to demonstrate it. In the Introduction to *Philemon* (AB 34C, especially in Section III), similar observations will be made.

3. In *Syb. Or.* III 345; V 318; VII 22–23, XII 280, the destruction of Hierapolis is mentioned (or lamented) together with that of the other cities.

about 150 C.E. demonstrate that at that time Colossae existed. Again, no local coins dated later than the middle of the third century have been found.

While therefore the earthquake in the Lycus Valley of 61/62 C.E. cannot provide evidence for the date and authorship of the letter to the Colossians, there is good reason to believe that Colossae was one of the least important places to which documents that were later canonized were ever sent. Among the letters collected in Rev 2–3, and among the Ignatian Epistles, there is no letter to Colossae. For a few centuries, Laodicea and Hierapolis became more or less famous episcopal sees, although their orthodoxy was less than reliable. Bishop Papias of Hierapolis (d. in 165?) became one of Eusebius' main sources of information on the origin of the canonical Gospels. But Colossae lost its bishopric to nearby Chonae and eventually vanished from the face of the earth.[4] Perhaps another earthquake or the Moslem conquest sealed its fate. Apart from some ruins not yet excavated and the inscriptions and coins already secured, only the epistle to the Colossians has spared it from oblivion.

II. PAGAN CULTS AND JEWISH PRESENCE IN PHRYGIA

"Phrygian Mysteries" were known and celebrated (occasionally condemned) before, during, and after the New Testament times not only in the towns of Phrygia but also in other regions of Asia Minor, in Greece, in Rome, and in several western parts of the Roman Empire. F. Cumont, who so far has made the greatest contribution to the description of these Mysteries, concedes that their internal development is not exactly known.[5]

---

4. See Lightfoot, pp. 45–72, for a sketch of the decline of Colossae between the first and seventh centuries.

5. *Les religions orientales dans le paganisme Romain*, 4th ed. (Paris: Librairie orientaliste, 1929), pp. 43–68. Cf. the English translation of the 2d ed. (1909), *The Oriental Religions in Roman Paganism* (Chicago: Open House, 1911), pp. 46–51. The progress made since A. Cumont is best represented by M. P. Nilsson, *Geschichte der griechischen Religion* II (Munich: Beck, 3d ed. 1974), pp. 622–701 (on the Phrygian Mysteries). Nilsson's A *History of Greek Religion* (Oxford: Clarendon, 1925, rev. ed. 1952) presents the results of Nilsson's research at an earlier stage and is, therefore, not used in this commentary. For a summary of Nilsson's thought see also his book, *Greek Piety* (Oxford: Clarendon, 1948). Other attempts to penetrate the structure of the changing kaleidoscope include R. Reitzenstein, *Die hellenistischen Mysterienreligionen*, 3d ed. (Leipzig: Teubner, 1927), pp. 92–191; F. A. Henle, "Der Men- und Mithraskult in Phrygien," TQ 70 (1888), pp. 590–614; M. Dibelius, *Die kleinen Briefe des Apostels Paulus erklärt*, HNT III 2 (1st ed. 1913), 85ff.; cf. 75; idem; "Die Isisweihe bei Apuleius und verwandte Initiationsriten," SHAW, phil.-hist. Klasse 4/1917 (Heidelberg 1917;

Among the names of the deities worshipped, Sabazius, Dionysus, Men, Attis, more rarely Mithras, figure prominently, and beside them the earth- and mother-goddess Cybele, upon whom honors formerly reserved for Anahita, the companion of Mithras in Persia, were conferred. Colossian coins of the Roman period show the names, symbols, or pictures of Isis, Serapis, Helios, Demeter, Artemis, and Men.

Forms of worship included procession and sacrifice, lamentation and jubilation accompanied by musical instruments, finally dances culminating in mutilation, even self-castration, performed in frenetic ecstasy. In colorful cults the fate and feats of deities who impersonated the changes of the year's seasons, of psychic experience, and of the human condition, found dramatic representation ("imitation"). Identification with the divine world order was sought through processions, dances, sacrifices, and other liturgical acts. Initiation in the timeless mysteries promised salvation from time- and earth-bound predicaments.[6] Some of the names and cults mentioned stem from the Phrygians' land of origin, Thracia. Sabazius was once an agricultural and medical deity, calling for bloody rites of purification and regeneration that were rejected and prohibited when they spread to Rome. At later times, Sabazius promised the souls of the departed a guide to the festival table set up in the other world. Men was a moon god; in company with the stars he controlled the heavenly world and the realm of the dead. The art of astrologers and the fixing of festival days were associated with his name.

The many names of male deities did not prevent their "syncretistic" contraction, conglomeration, and convergence (called "theocrasia") in the direction of monotheistic belief. Attis, for example, was assigned attributes of the Persian Mithras, that is, of the sun. Reverence was paid to many of the then known planets and stars—the influence of Chaldaean astronomy and astrology prevented their neglect—but the many heavenly bodies could be considered as no more than the halo of one supreme deity. Stoic utterances on the relation of Zeus to all things, and confessions proclaiming his oneness, uniqueness, and omnipotence, echo in the titles and acclamations given to one or another god.

All things, or the All (*pan*), were seen as dependent upon, and constituted by the deity or divinity, with or without personal qualities. Sometimes Attis (probably under Semitic influence) was called Hypsistos, "the highest [god]."

The worship offered to one supreme (male) god under many names seemed

---

repr. in idem, *Botschaft und Geschichte I* [Tübingen: Mohr, 1956], pp. 30–79; in the following quoted from the reprint as *Isisweihe*). Among the most recent commentators on Colossians, see J. Lähnemann, *Der Kolosserbrief*, SNT 3 (Gütersloh: Mohn, 1971, in the following quoted as *KolB*), pp. 83–87.

6. See the discussion of *mimēsis* (imitation) in AB, *Ephesians* 1 (1974), pp. 588–92, especially 590e. For the next paragraph, compare the discussion of "the Stoic omnipotence formula" in AB 34A, p. 177.

to conflict with the simultaneous adoration of the Great Mother, who received a share in the title "omnipotent." But eventually the cult of the male godhead, which sometimes was reserved for men only, was merged with the worship of Cybele, which was accessible to all people. The development of the Phrygian religion was not nearly completed at the time of the New Testament. The taurobolium, for example, a steer-offering which may have symbolized death, regeneration, and resurrection with the deity, a rite in veneration of Cybele, dates from the second century after Christ.

In summary, the religion of Phrygia proved capable of absorbing and assimilating whatever was offered by native traditions and current philosophical trends. Transient rulers with their armies, tradesmen with their caravans, sages of varying degrees of sincerity and wisdom, from many places—all left their mark upon the religion of the cities of Phrygia.

It is probable that alongside the typical Phrygian cults the classical deities of Greece and Rome also received some honors. Far and near political rulers were given divine titles, and religious ceremonies were observed in their honor. But religion of this sort may well have been limited to a relatively small circle of people, namely to officialdom and to a few public festivals.

Did Gnosticism also, as a late child of the Iranian Mystery of Redemption, together with a form of the myth(s) of creation (by a breakup of the original divine unity) and of redemption by a redeemed redeemer, play a vital role in Asia Minor during the first century after Christ? This question is still answered in contradictory ways. While it is obvious that Mystery Cults were *en vogue*, it is less than certain according to newer research that these cults were in essence a vehicle of those Gnostic ideas which became characteristic of a second century ecclesiastical heresy, and later of Mani's syncretistic redeemer myth.[7]

But one influence upon the Phrygian and the wider religious scenery cannot be doubted in light of extant literature, excavations, and coins: the Jewish presence in the cities of Asia Minor.[8]

One of the successors of Alexander the Great, Seleucus I "Nikator," in 312

---

7. Among the important newer contributions are R. McL. Wilson, *The Gnostic Problem* (London: Mowbray, 1958); idem, *Gnosis and the New Testament* (Philadelphia: Fortress, 1968); C. Colpe, *Die religionsgeschichtliche Schule* I, FRLANT 78 (1961); H. M. Schenke, *Der Gott "Mensch" in der Gnosis* (Göttingen: Vandenhoeck, 1962); ed. U. Bianchi, *The Origins of Gnosticism, Colloquium of Messina* (Leiden: Brill, 1967); ed. K.-W. Tröger, *Gnosis und das Neue Testament* (Gütersloh: Mohn, 1973); ed. W. Eltester, *Christentum und Gnosis*, BZNW 37 (1969); ed. U. Bianchi, etc., *Gnosis*, FS for H. Jonas (Goettingen: Vandenhoeck, 1978). See also the discussion of wider literature in AB 34, pp. 12–18 and the Topical Index in AB 34A, *Ephesians* 2, s.v. Gnosticism.

8. Pertinent among the ancient sources are, above all, Cicero *pro Flacco* XXVIII 68; Josephus *ant.* XII 119–28, 134, 138–53; XIV 110–13, 185–267; 306–23; XVI 160–78. Outstanding among secondary accounts are S. W. Baron, *A Social and Religious History of the Jews* I 1, 2d ed. (New York: Columbia University Press, 1952), pp. 169–71, 183ff.;

B.C.E. gained control over the territories which before 330 had been Persian, including Asia Minor. Jewish immigration, which was minimal before this time, was encouraged by him and rewarded by the grant of citizenship in the new cities founded by him (Josephus, *ant.* XII 119; *c.Ap.* II 39[9]). In Asia Minor and in their homeland, the Jews were assured of full religious freedom. Antiochus II (223–187) transplanted two thousand Jewish soldier-peasant families from Mesopotamia to the most important towns and fortresses of Phrygia and Lydia. According to Josephus (*ant.* XII 147–53) the Jews, as "loyal guardians of our [Antiochus'] interests," were to counteract rebellious tendencies in the native population. Since, in addition to free exercise of their religion, ample economic and financial privileges were granted to them, probably many Jews were comfortably situated and had no economic reason to complain about living in exile. Some of these settlers not only worked the royal domains, but in time became independent farmers, perhaps even great landowners. Tombstones found in Hierapolis, as well as Egyptian papyri and ostraca, reveal that there were Jewish merchants, artisans, physicians, and scribes, and salaried higher and lower officials. Some few were agricultural workers or, in rare cases, slaves. Socially, the Jewish population stood on the same level as the average people in their environment. A special "Jewish wealth was never a subject for anti-semitic propaganda" during the Hellenistic period, according to V. Tcherikover (see n. 8, p. 340). Exemption from military service was established officially only in 44/43 B.C.E. (Josephus *ant.* XIV 223–28).

Still, the Jews had to fight for their civic rights and privileges in Egypt (Philo *in Flacc.*; *de leg. ad Gajum*; Josephus *c.Ap.*) as well as in Asia Minor. Josephus takes pains to show that the Romans renewed the privileges granted by the Seleucids. Explicitly confirmed was, for example, the right of the Jews to send money from the province to Jerusalem, according to this author (*ant.* XVI 160–73). But the right confirmed by Emperor Augustus was not to the liking of every local ruler and Roman provincial officer. In vain the Jews of Asia Minor

---

E. Schürer, *History of the Jewish People* II 2 (Edinburgh: Clark, 1885), pp. 221–26, 255–91; R. Reitzenstein, *Mysterienreligionen* (see fn. 5), pp. 97–108, 141–54; V. Tcherikover, *Hellenistic Civilization and the Jews* (Philadelphia: Jewish Publication Society of America, 1959), pp. 269–377; M. Hengel, *Judaism and Hellenism* (Philadelphia: Fortress, 1974), I 261–309; II 199–205; ed. S. Safrai and M. Stern, *The Jewish People in the First Century* I (Assen: Van Gorcum, 1974), pp. 143–51, 184–215.

9. The moving story of the encounter of a Coele-Syrian Jew "who not only spoke Greek but had the soul of a Greek," and who on his journey through Asia Minor met Aristotle (as told by Josephus *c. Ap.* I 176–82) may sound too legendary to serve as evidence of a Jewish presence in Asia Minor before the times of the successors of Alexander the Great. But S. W. Baron (see fn. 8), p. 184, considers the anecdote "substantially authentic." V. Tcherikover (see fn. 8), pp. 328–32, questions the reliability of the information given by Josephus even about the time of Seleucus I Nikator; it is not (yet) confirmed by other writers or documents.

attempted to hide 800 talents from the eyes and fingers of the rebellious Mithradates VI Eupator (Josephus *ant.* XIV 110–13).[10] In 62/61 B.C.E. Cicero had to defend the propraetor of the province Asia, Flaccus, who by decree had prohibited transfer of gold to Jerusalem and had confiscated gold collected by the Jews in four centers, for example almost 100 pounds in Apamea, and more than 20 in Laodicea. If we suppose that the temple tax amounted to half a shekel (Matt 17:24) for male adults (women and children were exempt; no doubt there were tax evaders in those days too), out of a total 4–8 million Jews in the Roman Empire,[11] there may have been 10,000–11,000 tax-paying Jews in the region of Laodicea around 60 B.C.E. We may estimate that at least 500 of them were in Colossae. Whether they exerted a strong influence on the cultural, social, and religious life of the city is not known, but in Apamea, during the third century after Christ, the Jewish influence became so strong that the city's surname "chest" was explained as a reference to Noah's Ark, an equation confirmed by official coins. The *Sibylline Oracles* (I 261ff.) locate Mount Ararat in Phrygia near Apamea.

Modern descriptions of life, thought, and attitudes of the Jews living in dispersion throughout Hellenistic cities oscillate between two extremes, though they are mostly based on the same ancient sources.

On one side a picture is created by Jewish and Christian writers which identifies "Hellenistic Judaism" with almost total assimilation and acculturation. Reference is made to the attempts to sell Judaism to Egyptians and Greeks as the oldest and prototypical religion, and as one of the respectable philosophies. Indeed, there were trends in Egypt that manifested themselves in the building of Jewish temples in Elephantine and Leontopolis, and even in Jerusalem attempts were made at a far-reaching assimilation by a Jewish party, before the Maccabean revolt and the Hassidic renewal quashed the radical Hellenization of city and temple. Unquestionably, Hellenistic Judaism is "syncretistic" when Yahweh is placed in the company of other gods, or when one of the pagan gods is identified with him. The substance and form of Jewish worship and daily conduct yielded to foreign influence just as in the time of the pre-exilic prophets. Colossae and its environment were not excluded from this process.

Among some Jews and/or pagans living in the Phrygian cities or elsewhere

---

10. Perhaps the sum of 800 talents is the result of an overstatement. The worth of a talent, varying according to place and coinage, and according to metal and weight—and to the calculations offered in Dictionaries and Commentaries—ranges between $250 and $2500.

11. Philo *leg. in Gajum* 245 speaks of a vast number of Jews in the cities of Syria and Asia. S. W. Baron (see fn. 8), pp. 170–71, believes that there were 8 million Jews, forming one tenth of the population of the Roman Empire. On the basis of T. Mommsen's and A. v. Harnack's research, H. J. Schoeps, *Paul* (Philadelphia: Westminster, 1961), p. 262, arrives at the figure of 4.5 million, corresponding to 7 percent of all the people under the Roman eagle.

in Asia Minor, the god Sabazius and the Lord Sabaoth are no longer distinguished from one another. Among them "Lord Sabaoth" (= "the Lord of Hosts") is supposed to mean "the Lord who instituted the Sabbath"! Circumcision and dietary laws may have been associated with the mutilations and ascetic observances typical of the worship of the Phrygians. The dates of the new moon calculated by Men's astronomers may sometimes have coincided with those fixed by order of the Jerusalem priests. The joy expected by Jews at the Messianic Table seems to resemble the pleasures at the table of Sabazius, to which Hermes as "a good angel" led the souls of the departed pious. Does this mean that in Asia Minor, a portion of Judaism, partly under the influence of Iranian religion, was "dissolved in paganism," as Richard Reitzenstein affirms?[12]

On the other hand, polemics against the Jews like those of Tacitus indicate that, because of the distinctive traits of the God whom they worshipped, of the consciousness of special election, and of the concomitant aloofness *(amixia)* from outsiders, the Jews in the Roman Empire by no means impressed their Hellenistic contemporaries by their adaptability and their eagerness to assimilate. Rather, they were an offense to their neighbors.[13] Even Philo of Alexandria, who lived at the time of the apostle Paul and did much to reconcile Jewish faith with gentile philosophy in continuing a line that had started with late Jewish Wisdom literature, decried in most explicit terms the Mystery Religions *(spec. leg.* I 319–23). In resisting the pressures of pagan forms of worship, the Synagogues in the diaspora insisted upon circumcision, keeping the Sabbath, and dietary observances. They would not have admitted proselytes in great numbers, and proselytes would not have made pilgrimages to Jerusalem, unless Jews everywhere had been bent upon keeping the law, and with it their identity.

Therefore, another picture of Hellenistic Judaism has also been drawn, most emphatically by V. Tcherikover, M. Stern, and S. Safrai (see fn. 8). Although this picture contains some "individuals who felt drawn to the alien world outside, either because they deliberately rejected Judaism or because they wished to make their way in the surrounding world" and some other "intellectuals who gave the Torah an extreme allegorical interpretation," Stern and Safrai (p. 185) claim that "there was no general tendency to assimilation." On the contrary, the Law of God lived in the hearts and the temple of God dominated the

12. R. Reitzenstein (see fn. 5), p. 99. E. P. Goodenough, *By Light, Light* (New Haven: Yale University, 1935), pp. 263–64, calls, e.g., the mysticism promoted by Philo "for all its passionate loyalty . . . not fundamentally a Judaism with Hellenistic veneer: it was a Hellenism, presented in Jewish symbols and allegories. . . ."

13. See Tacitus *historiae* V 2–5, 8; *annales* XII 54, Plutarch *symp.* VI 160; Josephus *c. Ap.* II 6, 8, 10; Pliny *hist. nat.* XIII 4–46, and the descriptions of the anti-Semitism of the Hellenistic period by E. Schürer (see fn. 8), pp. 291–327 ("the feeling [was] not so much of hatred as of pure contempt," p. 297), and by I. Heinemann, in Pauly-Wissowa, suppl. vol. V (1931), pp. 3–43, especially pp. 31–43. M. Hengel (see fn. 8), p. 473, etc., discusses the ancient exponents of anti-Semitism together with recent literature.

worship and conduct of the dispersed Jews, despite all spiritualizing and universalist trends of the Hellenistic era. Indeed, prayers (see for example, 3 Macc 6:1–15); the hope for spiritual and physical return to the land of the Fathers (Philo *praem. et poen.* 113–117); pilgrimages of Jewish men, women, and children; the temple tax; tithes; and voluntary gifts sent to Jerusalem show that Jerusalem and the promise of a return were not forgotten (cf. Ps 137, Deut 30:4, etc.) Acts 2:10 mentions Jews from Phrygia who attend the Pentecost ("Weeks"-)Festival at Jerusalem, and according to Acts 21:27–30, it was "Jews from Asia (Minor)" who excelled by their zeal against the reputedly scandalous teaching and conduct of the apostle Paul vis-à-vis "the people and the Law and the place [= the temple]" of Jerusalem. In about 300 C.E. the Palestinian Rabbi Chilbo stated, "the wine from Phrygia and the baths of Diomsith (?) have ruined ten tribes of Israel" (b Sabb. 147 B, unless the place spelled "Prugitha" was situated in Palestine). At any rate, orthodox and orthopractical Judaism cannot be made responsible for the life led and the impression made by some syncretistic Phrygian Jews.

Hellenistic Judaism in Phrygia did not consist only of the extremes just described. However, so far nothing is known of a Jewish Wisdom School, an Essene settlement, or a famous rabbi resident among the tradesmen and craftsmen of Laodicea, Hierapolis, and Colossae. Yet it is reasonable to assume that currents and winds of many different sorts of Jewish doctrine and conduct reached these towns and influenced not only Jews but also gentiles. Whether some of these currents can be described as "Gnosticizing Judaism" depends to a large extent upon the definition of Gnosticism. Evidence for acquaintance of the Jews in Asia Minor with apocryphal and apocalyptic books is unattainable. Since most of these books were probably written only after 70 C.E., there is no need to believe that Colossae and its neighbors were influenced by their way of thinking. Both terms, "Hellenistic Judaism" and "Gnosticizing Judaism," are so full of obscure and contradictory elements that they contribute nothing to the elucidation of Jewish religious life and its relationship to the pagan environment in the region and time-span to which the epistle to the Colossians pertains. Only the fact that a "process" took place in which Judaism was not only influenced by, but also influencing, pagan cults in a "reciprocal penetration" (F. Cumont, pp. 63–64) is undisputed.

However, gentiles and Jews were not the only ones living in Colossae and its environment; Col 1:2; 4:13, 16; cf. 2:1 *var. lect.*, and the epistle to Philemon ascertain that as early as the fifties of the first century after Christ there were also Christian communities in Hierapolis, Laodicea, and Colossae.

III. THE CONGREGATION AT COLOSSAE

The church at Colossae, and probably also the congregations at Laodicea and Hierapolis, was founded by a man called Epaphras, who is mentioned nowhere in the New Testament except the two epistles sent to Colossae, that is, Colossians and Philemon. He is described as a gentile-born native of Colossae and hard working, beloved, and trustworthy fellow-worker, once also as a fellow-prisoner, of the apostle Paul.[14]

Although the name "Epaphras" is a well-known short form of Epaphroditus (BDF 125:1), it is most unlikely that Epaphras of Colossae is identical with the equally qualified and recommended Epaphroditus who, despite the struggle with almost mortal illness, served in exemplary fashion as a liaison between Paul and the Philippians (Phil 2:25–30; 4:18). It is hardly possible that the same person could have been associated so intimately with different congregations in widely separated areas as Macedonia and inland sites in Asia Minor. Fellow-workers of Paul such as these were more than simply agents of Paul. They also represented the members, special gifts, and needs of the congregations to the apostle.[15] Thus not only had Epaphras worked for the congregation and reported concerning it, but he also interceded for his fellow Christians as continuously as Paul (Col 1:7–8; 4:12).

Neither the Pauline epistles nor the Acts of the Apostles provide adequate information to establish the date of Epaphras' initial mission work. He may have returned to his hometown and the neighboring cities from the east, perhaps from Pisidian Antioch, in the late forties at the time of Paul's "first missionary journey." Luke sums up the missionary activity of the apostle and of his protector and friend Barnabas in Antioch (Pisidia), saying, "the word of the Lord spread throughout all the region" (Acts 13:2, 49). If the term "region" is interpreted very widely, it may include the Lycus Valley, even the tiny city of Colossae. Col 1:5–6 and 2:6 may confirm the report of Acts 13. In Colossae "the word of truth, the gospel . . . was heard . . . just as in the whole world [it was] bearing fruit and growing," "you received Christ Jesus as Lord." Was, as

---

14. Col 1:7–8; 4:12–13; Phlm 23. The theory saying that Epaphras was only a teacher in the congregation, not its founder, will be discussed in the Notes on 1:7.

15. In Col 1:7, the better manuscripts call Epaphras "a faithful servant of Christ on *our* behalf," but the variant reading, ". . . on *your* behalf," is supported by the contents of 1:8; 4:12–13. Correspondingly, the better readings of 4:8–9 describe Tychicus as a messenger who is to bring news of Paul *to* the congregation; the words "that he reassure your hearts" and "they [Tychicus and Onesimus] will make known to you all that has occurred here" support this. But other manuscripts express the hope of the apostle that Tychicus (and through him Paul) receive new information about the Colossian congregation. Paul himself may have insisted upon two-way traffic.

Col 1:7–8 appears to indicate, the gentile-Christian Epaphras the only evangelist of Colossae? In Col 4:10, Paul's co-worker Mark (who sends greetings and is about to visit Colossae) is introduced as "the nephew of Barnabas." This might reveal that Barnabas was known to the Colossians because he, too (before, during, or after Epaphras) had worked in Colossae, during Paul's first missionary journey.[16] However, wherever the Jewish Christians Paul and/or Barnabas preached the gospel, "many Jews and devoted proselytes" formed a core congregation (Acts 13:43), even though eventually Jewish authorities closed the synagogue doors to the heralds of the Messiah Jesus and had the missionaries expelled from the city limits (Acts 13:35–14:19). The Colossian church consisted only of gentile-Christians according to Col 1:21; 2:11, 13, and it cannot be proven that the polemics of Colossians are directed against Jewish or Jewish-Christian influences upon the congregation (see the next section). Therefore, Barnabas may never have been in Colossae; the Colossians might only have heard of him, just as they are now told in writing about two other important Jewish Christians, Mark and Jesus Justus (Col 4:10–11). If, in agreement with the exclusive mention of Epaphras in Col 1:7–8, Barnabas' visit in Colossae need not be stipulated, Epaphras' evangelistic work in Colossae must no longer necessarily be associated with the first missionary journey of Paul, and an alternative to Pisidian Antioch as the missionary base can be sought.

Indeed, the gospel may well have been brought to Colossae from the west, for example from Ephesus, in the early fifties. During Paul's "third missionary journey," before the apostle revisited the congregations in Greece founded during his second journey, he may have made Ephesus a theological training center and his missionary headquarters.[17] According to Luke, he taught for three months in the local synagogue, then for two years in the school of a certain Tyrannus, with the result "that all of Asia (Minor? or the Roman province?) heard the word of the Lord, both Jews and Greeks." An adversary of Paul, the silversmith Demetrius, made the following charge, "not only at Ephesus but almost throughout all Asia this Paul has persuaded and turned away a considerable company of people" (Acts 19:8–10, 26; cf. 20:31). These

16. As Bo Reicke, RevExp 70 (1973), p. 432, assumes.

17. Stimulated by int.al. W. Bousset, *Jüdisch-christlicher Schulbetrieb in Alexandria und Rom*, FRLANT, NF 6 (1915); R. Bultmann, *Theology of the New Testament* II (New York: Scribner's, 1955), p. 142; H. Conzelmann, "Paulus und die Weisheit," NTS 12 (1965/66), pp. 222–44; and E. Lohse, *Colossians and Philemon* (Philadelphia: Fortress, 1871; in the following: *Colossians*), pp. 181–82, Helga Ludwig, *Der Verfasser des Kolossenbriefes—ein Schüler des Paulus* (diss. Göttingen 1974, in the following: *Verfasser*), pp. 24, 193–231, has attempted to describe the origin and character of a Pauline school. Its eventual relationship with the production of letters such as Colossians and Ephesians will be discussed below, in Sections VIII–X, esp. fn. 101. Cf. R. Jewett, "The Redaction of First Corinthians and the Trajectory of the Pauline School," JAAR 44 (1978), 389–444.

statements, too, correspond to the description in Col 1:5–7, 23; 2:6–7 of worldwide and local teaching and reception of the gospel.

Whether founded on the earlier or the later occasion, the churches mentioned were no more than a few years old when Epaphras informed Paul about their "faith and love" (Col 1:4, 8). The epistle to the Colossians confirms the absence of any report in Acts of a personal visit of Paul to the churches of the Lycus Valley. Paul had only "heard" of their faith, and he prayed and suffered for them, although he had never met these Christians "face to face" (1:4, 9; 2:1).[18] In response to Epaphras' report, the epistle expresses thanks to God for the existence and the state of these churches. A splendid testimony for them precedes the less complimentary utterances that will follow: the Christians at Colossae and in its neighborhood "received" Christ and "heard [= obeyed]" the word of truth: their faith, love, and hope, tested by endurance, manifested their

---

18. Against an almost unanimous scholarly consensus, but supported by what S. E. Johnson in BA 13 (1950), pp. 4–5 (see fn. 1) calls a "good chance" (though it is "far less likely"), Bo Reicke, RevExp 70 (1973), pp. 432–33, believes that the Lycus Valley churches were founded during Paul's first missionary journey, and that Paul himself visited these young congregations during his third journey. He argues: (a) After crossing Galatia and Phrygia Paul passes "the upper parts" of Asia Minor on his way to Ephesus (Acts 18:23; 19:1), i.e., he followed the southern of the two parallel inner-Asiatic highways—the one leading through Colossae and Laodicea. (b) Paul's friendship with three Colossians (his fellow-worker Epaphras, Col 1:7–8; 4:12–13; Phlm 23; his convert Philemon, Phlm 10 and 19; and a local minister, Archippus, Phlm 2; Col 4:17); also Paul's acquaintance with a Laodicean lady, Nympha (Col 4:15), presuppose a visit of Paul to their places. (c) The mutual love and concern, evident between Paul and the Christians addressed by him, reveal previous personal contact.

In short, the term "those who have never seen me face to face" (Col 2:1), which convinces the majority of scholars of Paul's never having been at Colossae, describes according to Bo Reicke just some very recent converts, not the whole congregation. This interpretation distorts not only the meaning of the quoted words in their context but is marked also by other weaknesses. For the designations "Phrygia and the Galatian region" or "the Galatian region and Phrygia" (Acts 16:6; 18:23) need not mean the area east-northeast of the Lycus Valley from which Colossae, Laodicea, and Hierapolis can be reached on the southern highway. It is more likely that Luke uses this nomenclature for the northern parts of Phrygia which were incorporated in the Roman province Galatia, as e.g., J. B. Lightfoot, *Colossians*, pp. 24–28, and E. Haenchen, *The Acts of the Apostles* (Philadelphia: Westminster, 1971) in their comments on Acts 16:6 have shown. This region was situated far to the north of Pisidian Antioch; whoever intended to go from there to Ephesus would choose the northern inner-Asiatic trade-route, leaving it at Sardis to reach his goal. As for the individuals joined to Paul by warm friendship, he may have met them when they were visiting places outside Colossae and Laodicea. If the greeting chapter Rom 16 really is a part of Romans, then it demonstrates Paul's love and concern for co-workers and congregational ministers whom he may have known only by reports of others. The visit Paul plans to make to Colossae, according to Phlm 22, was—if ever—certainly not carried out before the writing of Colossians (see Section XI).

solid foundation in the "fruit-bearing and growing gospel." Not in vain are terms such as "fulfillment" and "perfection" used among the Christians in these places,[19] and Paul himself is "rejoicing to see how orderly and firm is their faith in Christ" (2:5).

In addition, the epistle contains traces of information on the composition, worship, organization, and daily life of the churches. The emphasis laid on the reconciliation of all powers, things, and persons through the crucified Christ (1:20, 22), and on the unity of Greek and Jew, circumcised and uncircumcised people, Scythians and Barbarians, freemen and slaves (3:11), makes it certain that all these groups, including children (3:20–21), were represented in the community, although the epistle addresses itself only to the local gentile-Christians (1:21, 27; 2:11, 13). The quotations made in the epistle from confessions, hymns, perhaps liturgies and catechisms show that preaching, teaching, counseling, creedal, confessional, or catechetical formulae, baptism, thanksgiving (most likely including the eucharistic meal), prayer, and hymn singing were part of the worship at Colossae as much as in the life of other churches. House churches existed in at least two private homes (Col 4:15; Phlm 2).

The delegation of special ministries to individuals is confirmed by the repeated mention of Epaphras (Col 1:7–8; 4:12), the special greetings to Nympha (4:15), and the exhortation directed at a certain Archippus (Col 4:17; cf. Phlm 2). Such ministries are enumerated and described more extensively in 1 Cor 3:4–15; 12:7–31; Rom 12:3–13. In Colossians there is, however, as yet no trace of a distinction between charismatic and institutional services, or between bishops and elders. This speaks for a rather early, certainly not for a post-apostolic, date of the letter.

Very little is known of the actual conduct of the church members. The counsels, commands, and prohibitions contained in the ethical part of Colossians (3:5–4:6) cannot be used for the reconstruction of the daily behavior of those addressed, for a schematic ethical instruction, applicable to all churches, although perhaps accentuated for the benefit of the Colossians, has been incorporated in the epistle, especially in the so-called "catalogues of vices and virtues" (3:5–17), and in the *Haustafel* (3:18–4:1). The emphasis laid here upon unity, love, and peace (3:5–15), and upon subordination to persons, namely, husbands, parents, and masters (not to institutions), reveals a specific danger threatening Colossae: an individualistic withdrawal from mutual responsibility, combined with a lust for emancipation at any price. While Colossians (except for the indications given in the greeting list (4:7–17 is limited to general exhortations, the epistle to Philemon discusses in some detail one specific and personal problem: how is Philemon, a member of the church at Colossae, to be true to his faith in dealing with the runaway slave Onesimus, who has recently

---

19. Col 1:2–11, 21–23; 2:5–7, 9, 19; 3:3–4; 4:12.

become a Christian? The picture of the congregations in the Lycus Valley, especially of the community in Colossae, nevertheless is incomplete, unless the existence and influence of a movement is mentioned that seemed alluring to the church while threatening it at its roots. Not all was well at Colossae.

IV. THE MENACE OF A RELIGION

In Col 2:4, 8, 16, 18 explicit warnings are given to the saints at Colossae about a great danger confronting them. Those whose faith, love, and hope have been recognized gratefully (1:2–8, 23) are threatened by "someone" who may persuade, catch, judge, and disqualify them by a "philosophy" (2:8). As is the rule in other Pauline letters (with notable exceptions in the Pastoral Epistles, for example 1 Tim 1:20; 2 Tim 2:17; 4:14), names of the potential or actual seducers are not mentioned. As in Galatians, Second Corinthians, Romans, and Philippians, the information given about their convictions and practices is far too spotty to provide a historian of religion with sufficient, clear-cut clues for an accurate derivation, description, and explanation of their "system of beliefs," if they had such a system at all.

Though in the vast literature devoted to the elucidation of the origin, character, and intent of the Colossian philosophy the designation "heresy" is used by preference,[20] not even this nomenclature is undisputable. Indeed, in Hellenistic times the term *hairesis* (heresy) was often used in a neutral sense to denote any school of thought claiming authority.[21] But as early as the New Testament, it bears a negative sense and means dissent or faction rending a community (Gal 5:20; 2 Pet 2:1). The pejorative sense became normative in ecclesiastical usage through Ignatius (Eph VI 2, Trall. VI I). Doctrines and members of a community deviating from and threatening the teachings held by a dominating group are called heresies and heretics respectively, even among Jews and Moslems. However, unlike the situation presupposed in other New Testament epistles containing the so-called *Gattung* "Ketzer-Polemik" (polemics against heretics), the threat which the letter to the Colossians faces probably

---

20. For the following, see the General *Bibliography* I and the Sectional Bibliography I, especially G. Bornkamm, "Die Häresie des Kolosserbriefes," in *Das Ende des Gesetzes* (Munich: Kaiser, 1952), pp. 139–56; J. Lähnemann, *KolB*, p. 104. Reference to a "Christology of the heretics" is made for instance by H. Hegermann, *Der Schöpfungsmittler im hellenistischen Judentum und Urchristentum*, TU 82 (1961), 164 (in the following: SpgM).

21. Stoicism, Cynicism, Sadducees, Pharisees, Christians, and others are described that way; see BAG, p. 23, for references among Greek writers, including Josephus and Luke (Acts 5:17; 15:5; 24:5; 26:5).

came from outside the congregation, that is, from Jews, from gentiles, or from people who considered themselves superior to any such distinction.[22] It is possible but not certain that the opponents had said a clear-cut "no" to the headship of Jesus Christ over all things (Col 2:19a). At the same time, the

22. According to W. Bauer, *Orthodoxy and Heresy in Earliest Christianity* (Philadelphia: Fortress, 1971), pp. 80–94, 192–93, 235, the churches of Asia Minor, including those situated in the Lycus Valley (and together with the Syrian and Egyptian churches) consisted of a majority of members who were considered heretics by orthodox theologians, churches, and synods; already at the time of the book of Revelation, heterodoxy threatened Pergamon, Thyatira, Sardis, and Laodicea (Rev 2–3), and Ignatius bypassed the Hierapolis and Colossae communities "in icy silence." Did, perhaps, Epaphras fail to eliminate a "worship of cosmic elements" that was offered at Colossae even before and while this co-operator of Paul preached there? Col 1:6–7 does not support this idea. E. Lohmeyer, *Die Briefe an die Philippen, an die Kolosser und an Philemon*, MeyerK IX (Göttingen: Vandenhoeck, 1930 and later editions, in the following quoted as *Kolosser*), pp. 3–8, avoids the word "heresy," but on pp. 99–100 agrees with Dib.-Gr., p. 38; M. Dibelius, *Isisweihe*, pp. 55–56, when he describes the Colossian Religion as a movement consisting of people outside *and* inside the congregation. If this assumption were valid, the letter to the Colossians would be engaged in a war on two fronts. J. Lähnemann, *KolB*, pp. 63, 75, 100, 104, 107, at first wavers between statements about the influence "upon" and "in" the church, then decides for an intramural heresy which is due to outside influence. Similarly E. Käsemann, RGG II (1958), 1728, declares that the "Christian" teachers stemmed from the environment of the church.

Clearer are the positions taken by, e.g., W. Schmauch, J. A. Stewart, and P. Vielhauer on one side, M. D. Hooker and W. Foerster on the other. Schmauch, *Beiheft* to E. Lohmeyer's commentary (1964), pp. 40–41, speaks of the scholarly consensus saying that a "Christian heresy" is being attacked in Colossians, not a pagan movement. Stewart, pp. 429–36, places the blame entirely at the door of Christians who sought to combine oriental and Jewish elements with their confession of Jesus Christ. Vielhauer, *Geschichte der urchristlichen Literatur* (Berlin: de Gruyter, 1975), p. 192, declares it for "certain that the opponents are neither Gentiles nor Jews but Christians, considering themselves true Christians." See also E. Percy, *Die Probleme der Kolosser-und Epheserbriefe* (Lund: Gleerup, 1946; in the following quoted as PKE, p. 142). This "consensus" is challenged by Miss Hooker, "Were There False Teachers in Colossae?," in FS for C. F. D. Moule, pp. 318, 326, 329, and W. Foerster, "Die Irrlehrer des Kolosserbriefes," FS für T. C. Vniezen (Wageningen: Veenmann & Zonen, 1966), pp. 72–73. The first puts into question the whole theory of a system of false teaching and an integrated heretical movement; she suggests that the epistle battles the pressure exerted by various beliefs and practices of the pagan and Jewish environment of the congregation, and Foerster places the whole movement outside the church, too.

Indeed, the judgment of those last-mentioned appears to be the best supported by the evidence at hand. The juxtaposition made in Col 2:8, "based on man-made traditions . . . and not upon Christ," and the accusation in 2:19 "he [the opponent] does not stick to the head [Christ]" do *not* demonstrate that the opposition claimed Christ for its foundation and head. Rather these texts speak of ignorance or neglect of Christ. The cunning persuasion mentioned in 2:4 need not yet have produced results in the

church members were in danger of succumbing to their dogmas (2:20b), though they had not yet fallen victim to their cunning persuasion (2:4,8).

What is actually known about the rebutted teachings? Because of the definite article used before the word "philosophy" in 2:8, many modern authors speak of "the (Colossian) philosophy." Three reasons make it advisable to call the movement "the Colossian Religion" rather than "philosophy": (1) in ancient, medieval, and modern *academic* parlance, philosophy has usually a narrow meaning: it is the science of the sciences; (2) the misunderstanding is to be avoided that the author of Colossians possessed or promoted a general antiphilosophical prejudice; (3) one of the senses which *philosophiā* had in the temporal and local environment of the early Christian congregations was equivalent to the English (as well as French and German) term "religion." A specific "type of religion" or "spirituality" is meant by the term in Philo's and Josephus' writings, for example (see fn. 32 for references). Its core was practiced reverence and piety, rather than abstract theories and thoughts, and hardly a tightly woven philosophical system. A survey of the available sources of information and their data, of the methods and results of their exploitation, and of suggested modern analogies is necessary for the detailed verse-by-verse commentary to be given later.

A. Sources

1. In the polemical part of Colossians (2:8, 16–23), fifteen words are used that occur nowhere else in the New Testament. In addition, the same section contains ten words nowhere else employed in the undisputed Pauline Epistles.[23] Indeed, "hapax-legomena" are found in all parts of Colossians, but their ratio to other words is almost twice as large in the polemical section. Among these words several, especially "philosophy" (v 8), "bodily" (v 9), "doffing," "stripping" (vv 11 and 15), "new-moon" (v 16), "worship," "initiation by visions," "voluntary worship" (v 18), "taste," "touch" (v 21), "harsh treatment of the body" (v 23) may stem from the vocabulary used in the self-description of the opponents. Even when in the same part of Colossians New Testament and Pauline terminology occurs, especially when reference is made to angels, traditions, statutes, commandments, and teachings (vv 8, 20, 22), dietary (and, perhaps, purity) laws (vv 16, 21), wisdom and humility (vv 23), essential

---

congregation, and the subjection to statutes as caricatured in 2:20 may have been an imminent danger, not an accomplished fact.

23. The problem of sources is discussed by J. Lähnemann, *KolB*, pp. 76–100, and is made an object of primary concern by J. J. Gunther, *St. Paul's Opponents and Their Background*, NovTSuppl 35 (Leiden: Brill, 1974), pp. 1–58.

The following statistical references are based upon R. Morgenthaler, *Statistik des neutestamentlichen Wortschatzes* (Zürich: Gotthelf, 1958) and E. Lohse, *Colossians*, pp. 85–87.

elements of the "Religion" are intimated. What emerges is the outline of a movement aiming at practical wisdom. This Religion takes the existence of angels and of the elements of the world equally seriously. It relies on tradition and statutes. It requires discipline and humility. It transcends sheer rationalism by its insistence upon truths sought and seen in visions. Finally, it prescribes festival days in order to harmonize faith and behavior with the cycles of the stars and of nature.

But the picture of the Religion, reproduced alone from Col 2, cannot be objective, complete, or coherent, because a strong bias is manifested in this chapter by the addition of negative evaluations. Even before explicit polemics start in 2:16, the propaganda made by the adversaries is described as an attempt to "outwit" the saints "by specious arguments" (2:4). Later, their procedure is equated with the intent to "captivate . . . judge . . . and disqualify" the saints (2:8, 18). Their "philosophy" is (by the interpretative conjunction "and") described as "meaningless deception" (2:8). Their tradition, commandments, and teachings are ridiculed as "man-made" standards (2:8, 22). Dietary prohibitions and the festival calendar are equated with a mere "shadow [-boxing?]" in 2:16–17, and commandments not to touch or taste certain things are said to pertain to no more than the way of digestion (2:22). Their humility is twice called arbitrary (2:18, 23); vision and initiation are defined as an unfounded inflation of the fleshly mind (2:18); the wisdom proclaimed is called a vain pretense, and the severity exercised against the body is condemned either as valueless for the needs of the flesh, or a self-satisfaction bare of any merit (2:23). Almost each of the seemingly descriptive terms used in 2:16–23 has a double sense: the literal and the caricature-like, ironic, and deprecatory meanings. Thus, an objective picture of the opposed Religion is as little intended and given in Colossians as is an impartial description of idolatry in, for example, Isa 44:9–20; Wis 12:23–15:19; Rom 1:18–32, or of Judaism in the Fourth Gospel.

2. This is obvious not only in the polemic part of Colossians but also in the introductory section 1:3–8; the homiletic, hymnic, and missionary paragraphs 1:9–2:5; the affirmative interlude among the polemic outbursts 2:9–15; the exhortations gathered in 3:1–4:6; and the concluding sentences 4:7–18. In these passages, too, elements are provided which may elucidate the essence of the Religion. In most of these sections, the words "wisdom," "mystery," "to reveal," "knowledge," "to know," "fullness," "to fill," "perfect," but also terms such as "creation," "to create," "principalities and powers," "head" and "body," "circumcision," and "Sabbath" are used so frequently or pointedly that they at least reflect a range of interest and perhaps the actual vocabulary of the opposed movement.[24] These terms also play an important role in the undisputed letters of Paul in which other adversaries are rebutted. Yet the emphasis and special

---

24. H. von Soden, *Die Briefe an die Kolosser, Epheser, Philemon, Die Pastoralbriefe* HBNT III I (Freiburg: Mohr, 1891; in the following: *Kolosser*), p. 11, argues that

sense given to them in Colossians presuppose most likely a special slant which they possessed in the language of the opponents.

The loaded words manifest that to the Colossian Religion belonged a belief in a supreme, perhaps monotheistic, deity and that this belief was combined with the conviction of the unfolding of the divine riches in a multiplicity of powers that exercise a mediating function between the heavenly and earthly spheres. Because all things created and perishable, especially body and flesh, were considered evil, redemption was sought from creaturely existence and from death. Wisdom and knowledge, growth and perfection counted as gifts of the ongoing revelation of divine mysteries and as benefits of cultic initiation and other exercises through which the tyranny of bodily matters was to be broken.

Was Christ identified as one of several mediators among the powers, either by the religious teachers outside the church, or by those Christians who were about to fall prey to their doctrines? An affirmative answer is suggested by the emphatic reference to the deity's "bodily" presence in Christ (2:9; cf. 1:19), to the achievement of reconciliation in the "body of flesh" and in the death of Christ (1:22), and to a worship offered in and through bodily actions and sufferings (see especially 1:24; 2:5; 3:5–4:6). These emphatic affirmations of Colossians may well be antitheses against the Colossian Religion. If so, they contribute to our knowledge of that religion and contribute to a sketch of its outlines, as it is here presented. One perspective may be added only tentatively: perhaps creaturely existence as such was considered a curse which could be escaped only by the souls' ascension to heaven; but an explicit statement confirming or contradicting this belief is not contained in Colossians. Equally, it is not safe to take Col 1:24 as evidence for saying the opponents spoke of things "lacking in Christ."

At any rate, the inclusion of the whole of Colossians among the sources serving the elucidation of the Religion permits at least one conclusion: not only the individual phenomena mentioned (haphazardly?) in 2:8, 16–23 but also a certain structure and coherence distinguished this Religion. It lived from the combination of *theology* (presupposing one supreme being manifested in many angels in the lower sphere of the universe), *soteriology* (the search for salvation through mediation between the visible and invisible realms), *liturgics* (insisting upon traditions, initiation, festivals, prostrations), and *ethics* (requiring disdain of the body, of fleshly pleasures, and of death). Elements of keen speculation, of mystical experience, and of harsh self-negation contributed to its emotional character.

Whatever the merits and credibility of such a summary of the Religion may

---

especially the numerous relative clauses found in Colossians affirm things that were denied by the Religion. Dib.-Gr.'s and E. Lohmeyer's commentaries presuppose that the hints given in Colossians are sufficient for the reconstruction of an adequate image of the opposition.

be, many blanks remain in the picture, as one example may illustrate. According to the proclamatory, perhaps hymnic statements of 1:19 and 2:9, it was God's pleasure to have all the fullness of the divinity dwell bodily in Jesus Christ. When this affirmation is examined in view of its implicit negations, it yields the following choices for the reconstruction of the Religion: the opponents taught that (a) the deity was subjected to a crisis when it *suffered* an emanation (among the Gnostics: an abortus) but did not *will* it: (b) only a *part* of the divinity went out from the godhead: (c) Jesus Christ was not the *only* location and manifestation of the loss suffered by the deity: and (d) whatever divine element was lodged in Christ, it was not *bodily* present in him. However, it can only be guessed that one or several of these four doctrinal variants (which indeed are found in Gnostic teaching of the second and later centuries) were really present and essential in the Colossian Religion.

The epistle to the Colossians demonstrates that the comprehensiveness, rationality, and emotionality of this religion looked attractive to the saints at Colossae, even though it required submission to fixed dogmas and rigorous discipline. This compelled the author of the epistle to formulate sharp warnings, biting sarcasms, and uncompromising refutations. Even more, it appears to have made him rethink his own creedal and ethical presuppositions, and to formulate new insights related to creation and reconciliation, revelation and tradition, knowledge and growth, fullness and unity.[25] Therefore the sarcastic remarks found in Col 2 need not demonstrate that the picture presented of the Religion is *only* a caricature, and that the writer was unable or unwilling to learn from the encounter. Though in 2:8 the author portrays the "elements" (respected in the Religion) and Christ (preached by Epaphras and Paul) as mutually exclusive criteria, in 2:17 he almost coordinates them by relating them as shadow to reality.

3. Sources other than the epistle to the Colossians have been tapped in order to shed additional light on the Colossian Religion. Various heresies are fought in the epistles to the Galatians, Corinthians, Romans, Philippians, in the Pastoral Epistles, and in the epistles of James, of John, of 2 Peter, of Jude, finally in the letters contained in Rev 2–3, perhaps also, though more indirectly, in the Synoptic Gospels and the Gospel according to John. Some of the apostrophized heretics appear to have emphasized primarily, or to have preached exclusively, either the divinity or the humanity of Christ. Concerning conduct, the extremes consisted of a legalism based upon the unshakable validity of some Mosaic commandments and of an enthusiastic libertinism appealing to the freedom brought by Christ the redeemer and pantocrator. Each type of Christology was combined with either the one or the other ethical model. Since the vocabulary, ideas, and practices of the Colossian Religion resemble, or are equal to, the New Testament descriptions of legalistic and/or docetic-Christological

---

25. This is the thesis of J. Lähnemann, *KolB*, especially pp. 114–15, 119, 134, 175.

types of heresy, the Colossian opponents have been considered more or less identical with the adversaries fought in Galatians or in the Gospel and the letters of John, for example.[26] Thus large parts of the New Testament have been treated as sources of information on Colossae. When[27] a convergence and combination of "Hellenistic philosophical Gnosis" with "Jewish-ethical praxis" in "Judaizing Gnosticism" is considered a sensible solution of the syncretistic process, then practically all traces of "heretical" or "heterodox" Judaism found in the New Testament (whether of the apocalyptic, Essene-Qumranite, sapiential, or mystical type) become additional resources. But the presupposition of this procedure, even the assumption that all heresies fought by Paul are basically identical, is questionable, as will be demonstrated when the results are compared (see Subsection C).

4. Contemporary and post-biblical information on the Colossian Religion has also been drawn from primary and secondary sources related to earlier and later Jewish and Christian sectarian movements, among them the Essenes and

---

26. Reference to world elements, angels, festivals, and circumcision invite the equation of the Colossian Religion with the Galatian heresy which is made by, e.g., H. Schlier, *Der Brief an die Galater*, MeyerK VII (4th ed., 1965), pp. 190–94; E. Percy, PKE, pp. 163–66; S. Lyonnet, in ed. U. Bianchi, *Origins*, pp. 544, 549; F. Zeilinger, *Der Erstgeborene der Schöpfung* (Wien: Herder, 1974 in the following: *Erstgeborene*), pp. 120–25, 133–36; J. Gunther (see fns. 23, 29, 33). If the Colossian and Galatian opposition to Paul was basically the same, an extended "South-Galatian hypothesis" might count Colossae among "the churches of Galatia" addressed in Gal 1:2. Colossians would then be no more than a sort of duplicate of Galatians. But as mentioned in Section I, since 49 C.E., Colossae was definitely part of the Roman Province of Asia, not of Galatia.

Is there evidence to assume that the Colossian Religion contained elements of the (Gnostic-)docetic Christology, against which implicitly all canonical Gospels, especially the Fourth, and explicitly the Epistle of John are fighting? (See fn. 36 for the names of scholars affirming or denying this hypothesis.) A connection of the church of Colossae with the western Asia Minor churches, especially with Ephesus (with which a strong tradition associates the Johannine Writings), and a similarity of the "heresies" emerging there and here, can be imagined, when, e.g., the verses Col 1:19–20; 2:9 are compared with the antidocetic tendency of John 1:14; 6:51–58; 19:34–35; I Jn 1:7; 4:2). The possible foundation of the Colossian church by a man coming from Ephesus (see Section III) and the parallel contents of Ephesians and Colossians could then be used to demonstrate that not only politically and administratively but also spiritually Colossae belonged in the western Asia Minor realm. However, the uniqueness of the Colossian Religion must not be obfuscated. For even if this Religion shared heretical doctrines with Ephesus and Galatia, it combined them in a unique way. For neither are the Galatians docetists, nor the Ephesians Judaizers.

27. With, e.g., E. Lohmeyer, *Kolosser*, pp. 3–8; G. Bornkamm, "Häresie," pp. 139–56; W. Schmithals, "The Heretics in Galatia," in idem, Paul and the Gnostics (Nashville: Abingdon, 1972), pp. 13–64.

other baptismal groups such as the Elkesaites, the originators of the Pseudo-Clementine Literature, and the documents and refutations of Gnostics such as Cerinthus, Marcion, Valentinus, and their followers.[28]

Since all of these groups show distinctive influences of pagan religion and philosophy, the evidence available through literature, excavation, and the reconstruction of the main religious and philosophical features and trends of the first century C.E. can prove as valuable for the description and understanding of the Religion of Colossae as the Jewish and Christian sources mentioned so far. Ancient Oriental cults and their continuation or revival in Mystery Cults, the role of indigenous deities and of their adaptation to the needs of a cosmopolitan era, classical philosophical systems and their variations in the form, for example, of Stoicism, Middle-Platonism, and Neo-Pythagoreanism; all of them vie for consideration. Only a complete description of the varieties of religions, philosophical offerings, and so-called magical practices available at the time when Colossians was written could do justice to the enormous amount of accessible information. A narrow-minded overexploitation of the first-named resources can be avoided when these sources are tapped. But since they are in endless supply, like the inexhaustible ocean, one can drown in the minutiae while looking for undisputably pertinent data.

B. Tentative Results

Frequently results of research are announced after primary, secondary, and tertiary sources have been distinguished, sifted, and evaluated, and after the history and context of the vocabulary, the motifs, the ideas, and the practices have been illuminated. A plausible, be it pleasing or distasteful, picture of the Colossian Religion can be reconstructed whenever three conditions have been met:

1. It must be held for certain that existing "parallels" or "affinities" in earlier, contemporary, or later documents demonstrate dependence.

2. An ingenious vision or predilection of the researcher for a certain religious or philosophical background, such as Iran or neo-Pythagorism, must be present in order to provide a running thread.

3. The scholar must possess the gift of systematic thought and a conviction that its results are applicable to historical research. Sometimes the question is taken seriously which (cultural, social, economical) need and which psychological disposition or mood influenced and determined individuals, groups, or masses which created or were allured by the religion in question.

---

28. Outstanding among many early and late attempts is still J. B. Lightfoot, *Colossians*, pp. 73–179.

Once these conditions are fulfilled, either the logical unity or the paradoxical composition of the system of beliefs and practices attacked in Colossians seems to be ready for an exact description. However, the results are of perplexing variety and often contradict one another, although there are signs of a growing consensus. A survey must suffice here.

1. At least four types of Judaism have been proposed as spiritual fathers and brothers of the Religion:

a. Just as in orthodox (rabbinic-pharisaical) *Judaism*, so in the Colossian Religion creation, revelation, tradition, knowledge (in the sense of an existential attitude of obedience, not just of intellectual insight), hope, circumcision, the sabbath played an important role.[29] But the Law and the Scriptures are neither mentioned nor explicitly quoted or interpreted in Colossians, and the asceticism mentioned in 2:21–23, including the possible prohibition of marriage, must have stemmed from other quarters.[30]

b. *Hellenistic Judaism*, especially of the type of Philo's philosophy, spoke of the mediation between the spiritual and the material realms and showed a tendency to equate the great drama of liberation with a mystery. It was concerned with the fight against fleshly passions, obeisance to liturgical rules, and the hope to ascend to the vision of God. Elements such as these form connecting links between Philo and the Colossian Religion. Cruder attempts at assimilation between diaspora Jews and their environment have been mentioned earlier.[31] But while Philo and Josephus indeed called the Pharisaical, Saddu-

29. Among most recent writers, W. Foerster, "Irrlehrer," pp. 74–76, has emphasized the connection of dietary laws, angelology, and other "shadow-" elements (cf. Col 2:17) with Old Testament traditions as they were continued or interpreted by Pharisaical Judaism. J. J. Gunther, *Opponents*, passim, has attempted to uncover the common Palestinian-Jewish background of all heresies refuted in Pauling epistles, including the Colossian Religion. Cf. fn. 33.

30. H. Hegermann, SpgM, p. 165, affirms, "in Colossae the main issue was not the law and the quest for righteousness"; while Paul meets the Galatians with the alternative, Either the Law—or Christ, in Colossians the choice has to be made between "the Head [= Christ] and the lower cosmic powers (2, 19)." Other differences between the Galatian and Colossian adversaries are mentioned by L. Goppelt, *Christentum und Judentum* (Gütensloh: Bertelsmann, 1954), p. 138–39.

31. See Section II, above, and the reference made there to M. Hengel's work. H. Hegermann, pp. 165–66, observes both, a substantial relationship and community of Paul's and Philo's stance against Mystery piety, and a harmony between Philo and the Colossian Religion concerning the function of stars and angels. For the latter, Hegermann quotes Philo *quaest in Ex* II 78, 81: *quaest in Gn* II 8; IV 9. J. Gewiess, "Die apologetische Methode des Paulus im Kampf gegen die Irrlehre von Kolossae," BibLeb 3 (1962), 258–70, believes that the Colossian "heresy" is Jewish in orientation and at the same time outfitted with Gentile astrological elements. W. L. Knox, *St. Paul and the Church of the Gentiles* (Cambridge: University Press, 1939), p. 149, judged in more general terms: "Colossae was the scene of an attempt to fit the Gospel into the

cean, Essene parties (and the Therapeutae) so many "philosophies," and while the Fourth Book of Maccabees called Judaism as a whole a philosophy,[32] they would hardly have considered and endorsed the Colossian movement as an expression of Jewish faith and worship.

c. *Sectarian Judaism* (if this term is considered meaningful at all before the formation of so-called "normative" orthodox Judaism) is represented by Qumran and apocalyptic or mystic groups. It includes features such as the following: consciousness of initiation into divine mysteries related to creation, redemption, and the end time; special respect for the guidance of angels; great concern with the festival calendar; and an ascetic discipline for those seeking perfection combined with humility. For these reasons a number of scholars explained the Colossian Religion as a derivative from, or a parallel movement to, the Therapeutae, the Essenes, or other esoteric circles.[33] Still, the conviction to

fashionable scheme of Hellenistic religion, as interpreted by circles which had a definitely Jewish character."

32. *Philo leg. ad Gaj* 156; *mut. nom.* 213; *vita contempl.* 34; *rer. div. haer* 80–82, esp. 80; Josephus *c. Ap.* I 178–82; *ant.* XVIII II (cf. XIII 171–73); *bell* II 119, 162–63; 4 Macc 1:1; 5:10, 22, 35; 7:7, 9, 21, 24; cf. LXX Dan 1:20. For Seneca *ep.* II 4, *philosophia* is a way of life. M. P. Nilsson, *Griechische Religion* II (see fn. 5), pp. 249–68 describes the "philosophy" of that period as a substitute for religion which, however, included religion and the gods. The judgment of E. Käsemann, "Kolosserbrief," RGG III (1959) 127–28, however, is too narrow; he believes that "in contemporary terminology" *philosophia* meant Mystery-Religion.

33. J. B. Lightfoot depended upon Philo and Josephus for his knowledge of the Essenes, whom he discussed extensively in order to illustrate the background of the Colossian philosophers. With some reservations, the lead given by J. B. Lightfoot, *Colossians*, pp. 73–101, is followed by, e.g., T. K. Abbott, *Colossians*, ICC, XLIX; R. Bultmann, *Theology of the New Testament* II (New York: Scribner, 1955), p. 149; W. D. Davies, "Paul and the Dead Sea Scrolls: Flesh and Spirit," in ed. K. Stendahl, *The Scrolls and the New Testament* (New York: Harper, 1957), pp. 166–70; S. Zedda, RivB 5 (1957), pp. 31–35; C. Daniel, RevQ 5 (1966), pp. 553–67; J. J. Gunther, *Opponents*. The special contribution of E. Lohse's commentary on Colossians (1971) consists in demonstrating how many elements of the description and refutation of the Colossians' "heresy" have stylistic and substantial precedents or parallels in the Dead Sea Scrolls. However, H. Braun, *Qumran and the New Testament* I, pp. 225–33, points out that despite some analogies the evidence of a decisive Qumran influence upon the Colossian heresy is "limited." W. Foerster, p. 79, concedes no more than a certain kinship with Qumran, but unlike J. B. Lightfoot and others, he will not call (Qumran) Essenism a Gnostic or proto-Gnostic movement. Additional titles and a summary information regarding Qumran influence on the letter closest related to Colossians, i.e., Ephesians, are found in AB 34, pp. 18–21, 405–6.

In his Yale dissertation, *A Re-examination of the Colossian Heresy* (1965, ref), F. O. Francis, and in his work on *St. Paul's Opponents* (1974), J. J. Gunther have drawn attention also to the impact of Jewish apocalypticism and mysticism as described by G. Scholem, *Major Trends in Jewish Mysticism* (New York: Schocken, 1946), pp. 40–79.

form a holy remnant in the critical end phase of history, the emphasis laid on thorough Scripture studies under the guidance of inspiration, the concern with the Torah and with purity, and the absence of the concepts "world-elements" and "fullness" form decisive differences between, for example, Qumran and Jewish apocalyptical circles on one hand and the teaching threatening Colossae on the other.

    d. The concepts *Gnosticizing Judaism* and/or *Jewish Gnosticism* appear to offer a patent solution to all problems. To some extent they embrace what has just been called "hellenistic" and "sectarian" Judaism. In Philo, as much as in

---

The sources from which Scholem draws for his fascinating reconstruction of Merkhaba Mysticism are very much like the Gnostic materials of the second and third centuries. There are striking resemblances consisting in the combination of humility, asceticism, entrance into the divine palace by visions, and ascent (of the soul). W. Foerster, "Irrlehrer," p. 75, points out that asceticism as a preparation for visions occurs also in, e.g., the apocalyptic book of 4 Esra. If only all those sources could be dated before or at the time of the emergence of the Colossian Religion. Then a historical dependence or common origin need no longer be put into doubt. This requirement is not fulfilled.

    Could the doctrines and practices refuted in Colossians have come from Jewish quarters and have gained influence over Christians of Jewish and pagan provenience? And was the necessary common respect of baptized Jews and Gentiles for the one root bearing both (cf. Rom 11:16) reason enough to prolong lines of *Jewish heresies?* Even if this were the case, the denotation of the Religion as offshoot of "heretical" or "heterodox" Judaism makes little sense. For not until at least thirty years after the writing of Colossians (see Section XI for a date about 61 C.E.) did Pharisaical-rabbinical teachers and liturgies begin to speak of *mînim* (heretics). Certainly the Maccabean revolt and the early Hassidic renewal, directed in the middle of the second century B.C.E. against the political, cultural, and religious Jewish assimilators of that time, offered precedents. Also the split between several Jewish parties ("philosophies") and communities at the time of Jesus were preludes to the sharp distinction between Jewish orthodoxy and heresy. Yet before the meetings of the Synods of Jamnia and Tiberias in the nineties of the first century after Christ, the split was not official.

    J. J. Gunther (see fns. 23 and 29) has added a special element to the discussion of the origin of the Gnostic Religion: the main culprit for all Christian heresies which are battled in the Pauline epistles, he finds in the *Judaism* of the Palestinian Judaeo-Christians. Gunther's thesis looks, as much as that of his predecessors and fellow-travelers, like a continuation or revival of the Church Fathers' and of later ecclesiastical anti-Judaism. It is still customary among Christian writers, and it has an appearance of scholarship to depict Jews and Jewish-influenced doctrines as chief threats and enemies of the gospel of Jesus Christ. Charlotte Klein, *Antijudaism and Christian Theology* (Philadelphia: Fortress, 1977), has collected shattering evidence of this form of anti-Semitism. But that believing and learned Jew has still to be invented who would accept responsibility for the Colossian Religion. The supposed origin and unity of the Religion on a Jewish basis may well be the result of scholarly vision and intuition. However, if this is the case, the judgment passed on visionaries in Col 2:18, 23 might be applicable. It is brief and has the wording "puffed up," and "sham wisdom."

31

the apocalyptic literature and in Qumran, traces or forerunners of the great second-century and later Gnostic systems have been discovered. Condemnation of the created earth, a dualistic worldview, the interest in good or evil powers ruling between God and man, the incorporation of Iranian and Platonic traditions, and finally novel interpretations of legal and other Scriptural passages reveal the distance of this sort of Judaism from all that looks distinctively Jewish in the sense of the orthodoxy established first after the Maccabean revolt, and then reinstituted after the destruction of the Second Temple. The explanation of the Colossian threat as a product of Jewish Gnosis has gained the upper hand in most recent literature. [34]

2. This does not mean that the presence of notoriously *pagan elements* has been or must be denied. Four of them are given special attention:

a. *Gnosis.* Since the Final Document of the Messina Conference on Gnosticism in 1966 proposed a clarification of nomenclature, it is no longer fitting to discuss a possible influence of "Gnosticism" upon the Colossian Religion or its refutation. Now (1) "Gnosticism" is the summary name describing a series of great systems of the second and later centuries, ranging from the Ophites to the Kathari to the Bogomiles and to more recent movements. In each case the first downward movement from the deity (with its catastrophic result: the origin of the present world) is counteracted by a second devolution or emanation: the coming of a revealer and of salvation through the knowledge which he conveys to those mindful of their original unity with a deity and striving for perfection. (2) "Gnosis" is an ideological concept describing confidence in the function or initiation of elect people in divine mysteries, as it is found in all cultural realms and in many periods. (3) "Pre-Gnostic" are called such themes and motifs as occur before the second century in Jewish phariseism and apocalypticism, in the Dead Sea Scrolls, and in Hellenistic quarters. (4) "Proto-Gnostic" are all Iranian, Indian, Platonic elements resembling Gnosticism in one or another aspect, but without maintaining a downward movement of the divine.

Correspondingly, a distinction is to be made between various sorts of dualism. "Dualism" may mean the assumptions that by definition the created

---

34. After J. B. Lightfoot, *Col.* (1875), pp. 3, 93, etc., had described the Essenes as an example of the Gnosticizing trend in Judaism, and H. J. Holtzmann, *Lehrbuch der historisch-kritischen Einleitung in das Neue Testament*, 1st ed. (Freiburg/Leipzig: Mohr, 1885), p. 268, had spoken more hesitantly of "Gnosticism in Judaic form," E. Lohmeyer, *Kolosser* (1930), pp. 3–8, und W. D. Davies (see fn. 33) followed their example. G. Bornkamm, "Häresie," made this solution so popular that most diverse scholars endorsed it: e.g., L. Goppelt, *Christentum und Judentum* (1954), pp. 125–43, especially pp. 137–40. W. G. Kümmel, *Introduction to the New Testament*, in FBK (Nashville: Abingdon, 1965), pp. 239–40; H. Koester, RGG III (1959) 18–20; S. L. Johnson, "Beware of Philosophies," BSac 119 (1962) 302–11; E. Yamauchi, BSac 121 (1964) 252; C. F. D. Moule, *Colossians*, p. 31.

world is bad, or that the originally good world has been spoiled by outer influences, or that there exists a metaphysical, dialectical breach between the spiritual and the material, the divine and the creaturely realms.[35]

The opponents fought in Colossians were distinguished by their enmity against (or contempt for?) the fleshly body, their striving for perfection, their pride in visions and special wisdom. Such elements do not have Jewish origins but may be called "pagan pre-" or "proto-Gnostic." Again, the veneration offered to angels and the absence of any explicit reference to the (imprisoned) soul of man signals an essential difference from the Gnosis of the type represented in the Corpus Hermeticum and from the second-century Gnostic systems.[36] Neither the classical Gnostic dualism nor a figure of a Redeemer is the dominating center or power-line in the structure of the Colossian Religion. Only confusion is generated when this religion is called a phenomenon of (Jewish or pagan) Gnosticism.

b. *Mystery Religions.* In Col 2:18 reference is made to visions that probably were connected with a ritual initiation into one or several Mystery Cults celebrated at Colossae. Humiliating exertions, abstention, fasting, even self-mutilations on an arbitrary basis (cf. 2:18, 23) could be part of those cults. Therefore the Religion of Colossae has sometimes been understood as belonging

---

35. See M. P. Nilsson, *Geschichte der griechischen Religion* II (fn. 5), pp. 581–622, especially p. 612; U. Bianchi, ed., *Origins* (1967), especially pp. XX–XXXII and 526. Cf. the titles listed in fn. 7.

36. In 1838, E. T. Mayerhoff, *Colosser* (1838), pp. 148–61, followed A. Neander's *Allgemeine Geschichte der christlichen Religion und Kirche* (1825ff.) when he identified the essence of the Colossian Religion with the teaching of the second-century Gnostic Cerinthus. F. C. Baur, *Paulus der Apostel Jesu Christi* (Stuttgart: Becker and Müller, 1845), pp. 421–26, called the constellation of powers, aeons, etc., a Gnostic feature, and discussed the affinity of Colossians to the teaching of the Valentinians. Both authors suggest a second-century date of Colossians. R. Bultmann, *Theology I* (1955), p. 133, calls the philosophy "Gnostic speculation;" cf. W. Schmithals (fn. 27).

Yet L. Mansoor, in U. Bianchi, ed., *Origins*, pp. 389–400, and W. Foerster, "Irrlehrer," pp. 76, 79, fight the notion that Qumran is to be called Gnostic or proto-Gnostic. The latter points out that some key terms of Colossians (such as "elements of the world" and "being filled") are not Gnostic. S. Pètremont, in U. Bianchi, ed., *Origins*, pp. 470–89, protests against using Colossians as evidence of an early Gnosticism. And while H.-F. Weiss, "Paulus und die Häretiker," in W. Eltester, ed., *Christentum und Gnosis*, BZNW 37 (1969) 116–28, especially 121–22, 126, readily acknowledges that second-century Gnosticism made use of a tendency in the epistle's doctrine on baptism (in Col 2:12), he denies any identity between them. M. Dibelius, *Isisweihe*, p. 66, calls the "heresy" a "germinal Christian-Gnostic formation," lacking "the pronounced dualism, the Gnostic Redeemer-figure, and therefore the Christian-Gnostic docetism." Cf. the end of fn. 187 for the names of the earliest Church Fathers who quote from Colossians in their fight *against* heresies.

in their community or neighborhood.[37] The polemics made in Colossians would in this case be a parallel to Philo's and the early Church Fathers' refutation of the pagan "Mysteries."[38]

This derivation and description need not exclude, or compete with, its Gnostic interpretation. In the current German literature on Colossians, the phrase "Gnosis in the form of a Mystery Religion" appears to express a consensus as strong as that reached upon its "Judaizing" character.[39] However, the exact meaning of the words *heoraken embateuōn* in Col 2:18 is so ambiguous, the available information on the essence of the Mystery Cults and their "theology" so scarce, the difference between some of them so great, their attestation so late, their spread in some cases so uncertain, and their collective incorporation among early Gnostic trends so dubious, that they cannot solve the riddle of the Colossian Religion.[40] Even if in Col 2:18 mystery terminology is used, this

37. M. Dibelius' *Isisweihe* (see fn. 5) is the foundation of this theory. A. Dietrich, *Eine Mithrasliturgie* (Leipzig: Teubner, 1903), had prepared the way toward a generalizing conception of the essence of "the Mystery Cults." Death and resurrection, rebirth and (divine) sonship, enlightenment and redemption, deification and immortality are considered by several scholars the key terms and topics determining all of them (cf. fn. 40).

38. Philo *cherub*, 40–52; *spec. leg.* I 319–23. See H. A. Wolfson, *Philo* I (Cambridge: University Press, 1938), pp. 36–38; H. Hegermann, *SpgM* pp. 9.47. Among the Church Fathers, Tertullian *de praesor.* is typical: the pagan mysteries are depicted as diabolic imitations of the divine.

39. Dib.-Gr., pp. 38–39; H. Hegermann, *Spg.M*, p. 161; P. Vielhauer, *Geschichte der urchristlichen Literatur* (1975), p. 194.

40. E.g., W. D. Davies, *Paul and Rabbinic Judaism*, 2d ed. (London: SPCK, 1955), p. 199, protests against R. Reitzenstein's (*Hellen. Mysterienreligionen*, pp. 169–85) simplistic conflation of Gnosis and Mystery Religions, and A. D. Nock, in his review of R. Bultmann, *Das Urchristentum im Rahmen der antiken Religionen* (Zürich: Artemis, 1949), see especially pp. 173–92), *Nuntius sodalicii neotestamentici Upsaliensis* (Lund, 1951), no. 5, pp. 35–40, is very critical of the underlying images of both the Mystery Cults and the alleged first-century Gnosticism. See also M. Hengel, *Der Sohn Gottes* (Tübingen: Mohr, 1975), pp. 45–59. Under the headline "*Synkretismus*," M. P. Nilsson, *Griechische Religion* II, pp. 581–622 and 622–701, discusses "Gnosticism" and "Mysteries" in separate sections; on pp. 685–86 he warns of fallacies in the approach to Mystery Religions.

Much of the available knowledge of the Mystery Religions is due not only to sculptures and inscriptions on unearthed altars that permit more than one interpretation, but also to early Christian writers. The latter show a tendency to select for their descriptions and polemics mainly such features as correspond to the faith and cultus of Christians. Modern authors, in turn, tend to disregard or to belittle basic differences among these religions though they were offshoots of *various* fully developed ancient cults. G. Wagner, *Pauline Baptism and the Pagan Mysteries* (Edinburgh: Oliver, 1967), has pointed out at least some of their fundamental differences. Besides, they did not flourish in the same periods. For instance, the Mythras, Cybele, and Attis Mysteries,

language does not demonstrate that indeed a mystery rite was performed by the opponents. Philo, for example, described Israel's redemption from Egypt, its sojourn in the wilderness, legislation, and entrance into the Promised Land as a mystery, and several Church Fathers interpreted the church sacraments in similar terminology. Often they do this in order to point out the *contrast* between the redemption and salvation by the God of Abraham and the Father of Jesus Christ respectively, on one hand, and the experience aimed for in Mystery Cults, on the other.[41] Though in substance the author of Colossians might well have agreed with them, the harmony of diction and intention is not sufficient evidence to prove that the Colossian opponents had formed or endorsed a Mystery Religion.

c. *Philosophy.* In a region close to Miletus and Ephesus (the birthplaces of the fathers of classical Greek philosophy, Thales and Heraclitus), the possibility cannot be excluded that a philosophical system, tainted as was commonplace in the Greco-Roman world by Eastern, such as Chaldean and Iranian, religious elements, has found an exponent in the Colossian Religion.[42]

Among the alternatives considered, preference has been given to the influence of Middle-Stoicism, as represented by Panaitius (185–110 B.C.E.?), by his pupil Poseidonius of Apamea (135–51 B.C.E.), and/or by the more rhetorical expressions of the same convictions by Cicero, Ovid, Seneca, Musonius, and Plutarch. These thinkers, each in his own way, combine the early Stoic notion of a universe headed, animated, and permeated by reason, with the appeal to consider human beings a microcosm and to make use of the free human will to master the lower elements and passions. Scholarly, psychological, physical, and historical studies were promoted and produced especially by Poseidonius.[43]

---

among them the *taurobolium*, appear to have been developed not earlier than the early third century after Christ and to have flourished only in the fourth (see J. Leipoldt, RGG, IV, 1960, pp. 1232–36, especially 1235).

41. See, e.g., Wis 14:22–23; Philo (fn. 38); idem, *deus immut.* 102–3; Justin Martyr *apol.* I 66; Tertullian *de bapt.; de praescr.* 40; Eusebius *vita Constanini* IV 61–62; Basilius of Caesarea *hom. XIII ad sanctum baptisma* 117 (MPG XXXI, pp. 223–43, 432). H. A. Wolfson, *Philo* I, pp. 36–38, 43–55; H. Hegermann (fn. 37); A. Kölping, *Sacramentum Tertullianeum* (Muenster: Aschendorff, 1948). While E. R. Goodenough, *By Light, Light: The Mystic Gospel of Hellenistic Judaism* (1935), pp. 11–47, is convinced that Philo so thoroughly endorsed the mysticism of the Mystery Religions that his teaching is no longer properly Jewish (see fn. 13), the Benedictine scholar O. Casel, "Liturgie als Mysterienfeier," *Ecclesia Orans* 9 (1923) 1–44; idem, *Das christliche Kultmysterium* (Regensburg: Gregorius, 1948), used the shadow/reality relationship intimated in Col 2:17 to declare the Mysteries as forerunners of a worship that reached its culmination in the cultus of the church.

42. In the C. F. D. Moule FS *Christ and the Spirit*, Miss M. D. Hooker has reopened the discussion of this aspect.

43. See M. Pohlenz, *Die Stoa* (Göttingen: Vandenhoeck, 1948), pp. 141–238; M. P.

Indeed, references are made in Colossians to the opponents' concern with the cosmos and all things (also to one deity at their head?), to the powers of the heavens and the elements of the world, and to the responsibility and capability of wise men to take proper (religious and ethical and scientific?) action against the perishable material body and its devious desires. Thus, a Stoic worldview, anthropology, and ethics may have influenced the Religion decisively.[44]

A Philosophical alternative is offered by the Pythagorean School(s). If the Colossian opponents were an offshoot of the Essenes, and if Josephus (*ant.* XV 371) was right in declaring the Essenes followers of the "way of life taught to the Greeks by Pythagoras," a connection could not be disputed. But because between about 300 and 60 B.C.E. nothing is known of the existence of a school or community of Pythagoras, it is unlikely that in this period Essenes or Therapeutes were influenced by them. Around the middle of the first century B.C.E., a revival of this almost distinct philosophy occurred, under the impetus of migrant preachers, among them miracle-doers like Appollonius of Tyana. Some claimed secret inside-knowledge of their divine master's doctrine. The neo-Pythagoreans' reliance on traditions which were derived from, or attributed to, Pythagoras; their conviction that mediation between the opposed heavenly and earthly realms is necessary, though evil *and* good powers may be operative in the earthly elements; finally, their quest for purity resemble tenets held by the Colossian opponents. A connecting bond between Pythagoreans and these Colossians may also have consisted of their common belief in a correspondence between macrocosm and microcosm, for example, between the large wild world and the tiny human beings. Those initiated were convinced that there existed an analogy between two pairs discernible in the universe as well as in human existence: just as the elements (stars) forming the upper world are related and opposed to the elements (fire, air, water, earth) of the lower world (with ether as a mysterious in-between), so the forces and virtues of the soul stand opposite weakness and vices of the mortal body. Although the affinities linking the Religion of Colossae to neo-Pythagorean teachings are closer than the links with the Essenes, the meaning of the term "elements of the world" in Col 2:8, 20 is still too obscure to permit more than a stimulating guess.[45]

Nilsson, *Griechische Religion* II, pp. 262–68. A crisp description of the "Stoic heresy" is found in, e.g., Epiphanius, *adv. haer.* I 5:1–3 (vid. I 12).

44. Above all, D. J. Dupont, *Gnosis* (Louvain and Paris: Nouvelaarts, 1949), pp. 419–93, etc., had drawn attention to the Stoic and Old Testament, rather than Gnostic, terms and thoughts that dominate the Pauline writings, including Ephesians and Colossians. C. B. Caird, *Paul's Letters from Prison* (1976), p. 164, prefers the uncertain theory that the Religion was "an amalgam of Stoic and Jewish ideas and practices," to "any loose talk about Gnosticism."

45. A neo-Pythagorean connection is discussed and rejected by J. B. Lightfoot, *Col.*, pp. 143–47; tentatively suggested again by E. Percy, PKE, p. 143; and reinforced by E. Schweizer, "Zur neuerer Forschung am Kolosserbrief" (since 1970), *Theologische Be-*

d. *Astrology, Magic, and Mysticism.* The concept "elements of the world" may designate stars. Certainly the festival calendar, especially the new-moon celebration (Col 2:16), is related to heavenly bodies; the mention of "shadow" in 2:17 (cf. Jas 1:17) may supplement the argument that astronomical research and astrological convictions and practices, perhaps combined with the notion of a merciless necessity and fate, were essential in the Colossian Religion. Magical performances are suggested by the possible references to the handling of physical elements, to the relevance of traditional formulae, to the cultic manipulation of demonic or angelic powers, and to the contemptuous attitude toward and harmful treatment of man's (soul and) body, as described in 2:8, 18, 20–23.[46] Finally the visions mentioned in 2:18, perhaps also the ascetic exercises destined for the mortification of the self (2:20–23), and the references in the nonpolemical parts of Colossians to perfection and fulfillment point to an underlying mysticism.[47]

There has been no dearth of brave efforts to define the origin and character of the Colossian movement—whenever it is placed into one or another pigeonhole under the Hellenistic religious and philosophical canopy. The wider the

---

richte 5 (Einsiedeln, 1976), pp. 163–89; especially pp. 174–79; idem, *Kolosser*, p. 104; idem, "Christianity of the Circumcised and Judaism of the Uncircumcised," in *Jews, Greeks and Christians*, FS for W. D. Davies (Leiden: Brill, 1976), pp. 245–60. Schweizer affirms that the first-century B.C. report of Diogenes Laertius VIII 24–33 on the neo-Pythagoreans (in Loeb's Classical Library, Diogenes Laertius II 341–49) contains "all" characteristics (except the Sabbath) of the Colossian heresy, especially the elements of the world, the ascent of the soul out of the present evil into the glorious upper world, dietary and sexual abstention, and the worship of angels. However, the text quoted by Schweizer does not mention angel worship; it indicates no more than worship of the Sun, of the Moon, of the Stars, and (in the afternoon) of the Heroes. In turn, Col 2:16–23 does not explicitly mention an ascent or transmigration of the soul and the flight out of this world. Further, Col 2 uses neither the numbers most important among the Pythagoreans (among them above all the figure 7), nor the "harmony" which is an essential element in Pythagoreanism of all periods. Finally, as will be shown in the interpretation of Col 2:8, 20, the terms "elements (of the world)" may have different meanings here and there.

Similar critical observations might be made in regard to J. Lähnemann's (*KolB*, pp. 93–94) references to Dio Chrysostomos' (ca. 40–120 after Christ) *oratio* 36. This text may illustrate how some Persian religious and Greek philosophical ideas could coalesce in a "philosophical worship of elements," but it does not demonstrate that the Colossian Religion derived from the same combination, for the identification of its "elements" with its "angels" is far from certain.

46. For a digest on the vast literature on astrology and magic in the Hellenistic period, see M. P. Nilsson, *Griechische Religion* II, pp. 268–81, 446–543.

47. See AB 34, pp. 385–88 and 419–20, for a discussion of the definition of mysticism and its influence upon some parts of the New Testament, also for a bibliography.

sources used and the information covered and exploited, the smaller becomes the willingness simply to equate the Colossian phenomenon with any one of the various Jewish and pagan options.

In rare instances the opinion is expressed that the Colossian Religion was a movement in its own right that cannot be subsumed among any of the known names and systems.[48] Still, without reference to the syncretistic history and nature of diaspora Judaism and of the philosophies and religions traceable in Asia Minor, it can hardly be described at all. In consequence, the Colossian Religion is considered a result of syncretism in which Jewish *and* pagan, philosophical *and* religious, scientific *and* superstitious theories and exercise are combined, compounded, mixed, or fused. Together with the names of deities, of religions, of philosophies or, instead, of fixation upon such names, summary abstract concepts, either alone or in various combinations are used, among them: Judaism, Hellenism, monotheism, syncretism, dualism, gnosticism, legalism, ritualism, asceticism, speculation, individualism, escapism.[49]

Some scholars select *one* of the terms used in Colossians in order to subordinate to it all phenomena of the Religion. The selection of a key-term permits them the reconstruction of a coherent, almost logical system. The cultus of element-angels (?), the quest after fulfillment and perfection by the divine fullness, and the search for a solution of the world's and life's great mysteries (for example, anxiety, death, and fate) in cultic experience and in the pangs of ascetic actions—these are among the preferred options. Others discern a dual, that is, a theoretical and a practical, aspect of the impugned philosophy: a paradoxical combination of Hellenistic-philosophical Gnosis and Jewish-ethical practice,[50] which forced the apostle to conduct a war on two fronts at the same time. A distinction of *three* or more constitutive elements separates (1) the theology of the Colossian Religion from (2) its doctrine on mediating agents in creation and redemption, and (3) the belief in the efficiency of cultic perfor-

---

48. See, e.g., J. Lähnemann, *KolB*, pp. 100–1.

49. A convenient survey of forty-four (!) identifications of the Colossian and other "heresies" is found at the beginning, and an enumeration of the prominent heretical elements amalgamated in Colossae at the end of J. J. Gunther's *St. Paul's Opponents*, pp. 3–4 and 314. According to this author, the quality and the impact of a movement appear to be determined by the *number* of doctrinal errors combined in it. In consequence, the Colossian "philosophy" would surpass the inherent wickedness and the actual threat of the heresies fought in the Galatian, Corinthian, Philippian, and other New Testament letters. Gunther's method of gauging religious doctrines and forms of worship and conduct is, perhaps, useful for (outdated) heresy trials. In such a trial, E. E. Ellis would probably contradict Gunther's testimony; for Ellis states (in the FS for M. Smith I, 1975, p. 296), "The Colossian situation is much less extreme [than the Galatian];" the "potentially dangerous errors [of Colossae]" deserve no more than "relatively mild admonitions."

50. Cf. E. Lohmeyer, *Kolosser*, pp. 6–8.

mances. Or cosmology, soteriology, and eschatology are placed side by side. Both the methods used and the results obtained so far can hardly be considered foolproof and final. In view of the ambiguity, multiplicity, and the various, sometimes late, dates of the sources, controversy about conclusions is inevitable. If in the Galatian heresy, for example, selected Jewish statutes played a major role, and if in the first two chapters of Hebrews a teaching is distinctly refuted that placed Christ among or under angelic powers, this does not prove that the same views prevailed in Colossae. Parallels, however numerous and astonishing, prove neither dependence nor identity. The distinction, enumeration, and comparison of single and combined words, ideas, and cultic performances may not be a suitable way to trace the root, and to describe the essence and vitality, of a movement. History of religion cannot be written solely on the ground of anatomical exercises and of the comparison of cuts and fragments. A living religion is greater than the sum of its parts; and its understanding calls for empathy and love for the believers rather than for a knife, an adding machine, and suitable labels. The definition of a religion by quoting historical names and by incorporating individual phenomena in timeless *-isms*, and the distinction of theory and practice, of theology and liturgics, or of cosmology and soteriology, etc., reveals more of the surgical skill and the synthetic gifts of Western scholars than of the character and faith of a religious group.[51]

As a consequence, the Colossian Religion remains an unsolved puzzle. While the available facts are insufficient to settle the issue, the only way to explain the subject is by close examination of every scrap of information provided by the text of the epistle. Barring the discovery of new pertinent data from outside sources, that remains the best procedure.

Or might there still be another access to the mysteries of this religion?

C. Modern Analogies

G. Bornkamm considers J. W. Goethe "the last, in any case probably the greatest, representative of the Colossian heresy."[52] W. Bieder describes the Colossian philosophy as an example of man-made religion which gives glory to man and enslaves him simultaneously, in contrast to the liberating faith in Christ.[53] J. A. Stewart sees in the Colossian opponents representatives of unethical mysticism and unmythical ethics as they are rampant even in today's

51. As M. D. Hooker in the FS for C. F. D. Moule, p. 327, observes.
52. G. Bornkamm, "Häresie," p. 156; cf. idem, "Ein Glaubensbekenntnis des alten Goethe," in idem, *Geschichte und Glaube* II (Munich: Kaiser, 1871), pp. 248–60. The reason given is Goethe's enthusiastic applause of the Hypsisterian sect in which Jewish, Asia Minor, Chaldean-astrological, and Persian (following Goethe, also Christian) elements were intertwined and mixed.
53. W. Bieder, "Die kolossische Irrlehre und die Kirche von heute," *Theologische Studien* 33 (Zürich, 1952), especially pp. 20–31.

churches.[54] E. Schweizer explains the philosophy as a product of the anxiety (*Angst*) caused by the powers of fate and expressed in psychic aggression and depression; people who consider forgiveness alone too small a comfort are attracted by it. The same author also states that the thoughts of P. Teilhard de Chardin seem to have a biblical foundation in Col 1:15–20, as long as the hymn contained in this text is not taken from the hands of the Colossian adversaries and corrected by interpolation and by its context 1:12–14, 21–23.[55] M. D. Hooker mentions the modern superstition and fatalism demonstrated by the role of horoscopes in the newspapers. K. Wengst, finally, unmasks the same religion as an ideology, formed to support the contemporary political, social, and economical ruling classes.[56]

Most, if not all, of these alleged modern anti-types of the Colossian prototype look fanciful. The underlying assumption that a modern man is, consciously or not, involved in the Colossian "heresy" can contribute to an actualization of the epistle. Certainly it would be stimulating and rewarding to evaluate P. Teilhard de Chardin's work in relation to the epistle. Is he, or where and when is he,

54. J. A. Stewart, "A First Century Heresy," SJT 23 (1970) 420–36, especially 435.

55. The presupposition of E. Schweizer, *Kolosser*, especially pp. 129–30, 217–21, may well be the existentialist interpretation of (Gnostic) mythology by, e.g., H. Jonas, *Gnosis und spätantiker Geist* I–II 1 (Göttingen: Vandenhoeck, 1954); idem, *The Gnostic Religion* (Boston: Beacon, 2d ed. 1963), pp. 320–40. This understanding of Gnosticism has been radically criticized by, e.g., A. D. Nock, in his review of H. Jonas' first-mentioned work in Gnomon 12 (1936) 605–12.

Reference to P. Teilhard de Chardin's possible affinity to the Colossian Religion is made by Schweizer, *Kolosser*, pp. 202–4, 216; idem, "Heil im Neuen Testament," *Kirchenblatt für die reformierte Schweiz* 130 (1974) 130–33, especially 132. More frequently, however, the question is posed whether or how the refutation of the Colossian heresy moves on lines similar to the cosmic Christology of Teilhard de Chardin. A. Feuillet, *Le Christ Sagesse de Dieu* (Paris: Gabalda, 1966; in the following: *Christ Sagesse*), pp. 243, fn. 1, 376–85, attempts to endorse Teilhard de Chardin, but expresses grave reservations. N. Kehl, *Der Christushymnus im Kolosserbrief* (Stuttgart: Katholisches Verlagswerk, 1967), pp. 25–26, 165, moves in the direction which also A. Vögtle, *Das Neue Testament und die Zukunft des Kosmos* (Düsseldorf: Natmos, 1969), pp. 12–13, 104–7, 213–20; has chosen: Colossians must be understood to speak only of *man's* salvation and of the eschatological *church*: the cosmological terminology of the letter has ultimately (only!) anthropological and ecclesiastical meaning. Thus, the salvation and the future of the world vanish from the agenda of theology.

56. M. D. Hooker in FS for C. F. D. Moule, p. 323. K. Wengst "Versöhnung und Befreiung," EvTh 36 (1976), 14–26, especially 15–17. In analogy, W. Klein, "Die antizipierte Entideologisierung," ZKTh 96 (1974) 185–214, sees in the fight against the world elements a rebuttal of *all* ideologized and absolutized creaturely spiritual forces. Perhaps he would include Socialism. C. F. D. Moule, *Colossians*, p. 159, is more reticent: he reminds the readers of present-day claims on wisdom, as made by "Christian Science" and "Theosophy."

nearer the Colossian Religion than its apostolic refutation? Still, this commentary has to deal primarily with the historical and literary problems of the epistle, not with its application to modern issues.

V. THE STRUCTURE, CHARACTER, AND PURPOSE OF COLOSSIANS

A. *The Structure*

The questions as to whether this epistle has a perspicuous logical structure at all, and what this structure eventually may be, are answered in various ways among the recent scholarly students of Colossians.[57] It may be appropriate to

---

57. W. Bujard, *Stilanalytische Untersuchungen zum Kolosserbrief*, SUNT II (Göttingen: Vandenhoeck, 1973; in the following: *Stil*), pp. 117–21, 153–59, 225–29, follows E. T. Mayerhoff, *Colosser*, p. 43, in affirming that Colossians as a whole has parenetical (hortatory, not dogmatic) character and style, and that its logical coherence is just as loose as that of the parenetical parts of the *homologoumena*. According to this view, a clearly structured systematic part, as it follows in most *homologoumena* upon the introductory thanksgiving, is missing in this letter. In his summary, Bujard speaks of a composition of sentences and greater units that is determined by loose word- or thought-associations, improvisations, arbitrariness, detours. He compares the author of Colossians to a man jumping haphazardly from one floe to another on an ice-covered stream (pp. 234–35). The absence of conjunctions and other words indicating a logical relationship (p. 53) and of sharp antithetical comparisons (pp. 111–15) is considered sufficient evidence to demonstrate the absence of sharp logical thinking—and to exclude Paul as an author (pp. 119–20). Similar is the opinion of C. R. Bowen, "The Original Form of Paul's Letter to the Colossians," JBL 43 (1924) 177–206, esp. 196, 198.

E. Lohse, *Colossians*, pp. 89–90, however, observes that "Colossians has a thoroughly unified structure from the point of view of form as well as that of content." On p. 3, he distinguishes together with, e.g., Dib.-Gr., p. 40; FBK, pp. 237–38; H. Conzelmann, *Die kleineren Briefe des Apostels Paulus*, NTD 8, 10th ed (Göttingen: Vandenhoeck, 1965), p. 130; E. Grässer, ZThK 64 (1967) 146; H. Ludwig, *Verfasser*, pp. 52–135, especially pp. 55–56, 133–34, a first great doctrinal and systematic part (chaps. 1–2) from a second parenetical half of the epistle (chaps. 3–4). These scholars see no reason to complain of a poor logic and structure of thought in Colossians. According to E. Lohmeyer, *Kolosser*, pp. 9–10, 15, too, Colossians has two main parts—but their length is less balanced. "Almost completely missing is the piece called in Romans and Galatians the theoretical part"; instead, there is an extended Introitus (1:1–29), followed by the (single) main part which deals with "Questions Related to the Congregation" (2:1–4:6), and by the Exit (4:7–18). F. Zeilinger, *Erstgeborene*, pp. 33–73, especially pp. 36–39, 72–73, discerns four topical discourses: (a) Christ and the Apostle, (b) Christ against the Heretics, (c) Consequences for the Unity of the Church (= parenesis), and (d) Personal Informations, centered in the utterances of Epaphras.

A much more artistic view of the structure is suggested by J. Lähnemann's *KolB*,

distinguish four main parts between the opening and the concluding verses of
Col 1:1–2 and 4:18. Both the frame and the main substance of parts I and IV of
the core of this epistle closely resemble other Pauline and NT letters. However,
the main parts II and III of Colossians are to a large extent unparalleled.

I	1:3–11	Thanksgiving and Intercession for the Spread of the Gospel and the Spiritual Growth of the Congregation
II	1:12–2:5	Hymnic and Didactic Praise of God, Christ, and the Apostolic Ministry, for the Reconciliation of All Things and Persons Through the Blood of Christ
III	2:6–3:4	In Opposition to Man-made Religion, Proclamation of Perfection and Life in Christ Alone
IV	3:5–4:17	General and Special Calls for True Worship and Participation in the Mission of the Church

The demarcations among these four parts are somewhat fluid: part I may
include 1:12–14; II may conclude with 2:3, or extend to 2:7; III may end with
2:23 so that IV begins with 3:1.

In "Colossians and Ephesians" (Section IX.B.3 below), the surprising
parallels and difference between the structure of these epistles will be pointed
out. The subdivisions of the main parts will be staked out in the commentary.

B. The Character and Literary Genus

Divergent ways have been chosen to describe the *Gattung* of the letter to
the Colossians. This epistle has been understood as a refutation, an apology, a
dialogue, and a pastoral essay. Because the third part of Colossians contains
sharp polemics against the Religion, and because at least implicitly the surrounding parts lay open the confessional ground and unfold the moral consequences of the rebuttal, the whole epistle appears to be conceived as a

---

pp. 58–62, who distinguishes three concentric circles: (a) the outer ring, consisting of
the opening and the conclusion (1:1–2; 4:7–18), (b) the middle circle unfolding the
doctrine of Christ and ethics (1:3–2:5; 3:1–4:6), and (c) the core: the polemic against the
philosophy (2:6–23). This form of structure can be described as a chiasm or ring
composition as it frequently occurs in poetic passages inside and outside the Bible. The
passage Col 2:6–23 is now no longer a dispensable excursus, digression, application, or
appendix in Colossians, but forms the core of this epistle. If further labors confirm the
presence of a chiastic or ring composition, their results might eventually contribute new
criteria to discover so-called interpolations or omissions in the text of Colossians, and
several earlier announced results might appear in a dim light. See also fn. 178 for
chiasms discovered in some subsections of Colossians, and fn. 65 for Lähnemann's
description of the logical structure found within small units.

refutation.[58] Indeed, in its dealing with the Religion of Colossae, the letter anticipates what in later centuries became a widespread type of literature. *Ketzerpolemik* is the avowed purpose of Irenaeus' "Against the Heresies," Tertullian's "Against Marcion" and *De Praescriptione*, and Hippolytus' "Refutation of All Heretics," for example. But if the earlier observation saying that the Colossian opponents probably were not Christians is valid, then the letter is not directed against "heretics" but against a menace coming from outside the church. Certainly there are no traces in this letter that would justify the vilification of heretics, not to speak of the heresy trials conducted in the church at later times.[59]

With the second-century and later "Apologies," the epistle shares the explicit anti-pagan polemic, including, at every more or less fitting occasion, the method of caricature and ridicule of the opponent, and of the insertion of preformulated ecclesiastical confessions and ethical counsels for the benefit of Christian readers.[60] But the absence of rationalistic arguments, above all of reasoning on the basis of natural religion (or of revelation in nature), of the "paradoxological" nature of miracles, and of the antiquity of the (Sinai-etc.) tradition, also the majesty, simplicity, and centrality of the testimony to Christ crucified and risen—all of this prohibits inclusion of Colossians in that *Gattung*.

The epistle differs widely also from dialogue literature,[61] ranging from Plato's dialogues to Justin Martyr's "Dialogue with the Jew Trypho," for example. Although it contains traces of entering and taking up (however critically) the opponents' language, questions, arguments, and affirmations, the opponent is not permitted to defend his cause. If the adversaries had claimed support from the Old Testament texts and their Jewish interpretations, the author would hardly have argued without explicit references to the Scripture and some literal

---

58. H. Ludwig, *Der Verfasser* (1974, see fn. 17), pp. 90–107, presupposes that there is a fixed *Gattung der Irrlehrerpolemik*.

59. For a description how, primarily in the ancient church of Rome, the demarcation line between orthodoxy and heresy was eventually drawn, see W. Bauer, *Orthodoxy and Heresy* (1972), chaps. V–X. P. Vielhauer, *Geschichte*, pp. 200–1, calls Colossians "not a real letter but a polemic pamphlet [*Kampfschrift*] in epistolary form" which makes shrewd use of pseudoepigraphic tricks.

60. B. Lindars, *New Testament Apologetic* (Philadelphia: Westminster, 1962), and J. Gewiess (see fn. 31), BibLeb 3 (1962), describe the Pauline polemic under the title "Apologetic." According to Gewiess, Paul's apologetics is unlike Origenes' against Celsus: the apostle does not attack his opponents directly, but seeks to build up the faith of the believer in a loving way: only indirectly (2:4, 8, 14–15, 22) does he engage in polemics. An opposite view of Colossians is represented, for instance, by GNT which, by means of English titles inserted between various sections of the Greek text, conveys the impression that this document has only an affirmative message to communicate.

61. E.g., J. Lähnemann, *KolB*, p. 63, speaks of a dialogue (*Gespräch*) between the writer and the readers.

or allegorical counter expositions (as they are found in Eph 2:13–19; 4:8–10; 5:30–32). Certainly it cannot be excluded that the author intended to engage in some sort of indirect dialogue with the "philosophers" of Colossae. But was he as willing, as some partners in the Dialogues of Plato, eventually to learn from, and to be changed by, the opinions of his adversaries? He does not directly address the creators or promotion of the "philosophy," but only the Christians tempted by that religion. If he possessed any openness and willingness to accept elements or angles of the Religion, his readiness was hidden under a rough shell.

While it is possible in the form of a letter to write and publish what in reality is a tract, essay, or treatise, in the case of Colossians the letter form is not just a matter of style, and therefore hardly a fiction. The opening section, the discourse on the very special suffering and commission of Paul among the gentiles, and the conclusion are both most personal *and* most closely related to the central hymnic and doctrinal parts of Colossians. The letter should be taken at face value: it is a pastoral confession and exhortation designed to meet the need of a congregation in acute danger. This document combines features of a personal letter with those of an official epistle.[62] Just as the canonical Gospels and the Acts of the Apostles are literature of their own kind, so are several New Testament epistles, and among them Colossians in particular, because it does not in abstract and timeless fashion discuss school opinions or battle Christian heretics, but meets a dangerous situation of unique kind.

C. The Purpose

The danger of this religion is met by means stronger than only explicit polemics and warnings. In this letter, confession, information, reflection, indoctrination, and exhortation are combined, and all are grounded upon Jesus Christ's unique dignity, work, and presence. Formulae, confessions, hymns are quoted or alluded to, and patterns of moral advice are used. It cannot be demonstrated that they have been artificially "Christianized"; on the contrary, it is obvious that in the form they have taken in Colossians, they make no sense whatsoever without their one center: Jesus Christ. The traditional materials incorporated in the letter most likely were known to the saints in Colossae, or else they would hardly have possessed evidential value. Formulations used in worship elsewhere could have been known and adopted in the Colossian church through Epaphras, the Colossian, and/or through other traveling aids of the apostle, through direct contact of other individuals or delegates with churches in the Asia Minor neighborhood, perhaps also through communication with

---

62. Cf. the Note on Col 1:1; for instances in nonbiblical literature see H. Kosken-niemi, *Studien zur Idee und Phraseologie des griechischen Briefes bis 400 n.C.* (Ann. Acad. Scientif. Fennicae, B 102:2, Helsinki 1956), pp. 201–5, cf. 91, maintains that there is no way to distinguish sharply between private and public letters.

the congregations in Syrian Antioch, Ephesus, and Jerusalem. In all these liturgical materials, and in great variation, Jesus Christ was praised as crucified and raised from the dead, as Lord over heaven and earth, good and evil, soul and body (cf. Phil 2:6–11; Heb 1:1–4; 1 Tim 3:16; Rev 1:4–6; 5:9–10, etc.).

By collection, interpretation, and accentuation of traditional materials, and by original contributions of his own which far exceed the work of a second-rate compiler or redactor, the author of Colossians has produced a document that depicts Jesus Christ as the beloved Son and total revelation of God, as redeemer who in eternity holds the whole created world (including the invisible powers) in his hand, as the mediator of forgiveness, reconciliation, and peace, and as guarantor of eternal and master of daily life. The writer intends to show that Jesus Christ triumphs over and outrules the complicated ways recommended or imposed by the Religion. Because positive affirmations outshine ironical and negative statements, the letter is a challenge to enjoy the freedom and peace brought into the world.

The way Colossians speaks of the reconciliation of all things, not just of humankind, is unique in the whole New Testament. This letter has particular substance and function which defy accommodation and subjugation to the contents and power of other parts of the Bible. The Old Testament contains many intimations regarding the cosmic rule of God and of the king whom he appoints, and in the New Testament, hints going in the direction of the Colossians' particularity are contained in the miracle and resurrection stories of the Gospels and Acts, in texts such as Rom 8 and Phil 2 among the undisputed Pauline letters, and especially in the book of Revelation. But a full-fledged "cosmic Christology" is developed only in Colossians and, although in less provocative form, in Ephesians.

Neither the enthusiastic Yes said to Jesus Christ nor the sarcastic No flung at the teachings and techniques of the adversaries permits the inclusion of this letter among those "elements" and "statutes" by which the opponents sought to catch and to fetter the saints. Intended is a reminder of the gospel of Jesus Christ, not the imposition of a law. The good news about the universal ruler and peacemaker, as proclaimed by hymns and preached by the apostle, is meant to supersede the dread of evil and the worship of good powers that make themselves felt between heaven and earth, their invisibility notwithstanding. Voluntarily borne suffering in Christ's service and the renunciation of vicious kinds of behavior replace trust in the saving value of self-castigation. Perhaps the opponents subscribed to a demonized worldview; certainly the epistle negates the divine character of the principalities and powers, and thereby de-demonizes the universe, including the human body. To the multiplicity of mysteries or to the mysterious initiation into the divine realm is opposed the one mystery of Christ. There is no longer a timeless tension between above and below, between spirit and matter, whereby miserable humanity is crushed and ground to dust. On the contrary, events have taken place in history, and certified proclamation has gone out which places human existence on a solid ground and gives it a sure hope. The positive statements of Colossians are distinguished by their radical Christocentricity on the one hand and their total application to the daily life of struggling humans on the other. All that is not related to Christ, or that fails to recognize his present rule over all, his uniqueness, and his sufficiency, is depicted as an anachronism. What was "once," "in the past," is valid no longer in the light of the "but now," the new aeon which has begun with Jesus Christ (Col 1:21, 26; 2:8–15; 3:7–8).[63]

Although the Colossian opponents, unlike the adversaries refuted in Galatians and Second Corinthians, appear neither to have attacked Paul personally, nor to have discredited his or his disciple(s)' teaching,[64] the letter contains reactions of a very personal character. It stresses the suffering apostle's authority, defames the opponents as puffed-up people, calls their religion a deception, and ridicules it on all levels (1:24–2:8; 2:16–23).

While interpreters of Colossians agree on summaries of this kind, their opinions vary in the presentation and evaluation of important details. One school maintains that the polemic is restricted to rash apotropaic gestures which, perhaps, reveal a partial misunderstanding of the opponents' Gnosis.[65] According to another, the epistle anticipates that "early-Catholic" buildup of the tradition of the church, of confessional formulae, of the apostolate, of the clergy, and of baptism, which (eventually enriched by the emphasis laid upon the monarchic episcopate and the privileges of other clergy) gained the upper hand in the epistles to Timothy and Titus, finally in 1st Clement and in the Ignatian Letters.[66] Widespread is, further, the opinion that the author of

---

63. As especially J. Lähnemann, KolB, pp. 52, 122–23, 129, 133–34 has pointed out: the many extras cultivated by the Colossian philosophers have an alternative "only in Christ" (p. 114). J. A. Stewart, SJT 23 (1970), 424, formulates the basic issue similarly: "Is Christ the whole of Christianity, or is he not?" According to C. F. D. Moule (Colossians, p. 163), "Christianity is Christ." Most of all, Col 1:15–22; 2:6–9, 11, 14–15, 17, 20; 3:1–4; 4:3–4 support this understanding. A description of the message of Colossians, gained by comparison with Ephesians, is offered below, in Section XI.B–C.

64. Only if it could be demonstrated that the "philosophers" had spoken of something "lacking in Christ," and that they explicitly disputed the "head"-ship of Christ (cf. Col 1:24; 2:19), would it be reasonable to presume that such an attack had occurred (cf. fn. 22, toward the end).

65. Initiated by E. T. Mayerhoff, Colosser (1838), pp. 33–34, and continued by E. Lohmeyer, Kolosser, pp. 3 and 100, this view was broadly unfolded by W. Bujard, Stil (1973). P. Vielhauer, Geschichte, p. 202, however, asserts that despite the occurrence of "some forceful invectives," the author's method of arguing is "to the point" (sachlich), and J. Lähnemann, KolB, p. 135, etc., discerns, at the side or under the cover of the main arguments, the polemic forms of (a) critical information, (b) positive response, and (c) blunt caricature, or summary conclusion.

66. In the wake of F. C. Baur and R. Bultmann (see the first pages of Section X,

Colossians, in trying to contradict his opponents, fell more or less victim to their teachings, foremost to their speculative cosmic notions and their dualistic Gnosticism.[67] Again, a more subtle judgment is passed when the possibility is left open that, just as the church discovered what it had to confess in struggling

below) the view is upheld by, e.g., E. Käsemann, "An Early Christian Baptismal Liturgy," in idem, *Essays in New Testament Themes*, SBT 41 (Naperville, Ill.: Allenson, 1964), pp. 149–64; W. Marxsen, *Introduction to the New Testament* (Oxford: Blackwells, 1968), p. 180. According to F. Zeilinger, *Erstgeborene* (1974), pp. 74, 137–77, etc., the core of the counterargument against the Religion is contained in the "baptismal theology" of Colossians.

67. Taking up an idea first expressed by F. C. Baur, M. Albertz, *Die Botschaft des Neuen Testaments* I 2 (Zollikon/Zurich: Evangelischer Verlag, 1952), p. 164, coined the phrase "anti-Gnostic Gnosticism" and declared the author of Colossians guilty of pursuing such a paradoxical goal. W. Schmithals, "Zur Herkunft der gnostischen Elemente in der Sprache des Paulus," in U. Bianchi, ed., *Gnosis*, FS für H. Jonas (Goettingen: Vandenhoeck, 1978), pp. 385–415, assumes that the (pseudonymous) author of Colossians became "to the Gnostics a Gnostic." E. Lohmeyer, *Kol*, p. 11, negates direct Iranian influence upon Paul, but affirms that "by way of Judaism" elements of Iranian cosmology and soteriology did reach the apostle. Dib.-Gr., p. 53, believes that the same Paul who was a Jew to the Jews and an outsider of the Law to those outside the Law in order to win people on both sides (1 Cor 9:19–23) became also "a Gnostic to the Gnostics" in order to convince them of his cause—though the present form of Colossians contains even more accommodations to Gnosticism that the apostle himself would have made. In a new variation the same charge is raised against Colossians by, e.g., E. Grässer, "Kol. 3, 1–4 als Beispiel einer Interpretation secundum homines recipientes," ZThK 64 (1967), 139–68, especially 152. H. M. Schenke, "Der Widerstreit gnostischer und kirchlicher Christologie im Spiegel des Kolosserbriefes," ZKTh 61 (1964), maintains that the author of Colossians was influenced by Gnostic Christology (p. 399), but sees in "the Christian-Jewish monotheism" and in the "faith in creation" saving features which did not permit the dualistic elements of the Gnostic Christology to become rampant; thus, one Christology struggles with another, with the result that the writer of Colossians, while he does not "actually fall prey to Gnosticism," yet represents a "moderate form of Gnosis" (pp. 402–3). W. Marxsen, *Einleitung in das Neue Testament*, 2d ed. (Gütersloh: Mohn, 1964), p. 158, is convinced that the author of Colossians did not really overcome the heresy, but advanced to no more than its (literally) "Christianizing usurpation" (Engl. trans., *Introduction to the NT*, Oxford: Blackwell, 1966, p. 183: "only takes it over and christianizes it"). H. Weiss, "Paulus und die Häretiker," represents a much more qualified view (see fn. 36), and similarly J. Gewiess (see fn. 31) affirms that the author of Colossians moves only to the brink of Gnosis, not into second-century Gnosticism. But S. Schulz, *Die Mitte der Schrift* (Stuttgart: Kreuz, 1976), pp. 91–93, returns to a more radical judgment: as the first member in the chain that leads within the NT Canon) on to Ephesians, to Second Thessalonians, to the Pastoral Epistles, and finally to the Acts of the Apostles, this epistle to the Colossians intends to fight Gnosticism. The means employed for this purpose is the confession of the congregation, guaranteed by apostolic authority (not by the justification doctrine based upon the cross of Christ). The author (working in Ephesus at about 80 c.e.) is all

47

against errors, so also the apostle had new questions posed and new horizons opened by the ideology and activity of the opponents.[68] Indeed, the designation of the Colossian adversaries' statutes as "shadow of the things to come" (2:17) expresses rejection. Yet it differs from the anathemata (curses) and strictures flung against the opposition in Galatia, Corinth, and Philippi.[69] In the verse-by-verse interpretation, special attention will be given to the fact that a rectified version of all that is rejected is included in the reconciliation of all things proclaimed in this epistle. However, before details of substance can be further examined, some urgent literary and formal problems require discussion.

VI. THE TEXT OF THE EPISTLE

"The various readings in this epistle are more perplexing than perhaps in any portion of St. Paul's Epistles of the same length."[70] "Of all the letters attributed to Paul, his letter to the Colossians contains proportionately the greatest number of textual problems."[71] These statements may overshoot the

---

the more "himself substantially influenced by Gnosticism." Much less prejudiced and complicated is H. von Soden's opinion (*Kolosserbrief*, 1891, p. 14): "Gnosticising inclinations of the authors [are] by no means demonstrated."

68. T. K. Abbott, *Colossians*, p. LVII; J. Lähnemann, *KolB*, pp. 114–15, etc.

69. Gal 1:6–9; 2:21; 5:12; 1 Cor 16:22; Phil 3:2. The character and style of meeting the opposition in Colossians does not seem to fit into any of the attitudes represented in the NT, regarding the relation between the gospel and pagan religion(s). G. Haufe, "Evangelium und Religion nach dem Neuen Testament," in Wiss. Zs. der Ernst-Moritz-Arndt-Universität Greifswald 24 (1975), 195–99, discerns four forms, each with its own limitations: (1) enthusiastic negation, approaching a dualistic worldview, and renouncing the attempt to take the opponent seriously (1 Cor 8:4; cf. Isa 41:23–29; Ps. 115:4–8), (2) demonological interpretation which could hardly convince those addressed (1 Cor 8:5; 10:14–21), (3) apocalyptic indictment, referring to the revelation of God (universal in creation and final in Jesus Christ), and lacking respect for the depth of Greek thinkers (1 Cor 1:21; Rom 1:18–32), and (4) apologetical search for contact, using pagan writings as a substitute for the OT and aiming at rational enlightenment about God's nature rather than at faith in Jesus Christ (Acts 17:22–31). Haufe suggests that ultimately types 3 and 4 are complementary, not mutually exclusive. A critical discussion of his typology appears necessary, but does not belong at this place.

70. J. B. Lightfoot, *Colossians*, p. 315. On pp. 312–22 the problems of Col 1:3–4, 7, 12, 14, 22; 2:2, 16, 18, 23; 3:16; 4:8, 15 receive intensive treatment.

71. B. M. Metzger, *The Text of the New Testament* (Oxford and Cambridge: University Press, 1964), p. 439. However, in his *Textual Commentary on the Greek New Testament* (London and New York: United Bible Societies, 1971), pp. 619–27, the same author discusses no more than the average number of variant readings in Pauline passages of the same length.

mark because the Pauline Letters have a common textual history and the transmission of Colossians in the various papyri, codices, and other sources bristles with the same idiosyncrasies as the textual tradition of the other letters. Some papyri and codices, minuscules, and patristic quotations, as well as the ancient versions, present a shorter, often more perplexing and difficult text, while others, by expanding the wording, are smoothing out, clarifying, or adapting to similar texts whatever appears rough in grammar, diverse from other letters, or dark and ambiguous in substance.[72] Terseness stands in contrast to verbosity, the unique in contrast to the typical in other Pauline letters; perhaps also the subtle opposes the simplistic, and the obscure is enlightened by the plain. The huge majority of textual variants moves back and forth between these alternatives. The per-page number and extent of variant readings offered in the Greek New Testament editions of Nestlé-Aland and GNT are about the same as in the other epistles.[73] However, there is a series of contradictions between the text represented by certain groups of manuscripts, sometimes of only a handful, against the great majority. These differences pose serious problems for both the translation and the exposition of the text.

Selected cases will subsequently be offered in which it becomes clear where the most important manuscripts contain divergencies touching upon substance. The concentration upon a selection bears the risk of subjectively influenced choices because it focuses primarily upon themes of theological relevance. Through the application of this method it can hardly be claimed that a significant contribution to the history of the text of Colossians is being made; nevertheless, at least some of the most important problems facing readers and expositors of this letter can be laid bare.[74]

---

72. In, e.g., Col 1:22, Papyrus 46, the codices Vaticanus, Boernerianus, and others have different passive forms of "reconciled." One of these forms corresponds to proper syntax, the other produces an *anakolouthon*. Both mean that God rather than Christ in the reconciler; cf. 2 Cor 5:18–20.

73. The text-critical data mentioned in the following, as well as the whole of this commentary, are based upon the 26th ed. of Nestlé-Aland (1979) and the 4th ed. of GNT (1980). According to R. V. G. Tasker, *The Greek New Testament* (Oxford and Cambridge: University Press, 1964), the NEB translators had to make major controversial decisions in their handling of the text of Colossians no more frequently than in the cases of other texts of the same length.

74. For the collection, comparison, and evaluation of the material here presented, two former assistants at Basel University, David MacLaghlan and Hans Rapp, have done extensive and intensive preparatory work.

The Greek text of the NT, as it is available today in print, is the result of the labor of generations of scholars who at first studied, compared, and collated only a few, finally over five thousand Greek manuscripts, and in addition, made use of the evidence of primary and secondary early versions, also of patristic and liturgical quotations of the biblical texts. In the latest printed editions, the Greek text of Colossians is derived from

COLOSSIANS

1. God Father, the Lord, and Christ. When references are made to "God Father" in 1:3, 12 and 3:17, in each case a different group of manuscripts has

the comparison mainly of the following thirty-seven MSS that are considered today as most important or interesting:

P⁴⁶ = Papyrus 46 (dated about 200 c.e.); P⁶¹ (around 700); B = Codex Vaticanus (4th c.); S = Cod. Sinaiticus (4th c., usually denoted by the Hebrew letter Aleph); A = Alexandrinus (5th c.); C = Ephraimi rescriptus (5th c.); I = Freerianus (5th c.); D = Claromontanus (6th c.); H = Euthalianus (6th c.); Psi = Athos Laurensis (8th or 9th c.); F = Augiensis (9th c.); G = Boernerianus (9th c.); the three majuscules 048 (5th c.); 0198 (6th c.); 0208 (6th c.). In the next rank: K = Mosquensis (9th c.); L = Angelicus (9th c.); P = Porphyrianus (9th c.) and the minuscules 33 (9th c.); 81 (11th c.); 104 (11th c.); 365 (13th c.); 630 (14th c.); 1175 (11th c.); 1241 (12th c.); 1506 (14th c.); 1739 (10th c.); 1881 (14th c.); 2464 (10th c.) and 2495 (14th or 15th c.). Finally, also 6; 323; 326; 424; 614; 629; 945.

In the Greek NT editions published before Nestlé 26th and GNT 4th ed., it was presupposed that among the Greek manuscripts, early versions, etc., at least three (if not four or five) text types (or groups or families) could be clearly discerned. The first was called "Alexandrian" (or "Hesychian," sometimes denoted by a Gothic letter H). A selected minority of manuscripts from this group was often considered the "best" among all existing ancient NT texts and was given the honorary title "neutral." The second type was named "Western"—it forms no more than a small minority, but some of its readings are exciting or suspect because they deviate drastically from the huge majority. The third group is labeled "Antiochian" (or Byzantine, or Koine, denoted by the siglum Byz or a Gothic K). It establishes the great crowd of textual witnesses. Among the manuscripts and early versions containing the whole or parts of Colossians, the Alexandrian group is represented by P⁴⁶ S B A C 33 and others; the Western by D d G g (also E e F f), the Old Latin and Old Syriac versions, and several Italian and African Fathers; the Antiochian by the codices K L and the vast Majority of the existing minuscules. On the basis of this grouping of manuscripts an often-followed criterion for selecting one among several competing readings of a word, phrase, or sentence was this: the best is that variant which is supported by the majority of text types rather than of individual manuscripts.

The two recent NT editions appear to drop the distinction between the mentioned text groups, especially the idea of a "Western" type and the summary contempt manifested for the Byzantine family. Nestlé and GNT now replace the relatively fixed earlier criterion of selection by a seemingly eclectic and certainly more elastic method which is named "local-genealogical." Decisions for a given reading are now made from one instance to another, based upon external and internal criteria—that is, depending upon geographical spread and logical priority. The best reading proposed after the application of this method to the text of Colossians differs in eight cases (1:3, 1:27, 2:12, 3:4, 3:6, 3:11, 3:22) from the 25th ed. of Nestlé. Its 26th ed. and GNT 4th ed. use the Gothic letter M, in the following reproduced by the letters Mjr, to designate a novel (and for each part of the NT different) group. Mjr is constituted for Colossians by all of the thirty-seven manuscripts mentioned above (unless specifically indicated by the editors) and by those not named in that list but containing the text of the Colossian passage in question (cf. the lists in Nestlé 26th ed., pp. 14*–15* and 684ff.). The methods and sigla employed in those editions are the most advanced and perhaps the best tools available

"God [the] Father."[75] Since invariably in these verses the language has a liturgical flavor (cf. also 1:2), the divergence may show inclination for, or reticence about, deviation from familiar (local?) parlance. On the other hand, these readings may reflect only a concern for clarity of expression. When God *and* Christ, God *or* Christ, or "the Lord" are mentioned in 1:2; 2:2; 3:13, 15, 16, 17, 22; 4:3, there occur not only (just as in all Pauline epistles) the varieties of composition and sequence of "Jesus," "Christ," and "Lord" with or without article but also distinct preferences for mentioning God or Christ, or for connecting both.

The most striking example is 2:2, where the words rendered in our translation "secret of God: of Christ" have no less than fourteen competing readings. Some have only "of God" or "of Christ;" others combine both by explanatory

---

today in Greek NT prints not exceeding 1000 pages. They are adopted in the following. However, in order to maintain contact with the far-from-outmoded earlier text-critical procedures used primarily in the Anglo-Saxon realm, and in order to enable owners of earlier Greek NT editions to check the evidence offered, the siglum Byz and references to the Alexandrian and Western text types have been retained. Since, in fact, Mjr corresponds in most cases to Byz, it will be mentioned in parentheses.

The sigla used, except for designating individual codices, are: P with a number always means Papyrus, min = one minuscle, mins = a plurality of them. The original script is indicated by an asterisk (* placed after the siglum of a codex), an exponent [1] or [2] or [3] indicates the hand of the first, second, or third correctors of a manuscript when such distinctions are possible; otherwise it is simply noted with an exponent [c] when an alteration of the text is due to a corrector.

Old Latin versions are represented by "it," the Vulgate by "vg" (vg[ms] stands for a single manuscript and vg[mss] for more than one manuscript, vg[cl] for the Clementine edition, Rome 1592). Agreement of "vg" with part of "it" is expressed by "lat," with all of "it" by "latt." The Syriac versions are represented by "sy." Since the "Old Syriac" Versions, i.e. the Syro-Sinaiticus and the Syro-Curetonianus from the last quarter of the second century after Christ, do not contain the Pauline Epistles, in this commentary "sy" stands mainly for the Peshitta (fifth century) and for the Harclean version (seventh century). The + sign signals words added; the − sign indicates words missing in the reading of the manuscript in question. An exponent [vid] means "apparently."

The manuscripts P[46] and B, and also S* and 1739 (in some instances, especially when their testimony is supported by lat), may well be the best textual witnesses for Colossians, that is, standing closest to the autograph of the biblical author. Yet even when their readings agree, they cannot automatically be placed above other witnesses—for reasons to be shown, later, in the commentary. In the cases where Nestlé and GNT do not have variant readings listed in this section of the Introduction, or later, either C. R. Gregory, *Canon and Text of the New Testament* (New York: Scribner, 1907), pp. 207–8, or the Beuron edition of the *Vetus Latina* XXIV 2 (Freiburg: Herder, 1969–71), pp. 311–520, or references made in commentaries such J. B. Lightfoot's and T. K. Abbott's were used. An *editio major* of Nestlé 26th ed. is in preparation.

75. Cf. AB 34, pp. 71–72, for variations of the phrase and of its appositions "of ours," "of our Lord," etc.

additions such as "of God which is Christ," "of God which concerns Christ," "of God who is in Christ Jesus," "of God and Christ," "of God (and) the Father of (our Lord) Christ (Jesus)."[76] Since the secret was kept hidden and finally was revealed by God, and since in 1:27; 2:3; 4:3[77] the substance of the secret is plainly identified with Christ, the text offered by a minority (P[46] B vg[mss], supported by Hilary, Pelagius, and Pseudo-Jerome, for example, by representatives of the so-called "neutral" text, *and* by "Western Fathers"—also by Clement of Alexandria; cf. 2:23) probably deserves preference. Only this reading can account for the emergence of the several variants; it appears to be the *lectio originalis* because all other readings look like explanatory derivations.

In 3:13, "the Lord" or "Christ" or "God," or "God in Christ" has forgiven; in 3:15, the "peace of Christ" or the "peace of God" shall arbitrate; in 3:16, the "word of Christ" or "of the Lord" or "of God" is mentioned; in the same verse, praises are to be sung to God or to the Lord; in 3:17, all is to be said and done in the name "of the Lord Jesus" or "of the Lord Jesus Christ" or "of Jesus Christ;" finally in 3:22 "the Lord" or "God" is to be feared.

Since in each case of the variants (especially of those selected from Col 3), different manuscripts, in association with these or with other manuscripts, contain a given reading, there is no indication of a fixed preference for distinguishing or identifying God and Christ, for the selection of the title Lord (for God *or* for Christ) in early or late, Eastern or Western text groups, or in individual papyri and codices such as P[46] and S, B, and A. The early (second-century) and the classical (fourth-, fifth-, and sixth-century) Christological controversies which might have influenced the choice of wording in texts bespeaking the divinity of Jesus Christ have apparently left no traces in the textual variants of the mentioned verses in Col 2–4. Unlike those modern Bible commentators who sometimes (see, for example, R. Bultmann on John 3:5, and the exposition of Col 1:15–20 below) decry as interpolations words of the Bible that do not suit their views of historic development or their dogmatic inclinations, the ancient copyists of Colossians appear to have reproduced with reverence the letters before them, without engaging in willful or tendentious manipulations of the descriptions of God and of Jesus Christ. A doctrinal tendency is, however, clearly recognizable in the insertion or omission of "not" in 2:18, in the context of sketching a feature of the Religion (see below under 3b).

---

76. See B. M. Metzger, *Text* (see fn. 71), pp. 236–37. Since nine out of a total of fifteen variants are found in ancient versions, and one only in a Church Father, GNT 1st ed. had good reason to offer only eleven and Nestlé 26th ed. only eight. Corresponding, though less rich in variations, is the textual tradition of the words "church of God" (". . . of the Lord," ". . . of the Lord and God") in Acts 20:28.

77. In 4:3, codex B*, together with a few other manuscripts, has "secret of God," all others "secret of Christ."

2. *Biography.* (a) In the text version of Col 1:7 offered by P[46] S* A B D* F G mins 326* 2495, Epaphras is a servant of Christ on behalf of the apostle (and of Timothy, cf. 1:1?); but he is servant of Christ for the benefit of the Colossians or representing them before Paul in S[2] C D[2] Psi mins 33 1739 and at least sixteen others. (b) The purpose of Tychicus' assignment is to bring news about Paul to the Colossians (4:8), but according to P[46] S[2] C D[1] Psi Byz (Mjr) some lat sy, Tychicus is to bring a report of the Colossians to Paul. (c) Also in 4:8, following S*, the Colossians are to learn about themselves (!) through this messenger. But the explicit and textually uncontradicted context of 4:7 (cf. Eph 6:21–22), "Tychicus will make known to you all about my affairs," recommends the reading of P[46] A B D*, etc., more than the variant version "your affairs." The Colossians are to be given information about Paul. (d) In 4:15 the name "Nympha(s)" is treated (according to the gender of the personal pronoun used in the same verse) as a woman's name by B 6 1739 1881, as a man's name by D F G Psi Byz (Mjr) some lat sy, and as a couple's name in S A C P 33 etc.: the church meets in "her," in "his," or in "their" house. A pro- or anti-feminine stance is hardly to be culled from, or constructed to be, the reason for these differences. (e) After 4:18 K L and others have the subscript "written to the Colossians from Rome (and to be delivered) through Tychicus and Onesimus." S B C D and others have "to the Colossians." A B[1] P have "written (—A) to the Colossians from Rome."

3. *Description of the Religion.* (a) In their rendition of 2:12, P[46] S[2] B D* F G and some mins latt speak of a "washing" *(baptismos)* in which the saints are buried with Christ. Perhaps this unusual name for baptism contains an allusion to purification rites performed in the frame of the Religion (similar, for example, to Qumran usage), although no other verse of Colossians refers to such rituals among the opponents. But the majority of manuscripts use the specifically Christian form: baptism is denoted by *baptisma*. Nestlé, twenty-sixth edition, considers "baptismos" as the more original reading. (b) In 2:18 S[2] C D[2] F G Psi Byz (Mjr) lat sy read "he has *not* seen a vision when he was initiated." This denial of visions experienced by the adversaries stands in opposition to the reading of (more recommendable) other witnesses that affirm the boasting about of visions among the adherents of the Religion. (c) In the last part of 2:23 (unlike the testimony of the other MSS) P[46] B 1739 it and vg[mss] may indicate by the omission of "and" before "harsh treatment" that the bodily discipline was the essence of, not an accessory to, that "arbitrary religion" and "mental [so F G it] humility" which were considered necessary for the achievement of high spiritual goals (for example, of visions). Still, the epistle does not explicitly establish a causal connection between the negation of the flesh and the purification of the perfection of the spirit.

4. *Personal and Relative Pronouns.* In their use of pronouns at least five times, in 1:7,12; 2:13; 3:4; 4:8, important individual manuscripts or groups of

them are at variance.[78] Some read "us . . . our," others have "you . . . your." The first and the last of the five instances have been mentioned under no. 2: they concern biographical matters. In 1:12; 2:13; 3:4, only the form, not the substance, of the utterance is varied: one group reproduces the liturgical (hymnical or confessional) "we" and "our," the other has the proclamatory (or hortatory) "you" and "your."

Colossians almost overflows with relative clauses of hymnic-doxological or logical-explanatory character. Sometimes ancient manuscripts disagree in the tradition of the pronoun opening these clauses. (a) In 1:27 some texts have (literally) "the secret who is Christ," others ". . . which is Christ." (b) Equally in 3:14 one group has after "love" the neuter, another the masculine, a third the feminine pronoun. In all cases, what looked to one group like poor grammar and syntax was by the other favored as a (grammatically correct) attraction of the relative pronoun. (c) Misreadings or, again, varying judgments of proper grammar may be at the root of the singular or plural relative pronouns chosen in 2:17 and 3:6. (d) In 2:2 only D*, one ninth-century Old Latin version, and some vg^{mss} as well as Pelagius and Augustine support the substitution of "the secret of God which is Christ" for the reading of P[46] and B vg^{mss} ". . . of God: of Christ." (e) Most puzzling is the minority reading "which is the head" replacing "who is the head" in 2:10. Did the minority group of manuscripts follow a tradition which said that in the fullness of the divinity (rather than in Christ) the Colossians were fulfilled, and that the fullness is the head? Or was a fragment of the liturgical text (describing Christ, not the fullness) interpolated into Colossians at some stage of the composition of Colossians, even to the detriment of correct grammar?

At any rate, no traces are visible of a stable course chosen by a given number, character, or group of manuscripts which would prefer masculine or neuter, singular or plural pronouns in hymnic or didactic relative clauses.

5. *Short Forms.* In a majority of cases, the shortest text of the epistle is found in P[46] and B.[79] Rather frequently, although rarely in matters of brevity,

---

78. It is found in P[46] B D F G but contradicts the text of the corrected P[46] and of S A C Psi, Mjr, and part of the old Latins.

79. Exceptions in which (the) "best" manuscripts contain a more extended text include 1:12 (P[46] 1175: + "and" before "give thanks;" P[46] B: + "at the same time" after "give thanks;" B: + "who called us and" before "who gave us the title;" the other manuscripts have either "gave us the title" or "called us," but never a combination of both. At this place B seems to make a compromise, as if tired of preceding battles); 1:18 (P[46] B 1739 and other mins: + article before *arche* [in our translation: "source"]); 1:20 (P[46] S A C D^1 Psi 048 [Mjr] sy, in this case against B D* F G I L 1739 and other mins latt: "through him" is repeated [in our translation the repetition is rendered by "alone"]); 2:2 (S and others: + "father" after "God"); 2:7 (B D2 H Byz [Mjr]) it sy: + "in which [faith' " after "abundantly," and S^2 d* it vg^{cl}: + "in him [= Christ];" 3:16 (P[46] S^2 B D* and others: + article before "grace").

these two manuscripts contain traditions that are also reflected in S* and/or in S* and min 1739.

Short forms of the text include the following substantial differences from longer formulations: (a) In 3:15, P⁴⁶ B 6 1739 1881 read "in [a, or your?] body" instead of "in one body." (b) Regarding 2:2, see #4(d) above. (c) In 3:5, P⁴⁶ F G omit "evil" before "desire;" indeed, in Stoic literature, "evil" is dispensable, but since in the Pauline letters "desire" does not always have a bad connotation, the specifications found in the other manuscripts are not superfluous. (d) In 3:22, P⁴⁶ and a few mins do not contain the words: (obey) "in every regard;" thus the stricture given to the slaves is less absolute. (e) In the same verse, P⁴⁶ A B D F G and others have the singular, not the plural, expression for "putting on a show"; the difference between total attitude and individual acts may be at stake (cf. the difference between "sin" and "sins"). [80] (f) After 4:18, P⁴⁶ and a few mins have no subscript; indeed, the addition of a subscript to this and other letters is most likely the contribution of a post-Pauline collector's or editor's, not from the author's hand.

6. *Long Forms.* Among the prominent manuscripts, in the majority of cases (but not, for example, in Col 3:4 where A and some mins omit "with him") S D A C G present a longer text. Also the Byz group with their vast following among the mins has many expansions. Not just stylistic, but contextual questions are raised by the various readings offered in the passages which were listed under #5 and also in Col 1:23, for example (S² D² Psi Byz [Mjr], etc., have "of the whole creation" instead of "of all creation"); 2:2 (A C H 33 81 have "the whole riches" instead of "all the riches"); 2:7 (S² D* it vg^cl sy add "in him" after "abundantly"); 3:8 (F G it vg^mss "shall not proceed"); in reproducing 3:18–19, D* F G L it sy or/and a great number of mins add "your" or "your own" to the nouns "husbands" and/or "wives." The personal pronouns do not change the meaning but underline the obvious: the commandments of subordination and love pertain only to those joined by marriage, not to the general relationships between adult males and females; 3:23 (A has "as such who serve the Lord," instead of "for the Lord"); 4:3 (A adds "in *parrhesia*" [freedom of speech, boldness] before "to tell the secret"); 4:18 (S² D Psi Byz [Mjr] lat sy: + Amen).

7. *Apparent adaptations* of the text of Colossians *to the wording of Ephesians* serve more often to emphasize given points than to change the substance. They are found in 1:2 cf. Eph 1:2 (S A C F G I P Byz (Mjr) it vg^cl sy: + "and

---

80. Short formulations of perhaps trivial character include 1:4 (B: − "which you fostered"), 1:9 (B K vg^ms: − "and to ask"); 1:18 (P⁴⁶ S* 2495* Irenaeus: − "from" before "the dead," resulting in "[the first-born] *of* the dead"); 1:27 (P⁴⁶: − "the glory of"); 2:15 (P⁴⁶ B vg^ms: + *kai* [even, also, and] before "he exposed them"); 2:23 (P⁴⁶ B 1739 it vg^mss: − *kai* before "harsh treatment"); 3:12 (B 6 33 + *kai* before "beloved"); 3:23 (P⁴⁶ B 1739: − *kai* before "not for men").

from the Lord Jesus Christ"); in 1:4 cf. Eph 1:15 (D² Psi Byz [Mjr]: "love for all the saints," instead of "love which you have for all the saints"); in 1:14 cf. Eph 1:7 (a few mins and versions add "through his blood" after "freedom"); in 1:26 cf. Eph 3:5 (G adds "apostles" after "saints," so as to read "holy apostles"); in 3:6 cf. Eph 5:6 (S A C D¹ F G I Psi Byz [Mjr] lat sy insert "upon the rebellious" after "wrath of God"); in 3:8 cf. Eph 4:29 (F G it vg^mss: + [from your mouth] "it shall not proceed"); in 3:21 cf. Eph 6:4 (A C D* F G L 33 1739) and many other mins have "irritate" instead of "provoke to quarrel").

8. *Other Peculiarities.* In the title of Colossians (cf. Col 1:2), P⁴⁶ B A I K and many others have *Kolassaeis* (Colassians in Engl. tr.), reproducing a spelling customary no earlier than the third century after Christ. Further variants include 1:14 (B: "we have seized [or accepted, taken hold of] freedom," instead of the familiar "we possess . . . ," cf. Eph 1:7⁸¹); 1:14 (D*:—"the forgiveness"); 1:22 (S A and others: "through *his* death"); 1:23 (A: "herald and apostle and servant," instead of "servant" or "herald and apostle"); 2:10 (S*: "head of the whole government [or source, or beginning?] of the church"; D*: "head of every church," instead of "head of every government and authority"); 2:15 (G: "stripped the flesh," instead of "stripped the governments and authorities"); 3:8 (G: "in every regard," instead of "all these things"); 3:11 (D* F G 629 it vg^mss have "male and female" before "Greek and Jew." In Gal 3:28 "male and female" follow after "Jew and Greek"); 3:13 (F G: "wrath" [*orgēn*] instead of "reason to complain" [*momphēn*]); 3:14 (D* F G it vg^mss: "bond of unity" [cf. Eph 4:3,13], instead of "bond of perfection"); 4:13 (D² Psi Byz [Mjr] sy: "has much zeal," instead of "labors hard").

None or few of these variants may look dramatic at first sight. However, all of them express early church attempts at understanding or interpreting the text of Colossians. The variants are a first commentary which must hold priority over all expository notes and comments added at later times. In the exposition of individual verses it will become clear that sometimes decisions in favor of one of the extant text forms remain tentative. Textual criticism imposes upon the expositor a burden of humility. Since he does not hold in his hands a text standing beyond any question and doubt, he cannot claim infallibility either for traditional interpretations or for the exposition he offers.

VII. VOCABULARY AND STYLE

In many instances the vocabulary and the diction of Colossians share in the peculiarities of the language of Ephesians.⁸² Some nineteenth- and twentieth-

81. The obvious error contained in AB 34, *Ephesians 1*, 83 fn. 42, must be corrected: the Greek form *eschomen* is (second)aorist, not future.

82. See AB 34, pp. 4–6. To the literature there mentioned is to be added A. van Roon, *The Authenticity of Ephesians*, NovtSup 39 (Leiden: Brill, 1974), pp. 110–212.

century books on Colossians make decisions on authenticity or spuriousness primarily on the basis of word statistics.[83] This method may have its merits but also suffers from oversimplication of difficult issues and all too rashly drawn conclusions. Recent philological research begins to provide evidence that an author need not be tied down to only a single vocabulary and one sole form of diction. Charles Muller, an expert in modern linguistics, is probably right in affirming that there are too many lacunae in our knowledge of the mechanism of language and speech to permit fruitful attempts at the solution of questions of the date and author of given documents.[84] His warning has to be kept in mind.

A comparison between the vocabulary, diction, and logic of Colossians and the language of other Pauline letters need not be prejudiced by fixed assumptions regarding the spuriousness of Ephesians, Second Thessalonians (the whole or parts of First and Second Timothy, and of Titus), and the authenticity of Romans, First and Second Corinthians, Galatians, Philippians, First Thessalonians, and Philemon. For the sake of convenience, the seven last-mentioned "undisputed" letters will be treated as a unit under the name *homologoumena* in the following discussion. Only linguistic observations will be made to avoid, as far as possible, the intrusion of circular arguments.

The vocabulary of Colossians contains forty-eight words that do not occur in the other Pauline letters; thirty-four of them are not used in the rest of the New Testament (such as, "to make peace," "philosophy," "to be arbiter," 1:20; 2:8, 23; 3:15). Almost half of these *hapax-legomena* are found in the polemical part of Colossians. Many, if not all, of them are most likely picked up from the vocabulary of the opposed religious movement, or they are coined to describe or to caricature it. The rest are almost equally divided between the intercessory and liturgical first part, and the hortatory and ministerial last half of the letter. In these sections the strange vocabulary occurs more often in passages taken up from tradition, than in those freely formulated by the author. Just as in the case of Ephesians, the number of *hapax-legomena* corresponds proportionally to their number in Romans, Galatians, and Philippians, for example. Each author has a reservoir of words at his disposal out of which he uses only a selection for particular purposes. Remembrance of formulations coined by others augments his vocabulary or makes him reticent to use certain terms. The need to

83. E. T. Mayerhoff, *Colosser* (1838); H. J. Holtzmann, *Kritik der Epheser- und Kolosserbriefe* (Leipzig: Engelmann, 1872), pp. 99–121; R. Morgenthaler, *Statistik* (1958), pp. 15, 17, 23–25, 28, 38–40, 44–49, 53–54, 164, 175–180; E. Lohse, *Colossians*, pp. 84–91; W. Bujard, *Still* (see fn. 57); H. Ludwig, *Verfasser* (1974), pp. 8–51.

84. C. Muller, *Initiation à la statistique linguistique* (Paris: Larouse, 1968), p. 13. W. Richter, *Exegese als literarische Wissenschaft* (Göttingen: Vandenhoeck, 1971), pp. 49–72, especially 55, pleads against the insulation of individual words from their context. His interest lies more in general questions of literary criticism than in the narrower question of authorship.

communicate with specific people may have the same double effect. The author of Colossians reveals linguistic skills, perhaps by coining some words that were new to him or to those addressed, certainly by using some terms that occur only outside, and others that appear only inside, the Septuagint.[85]

The choice of a particular vocabulary is most conspicuous whenever figurative speech is being used. Indeed, a series of picturesque images sometimes interrupts the flow of less artistic discourse and trite or pompous words. Vivid are the utterance on the flow of God's fullness upon and into Jesus Christ (1:19; 2:9), the description of Christ's death as a circumcision of humankind (2:11),[86] the interpretation of forgiveness as a destruction and crucifixion of an IOU (2:14), the picture of a victory parade which shames the vanquished (2:15), the caricature of the inflated visionary (2:18), and the biting mimicry of ascetic exercises (2:20–23). Obviously, a master of imagination and language is at work, rather than a slavish or mediocre pupil who just imitates his master's voice.

Certain words are used proportionally more often than in other Pauline epistles, or they have a sense that looks different from typically Pauline usage. Main instances are *mysterion* (secret, or mystery?), head, body, fullness, fulfill, reconcile, *oikonomia* (administration, or plan?). Such terms are singled out by interpreters as indications of the non-Pauline origin of Colossians.[87]

On the other hand, favorite Pauline nouns and verbs (with over thirty

---

85. Cf. fn. 190. Newly created words are: "make you his prey" (2:8), "(the) putting off" 2:11, 15; 3:9; (literally) "wanton religion" (in our version of 2:18: "arbitary religion"). Not used in the LXX are ten words, among them "divinity" (2:9), "bodily" (2:9), "act (3:8)." Only in the LXX is "making peace" found (Prov 10:10; but Aqu., Symm., Theod. have it also in Isa 27:5).

86. The exposition of 2:11 will be discussed below, in the Notes and Comments.

87. C. L. Mitton, *The Epistle to the Ephesians* (Oxford: Clarendon, 1951, in the following: EE), pp. 82–97, endorses and enriches arguments produced tentatively (regarding Ephesians only) by M. Goguel, *Introduction au Nouveau Testament* IV 2 (Paris: Leroux, 1926), pp. 466–67, and with full conviction by M. Dibelius, *Kolosser* (1927), pp. 63–65; cf. E. Gaugler, *Der Epheserbrief* (Zurich: EVZ, 1966), pp. 11–14. But already H. J. Holtzmann, *Kritik der Epheser-und Kolosserbriefe* (Leipzig: Engelmann, 1872), p. 59, would not know of such reasoning. Similarly, e.g., E. Percy, PKE, pp. 379–86; P. Benoit, "Corps, tête et piérôme," RB 63 (1956) 5–44, especially 37, 40–41 (repr. in idem, *Exégèse et théologie* II [Paris: du Cerf, 1961], pp. 107–53); and A. Feuillet, *Christ Sagesse*, pp. 277–319, question these arguments because in several cases they are based on prejudices. Does e.g., *oikonomiā* really mean "plan" in Ephesians, so much so that it is identified with a hidden "mystery," while in Colossians (just as in the undisputed Pauline letters) it signifies "stewardship" or "administration?" For an answer see AB 34, pp. 86–88, 127–28. Or does *sophia* (wisdom) have contradictory meanings in diverse Pauline writings? J. B. Polhill, "The Relationship Between Ephesians and Colossians," RevExp 70 (1973) 439–50, especially 443, does not question differences but observes that in closely connected verses such as 1 Cor 1:21 and 1 Cor 1:24 *sophia* has different meanings.

occurrences in the *homologumena*) are missing in the vocabulary of Colossians. Among them are righteousness, law, to reckon, to write, to boast, (the address:) brothers, children, or beloved ones. Also the less frequently used but still typically Pauline terms to justify, to believe, freedom, obedience, the cross, (Holy) Spirit, revelation, to reveal, salvation, to save, community, building, and the singular "sin" cannot be found in this epistle. Thus it is quite evident that the doctrine of justification is not the central topic of Colossians. However, since the count of missing terms is an argument from silence, it has little or no weight for the question of authenticity.[88] In the case of Colossians, absent terms are counterbalanced by the presence of about fifty of Paul's favorite words, such as the nouns love, brother, truth, apostle, glory, power, peace, church, work, gospel, world, flesh, grace, and the verbs to die, to live, to greet, to admonish.[89]

Regarding less weighty words (articles, pronouns, prepositions, conjunctions), the following observations may be relevant:

1. *Additions* to New Testament, especially to Pauline, vocabulary: (a) among the New Testament writings only Revelation and Ephesians surpass the Colossian ratio of the occurrence of *articles* per hundred words; (b) the *emphatic "he" (autos)* is often used in acclamations; then it means "*he is the one who.*" Only in the Gospels, Acts, and the Johannine Epistles is the proportion of occurrences even greater than in Colossians; (c) at the end of sentences, at least

---

88. No one would dare to dispute the genuineness of First Thessalonians and First Corinthians because in the totality of their twenty-one chapters the word "righteousness" is used but once (in 1 Cor 1:30). "To justify" does not occur in First and Second Thessalonians, Second Corinthians, and Philippians. "The Cross," though it holds a central position in the theology of Paul, is missing from both Thessalonian letters, and also from Second Corinthians (but "to crucify" occurs in 13:4), Romans, and First and Second Thessalonians: There is no references to "salvation" in First Corinthians and Galatians, or to "saving" in Galatians and Philippians. Lacking is the address "brothers" between Rom 1:13 and 7:1, and in Second Corinthians it occurs only in 1:8; 8:1; 13:11; this means, Paul has occasionally written five or six successive chapters (more than the four chapters of Colossians!) without using this rhetorical device. Finally, the terms "to boast" and "to reckon" seem to be indispensable in Paul's theology; but the first is prominent only in Second Corinthians, the second only in Romans and Galatians. Therefore, the absence from Colossians of the terms mentioned proves nothing.

89. When the number of all the nouns and verbs used in Colossians is counted, the resulting ratio is 166:137, i.e., about six to five in favor of the nouns. The overall ratio of nouns and verbs in the New Testament as a whole, and in Second Corinthians, Romans, Philippians, Philemon in particular, is about 1:1. But Ephesians surpasses Colossians with a ratio of 3:2; and Galatians forms the opposite extreme with a relationship of about 2:3 (see R. Morgenthaler, *Statistik*, p. 164). In speech and script, preponderance of nouns over verbs often has an unequivocal effect: at the expense of fluent and/or dramatic style, the diction becomes descriptive, formal, ponderous. Still, there are exceptions: at various occasions and in several parts of a written composition or a speech, the same author can use nouns and verbs in most diverse ratios.

seven times, a statement is specified by the *addition of "in"*, followed by an abstract word or by the name of Christ, such as "in truth," "in the spirit," "in the light," "in power" (1:6, 8, 9, 12, 29, etc.; in our translation these appendices are sometimes freely rendered); the verbs to walk, to build upon, and to fill are connected with "in Christ" in 2:6–7, 10; (d) *relative clauses*, introduced by "who is," "which is," etc., are appended for various purposes[90]; (e) after the relative pronoun, after the conjunction "just as," and/or before personal pronouns, Colossians often has a puzzling *kai* (and, also, even); (f) in this context belongs the frequent use (thirty-nine times) of *pās*, which is matched only in Ephesians and Philippians; the singular of this word often denotes "each" and the article and/or the plural signal the meanings "the whole" or "all [persons or things]"; surprisingly frequent is, however, the connection of *pās* with an abstract, such as with wisdom (1:28; 3:16; and understanding, 1:9), good pleasure (1:10), power, endurance, and patience (1:11), fullness (1:19, with article) riches (2:2; var. lect.: with article); the pleonastic *pās* is found only in the first two parts of the epistle; its meaning is quantitative and/or qualitative, and in many cases it poses serious problems to a smooth translation (see Comment III on Col 1:3–11).

2. *New Testament*, especially favorite Pauline connecting *words not used*: (a) the occurrences of the conjunction *de* (but, and, that is) with which Galatians and First Corinthians bristle, stand in Colossians (and Ephesians) far below the Pauline average; the same is true of the emphatic "but" *(alla)*; (b) missing are several *conjunctions*, such as "for," "therefore," "because," and other words indicating a *logical* connection such as "much more," "not only–but also," "either-or," "neither"; among the occurrences of "if," no use is made of "if not," "if someone," "even if," "if indeed"—but some of these are absent also from several *homologoumena*; (c) the sharp negation "far be it," which elsewhere is characteristic of direct polemics, is absent from Colossians; (d) when an

---

90. The Greek concordance of C. H. Bruder (Leipzig: Bredt, 1867), pp. 250–54, lists sixteen occurrences. Three groups can be distinguished: (1) doxological use in Col 1:15, (18?), 27; 2:3, 10; 3:1; also 2:2 var. lect.; (2) explanatory use in 1:18 (?), 24; 2:3, 17, 22, 23; 3:5, 14 (cf. 20); (3) biographical use in 1:7; 4:9. Though less frequently, Ephesians also is inclined to employ similar relative clauses: there are four doxological and three explanatory occurrences, while in the sixty-four chapters of the letters to the Thessalonians, Corinthians, Galatians, Romans, Philippians, and Philemon, only eighteen cases occur, mostly of the doxological type. Whether some of these appended clauses have to be considered marginal notes made by readers of the manuscripts and erroneously incorporated into the original text by well-meaning copyists cannot be decided on the ground of a modern reader's conviction or feeling regarding the style proper to the author. Only manuscript evidence, i.e., the increase of relative clauses in variant readings of ever later manuscripts, would confirm the interpolation theory—in fact, it fails to do so. On the other hand, the author himself may, on second reading of his work, have made additions.

infinitive of purpose is (loosely) joined to a (preposition and) statement, the article is, contrary to customary Pauline usage, omitted.

Considering the weakness of arguments from silence, no further examples of this sort need to be added.

3. *Stylistic Features.* The increased or reduced vocabulary influences the style. Samples taken especially from the first chapter of Colossians may serve to illustrate this fact: (a) *repetitions:* "praying," "hearing," "fruit-bearing," "growing," etc., in vv 4–6 and 9–11; cf. the triple repetition of "each man" in v 28[91]; (b) *synonyms* or closely related terms, combined by "and" or in blunt juxtaposition, are often found: "bear fruit and grow" (vv 6 and 10), "faith . . . and love . . . through hope" (vv 4–5), "hear and come to know" (v 6), "praying and asking" (v 9), "Spiritual wisdom and understanding" (v 9), "freedom, the forgiveness of sins" (v 14), cf. "his body, the church" (v 18), (literally) "holy and blameless and beyond reproach" (v 22), (literally) "founded and firm and not moved" (v 23), "ages and generations" (v 26); (c) cognation (use of cognates) is a well-liked rhetorical means, and is employed not solely for sound effect: (literally) "empowered with power" (v 11); cf. (literally) "energy that gives energy" (v 29); "circumcised with a circumcision" (2:11) etc.; (d) *genitive appositions:* (literally) "of the word of the truth of the gospel" (1:5); "a share of the saints' allotment" (v 12); (literally) "the kingdom of the son of his love" (v 13); cf. (literally) "the blood of the cross of his" (v 20); (literally) "riches of fullness of understanding (2:2); (e) *infinitive appositions:* (literally) "so that you walk" (v 10); cf. "to present you" (v 22), "to pay out" (v 25); (f) *participle apposition:* (literally) "having heard," "having also revealed," "having made

---

91. Examples of other repetitions in Colossians are collected by E. T. Mayerhoff, *Colosser*, pp. 45–49; H. J. Holtzmann, *Kritik*, pp. 121–30; H. Hegermann, *SpgM*, p. 167; W. Bujard, *Stil*, pp. 86–100; and others. To be mentioned are: hope and gospel (Col 1:5 and 23); thanking the Father (1:3 and 12); (in the past) but now (1:21–22 and 26); in the flesh (2:1 and 5); not judge and not disqualify (2:16 and 18); thanksgiving (3:15 and 17); recommendations of Tychicus and Onesimus (4:7 and 9). Some of these doublets may be neither rhetorical, nor logical, nor signs of mutual dependence of Colossians and Ephesians nor of interpolations from one letter into the other. Rather may they be intended explicatory repetitions or self-quotations of the author. In the latter category certainly belong the characterizations of Epaphras and Tychicus (Col 1:7 and 4:7); the references to the (literally) "first-born of all creation" who "exists before all things" (1:15 and 17); to heaven and earth (1:16 and 20); to principalities and powers (1:16 and 2:15); and to the whole world and all creation under heaven (1:6 and 23). Repetitive is also the mention of fullness in him (1:19 and 2:10); filled in him, consummated in God's will (2:10 and 4:12); perfect (1:28 and 4:12); rooted and founded (1:23 and 2:[2]7); hidden and revealed (1:26–27 and 2:2 and 3:3–4); preaching, teaching, and advising in wisdom (1:28 and 3:16); future presentation as blameless and perfect (1:22 and 28; cf. 4:12); enjoyment of the riches of understanding and knowledge of the secret (2:2a and b); circumcision of Christ, not handmade circumcision (2:11a and b); humility and worship (2:18 and 23); etc. Cf. Section IX.D below, especially fn. 167.

peace" (vv 4, 8, 20); just as in Ephesians, participles in the nominative case continue a sentence about three times more frequently than in the *homologoumena*, (cf. fn. 120); (g) *appositions* to complete statements *introduced by "in"* or other prepositions [see #1(c) in this section]: for example, "with joy" (v 11); (h) *accumulation of prepositions* such as "about," "through," "in," "for" (vv 3–8, 12–13, 15–17, 19–20); (i) *acclamation style* [vv 7, 15, 17; cf. above 1(b)]; (j) *relative clauses* (vv 4–9, 13–14); added may be the three clauses beginning with "just as" [vv 6–7; cf. 1(d)]; (k) *pās* [each, all, whole, in vv 4, 6, 9–11, 15–20; cf. 1(f)]; (1) *logical* connecting words: "therefore," "for," "in order to," [only in vv 9, 16, 18–19; cf. 2(b)]; (m) *long sentences* [see (literally) v 3–8, 9–20; cf. 2:8–15; in our translation they have been subdivided into shorter units].

The same stylistic characteristics are dominant in Col 2 and in the first and second parts of Ephesians (Eph 1:1–4:24). But in the *homologoumena*, in Col 3–4, and in Eph 5–6, they occur less than half as often, with the exception of a few short prayerlike and hymnic subsections.[92] Indeed, the listed stylistic elements can be called liturgical and hymnic, or more caustically: pleonastic and baroque. Closest almost contemporary analogies are found in the *Thanksgiving Psalms* and in the final parts of the *Manual of Discipline* of Qumran.[93]

Still, the study and description of the style of Colossians presented here cannot be called complete and satisfactory. A truly comprehensive or holistic analysis of the vocabulary and style of the document would have to include the observation, comparison, effect, and evaluation of the sound and rhythm of the language, of the structure of the epistle *in toto* and in details, and of chiastic arrangements of lines and thought in particular (see fn. 57, at the end). Not less important is the triangular interaction between (1) a specific, dominating person and cause (in the case of Colossians, of Christ crucified who, by the power of resurrection, rules the world, the church, and the life of each believer), (2) the biographical and psychic condition of the writer, and (3) the cultural and social predicament and aspirations of the addressees.[94] Far too much is still unknown or has not yet been sufficiently scrutinized to permit the drawing of an objective picture and of final conclusions. However, in view of observations made on ancient and more recent writers, one judgment appears tenable: "The same

92. E. Percy, E. Lohse, W. Bujard, H. Ludwig, and A. van Roon have demonstrated this in the works mentioned in fns. 82 and 83.

93. A comparison of the features typical of a hymn, as enumerated in AB 34, pp. 6–8, shows several common traits. Parallels in the diction and style of the Qumran literature have been pointed out by K. G. Kuhn, "Der Epheserbrief im Lichte der Qumrantexte," NTS 7 (1960/61) 334–46 (Eng. trans. in J. Murphy-O'Connor, ed., *Paul and Qumran* (Chicago: Priory Press, 1968), and emphasized by E. Lohse, *Colossians*, pp. 88–89; 181, n. 11. They do not demonstrate direct dependence.

94. W. Bujard, *Stil*, especially pp. 130–46, 165–93, 220–23, bravely seeks to plough new ground by calling for a holistic *(ganzheitliche)* literary method of analysis. But the results of his inquiry are not convincing; cf. fn. 57.

author may have command over more than a single literary style."[95] In consequence, the *caveat* of F. W. Kümmel regarding authenticity verdicts on Colossians is to the point: "the language and style of Colossians . . . give no cause to doubt the Pauline origin of the Epistle."[96]

The reaction of the first readers to the language of Colossians is not known. The responses of modern students to its style vary greatly. J. B. Lightfoot observes a "certain ruggedness of expression," a "want of finish often bordering on obscurity," a "diminished fluency" and "compression of thought," but "no want of force." A. Deissmann compares Colossians to a fugue of J. S. Bach, and C. R. Bowen passes the hard judgment that "the movement of expression is slow, even sluggish, heavy, involved"; "the sentences . . . simply drag on from one idea to another"; "the end . . . has no remotest relation to its beginning"; "this Paulinist editor is not very original or very clear in his intellectual grasp." Obviously, Bowen feels highly superior! Even without the benefit of the Qumran materials discovered since 1947, E. Lohmeyer followed hints given by E. Norden and A. Debrunner in 1930 and recognized the characteristics of Semitic religious language, which is free from the dictates of Greek syntax and the urge for logical syntactical concatenation, and yet displays "a living unity," produced by "a pathetic breath." W. Bujard, however, is shocked by the erratic character and other deficiencies which he finds in the logic of this epistle.[97] Despite the gap of many centuries and the unusual style of Colossians, this epistle can still provoke more than just one passionate reaction.

A look at non-Pauline materials incorporated in Colossians, and consideration of the relationship of this epistle to Ephesians, help to reveal possible sources of the linguistic features just sketched.

---

95. A. van Roon, *Authenticity*, p. 209; cf. the titles listed in fn. 84. J. A. T. Robinson, *Redating the New Testament* (London: SCM, 1976), p. 70, speaks of Paul's "highly diverse and adaptable manner of speaking and writing for wider audiences" and again of his special style in addressing subordinate clerics, (e.g., in the farewell discourse in Acts 20, and in the Pastoral Epistles).

96. FBK, p. 241, E. Käsemann, "Epheserbrief," RGG II (1958) 517–20, especially 519, remarks about Ephesians, "Lexical and stylistic arguments, taken by themselves, do not possess the weight [to disprove Pauline authorship] which was earlier attributed to them." Instead, theological differences between Colossians and Ephesians, and between these two letters and the *homologoumena*, are considered sufficient evidence to solve the problem of dependence and authenticity of Colossians and Ephesians. See below, Sections IX and X.

97. J. B. Lightfoot, *Colossians*, pp. 191–92; A. Deissmann, *Paulus*, 2d ed. (Tübingen: Mohr, 1925), p. 87, fn. 1; C. R. Bowen [see fn. 57, JBL 43 (1924) 196, cf. 198, commenting on Col 1–2]; E. Lohmeyer, *Kolosser*, p. 13; E. Lohse, *Colossians*, p. 89; cf. BDF 458, 464; W. Bujard's opinion (*Stil*, passim) was mentioned above, in fn. 57.

VIII. THE WEIGHT OF TRADITIONAL MATERIALS

Colossians contains allusions to elements of the Colossian Religion, which probably are related to or drawn from one or several ancient religions and philosophies; to the Old Testament and its learned, ethical, and liturgical interpretation by Jews; to confessions, liturgies, and moral instructions used among Christians; and to utterances made in the Pauline *homologoumena*.

1. *Elements of the Religion.* In Sections IV, V, and VII, two observations were made which do not need to be documented again: (a) the letter makes use of terms and thoughts of the Religion against which the battle is waged; (b) despite the radical No said to the Religion, in order to present its message the epistle takes up some of the problems and questions posed by it. Irony is cunningly employed—and yet the author also cares for the "shadow" of the reality which he perceives in the Religion (2:17).

2. *Old Testament and Judaism.* Because in other letters the transmitted Holy Scriptures of Israel play a prominent role in the unfolding of Paul's message, extensive references to the Scriptures should be expected also of Colossians. All the more surprising is the absence of any quotes from the Law, the Prophets, the Writings, and from apocryphal books. Indeed, Old Testament wording (although not exactly following the LXX, but perhaps in line with a wording used in diaspora Synagogues) is apparent when "the hidden treasures of wisdom," "man-made commandments and teachings," the "sitting at God's right hand," "the image" of the Creator, and the impartiality of the Judge are mentioned.[98]

---

98. Isa 45:3 (also Prov 2:3–4) in Col 2:3; Isa 29:13 in Col 2:22; Ps 110:1 in Col 3:1; Gen 1:26–27 in 3:10; Deut 10:17 in Col 3:25. C. Maurer, "Der Hymnus von Epheser 1 als Schlüssel zum ganzen Brief," EvTh 11 (1951/52) 151–72, especially 158, speaks of eight OT parallels and quotations in Colossians, and compares them with the forty-two found in Ephesians. E. E. Ellis, *Paul's Use of the Old Testament* (Edinburgh: Oliver & Boyd, 1957), pp. 153–54 lists most of the correspondences just enumerated, and he interprets them (on pp. 128–29) on the basis of the contrast *and* the complementary character of "shadow and reality" in Col 2:17; he finds in them an expression of the OT-NT typology, i.e., of the "dispensational and economic relationship [of OT words and events] to the corresponding NT facts. But while he avers the fundamental harmony between Colossians and Paul's *longer* letters to the Galatians, Corinthians, Romans—to which Hebrews and First Peter might well be added—he also notes a difference (on pp. 32–33): in his *shorter* letters Paul is concerned with one or two pressing questions, not with the unfolding of all the "regulative authorities." Ellis concludes that really representative of Paul's theological method are only his capital letters. O. Michel, *Paulus und seine Bibel* (Gütersloh: Bertelsmann, 1929), p. 122, argues that in some cases it was "urgently necessary" for Paul to avoid references to the OT, and he seems to suggest that Colossians and Philemon were such cases. H. Weiss, "The Law in the Epistle to the

Missing are, however, not only introductory quotation formulae such as "it is written" or "he says," but also extensive or subtle attempts at exegetical arguments.[99] The same observation applies to Luke's rendering of the apostolic speeches before the gentile audiences of Lystra and Athens (Acts 14:15–17; 17:22–31). Yet in Colossians, the absence of Scripture citations and arguments is not necessarily due to the gentile origin of those addressed. The letter to the Ephesians presupposes the same provenience of the readers (Eph 2:1–2, 11–13; 4:17–19; 5:8) and still engages with zeal and skill in not fewer than four intensive discourses on Scripture.[100] In Ephesians, the specific topic of the epistle (such as the unity of the people of God, created by the unification of Jews and gentiles through the Messiah promised to Israel) was the reason why the author *could* not convey his message without constant reference to the Old Testament. A translation of Ephesians which seeks to correspond to this concern has therefore to render the title *ho Christos* "the Messiah," not "Christ." Equally, the emphasis laid in Romans and Galatians upon the unity of the promise given to Abraham and its fulfillment in the freedom of gentile-Christians from the Law called for extensive Old Testament quotations and expository arguments. But in Colossians, just as in the undisputed Pauline First Letter to the Thessalonians and the Letter to the Philippians (cf. the Johannine Epistles and the book of Revelation), other themes are unfolded in other ways. In the case of those writings, *ho Christos* need not necessarily be rendered "the Messiah [of Israel]," although in the theological exposition the continuous solidarity of Jesus Christ, and of faith in Christ, with Israel can never be overlooked or negated.

What can account for the deviation of Colossians from the prevailing Pauline practice? If the hypothesis could be upheld that orthodox Jews, Jewish Gnosticism, or gnosticizing Judaeo-Christians, if not judaizing gentile-Christians, were responsible for the Colossian Religion, an answer might be at hand: the author of Colossians may have disdained all things Jewish so totally that he was unwilling to meet his opponents on their own ground. This explanation

---

Colossians," CBQ 34 (1972) 294–314, especially 306, believes that the pseudonymous author of Colossians, unlike Paul in Gal 3 and Rom 4, did not wish to point *backward* to the promise given to Abraham, because he was totally devoted to apocalyptic and wisdom traditions. Cf. also S. Lyonnet, in U. Bianchi, ed., *Origins*, p. 55, and C. R. Bowen (see fn. 57), p. 193. The bibliography pertaining to Paul's use of Scriptures which is contained in AB 34, p. 407, calls for at least two supplements. While J. Blank, "Erwägungen zum Schriftverständnis des Paulus," in *Rechtfertigung*, FS für E. Kaesemann (Tübingen: Mohr, 1976), pp. 37–56, does not really initiate new insights, L. Gaston, *Paul and the Torah* (Vancouver: University of British Columbia Press, 1987), takes very bold steps to demonstrate the unity of the Torah's and Paul's intentions.

99. Except perhaps in 1:15–20; see C. F. Burney, "Christ as the ΑΡΧΗ of Creation," JTS 27 (1926) 160–77. Cf. fn. 103.

100. See the commentary on Eph 2:14–18; 4:8–10; 5:31–33; 6:2–3 in AB 34 and 34A, pp. 267, 276–79, 430–34, 472–77, 637–50, 720–38.

cannot be considered satisfactory for precisely the so-called "Judaistic" opposition, refuted by Paul in Galatians and Romans, is attacked on the ground of Scriptural arguments! Also it was shown above, in Section IV, that the classification of the Colossian Religion among Judaistic trends is far from demonstrated.

One of the reasons for the absence of Old Testament citations in Colossians may be this: the author, in being confronted with a religion emphasizing "tradition," "dogmas," and (doctrinal?) "elements" (2:8, 20), did not wish to argue like a scribe who insists upon his choice of Scripture texts just as a lawyer is wont to insist upon particular citations from a book of law; neither did he intend to claim for himself a superior understanding of the writings (but cf. 1 Cor 9:9; Eph 5:31–32, for example). All too easily sentences quoted from the Old Testament might have looked like the "world elements" which held a high rank in the opponents' Religion, or like "letters" that "kill" (cf. 2 Cor 3:6; Rom 7:6). In Colossians, the apostolic and congregational confessions of Christ crucified and risen are, as it were, precursors of the New Testament canon and the later Creeds of Christendom; they have taken the place of explicit references to the (Old Testament) Scriptures.

This substitution is a bold step which hardly would have been taken by a person uncertain of his own authority. Is, as recent work on Colossians affirms, a fixed "Pauline School" tradition responsible for this letter? If this were the case, the use, quotation, and interpretation of Old Testament (and some apocryphal) texts, perhaps culled from a "Book of Testimonies," would not have been missing. For the Letters of Paul demonstrate clearly that the headmaster of the supposed school was wont to teach and exhort on a Scriptural basis.[101]

Despite the absence of formally introduced citations from Colossians, many indirect references point to the Scriptures themselves and to the history, life, liturgy, and interpretations of the Jewish people. In this letter the faith of the Fathers and the worship of the children is not a weapon to wield, but the colorful background against which, and the spiritual climate in which, the author lives and wants his addressees to move. It is the special merit of E. Lohmeyer's commentary to have pointed this out. Perhaps one day Jewish scholars (who alone can be competent in such matters) will arrive at the conclusion that the author's No to the Colossian Religion proves him to be a

---

101. The school theory is represented by P. Benoit, "Rapports littéraires entre les épîtres aux Colossians et Ephésiens," in *Neutestamentliche Aufsätze*, FS für J. Schmid (Regensburg: Pustet, 1963), pp. 11–22, especially pp. 21–22; repr. in idem, *Exégese et théologie* III (Paris: du Cerf, 1968), pp. 318–34, especially pp. 333–34; idem, "L'hymne christologique de Col 1, 15–20," in J. Neusner, ed., *Christianity, Judaism and Other Greco-Roman Cults*, FS for M. Smith I (Leiden: Brill, 1975), pp. 226–63, especially pp. 253–54; H. Ludwig, *Verfasser*; H. M. Schenke, "Das Weiterwirken des Paulus und die Pflege seines Erbes durch die Paulusbriefe," NTS 21 (1975) 505–18; E. Schweizer, "Zur neueren Forschung," (see fn. 45), p. 168.

hundred times better Jew than his opponents allegedly were. For this author had a far more faithful concept of Old Testament festival traditions, of circumcision, of the co-inheritance of creation and redemption, and of ethics than Jewish or Christian heretics fostered.

Among the outstanding examples of the harmony between Colossians and living Jewish faith, at least the following deserve mention:

a. As P. Schubert has shown, "thanksgiving" in epistolary form (such as Col 1:3–12) is a Greek-Hellenistic rather than a traditional Jewish feature.[102] Even if it differs in form, the thanksgiving offered and encouraged in Col 1:3ff. and 12ff. expresses substantially the content of Old Testament Thanksgiving Psalms (such as Ps 22:22–31), and of the Qumran *Hodayoth*, as well as of modern Jewish prayer books. The exemplary function of God's mercy, shown foremost (for the benefit of all the world) to his elect people, establishes the connection between Colossians and the biblical Psalms, and the emphasis laid on knowledge has analogies in Prophetic and Qumran literature.

b. The reference to the inheritance granted, to the redemption from darkness, and to the transplantation into the realm ruled by God's Son (1:12–13) resumes the traditions of the promise of Canaan, the Exodus from Egypt, and the occupation of the Land.

c. Allusions to the celebrations, sacrifices, and prayers of the Day of Atonement are certainly made in 1:14, where redemption (freedom) and forgiveness of sins are mentioned. Prayers offered at this festival, perhaps also elements of the liturgy of New Year's Day, and learned or speculative interpretations of those celebrations appear to be taken up in the hymn, Col 1:15–20.[103] At the beginning of the two strophes that are sometimes distinguished in that hymn (to be discussed later), certain rabbinical paraphrases of texts chosen from the creation story (Gen 1:1, 26–27) may be reflected and corrected, as C. F. Burney has shown (see fn. 99).

d. The same hymn combines creation and redemption in a way which has its closest correspondence in Old Testament priestly and prophetic theology.[104] Instead of being related like universal cause or logical presupposition to particu-

---

102. *Form and Function of Pauline Thanksgiving,* BZNW 20 (1939); see AB 34, pp. 160–62.

103. E. Lohmeyer, *Kolosser,* pp. 40–46, 52–54. Lohmeyer's suggestion (p. 44) that the festival of the New Year's Day is to be included in the background of the hymn 1:15–20, too, has been elaborated upon, with special reference to Philo's interpretation of that festival in *spec. leg.* II 188–92; cf. I 210, by S. Lyonnet, "L'hymne christologique de l'épître aux Colossiens et la fête juive du Nouvel An," RSR 48 (1960) 93–100.

104. Most important are Gen 1–2; Isa 41:10–20; 45:6–13; Ps 74; 89; 102; Prov 8:22–31; Wis 7:17–30; 10:1–12:2. Cf. G. von Rad, *Old Testament Theology* I (New York: Harper, 1962), pp. 136–60; idem, "The Theological Problem of the Old Testament Doctrine of Creation," in idem, *The Problem of the Hexateuch and Other Essays* (Edinburgh and London: Oliver & Boyd, 1966), pp. 131–43.

laristic evidence of mercy and grace, creation is here depicted as a redemptive event, and redemption as a creative feat. The references made to the (potentially or actually inimical) created "heaven and earth" rather than to an imperishable "world" (= the *kosmos*, which among pagans of that period is identified with a deity, or includes the gods, or is a unified whole in and by itself) are distinctly opposed to pantheistic and to dualistic worldviews. Old Testament and Jewish doctrines are led to a culmination in Colossians. The equation of Wisdom, Logos, (Son) Image of God, Head, Prime and Last Man which is presupposed in 1:15–20, also in 2:3 and 3:9–10, is not an invention of the author. It has its roots in Old Testament and later Jewish traditions as they are represented not only in the Proverbs and the Wisdom of Solomon but also in Philo.[105]

e. A very positive attitude to a specific understanding of circumcision, anticipated by Old Testament strictures against reliance upon purely fleshly circumcision, is manifested in Col 2:11.[106] The limited value attributed to festivals and to abstention (probably also to purity laws), to angel worship and to a fake wisdom in 2:10, 18, 21, 23, is not in conflict with an affirmation of a worship in spirit and in truth, in agreement with Old Testament prophets. The notion of God's dwelling in a human being and of his filling the sanctuary (1:19; 2:9–10); the identification of faith with stability and firmness (1:23; 2:5, 7); the call to missionary existence of the whole congregation (4:5); the emphasis on teaching and on fidelity to a given tradition (2:7–8), rather than to the whims of man-made doctrines (2:4, 8, 23)—these and other features reveal how solidly Colossians is founded in prophetic, priestly, and rabbinical traditions.

To point out the relation of the author to this heritage is not simply a matter of tracing historical origins or literary parallels. But the message of Colossians lives and draws from the ground upon which it is built. "You share of the richness of the root of the olive. . . . You do not carry the root but the root carries you" (Rom 11:17–18). The teaching of Colossians on the relationship between the church and Israel will be further discussed below, in Section IX.C.5. pp. 95–96.

The substance of the many vital elements which Colossians has drawn from Judaism is much weightier than has been reflected in recent literature on the subject, especially when attention was focused all too exclusively upon the reception of formulated creeds and catechetical materials of Christian origin.[107]

---

105. A rich collection of pertinent materials and important reflections is made by A. Feuillet, *Christ Sagesse*, pp. 153–273, and H. Hegermann, *SpgM*, passim.

106. Cf. Lev 26:41; Jer 4:4; 9:25–26; Deut 10:16; 30:6; Ezek 44:7.

107. The form-critical observations made by e.g., E. Käsemann, "Kolosserbrief," RGG III, pp. 1727–28; E. Lohse, *Colossians*, p. 2; and J. Lähnemann, *KolB*, p. 28, are restricted to elements adopted from the (pre-Christian and Christian) opponents, from hymns, confessions, and liturgies, and from parenetical (hortatory) traditions which only to a limited extent are considered Jewish.

Still, the contribution of church tradition to Colossians must not be underestimated.

3. Ecclesiastical Elements. Alongside the Old Testament lines of thought and Jewish traditions which are continued in Colossians stand confessional, liturgical, and hortatory ("parenetical") voices, perhaps also texts whose origin is most likely to be sought in the congregations not only of Palestine and/or Syria, but also of Asia Minor, Macedonia, Greece, and perhaps even Rome. Among the Colossian borrowings from the hymnic and confessional materials, the Christological passages 1:15–20 and 2:9–15 are outstanding. Sometimes they are considered parts of a baptismal liturgy, as will be shown later. Traditional parenetical patterns and contents have been discovered in the *Haustafel* 3:18–4:1, and in the general admonitions found in 3:5–17 (perhaps, again, with an allusion to a baptismal instruction in the imagery of "stripping off the Old" and putting on "the New Man" in 3:9–10, 12).

The reason for and intention behind these endorsements may be manifold: fidelity to an authority considered superior; lack of originality on the part of the writer; satisfaction and consensus with the best possible way of formulation; appeal to a tradition recognized as valid criterion among the readers. It has been suggested that either by the arrangement, or by the frame in which the references are made, or by alterations of the traditional formulations, the author has bent the quoted texts so as to suit his own theology.[108] Later in the commentary, this theory will be tested, case by case.

Does the author's reliance on churchly traditions reveal one aspect of his victimization by the opponents whom he battles? Indeed, the antagonists at Colossae did rely upon traditions and did impose upon their followers dogmas and man-made teachings (2:8, 20, 22). And Paul himself leans on a tradition "which I have received and also have delivered" to the congregation (1 Cor

---

108. E. Schweizer, *Kolosser*, pp. 45–80; idem, "Zur neueren Forschung," (see fn. 45), pp. 181–85, explains the contents of 1:12–14 and 1:21–23 as a correction of the hymn 1:15–20 and follows the host of those commentators who call at least four clauses "interpolations": the words (1) (following after "the body," in v 18, literally) "which is the church"; (2) (after "from the dead," in the same v) "to be in person the universal sovereign"; (3) (after "through him alone" in v 20) "through the blood of his cross"; and (4) the lists of the "things . . . in the heavens and upon the earth" (in vv 16 and 20). Acting as a "redactor" of the tradited song, so Schweizer assumes, the author of Colossians, if not a later corrector, made the hymns suit the purpose of the epistle. Thus scholarly redaction-criticism crowns the results of form-criticism: the recognition of the hymnic character of 1:15–20. In this process the question remains unanswered, how an author could hope to persuade the threatened Colossian Christians of his own (orthodox and tradition-sanctioned) stance while he arbitrarily changed a text supposedly known and respected among those addressed? J. Lähnemann, *KolB*, p. 35, asserts that the writer of Colossians "deals very freely with the utterances of the hymn," and that "it can hardly be maintained that [he] appeals to it because it possesses recognized authority."

11:2, 23; 15:1–3). This holds true not just of his communication with one church. Without saying so explicitly, he incorporates formulae developed in the churches of Judaea and outside Palestine in several, if not all, of his letters.[109] To say it with the unique formulation used in Rom 6:17, all Christians and all churches were "committed to the [given!] standard of teaching."

It looks as if two types of traditionalism (*Traditionsprinzip*), that is, Paul's and the opponents' versions, had flowed together and been melted into one in the epistle to the Colossians. In 2:6 the technical rabbinical term "you received" appeals to what the Colossians have been "taught" and have "learned" are found in 1:7, 28; 2:7; cf. 3:16. Whether this reliance on tradition, teaching, and learning stems from Judaism, from a philosophical school, from a Mystery Religion, or from Gnosticism makes little difference: traditionalism appears triumphant wherever it is presupposed that there exists at a certain place a deposit of formulated truth (called a depositum fidei in the early church, with reference to, for example, 1 Tim 6:20), and that fail-safe channels have been established to guarantee its verification, transmission, and distribution. For E. Käsemann and others, therefore, the conclusion seems inevitable that Colossians helps to lay out the route and takes the first steps on the road which leads to the even stronger traditionalism and institutionalism of the Pastoral and the Ignatian Epistles; the apostle Paul, however, *cannot* have been guilty of the choice made in favor of that deplorable way; therefore he *cannot* have written Colossians, and the case for the spuriousness of this letter thus seems to be proven beyond doubt.[110]

A tamer conclusion, based, however, on the same theological presuppositions, is drawn by those who consider it likely that already during Paul's lifetime an overeager (or insecure?) disciple of Paul was convinced that the truth of the gospel needed the support of two or three pillars in combination: the authority of the apostle, the tradition of the church, and the miracle of baptism.[111]

These arguments and conclusions have not been left unchallenged. Colossians is considered Pauline, or at least is moved much nearer the apostle's own theology, when stress is laid on the statement "just as you received Christ Jesus as [the only] Lord, walk in his way" (2:6). Evidently, Jesus Christ himself is not simply identified with confessional formulae and apostolic doctrines, but he is in person the one "tradition" which the congregation is to follow.[112] Also it

---

109. Rom 1:3–4; 3:24–26; 4:25; 6:3a (also 11:25–26?); Phil 2:6–11 are examples from the undisputed Pauline epistles.

110. The idea of a basically post-apostolic and un-Pauline character of the emphasis on tradition and authority has been powerfully proposed by E. Käsemann, "Baptismal Liturgy" (see fn. 66). Cf. K. Wegenast, *Das Verständnis der Tradition bei Paulus und in den Deuteropaulinen*, WMANT 8 (Neukirchen, 1962), pp. 128–30; W. Marxsen, *Introduction* (see fn. 66), pp. 180–81.

111. E. Lohse, *Colossians*, pp. 177–83; H. Ludwig (see fn. 17); and others.

112. H. Löwe, *Christus und die Christen* (diss., Heidelberg, 1965), p. 205 (ref),

---

cannot be proven that in Colossians church confessions and apostolic authority have really superseded the authority of the Old Testament and other bonds linking the church with Israel.

Again, the letter to the Colossians lays special emphasis on the ministry of the apostle Paul.

4. *Pauline Utterances.* The epistle to the Colossians contains not only a singular exaltation of the apostle's ministerial suffering (1:24) which supports the weight and dignity of the apostle's spoken words when he is present, and of his written words when he is absent in body (2:5; 4:16). The fact that unlike Eph 3:5 (cf. 2:20; 4:11) he is not one among several, but *the* herald of the revealed secret and *the* exemplary servant of the gospel *par excellence*, even of Christ among the Gentiles, is underlined throughout this epistle (1:23–2:5; 4:3–4). The structure of this document includes, along with many building stones shared with Ephesians (see Section IX of this introduction) almost innumerable thoughts and formulations that resemble, or are equal to, parts of the *homolo-goumena.* Just as the other materials incorporated in Colossians, so also the Pauline elements appear in suitably adapted form. At least one expositor calls the result "the Testament of Paul."[113] Whether Colossians was written by Paul himself or by one of his disciples, its intention includes a confirmation and reinforcement of the apostle's authority, not a correction of his teachings. The Colossians are made aware that the testimony given by Paul *to Christ* and spread around by his co-operators is that firm foundation which is the only alternative to the slippery ground offered by the adherents of the Religion.

Still, unlike the doctrinal orthodoxy and the hierarchical order which in some parts of the epistles to Timothy and Titus, and even more conspicuously in the letters of First Clement and Ignatius and in the writings of Hermas, seem to serve as guarantors and guardians of tradition, in Colossians it is not formulae, texts, and men which bear this burden and honor; rather, the secret, wisdom, and gospel of Jesus Christ, or more briefly, Jesus Christ himself, are here the criteria of truth, the mediator of salvation, and the way to obedience and perfection.[114] To adhere to a tradition (2:8), or to be entrusted with a ministry (4:17), does not automatically secure true faith or faithful fulfillment of the

---

fights the notion of a coordination of church confession and the apostolate as twin pillars of authority, and J. Lähnemann, *KolB*, pp. 28, 33, 48, 111–15, 150–51, 162, 171, insists that, in Colossians, unlike the letters to Timothy and Titus, it is simply the actual growth of the congregation (not a liturgically fixed tradition) that is proclaimed as an alternative to the tradition of which the Colossians Religion boasted.

113. F. Zeilinger, *Erstgeborene*, p. 72, speaks of a "testament" and of Ephesians as its "execution." G. Bornkamm, "Der Römerbrief als Testament des Paulus," in idem, *Geschichte und Glaube* II, BEvTh 53 (Munich: Kaiser, 1971), pp. 120–38, has reserved the title "testament" for Romans, and a few others have attributed a similar character to Ephesians; see AB 34, 56–59.

114. Col 1:22, 27; 2:3, 6, 8; 3:1–4, 11, 17; 4:3. Unlike E. Käsemann, J. Lähnemann,

expectations attached to them. Rather, the tradition of Christ is carried on by prayer for the spread of the gospel; by faith, love, and hope; by the growing knowledge and obedience of the congregation which God alone provides (1:4–6, 9–11; 4:2–4); and by the mutual teaching and counseling of each church member (3:16).

In view of the presence and weight of the great number of traditional elements in Colossians, the writer of this letter (just as the author of Ephesians, according to E. J. Goodspeed) appears to resemble a collector and compiler. But the test of an author's originality and creativity lies not in the scarce or abundant endorsements of other people's words, formulations, and ideas, but in what he makes of given materials. Colossians is clearly dialogical in character, although it does not make use of the diatribal style (interjected questions and sharp answers) found in undisputed Pauline letters. In the process of teaching, the author is above all a listener. Instead of claiming originality, he seeks only to serve a person and a cause that stand above him and the congregation, uniting both under the aegis of mercy and judgment.

A special problem is, however, posed by the resemblance between this epistle and Ephesians.

IX. COLOSSIANS AND EPHESIANS

In form and substance, the epistles to the Colossians and to the Ephesians resemble twins. However, their unity is not without striking marks of diversity. Both their resemblance and their difference create problems as they are known from, for example, the comparison of the Synoptic Gospels with one another, and of First Peter with James.[115] Is Colossians or Ephesians more original—

KolB, pp. 58 and 115, underlines the differences between Colossians and the Pastoral Epistles. See also K. H. Rengstorf, TDNT II, 147.

115. See Bibliography II. Intensive preparatory work for the following, including the suggestion of tentative conclusions, was made by my former assistant at Pittsburgh Theological Seminary, Rev. Archibald M. Woodruff, Ph.D.

In addition to the Colossian-Ephesian relationship, the parallel features connecting Colossians with the Pastoral Epistles (to Timothy and Titus) require special study. E. T. Mayerhoff, *Colosser*, and H. J. Holtzmann, *Kritik*, have given full attention to the latter. A triple (triangular) relation between Colossians/Ephesians/Pastorals is indicated by (1) similar or identical data concerning sojourns and travels of Paul's cooperators; parallel utterances on e.g. Tychicus are made in Col 4:7–8 // Eph 6:21–22 // 2 Tim 4:12; other biographical elements will be discussed in connection with the date of Colossians, in Section XI, below; (2) the mention of Paul's bonds (Col 4:3, cf. 4:10 // Eph 3:1; 4:1; 6:20 // 2 Tim 1:8); (3) the parenetical form of *Haustafeln* (Col 3:18–4:1 // Eph 5:22–6:9 // 1 Tim 2:8–15; 6:1–2; Titus 2:1–10; cf. 1 Pet 2:18–3:7); (4) details such as the pejorative use of "doctrine" (Col 2:22 // Eph 4:14 // 1 Tim 4:1). While Ephesians, in particular, corresponds to the Pastorals in the use of the denotation "Devil" (Eph 4:27; 6:11 // 1 Tim

perhaps authentically Pauline—so that one of the two is dependent on the other? Or were both written either at about the same time by one author, or by different authors who both used the same oral and/or written instructions or prototypes? Resemblance, relation, and dependence will here be treated as one issue, authorship as another, despite the complementary nature of both. Observations and tentative conclusions concerning the first complex of questions may contribute decisive elements to solve the second in an unprejudiced and noncircular way.[116] At the opening of the next section, a minimum number of indications will be given regarding the relevance of the dependence and authenticity question for the exploration and description of Pauline theology.

In this section, the sigla C and E will be used for the letters to the Colossians and Ephesians respectively.

A. Four Case Studies

A biographical, a hymnic, a doctrinal, and a parenetical passage from C are suitable examples to illustrate the problems of unity with and diversity from E.

1. *A Biographical Text.* The special relationship between C and E is epitomized by the almost identical wording of two passages near the end of the two letters. A literal translation in which the words or phrases distinguishing C from E are underlined permits the following synopsis:

3:6–7; 6:9 var. lect.; 2 Tim 2:26), which is not found in the *homologoumena*, and of the verbal form "those hearing" (Eph 4:29 // 1 Tim 4:16; 2 Tim 2:14), only Colossians shares with the Pastorals references to a hope or crown (literally) "deposited" (in the heavens, Col 1:15 // 2 Tim 4:8). The asceticism refuted in Col 2:22–23 may be similar to that fought in 1 Tim 4:3, 8, but appears to be different from the abstention (only?) from meat discussed in Rom 14:1–15:7. The "struggle," mentioned in Col 2:1 // 1 Tim 4:10; 6:12; 2 Tim 4:7, recurs only once in the *homologoumena*, in Phil 1:30."

The verbal and thematic kinship connecting Colossians and the undisputed Pauline letters is evident in the synoptic presentations of texts offered, e.g., by J. Moffat, E. J. Goodspeed, and C. L. Mitton (see fn. 123). The Ephesian and/or the *homologoumena* connection(s) have been discussed extensively, by W. Hönig, "Uber das Verhältnis des Epheserbriefes zum Briefe an die Kolosser," ZWiss Theol 15 (1872) 63–87; C. R. Bowen, (see fn. 57); and E. P. Sanders, "Literary Dependence in Colossians," JBL 85 (1966) 28–45. Sanders emphasizes the special relation between Colossians and Philippians; cf. H. v. Soden, *Kolosser*, pp. 13–15; T. K. Abbott, *Colossians*, pp. LVIII–LLX. See also fn. 162. Among more recent works, the books of J. Lähnemann, H. Ludwig, and A. van Roon illustrate the compatibility of vocabulary, style, and teaching of Colossians with, e.g., Romans and Philippians. E. Lohse, *Colossians*, p. 182, lists not fewer than ten structural and material elements common to Colossians and Romans.

116. According to Dib.-Gr., p. 83, "the relationship of Ephesians to Colossians is the [starting, or Archimedean?] point from which the question of authenticity has to be answered."

Col 4:7–8	*Eph 6:21–22*
v 7 *All* about my affairs	v 21 *In order that you,* *too, have knowledge*
	about *me,* how my affairs *stand . . .*
will make known to you, Tychicus the dear brother and faithful servant *and fellow slave* in the Lord	will make known to you Tychicus, the dear brother and faithful servant in the Lord.
v 8 For this very purpose I have sent him to you that you may know our situation	v 22 For this very purpose I have sent him to you that you may know our situation
and that he reassure your hearts	and that he reassure your hearts
v 9 *with Onesimus our faithful and dear brother who is one of yourselves. All that has occurred here they will make known to you.*	

These two biographical sections presuppose the same situation and expectation of the apostle Paul. Thirty-two identical Greek words are used in the same order. Eph 6:21 contains a mangled ("anakolouth") sentence structure and is more wordy than Col 4:7. In turn, Col 4:7 describes Tychicus more fully, and Col 4:9 adds a reference to the fellow messenger Onesimus, the Colossian runaway slave who was the reason for Paul's writing to Philemon. If the quoted passages were variant readings of the same text in one and the same epistle, traditional criteria of textual criticism would probably lead to the following verdict: Col 4:7 is secondary. For it is more likely that the rough reading of Eph 6:21 was smoothed out by a later copyist than that a proper sentence structure was truncated. However, the fuller description of Tychicus in Col 4:7 can either be ascribed to a secondary extension of the crisper Ephesian text, perhaps made in the interest of the plea for the "slave" Onesimus in Phlm 11–20, or Eph 6:21 might be the result of a secondary concentration upon the essential.

Nevertheless, criteria and counsels applicable to text criticism are far from foolproof for the comparison and explication of Col 4:7–9 and Eph 6:21–22.

Insulated from other standards, they cannot demonstrate whether one or two authors are responsible for the discrepancies, and which of the two documents is prior. Other parallel passages in the two epistles call for additional considerations.

2. A *Hymnic Text.* When Col 1:20 is compared with Eph 2:13–16, the essential harmony between the substance of the shorter and the longer statements strikes the eye. Identical words are used and the same topic, unification, is treated in C and E—although there are also slightly different formulations and changes in the sequence of individual elements.

The present Greek text of Col 1:20 says (literally): ". . . *through him* [Christ, God wanted] to *reconcile all things* to himself, *pacifying* through the *blood of his cross, through him,* be it *those on earth or those in the heavens.*"[117] The italicized words point out at least five puzzling features of this verse[118]: (a) A very rarely used compound verb, peacemaking, is used which here was rendered "pacifying" in order to suit the following accusative object "those on earth" etc. (b) Reference is made to reconciliation and peace, though in the foregoing vv 15–19 the reader had not been prepared for reconciliation by any explicit mention of conflict or war. (c) The expression "the blood of his cross" may not have sounded as conducive to speaking of the "bloody cross" as it sounds to the ears of all those avoiding cursing. Although the author certainly intended to speak of no more than of "His blood shed on the cross," the formulation chosen by him is outright ugly. (d) The repetition of "through him" in the middle of the statement is not only superfluous but embarrassing. (e) The apex of the whole sentence is clearly stated, "all things . . . on earth and in heaven" are to be reconciled; however, the Colossian context (1:12–14, 21–23) speaks only of the redemption and reconciliation of *persons.*

Light falls upon and into the puzzling elements of Col 1:20 as soon as this verse is explained as a conflation of Eph 1:10 and Eph 2:11–16. In the following, underlinings mark the vocabulary common to these verses in E and C. The first Ephesian text (1:10) affirms, "all things have to be comprehended *under one head,* the Messiah—*those in heaven and upon the earth—under him*" and they are echoed in the Colossian puzzle (d) and (e). In the second passage (Eph 2:11–18), E first depicts separation, estrangement, enmity between Jews and gentiles by its reference to mutual name-calling, to political and spiritual division, to a wall of hostility, and then praises the Messiah as the one person *who* reconciled the two groups and *made peace* between them, by creating one

---

117. Operations, especially excisions, carried out by modern commentators in order to restore a more original reading (cf. fn. 108), will be discussed below in the Notes and Comments.

118. In the following, arguments of J. Coutts, "The Relationship of Ephesians and Colossians," NTS 4 (1957/58) 201–7, are reproduced in abbreviated form, with minor additions and alterations.

new man through his *blood*, his flesh, his own body, the *cross*, the killing. Puzzles a, b, and c of the Colossian parallel verse look soluble against this background.

In summary, it appears that the beautiful, detailed, logical, climactically structured sequence of the prose and hymnic utterances in Eph 2:11–16 have been excerpted, and that the excerpts have been condensed in one brief sentence in order to give Col 1:20 its present shape. In addition, Col 1:22 takes up from Eph 2:14, 16 the terms "body" and "flesh," and the same Colossian verse speaks simply of Christ's "death" while Eph 2:16 more verbosely affirms that "in his own person Christ has killed the enmity." It is hard to imagine that out of the haze and maze of Col 1:20 (and 22) the separate and lucid verses Eph 1:10 and 2:11–16 should have been spun. It is more probable that C intended to make a drastic contraction of E's clear utterances, and in so doing created the obscure verse 1:20. Still, closely related or very similar hymns, or early and late forms of one and the same hymn, might also have been used by the author or authors of both C and E.

3. *A Doctrinal Text.* Col 2:19 and its parallel, Eph 4:15–16, seem to have been singled out by Martin Dibelius for two reasons: to answer the question of the C/E interrelation and to solve the problem of authenticity of one or both of these letters. Indeed, these issues are most acute when the verses mentioned are compared. In the following, Edgar J. Goodspeed's version and linear juxtaposition are reproduced in combination with the main underlinings of the word and phrases common to C and E, as they were contributed by C. Leslie Mitton.[119]

Col 2:19	*Eph 4:15–16*
v 19 a . . . not holding fast	v 15 [that we] speaking the truth in love
	may grow up in all things into him
the head	who is *the head*, even Christ;
v 19 b *from whom all the body* being *supplied* *and knit together* *through the joints* and bonds	v 16 a *from whom all the body* fitly framed *and knit together*
	v 16 b *through* that which *every joint supplieth*

119. M. Dibelius, *Epheser* (1927), pp. 63–65; Dib.-Gr. (1953), pp. 83–85; E. J. Goodspeed, *Key* (1956), pp. 42–44; C. L. Mitton, EE (1951), 301; H. Hegermann, SpgM, p. 154; and others. Goodspeed's synopsis is here reproduced, except for the references he makes to Col 1:10b, 18a, 29b, i.e., those texts in which C, apart from 2:19, contains parallels to Eph 4:15–16.

Col 2:19	Eph 4:15–16
	according to the working in due measure of each several part,
v 19 c increaseth with *the increase of God*	v 16 c maketh *the increase* of the body unto the building up of itself in love.

In the freer but perhaps more palatable version of Eph 4:15–16 which is proposed in AB, *Ephesians*, the two Ephesian verses say, "[15] By speaking the truth in love we shall grow in every way toward him who is the head, the Messiah. [16a] He is at work fitting and joining the whole body together. [16b] He provides sustenance to it through every contact according to the needs of each single part. [16c] He enables the body to make its own growth so that it builds itself up in love."

What in the two texts quoted is affirmed in regard to the activity of the head and to the composition, nourishment, and increase (or growth) of the body, includes the following five differences:

a. *Grammar.* In Col 2:19b the gender of the relative pronoun *(ex)hou* is considered masculine and rendered "(from) whom" in Goodspeed's and other versions. The form used in the Greek original might be neuter ("from which") as well as masculine. However, a careful or pedantic grammarian would call for the feminine gender *(ex hēs)* because the relative pronoun refers to the preceding Greek feminine "head" *(kephalē)*. The grammatical jolt offered by C[120] is

---

120. An analogous jolt appears to consist of the masculine plural present participles such as (literally) "fruit-bearing," "growing," "joining together," "teaching," "advising," "singing" (Col 1:10–12; 2:2; 3:16; see H. J. Holtzmann, *Kritik*, p. 112). The nominative forms of these participles are in extreme tension with the grammatical requirements of their respective contents. But no variant reading seems to exist which attempts to correct the grammatical and syntactical lapses. A convincing explanation of the sense of these participles has been given by D. Daube, "Participle and Imperative in I Peter," Appended Note in E. G. Selwyn, *The First Epistle of St. Peter* (London: Macmillan, 1947), pp. 467–88; idem, "Haustafeln," in idem, *The New Testament and Rabbinic Judaism* (London: Athlone, 1956), pp. 90–105; see also the references given in AB 34, p. 372, fn. 23. The so-called "absolute participles" which occur in the *homologoumena* and in First Peter as well as in CE, are (though they are not found in the *Pirke Aboth*) a typically rabbinical form of admonition. They express an appeal to the honor of those addressed and call for voluntary obedience as it befits, e.g., a prince, not the slavish attitude of an underling. In Col 1:23; 2:7; 3:9–10, 17, 22; 4:2, 5, the nominative plural forms of the participles happen to fit in the context but still possess the rabbinical character just mentioned.

avoided in the variant reading of D*, probably in the Greek text used for the Syro-harclensian version (early seventh century), and in the parallel text in E (4:15–16): all of them contain the explicatory "Christ" after the Greek feminine "head" and before "from whom." Therefore, the English version "from whom" is strongly recommended by the variant readings and by E: it catches exactly the meaning of the whole sentence. Why, however, do the huge majority of the C manuscripts offer a text that sounds like an insult to careful diction? Two answers seem possible: (1) the author of C may have intended to use the (perfectly legitimate) *constructio ad sensum*—which was later corrected for the sake of clarity and beauty by E and by the variant reading(s) of C. E would then be later than C. (2) C and E may have used a traditional oral formula or written text which mentioned "Christ" explicitly before the beginning of the relative clause. In this case E would stand nearer the common source (the so-called "*Vorlage*") of C and E because it contains the reference to "Christ." From "nearer the *Vorlage*" to "older" is only a small step. On the other hand, the "later" C would then have omitted what looked superfluous, but with the omission of "Christ" would have incurred the risk of hurting pedantic linguistic feelings. A decision for either one of these possibilities cannot be made on philological grounds.

b. *Omissions.* The Colossian text is not only shorter but also less rich in substance than its Ephesian twin. Eph 4:15–16 expresses at least five ideas not found in Col 2:19, although some of them are reflected elsewhere in C: (1) The saints "grow up . . . *into* the head," vid. the body "grows *toward* Christ" (Eph 4:15b), not only "*from* him." (2) The body is "fitly *framed and* knit together," not only "knit together." (3) The contribution of "each several part [var. lect. of Eph 4:16b: of each member]" of the body is strongly emphasized; the energy flowing from the head does not exhaust itself but engenders and inspires energy also in the body and its members; in consequence, the body (itself!) "makes the increase of the body" in order to "build up itself." It is not only a passive recipient in Eph 4:16c. (4) A clear distinction is made in the Greek text, although Goodspeed's version does not show it, between the composition of the body by Him (alone) who "frames and knits it together" and the "supply" (vid. "sustenance"), provided to it "through the joints;" in Col 2:19b the order of these two actions is reversed and both are performed by Christ "through the joints." In summary, C and E make clear that the church lives and grows only "from" Christ's power and care, but E has particular things to say about the church's own life under her head.

c. *Additions.* In two instances, Col 2:19 has longer and fuller expressions than Eph 4:15–16: (1) The body is supplied not only through joints but also through "bonds" (vid. "ligaments"). This may indicate that C understood and used the Greek noun *haphē* (which in our version of Eph 4:16b, in agreement with the widespread abstract sense of the word, was rendered "contact") in a specific (physiological), that is, "joint" sense. Thus, C attributes greater weight to the mediating function of certain (clerical?) church members than E, which describes the contact between each and every church member as the means "through" which the church receives supply from her head. (2) The use of cognate vocabulary in the expression "increase with the increase of God" (vid. [literally] "growth with a growth of God") in Col 2:19c reveals an attempt at rhetorical richness. In substance the phrase corresponds to I Cor 3:5–7: whatever the merits of servants who plant and water in God's plantation, God alone "gives the growth." Thus, in C, once again, the sufficiency of God's care and power is underlined, although not in a way that would exclude the church's own growth "into" or "toward" her head which is proclaimed in Eph 4:15.

Dibelius and in his wake many others believe that Col 2:19 still expresses (in slightly Christianized form) the Orphic-Stoic notion of the world being the body of the deity. The same background is discovered in the hymn Col 1:15–20, which is said to have become Christian only by the interpolation of "the church" after the words "his body." While Dibelius considers recourse to the original pagan notion appropriate for the dispute of the author of Colossians with the Colossian Religion, there are serious alternatives to his derivation of the concept "head" and "body."[121]

d. *Perspicuity.* Col 2:19 is clearer and reads more smoothly than its parallel in E. Despite some additions, C is shorter and lacks the immensely complicated conglomeration of ideas that characterizes Eph 4:15–16 in the Greek original, and that has required four independent clauses in the English version proposed in the AB. At this place E makes many points while C is to the point.

e. *Function.* The whole verse Col 2:19 or part of it seems to fit so poorly in the midst of the deprecatory statements made about the Colossian Religion in Col 2:16–18 and 20–23, that it invites being dubbed an interpolation, borrowed from the common *Vorlage* of C and E, or from E, whether it be attributed to the less than careful author of C himself or to an anxious or zealotic, although well-meaning, editor. The positive statement of Col 2:19b, describing Christ's relationship to the body, is suspended on the condemnation found in 2:19a: "[the opponent] does not hold fast "the head." But the parallel verses Eph 4:15–16 form a well-fitting segment of the circle of thoughts devoted in Eph 4:1–24 to the constitution of the church and the gift of new life. Certainly Col 2:19 and Eph 4:15–16 contain the same substance and most valuable information phrased in almost identical vocabulary. However, what in C is used as a sledgehammer in order to warn and destroy serves in E as a building stone. Who can say whether in this case the hammer or the stone is prior?

4. *A Parenetic Text.* Col 4:2–6: "[2] Persevere in prayer. On the basis of

---

121. Dib.-Gr., pp. 36, 84. See the Comment "Head, Body, and Fullness" in AB 34, pp. 183–210.

thanksgiving watch [out for the Lord]. [3] At the same time pray especially for us that God may open the door [of speech] to tell the secret of Christ. For this I am bearing chains: [4] to reveal it the way I must tell it. [5] Wisdom shall direct your ways among those outside. Redeem the time. [6] Grace shall always qualify your speech [as] the salt that seasons it so that you know how to answer in each case each person, at each occasion." In these five verses, at least three themes can be discerned which are also discussed in Eph 4:29; 5:15–16; and 6:18–20, although in reverse sequence and interrupted by extensive discourses on other topics. The three subject matters are: (a) participation of the saints by constant prayer in the missionary function of the apostle, that is, in the publication of the revealed secret of God; (b) wise conduct and use of the remaining time; (c) edifying speech.[122] In E, each of these themes has its beautiful and logical place within the closely knit structural webs of three different and separate parenetic units. But in C, the three topics are drawn together to form one single net. It is improbable that E is the work of a later author who, by pulling main threads out of the artistically structured ethical summary of Col 4:2–6, destroyed that handy piece of a catechism, and then used the material gained to create three entirely new patterns. Rather, the author of C might have culled those elements from E which appeared most useful for combination and insertion in a more concise artwork of his own.

There are more commentators teaching the dependence of E on C than the reverse relationship, but the last case study tends to weaken the theory of E's dependence on C. If C did not exist at all and, therefore, did not invite comparison with E, no reader of Eph 4:29; 5:15–16; 6:18–20 would consider these verses haphazardly separated from one another and wantonly interpolated in their present context. Still, the four direct comparisons made between C and E texts fail to encourage a definite decision in favor of the priority of either C or E. Fortunately there are also other methods to be applied and criteria to be considered.

B. Comparison of Vocabulary, Style, and Structure

1. *Vocabulary and Style.* Apart from the verses treated previously, several times in C and E up to seven identical words are used in the same sequence. The same thoughts, on the other hand, are occasionally expressed in slightly different wording.[123] Each letter has its own number of *hapax-legomena*, and it

---

122. Peculiarities of the treatment of the last-mentioned topics in C and E, e.g., the occurrence of the perplexing terms (literally) "building up the need" in Eph 4:29, and "those outside" in Col 4:5, are discussed in the Notes to E and C respectively.

123. Following M. Goguel, FBK, p. 253, mentions the fact that 73 out of 155 verses of E have verbal parallels in C. A basis of this count is the list of 39 parallel passages first composed by W. M. L. De Wette, *Einleitung*, 4th ed., 1842, pp. 259–63 (only Greek

was stated before that some commentators put much stress upon the different meanings of terms such as *mystērion* (mystery or secret), fullness, *oikonomia* (plan or administration), body, to reconcile when they are used in E and C respectively (see fn. 87). In Section VII of this Introduction that dealt with Vocabulary and Style of C, it was already observed that the diction of C agrees in decisive instances with that of E. In some cases, there are only variations in vocabulary which do not affect the sense even though they exhibit different emphases.[124] Elsewhere, one of the epistles either has better grammar and syntax, smoothing out rough diction, or clarifying obscure expressions.[125] The terminology chosen and the transition first from prayerlike to hymnic, then

text); 6th ed., 1960 (also German trans.), which was taken over by, e.g., H. J. Holtzmann, *Einleitung* (see fn. 34), p. 278, and T. K. Abbott, *Colossians*, p. XXIII. Following C. L. Mitton's count (EE, p. 57), a quarter of the vocabulary of E is shared with C, and a third of that of C occurs in E.

Most convenient for the comparison of the Greek texts is C. L. Mitton, EE, pp. 279–321; the English texts are printed in parallel columns by E. J. Goodspeed, *The Meaning of Ephesians*, pp. 82–165; idem, *Key*, pp. 2–74. For an extensive discussion, H. J. Holtzmann's *Kritik* is still fundamental; see also E. Percy, PKE, pp. 386–428.

124. In this and in the following fns. only examples typical of one or another aspect will be presented.

The two Greek words for "new" (*neos* and *kainos*) are exchanged in Col 3:10 // Eph 4:24 (cf. 2:16; but Col 3:10 contains *anakainoō*, to "renew"). Col 2:13 says "you" while Eph 2:5 has "we." The secret was hidden from eons and generations, and it was revealed to the saints according to Col 1:26, but Eph 3:5, 9 mentions the hiding from generations and from eons in separate verses and speaks of its revelation only to the "holy apostles and prophets." According to Col 3:5, greediness is idolatry, following Eph 5:5 a greedy man is an idolator. Col 3:12 lists five, Eph in different contexts (4:24, 32; 5:9) three good attitudes. In Col 3:13 "just as" and "so also" follow logically upon one another; in Eph 4:32 the logic is maintained, but "just as" seems also to serve as introductory formula of a quotation. For a summary of more stylistic observations, see E. Percy, PKE, pp. 430–32, and—with *caution!*—the monograph on the style of C by W. Bujard (see fn. 57).

125. The style of C *is better than that of* E in Col 3:5 ≠ Eph 5:5 (correct gender of the relative pronoun in C); Col 3:23 ≠ Eph 6:8 (in C: "whatever you do" is followed by a smooth continuation, instead of E's clumsy and faulty sentence structure [literally] "for each, when he does something good, this he will receive"); Col 3:18 ≠ Eph 5:22 (C: "it is fitting in the Lord," against the ambiguous short-formula of E: "as to the Lord"); Col 4:7–8 ≠ Eph 6:21–22 (as stated earlier, C has a straightforward clause instead of E's broken sentence).

E looks like an improvement upon C in Eph 4:15–16 ≠ Col 2:19 (E has the correct gender of the relative pronoun); Eph 2:13–19 ≠ Col 1:20 cf. 3:15 (E fully explains, through the description of estrangement and hostility, why the making of peace through Christ is necessary, while C surprises its readers with the sudden reference to peacemaking); Eph 2:14–15 ≠ Col 2:14 (in E the Law, the statutes, and the middle wall are clearly identified, while in C the relation between the IOU, the [Law and the] statutes, and the [literally] "removing from the midst" is obscure and comes as a surprise); Eph

from strictly personal to traditional hortatory styles, including the sequence, first baroque features, then crisp commandments, confirm the twin look of C and E and distinguish them from major portions of the *homologoumena*.[126]

After the application of form-critical rather than linguistic criteria, the priority (at least of parts) of C and E was discussed on a partly new basis. A. Seeberg (*Der Katechismus der Urchristenheit*, 1903) had initiated the search for parenetic traditions which was taken up by, inter alios, M. Dibelius in his commentaries on James (1921) and Colossians (1927) and found its first full-blown exponent in H. Weidinger's *Haustafeln* (1928). Since then, it was often repeated that C represents an older and more original form of counseling for the benefit of husbands and wives, parents and children, masters and slaves. Later, the form- and tradition-critical study of New Testament hymns has yielded the (tentative) result that E reproduces hymnic materials in an older form.[127] In Eph

---

5:1–12 ≠ Col 3:13 (E illustrates the call extended in Eph 4:32 to "forgive one another just as God has forgiven you in Christ" by a long excursus on the transforming power of the light [of God]; C adds the casuistic words "when one has a reason to complain against someone else" and quickly passes on to another topic); Eph 6:19 ≠ Col 4:2 (E: the door to be opened is the apostle's mouth; C seems to leave it open whether a door on the side of the recipients is in mind).

126. In E. Lohse, *Colossians*, p. 86, a list of those ten words (among them: "to be alienated," "to be rooted," "to raise and to make alive together," "growth," "hymn," "eye-service") is found which do not occur in the NT outside C and E. In addition, another list names those fifteen terms (such as: might, mind, to dwell, to lodge, to be grounded, song, to sing) that recur in the New Testament, yet not in the *homologoumena*. Eleven other words (to enable, steadfast, to bury with, to triumph, to be puffed up, fairness, and others) connect C more closely with the undisputed letters than with E.

127. Concerning parenesis, see E. Käsemann, RGG II 519; Dib.-Gr., p. 49; FBK, pp. 243, 253; K. G. Kuhn, NTS 7 (1960/61) 334–46, especially 338; E. Kamlah, *Die Form der katalogischen Paränese* (Tübingen: Mohr, 1964), pp. 31–32.

In regard to hymns, see G. Schille, *Frühchristliche Hymnen* (Berlin: Evangelische Verlagsanstalt, 1965), pp. 33, 54–56; J. T. Sanders, "Hymnic Elements in Eph 1–3," ZNW 56 (1965) 214–32; N. A. Dahl, *Kurze Auslegung des Epheserbriefes* (Göttingen: Vandenhoeck, 1965), p. 8; idem, "Der Epheserbrief und der verlorene erste Brief des Paulus an die Korinther," in *Abraham unser Vater*, FS für O. Michel (Leiden: Brill, 1963), pp. 71–72.

However, following a hint given by H. Weidlinger in *Die Haustafeln* (Leipzig: Hinrichs, 1928), Dib.-Gr., pp. 91–92, gives a warning: too little is known about the pre-Colossian and pre-Ephesian forms of parenesis to use the form of the parenetical material found in C and E as evidence of the priority of one letter over the other. Cf. also W. D. Davies, *Paul and Rabbinic Judaism*, pp. 123–27.

Insights derived from the study of the form and the dates of OT hymns, e.g., the Song of the Sea and the Song of Deborah and their relation to the preceding prose accounts of historical events (Ex 14–15; Judg 4–5), may be applied to the evaluation of the hymns in C and E. But the time span covering the origin of the New Testament books is so much shorter than each one of the great periods of the history and literature

2:14–18; 5:25(–27) and 1:20–22; 2:4–10, for example, E *sings* about Christ's death and resurrection, while in Col 1:21; 2:13; 3:1–4 the tone of a preacher prevails. Indeed, the picturesque Ephesian image of the broken wall (2:14) has its vivid counterparts in the metaphorical utterances of C about the wiped-out and crucified IOU and the triumphal procession (2:14–15). But the exhortation of Eph 4:25–6:9 is more explicitly related to Christ and contains more affirmative and explanatory counterweights against mere prohibition than the section Col 3:5–4:1. A decision on the priority of either C or E obviously cannot be based on such stylistic observations.

2. *Conflation.* Sometimes in one of the two epistles, several words, verses, or thoughts found in the other appear to be drawn together ("telescoped") into a shorter unit. This conflation has been called "one of the most important, and significant, characteristics of the interdependence."[128] E. J. Goodspeed in his synoptic tables (see fn. 123) and others before and after him have shown that C contains verbatim excerpts or free borrowings from the *homologoumena*. The performance and the result of the collector's work was ascribed either to Paul or to one of his disciples. At any rate, what was considered patent in the case of C is even more so with E. The author of the latter may have used, excerpted, and condensed a copy of the Pauline *homologoumena* and of C. Here he copied, and there he paraphrased in accordance with his own understanding of the *Vorlage*, but on occasions he also inserted an original thought. Thus he fabricated his own summary of Pauline teaching, as it is now known under the name of E. Especially C appears to have been close to his heart for again and again it seems that the author of E selected two or three verses out of separate contexts in C, and created out of them a new sentence or unit.[129] But when an examination is made in the reverse direction, the opposite thesis can emerge as well: the author of C may have contracted materials stemming from E. Certainly he has added not only elements drawn from the *homologoumena* but also words and thoughts of his own.[130] In addition, on several occasions either one of the authors of C and E or both may not be dependent on another document but

---

of Israel that the criteria useful for Old Testament research cannot simply be transferred to NT studies. Cf. fns. 173 and 174.

128. C. L. Mitton, p. 64, cf. pp. 65–81, 243–44, etc.

129. Eph 1:7 appears to be composed out of Col 1:14 and 20 (common are the terms, freedom through blood); Eph 1:10 out of Col 1:16 and 20 (heaven and earth, one head); Eph 1:15–16 out of Col 1:4 and 9 (hearing, faith, love, intercession); Eph 1:18 out of Col 1:5, 13, and 27 (hope, light); Eph 1:21 out of Col 1:16; 2:10 and 15 (powers); Eph 1:23 out of Col 1:19 and 2:9–10 (fullness, filling).

130. Col 1 exemplifies how one Colossian text may look like a conflation, contraction, or extract from several Ephesian elements: Col 1:16 out of Eph 1:10, (21) and 4:9–10 (common are: heaven and earth, etc.); Col 1:20 out of Eph (1:14?) 2:13 and 16 (peace-making by blood on the cross); Col 1:21 out of Eph 2:(1), 12 and 4:18 (estrangement); Col 1:22 out of Eph 1:4; 2:16 and 5:27 (reconciled, spotless); Col 1:25 out of Eph

may rather repeat or quote words, formulations, and thoughts uttered earlier in the same letter. Self-quotes must not be excluded in the dependence discussion; they can show that C is as much dependent on C, and E on E, as both also depend on the *homologoumena*. Since E is longer than C, repetitions are bound to be more frequent in E.

The problem of conflation is as complex as the appropriate kind of test. Statistical observations must be combined with the consideration of possibilities and the weighing of probabilities, a rather unpleasant and seemingly less than lucid method.

For a brief illustration, in the following, those passages in C and E are chosen which describe the status and conduct of the Christians by the ("absolute") participles "founded," "rooted," "joined [or knit] together," "built upon," "built together." For our test, Col 1:23 will be called A; Col 2:7 = B; Col 2:19 = C; Col 2:2 = D; Eph 2:20–22 = X; Eph 3:17 = Y; Eph 4:15b–16 = Z.[131] "Founded" in A and Y; "rooted" in B and Y; "joined," together with "in love," in D and Z, without "in love," in C; "built" in B and X (two times). The Colossian D may be a conflation of the Colossian A and B, mutually canceling each other out for an answer concerning priority. But it can be argued: (a) if C is prior, then (elements out of) ABC were conflated by the author of E to yield X; ABD to produce Y; and BCD to issue in Z; (b) if, however, E is prior, Y inspired A, (elements of) XY were combined to form B, and Z found reception in C and D. The second assumption (b) is superior to (a) because of its greater simplicity. It reckons with a smaller number of conflations and explains the repetitions found in E as self-quotations.

Even this is explicitly affirmed in Eph 3:3: "as I have briefly written above, the secret was made known to me by revelation." The "above" statement to which reference is made in this verse is much more likely to be found in Eph 1:9–10 than in other Pauline letters (for example, Gal 1:1–16; 2 Cor 12:1–4) or in Col 1:26; for the other Pauline texts are not "brief" nor can their knowledge be presupposed in Ephesus around 60 C.E. Col 1:26 is hardly the source of Eph 3:3–5; for the Colossian text speaks of the revelation of the secret to "[all?] the saints," not only to Paul and the "holy apostles and prophets." Still, the reference to conflations provides as little a clear-cut answer to the dependence

3:2, 7, and 8 (gift to the apostle); Col 1:26 out of Eph 1:9; 3:5, 9–10 (formerly hidden secret, now revealed); Col 1:27 out of Eph 1:9; 18; 3:6, 8–9, 16–17 (Christ, the secret and hope for the Gentiles [or among them], in the hearts). Though C is shorter than E, more than elsewhere in Col 1, the condensations of Ephesian passages (or the allusions to them) outnumber the conflations of Colossian materials found in E.

However, this fact may not only be explained by dependence of C upon E. Just as C, so also E may repeat or quote itself whenever a later passage resembles an earlier one.

131. A discussion of these passages and their relevance for the dependence question is found in, e.g., H. J. Holtzmann, *Kritik*, pp. 50–71; E. Percy, PKE, pp. 378, 410–11; C. L. Mitton, EE, p. 66; J. Coutts, NTS 4 (1957/58) 201–2.

question as the appeal to stylistic observations. The priority of C is *not* obvious; E may still be a source of C.

Will another method lead to more cogent results?

3. *Structure.* The order or sequence of the various *greater* units in C and E is in "a rough correspondence."[132] *Unique* passages are inserted into the common total structure of C and E at about the same places and with analogous intentions. As shown in Section V.A (above pp. 41–48, especially in fn. 57), the great units have been delimited with various results and given different titles; for better comparison with the structure of E, the demarcations and headlines of the several parts are now (slightly) changed. Reduced to a simple form, and omitting the openings and conclusions of C and E, the following structure can be observed:

Common Part I (Col 1:3–11 // Eph 1:3–18)
Thanksgiving and Intercession[133]

Special Matters A
The Effect of Christ's Resurrection and Death

Col 1:12–23: Hymn and comments on Christ's work in creation and redemption, mentioning his resurrection, his death, and the church together with the world as beneficiaries of the peace made.

Eph 1:19–2:22: Hymns and comments on the resurrection of Christ and with Christ, on the death of Christ, and on the unification in peace of Israel and the gentiles.

Common Part II (Col 1:24–2:5 // Eph 3:1–13)
The apostle, privileged by Revelation and proven true by suffering, in the service of the church that includes gentiles.

---

132. C. L. Mitton, EE, p. 64. E. Lohse, *Colossians*, p. 182, and others attribute this order to a "school tradition"; cf. fn. 101. E. Percy, PKE, pp. 362–72, in concentrating his attention upon smaller units in C and E, recognizes a substantial structural harmony only in the case of the *Haustafeln* Col 3:18–4:1 // Eph 5:21–6:9; cf. W. Munro (see the end of fn. 162). The different sequence of the small units discerning the reconciliation of all things and of mankind was discussed in Subsection B.2, pp. 83–85.

133. The Great Benediction Eph 1:3–14 is part of the Thanksgiving Eph 1:3–18 (if not 1:3–3:21; see AB 34, 53–56, for a discussion of the structure of E). Yet it may also be singled out and called a proëm. As such it could be an insertion made by the author of E between the opening and the first part of E (i.e., between 1:1–2 and 1:15–3:21). C. Maurer (see fn. 98) considered 1:3–14 "the key to the whole epistle to the Ephesians). Equally, Eph 1:3–14 might have been the basic text on which the author of C was elaborating when he wrote the first part of his epistle (Col 1:3–23).

Special Matters B
The True and the False Community of Worshippers

Col 2:6–3:4: Polemics against the Colossian Religion, interrupted by the evangelistic passages 2:9–15, 19bc, and 3:1–4 describing the "filling" of the saints and their heavenly calling.

Eph 3:14–4:16: Prayer for perfection, and description of the church's constitution, interrupted by a crisp No to heretics in 4:14.

Common Part III (Col 3:5–4:1 // Eph 4:17–6:9)
General ethics founded on the contrast between the old and the new man, and special commands in the form of *Haustafeln*.

Special Matters C (Inserted into Part III)
Christocentric Conduct

Col 3:11: Unity of all separated groups, in Christ; in 3:22–4:1 emphasis on the slave-master relationship.

Eph 5:21–32: the Christological foundation of the husband-wife relation, supported by allegorical Scripture interpretation.

Common Part IV (in Col 4:2–6, 7–8 // Eph 6:21–22, 18–20)
The participation of the congregation in mission, by prayer and the commission of Tychicus.

Special Matters D
Personal Greetings, or Call to Arms

Col 4:9–17: Recommendation and love of persons near Paul and in the Lycus Valley.

Eph 6:10–17: the Spiritual armor.

Thus peaceful E ends on a bellicose vein, while polemical C concludes its message in warm tones—a paradox which forbids simplistic characterizations of either epistle.

The comparison of the structure of C and E yields four options for explaining the relation between C and E: (1) the same author (Paul or an imitator) used the same outline twice but added for the writing of each letter specific arguments and applications; (2) one author used the composition of another, making changes, including additions and deletions, to meet the needs of the recipients he had in mind; thus C is prior to E, or vice-versa; (3) the original Pauline text of C (*"Ur-Kolosser"*) was elaborated upon by the author of E, and E was used for making interpolations in Ur-Colossians ("interdependence"). (4) A (lost) draft of the apostle or an oral school tradition was used by the writers of both letters. Options 1, 2, and 4 actually contain two variants each, yielding a total of seven possibilities to explain the C-E relationship (see Subsection D below, pp. 101–12). C. L. Mitton observes that the subsections Col 2:7–14 and 3:5–12 "break up the orderly sequence of progression," and H. J. Holtzmann is convinced that whenever the order of C is interrupted by E, a trace of the *shorter,* original, and authentic Colossians becomes visible.[134] But just as in Synoptic research the order of pericopae (especially the fact that Matthew and Luke never agree against Mark in the sequence of passages that have Markan parallels) can be used to demonstrate the priority of Mark as well as his posteriority to the fellow evangelists, so the structure of C and E in their present form is inconclusive for the question of priority.

Left over is still an entirely different approach: a comparison of the message or doctrine of the two epistles. Since C and E are theological documents, the literary and historical study of these texts requires a penetration into strictly theological problems.

C. Nuances in Common Doctrine

Outstanding among the doctrinal elements common to C and E are the descriptions of God the Father and Jesus Christ in terms of glory, riches, power, fullness, grace. In C, just as in E, much is said about the revelation of the one secret and wisdom of God which through Jesus Christ has taken place now and has antiquated the former hiddenness of the mystery and the estrangement of the gentiles. The body and blood, the cross, and the death of Christ are praised as the efficient means of reconciliation and peace for all men, even for all things.

Numerous are references to heaven and earth, to principalities and powers, and to their subjugation to one head: Christ. He was before and he is above the whole creation for he was raised from the dead and exalted at God's right hand to appear again in glory. In a particular way he is head of his body, the church.

Similar, and often identical, are the descriptions of the past, present, and future of the congregation and its members. Here and there, former gentiles who were dead in sins and then were resurrected with Christ are addressed. The address in the form of a writ follows upon the true word, the gospel, which was first revealed to, and preached by, the apostles. The apostle Paul suffers gladly for his ministry to the church. A foundation was laid, knowledge was imparted, hope was given, and forgiveness was granted in order that all the saints might attain perfection before God's eyes; grow in insight, mutual love, and good works; and bear testimony to the world by their conduct. In the context of

---

134. C. L. Mitton, EE, p. 64; H. J. Holtzmann, *Kritik*, pp. 5, 130.

ethical exhortation, both letters speak of the Old and the New Man and list works typical of the two key persons which have to be doffed and donned respectively. Both contain so-called *Haustafeln*, both remind in passing of baptism,[135] and both call to thanksgiving, hymn singing, and prayer.

On frequent occasions, not only are special shades of color or tone given to a topic and its presentation, but a variance in doctrine itself cannot be ruled out.

Without parallels in C are, for example, the extensive descriptions of the unification of Jews and gentiles, of the husband-wife relationship, and of the spiritual armor in Eph 2:11–22; 5:22–33; 6:10–17. Absent from E are the hymn connecting creation and redemption, the extended polemic against a Religion, the reference to dying with Christ, and the personal greetings in Col 1:15–20; 2:8, 16–23; 4:10–17.

The variations found in the epistles may be the result of developed insight—in some cases they may be complementary; in others they seem to be in contradiction. Certainly the centrality of Jesus Christ and the cruciality of his eternal unity with the Father, also his incarnation, crucifixion, resurrection, ascension, and his rule at the right hand of God over church and world, constitute the common and decisive message of both epistles. Through Christ, God is, and does, and rules "all in all" (Eph 1:23; Col 3:11, etc.). However, by different means various thoughts are emphasized and new aspects are opened. Among the themes in question, Christology (the teaching on Jesus Christ and his work in relation to God, the universe, and the Church) is decisive for all that is added concerning the Spirit, the world, the church, eschatology (teaching on the last things and the end time), the ministry, and the conduct of the saints.

1. Christ's Person and Work. In almost identical terms the passages Col 1:20, 22 // Eph 2:16 and Col 3:17 // Eph 5:20 speak of the reconciliation and peace established by God through Christ, and of the thanksgiving which the saints offer to God through the same Lord. These passages exemplify what both letters intend to affirm: there is no other mediator but Christ. God reconciles "through" the same person "through whom" (or "in whose name") also the saints offer their prayer. God and man—in the words of 2 Cor 1:20 the fulfillment of God's promise and the pronouncement of the human amen in response to God—are present and united in Christ. However, Christ's oneness with God, as well as his unity and solidarity with mankind and with creaturely existence, are described with different emphases.

In Col 3:16 only God, but in the parallel Eph 5:19 the Lord (= Christ) is praised in hymns, in Col 3:13 forgiveness is granted by the Lord, in Eph 4:32 by God in Christ. Thus in the first case C, in the second E, has "the Lord" or "Christ" instead of "God." In Eph 3:9, cf. 1:4, God is the creator of all things,

---

135. The relevance of baptism for the main theological argument is specifically emphasized by F. Zeilinger (see fn. 26); E. Käsemann, "Baptismal Liturgy," (see fn. 66) and J. C. Kirby, *Ephesians, Baptism, and Pentecost* (Montreal: McGill University, 1968).

but Col 1:15–17 extols Christ's role in creation. In turn also Eph 2:15 calls Christ the creator—of the New Man. According to Col 1:19, 2:9–10, God's fullness fills first Christ, then also the church, while the verses Eph 1:22–23; 3:19; 4:10 speak only of Christ who fills both, the church and all things, omitting a reference to Christ who is being filled. Thus C avoids the idea of a cosmic pantheism, at the expense of an all-too-close connection between God and the world of powers and things, but E resists an interpretation suggesting that God might have lost himself or part of his fullness in favor of the church and the world. The residence of God's fullness in Christ's "body of flesh" is emphasized repeatedly in C (1:19, 22; 2:9), while "his (Christ's physical, biological) body" is mentioned only once in E (2:16). C lays particular stress on God's might and right over the creaturely body perhaps in order to refute the idea of a flight out of the body for attaining salvation for the soul alone in another world, as suggested by the Colossian Religion. E, however, has references to the cooperation of Christ and the Spirit (for example in 2:18) which are without parallels in C (see Subsection 3, below, pp. 92–93).

Several passages in *Colossians* appear to give greater glory to Christ than their Ephesian parallels. According to C. L. Mitton and others, only in C (1:26–27; 2:2; 4:3) is Christ himself the mystery of God in essence, while in E (1:9; 3:3–4; 6:19) God's plan is meant by *mystērion*.[136] No explicit parallels are found in E to Col 2:3, where all treasures of wisdom are placed in Christ, and to Col 1:15–17, which describes Christ in a terminology used formerly (in Prov 8:22–31 and Eccl 7:22–30) only of the pre-existent Wisdom. Only C (2:11) speaks of a "circumcision not hand-made," even of "the circumcision of Christ" by which the saints were circumcised; E (2:11–19), however, apparently related Christ more indirectly to those having and those lacking "circumcision in the flesh." Resurrection is imparted only "together with Christ," according to Col 2:12–13; 3:1; yet Eph 2:1–6 insists that the resurrection and enthronement in heavenly places have been received "together with the Messiah" *and* with the Jews, who were formerly as dead in their sins as the gentiles. Col 2:7 describes the saints as (literally) "rooted and founded in Him [Christ];" Eph 3:17 urges them to be "rooted and founded in love."

Still, on other occasions *Ephesians* outflanks C by Christocentric statements of its own. Christ is the peacemaker in both letters (Col 1:20 // Eph 2:15). Nevertheless, he is the prime herald of peace only in Eph 2:17, while in Col 1:7, 23–29; 4:7–17 other preachers, teachers, and functionaries are mentioned (compare with this Eph 3:1–13; 4:11). Thus in E, most prominently in 1:10, all matters regarding "administration" are first placed in the hands of Christ. Correspondingly, Eph 2:14 is bold enough to call Christ in person (literally) "our peace," unlike Col 3:15 which bids that "the peace of Christ [or the peace which is Christ?]" shall be arbiter in the hearts of the saints. In Eph 4:13 the

136. C. L. Mitton, EE, pp. 86–91; for other judgments, see fn. 87.

Messiah alone is called "perfect," and in 1:4; 5:27 perfection as well as blamelessness are gifts still to be received by the saints. Yet according to Col 1:22–28; 4:12, not only is perfection "in Christ" preached to each man and promised first of all to the saints, but God is also asked to make the members of the church "stand fast as perfect and consummated people." "The Inner Man" (that is, the Messiah) shall dwell in your hearts," says Eph 3:16–17, but Col 3:16 asks that the "word of Christ [or the word which is Christ?] shall reside" in the saints. In Eph 2:5–6 the co-resurrection with Christ is described as an event taking place exclusively "in the Messiah."[137] Despite the baptismal-liturgical origin sometimes asserted for this text and its context, baptism is not explicitly mentioned here, but Col 2:12–13 speaks of baptism and thus seems to locate co-resurrection in baptism. Whether this transfer of the miracle from the hands of Christ into the mystery of a sacrament is really meant in C will be discussed later in the Notes and Comments.

Despite the limited size of both epistles, their picture of Christ contains many additional shades of difference, for example, in details pertaining to Christ's pre-existence, to his word, to his function in ethics, and to the last judgment. But at this place only an additional aspect is to be pointed out. Terms such as "making peace" (Col 1:20 // Eph 2:15), "kingdom of his beloved Son" (Col 1:13), "head over all things" and "head of his body: the church" (Col 1:18, 2:10, 19 // Eph 1:10, 22–23, 4:15–16) reveal that (in Christ's work) power and love are combined in a unique way. At the same time, this Christ manifests his indisputable and eternal dominion by imposing peace even upon inimical creatures, and by demonstrating a love which calls for the response of love among those reconciled. How are power and love interrelated when they affect the manifold creatures of God?

2. *Power and Love.* One prominent motif running through E and C is this: the whole of creation, all powers are subjugated to Christ by God—without their consent. They were not consulted about whether God should send his Son and raise him after he had completed his work by his death on the cross. No hint is given that faith, love, and hope are expected of "all things," or that there is a spirit in or of all things which by the (Holy) Spirit can be so moved that it gives an answer to God and Christ by full trust and voluntary self-subordination. Certainly God's intimate care of all things and all powers was manifested. For the body in which God's fullness dwelt was physical, the death of Christ was real death, and the chaos among the revolting powers against God was redressed in order to establish the goodness of *all* creation. Eph 1:19–21 describes God's legitimate power as an almost brutal force, and Col 1:15–20 shows that what

---

137. Two passages in E (1:13–14; 4:30) mention the (live-giving) "seal of the Spirit"; the other Ephesian references to the Spirit (see fn. 142) harmonize with the close connection between Christ and the Spirit in 2 Cor 3:6; Rom 8:11; cf. 1 Tim 3:16; John 6:63; 1 Pet 3:18.

was created in, through, and for Christ has as little free choice as, to use a favorite Biblical image, the pot has against the potter.[138] Indeed among God's creatures humanity also profits from the almighty power of God exerted in Christ (Col 1:29 // Eph 3:20). But in addition, here men, women, and children enjoy great preference: the gospel is preached to them, they are called upon to respond to God by voluntary submission as manifested in faith and hope and love. While all things experience the *power* of God's love, humankind is granted the privilege to understand, to accept, and voluntarily to reciprocate the *love* of God's power and to address God as Father through the Spirit (Rom 8:14–16).[139]

In unfolding this distinction, C and E set their own accents. The body, blood, cross, and death of Christ are related only to the redemption of the saints in E (1:7; 2:13, 15–18; 5:2, 25). C, however, speaks of two dimensions of Christ's sacrifice: through "the blood of his cross" *all things* in heaven and upon earth are reconciled and all powers are defeated (1:20; 2:15), *and* "in his fleshly body" through his death he forgave the sins of *the saints* and reconciled them to God (1:14, 22; 2:14). In E (1:18–2:10), only Christ's resurrection pertains to both the subjugation of the powers and the salvation of the saints.

In *Ephesians,* first (1:4) the eternal election of the saints is depicted as the secret and essence of the eternal God's love of his eternal Son: then only (in 1:10) are mentioned the dominating and unifying function and office of Christ in regard to "all things . . . in heaven and upon earth." Thus, the line of thought leads from the saints to all things—but immediately after 1:10, in 1:11–18, it returns to the saints. It does so a second time when, after a new section describing the power displayed in Christ over all forces and all things (1:19–22a), the text again concentrates attention on the church (1:22b–2:22). Similarly the same topics follow one another in Eph 4:1–16. The first eight verses speak of the conduct, confession, grace pertaining to the saints; 4:9–10 takes up hints contained already in 4:6, 8 regarding God's and Christ's relation to all things and places: the "filling of all" is mentioned; finally 4:11–16 discusses anew the life of the church. According to Eph 2:7, the church is a sample of the riches of God's mercy presented to all powers, and following 4:9–10 the church is God's herald to the powers, announcing to them the wisdom of the creator of all things. Toward the end of the epistle (Eph 6:10–17), the still existing tension between the invisible evil powers of the universe and the saints becomes visible; the saints are equipped to resist their attack (cf. Rom 8:33–39).

Colossians, in turn, starts out with a sequence that reverses the order of Eph 1:4 and 10. In the hymn Col 1:15–20, the creation and sustenance of all things and powers through Christ are mentioned before the text speaks of Christ's rule over the church (see 1:15–18); in 1:20, the reconciliation of all things concludes

---

138. See, e.g., Isa 29:16; 45:9; Jer 18:6; Rom 9:20–23.

139. The dialectic between love and power was discussed in AB 34, 129, and the difference between forced and voluntary subordination in AB 34 A, pp. 708–15.

the praise of Christ. More complex, though skillfully organized, is the context surrounding this hymn: Col 1:12–14 and 1:21–23 describe the redemption of the saints. The structure of 1:12–23 is, therefore, not essentially different from the movement of thought discernible in Eph 1: church → all things → church → all things → church. In the section Col 2:9–15, the stream of argument flows from the divine fullness in Christ to the filling of the saints, then to the dominion over all powers (vv 9–10); finally, a second time, from Christ's circumcision, death, and resurrection to their benefit for the saints, and (as culmination and climax) to his victory over the powers (vv 11–15).

In its statements on the powers and all things, C speaks more emphatically of their creation and reconciliation through Christ. The creation of all things is mentioned only in passing in Eph 3:9, and their unification and reconciliation are mentioned very briefly in Eph 1:10; 2:14; 4:9–10. The author hurries on from the mention of all things to preaching the salvation of all people.[140] On the basis of such observations, the impression was created that C is more cosmological, E more ecclesiastical in the depiction of the extension and effect of Christ's work.[141] While a comparison of the Ephesian and Colossian passages just discussed does not support this generalized judgment, it is indisputable that E emphasizes the reconciliation of the gentiles with the Jews, and of both, gentiles and Jews, with God (2:11–19; cf. 1:12–13; 3:6; also Col 1:27–28; 3:11), while C (1:20; also Eph 1:10) proclaims in particular the reconciliation and pacification of all things in heaven and upon earth.

Other themes treated with fine distinction in the two letters are related like spokes connecting the hub and the rim of a wheel.

3. *The Spirit.* E refers rather frequently to the work of "the (Holy) Spirit (of God)."[142] C mentions the Spirit explicitly only once, and more indirectly

---

140. It is possible that in Eph 2:14–18 the transition of the Greek wording from the neuter "both" to the masculine "both" (from *amphotera* to *amphoteroi*) means a progress of thought from "all things in the heavens and upon the earth" (Eph 1:10) or from good and evil "powers" (Eph 1:21; 2:7; 3:10) to "those near [= the Jews]" and "those far [= the gentiles]." In this case, E, too, concentrates its attention upon the church, (temporarily) at the expense of "all things," including the "powers."

141. So, e.g., A. Feuillet, *Christ Sagesse*, p. 318, and E. Gaugler, *Epheserbrief*, pp. 11–12. Indeed, when a key passage such as Col 1:15–20 (except for its context 1:12–14, 21–23) is compared with Eph 2:11–22 (forgetting Eph 1:10; 2:7; 3:10; 6:10–17), this distinction is confirmed. But much depends on which passages are selected for a test.

142. There are fourteen main passages of E mentioning the Spirit (1:13–14, 17; 2:18, 22; 3:5, 16; 4:3–4, 30; 5:[9, var. lect.], 18; 6:17–18; cf. "Spiritual" in 1:3; 5:19. The sections or verses 1:3–14, 15–23; 2; 18, 20–22; 3:1–9, 14–19; 4:4–6, 30–32; 5:18–20 look like anticipation of the later church doctrine on the trinity of God the Father, the Son, and the Spirit. Several Ephesian verses speak of man's spirit, and some others (e.g., Rom 8:16) attest to the interrelation between both, as a result of God's revelation and grace.

twice.[143] However, the particular references to God's power (in Col 1:11, 29; 2:12) and to the fullness (*plērōma*, in Col 1:19 and 2:9) may substitute for the mention of the "Spirit" in the undisputed epistles).[144] The single occurrence of the word "Spirit" in C does not demonstrate that the author of this epistle, unlike Paul, fostered misgivings about the Spirit; also it does not imply that C fails to make any contribution to the later church doctrine(s) of the Spirit. Concern for the Spirit and corresponding spirituality are not recognized by the presence or absence of a specific vocabulary but find many forms of expressions.

4. *The World.* In E (1:4; cf. 2:2, 12) the noun *kosmos* is used to describe

---

143. Col 1:8 speaks of the Spirit (of God), and the adjective "Spiritual" occurs in 1:9; 3:16. E. Schweizer, "Christus und Geist im Kolosserbrief," in *Christ and Spirit in the New Testament*, FS for C. F. D. Moule (Cambridge: University Press, 1973), pp. 297–313; cf. idem, "Zur neueren Forschung" (see fn. 45), pp. 163–91, especially pp. 169–70; idem, "Christology in the Letter to the Colossians," RevExp 70 (1973) 451–67, especially 462–63, attributes the absence of references to the Spirit in Colossians (1) to a decline of interest in the Spirit in "a later period" and (2) to the Spiritual claims made by enthusiasts. Still, it is a problematic procedure to combine an argument from silence with the assumption that at the same time the interest in the Spirit was slackened *and* enthusiasts were present in Colossae, if not in the whole region. On the one hand, the Montanist movement disproves a reduced concern for the Spirit among the Christians in Asia Minor of "a later period." On the other hand, it is by no means demonstrated that the Religion threatening the Christians of Colossae boasted of the possession of the Spirit. In Corinth there were enthusiastic Christians, drunk with the Spirit as they prided themselves; but this does not prove the presence of the same phenomena in Colossae. Though "Phrygian Mysteries" included processions of people equipped with tambourines, etc., and at times culminated in ecstatic actions, there is no evidence that the Colossian Religion was part of an enthusiastic trend. Even if it be assumed that a dangerous Spirit movement was rampant outside Corinth, too, e.g., in Galatia and Rome, the letters to the Galatians, Corinthians, and Romans show that the presence of enthusiasts among those addressed does not prevent Paul from speaking explicitly and extensively of the Spirit. Indeed, in his commentary on Colossians (1976), pp. 21–22, Schweizer denies, while on pp. 134, 145, 149, and 164 he seems to affirm, enthusiastic traits of the Colossian "philosophy."

The assertion (made by Schweizer on p. 39) that Christology rather than pneumatology (doctrine of the Spirit) provides criteria to discern true from false doctrine, it appears to be supported by the First Epistle of John more than by, e.g., John 14–16.

144. God's power is equated with the Spirit in, e.g., 1 Thess 1:5; 1 Cor 2:4; Rom 15:13, 19; Acts 1:8; 10:38; cf. Eph 6:10, 17. After already G. Münderlein, "Die Erwählung durch das Pleroma," NTS 8 (1962) 264–76, had established the connection between *plērōma* and Spirit (or glory, or wisdom) of God (cf. AB Ephesians I, pp. 203–4), A. J. Bandstra, "Pleroma as Pneuma in Colossians," in *Ad Interim*, FS for R. Schippers (Kampen: Kook, 1975), pp. 96–102, has, again, argued in favor of the thesis that in Col 1:19; 2:19 *plērōma* "may be a remarkable designation for the cosmic Spirit of God," i.e. "the Spirit in redeeming action." Less persuasive is his conclusion that this Spirit "became a spiritual body."

the universe of created beings in heaven and upon earth, but in C (1:6; 2:20b; cf. 1:23) only the realm "under the heaven" is denoted by it.[145] Does E make a concession to Greek and/or apocalyptic Jewish vocabulary which C avoids? Certainly with its variations on the biblical terminology "heavens and earth" (see Gen 1:1, etc.) in 1:10; 3:15; cf. 1:21c, E confesses that it does not intend to deviate from the biblical ground: the world is not a monolithic whole but includes a tension between above and below, things not seen and things that are seen, both of which God alone can control, just as the verses Col 1:16 and 20 affirm. But in regard to the invisible part of creation, E contains affirmations that are not found in C. E speaks of both, (literally) "the heavens," and "the heavenly places." In the latter are gloriously seated not only the Lord, but also his elect Son, and his chosen people; from there not only God's blessings radiate; but there also reside good and evil forces (Eph 1:3,20; 2:6; 3:10; 6:12). C, however, mentions the "above" and (literally) "the heavens" exclusively as the place of the Lord, the repository of hope, and the operational sphere of good and evil principalities and powers. The different terminology found in E is puzzling but offers no reason to call the doctrine on heaven contained in one epistle more "mythological" than that of the other.[146]

The same is true in regard to another concept used to describe the whole world. Some scholars are convinced that a pagan tradition is incorporated in an earlier or even in the present form of C (especially in 1:18 and 2:19) that calls the visible and invisible world the "body" of a supreme deity. They argue, for instance, that E presupposes the separation *from* the Orphic-Stoic equation (saying that the world is the body of the deity), and *toward* the ecclesiastical identification of the church alone with the body of Christ, while C has not yet taken that step.[147] This view, also, will be subject to closer examination in the commentary.

145. It is unlikely that the term "elements of the world" in 2:8, 20 means heavenly bodies, that is, stars or invisible powers. See the commentary on 2:8, 20 for other options.

146. In Eph 1:3, 10, 20; 2:6; 3:10, 15; 4:10; 6:9, 12; Col 1:5, 16, 20; 4:1, var. lect.; cf. Phil 2:10, always the plural "the heavens" is used, but twice, in Col 1:23 and 4:1, the singular. In AB 34, in the exposition of Eph 2:11–22, the opinion of H. Schlier, *Christus und die Kirche im Epheserbrief*, BHT 6 (Tübingen: Mohr, 1930); repr. 1966, pp. 18–26; idem, *Der Brief an die Epheser* (Düsseldorf: Patmos, 1958), pp. 127–33, was examined which suggested that E included in its teaching on a destroyed "wall" the Gnostic-mythological idea of a *horos* separating the world of the divine powers from the dark realm of creaturely existence. In no case do the "heavenly places" mentioned in E occupy a middle, be it mediating or obstructive, position between heaven and earth. The Hebrew *pluralia tantum šāmayim* (heavens) and the apocalyptical and rabbinical references to several heavens, however influenced by Canaanite mythology, speak against a derivation of the CE terminology from a Gnostic mythological doctrine of creation in the sense of a cosmic split and fall, followed by redemption of the soul.

147. See the comment of "Head, Body, and Fullness" in AB 34, 183–210. The reputed gloss, (His body): "the church," in Col 1:18 will be discussed in the commentary,

More certain than attempts to speak of a closer kinship of C to pagan mythological cosmologies than is found in E is the assumption that, in both epistles, just as in the Old Testament and in Jewish writings, the term "all things" *(ta panta)* is a synonym or parallel of the expression "heaven and earth" and includes all "powers." The unanimous witness of C and E concerning the world affirms that there is more between heaven and earth than meets the eye, even that which in modern terminology is called the (invisible) "structures and institutions" of social, individual, historical, physical, and spiritual human existence.[148] But only C (2:18; cf. 2:23) mentions "angels," and only E (4:27; 6:11; cf. 2:2) the Devil.

In their teaching on the mortality of the body and the vicious force of the flesh, as caused by the sway which "sins" hold over mankind, and as enhanced rather than overcome by religious rituals such as circumcision, the two letters fully agree. Still, only C (2:18, 23) speaks ironically of the "mind of the flesh" and the "stilling of the flesh." These examples suffice as signals of the "worldviews" of C and E.

5. *The Church.* In agreement with most of its occurrences in the *homologoumena*, the world *ekklēsia* (church) denotes a local congregation in C; it is specifically employed for a house church, in Col 4:15–16 and Phlm 2. But in Col 1:18, 24, just as always (nine times) in E, this term means "church universal." As earlier observed, both E and C call the (universal) church "body of Christ," and both insist upon the fact that the subjection of the church to her head, Christ, takes place in the frame of the worldwide establishment of Christ's monarchy: he is also the head of all things (Eph 1:23; Col 1:15–18, etc.). But C (2:19 speaks in a way of the ("vertical") relation between head and body, for example, between Christ and his church, which does not make explicit the ("horizontal") coordination of the several members of the body which is emphasized with force in the Ephesian parallel text (4:15–16). Further, E (4:1–16) speaks in tones of praise not only of the unity but also of the *diversity* found and sustained even within the church. C (3:11, 15), although it is aware of the variety and diversity of persons and ministries belonging in the church, rejoices more exclusively in her *unity.*

The emphasis with which E, especially in 2:11–22, preaches and sings about

---

where also pertinent literature will be mentioned; some of the problems of Col 2:19 were discussed among the case studies at the beginning of this section (see pp. 76–80). E.g., W. Bousset, *Kyrios Christos* (Nashville: Abingdon, 1970), p. 364, argues that the difference between the concept "church" in C and E "proves beyond any doubt that the two epistles come from different authors," and H. Schlier, *Epheser*, p. 93, explains the variance between the wording of Col 1:24 ("His body which is the church") and Eph 1:22–23 ("the church which is His body") in the sense mentioned. Compare, however, F. C. Synge's opinion, quoted below in fn. 161.

148. Exegetical arguments for this interpretation have been collected in AB 34, pp. 170–83, in the comment on "Principalities, Powers, and All Things."

the assembly of Jews and gentiles in the church, the house and temple of God, has no parallel in C, although in the latter epistle (1:6, 23, 26–28; 2:11, 13) the surprise and joy at the admission of uncircumcised gentiles to the community of the saints are expressed. E mentions in the same text the estrangement of the gentiles from both God (cf. 4:18) and Israel, and their reconciliation by adoption and naturalization into the covenant of peace with God and Israel. According to C (1:20–22), however, the estrangement and enmity existed in the mind and the works of each gentile; it meant separation from God, requiring reconciliation with Him alone. Thus in C, Israel is not explicitly called the forerunner and partner of the gentiles in God's covenant, and reconciliation with God has a slightly individualistic overtone, which is not characteristic of the social concern of E.[149]

On the other hand, both letters resemble the self-description of the Qumran community when they call the saints a plantation and building, rooted in and founded on solid ground (Col 1:10, 23; 2:7 // Eph 2:20; 3:17). But only in E (2:20–22) is the building explicitly called a "temple of God" in which Jews and gentiles are "fitted and built together" in Christ, growing toward the "capstone, Christ." Also the beautiful description of the common worship of the reconciled Jews and gentiles which is found in the words "through Him and in one single Spirit the two have free access to the Father" (Eph 2:18), is unparalleled in C. Further, a difference is apparent also in Col 2:12–13; 3:1, where C reminds of the resurrection "with Christ," while E (2:5–6), as was already mentioned, speaks of a resurrection effected "in the Messiah" which is a co-resurrection with both the raised Christ and the Jews who were formerly dead in sins. E (2:6) surpasses C by adding to the co-resurrection a co-enthronement. But only C (2:20; cf. 3:3) speaks of "dying with Christ," and (in 2:11) of a circumcision with Christ's circumcision. Correspondingly C emphasizes mortification (cf. 3:5) where E sings of glorification. The explicit references of E to the "seal of the Spirit" (1:13; 4:30) may belong in this context.

With the references to resurrection, enthronement, and the Spirit, the next common theme of CE has come into focus.

6. *The End Time (Eschatology).* According to C (3:1–2), only one person is enthroned "above . . . at the right hand of God," Christ, and the saints are encouraged to "search for" and to "keep their minds on the things above," only at the day of Christ's parousia (the so-called "second coming") "will they be

---

149. This does not mean that C, by its omission of explicit references to Israel and the Scriptures, presupposes that the "kingdom of the beloved Son" (1:13) was depopulated of its Jewish members in order to permit the transplantation of pagans upon its ground, and that the Scriptures were torn up rather than fulfilled by Jesus Christ's coming. In Section VIII.2 (pp. 64–69) it was shown how inseparably the message of C is connected with the promises given to Israel. Not even by implication does C consider the church a substitute or legitimate successor of the people that was first elected by God.

revealed with Him in glory." E (2:6) seems to have anticipated that day when it speaks of the saints' co-enthronement here and now. Would it therefore be appropriate to speak of an ecclesiastical triumphalism of E?[150] Certainly both epistles contain elements of "realized eschatology." The letters presuppose that the secret hidden in the past is now gloriously revealed and preached in all the world (Eph 3:5 // Col 1:26). They affirm that the power (and/or the Spirit, see 3, above) is manifested in the congregation. They tell the saints that they have already been raised from the dead, together with Christ (Col 2:12; 3:1–4; Eph 2:5–6). Obviously they proclaim in unison that the end is at hand and the future is already present, according to both epistles.

Yet slightly different structures have been built upon the common basis. E points to the hope given to Israel's Fathers and fostered by the Jews alone (1:12; 2:12). This hope is fulfilled with the coming of the Messiah, although a hope remains also for the Christians, together with the necessity of their moving forward toward a perfection still to be attained (1:18; 4:13; 5:26–27). In turn, C (1:5, 23, 27) speaks exclusively of the sure hope of the Christians. In order to avoid any possessive boasting among the saints, C describes this hope not only in futuristic but also in geographical terms. Hope is "kept safe [literally: deposited] in heaven," "all treasures of wisdom and knowledge are [still!] hidden in Christ" who is "above" and "with whom the life of the saints is [still!] hidden in God" (Col 1:5; 2:3; 3:3).[151]

Does this imply that only in C (3:1–4) are the saints encouraged still to wait for the parousia, while E reveals its post-apostolic origin and character by its silence on that topic? In our interpretation of Eph 4:13 it was shown that E is no less concerned with the future appearance of Jesus Christ than C.[152]

Finally, some passages in C contain even more strands of "realized eschatology" than E. For C affirms not only (in line with its "theology of hope") that the saints are still to be "filled with knowledge" in order to appear on the Last Day holy, spotless, perfect before God (1:9, 22–23, 28), it also states jubilantly that they are already "filled" with God's fullness in Christ (2:9–10). Its author

---

150. See the comment, "The Presence of the Future," in AB 34, pp. 115–19, and the strictures on an ecclesiastical triumphalism in AB 34A, pp. 484–97.

151. The concept of "hope" as it is presupposed and developed in C has been exposed to severe (theological) criticism, followed by the verdict that Colossians is not authentically Pauline. See G. Bornkamm, "Die Hoffnung im Kolosserbrief," in *Studien zum Neuen Testament und zur Patristik*, FS für E. Klostermann, TU 77 (Berlin: Akademieverlag, 1961), pp. 56–64; repr. in idem, *Geschichte und Glaube* II (see fn. 113), pp. 206–13; cf. the essay of E. Grässer on Col 3:1–4 mentioned in fn. 67. Both authors take offense at the geographical (rather than temporal or existential) description of the character of hope. See Comment II on 1:3–11.

152. There it has been proposed that the Perfect Man whom the saints are to meet is Jesus Christ in his Second Coming, just as in the Parable of the Ten Virgins (Matt 25:1–13) and in the vision of Christ's parousia in 1 Thess 4:13–17.

takes comfort in Epaphras' prayer that they "stand fast as [already] perfect and consummate people" (4:12). Thus it is not advisable to call the eschatology of C more primitive, more futuristic, or merely geographical.

7. *The Ministry.* In the service of the comprehensive ministry of Jesus Christ, the only mediator of creation and redemption between God and his human, spiritual, and material creatures, stand many ministries, including the ministry of the whole church and of each one among the saints, according to CE and the *homologoumena.* All Pauline epistles give the apostolate of Paul a unique place but attribute also high and indispensable functions to other servants of Christ. They range from the co-authors to the carriers of the epistles, and from bishops (Phil 1:1) to hospitable housekeepers. But unlike C (1:1, 7–8; 4:10–17), E does not speak of the contribution (as a scribe or a secretary?) of Timothy, neither does it recommend special congregational functionaries or convey personal greetings. An exception is Tychicus, whose name and function are mentioned in E (6:21–22). When E offers a list of ministers of the Word, they are anonymous. All the more it is emphasized that all of them are appointed by the exalted Christ (Eph 4:7–11).

C is at variance with E because it does not restrict the revelation of the formerly hidden secret to "apostles and prophets." The secret was manifested to "[all] the saints" (Col 1:26 // Eph 3:5). C does not speak of the foundation of the church upon apostles and prophets. Perhaps because of the visions emphasized by the Colossian opponents (Col 2:18), a reference to New Testament prophets (who might have spoken of visions of their own) is not included in C.

According to this epistle, the ministry entrusted to persons in Christ's service is directed toward "each human being," and to the members of the congregation specifically (Col 1:28; 3:16; 4:3–5, etc.). The world or the powers are not addressed by it, although they form the stage and background of the missionary and pastoral work (Col 1:6, 23). However, in Eph 3:10 the whole church is given a missionary task for the benefit of the powers: "The manifold wisdom of God is now to be made known through the church to the governments and authorities in the heavens."

Although E as well as C build upon the authority of the apostolate, of hymns, confessional formulae, and traditions (Eph 4:20–24 // Col 2:7–8; 3:9–10, etc.),[153] the Ephesian emphasis on the Spirit and on prophets, also on the inspiration of all the saints (1:17), permits more openness, freedom, and variety in the church. Correspondingly, the dignity of the apostolic ministry, above all of the suffering of Paul, is emphasized more in Col 1:24, 28–29; 2:5; 4:16 than in Eph 3:1, 13; 4:1.[154] Only toward the end of E (6:18–20) is Paul's captivity mentioned in even stronger terms than in Col 4:3 and 10.

---

153. See Sections VII.3 (pp. 61–63) especially fns. 110 and 112, for controversial opinions and literature on these elements in C and E.

154. H. Ludwig, *Verfasser*, p. 88, believes that the author of C intentionally composed out of "the several elements of the Pauline self-understanding . . . a changed

But CE agree when they discuss the ministry of each saint in closely related contexts. *Mutual* subordination is prescribed in Eph 5:21, *mutual* teaching and advising in Col 3:16. Perhaps the double term "joints and ligaments" in Col 2:19 contains a clerical overtone (see above, in Subsection A.3(c), pp. 78–79), while in E (5:25–27; unlike, for example, John 3:29; 2 Cor 11:2) no intermediary agent between Christ and the church is mentioned. According to Eph 6:10–17, *each* saint wears the spiritual armor of an officer.

8. *Ethics.* In C no less than in E, the subordination of individual and communal exhortation ("parenesis") under the proclamation of God's saving acts is as strictly upheld as in the *homologoumena*. No imperatives are given except on the basis of indicatives! Obedience is the gift of God's grace, not a way to earn it! But both letters share also with the Pauline *homologoumena* certain emphasis on good works, on threatening wrath, and on promised reward in the Last Judgment.[155] Also, both mean a share in the life of God and a conduct on the ground of grace by "knowledge" and "wisdom," following the way pointed out by God, not just intellectual enlightenment and insight into one truth or another.[156]

However, C (1:9–10; 2:2) speaks loudly and clearly of an increase in the knowledge that is hidden in Christ, and it aims at full understanding on the part of the saints, while E (1:17; 3:18–19), fully aware of the continuous need of the ever-new gift of wisdom and knowledge, affirms that the material offered to the knowledge of Christ's love is so immeasurable and inconceivable that it surpasses all knowledge. Still, only E (3:10) states that the "wisdom of God" is to be made known to the powers through the church. In turn, only C (1:6, 10) combines fruit-bearing and growth (in a sequence which differs from biological observation!).

A few early manuscripts of Eph 1:15[157] attest to a meaning of "faith" which includes faithfulness (that is, loyalty and love) to both God and the saints, but the Colossian parallel (1:4), together with the later manuscripts of E, add "love"

---

image of the apostle": no longer holds the apostle a place "above the co-operators," for now he stands (only!) at their side. It would be difficult to demonstrate that this is really the intention of C.

155. See, e.g., Eph 2:10; 5:6; 6:8–9 // Col 1:10; 3:6; 3:25–4:1. In the comments on "God's Work, Works of Law, and Good Works" and on "Proclamation, Exhortation, and Vocation" in AB 34, pp. 242–51; 34A, pp. 453–62, it was shown that there exists no contradiction between the Pauline doctrine on justification by grace alone, "without works of the Law," and the emphasis placed on works and on the Last Judgment in C and E. See Gal 6:7–10; 1 Cor 3:12–15; Rom 2:5–11; 12:1–2, etc.

156. Col 1:9–10, 26–29; 2:2–3; 4:5 // Eph 1:17–18; 3:5–10; 5:15–16. The Old Testament and intertestamental roots of this concept of knowledge and wisdom are discussed in AB 34, pp. 119–23.

157. P46 B S* A, also mins 33, 365, 1739 Jerome and others, omit the reference to love.

toward the saints, to "faith [in God]." While in C (3:14) love is the "bond of perfection" among the saints, E (4:3) mentions a bond of "peace" which according to Eph 2:14–19 also embraces people who once were "far," that is, gentiles.

The missionary responsibility of the whole congregation which is strongly emphasized in E (5:8–13) is not totally absent from C. But the term "those outside" used in Col 4:5 (just as in 1 Thess 4:12; 1 Cor 5:12–13) to denote non-Christians does not occur in E, and the summary way chosen in Col 4:3–6 to describe the missionary task of each church member is unlike E. C lacks the warmth with which Eph 2:13, 17, 19 speaks of those far away and of the strangers, and it does not burn with the zeal shown in Eph 3:10; 5:8–13; 6:18–20 for the mission entrusted to the whole church and each Christian. Was the threatened church of Colossae less capable than its Ephesian sister of engaging in active mission work? A definite answer to explain the difference between C and E can hardly be given.

Yet another contact between the saints and the world, in essence at least as related to mission as the one just mentioned, cries out for full recognition at this place. The *bodily* presence of God's fullness in Christ, Christ's crucified *body* of flesh, and the *body*, that is, the bodily life in which the saints are to serve the Lord, are placed in the foreground in Col 1:22; 2:9, 11, 23; cf. 2:17; 3:5, that is, four or six times. But the earthly human body is mentioned only once in E, in 2:16. It is therefore probable that only C fights the denigration and depreciation of the physical body and the bodily life. It is possible that the Colossian Religion considered the physical body fit for nothing better than destruction because it was composed of earthly "elements" (2:8, 20?). At any rate, Col 2:23 speaks of the "harsh treatment of the body," which reflects the utter disdain of the opponents, fostered perhaps (in docetic fashion?) against a redeemer appearing in bodily, material shape, and certainly expressed in rigid forms of asceticism. C meets this feature of the Religion by the message of the "bodily" incarnation of God's fullness, of Christ's sovereign dominion, and of his peace-making reconciliation which comprehends not only all heavenly but also all earthly "things" (Col 1:15–20, 2:9). Since the reconciliation was carried out in Jesus Christ's "body of flesh," the saints are entitled and encouraged even in their bodies, in their various physical, psychical, and social predicaments, to kill obnoxious attitudes and to serve the Lord (Col 3:5–4:1).

In other words, the body of each saint constitutes and reveals his belonging in the world of "all things." Inasmuch as this body is corrupted by sin, it can only and must perish. But now God has revealed and triumphantly established his might and right over all creatures, including the human body. Therefore, the saints in every aspect of their creaturely existence, not just their minds or souls, are saved and called upon to worship their creator and redeemer. The same message and challenge has a prelude, is given support, or finds an echo, also in E.[158] But E does not play this tune *fortissimo* as does C.

_____

158. Eph 1:19–21; 2:15–16; 4:25–32; 5:21–6:17.

The positive attitude of C toward the body has a negative complement: only C (2:[11], 20, 3:3a, 5) speaks of the death of the saints with Christ and contains a full-blown declaration of war against the "members . . . that are on earth." Service *in* the body does not mean service *to* the body, but presupposes a "stripping off the Old Man" (Col 3:9 // Eph 4:22), and a battle to death against the viciousness of its members. Catalogs of vices and interspersed prohibitions outnumber the good works enumerated in Col 3:5–13. This distinguishes C from the more balanced and evangelically motivated calls to decision found in E (4:25–32).

The topical comparison might be continued. This method is rewarding for acquiring a sensitivity for the idiosyncrasies of C and E, and for their common message; but it illustrates and poses rather than solves the problem of their interrelation. If the facts presented permit any conclusions at all, they are these: the same doctrine of God's and Christ's power and love in relation to all things, all powers, and all men and women is presented in both epistles. A value judgment, declaring one presentation superior to the other, is beyond a commentator's task and competence; also, it is impossible to decide whether the substance of one of the two letters is nearer the undisputed Pauline doctrine contained in the *homologoumena*.

D. The Question of Dependence

While a close relationship between C and E is certain, the question whether the dependence of one or both of these letters can be demonstrated is as yet open.[159] Whenever *literary* dependence was made the working hypothesis for studying the relationship between C and E, one of the following alternatives emerged:

1. E is an elaboration on C.[160]
2. C is an abbreviation and polemical application of E.[161]

---

159. Among the summaries of the discussion are J. T. Sanders, "Hymnic Elements" (see fn. 127), pp. 101–4; J. B. Polhill, "Relationship," RevExp 70 (1973) 439–50; A. van Roon, *Authenticity*, pp. 4–8. The following is an elaboration on the possibilities enumerated above, on pp. 101–4; literary forms of dependence are now separated from several possibilities of nonliterary relationship.

160. W. M. L. De Wette's, F. C. Baur's, and H. Milgenfeld's *Einleitung*, pp. 663–75, conception of the priority of C was undergirded with additional arguments by W. Ochel, *Die Annahme einer Bearbeitung des Kolosserbriefes im Epheserbrief, in einer Analyse des Epheserbriefes untersucht*, Diss. (Marburg, 1934). He believed that E was meant to replace C. The judgment, C is prior, is widespread and often combined with the verdict, C is authentic—so much so that the list of names to be presented in Section X.C (pp. 121–22) includes those commentators who decide for the priority of C. The same applies to the following options: see the names listed in Sections X.C–D (pp. 121–25).

161. E. T. Mayerhoff, *Colosser*, pp. 103, 109–110, 143, 147fn.; J. Coutts, "Relationship," NTS 4 (1957/58) 201–7, on the basis of observed conflations of Ephesian passages

3. A short (lost) Ur-Colossians was written by Paul. This script was then used by another author for the writing of E. Finally, this "other author" interpolated parts of E into Ur-Colossians, giving it the form in which C was canonized. The term "(mutual) interdependence" sums up this solution.[162]

4. Two authors other than Paul wrote E and C, using independently of

---

in C; F. C. Synge, *St. Paul's Epistle to the Ephesians* (London: SPCK, 1941), pp. 69–75, considers "Body *(sōma)* of Christ" a vivid simile in E, recalling the literal meaning of "body," but a "pure metaphor [presupposing that it means the church]" in C. The same *sōma* passages as quoted by Synge are used by H. Schlier with the opposite result, see fn. 147. M. Goguel, "Esquisse" (1935, see fn. 124), unlike idem, *Introduction* (1926), holds that E was written first, by Paul, as a general letter to the churches of Asia, followed by C, which also is genuinely Pauline. Then an editor, using C, tampered with E. However, A. van Roon, *Authenticity*, pp. 144, 426, 436, tentatively decides for the priority of E; he reckons with one and the same author, working at about the same time on both manuscripts. If the letter to the Laodiceans mentioned in Col 4:16 could be proven to be what was canonized under the name "Ephesians," at least the priority of E would be certain, as W. Marxsen, *Introduction*, p. 191, observes.

162. H. J. Holtzmann, *Kritik*, passim; idem, *Einleitung*, pp. 277–81; J. Weiss, *Earliest Christianity* I (New York: Harper Torchbook, 1937), p. 150; C. Masson, *Colossiens* (1950), passim, especially p. 159.

In his *Kritik*, Holtzmann's Ur-Colossians consisted solely of Col 1:9b–12, 14–24, 26–28; 2:2b–3, 7a, 9–11, 15, 17–19, 22–23; 3:1–2, 4–11, 14–16, 18–25; 4:1, 9, 15–17; but in his *Einleitung*, some of these elements, i.e., Col 1, 14–22; 2:6, 9–10 were considered non-Pauline additions. C. Masson's Ur-Colossians contain the smallest number of verses proposed: 1:1–4, 7–8; 2:6, 8–9, 11a, 12a, 16, 20–21; 3:3–4, 12, 13a, 18–22a, 25; 4:1–3ab, 5–8a, 10–12a, 14 (-15), 17–18. A solution on the Holtzmann-Masson line is favored by P. Benoit, *Les épîtres de Saint Paul aux Philippiens, à Philémon, aux Colosiens, aux Ephésiens*, La Sainte Bible (Paris: du Cerf, 1949, cited as *Colossians* in the following), pp. 85, 159; idem, "L'hymne christologique" (see fn. 101), 253–54, 258–59.

While H. J. Holtzmann's main work was appearing in print, W. Hönig, "Über das Verhältnis" (see fn. 115) also assumed that C contained interpolations. But Hönig found the origin of the interpolated words, sentences, and thoughts in the *homologoumena*, not in E. While H. v. Soden, too, in his essays on C in the *Jahrbuch für protestantische Theologie* II (1885) 320–68, 497–543, 672–702, had considered Col 1:15–20 as a later insertion, he abandoned that view in his *Kolosser* (1891), p. 31, but returned to his former judgment, again, in 1905, in his *Urchristliche Literaturgeschichte*, pp. 51, 53.

According to C. R. Bowen, "Original Form," JBL 43 (1924) 177–206, the authentically Pauline Ur-Colossians was augmented by a disciple of the apostle who early in the second century added to Paul's composition the polemical parts. On the basis of the interpolated Colossian text, so he argues, E then was written. P. N. Harrison, "Onesimus and Philemon," ATR 32 (1950) 268–82, concurs with the theory of the inserted antiheretical materials, yet not with the mentioned explanation of the origin of E. In turn, E. P. Sanders, JBL 85 (1966) 28–45, suggests that Col 1:1–3:10 is a conflation

one another the same or slightly varying (forms of) liturgical and parenetical materials.[163]

Already long before, but with new arguments after the development of form- and tradition-critical research, several solutions were proposed which renounce the idea that C and E owe their origin to copying done from one or several written sources. *Oral* or mental dependence can be emphasized, at the expense of literary copying from a completed document.[164]

5. One author, whether Paul himself or a disciple, wrote both epistles in close succession or at the same time, formulating the same thoughts in slightly varied wording.[165]

---

constructed out of Pauline elements, increased by extensive interpolations, while only Col 3:11–4:18 may contain genuine ethical and greeting materials. In his commentary on Ephesians (1941), p. 69, F. C. Synge speaks for some earlier and later expositors when he sees only in Col 4:10–18 an authentic Pauline fragment. Following W. Munro, "Col III.18–IV.1 and Eph V.21–VI.9," NTS 18 (1972) 434–47, the *Haustafeln* are a late interpolation in both C and E.

163. H. J. Holtzmann, *Kritik*, p. 36. In his commentary on C of 1927, p. 70, M. Dibelius spoke only of parenetical material, but Dib.-Gr. (1953) added to it hymnic traditions as being used by both authors. E. Käsemann, "Epheserbrief," RGG II, p. 519; idem, "Kolosserbrief," RGG III, p. 1727, and newer commentaries such as E. Lohse's concur with the distinction of these two basic types of incorporated materials. According to N. A. Dahl, "Der Epheserbrief und der verlorene erste Brief des Paulus," (see fn. 127), pp. 71–72, sometimes C, sometimes E offers the material in an older form; e.g., the parenesis of Col 3:5ff. is more influenced by the situation of the addressees than its parallel in Eph 5:3ff.

164. General criticism against explaining harmony and difference by reference to one or another *literary* relationship has been formulated by, e.g., J. B. Polhill, "Relationship," pp. 449–50; H. Ludwig, *Verfasser*, p. 24; A. van Roon, *Authenticity*, pp. 416–17, 426, 429.

165. Col 1:1, 23; 4:18 and Eph 1:1; 3:1 affirm explicitly that Paul wrote each letter. C and E would not have been canonized without the conviction that both were authentic. In the tradition of the church this was not disputed until in 1824 L. Usteri, *Die Entwicklung des paulinischen Lehrbegriffs* (Zürich: Orell Füssli, pp. 2–8), and in 1826 W. M. L. De Wette questioned the authenticity of E, and in 1838 E. T. Mayerhoff followed suit regarding C.

A common author of C and E, different from Paul, was proposed by F. C. Baur, *Paulus* (1845), pp. 448–49, 455–57; H. J. Holtzmann, *Kritik*, pp. 46–47, 64–65; P. Pokorný, *Der Epheserbrief und die Gnosis* (Berlin: Evangelische Verlagsanstalt, 1965), p. 13; tentatively also by G. Schille, "Der Autor des Epheserbriefes," ThLZ 82 (1957) 325–34, especially 333–34; idem, *Frühchristliche Hymnen* (1965), p. 33; A. van Roon, *Authenticity*, pp. 417, 419, 431. E. Gaugler, *Epheserbrief* p. 12, prefers the assumption that one author wrote in close succession first C, then E, but will not decide whether it was "the apostle himself or a disciple of Paul or a total stranger."

6. The author of E knew C most intimately, as if by heart; he used a copy of C only when he wrote Eph 6:21–22.[166]

7. During Paul's lifetime, different secretaries or disciples of Paul, or after Paul's death, different members of his "school," with or without the help of a Pauline oral or written outline but acquainted with Paul's teachings and his undisputed letters, wrote the two letters (see fn. 101). If they worked as Paul's secretaries, their dependence on their master can have had different forms.[167]

In view of the great number of these possibilities, and of the conflict among the various theories formed on their basis, it is not astonishing that a last group of scholars considers the question of dependence, and sometimes the problem of authorship as well, insoluble, and perhaps ultimately irrelevant. The inclination appears to be rising to give up and bury the whole literary quest for authentic Pauline letters because even for the *homologoumena* a creative cooperation of secretaries, pupils, or transmittors cannot be excluded.[168]

In the following discussion, first the various successive or competing modern schools and their criteria for finding a solution will be enumerated. Then a summary and evaluation of the answers will conclude the prelude to the authenticity question.

1. Literary Criticism. After more than a hundred years of intensive philological, historical, and theological studies in the interrelation among the

---

166. E. J. Goodspeed, *Key*, p. XII; idem, *Meaning of Ephesians*, pp. 5, 46–47.

167. The secretary hypothesis was proposed for the origin of E as early as F. E. D. Schleiermacher, *Einleitung ins Neue Testament*, ed. G. Walde (Berlin: Reimer, 1845), pp. 161–66, and more recently extended to Colossians by, e.g., P. Benoit, "Rapports Littéraires" (see fn. 101), pp. 21–22; idem "Introduction to the Letters of Saint Paul," in JB, NT (New York: Doubleday, 1966) pp. 253–66, especially p. 261; G. H. P. Thompson, *The Letter of Paul to the Ephesians* (Cambridge: University Press, 1967), pp. 9, 12, 16, 19. Also A. van Roon and E. Schweizer embrace this solution. See fn. 197 for the names of the secretarial aides suggested in newer literature. But E. Percy, PKE, pp. 421–22, thinks that more questions are posed than answered by this hypothesis, and E. Lohse, *Colossians*, p. 181, fn. 10, attributes it to "embarrassment" on the part of the commentators (*eine Verlegenheitslösung*). R. Morgenthaler, *Statistik*, p. 58, enumerates five ways in which an *amanuensis* or *famulus* may have worked: (1) following complete dictation by the apostle, (2) following dictation of parts only, (3) following general directions received, (4) elaborating on an original script of Paul, by making changes and additions, (5) creating without authorization a document which was mailed under the name of Paul. Cf. AB 34, pp. 40–41.

168. So, e.g., Dib.-Gr., p. 83 ("a problem, perhaps insoluble, but never a strict proof of spuriousness"); A. van Roon, *Authenticity*, passim (regarding E); cf. W. Marxsen, *Introduction*, p. 181; J. B. Polhill, RevExp 70 (1973) 444, 449; J. Lähnemann, *KolB*, pp. 177–82; E. Schweizer, *Kolosser*, p. 25.

("synoptic") Gospels of Matthew, Mark, and Luke, no method used in theological schools has as yet proven fail-safe, successful, and convincing to determine
the temporal and literary relationship between two or more undated documents
that are as similar and dissimilar to one another as the Synoptic Gospels. Always
dogmatical or other *a priori*, plain traces of a *tour de force*, inexplicable details,
and blank spaces remained visible on the map and called for subtle or crude
counterargumentation.[169] Indeed, the methods of literary criticism which were
developed for research in the Gospels can be and have been applied to the C-E
dependence problem. But their fruitfulness is as unconvincing as the uncritical
transfer of the rules of textual criticism to this issue. For example, the vocabulary, the style, the biographical data, and many doctrines characteristic of C and
E are so similar, and the divergent elements in diction and substance can so
easily be explained by the specific situations addressed in C and E respectively,
that they alone yield no reason to deny simultaneous authorship by one and the
same person. Also there is no unequivocal evidence of literary dependence of
one letter upon the other, or of both on third sources.

2. *Historical Criticism.*   Research done in the historical setting of C and E
appeared to confirm what on the basis of literary criticism at best could be
guessed. The history of religions showed to E. T. Mayerhoff that Corinthian or
other Gnosticism was refuted in C; therefore, this epistle had to be dated in the
second century and to be dependent on E. Still, this supposedly exact delineation of the Colossian Religion has not remained unchallenged.[170]

The history of the early church, especially of its self-understanding, its
relation to the Jews and to the Law, its ministry, and the developing doctrines
on Christ and eschatology were scrutinized for finding out whether C fitted
better in a phase of the apostolic, late-apostolic, or post-apostolic period than E,
or vice versa. However, because the same epistles were used as sources for

---

169. One of the latest thorough works on the origin of the Synoptic (and Johannine)
Gospels, under the point of view of literary dependence, is P. Benoit and M.-E.
Boismard, *Synopse des quatre évangiles* II (Paris: du Cerf, 1972), especially pp. 15–55.
The authors reconstruct four documents, rather than the widely accepted pair of Q and
Mark, from which (by ways of four separate intermediate proto-Gospels, and with the aid
of special sources accessible to each one of the four evangelists) the four Gospels came
into being. Presupposed in this reconstruction is the conviction that a combination of
word counts with the theory of *literary* dependence can solve the problem of the Gospels'
unity and diversity. In his review of Benoit's and Boismard's work in JBL 94 (1979)
128–32, E. P. Sanders has reproduced the chart drawn by Boismard (on p. 17) which is
meant to elucidate the (most complicated!) interrelationship between the reputedly
earliest sources, the intermediate stages, and the Gospels in their present form.

170. Pioneering in tracing the heresies back to the early days of Christianity was and
still is the earlier mentioned work of W. Bauer, *Orthodoxy and Heresy* (German original,
1934; Eng. trans., 1972); cf. S. L. Greenslade, *Schism in the Early Church* (London,
SCM., 1953); also H. Koester, "Gnomai Diaphorai," HTR 58 (1965) 279–318.

defining what was called apostolic, late-, or post-apostolic, this historical argument was circular. Also the picture created of the various phases of constitutional or doctrinal development of the church has been so strongly influenced by personal predilections or prejudices of the commentators that the results for placing and dating of this or that epistle are not free of the suspicion of a *petitio principii*. It is still possible that so-called "late" patterns of organization, heretical movements, and theological conceptions coexisted with undisputedly early elements. Therefore, many present-day distinctions between early and late historical developments are unsafe criteria for dating C and E, and for determining the sequence of their writing.[171]

3. *Form, Tradition, and Redaction Criticism.* With the help of new methods of scholarly New Testament study, developed since the twenties of this century, contributions to the elucidations of both letters were made as described

---

171. Arguments in favor of a very complex picture of organization, life, and teaching of the earliest churches include the following:

1. Bishops are mentioned as early as the Pauline *homologoumena* (see Phil 1:1); e.g., B. H. Streeter, *The Primitive Church* (New York and London: MacMillan, 1929), pp. 48–57, laid emphasis on the different forms of church order that coexisted at the same time.

2. A combination of legalism and libertinism existed already in the Galatian churches. W. Schmithals, *Gnosticism in Corinth* (Nashville: Abingdon, 1971); idem, *Paul and the Gnostics* (Nashville: Abingdon, 1972), lacks a historical basis when he equates the substance of the opposition to Paul with that of second-century and later Gnosticism. However, a partial anticipation of the composite and sometimes bifurcated teaching of some Gnostic groups may have taken place.

3. Elements of the "highest" and reputedly latest Christology [see, e.g., O. Cullmann, *Christology of the New Testament* (Philadelphia: Westminster, 1954), pp. 247–328] are found in Matt 11:25 // Luk 10:21–22, that is, inside the so-called "Q document" which—if it ever existed at all—would have to be dated in one or another stage of redaction about 50 C.E. The same or an analogous "high" Christology is also unfolded in the hymn Col 1:15–20, to which an early date has to be attributed if the author of C intended to quote it as an authority for his readers.

4. Explicit references to the parousia occur only rarely in Luke's reports on the life and teaching of earliest Christianity—though Acts 1:11; 3:20–21; 17:31 form remarkable exceptions. Different views of this fact are represented by, e.g., T. F. Glasson, *The Second Advent*, 3d rev. ed. (London: Epworth, 1963) and J. A. T. Robinson, *Jesus and His Coming* (London: SCM, 1957); idem, "The Most Primitive Christology of All," in idem, *Twelve New Testament Studies*, SBT 34 (1962) 139–53, on one hand, and by E. Grässer, *Das Problem der Parusieverzögerung*, BZNW 22 (3d ed., 1977), especially pp. 204–15; idem, *Die Naherwartung Jesu*, SBS 61 (1973), on the other. Though the judgment of Dib.-Gr. (p. 53) that, in view of the fallible nature of stylecritical arguments, aspects of the history of theology (and of religions) are decisive for a judgment on the authenticity of C, has been respected in the recent decades, especially by some German scholars, it cannot be normative forever. For as yet the history of theology and of religions contains too many secrets to be used as foolproof datebook.

above, in Section VIII (pp. 78–90). There the fact and the modes of the incorporation and redaction of traditional materials in C were discussed.[172] But the existence of a flourishing Pauline academy at Ephesus can only be guessed; it has not yet been demonstrated by archaeological research or unambiguous other means. Indeed, formulae, hymns, and exhortations may be quoted or adapted by the writer and/or redactor of either C or E, or of both. But their original forms have only been reconstructed, not actually discovered on, e.g., ancient tombstones or in some long-known or recently discovered documents. Thus the gaps left open by the application of the historical- and literary-critical methods have not really been filled and the hypotheses (called "results") of the respective schools are not yet verified. While, for example, G. Schille seems to argue that the more a document quotes an early form of a hymn, the older it must be, C. Maurer and P. Benoit assume that the presence of a hymn can be evidence of a document's secondary character.[173] Is E therefore older than C because at places it sings, where C preaches? If only the same criteria could be applied to prose and hymnic sections in C and E as are used for describing the Song of the Sea (attributed to Moses and Miriam), and the Song of Deborah in their relation to the prose reports on the crossing of the Sea of Reeds and the battle at the foot of Mount Tabor, or for illuminating the interrelation between poetic and didactic passages in the same prophetic book.[174] But the time span within which the New Testament books were written is probably too short to

---

172. Cf. the analogous introductory Section II in AB 34, pp. 6–10.

173. G. Schille, *Hymnen* (see fn. 127). C. Maurer, "Der Hymnus von Epheser 1" (see fn. 98), concludes his essay stating that form and contents of the "hymn" (Eph 1:3–14) indicate the posteriority of E in relation to C and the Fourth Gospel. He assumes that the fight against the Gnostic Redeemer is presupposed in E (and therefore belongs to an era long past), so that nothing is left but to think over the questions raised by Gnosticism in terms of the congregation's stance. P. Benoit, in his discussion of the Christological hymn of Col 1:15–20 (see fn. 101), p. 250, asserts that after the completion of an early form of C by Paul, and of E by an *amanuensis* of Paul, the apostle himself composed a poetic summary of his prose teaching in C; he used the earlier hymn Col 1:15–17 as a pattern for his original contribution, Col 1:18–20, and he inserted—as a latest act of redaction—Col 1:15–20 into his earlier draft of C.

174. Cf. F. Crüsemann, *Studien zur Formgeschichte von Hymnus und Danklied in Israel* (Neukirchen: Neukirchener Verlag, 1969), especially 1821. According to D. N. Freedman and F. M. Cross, "The Song of Miriam," JNES 14 (1955) 237–50, the Song of the Sea (Ex 15:1–18) is older than any other written tradition of Israel's early history. But following M. Noble, *Das zweite Buch Mose*, ATD II (Göttingen: Vandenhoeck, 1959), pp. 96–100, the hymnic-liturgical character of the same song demonstrates that "Ex 15:1–19 is a relatively young piece which [however] does not permit a more specific dating of its origin." The controversy is as yet unsettled in this case, but less frustrating in another: The Song of Deborah (Judg 5) is extensively discussed by, e.g., C. F. Burney, *The Book of Judges* (London: 1903; repr. New York: KTAV, 1970), pp. 78–176, especially pp. 78–83, 94–102, and A. Weiser, "Das Deboralied," ZAW 71 (1959) pp. 67–91.

permit the same processes and changes of traditions as reflected in many parts of the Old Testament. The many questions still unanswered by the Old Testament scholars who have vast amounts of study material at hand can hardly find an easy solution in New Testament research with its very restricted field of operation.

4. *Structuralism.* Left over as a method for scrutinizing the relationship between C and E are criteria which might summarily be called "structuralistic" although to a considerable extent their discovery and application antedates the challenges, theses, and claims which have issued from the Structuralists' citadels at Warsaw, Vienna, Paris, and Geneva. While a structuralistic approach need not necessarily introduce a part or all of the philosophical presuppositions and the technical terminology characteristic of the majority of the representatives of Structuralism, it cannot be carried out without frequent recourse to the questions, standards, observations, and conclusions that have distinguished preceding schools of scholarly criticism.[175] Outstanding are the following criteria:

a. The change of *vocabulary* and of *word meanings*—even if it could be demonstrated that C uses Pauline words in a more typical Pauline sense than E—is evidence neither of a falsifier nor of a different author but often of a creative writer. Such an author takes up the vocabulary of the people whom he addresses, and his use of given words is determined each time anew by the whole sentence or context in which they occur, not by a narrow dictionary definition.[176]

b. The *doublets* and *repetitions* in C, including intended self-quotations or clarifications, have been considered by E. T. Mayerhoff, H. J. Holtzmann, and C. Masson as a sign of total or partial dependence of C on E. For the majority of other scholars they are part of the baroque style of Paul or the pseudonymous writer of C which was imitated by the author of E.[177] An examination of the occurrence and function of double expressions and of the resumption of

---

Today the opinion prevails that the Song of Deborah is older than the prose narrative in Judg 4. As to prophetic books, S. Herrmann in his report on "Forschung am Jeremiah-buch," ThLZ 102 (1977) 481–90, illustrates how manifold are as yet the solutions offered for deciding on authenticity and age of the poetic passages in the book of Jeremiah, once they are separated from the prose sections; unquestionably, many prose texts have a later date than poetic passages, but not all that is poetic is necessarily older or genuine.

175. H. J. Holtzmann, *Kritik*, pp. 25–26, and M. Bujard, *Stil*, passim, especially pp. 11–19, 220, have called for holistic methods. At this place, also J. Lähnemann's and F. Zeilinger's works have to be recalled. With greatest care they attempted to display the main structure and substructures of C (see fn. 57).

176. See fn. 87 for M. Goguel's, M. Dibelius', and C. L. Mitton's arguments to the contrary, and for the names of scholars who, long before the rise of structuralism, have announced doubts about their validity.

177. A list of repetitions and doublets is presented in fn. 91. E. T. Mayerhoff, *Colosser* pp. 46–48, had assumed that the author of C substituted synonyms and

thoughts in liturgies, in hymns, in artistic and common prose, and of the clarification of earlier mentioned thoughts in letters and other literature of friendly-affirmative or polemic character cannot be made here. It would certainly show that literary dependence or interdependence is only one among many possibilities in explaining the phenomenon. Sometimes rhymes, produced by the choice of similar words, grammatical forms, or accentuation, are intended to create pleasant sounds. At other or at the same occasions, kaleidoscopic variations or clarifying expositions of given concepts or ideas are presented either to evoke the feelings of harmony or symmetry with accepted tenets, or to answer the provocation caused by the opposed movement. Instead of a linear or prosaic (Western) logical deployment of an argument, often the (more Oriental) artistic means of chiastic arrangement of ideas can be observed, for example, the pattern of *inclusio,* where thought or word A leads to B, and after a repetition of B the argument is concluded with A.[178] This feature and more complex variations of it look redundant or irritating only to such readers who are blind and deaf to the *parallelismus membrorum* characteristic of Semitic and especially to Near Eastern poetry. In the similarities between C and E, they play a much larger role than a possible mechanical literary dependence.

   c. *Grammatically* correct (for example, harmonious with classical Greek)

---

tautologies for quality of thought (suffering from *Gedankenarmut* as he was) and M. Bujard, *Stil,* pp. 87–100, etc., attributed the duplications to a loose association of ideas, a fixation upon formulations given by a tradition, and a lack of mental mobility. However, the same author observes what H. Hegermann, *Schöpfungsmittler* (1961), already had stated: in C, repetitions of expressions and thoughts are "about as frequent" (p. 97) as in the *homologoumena,* where they serve the logical continuation of Paul's reasoning. Hegermann (p. 167) speaks of the tension and combination found in C between thanksgiving for the redemption of the saints on the one hand, and warning of the threatening danger on the other.

178. Attempts have also been made to reveal a poetical-dramatical, especially a chiastic, order of topics within individual parts of Colossians. G. Giavini, "La struttura litterarea del inno cristologico de Col," RivBibl 15 (1967) 317–20, sees a correspondence in C (Col 1:12–14), B (1:15), A (1:16a) to, A' (1:16bc, 17), B' (1:18 [a]b), C' (1:19–20a), in which Christ forms the radical center in A and A' (1:16–17). P. Lamarche "La structure de l'épître aux Colossiens," *Biblica* 56 (Rome, 1975) 543–63, observes chiasms in the parts I and II of the epistle (found in 1:1–20, and 1:21–2:15) respectively, which precede the application presented in part I (2:16–4:1) and the conclusion found in part IV (4:2–18). Part I announces the three themes—Thanksgiving, Prayer, and News Received—and develops them in reverse order; similarly, part II first only hints at Transformation by God in Christ, Warning, and Proclamation of Hope, then treats these three topics in the opposite sequence. For the whole of an epistle, i.e., for Galatians and for each one of its major parts and minor subsections, a chiastic reconstruction has been offered by J. Blight, *Galatians in Greek* (Detroit: St. Paul's Publication, 1966), and for the Lukan Travel Narrative (Luke 9:51–18:28) and some of its major parables, by K. E. Bailey, *Poet and Peasant* (Grand Rapids: Eerdmans, 1976), pp. 79–206. In all cases, the

word forms, proper or pleasantly alternating *syntactical* connections of words and clauses, and *logically* conclusive associations of one statement with another—all such features occur in C and E with the same high or low frequency. It is impossible to decide whether poor diction and logic of one epistle was improved by the secondary letter, or whether by abbreviation or prolongation the later epistle truncated the originally fluent text of the first, in the service of concerns higher than grammatical and rhetorical. Whenever selections of examples were made to demonstrate the priority of C over E, the various options presented by Koine-Greek, Semitic poetry, and logical-doctrinal concatenation may have been too little respected or too much limited under the influence of popular or individual prejudices.

d. The *parallel structure* of the main parts of C and E was already discussed in Subsection B (pp. 80–87), with the conclusion that the structural comparison of C and E yielded as little indisputable evidence in favor of the priority of C or E, as the case studies and the linguistic and doctrinal inquiries.[179]

5. *Psychological Reasoning.* Psychological explanations can be found to justify almost any theory of relationship and dependence between the author(s) and the two letters. Sometimes they appear to be used by modern scholars to bolster decisions already made on other grounds, or they reveal more about the scholar's psychic reaction to the letters than about the letters and their author(s) themselves.

H. J. Cadbury would like to meet the modern scholar's reluctance to live with indecision and complexity, yet feels forced to affirm that the problem of the authorship of E "ultimately lies" in the "obscure area of psychological probability." F. C. Synge, admitting that Paul "could have written Ephesians," opines that if the apostle also wrote Colossians, "it must have been in a mood of dejection and lethargy." Opposite results are attained when (consciously or not) one or another of the variant readings of Luke 5:39 is considered applicable to the solution of the C-E problem. Then either "the old is good" or "the older is milder." C does indeed taste "old" and "good" (or at least: better) because its Christocentrism is reminiscent of Paul's Christocentric teaching in the *homologoumena*, and the ecclesiasticism of E, with its alleged advocacy of a late- or post-apostolic institutionalism, is found guilty of "weakening of argument" (E. Käsemann) and must take the back seat. Or it is assumed that peaceful and mild E must have been written by an author mellowed through old age to the extent that he has given up the grim battles fought against heretics in younger years. The poor old man has lost his teeth! Whether a poor Paulinist

---

skill of the expositors deployed in pointing out or in constructing chiasms may be more obvious than the intention and artistry of the biblical authors themselves.

179. H. J. Holtzmann, *Kritik*, p. 130, observes that both letters contain "characteristics of the primary and secondary" and he includes linguistic theological traits in this observation.

or Paul himself is considered the author of C or E, or of both C and E—in any case the verdict, C is prior, then is determined either by the dogma of a primitive historicism (saying that what is older is more reliable and true) or by the prejudice of people considering themselves young (expressed by their contempt of older persons). K. Staab who considers C and E—the latter with additions made by a pupil—as genuine as Philemon, does not acknowledge a basic distinction between C and E: "[the apostle] has become old (Philemon 9), but in his soul a youthful fire is still burning, and it breaks forth [in Colossians and elsewhere] when he sees his flock menaced by Judaizing agitators (Phil 3, 2)."[180]

Although wine tasting and testing, psychological and gerontological research can be performed ritually, artfully, and scientifically, arguments such as those just mentioned cannot have the last word in the solution of literary and historical problems of biblical interpretation. The essence of both creative persons and historical events or sequences (including the writing of letters) contains not only surprises but also paradoxes beyond the limits of psychological diagnosis and prognosis.

6. Doctrinal Preferences. Probably few scholarly readers of C and E would like to admit that their criteria, methods, and results are an effect of their own predispositions. Invariably, the influence, if not pressure of their national, cultural, denominational background, not to speak of their academic training and theological coinage, is reflected in their findings regarding matters literary and historical. For almost a hundred and fifty years, German-speaking Protestant scholars have more often turned to radical criticism of traditional opinions than their Anglo-Saxon, French, or Roman-Catholic colleagues. Some of the latter have shown more readiness than the former to be aware of potential prejudices and to be critical not only of the tradition but also of some dogmas of biblical criticism, including the necessity to follow the trend to call C prior, or to consider only C authentic, at the expense of E. When, for example, the fixed idea is dominant that a document has to contain or express, in so many words or in tolerably analogous terms, the "doctrine of justification" in order to be authentically Pauline, or when a specific historical view of the development of early church doctrine and organization is declared the bedrock of all scholarly biblical work, then C has to be a suspicious halfway house between the *homologoumena* and E.[181] But even loaded theological predilections and preju-

180. H. J. Cadbury, "The Dilemma of Ephesians," NTS 5 (1958/59) 91–102, especially 92; F. C. Synge, *Ephesians*, p. 70; E. Käsemann, RGG III, p. 1728; K. Staab, *Gefangenschaftsbriefe*, pp. 72, 115–19, 168–69.

181. According to H. von Soden, *Kolosser*, pp. 11–15, "the substance of the statements" *(die sachlichen Aussagen)*, not the "formalia" of C, are decisive for the question of authenticity. Reference to E. Käsemann's similar judgments was made in fn. 96. Käsemann believes that the theology of C stands closer to the *homologoumena* than the intention and message of E. Still, he observes so much of a "weakening of theological

dices, also elaborate depictions of historical processes, are sometimes subjective. Just as in the case of E, so also a new commentary on C has to ask for more than a repetition and confirmation of conservative or critical beliefs.

E. Summary

The criteria mentioned in the foregoing have been used individually or in combination, with a rough hand or with subtle skill. The results achieved by their application can now be summed up in a few lines. In some instances, arguments not yet mentioned explicitly will be added. Among the reasons given for the priority of C over E, making E dependent on C, and among the arguments for the opposite and for a third solution, the following are prominent.

1. *In Favor of Colossians:* C addresses a local church, as does the majority of the *homologoumena*, specific needs are met, greetings similar to those in Philemon are extended; E has been intended to substitute for C: the vocabulary of C, its meaning, and the theology expressed by it are (more) like Paul's in E; the crisp brevity of C becomes tiring verbosity, clear passages of C are obscured, or obscure passages are clarified; E disrupts the coherent structure of thought which distinguishes C; in C, hymns are directed to God, not to Christ, moral exhortations (specifically the *Haustafeln*) are "less Christianized" than in E; a primitive, pagan, cosmic understanding of the world as the deity's body remains perceptible while the conviction that only the church is the body of Christ is certainly preached in the present text of C, but unlike E, not yet presupposed; the elements of realized eschatology have not yet totally eclipsed the futuristic strands.[182]

2. *In Favor of Ephesians:* Arguments such as the following are being used: what is called the (earlier written!) letter to the Laodiceans and was actually written *before* C, according to Col 4:16, is actually identical with E or has E for its basis; many homiletic Ephesian passages look older than their shortened dogmatic and moralistic Colossian counterparts; the hymns in E have a more ancient form; the Colossian parenesis consists of excerpts from the discourses on ethics in E; C condenses the peaceful Ephesian letter and presses it into battle service against a (post-apostolic) heresy; the teaching of the unity of Jews and

---

argument" and so many stamps of the post-apostolic period that he feels compelled to dispute the authenticity of this letter. Further examples of theological criticism leveled against C will be given at the beginning of Section X.

182. H. J. Holtzmann, *Kritik*, pp. 55–61, lists Col 1:1–2 // Eph 1:1–2; Col 1:3–5, 9 // Eph 1:15–18; Col 1:5 // Eph 1:3, 12–13; Col 1:25, 29 // Eph 3:2,7; Col 2:4, 6–9 // Eph 4:17, 20–21; Col 4:5 // Eph 5:15–16; Col 4:6 // Eph 4:29 to prove such points. The remarks of E. Lohse, *Colossians*, p. 4, "In certain passages Ephesians reads like the first commentary on Colossians, though admittedly it does more than explicate the thoughts of Colossians," contains a necessary correction of superficial distinctions between E and C as they have been made—mostly at the expense of E.

Gentiles is earlier than the generalization about heaven and earth because the particular and the concrete precede the abstract; the cosmic Christology of C is farther removed from the anthropological orientation of the witness given to Christ in the *homologoumena* than the ecclesiology of E, which focuses upon the unification of mankind by God's grace, and upon the edification and mission of the church.[183]

Because in the arguments for the priority of either C or E stronger and weaker reasons are found on both sides and in approximate balance, it was necessary to ask for other solutions to the problem:

3. *In Favor of Mutual Interdependence*: H. J. Holtzmann and C. Masson, followed by others, have plowed old and new ground by their ingenious theory and skillful elaboration of the sequence U-Colossians → E → C. Still, in many decisive details their observations and conclusions are so divergent and disregard so obviously the early date of C (for which arguments will be proffered in the next Section) that their theory could not marshal acceptance but called for still another explanation of the special C-E relationship.

4. *In Favor of Common Dependence* upon third materials: The reconstruction of early Christian hymns, liturgical forms, parenetical patterns, and a Pauline school has been promoted with energy and skill, foremost by German-speaking scholars. But the feasibility of the exact reconstruction of oral or written traditions, the assumption of the existence of a sort of academic education and mission center, and the reliability of the results achieved on the basis of these constructs are at present no more than working hypotheses.

Inevitable is the conclusion that the cause and character of the interrelation of the two epistles is still unsolved and may well remain unsolved, unless archaeological findings or an as yet undeveloped new hermeneutical method can produce new facts or develop new criteria. For the time being, unity and diversity of the epistles need not necessarily be explained by a one-sided or mutual literary dependence. Under the influence of the same predicament and of a good memory, even the Tychicus passages (Col 4:7–8 // Eph 6:21–22) may have been written down in almost identical wording. Momentary contingencies other than initial confusion and later syntactical puritanism can sufficiently explain the presence or absence of *anakoloutha* in the same author's dictation or handwriting. This applies also to the handling of vocabulary and theological themes in both epistles. Tensions and irreconcilable contradictions exist between several of the seven possibilities mentioned above (on pp. 101–4) to solve the dependence problem. Complicated routes have been constructed and followed

---

183. H. J. Holtzmann, *Kritik*, pp. 46–55, speaks of an ill-fitting new context, a dropping of ornaments, but also of a loss of richness in C when he compares Col 1:22 with its parallel Eph 1:4; Col 1:13–14 // Eph 1:6–7; Col 1:26; 2:2 // Eph 1:3, 5, 9; Col 1:23; 2:2, 7 // Eph 3:17–18; 4:16; 2:20; Col 2:19 // Eph 4:16; Col 3:9–10 // Eph 4:22–24; Col 3:16 // Eph 5:19.

in order to verify one or another hypothesis. The most sober and plausible explanation of the unity and diversity of C and E may still be found on a simple path leading through the literary and theological thickets: at about the same time, but in addressing different congregations in different situations, one and the same author wrote both letters.

Is it still possible to assume that Paul himself was this author?

X. THE PROBLEM OF AUTHORSHIP

The substance of the preceding Sections III–IX has immediate bearing on the question whether Colossians is to be treated as a genuine Pauline product or as the work of a contemporary or later admirer of the apostle. Since in most scholarly discussions the problems of the kinship between Colossians and Ephesians and of the authorship of both epistles have not been clearly separated, Bibliography II applies also to this section although occasionally other titles will have to be mentioned.

A. The Case Against Colossians

The question of Pauline authenticity is not a matter of antiquarian curiosity, scholarly pendantry, or idle luxury. Ever since, on literary and historical grounds, the secondary and spurious origin of Colossians was "discovered" or "demonstrated," cumulative experience has shown that the verdict "inauthentic" leads to a depreciation and devaluation of some elements, at times even of the essential substance and character of this letter. Sachkritik (substance criticism) against the alleged or actual universalism, demonology, and moralism of Colossians was sometimes the result of the literary and historical verdict. The work of a disciple of Paul could not command the same respect as the work of the master.[184]

More often, especially in more recent historical-critical literature, it is conceded that literary and historical reasons do not suffice to prove the spuriousness of Colossians. Instead, the doctrines contained in this letter are declared irreconcilable with Paul's teaching, and now on *this* basis the theory of

---

184. Most of these charges are directed against both Colossians and Ephesians; see R. Bultmann, *Theology of the NT* II (1955), pp. 127–38 (especially p. 133), 144–54 (especially p. 149), 175–83, 186. Cf. fns. 66 and 181. The most radical among Bultmann's fellow executors of these two and other NT "Deutero-Pauline" products is S. Schulz (see fn. 67). It seems that he charges that about nine tenths of the NT have defected from (the Lutheran-Bultmannian concept of) justification, and therefore have denied and belied the only true proclamation of salvation.

spuriousness is developed (see, for example, fn. 96). The indictments formulated against Colossians, for instance, by Rudolf Bultmann have been copied or imitated by a great number of followers, and not only by those who belong in his school. Bultmann's opinion can be summed up this way: Colossians promotes a Christian Gnosis; a static and orthodox concept of faith rules the day and is combined with an undeveloped feeling for its existential essence; sin is not taken seriously enough—or else there would be no restriction to the plural "sins"; a tradition-bound authoritarianism and clericalism have crept into the preaching of the gospel and claim apostolic origin; a speculative conception of the relation between the (pre-existent) Christ and the cosmos, that is, a mythological doctrine of creation and redemption, is developed as revealed by the inclusion of angels and demons; ethics are produced in the poor form of moralism, as manifested by the return to the equivalent of (Jewish) "good works" and the abundance of prohibitions; finally, eschatology is transformed into a means to extol the effect of baptism and of the church as a saving institution.

In brief, so affirm the members of this school of thought, Colossians presents no more than a "somewhat faded Paulinism" and must be understood as part of that sorrowful process which ruined the majesty of the theology of Galatians and Romans, and led into the abysses of the Pastoral Epistles and other post-apostolic, early-catholic writings such as the earlier-mentioned products of First Clement, Barnabas, Ignatius—not to speak of Hermas and the Apostolic Constitutions. Within the New Testament, Colossians now becomes an example of how *not* to do theology, at least when you are a Protestant. The incorporation of this letter into the canon can then at best be understood as the planting of a warning signal, and at worst, as a mistake by which the church is led into temptation. There are no reasons to assume that the Synods which "received" Colossians into the collection of canonical books (called the New Testament) possessed infallibility in matters of apostolic origin and constructive usefulness.

However proper or precipitous *Sachkritik* of the sketched type may be, it is based upon some historical judgments to which attention must now (again) be drawn. In Section IV it was shown that exactly those elements have been considered essentials of the Colossian Religion (speculation, Gnosticism, mythology, legalism, traditionalism, etc.) which according to Bultmann, his forerunners, and his followers are characteristic of the message of Colossians (and Ephesians)—and defile it. This means that the author of the letter is considered a victim of the Religion that he intended to resist, or in other words, that Colossians exemplifies the failure of a mission. The term "anti-Gnostic Gnosis [of Colossians]" is a beautiful summary of this opinion (cf. fn. 67). How could anybody be so foolish as to presume that the Devil might be expelled with the help of Beelzebub? The handwriting of the apostle Paul is recognized by the persuasive way in which he refutes the (Gnostic-enthusiastic and/or Jewish-legalistic) heresies in his letters to the Galatians, Corinthians, Romans, Philippians. The same man cannot be imagined to have fallen into the trap set by opponents as dangerous as the Colossian philosophers. Therefore, Paul cannot have been the author of Colossians—this is the core of an argument built upon the premise that "what must not be, cannot have occurred."

Not only is such reasoning questionable, but two of its presuppositions are less than sufficiently confirmed: (1) the assumption that Paul never might have failed, and even more (2) the conviction that Colossians is the product of a man victimized by the Colossian Religion. Those assuming that an interpretation of Colossians requires criticism of the message attributed to Paul in this letter might unconsciously have chosen sides with the promoters of the Religion who also might have stood in opposition to the message brought to them by Paul's trusted disciple, Epaphras. Unwillingness to learn more and better about the breadth and depth of the gospel preached by Paul may be the decisive motivation in either case.[185]

In turn, mistakes and contradictions found among the disputers of the genuineness of Colossians do not suffice to demonstrate that the letter is authentic. Other main arguments pro and contra still deserve a hearing although the majority of them were mentioned in passing in the preceding sections.

Col 1:20	*Eph 2:11–16*
20 and to reconcile through Him with Him all things, by creating peace through His blood of the cross, through Him, be it that, which is on earth, be it that, which is in the heavens.	[11]Remember, then, that in the past [and] in the realm of flesh you, the Gentiles—called The Uncircumcision by those who call themselves The Circumcision, that handmade operation in the realm of flesh . . . [12][Remember] that at that time you were apart from the Messiah, excluded from the citizenship of Israel, strangers to the covenants based upon promise. In this world you were bare of hope and without God. [13]But now you are [included] in the realm of the Messiah Jesus. Through the blood of the Messiah you who in the past stood far off have been brought near. [14]For [we confess] He is in person the peace between us.

185. Analogous arguments concerning Ephesians have been offered in AB 34, pp. 41–50.

Col 1:20	*Eph 2:11–16*

He has made both [Gentiles
and Jews] into one.
For he has broken down the
dividing wall,
in his flesh [he has wiped out
all] enmity.
¹⁵He has abolished the
law [, that is, only] the
commandments [expressed]
in statutes.
[This was] to make peace by
creating in his person
a single new man out of the
two,
¹⁶and to reconcile both to God
through the cross in one
single body.
In his own person he has
killed the enmity.

B. For Authenticity of Colossians and Ephesians

The Epistle to the Colossians itself, not only the (more or less extended) titles which in the ancient manuscripts and in the versions of all periods are prefixed to it, affirms Pauline authorship. The recommendation of Tychicus and Onesimus, and the Greeting List (Col 4:7–17) contain biographical information which in substance and character closely resemble the content of the letter to Philemon, whose authenticity is not disputed. The presentation of Paul's high and full apostolic self-consciousness in Col 1:24–2:5; 4:3–4 complements the substance of Gal 1; 2 Cor 3:10–13, for example, but does not exceed or caricature it. In the post-apostolic period Colossians is solidly attested as a work of Paul, although the attestation is slower, later, and less frequent than that of the *homologoumena*. Perhaps 1 Clement, Barnabas, Ignatius, Justin Martyr, the Odes of Solomon knew and used Colossians as a Pauline letter.[186] Certainly

---

186. It is unlikely that the "bond *(desmos)* of God's love" mentioned in 1 Clem. 49:2 refers to (literally) the "love which is the bond of perfection" in Col 3:14. The expression "all things are in Him and for Him" (Barn. XII 7) may or may not recall Col 1:16. The formulae "things seen and unseen" in Ignatius *Trall* V 2; *Rom* V 3; *Smyrn.* VI 1; "steadfast . . ." or "firm and unchangeable in faith" in Ignatius *Eph.* X 2; Polycarp *Phil.* X 1; finally the equation of avarice with idolatry in Polycarp *Phil.* XI 2, need not be intended allusions to Col 1:16, 23; 3:5. The first expression is a widespread formula, the others may stem from Jewish or ecclesiastical compositions whence Ignatius, Polycarp,

Marcion and other Gnostic heretics, as well as the Church Fathers, Irenaeus, Tertullian, Clement of Alexandria, Origen, the *Marcionite Prologues*, the *Canon Muratori*, and later canonical lists did quote from it or count it as canonical.[187] Nevertheless, there is good reason to observe that "in spite of its

---

and the author of Colossians may have borrowed them independently of one another. Justin Martyr *dial.* 84:2; 85:2; 100:2; 125:3; 138:2, calls Christ the "firstborn of all works," ". . . of every creature," or ". . . of God and all creatures." The omission of the article in the Greek text, between "all" and "creature," hardly suffices as evidence of Justin's dependence on Col 1:15. None of the authors mentioned affirm that they are quoting, be it a letter of Paul or another tradition or document. The *Didache* and the *Shepherd of Hermas* show nowhere any resemblance to Colossians. In the *Odes of Solomon* (XVI 18), the pre-existence of the "Lord . . . before anything was at all" is clearly asserted. This idea may be influenced by one or another part of the New Testament; it may stem from Col 1:15–17. But its source might just as well be John 1:1–4 or Heb 1:1–4 or Matt 11:27 (not to speak of Prov 8:22 or Wis 7:22 and Jewish texts speaking of the pre-existence of the Torah).

A convincing reason for the absence from the Apostolic Fathers of exact Colossian quotes and unambiguous allusions to Colossians has not yet been found. Even Ephesians and the Pastoral Epistles had a much better press. T. K. Abbott (*Colossians*, p. L) guesses that the "controversial" substance of Colossians made its use "less familiar to those [congregations or ecclesiastical writers] who had no concern with the heresies with which it deals." However, in not being quoted early and widely, Colossians shares the fate of several *homologoumena*. They, too, had to wait for the (re)discovery of Paul by Gnostics such as Marcion, and by orthodox authors of the caliber of Irenaeus and Augustine. Thus, there *are* other reasons to explain the late attestation of this letter than an alleged spurious late-second-century origin by which F. C. Baur sought to account for the silence.

187. Marcion quotes from every chapter of Colossians but omits (or deletes) in, e.g., Col 1:15–17 the statements about Christ's function in creation, and in 2:17 the utterance about the (literally) "body" which is Christ. In 4:14, after the mention of Luke, the words "the beloved physician" are missing. See A. v. Harnack, *Marcion: Das Evangelim vom fremden Gott*, 2d ed. (Leipzig: Hinrichs, 1924), pp. 51, 121*–124*, 129*. Among the Gnostic groups, the Valentinian School made intensive use of Colossians; for in this letter its great teachers believed that they could find support for their theory of eons, vid. principalities and powers, that either constituted the divine *plērōma* (fullness) or formed a separating wall between the deity and the realm of creation (see AB 34, pp. 12–18, 171–72, 200–3 for references). Gnostic texts which capitalize on the "resurrection by baptism" supposedly taught in Col 2:12 are collected by H. Weiss in his essay "Paulus und die Häretiker," (see fn. 36), pp. 121–26. References to the Gnostic use of all chapters of the Pauline letters have been gathered by Elaine H. Pagels, *The Gnostic Paul* (Philadelphia: Fortress, 1975); for the epistle to the Colossians, see pp. 137–40, cf. p. 29. Among the earliest Church Fathers using Colossians as a canonical book are: Irenaeus *adversus haereses* II 22:4; III 14:1, etc.; Tertullian, passim; Clement of Alexandria *stromateis* I 1, 15:5, etc.; Origen, e.g., *contra Celsum* V 8 and *passim*; in *Joannem commentarii* I 17 and *passim* (see the Indices of Biblical Passages in, e.g., H. Chadwick,

118

Christological relevance, in the Patristic period, the letter to the Colossians takes a place behind the better-liked Ephesians."[188] Frequently quoted are no more than relatively few verses of Colossians, such as, 1:15–18, 20–24; 2:8–15; 3:1–4. But the scarcity of explicit references to Colossians in the early church is not caused by doubts about the letter's authenticity. The debate on its genuineness started no earlier than 1838 with the publication of E. T. Mayerhoff's brief but incisive and stimulating work, *Der Brief an die Colosser.*

Among the modern scholars who tentatively or with firm conviction still uphold the authenticity of both Colossians and Ephesians are C. B. Caird (pp. 11–29, 155–57), L. Cerfaux, M. Goguel ("Esquisse," conceding anti-Gnostic interpolations in Ephesians) E. Percy, E. F. Scott, G. Schille (*Hymnen*, p. 33), H. Schlier, and K. Staab (pp. 72, 115–19).[189] For instance, they argue

Origen: *Contra Celsum* (Cambridge: University Press, 1953), p. 530, and ed. E. Preuschen, *Origenes* IV, GCS (Leipzig: Teubner, 1903), p. 593.

188. H. J. Frede, "Epistula ad Colossenses," in ed. Erzabtei Beuron, *Vetus Latina* XXIV 2, fasc 4, p. 274. On pp. 290–304 of the same work, the place of Colossians in the collection of the Pauline letters (that is, in the canon shaped or used by the Fathers) is discussed. While in most cases the length of the Pauline letters determined their placement in the canonical lists, assuring Romans the lead position, Marcion, the Marcionite Prologues, the Canon Muratori, and a few others appear to have decided in favor of a chronological order—which meant a dethronement of Romans, mostly in favor of Galatians. Unlike the epistle to the Hebrews which, whenever it was considered Pauline and canonical at all, was assigned most diverse locations, the letter to the Colossians maintained a fairly stable position. Except in the ninth-century Codex Syr. 10, it is always found *after* Ephesians. Sometimes (as in the case of Marcion and the Marcionite Prologues) Colossians follows immediately upon Ephesians. More often, (Galatians and) Philippians (occasionally also First and Second Thessalonians) stand between the two. Athanasius' Easter Letter of 367 c.e. appears to have established the sequence Ephesians-Philippians-Colossians which became normative in the official canons of the Eastern and Western churches. The stichometric length rather than the chronological date of the epistles appears to have been the final criterion of the arrangement. Hebrews, however, was given a place at the end of the Pauline letters because a concession seemed appropriate to the misgivings of the Western churches regarding its authenticity.

189. Page references in parentheses concern works listed in the Bibliographies I and II. When they are omitted, either the whole pertinent part or excursus in an author's Introduction to his Commentary, or an earlier mentioned monograph on a Colossian problem, is meant. Most names and works are mentioned in fns. 160–68.

Further supporters of the authenticity of Colossians and Ephesians are P. Benoit, *Aux Colossiens* (1949), pp. 9–11, 74, 77–78; F. F. Bruce, *Commentary on the Epistle to the Colossians* (Grand Rapids: Eerdmans, 1957), pp. 172–73; idem, "St. Paul in Rome III; IV; BJRL 48/2 (1966) 268–85; 49/2 (1967) 302–22; R. M. Grant, *A Historical Introduction to the New Testament* (London: Collins, 1963), pp. 195–97, 200 (Bruce and Grant speak only tentatively regarding Ephesians. Benoit believes that in Ephesians the helping hand was given "more freedom," but that "the thought and heart of S. Paul"

that Colossians presupposes the same external situation and the same attitude to slavery as the letters to Philemon, and that neither the "proto-Gnostic" character of the Colossian Religion nor the use of the epistle to the Colossians by second-century Gnostics for their own purposes prove spuriousness. As to strange forms of diction, minor and major Pauline stylistic peculiarities, together with liturgical and parenetical elements occur in Colossians just as in the uncontested Pauline letters.[190] Logic and rhetoric of Colossians are far from arbitrary, confused, and generally poor. For the structure of the epistle as a whole and the substructure of its parts with their ever new sequence of formulated intention → careful indoctrination → summarizing conclusion reveal that a skillful writer is at work—even the man known under the name of Paul. In writing Colossians, the apostle saw as little reason as in the writing of the *homologoumena* to abstain from the combination of (1) carefully spun out reasoning, (2) lengthy, repetitious, parallel, or chiastic formulations and arguments, and (3) dramatic interruptions or outbursts in the form of *anakoloutha*.[191] Concerning the use of

---

remained intact); A. F. J. Klijn, *An Introduction to the New Testament* (Leiden: Brill, 1967), pp. 105, 117; W. Michaelis, *Einleitung in das Neue Testament* (Bern: Evang. Gesellschaft, 1946), pp. 218–20; J. A. T. Robinson, *Redating* (see fn. 95), pp. 61–65, 193; H. Schlier, *Epheser*, pp. 23–28, 280; cf. BDF 458.

190. *Minor* stylistic features: the pleonastic *kai* (and, too, just, even) after "therefore" (Col 1:9; cf. 1 Thess 2:13; 3:5; Rom 13:6); the term "his saints" (borrowed from the LXX; Col 1:26; cf. 1 Thess 3:13; 2 Thess 1:10); *charizomai* instead of *aphiēmi*, in the sense "I forgive" (Col 2:13; 3:13; cf. 2 Cor 2:7, 10; 12:13); *en merei* in the sense of "regarding" (Col 2:16; 2 Cor 3:10; 9:3; literally "in part of"); "each good work" (Col 1:10; cf. 2 Thess 2:17; 2 Cor 9:8). These examples are proffered by FBK, p. 241. If an imitator of Paul had been at work, he would probably have taken pains to avoid idiosyncrasies of his own and to use preferably peculiar stylistic characteristics of his master.

Major style elements: Proceeding from one of his letters to the next, Paul did remember or appropriate to himself an additional vocabulary and variant word meanings, stemming from either his Jewish and Greek education, or his continued study of the Old Testament and of Jewish (and Greek?) writings, or from his daily encounters and experience as a missionary, or originating from early church tradition or from the community of those addressed in the epistles. The apostle was capable of falling into rhythmic diction, even into hymnic forms of speech (cf. fn. 85). In person he exemplifies the observation made in 1 Cor 14:26, "when you come together, each one has a psalm," and the command given in Col 3:16, "teach and advise one another in all wisdom . . . singing gracefully." This is certainly the case in the undisputed passages Rom 8:38–39; 11:33–36, and above all in 1 Cor 13, the great paean on love. It was repeatedly stated that in Col 1:15–20 Paul may quote a hymn in use in one or several churches and known to the Colossians beforehand (cf. Section VIII). But also outside those verses, in, e.g., Col 1:10, 11, 24–26, his style is artistic and hymnodic as shown foremost by the "parallelism of members" (in synonymous, explicatory, or contrapuntal form). For the occurrence of doublets and repetitious expressions, see fns. 91 and 167.

191. In fn. 57 it was shown that the wild accusations of M. Bujard against the logical

liturgical elements, the concatenation of originally Pauline statements in preaching style with the quotation of materials that were probably known to the congregation (for instance, in Col 1:12–23) is also found in Phil 2:1–11 and Eph 1:3–14; 2:4–10, for example.[192] If the *Haustafel* of Col 3:18–4:1 were a post-apostolic product, certainly it would have been even more "Christianized" than that of Ephesians.

The cosmic Christology, the hope to which appeal is made, and the functions attributed to the apostle, the church, and their ministers unfold and develop (but fail to contradict) the teaching on the relationship between God, Christ, and the universe of creation, as presented for instance in Rom 8:19–24, 29; 1 Cor 2:8; 8:6, 2 Cor 3–4; Gal 1:12–15; 4:3, 9; Phil 2:10.[193] Certainly arguments regarding wisdom and mildness, or exhaustion and debilitation, of the aged Paul cancel each other out as flatteries or insults offered to an old man. Great is, however, the probability that Paul and his thinking were developing and growing over the years of his ministry. Having recourse to a secretary or disciple in order to find an excuse for the alleged stylistic and doctrinal weaknesses of the epistle barely covers the unwillingness of commentators to expose themselves to a document that challenges traditional views of Paul's theology. A *famulus* or imitator of Paul would have taken pains, above all in the opening and concluding lines of the epistle, not to deviate as freewheelingly from Paul's epistolary style as does Col 1:1–2 and 4:18. Thus, some differences between Colossians and the *homologoumena* speak louder in favor of Colossians as a product of the creative mind of Paul than do the obvious harmonies.

C. For Authenticity of Either Colossians or Ephesians

In suitably reduced form, the reasons just mentioned to support the genuineness of both Colossians and Ephesians have also been proffered to favor solely the authenticity of Colossians, int. al. by F. W. Beare (IB X, 604–5), P. Benoit (see fns. 101 and 173), C. R. Bowen (except for Col 1:15–20 and the polemical parts of Col 2), F. F. Bruce (see fn. 189), W. M. L. DeWette, Dibelius, and H. Greeven (pp. 53, 83–85), E. J. Goodspeed (*Key*, pp. V–XVI), H. Hegermann (*Schöpfungsmittler*, pp. 88, 154, with reservations), N. Hugedé, N. Kehl, J. C. Kirby (*Ephesians, Baptism*, pp. 165, 169–70; cf. p. 51), J. Knox, (interpolations are recognized), W. L. Knox (in *Gentiles*, pp. 177ff., especially p. 184), W. W. Kümmel (FBK, pp. 240–44), J. Lähnemann (*Kolosserbrief*, pp. 29–30, 163–68,

---

order of individual sentences and drawn-out thoughts cannot be upheld in the light of, e.g., J. Lähnemann's and F. Zeilinger's work.

192. In the passages mentioned, Phil 2:1–5; Eph 1:10–13; 2:8b–9 have the prose style of homiletical speech; the other verses appear to contain quotations from hymns.

193. See, e.g., FBK, pp. 242–43; N. Kehl, *Der Christushymnus* (see fn. 55), pp. 49, 92.

174–76, 181), C. L. Mitton (*Ephesians*, pp. 35–77, 111–18, 243–55), J. Moffat, C. F. D. Moule, E. Norden, W. Ochel, B. Rigaux, D. F. Schleiermacher, H. von Soden (*Briefe*, pp. 10–15), K. Staab, H.-A. Wagenführer, R. R. Williams (the latter by implication).[194]

Their reasons for separating genuine Colossians from pseudonymous Ephesians are based less upon linguistic and stylistic, than on historical and theological observations. The nuances described in Section IX.B are considered evidence of a greater proximity between Colossians and the *homologoumena* than between Ephesians and the undisputed letters.

Much less successful in gaining widespread adherence has been the minority which affirms that the letter to the Colossians is spurious and dependent on the genuine epistle to the Ephesians. E. T. Mayerhoff, F. C. Synge, J. Coutts, and (very timidly) A. van Roon are its chief exponents (see fn. 161). The poor numerical representation of this school of thought need not demonstrate that their reasoning is defective. Certainly the relatively late attestation of Colossians speaks in their favor but is an argument from silence. Their strength lies in the fact that they have used the same criteria and tests for deciding on priority as the scholars of group C, only in reverse orientation and with opposite results. In the preceding Section IX some case studies and arguments in their favor were produced, even at the expense of the weaker points in their procedure. Even so, uncontradictable evidence has not been forthcoming.

A common weakness of groups C and D consists in their failure to demonstrate why Paul, if he wrote one of the two letters (including its formal and material discrepancies from the *homologoumena*), could not also and just as well have written the other. Even this weak point is taken most seriously by the next school.

D. Declaring Both Letters Spurious

Most scholars go all the way in declaring both Colossians *and* Ephesians post-apostolic fabrications, but some allow Colossians a place in the late-

---

194. The observation of E. Käsemann, RGG III (1959) 1727, saying that "today, the authenticity of Colossians is almost generally recognized," may have been valid for French and Anglo-Saxon research, certainly not for the members of the Bultmann school. E.g., J. M. Robinson, "A Formal Analysis of Colossians 1:15–20," JBL 76 (1957) 270–92, 287 fn. 21, considers "the general tendency of German scholarship to reject Colossians as non-Pauline" a complication of the task of interpreting this letter.

Among the titles not yet or only seldom mentioned in the foregoing are J. Moffatt, *Introduction* (1911), p. 375; E. Norden, *Agnostos Theos* (Leipzig: Teubner, 1913), p. 251, fn. 1; B. Rigaux, review of F.-J. Steinmetz, *Protologische Heilszuversicht* (1969), in Bibl 52 (1976) 281–83; A. Wagenführer, *Die Bedeutung Christi für die Welt und für die Kirche* (Leipzig: Weyand, 1941), pp. 121–44; R. R. Williams, "The Pauline Catechesis," in ed. F. L. Cross, *Studies on Ephesians* (London: Mowbray, 1956), pp. 89–96, especially p. 96. To those who will not exclude the cooperation of a pupil of apostolic period and yet attribute it either to an able and faithful, or to an early catholicizing, disciple of Paul.

In summing up and augmenting the literary, the historical, and the paramount theological judgments of F. C. Baur, A. Hilgenfeld and O. Pfleiderer, R. Bultmann has spoken with such finality on the spuriousness of both letters that (even without the contribution of essentially novel arguments and reflections) the Martburger's opinion was taken up by people of most varied theological orientation: G. Bornkamm, E. Käsemann, H. Conzelmann, E. Schweizer, H. J. Gabathuler, W. Marxsen, E. P. Sanders, E. Lohse (*Colossians*, pp. 177–83), W. Bujard, H. Ludwig, P. Vielhauer.[195]

The verdict against both letters need not necessarily imply that the pseudonymous authors of Colossians and Ephesians are considered falsifiers, and that their products are maligned as counterfeits. Studies in ancient secular, Jewish, and ecclesiastical pseudepigraphy have shown that there were many reasons and motivations to create and to circulate documents under an assumed name. Decisive were not only personal, group, or academic interests, such as the desire to cheat others or to augment the writer's glory and gain, to satisfy an animosity against adversaries, to demonstrate the ambiguity of an opposing doctrine, to fill gaps in the local or the scholarly tradition. Much more pseudonymous documents, especially letters with philosophical content, were set in circulation because disciples of a great man intended to express, by imitation, their adoration of their revered master and to secure or to promote his influence upon a later generation under changed circumstances. In addition, among Jews and Christians the respect for the operation of God's Spirit could be a reason to withhold or hide the actual human author's name.[196] Therefore, in following

Paul in the writing of Ephesians belongs K. Staab, *Gefangenschaftsbriefe*, p. 118. D. F. Schleiermacher, *Einleitung* (1845), pp. 163–66, tentatively identified Tychicus with that disciple, on the basis of Col 4:7–8 // Eph 6:21–22; cf. fns. 167 and 197.

195. F. C. Baur, *Paulus* (see fn. 155); R. Bultmann (see fn. 184); G. Bornkamm, "Häresie" (see fn. 20), p. 139, fn. 1; E. Käsemann, *Leib und Leib Christi* (Tübingen: Mohr, 1933), p. 143; idem, RGG II, pp. 518–19; III, pp. 1727–28; H. Conzelmann, NTD 8, pp. 56–57, 141–42; idem, *Grundriss der Theologie des Neuen Testaments* (Munich: Kaiser, 1967), pp. 344–47; E. Schweizer, "Zur Frage nach der Echtheit des Kolosser- und Epheserbriefes," in idem, *Neostestamentica* (Zürich: Zwingli, 1963), p. 429; H. J. Gabathuler, *Jesus Christus Haupt der Kirche—Haupt der Welt* (Zürich: Zwingli, 1965), p. 145; E. Lohse, *Colossians*, pp. 177–83; W. Bujard, *Stil*, p. 62; P. Vielhauer, *Geschichte der urchristlichen Literatur* (1975), pp. 197–200.

196. K. Aland, "The Problem of Anonymity and Pseudonymity in Christian Literature of the First Two Centuries," JNTS 12 (1961) 39–40; H. R. Balz, "Anonymität und Pseudepigraphie im Urchristentum," ZThK 66 (1966) 403–36; H. Hegermann, "Der geschichtliche Ort der Pastoralbriefe," in idem, *Theologische Versuche* I 2 (Berlin: Evangelische Verlagsanstalt, 1970), pp. 47–64; W. Speyer, *Die literarische Fälschung im Altertum*, HBAW I 2 (München: Beck, 1971), pp. 105–6; 131–303. Among the means employed for giving a pseudonymous document the ring of authenticity, N. Brox, "Zu

the Jewish legal maxim, "the one sent by a man is as the man himself," Paul himself may have charged, inspired, or permitted his pupils to write in his name.[197] However, the verdict "spurious" has drawn after itself those deprecatory theological judgments and that hardening of the heart against the substance of Colossians which were described earlier in this section.

There have also been some arguments other than theological leveled against the Colossian and Ephesian letters. Against those willing to save at least the authenticity of Colossians, it is argued: the letter form of Colossians is artificial, it was stimulated with the help of those excerpts from Philemon which now dominate Col 4:9–17, but the falsification is revealed by the omission of the announcement of Paul's forthcoming visit to Colossae (Phlm 22). Other literary and stylistic arguments have been discussed in Section VII. Historical reasoning points to the second-century origin of the Gnostic Religion of Colossae (see

---

den persönlichen Notizen der Pastoralbriefe," BZ 13 (1969) 76–94, notes the insertion of personal notes, e.g., the request for the forgotten cloak and for the sending of books (2 Tim 4:13), as well as the wish to meet the correspondent again. According to Brox, such things are literary *clichés* which, especially in the case of the Pastoral Epistles, prove rather than disprove the lack of authenticity. Nevertheless, Brox fails to demonstrate why some of the personal notes in the *homologoumena* do not compel him to come to the same conclusion.

197. See *Berakot* 5:5 (34b); cf. StB III 2–4; TWNT I 413–20. Names of scholars who formed or endorsed the "secretary hypothesis" were mentioned in fn. 167. Proposed as candidates have been Timothy (who indeed is mentioned as co-author in Col 1:1) first by E. Renan, *Antichrist* (French original, 1873; Eng. trans., Boston: Roberts, 1897), pp. 91–94; and recently again by H. Ludwig, *Verfasser*, pp. 63, 198–99; E. Schweizer, "Zur neueren Forschung" (see fn. 45), p. 173; idem, "The Letter to the Colossians "Neither Pauline nor Post-Pauline?" in *Pluralisme et écumenisme en recherche théologique*, FS for S. Dockx (Gembloux: Duculot, 1977), pp. 3–16; idem, *Kolosser*, pp. 25–27. Already P. Ewald, *Die Briefe des Paulus an die Epheser, Colosser, Philemon* KNT X (2d ed., 1910), had suggested Timothy—but he presupposed authentically Pauline initiative, outline, control, and conclusion of the letter; cf. M. Goguel, in his *Introduction*. W. Marxsen, *Introduction*, and A. Suhl orally (as quoted by J. Lähnemann, *KolB*, pp. 181–82) prefer to nominate Epaphras because of the prominence he is given in Col 1:7–8 and 4:12. Thus, Colossians is considered a shrewd self-recommendation of Epaphras, who capitalized upon the confidence which once upon a time the apostle Paul had placed in him.

Some of E. Percy's criticisms still hold water: Why should Paul have written only one of the two letters to the Ephesians and Colossians, and have delegated the writing of the other to a co-operator, and why should the pupil have taken so many liberties over against the work of his master (PKE, pp. 421–22)? It might be added that this aide of the apostle would have outshone or overshadowed his revered hero. It is probable that historical pursuits, such as the hunt for an author of Colossians other than Paul, cannot be successful when methods and aspirations of present-day academic lecturers and theological schools are considered the only viable options.

Section IV) and to the sub-apostolic emphasis given to the apostolate, to the weight of tradition, or to the authority of members of Paul's school (see Section VIII). But it was argued before that neither the options open to Paul's diction, nor the historic developments of the early church and its theology, nor the length and breadth of Paul's specific message are so completely known and so safely under the control of modern scholars as to permit final verdicts on the basis of either literary, or historical, or theological arguments.

E. Recognizing Authentic Fragments

The procedure of those who assume that inside the present spurious shell of Colossians lie fragments of an authentic kernel is much more circumspect than the methods employed by all schools mentioned previously. In fn. 162 it was shown which passages were singled out as genuine under the leadership of H. J. Holtzmann and C. Masson, by P. Benoit, C. R. Brown, M. Goguel, P. N. Harrison, W. Hönig, E. P. Sanders, F. C. Synge.

H. J. Holtzmann spoke of the "double-face" (*Doppelgesicht*) of Colossians and meant to say that this epistle (as well as Ephesians), with its "characteristics of the primary and the secondary," is "simultaneously Pauline and non-Pauline."[198] The complex nature of the Holtzmann-Masson theory, the often contradictory results of their labors, and the short time available for the transition from Ur-Colossians to Ephesians and back to Colossians militate against the identification of Colossians with a patchwork produced by a skillful redactor. Above all, the logical and intricate structure of Colossians, both as a whole and in its several parts, contradicts the scholarly verdict.

In consequence, the most solid and safest working hypothesis for the reading and exposition of Colossians is still the assumption that it was Paul who wrote, or rather dictated, the whole letter himself, and that eventual revisions, made by one or several aides before its delivery to those addressed, were executed at his command or with his approval. Even in the face of the critical work done by and since E. T. Mayerhoff in 1838, the maxim still stands: *in dubio pro reo*, or "innocent till proven guilty."

This commentary presupposes that Paul was the author who wrote both Colossians and Ephesians, at about the same time. Their formal and material similarities and differences stem from the consistent and continuous, yet also free and developing, mind of the apostle, who faced to the best of his gifts and capabilities the problems of the people whom he had to address. Similar issues

---

198. Cf. *Kritik*, p. 130; on pp. 305–6, and in his *Einleitung*, pp. 268, 280, H. J. Holtzmann adopts the terms *Doppelgesicht* and *doppeltes Gesicht*, which were coined by H. G. A. Ewald in his review of Holtzmann's *Kritik* (Goettingische gelehrte Anzeigen 1872 II, pp. 1619–31, especially 1616–21). Holtzmann observes the same feature in the *homologoumena*, e.g., in Rom 1:3–4; 9:5; 1 Cor 8:6; 2 Cor 4:4–6; 5:17; 8:9.

were treated in similar diction and met by similar arguments. Divergent local conditions and problems called for different emphases and details.

Paul at times used his own language, with the idiosyncrasies revealed in his other works, at times the confessional, liturgical, or parenetic diction of pre-Pauline and Pauline churches, and again at other times the phraseology generally accepted by the group being addressed. As novel issues turned up, they helped the apostle to rethink and to formulate in new terms his message of Jesus Christ.

XI. DATE AND PLACE

Even with the affirmation of Pauline authorship, the question of the date and place of origin of Colossians is not automatically answered. Three occasions in Paul's life appear to provide a suitable setting for the composition of Colossians: Ephesus, between 52 and 54 C.E.; Caesarea-on-the-Sea, between 58 and 60; and Rome, between 61 and 63 (or 60 and 62?).[199] The subscript of

---

199. a. The following voices speak out for *Ephesus*: In the ancient church, the *Marcionite Prologues* 64, found in, e.g., ed. E. Preuschen, *Analecta*, Kürzere Texte zur Geschichte der alten Kirche und des Kanons II (Tübingen: Mohr, 1910), pp. 85–87; or in A. v. Harnack, *Marcion*, pp. 129*, 136*–38*; or in Eng. trans. in D. J. Theron, *Evidence of Tradition* (Grand Rapids: Baker, 1958), p. 81. Among newer scholars: A. Deissmann, "Zur ephesinischen Gefangenschaft des Apostels Paulus," in *Anatolian Studies*, FS for W. M. Ramsay (Manchester: University Press, 1923), pp. 121–27; idem, *Light from the Ancient East* (New York: Doran, 1927), pp. 137–38; idem, *Paul* (London: Hodder & Stoughton, 1926), pp. 17–28; C. R. Bowen (see fn. 57, p. 187); Dib.-Gr., p. 52; FBK, pp. 229–35, 244–45; E. Lohse, *Colossians*, pp. 166, 182fn. (if Colossians were authentic); N. Hugedé, *Colossiens*, p. 11; A. F. J. Klijn, *Introduction*, p. 105; W. Foerster, "Irrlehrer" (see fn. 22), p. 80. The basic works favoring Ephesus are still W. Michaelis, *Die Gefangenschaft des Paulus in Ephesus* (Gütersloh: Bertelsmann, 1925); idem, *Einleitung in das Neue Testament* (Berne: 1946), pp. 200, 211–20, 267–69, and G. S. Duncan, *St. Paul's Ephesian Ministry* (New York: Scribner, 1930); idem ET 67 (1955/56) 163–66; NTS 3 (1956/57) 211; 5 (1958/59) 43–45.

b). *Caesarea* is the choice of W. M. L. De Wette, *Lehrbuch der . . . Einleitung* (6th ed., 1860), p. 303; E. Haupt, *Die Gefangenschaftsbriefe* (Göttingen: Vandenhoeck, 1902), p. 12; E. Lohmeyer, *Kolosser*, pp. 14–15; M. Gouguel, "La date et le lieu de la composition de l'épitre auz Philippiens," RHR 66 (1912) 330–42, especially 333; idem, *Introduction* IV 2 (1926) 426–30; M. Dibelius and W. G. Kümmel, *Paul* (Philadelphia: Westminster, 1953), pp. 138, 146; FBK, pp. 138, 146; Bo Reicke, "Caesarea, Rome, and the Captivity Epistles," in *Apostolic History and the Gospel*, FS for F. F. Bruce (Grand Rapids: Eerdmans, 1970), pp. 275–86; idem RevExp 70 (1973) 433–38; idem, "Chronologie der Pastoralbriefe," ThLZ 101 (1976) 81–94; J. A. T. Robinson, *Redating the New Testament* (1976), pp. 65–67; A. van Roon, *Authenticity*, pp. 204, 341.

Colossians, found in a small group of manuscripts, mentions Rome. It is supported by statements made, during the fourth century, by Jerome, John Chrysostom, and Theodoret. But it does not occur in the better text tradition of the epistle, and it is so obviously the annotation of a collector or editor of Paul's epistles that it cannot displace other proposed locations and dates. Nevertheless, it may preserve a trustworthy tradition, especially if other evidence supporting Rome can be produced.

As Col 4:3, 10, 18; cf. 1:24 clearly state, Paul was imprisoned while he wrote Colossians. In Acts (23:23–26; 28:14–31) Luke describes two extended stays of Paul under guard which occurred toward the end of the apostle's life in Caesarea and Rome; in the chapters devoted to Paul's "third missionary journey," especially to Paul's 2½-year sojourn in Ephesus (rounded up to 3 years in Acts 20:31), an Ephesian imprisonment is not mentioned (see Acts 19:1–20:1). On the other hand, Paul himself speaks of several imprisonments and many other mortal dangers endured "in Asia (Minor)."[200] The political authorities of Ephesus, the capital of the Roman province Asia, may have treated Paul no friendlier than those in other Asian places. Therefore, there are tales of three cities from which Paul may have written Colossians. Which arguments speak for a decision in favor of one of the three?

The strongest *reason for Ephesus* is geographical: the distance between Rome and Colossae, whether covered on the land route alone (except for the crossing of the Bosporus) or by sea and land, is so enormous that two things are hard to imagine: (1) how would the fugitive Onesimus have mastered 900 miles (as the crow flies) in order to come to Paul, without starving or falling into the net of the police, and (2) how could Paul speak of imminent visits by Mark and himself at Colossae (Col 4:9–10; Phlm 10, 22)? The relatively short distance between Ephesus and Colossae (90 miles) facilitates such moves in either direction.

But geography does not suffice to make a final decision. There is no clear-

---

c). Among recent scholars who have decided for *Rome* are P. Benoit (see fn. 189), F. F. Bruce, (see fn. 189), G. B. Caird, *Paul's Letters from Prison*, pp. 2–6; R. M. Grant, *Historical Introduction*, pp. 192–93; W. L. Knox; J. Lähnemann, *KolB*, pp. 177–81 (if Colossians be authentic); J. B. Lightfoot, *Colossians*, pp. 32–33; C. F. D. Moule, *Colossians*, pp. 21–25; E. Percy, *PKE*, pp. 467–74; J. Schmid, *Ort und Zeit der Paulinischen Gefangeschaftsbriefe* (Freiburg: Herder, 1931), pp. 130–47. K. Staab, *Gefangenschaftsbriefe*, p. 118, assumes that Ephesians, Colossians, and Philemon were written within a few days in Rome, between 61 and 63, and that Philippians stems from a later date, but from the same city.

200. 1 Cor 15:32 mentions (symbolically?) a fight of Paul with wild beasts in Ephesus. 2 Cor 1:8–11 speaks of tribulations, burdens, despair of life, and "this kind of death" suffered "in Asia," from which the apostle once was rescued and trusts to be rescued again. In 2 Cor 6:4–5, among other evils endured, "beatings and imprisonments" are listed, but a location is not mentioned. The same is true of 2 Cor 11:23, where Paul claims to surpass other "servants of Christ" by the hardness and frequency of his troubles,

cut proof of an extended Ephesian captivity of Paul either in Paul's letters or in the Acts of the Apostles. Luke was near Paul when Colossians was written (Col 4:14; Phlm 24; cf. 2 Tim 4:11); but those parts of Acts in which Luke reports his personal experiences (using the pronoun "we") do not include the time which Paul spent in Ephesus. Therefore, it is unlikely that Luke was with Paul in Ephesus. Finally, an Ephesian date of Colossians, and eventually of Ephesians too, would place these letters not only too near, but actually before or between the writing of the Corinthian and Roman epistles.[201] It defies imagination, reconstruction, and description how Paul's diction and theology should have developed from the Thessalonian epistles directly to the captivity letters, and from there to the capital letters. Only the theory of a return of Paul to the east after his (first) Roman captivity, and of an imprisonment at Ephesus at that occasion, could place the origin of Colossians in an Ephesian prison. The discussion of this special theory belongs in the exposition of the epistles to Timothy and Titus.

Reasons for Caesarea are to a large extent built upon the combination of biographical information contained in all Pauline epistles (including the Pastoral Letters) and the fact that the distance between the Lycus Valley and the Palestinian harbor town Caesarea (about 350 miles) can be covered, with all deliberate speed, in a useful and predictable time span. Not only the letters to the Colossians and to Philemon but also Philippians and Second Timothy contain intimations regarding planned or actual journeys. Bo Reicke has so conflated these hints that a complete picture emerges of movements to and from the imprisoned Paul, a picture which appears to reveal the Caesarean origin of Colossians, Philemon, Philippians, Second Timothy—and of Ephesians:

1. At a certain point toward the end of his life, Paul experienced an extended captivity *for the first time.* There is no solid reason to question the account of Acts saying that Paul stayed for two years in a Caesarean prison. Since no earlier than in the letter to Philemon (v 9), Paul describes himself as "an ambassador but *now also* a prisoner for Christ," this letter was written from Caesarea.

2. The same applies to the letters to the Colossians, to the Ephesians, and to the Second Epistle to Timothy, as shown by a comparison of the biographical hints concerning the friends surrounding and serving the imprisoned apostle, especially by a conflation of Col 4:10–14 and Phlm 23–24. Corroborated even by Philippians (notwithstanding the special problems of this epistle in regard to its unity and date or concerning dates of its several parts), a clear consequence

---

imprisonments, beatings, and "deaths" (sic). 2 Tim 3:11 speaks of persecutions and sufferings endured in (Pisidian) Antioch, Iconium, and Lystra.

201. E.g., R. Jewett, *A Chronology of Paul's Life* (Philadelphia: Fortress, 1979), pp. 100–4, places Colossians in the winter 55/56 "from Asian imprisonment" between First/Second Corinthians and Romans.

of events during Paul's two Caesarean years seems to emerge. Among Paul's co-operators, Timothy first served as co-author of Philippians, Colossians, and Philemon (see Phil 1:1; Col 1:1; Phlm 1:1). The apostle hoped within useful time to send Timothy to Philippi, and he expected from him (that he would return and bring) good news about that congregation (Phil 2:19). After Timothy had left, Paul wrote Ephesians without the aid of this beloved co-worker (Eph 1:1 mentions only Paul). Together with the as yet undispatched letters to the Colossians and Philemon, Ephesians was entrusted to the hands of Tychicus, who was charged to bring these three epistles to their destination and to complement their substance by his own oral report on Paul's situation and work. The variant reading of Col 4:8 affirms that what Tychicus eventually learned about the Colossians, this he also was to report back to Paul. But in actuality, it is not certain whether Tychicus ever made a return trip. At any rate, together with Tychicus, the runaway slave Onesimus was to travel (by way of Ephesus, 2 Tim 4:12) to Colossae (Col 4:7–9). Paul hoped that Philemon, the owner of Onesimus, would receive the fugitive as a member of the congregation and set him free for service at the apostle's side (Phlm 10–21). Once Paul "had sent Tychicus to Ephesus," Second Timothy was written (2 Tim 4:12).

3. In the meantime, one of Paul's friends and companions, Demas, had turned apostate (compare Col 4:14; Phlm 24 with 2 Tim 4:10b). Epaphras, the founder of the congregations in the Lycus Valley, who was free at the time Colossians was written, had been committed to the same prison in which Paul was already detained (compare Col 1:7–8; 4:12 with Phlm 23). The Macedonian Aristarchus (mentioned in Acts 19:29; 20:4; 27:2), however, had gone the opposite way: from prison into freedom (4:10; Phlm 24). Details concerning other companions of Paul such as Luke and Mark (Col 4:10, 14; Phlm 24) might complete the picture.

Indeed, these arguments are well suited to be added to those mentioned earlier in order to refute the Ephesian hypothesis. While he is traveling or imprisoned, and when he is free to dictate or write the letters, Paul keeps up communication between himself and Ephesus. Certainly the prison from which he writes a letter to Ephesus and sends a man to the same city cannot be sought at Ephesus. On the other hand, when round-trip travels are expected in the foreseeable future (certainly in the case of Onesimus, probably in the case of Timothy, perhaps in the case of Tychicus, too), and when the prospect of a Pauline visit at Colossae in Philemon's house is as good as the petition for preparation of quarters in Phlm 22 indicates—then the great distance between a *Roman* prison and Asia Minor creates difficulties for the Roman hypothesis. All of this speaks in favor of a Caesarean origin of Colossians.

Yet, it is not sure whether Second Timothy really can be placed in the midst of the other so-called "Captivity Letters," and whether it can be proven beyond reasonable doubt that all of them were written in Caesarea and are authentic. There are (1) biographical problems, related especially to travels of Paul and his co-operators, (2) the possible development of Paul's diction and style, and (3) different theological emphases in the five letters presumed to have about the same date. The consideration of all of these topics makes the Caesarean solution questionable, though not impossible for the following reasons:

1. If, in deference to a decision of the Papal Bible Commission of 1913,[202] or on other grounds, the Pastoral Letters are considered genuinely Pauline, allowance must be made for the release of the apostle from his "first Roman imprisonment" and for one or several travels of Paul from Rome to northern Greece, Asia Minor, Crete (not to speak of Spain) and back to Rome, where his second incarceration ended with his execution. So far, attempts at reconstructing these journeys have led to a variety of conflicting results. As to the travels of Paul's aides, it is uncertain whether intimations, for example, regarding Timothy in Phil 1:1; 2:19 and 2 Tim 4:9, 12, can be so conflated and harmonized with those of Colossians (1:1, and by silence of Eph 1:1) as to reproduce an unbroken chain of events, originating in Caesarea. While passages in Philippians, Philemon, Colossians, and the Pastoral Epistles express Paul's expectation or command that one or another fellow-worker come or go here or there, it is not sure whether and when such journeys actually took place. The assumption that all went according to plan is not supported by the available evidence regarding Paul's own travel plans, promises, and accomplishments.[203]

It can be assumed as certain that Colossians and Philemon stem from the same date and place. Five identical persons are mentioned who join the captive Paul in his greetings (Col 4:10–14 // Phlm 24): Luke, Mark, Demas, Aristarchus, and Epaphras, who is a fellow prisoner according to Phlm 24, while Aristarchus shares the imprisonment following Col 4:10). Onesimus and probably Tychicus, too, although he is not mentioned in Philemon, are still with Paul but are dispatched together as letter carriers, with warm recommendations (Col 4:9 // Phlm 12–17). Timothy is co-author of both Colossians and Philemon. But

---

202. See *Enchiridion Biblicum* (Naples and Rome: Auria & Arnodo, 1961), pp. 129–30, pp. 407–10.

203. E.g., 2 Cor 1:15–18; Rom 1:10–13; also Rom 15:24; 28? see J. A. T. Robinson, *Redating*, pp. 71–72, for an enumeration of different proposals. As stated earlier, the arguments in favor of Caesarea, as they were reproduced on the foregoing pages, are those in substance collected and upheld by Bo Reicke. But on several occasions—though Robinson endorses just these cases—Reicke's reasoning is less than convincing. E.g., in ThLZ 101 (1976) 90, he interprets the words, "when he [Onesiphoros] arrived in Rome he searched for me eagerly and found me" (2 Tim 1:17) as meaning that Onesiphoros looked for Paul in Rome and found him—in Caesarea (!). Caesarea, rather than Rome, is therefore considered the place from which Second Timothy, and with it, the other Captivity Letters, were written. An equally strained exposition is found on p. 86. The clause "I left you in Crete" (Titus 1:5) is supposed to mean that Paul, from a faraway place, assigned Titus to his position on the island, rather than that Paul was in Crete and left from there without Titus.

while the names of Luke, Mark, Tychicus, Demas, and Timothy also occur in Second Timothy, only in one case is an individual's specific function the same as in Colossians/Philemon: Tychicus is being sent to Ephesus (2 Tim 4:12). On the other hand, in 2 Tim 4:9–12, 21 Luke is alone with Paul, Mark has to be brought to Paul, Demas has defected, and Timothy is given counsels and urged to visit Paul in a manner that presupposes a preceding extensive separation from Paul. In conclusion: the biographical indications urge placing Second Timothy considerably after Colossians.

Even more important may be the apostle's statement about his possible death. In Philippians he expresses his readiness to die in performing his ministry (Phil 1:20–23; 2:17–18; 3:10). In Colossians (Philemon, and Ephesians) he speaks with joy of his imprisonment and sufferings (Col 1:24; 4:10, 18)—without facing death in the near future. But when writing Second Timothy, he expects to die very soon, after he has barely escaped the "lion's jaws" (JB), that is, the first hearing before a Roman court (2 Tim 4:6–8, 16–17). There is no evidence that during the Caesarean captivity, before or after Paul's appeal to Caesar, the apostle's predicament ever changed so drastically as to give cause to the words "the hour of my departure is upon me" (2 Tim 4:7 JB). If therefore Second Timothy is treated as genuine in substance, it cannot be allocated to Caesarea, but belongs in the latest Roman period of Paul. In this case Colossians, too, could have been written in Rome, though Caesarea still remains possible.

2. Remarkable differences distinguish the *style*, tone, and temper of the three groups of writings which may be discerned among the letters allotted to the Caesarean captivity: (a) The doctrinal and the parenetical parts of Philippians resemble closely the diction of the *homologoumena*, especially Galatians and Romans. (b) The abundance of liturgical-hymnic and formalized-ethical elements in Ephesians and Colossians welds these two letters together into a group of their own. (c) Second Timothy, with its traits of pagan-secular and religious style, is justly embedded among the other Pastoral Epistles, First Timothy, and Titus. Philemon stands somewhat nearer the exhortations found in the *homologoumena* (including Philippians) than the corresponding sections in Colossians and Ephesians.

In Section VII (pp. 56–63) it was shown that stylistic differences between the *homologoumena* on one hand, and Ephesians/Colossians on the other, do not suffice to demonstrate the spuriousness of the latter. As was earlier observed, in addressing or in writing to different audiences, and in treating various topics, one and the same author may well have chosen different words (or used different meanings of the same words) and composed them in manifold forms of expression and sentence structure.[204]

But even if Paul possessed an admirable flexibility to meet the needs of the

---

204. J. A. T. Robinson, *Redating*, pp. 70–71, 76, 83, seems to speak out of his own past experience as the author of careful and stimulating NT essays, and of battle cries

moment, his style may also have changed from one period of his life to another.[205] It is more likely that the three groups of writings originated not at the same time but rather from the periods of the Caesarean and the first and the final Roman imprisonments, respectively.[206] Just as First Timothy and Titus belong in the period(s) Paul spent in Rome, so also Second Timothy may have originated in that city. They were separated from the writing of Colossians (Philemon, and Ephesians) by almost two years, if there was only one long-term Roman captivity. They were written after an even longer time, if there were two prison terms, with extended traveling during the interval. Nevertheless, if secretaries or later disciples of Paul were the authors of Colossians, Ephesians, and the Pastoral Epistles, the different styles would no longer provide an argument for different dates and locations.

3. Concerning theological *substance*, the theme of Jesus Christ's present and future rule over the whole cosmos and all powers and things may serve for exemplification. The cosmic praise of Jesus Christ's Lordship at the end of the hymn Phil 2:6–11 corresponds to the hymnic and prose utterances about the creator, reconciler, and unifier which are found in Ephesians, Colossians, and the Pastoral Letters. However, there is a difference between the strictly eschatological-futuristic affirmations of Philippians, which approximate those of, for example, Rom 8:19–25 and 1 Cor 7:26–31; 15:25–28, and certain passages in the later letters. In Ephesians and Colossians, it is proclaimed that the saints have already been raised with Christ, and all things, including the

---

such as "Honest to God," finally as a bishop, when he affirms that Paul "would not be the last church leader" who in addressing subordinate clergy used a style which "differed markedly from his already highly diverse and adaptable manner of speaking and writing for wider audiences." Robinson takes up and goes beyond a suggestion of Reicke in saying about the Pastoral Epistles: Paul spoke "very much as the director of operations . . . like a general reporting on the movements of his commanders in the field . . . or the head of a missionary society giving news of his staff . . . more like the charges composed by a modern missionary bishop for an archdiaconical visitation" for which he uses "earlier material . . . prepared . . . for spoken exhortations to church leaders." Thus an image of Paul is created after the likeness of a high Anglican churchman.

205. When, e.g., a resounding liturgical tone and a sophisticated composition of well-known formulae is made the criterion of beauty and truth, he changed for the better. But his development is regretted when conformity with, or deviation from the vocabulary and doctrinal style of the justification doctrine is used as a measuring stick.

206. The fact that Paul and Timothy are co-authors of both, Philippians and Colossians, and that these two letters engage in sharp polemics, does not demonstrate their origin at the same time and occasion. Timothy is also co-author (with Silvanus) of First and Second Thessalonians, and of Second Corinthians. Only the simultaneous writing of Colossians and Philemon cannot be disputed. In each case, Timothy appears to have gone along with Paul's changing style, rather than to have imposed upon the letters he helped to compose a distinctive style of his own.

powers, are now reconciled with God.[207] Among scholars, a doctrine which anticipates the fulfillment of promises given for the future and places their realization into the present time, is being called "realized eschatology." For the development of Paul's thought from Philippians to the composition of Colossians and Ephesians (not to speak of the Pastoral Letters), not only the temporal distance between his stays in Caesarea and in Rome, but also the impact of the experienced "unhindered" gospel proclamation in the world's capital (Acts 28:31) offers a plausible explanation, although not a proof.[208]

Before new evidence and arguments are brought up for consideration, the issue "Caesarea or Rome?" will remain open. For the conditions of both Paul's Caesarean and (first) Roman detentions were relatively clement. According to Acts 24:23 and 28:16–31, Paul was permitted to accept the service of visitors and to continue his mission work, either in person or by the writing (or dictating) of letters or by receiving and dispatching aides.[209]

During a part of his Caesarean captivity,[210] as well as at the beginning of the years spent in Rome, there were still hopes for a gracious treatment by the Roman officials; otherwise Paul would not have fostered the expectation of release after a short spell or considered a forthcoming return to Macedonia and Asia Minor (Phil 2:24; Phlm 22). The disappointment implicitly expressed in Col 4:11 at the small number of Judaeo-Christians supporting Paul's person and cause seems to speak in favor of Caesarea. But after the overture made in the epistle to the Romans, and orally, according to Acts 28:17–24, to win the Roman Jews for the gospel, Paul had no less cause for grief in Rome.

The *reasons for giving preference to Rome* consist mainly of the evident weakness of the arguments used for Ephesus, and of the objections that can be raised against a definite decision for Caesarea. The first written tradition allocating Colossians to any place is found in an interpolation inserted into the fourth-century Codex B; Codex A and a few later manuscripts contain the same remark: it avers that Colossians was written in Rome. As Acts 28:28–31 intimates, the amount of freedom granted to the apostle at the beginning of his stay in Rome, for example, during the "first Roman captivity," was greater than the privileges he enjoyed at Caesarea. The joy expressed in Col 1:6, 23 at the

207. In these two letters, however, futurist statements are not simply suppressed, as, e.g., Col 3:1–4; Eph 4:13 (see AB 34, pp. 115–19; 34A, pp. 484–96). The same is true of the Pastoral Letters.

208. Among other reasons brought forward against Caesarea (e.g., by E. Lohse, *Colossians*, p. 166), some are not convincing: the silence of Acts 23:23–26:32 on those co-operators who are mentioned in Ephesians, Colossians, and Philemon, and the supposed lack of space in the small harbor town for the mission work in which Paul's companions were engaged.

209. By Phil 1:12–17; Col 4:3–4 // Eph 6:19–20, the report of Acts is confirmed.

210. Before he had appealed to Caesar (Acts 25:11) and thereby lost every chance of a quick release.

preaching and fruit-bearing of the gospel "in the whole world," "in all creation under heaven," seems to correspond exactly to the account Luke gives in Acts 28:31 about the Roman situation: Paul was free enough "to proclaim the kingdom of God and to teach about the Lord Jesus Christ with all openness unhindered."

In such a situation, the older or more recent, firm and yet repeatedly changed travel plans, including Spain in the west (see Rom 15:24, 28) and Colossae in the east (Phlm 22), were not an absurdity—as long as there was hope for a good issue of the Roman trial. The Roman date of Colossians allows time for the stylistic and material differences between Colossians and Ephesians on the one hand, and the *homologoumena* (including Philippians, which may have been written at Caesarea) on the other. If it is true that Colossae was damaged or destroyed by an earthquake during Nero's reign, that is in 61 or 62 C.E., the absence of a reference to the catastrophe would urge a date no later than these years.

Whether the probable origin of Colossians in the Hellenistic world capital corresponds to the substance of the document and makes it as important as any one among the so-called "capital letters" of Paul (to the Galatians, Corinthians, and Romans), this remains to be shown in the Notes and Comments.

COLOSSIANS
TRANSLATION WITH
NOTES AND COMMENTS

◆

I. THE EPISTOLARY ADDRESS (1:1–2)

1 From Paul, who by the will of God is apostle of the Messiah Jesus, and from Timothy, our brother. 2 To the saints at Colossae, who are true brothers and who confess the Messiah as Lord. Grace to you and peace from God our Father.

NOTES

1:1 *From Paul.* The Pauline letter formulation is reminiscent of the Near Eastern Jewish custom of the opening address, while, by contrast, to the Greek style[1] the sender is named first, then the addressee, after which a *chairein* (a proffered greeting) is added (e.g., in the NT: Acts 15:23; Jas 1:1). The division into two parts is characteristic: the sender and recipient are named, followed by a blessing in the form of an address (cf. in the OT: Dan 3:31). Both kinds of introductions can be embellished, but the basic structure remains consistent.

K. Berger pointed out that this Pauline introductory paragraph must have seemed "strange," "archaic," and at any rate "highly unusual" to his Hellenistic contemporaries. He attributes more significance in his interpretation of early Christian letters to the "literary fixed speech of theologically connected figures of authority in Judaism (prophetic letter, testament, apocalypse)" than is generally customary, and he finally defines the genre of apostolic letters as a "Literary set, addressed apostolic speech."[2]

---

1. See esp. E. Lohmeyer, "Probleme paulinischer Theologie, I, Briefliche Grussüberschriften," ZNW 26 (1927) 158–73; G. Friedrich critically illuminates Lohmeyer's thesis on the Pauline epistolary heading in ThLZ 81 (1956) 343–46; K. Berger: "Apostelbrief und apostolische Rede. Zum Formular frühchristlicher Briefe," ZNW 65 (1974) 190–231; G. J. Bahr, "Paul and Letter Writing in the First Century," CBQ 28 (1966) 465–77.

2. Compare K. Berger, op. cit., pp. 197, 231.

who by the will of God is apostle of the Messiah Jesus (literally: apostle of Christ Jesus according to the will of God). Although there is no indication in Col that the position of Paul as apostle is in question, we find the "title" apostle in v 1.[3] This is not surprising. The bare title, or the assumption of one, does not establish authority. Paul is apostle,[4] even though he persecuted the community of God, or more precisely, the former persecutor of the community is now the apostle of Jesus Christ. Decisive is not only the fact that the *apostle* Paul is writing to the communities as though the persona were distancing himself from the title or as though the title were the primary factor, but also the fact that the apostle *Paul* is writing. That he, and specifically he, is apostle, is already the gospel. This was deeply impressed into the consciousness of the young church even though the pastoral letters are to be attributed to a generation after Paul. Thus, according to 1 Tim 1:16 we see in Paul an example of the people *to whom* the gospel is applicable and thus what the gospel is as well. Authority is thereby not created by the title of its proclaimer, but is already proven as gospel by the choice of its proclaimer.[5] It substantiates itself on its own (cf. esp. 1:6). The "apostolic self-consciousness"[6] can also be understood on this basis. And thus it is also understandable that Paul can omit the designation "apostle" completely (1 Thess 1:1; 2 Thess 1:1) or he can replace it with "servant" *(doulos)* or "prisoner" *(desmios)* (cf. Phil 1:1; Phlm 1:1), without diminishing the authority of his message.

The expression *"by the will of God"* should not be understood polemically. Rather, it emphasizes the enormity that is at the basis of the combination "Paul—Apostle." It refers expressly to the will of God,[7] to the fact that Paul is a proclaimer of the Gospel. "By the will of God" means, further, that Paul did not undergo a "religious conversion" when he changed from persecutor to

---

3. In 1 Thess 1:1, we find only the name "Paul" next to Silvanus and Timothy. In Phil 1:1, Paul calls himself (as well as Timothy) "servant of Christ Jesus" *(doulos)*, in Phlm 1 "captive of Christ Jesus" *(desmios)*.

4. For "apostle," cf. M. Barth, AB 34, pp. 356–66; J. A. Kirk, "Apostleship since Rengstorf: Toward a Synthesis," NTS 21 (1975) 249–64 gives an overview of important NT declarations on thematics and on the research of the "last 40 years" (to 1975), and in addition, on an interesting theme of its own. Compare also E. Schweizer (pp. 31f.).

5. Compare 1 Cor 15:8f.; Eph 3:8. Weakness is precisely a sign of the Pauline apostolic office (1 Cor 1:26–29; 2 Cor 12:9f.). It is also the work of God, and he is thanked for this whenever the word of the divine sermon is not perceived as simply the word of the human being, but rather as the word of God (1 Thess 2:13).

6. For "apostolic self-consciousness," compare K. H. Rengstorf, ThWNT I, pp. 438–44.

7. The idea of a divine world plan, into which Paul inserts himself (K. H. Rengstorf, ThWNT I, p. 440), does not appear to be of primary consideration here. Compare M. Barth, AB 34, p. 65.

apostle of Christ Jesus. He still served the same God, before and after, whom he wanted or meant to serve before his commission.[8]

As in the corresponding passage of most of his epistles[9] (only Gal and in the pastoral letters only Titus are exceptions), Paul places the name Jesus before *Christos* in his Colossian prescript.[10] It cannot be precluded, since the article is missing before *Christos* in the Greek, that *Christos* has become a proper name. A title can be used without an article in Greek or in Hebrew.[11] On the other hand, proper names can also be used with articles (cf. for example Rom 8:11 ⟨vl⟩; Gal 6:17). Even if it were possible and even probable to translate *Christos* here as a proper name, as is usual and most frequent in Paul,[12] this should not be viewed as an alternative to the "titular" significance. Just as in Paul there is no salvation in Christ by excluding the Jews, so also there is no designation *Christos* without considering the Jewish Messiah (cf. Comment V to 1:9–23). Specifically because Paul uses *Christos* as a proper name, Paul emphasizes the fact that the Jewish title "Messiah" is inseparable from and is now tied solely to this Jewish Jesus. In order to mark the either/or between proper name and title beforehand as a wrong proposition, the title *Christ* has been translated as "Messiah," especially also because Paul understood the word as a proper name.[13]

and from Timothy. The unusually close relationship between Paul and Timothy makes it conceivable that *this* co-worker appears as co-sender. They have shared sorrow and joy, thanks and petitions, and many other things that characterized their relationship to the communities entrusted to them. Beyond that, it is pertinent that Timothy wrote Colossians from Paul's dictation, since Col 4:18 refers specifically to the fact that the letter was not put down on paper by Paul personally. There is no mention of a scribe, and since there is fair certainty of a co-worker with Paul who wrote the letter, we may presume that Timothy assumed this role[14] (cf. Comment I).

our brother (literally: the brother). Paul does not name any of his co-senders

---

8. Compare K. H. Rengstorf, ThWNT I, p. 439. See especially K. Stendahl, *Der Jude Paulus and wir Heiden. Anfragen an das abendländische Christentum* München: Kaiser, 1978, pp. 17–37, esp. pp. 17–25. Compare also 2 Tim 1:3.

9. According to the reading preferred in Nestlé-Aland.

10. References for the names and titles of Jesus are indicated by M. Barth, in AB 34, p. 66, fn. 6.

11. John 4:25; see A. S. van der Woude, ThWNT IX, p. 500; W. Grundmann, ibid., p. 533.

12. See esp. W. Grundmann, ThWNT IX, p. 534–36.

13. The idea that the office is to be emphasized in favor of the person (P. Ewald, p. 61) is questioned in Gal 1:1.

14. Compare esp. G. J. Bahr, "Letter Writing," op. cit.—There is no Pauline Epistle extant in which *only* Paul is mentioned in the heading *and* in which a passage in the epistle is expressly noted as written in his own hand, so that one could conclude that the scribe of the epistle was left unmentioned. Most likely, even Gal is also not an

"apostle" along with himself in any of the superscripts of his letters.[15] As also in 2 Cor 1:1, Timothy is called "the brother"[16] and Paul "apostle" in Col. A possessive pronoun ("my" or "our" or specifically "your"), as in a similar context in 2 Cor 2:13 or 1 Thess 3:2, is missing here.[17] That is probably due to the fact that an emphatic "my" or "your" is not implied, but rather the obvious "our" which was omitted.[18] We find this explicitly in 1 Thess 3:2.

Timothy is not "only" called brother because Paul alone is *the* apostle, or even because Paul's co-worker receives his legitimacy only from the community because of the apostle, and thus his authority.[19] Paul uses the title "apostle" because, as previously mentioned, this distinction lies in the fact that, to him, the least of all the apostles, the former persecutor of the communities, to him was entrusted the gospel for the gentiles. This is to be a signal for the Jews and for the gentiles. The "title" brother thus does not demarcate Timothy from Paul in any hierarchical way,[20] but rather it places the co-worker *alongside* the apostle: Timothy *serves with* Paul in the gospel (Phil 2:22); neither the one who plants nor the one who waters is worthy, but God alone ordains growth (cf. 1 Cor 3:5ff). We should not suppose a subordination here, but rather a coordination regarding the evaluation of service, and of a superordination of the grace and love of God over all humanly hierarchical ambitions, because God calls a sinner like Paul into his service. Thus the title "brother"[21] is used here to designate a

exception, even though Gal 6–18 seems to indicate that Paul had written the entire epistle in his own unskilled hand, rather than that he only appended his own written summary to the letter (compare G. J. Bahr, op. cit., p. 466).—We cannot ascertain a better conclusion from the dearth of Pauline material left for comparison, but contrary assumptions seem even more hypothetical. Even mention of Sosthenes in the heading in 1 Cor, who is not named again in the entire NT (except in Acts 18:17), can best be explained by the fact that he wrote down the epistle according to Paul's dictation.

15. Differently, however, in the course of the epistle, compare 1 Thess 2:7.

16. "Brother," without any kind of additional explanation, is otherwise used to refer to the following persons named by Paul: Quartus (Rom 16:23), Sosthenes (1 Cor 1:1), Apollos (1 Cor 16:12), and Timothy (Col 1:1; Phlm 1). The sense that all those named—except Quartus, of whom we know nothing further in the NT—are Jewish-Christians would be a coincidence. At any rate, it cannot be claimed that Paul used the designation "brother" in order to give special emphasis to a brother as a Jewish-Christian (compare Col 4:10f. with Phlm 23f.).

17. So also Eph 6:21; Col 4:7, 9.

18. For similar reasons, the possessive pronoun is not used in 1 Tim 1:2 (compare 2 Tim 1:2; Titus 1:4). In 2 Cor 2:13, it reads "my brother," not because the reference to the community is of primary concern, but rather because Paul is *concerned*, since he cannot find his brother.

19. Compare R. P. Martin, NCC 44; E. Lohmeyer, p. 17; W. Bieder, p. 10; esp. E. Schweizer, p. 33.

20. Compare esp. J. A. Kirk, "Apostleship," op. cit., esp. pp. 261–63.

21. To the question whether "brother" was a special designation of office, compare E. E. Ellis, "Paul and His Co-workers," in his *Prophecy and Hermeneutics in Early*

"colleague/co-worker."[22] Perhaps Paul chose the word "brother" purposely to convey this concept as it was perhaps used in the correspondence of kings, where the title is used to address persons of *equal* rank.[23]

2 *To the saints at Colossae, who are true brothers* (literally: to the holy and faithful brothers in Colossae). The manner of writing the name *Colossae* is not uniform. In a few old and important manuscripts, in Papyrus 46 (ca. 200 C.E.), in the Codex Alexandrinus (fifth century), in a correction of Codex Vaticanus (fourth century), we find *Colass-*. In Codex Sinaiticus (from the fourth century) we read *Coloss-* in the epistolary address, but in the edition of the scribe of this manuscript, which was inserted below the text, we read *Colass-*. *Colass-* is also used as a variant in Herodotus and Xenophon.[24] Evidently both forms were in use, making it difficult to assess which form Paul used.

In the epistolary address of Col, the recipients are not designated as *ekklēsia* (church). But as is clear from 1 Cor 1:2, *tois hagiois* (to the holy ones) is a paraphrase for *ekklēsia* without a significant difference.[25]

In light of the grammatical construction in which the article precedes the expression without repeating it, we can consider *hagiois* an adjective of "brothers." It is true that, in the other Pauline epistolary introductions, *hagioi* is always used expressly as a substantive,[26] but in this case, that observation does not permit a definite conclusion. Since the address *adelphoi* (brothers) is specific to Col, Paul can emphasize this distinction by subordinating the normally emphatic *adelphoi* adjectivally to the substantive *hagios*.

If one translates *hagios* substantively ("to the saints"), then the "and" must be understood as an "explicating and" called a *kai exepegeticum*, which has the significance of "and that is." In this case, it is not unusual that the article before *pistois* (faithfulness) is not repeated.[27] Above all, in the choice of the translation "to the saints at Colossae, specifically to the faithful brothers," we prevent the

---

Christianity, NT-Essays, WUNT 18 (Tübingen: Mohr, 1978, pp. 3–22 (= NTS 17 (1970/71) 448ff.).

22. As elsewhere in Greek, compare LSLex, p. 20. In the OT, compare, for example, 2 Kgs 9:2; Isa 41:6, where the limitation of meaning for "colleague" is fluid.

23. Compare LSLex, p. 20; in the OT: 1 Kgs 9:13; 20:32f.; also Num 20:14.

24. Compare H. A. W. Meyer, p. 218; T. K. Abbott, p. 193.

25. In the heading, we find *ekklēsia* (community) in: 1 Thess, 2 Thess, Gal, (Phlm next to single individuals, who are named as recipients); *ekklēsia* with additional material in: 1 Cor, 2 Cor; *ekklēsia* is lacking in the heading in: Rom, Eph, Phil, Col. The observation of J. B. Lightfoot (p. 198), that *ekklēsia* is included in the later epistles but no longer after Rom, needs to be corrected because of Phlm 1:2.—Even in the list of greetings in Col (4:15f.), a house community and a place community are designated by *ekklēsia*.

26. Rom 1:7; 1 Cor 1:2; 2 Cor 1:1; Eph 1:1; Phil 1:1.

27. Even otherwise, Paul uses the additional designations of the communities in the heading without the article. Compare Rom 1:7; 1 Cor 1:2.

misunderstanding that Paul is writing to different groups within the community of Colossae. Such an assumption, however, which would signify that Paul formulated his address in a polemic fashion,[28] can hardly be justified. There is no indication of this in Col because Paul does not argue with opponents within the community, as we shall discuss later (cf. Comment V.3 to 2:6–23). Even the significance of the word "saints" makes such an interpretation improbable. Paul does not mean a moral quality, but rather the quality of being chosen by God (see below). Also significant is the fact that in other cases we know Paul reprimands community members who are not living in accordance with their chosen faith, and dissuades them, but he does not simply pass them over (cf. esp. 1 Cor 4:14f.).

With the designation "saints," Paul characterizes the recipients of the epistle as the chosen ones of God, just as he also is apostle by the will of God. And just as Israel is holy on the strength of God's choosing (cf. esp. Deut 7:6–8; Isa 62:12), thus also is the community at Colossae (cf. 1:12, 26 and Comments V to 1:9–23).

and who confess the Messiah as Lord (literally: in Christ). The chosen paraphrase of the Greek *en christō* is elucidated further in Comment III. Because *en christō* (in Christ) is generally a fixed expression in Paul (cf. Rom 8:1; 16:3, 7, 9, 10, cf. 16:8, 11, 12, 13; 1 Cor 1:2, 30 etc.) and Paul also uses "pistoi adelphoi" (faithful brothers) without the addition *en christō* as a praiseworthy designation for his co-workers, it is not probable that *en christō* refers to the adjective *pistos* to indicate the object of "faithfulness." The meaning of "faithful in Christ" could be justified on the basis of LXX Ps 77(78):22; Jer 12:6; Mark 1:15; John 3:5, but cannot be confirmed in the Pauline epistolary.[29]

We can recognize a chiasm in the Greek text in the choice of the substantive translation of "saints,"

(lit.) to the   in Colossae saints . . .
       (to) the faithful brothers in Christ.

However, this stylistic form is incomplete, since *adelphois* (brothers) comes after *pistois* (faith). We need to be cautious about reading too much into this stylistic feature.

Grace to you and peace from God our Father. Form, function, and significance of the blessing formula in the Pauline and Petrine epistles are discussed

---

28. For this interpretation, compare J. B. Lightfoot, p. 198; A. Lindemann, p. 16.

29. 1 Cor 4:17 and Col 4:7 refer more to the *faithfulness* of the co-workers than to their "faith in . . ." Even the declarations of Paul which contain the expression *pistis en* (Rom 3:25; Eph 1:15; Col 1:4, in the Pastoral Epistles 1 Tim 3:13; 2 Tim 3:15) do not unambiguously support the meaning "faith in . . ." Unambiguous is the expression in 2 Tim 1:13, where the meaning "to believe in . . ." is excluded.

in AB 34, pp. 71–75. The blessing formula is purposely not interpreted in light of requests found in the beginning of extra biblical Greek letters. Rather, its use can be traced back to the community worship service. Moreover, in the OT precedents, "grace" and "peace" have the same relationship to each other as "covenant" and "life;" gentiles are included in grace and peace which are given through the Messiah.

The detailed peace-blessing is distinctive of the apostolic letter and is absent even in comparable Jewish letters of the period.[30] When Paul bestows *grace* upon the addressees, he is not thinking only of forgiveness of sins. The concept incorporates much more. For him, the attitude (of God) is fundamental, the one which is purely of a giving nature (cf. Rom 4:4; 11:6; Eph 2:4f.). It becomes substantive in all areas of life, becomes visible and concrete, remains not only a posture but at the same time is the gift itself. The sermon of the gospels *is* grace (Col 1:6); likewise it is recognition (2 Cor 8:7); but even the collection made by the community for brothers in distress is termed "grace" (2 Cor 8 passim). The material things necessary for the sustenance of life (2 Cor 9:8) are called "grace." The strength of God provided to those enduring tribulation is termed "grace," so that one may be fearful without despairing, oppressed without succumbing (2 Cor 4:7–16). All this and more is encompassed in the blessing formula of grace to the church at Colossae.

Peace (eirēnē) does not mean peace of the soul in the sense of a psychological and individualistic meaning, although this meaning occurs in LXX Lam 3:17; Hag 2:9). Rather, it signifies the condition of harmony, wholeness, and contentment between God and humankind or between human groups one with the other. The consideration that exclusion and separation have been surpassed stands in the forefront (cf. Notes to 1:20f. and 3:15).

This blessing formula in Col is the shortest in the Pauline epistles after 1 Thess.[31] The usual closing "and from the Lord Jesus Christ" is missing in the important manuscripts, as for example in Codex Vaticanus and Minuscule 33, while we have it in other good texts (Codex Sinaiticus, Codex Alexandrinus, Codex Ephraemi Rescriptus). The shorter form is probably the original one. However, it is difficult to find theological reasons for the "incompleteness" of the blessing formula. Other remarks in Col would contradict the notion that at this place the significance of Christ was intentionally reduced.

---

30. Compare K. Berger, "Apostelbrief," op. cit., pp. 196f. Berger also considers it possible that the apostolic epistle with its introductory blessings assumes an older oriental epistolary style in order to emphasize its official character; however, he points out that the introductory blessings were found in private letters just as frequently in ancient times (p. 197).

31. Neither God the Father, nor Christ, is mentioned here.

COMMENTS I–IV TO COL 1:1 + 2

I. Timothy, Co-worker of Paul, and the Question of Authorship

Timothy is a disciple from the city of Lystra or Derbe in Central Asia Minor. He has a good reputation among the brethren and Paul chose him in the first phase of his Second Missionary journey as his traveling companion. According to the report in Acts, Paul and his companion wanted to give the already existing congregations the so-called "Apostolic Decree" (Acts 15: 23–29). In this decree, the gentile Christians were absolved from the obligation of circumcision, among other matters. When Paul had Timothy circumcised anyway, for the sake of the Jews in and also outside the community, he did not depart from the principles of the "Apostolic Decree." Timothy was not a gentile Christian, but rather the son of a Jewish mother[1] (and a Greek father) and thereby an Israelite according to Jewish law.[2]

Luke does not mention Timothy in connection with Paul and Silas in prison at Philippi, and according to the report in Acts we do not discover any further details of his activity in Thessalonia, though very probably he was among the companions of Paul in both locations (cf. 1 Thess 1:1; 2:1 + 2). When Paul then moved on from Beroea to Athens (Acts 17:14), Silas and Timothy remained behind in Beroea. They followed later and met the apostle again in Corinth.[3] During the two-year stay in Ephesus (Acts 19), Timothy is mentioned along with Erastus as one of those who *served* Paul. We also have reports that Paul sent both of them ahead to Macedonia (Acts 19:22; 1 Cor 4:17; 16:10). Timothy was also among Paul's companions on the subsequent trip to Jerusalem (Acts 20:4). If the Col and Phlm Epistles of Paul were written in Rome, then Timothy was a companion of Paul there, although Acts does not mention him there (Acts 27:2). Timothy was also in captivity with Paul when the epistle to the Philippians was written. He was to maintain communication between the captive apostle and the community (Phil 1:1; 2:19).

In his letter to the Philippians, Paul recommends Timothy to the commu-

---

1. We find still further indications in the Pastoral Epistles: The author of 2 Tim indicates the names of Timothy's grandmother (Lois) and of his mother (Eunice). Accordingly, he points out their unadulterated faith (2 Tim 1:5), as also the fact that Timothy has been raised in the Jewish faith (3:15). We can deduce from 1 Tim 1:3 that Timothy occupied a responsible position in the community of Ephesus. In 1 Tim 1:18, we are reminded of earlier predictions that pertained to Timothy, and the text deals with the gift of God which Timothy received by the laying on of Paul's hands (2 Tim 1:6). Heb 13:23 mentions the end of an incarceration for Timothy.

2. Compare St.-B. II, p. 741.

3. The statements in 1 Thess 3:2, 6 differentiate themselves here from those in Acts: Timothy is sent from *Athens* to Thessalonica. Compare also W. G. Kümmel, *Einleitung in das Neue Testament* 18th ed. (Heidelberg: Quelle und Meyer, 1973), p. 222.

nity in a manner that reveals an especially close relationship between this co-worker and Paul, which places him prominently above the group of companions. Timothy's thinking is more like Paul's than any of the others; he alone can provide for the community, since Paul is in captivity. The Philippian church knows him as a proven co-worker of Paul, a trusted child of the father, a servant to the gospel along with Paul (Phil 2:19–22). In 1 Cor 4:17, Paul calls him his beloved and faithful child. He is not concerned for himself but only for that which serves Jesus Christ. Toward this end, he works in Corinth with Silas for their sustenance, so that Paul is completely free for the dissemination of the Gospel (Acts 18:5). But he is not a subservient helper[4]; he also preaches of the Son of God, alongside Paul (2 Cor 1:19). He receives the accreditation from Paul to teach the communities in the same way that Paul does himself (1 Cor 4:17); he carries out the work of the Lord as does also Paul (1 Cor 16:10). And in 1 Thess he is called "apostle" by Paul (cf. 1 Thess 2:6f. and 1:1).

In Col, Timothy is mentioned only in the preface; his name does not appear in the greetings at the end of the letter. This is generally true for the closings in Paul's letters unless Paul expressly indicates by name that he has added the concluding greeting with his own hand. The fact that the relationship of Timothy to the community of Colossae is not explained more precisely in the course of the epistle, in contrast to the (co-)senders of the other Pauline epistles,[5] simply indicates that there was nothing further to clarify.

Why is Timothy even mentioned in the preface of Col? Of course, the community will thus have discovered that Paul was not alone in his captivity. But such information could more likely be expected in a greeting at the end of the letter. Also, Paul will hardly have wanted to undermine his authority by naming his co-worker. Then he should have also mentioned the other *co-workers* in the preface who are mentioned in the greetings at the end (Col 4:7ff.). The argument that Timothy had a special part in the formulation of the letter is not likely. On the other hand, he disappears completely into the background in the course of the letter to the Colossians (see also Phil 1:3–6 and passim). Throughout, Paul writes in the first-person singular (Col 1:23–25, 29; 4:7–19; cf. 1 Thess 1:1; 3:2–6; Phil 1:1; 2:19–24). On the other hand, there is little point in attributing stylistic and theological peculiarities in a letter to a co-author who is an unknown quantity in this regard. In addition, there are no uniform

---

4. For a child-father image, see above all Gal 4:1–7: intended is precisely not a relationship which can be delineated by such key concepts as "minor," "dependent," "under-age," "subject to authority."

5. In 1 Cor, Sosthenes is named in the heading, but there is no further reference to him in the epistle. In addition, Paul writes in the first-person singular after 1:4. If we assume that we are dealing with the head of the synagogue, then this man is well known to the Corinthians. This is also the case concerning the relationship between co-senders and recipients in 2 Cor (see 1 Cor 4:17), Phil (see 1:1; 1:19), and 1 + 2 Thess (see Thess 1:1, 3:2, 6; Acts 17:4).

peculiarities in the letters in which Timothy is mentioned in the preface which would justify regarding him as a co-author of the letter.[6]

Was he then, perhaps, the author of the epistle to the Colossians under a pseudonym? His close relationship to Paul makes this plausible but the following arguments need to be weighed:

1. Col 4:18 explicitly mentions Paul's greeting *in his own hand*, although that is not his normal procedure in all of his epistles. The phenomenon of pseudonymity can be explained without bringing in moral considerations and arguments.[7] But a manuscript forgery leads to the assumption that a clever trickster is at work.

2. It would also be extraordinary for Timothy to name himself as co-author in the preface if he were also the pseudonymous author of the epistle. As far as we are aware, this would be without parallel in pseudonymous literature.

3. If the author with the means to falsify the manuscript attempted to deceive the readers about its true authorship,[8] then it is incomprehensible that he would have neglected the "best" possibilities, for example imitating the typical Pauline style, especially in the preface (see Notes).

E. Schweizer offers a solution which has the advantage of the authorship of Timothy without its associated problems. He rejects a pseudonymous author, because a "clever falsification of this nature in a letter by a person who is still in close proximity to Paul would presumably be under suspicion immediately." This would be incomprehensible to him (p. 24). Thus he presumes that Timothy wrote the letter in both their names, since the conditions of Paul's incarceration would not have permitted Paul to write the letter himself. Finally, he speculates, Timothy presented the letter to Paul for his signature (p. 26).[9]

The problems are thus solved in an impressive and yet purely hypothetical manner. Besides that, one could argue that there is hardly a clue for the assumption that Paul's conditions of imprisonment correspond to E. Schweizer's description; the contrary is rather the case. In addition, we are on completely uncertain ground here in terms of solving the theological and stylistic problems in Col if one were to presume Timothy as the author (see above).

II. Co-workers Among Themselves

Paul calls the recipients of his epistle "true brothers." In doing so, he uses an expression which he otherwise employs to praise and highlight his co-

---

6. For the "hypothesis on the secretary," compare esp. W. Michaelis, *Einleitung in das Neue Testament*, 2d ed. (Bern: BEG Verlag, 1954), pp. 242–44; W. G. Kümmel, *Einleitung*, op. cit., pp. 329f. See also E. Lohse, p. 34, par.3.

7. Compare J. Gnilka (pp. 23f.). Further references are indicated there.

8. A comparison of the lists of greetings of Col and Phlm is also instructive. Reversals and changes would also point in the direction of a clever falsification. Compare E. Schweizer (p. 24).

9. The number of Paul's co-workers and visitors, as well as the substitutions of those

workers.[10] It seems as though Paul expressly did not want to write as a "superior" to his "subordinates." This impression is further enhanced if one is allowed to view Paul in this position on the basis of his statements in Eph 4:12. According to the latter, the apostles, prophets, evangelists, and shepherds are to equip the saints in the service of the work of erecting the "body of the Messiah." The "saints at Colossae" are thus co-workers with Paul in order to serve the gospel together with him. All those addressed in Col are included, be they men or women, children or parents, slaves or masters.

In Col it is clear already in the Epistolary Address, more so than in any other Pauline epistle, that we are dealing with a message from brothers to brothers. They are hardly referred to as brothers for stylistic, rhetorical, or emotional reasons. For one thing, the letter to the Galatians shows that it was not Paul's habit to win his readers through praise where this was basically not applicable. In Col, Paul did not have to come to terms with grievances in the community which would forbid his use of the address of "true brothers." Paul is able to rejoice in the orderly and steadfast loyalty to Christ in this community (2:5), even while he is concerned by specific threats and exposure from external and anonymous sources.

Aside from that, he speaks in his blessings not only of "brothers," but also of "God, *our Father*" and in the following verse of "God the Father of our Lord Jesus Christ."[11] Since the sender and the receivers have God in common as their Father through their common Lord, the Messiah (cf. 1:12–14 and Comment II to 1:3–8), they are brothers among themselves in order to serve God together.

III. Brothers "in Christ"

The direct context does not give a clue to determine clearly what Paul means by his often-used phrase *en christō* (in Christ) in Col 1:2. We can find a rich assortment of varying interpretations in the commentaries.[12]

The preface of 1 Cor may help to clarify the meaning of this formula which

---

who share his imprisonment, are rather more indicative of the loosely regulated conditions of imprisonment, just as they are reported in Acts 28:16, 30.

10. Compare Col 4:7, 9; Eph 6:21.—*Pistos* without the addition of "brother" is used to describe a faithful servant in Col 1:7; compare 1 Cor 4:2, 17. *Pistos* seldom has the meaning denoting "faith": 1 Cor 7:14 v. 1; 2 Cor 6:14; Gal 3:9; compare also 1 Cor 7:12–15, and others, where *apistos* means "unfaithful."

11. Compare Gal 3:26; Rom 8:15, 29.

12. The various possibilities of interpreting *en christō*, whether these are mythical, mystical, existential, eschatological, judicial, ecclesial, sacramental, local, or historical, have been pointed out and discussed by M. Barth in AB 34, pp. 69–71. Compare also F. Neugebauer, *In Christus. EN CHRISTO. Eine Untersuchung zum Paulinischen Glaubensverständnis* (Göttingen: Vanderhoeck & Ruprecht, 1961).

characterizes the community in the introduction of the epistle. Paul writes to the community in Corinth and includes everyone in the circle of recipients "who call upon the name of our Lord Jesus Christ." By that, he has obviously given the signal that singularly determines the recipients of his letter. Against the background of 1 Cor 8:5, it is even more clear what is meant by "calling upon the name of our Lord Jesus Christ," even if there are many lords in the world, "*we* still have only . . . *one* Lord, Jesus Christ, through whom all things are and we through him." Presumably the "in Christ" in the salutation of Col is a shortened form of the more explicit predication in the salutation of 1 Cor.

We should consider a further factor of the address to "true brothers *in Christ.*" The connection with these brothers, the special commission to write to them and to exhort them, is based on this appellative to a greater extent than upon the title "apostle."

This becomes clear when one considers excerpts from 2 Cor 5. There, Paul describes his (missionary) mandate to be a messenger in the place of Christ (2 Cor 5:20). His mandate is based on "the fact that when *one* has died for all, then they have *all* died . . . so that the living (!) do not live for themselves but for him who died for them and rose again" (2 Cor 5:14f.). All people have thus died with Christ and are therefore reconciled to God. Paul summarily circumscribes these facts in 2 Cor 5:17 as "being in Christ." Paul is now commissioned to ask the reconciled to let themselves be reconciled to God, meaning that they are to live for him who has also reconciled them.

IV. Conclusion

The significance of the preface is not restricted simply to naming the sender and receiver. Rather, it already contains deep theological statements. The meaning of "gospel" is pregnantly expressed in these first two verses of Col.

Paul, the *former persecutor* of the community of God, has been *called by God*—he is called apostle. He, his co-worker Timothy, and the recipients of the letter are *brothers*, co-workers in the service of one Lord. This gives expression to the term "true brothers," which is otherwise reserved for the laudatory elevation of the trusted companions of Paul. He thus avoids hierarchical implications.

All this is possible because *God*, whom Paul had already recognized before his conversion, has become Father of them all.

His blessing becomes visible in this relationship to Paul and in the brother and sisterhood of God's children as well as in all the blessings that God confers upon his community. And it is the strength of this blessing which protects the community from all dangers which Paul will describe in the epistle.

II. THANKSGIVING, INTERCESSION, AND HYMN (1:3–23)

1. Thanksgiving (1:3–8)

3 We thank God the Father of our Lord Jesus (Christ) always for you in our prayer. 4 Because we have heard of your faithfulness to the Messiah Jesus, that is the love that you have for all the saints, 5 because of the hope that is securely stored up for you in heaven. Of this you have heard previously through the word of truth, (namely) the gospel. 6 This came to you and became at home with you as it also continuously brings forth fruit and grows in the whole world, as also among you, since the day when you heard and knew the grace of God as truth. 7 As you (certainly) learned it from Epaphras, our beloved fellow servant. He is a faithful servant of the Messiah in our place; 8 and he has also reported to us of your love which is a gift of the Spirit.

NOTES

In the beginning of most Pauline epistles, there is an expression of gratitude[1] or a eulogy (as in 2 Cor) or both (as in Eph). The letter to the Galatians is an

---

1. P. Schubert, *Form and Function of the Pauline Thanksgivings*, BZNW 20 (Berlin: Töpelman, 1939), worked out two main types for the Pauline statements of thanksgiving, with the following formal designations: In type 1a—to which also Phlm, 1 Thess, and Phil belong in addition to Col (the "more personal epistles")—two or three participial constructions follow the finite verb *eucharisteō* (to thank). A final sentence follows these participials without exception, and is subordinated to them. Type 1b characterizes the "less personal epistles" (1 Cor, Rom, 2 Thess): The main sentence with the finite verb *eucharisteō* is followed by a causal subordinate sentence introduced by the conjunction *hoti*, and a subsequent sentence introduced by *hōste* is dependent on that.—Both types, in mixed fashion, are found in Rom, but also in 1 Thess, so that their existence cannot be explained chronologically. According to P. Schubert, the function of the thanksgiving consists in the fact that they introduce the main themes of each epistle. An exhaustive comparison of these observations with the "pseudo-Pauline epistles," the remaining Christian literature of the First and Second Centuries, the LXX, Philo, Epictetus (and the Stoa in general), the inscriptions, and the papyri, lead Schubert to conclude that the thanksgivings are not to be understood liturgically in form and function, but that they can rather be explained in the context of the Hellenistic letter formulations.—For a critique of these results, see, among others, J. M. Robinson: "Die Hodajot-Formel in Gebet und Hymnus des Frühchristentums, in FS für E. Haenchen, *Apophoreta*, BZNW 30 (Berlin: Töpelmann 1964), pp. 194–235; P. T. O'Brien: "Thanksgiving and the Gospel in Paul," NTS 21 (1974/75) 144–55 (further references there, esp. p. 145, fn. 9). Compare also J. Gnilka (p. 29), who prefers to use community epistles from the Judaic

exception (as is also the letter to Titus in the so-called Deutero-Pauline literature). In Gal we find instead an expanded blessing formula that culminates in a doxology.

The expression of gratitude in Col consists of a single long sentence (vv 3–8). The verb *eucharistoumen* (we thank) is at the beginning (v 3) and is augmented by the participle *proseuchomenoi* (praying). After the thanksgiving in vv 3–8, this verb "to pray" is then used again in v 9, followed by the intercession. This intercession flows into another thanksgiving in v 12, now in the form of a hymn. The ending of the expression of thanksgiving, which includes the intercession, is difficult to determine. A clear conclusion is only distinguishable in v 23. Verse 24 begins a new theme,[2] but now we return to vv 3–8.

The occasion for thanksgiving is expressed in v 4. Paul and Timothy have heard of the faithfulness and the love of the Colossians. "Love" is the cue for a new declaration in v 5, which begins with the relative clause "which you have for all the saints because of the hope. . . ." "Hope" is the connecting link for the next thought which is amplified in the relative clause in v 5b, "which you have heard before. . . ." In this explanation, Paul considers it necessary to describe still further the "word . . . which has to come to be at home among the Colossians"; he adds a comparative phrase, "as also in the whole world. . . ." In

---

realm for comparing the statements of thanksgiving in the Pauline epistles, where prayers as well as remembrances can be found (ApkBar syr 78:3; 86:3; 1 Macc 12:11; 2 Macc 1:3–5), since, in the Hellenistic comparative material, we are dealing with letters to individual persons and since the thanksgiving appears to operate almost exclusively on a formulaic basis. Schubert does not work out formal characteristics for the ending of the statements of thanksgiving precisely. Among others, J. T. Sanders dedicated himself to this task: The Transition from Opening Epistolary Thanksgiving to Body of Letters of the Pauline Corpus, JBL 81 (1962) 348–62. J. L. White added a correction: "Introductory Formulae in the Body of the Pauline Letter," JBL 90 (1971) 91–97. For the transition from the introductory material to the main component in Hebrew and Arabic epistles, see D. Pardee: "An Overview of Ancient Hebrew Epistolography," JBL 97 (1978) 321–46, esp. 339f. For this topic, compare also M. Barth, AB 34, pp. 160–62, and T. Y. Mullins: "The Thanksgiving of Philemon and Colossians, NTS 30 (1984) 288–93.

2. J. L. White, "Introductory Formulae," op. cit., worked out six different formulae, which introduce the main portion of the uncontested Pauline epistles (homologumena), and which would thus permit also recognition of the end of the introductory components of the epistles. He calls one of these formulae "joy expression" (pp. 95f.). Even if the format does not correspond to that in Col 1:24, there is still agreement in the item—P. Schubert, *Form and Function*, op. cit., pointed out the eschatological end-climax as characteristic for the ending of the thanksgiving, which he views as achieved in Col with 1:13f. But he hesitates to accept the ending here, since 1:15–20 is closely linked to 1:12–14. Thus he indicates Col 1:23 as an alternative for the ending of the thanksgiving in Col (p. 6). In favor of this argument is the fact that 1:22 reaches an eschatological climax.—The length of such a thanksgiving would not be unique, since it is surpassed in 1 Thess, where it continues from 1:2 to 3:13.

this extended train of thought, Paul reminds the Colossians that they (literally) "have heard and recognized the grace of God in truth," and he takes this expression as the occasion for further exposition, which is again introduced by the comparative particle "as" *(kathōs,* v 7). The structure of this thought process (vv 3–8) can be represented schematically as follows (the catchwords that form the links for a new exposition between the units are underlined):

V 3	we thank . . . praying
v 4	having heard . . . of the *love*
vv 4 + 5	which *(hēn)* you have heard . . . because of the *hope* . . .
vv 5 + 6	which *(hēn)* you have heard in *the word which has come to be at home with you* . . .
v 6	as *(kathōs)* also in . . . since . . . you *heard and recognized the grace of God in truth*
vv 7 + 8	as *(kathōs)* you have learned . . .

The reader-listener is carried along from one thought to the next. It is not necessary for him to have an overview of the entire sentence in order to understand it. That is true first of all for the sequence of thoughts. Understanding the content of the individual thoughts is more difficult, because attributes are attached within the subunits of thought that compound the difficulties of the exegesis, as we will discover. Thus, unambiguous interpretations are hardly possible.

In the course of the exegesis, it should become clear whether we have a distinctive stylistic example for the whole epistle in these verses, which might give us a basis for excluding Paul as author.[3] The style of these verses is certainly a departure from the prevailing pattern of the Pauline epistles regarded as genuine by all scholars. However, we should bear in mind that a prayer has been inserted into the epistle to the Colossians. So-called "rules," valid for other

---

3. W. Bujard, *Stilanalytische Untersuchungen zum Kolosserbrief als Beitrag zur Methodik von Sprachenvergleichen,* StUNT 11 (Göttingen: Vandenhoeck & Ruprecht, 1973), sees a good example in this passage for the connecting style which differentiates Col from the Pauline epistles (p. 73), because the logical connections of the individual sentences and sentence components to each other are not given unequivocal and clear expression (p. 79). In his analysis of Col 2:6–15, W. Bujard comes to the conclusion that the connecting style gives expression to a freer train of thought (p. 86). He considers his viewpoint further confirmed by the fact that instead of continuing repetitions, we find indicators which are to be interpreted as "recourses." The repeatedly used word combinations which occur in this way would indicate "a deficiency in the author of Col in flexibility of thought and formulation" (p. 100).

stylistic forms, are not obligatory upon prayers, hymns, etc.[4] When "the mouth overflows with the contents of the heart," we should not expect a strictly logical development of thought, but rather an "associative" and "abundant" style.

3 *We thank God the Father of our Lord Jesus (Christ)*. The question is whether, in the plural formulation of "we thank . . . ," we are dealing with a "literary plural" in which Paul has only himself in mind, or whether the apostle refers to himself and Timothy, or specifically to his other co-workers. We will deal with this question in Comment I.

The thanksgiving is directed to God in all the Pauline epistles.[5] An exception, if we presume that Paul wrote the epistle, is 1 Tim. God, as the recipient of thanksgiving, is usually designated by the short expression *tō theō*, or *tō theō mou* (1 Cor; Phil; 1 and 2 Thess; Phlm). In the letter to the Romans, this expression is supplemented with "through Jesus Christ." (See also Col 3:1.) The author of 2 Tim adds a relative clause, "whom I serve with a pure conscience, as did also my ancestors." In the letter to the Ephesians, the addressee of the prayer is not mentioned at all, but the purpose of the prayer is mentioned in a closing sentence in which the reference is to "God of our Lord Jesus Christ, the Father of glory" as the giver of all that is requested (Eph 1:17). In 2 Cor, we have a glorification instead of a thanksgiving. It is directed to "God and (namely) to the Father of our Lord Jesus Christ." This long formulaic prayer address is very reminiscent of the epistle to the Colossians. Here, also, we can justify the supposition that this pattern is the basis for the prayer formulation of the pre-Christian worship service. If there was an abbreviated form of the blessing formula in v 2, then we find an extended form of the prayer formula in v 3 (cf. Comment II.)

A few of the less reliable manuscripts add an article before "Father," but important key texts like Codex Sinaiticus (fourth century) and Codex Alexandrinus (fifth century) indicate "and" instead. The best textual evidence among the majuscules (see the Introduction, Section VI), the Codex Vaticanus (fourth century) reads Father following God, without the article. The same is most

---

4. See esp. E. Percy, *Die Probleme der Kolosser-und Epheser-briefe*, SHVL 39 (Lund: Gleerup, 1946), pp. 43ff. (subsequently cited: PKE). E. Lohmeyer (p. 20) points out that despite references to epistle style in antiquity, the thanksgivings are intended liturgically. A prayer follows the blessing in the Jewish, as well as in the Christian, worship services. E. Lohmeyer argues that the entire section is segmented into four three-liners, with a verb in the beginning of each segment, and in each line he again differentiates three segments.—The train of thought into which the reader-listener is brought and which the sentence construction does not permit to be viewed in its totality, however, causes us to question whether Lohmeyer recognized intentionality on the part of the author in this passage.

5. For the question as to whether the veneration of Jesus existed in the Christian worship service in the NT communities, compare G. Lohfink, "Gab es im Gottesdienst der neutestamentlichen Gemeinden eine Anbetung Christi?" BZ.NF 18 (1974) 161–79.

probably true of the Papyrus 61, and also of the very important Minuscule 1739 (see the Introduction, Section VI).

In Greek, the article is required before the noun "Father," and thus the rendition as we find it in Codex Vaticanus is exceptional. Normally Paul uses the connecting "and" in other similar instances between the substantives "God" and "Father," which makes the repetition of the article unnecessary (cf. Rom 15:6; 1 Cor 15:24; 2 Cor 1:3; 11:31; Eph 1:3; 5:20; also 1 Peter 1:3; Rev 1:6). The unusual variant also occurs in Col in 1:12, 2:2, and 3:17. It is noteworthy that we do *not* have the "and" in 1:3 in Codex Sinaiticus and Codex Alexandrinus, but we do have it in 3:17. This Greek anomaly is best explained as an influence from the Hebrew, because in Hebrew the first (construct) noun is not determined in the genitive construction.[6] This explanation does not apply to 3:17, since a genitive construction is not used there. In our verse (1:3), our explanation would be supported by the fact that this unusual formulation was the original phrasing and was corrected subsequently.[7]

In Codex Vaticanus and in Minuscule 1739, the designation "Christus" after the name "Jesus" is absent. This reading is so unusual that we suspect, along with C. F. D. Moule (p. 48), that it is original for exactly that reason.

Paul does not follow the ancient Hellenistic epistolary style when he thanks God at the beginning of his epistles. In Col it becomes clear how important the thanksgiving is to him because he repeatedly invites the recipients of the epistles to offer their own prayers of thanksgiving (1:12; 2:7; 3:15, 17; 4:2).[8] Paul himself provides a striking example of this practice in this epistle, especially when we note that the prayer extends to 1:23. Paul places the thanksgiving at the beginning of most of his letters. He makes it clear that all the benefits that accrue to the community are not derived on the success of his mission or his personal fame. Paul and his co-workers do not view themselves as the givers. Rather, they perceive themselves very consciously as those who are among the recipients.[9] In this equality they all want and should be giving thanks.

always for you in our prayer. A few manuscripts render *hyper hymōn* (for you), others *peri hymōn* (concerning you). Both variants are well attested. In both cases, the sense is the same, because in the NT *peri* often takes the place of *hyper* (cf. BDR 229.1; 231). We have *hyper hymōn proseuchomenoi* in v 9

6. Compare BDR 259.

7. H. A. W. Meyer (p. 219) is of the opinion that the "and" is original and that it was technically omitted after the immediately preceding *apo theou patros hemon*, where there is no "and" between "God" *(theou)* and "father" *(patros)*.

8. To this frequent exhortation of saying thanks, we find parallels in Paul only in 2 Cor 1:11; 4:15; 9:11–12; Eph 5:4,20; Phil 4:6; 2 Thess 5:18.

9. We find a similar thought in Rom 1:11 + 12. Paul writes to the Romans that he would like to come in order to convey something to them in terms of spiritual gifts so that he can strengthen them. Then, however, he corrects himself, "that is, that we may be mutually encouraged through your and my faith. . . ."

without text variants. That is why we assume that v 3 was probably originally *peri* and was then corrected from v 9.

The adverbial determinant "always" can modify "to thank" or the participle "praying," as well as both verbs. In the prayer of thanksgiving of 1 Cor and 2 Thess, "always" clearly modifies "to thank." In Eph we read "I do not cease to thank. . . ."

Just as Paul intends unceasing petition in v 9, he probably speaks of continuing thanksgiving in v 3. We cannot definitely decide whether he means a faithful regular remembrance here, or a prayer of 24-hour-per-day duration.[10] In any case, we should not choose the possible translation "always when we pray" which can easily give the impression of fixed prayer times. Paul could then give the impression that the text needs to be interpreted as separating "official and private areas," "liturgical and private life."[11] The assertions of Paul in other epistles speak against such a separation, which would let us think of a continuous prayer lasting the entire day (Eph 6:18, 1 Thess 5:17; 2 Thess 1:11; cf. also Rom 12:12; Col 4:2). Accordingly, Paul would enter into prayer of thanksgiving and intercession for the saints, whether he is working as a tentmaker or traveling, whether he is preaching or lying in chains for the gospel. A good solution seems to be not to make a decision for one or the other possibility in the translation, and to render the participle by "in our prayer."

The expression "for you" can also refer to either one of the verb forms. It probably belongs with "we thank." Otherwise it would emphatically precede the participle, as though Paul wanted to say, "for you, in contrast to others, we always give thanks." There is no indication of such a contrast, for instance as though he could not give thanks for the community in Laodicea where the epistle to the Colossians would also be read (4:15).

4 *Because we have heard of your faithfulness to the Messiah Jesus.* The faith of the Christians in the cosmopolitan city of Rome is renowned in the "whole world" (Rom 1:8), and the faithful in the large and important trade city of Thessalonica have also become a model for the Christians in outlying areas (1 Thess 1:7). Good reports have also reached far beyond the community of little out-of-the-way Colossae, yes, even to the capital of the Roman empire, if Paul composed Col in Rome.

Pistis en should be translated analogously with the adjective *pistos* in v 2 as "faithfulness to."[12] This is preferable because the *pistis* of the Colossians is

---

10. In Rom 1:9 + 10, "continuously" and "always" refer to the fact that Paul has not ceased to pray about being able to come to Rome. Whether he means by that fixed times for prayer cannot be determined from this passage. We find the same reference in 1 Thess 1:2–3; 2:13; Col 1:9.

11. Compare E. Schweizer, p. 35.

12. In Rom 1:8 also, *pistis* is possibly used in a similar sense, where the subject concerns *pistis en allēlois*, which could possibly be translated as "mutual faithfulness."

represented by a relationship of faith by "love to the brothers." *Pistis* therefore obtains its significance here, as also in other passages in Paul, from the Hebrew *ʾemunah* (faith, loyalty). An example from the epistle to the Romans may make this clear. In Romans 3:3–4, Paul refers to the *pistis* of God. Here the noun designates the faith relationship of God to his people, his truth and loyalty toward his (covenant) promises. This divine *pistis* is the example for Paul of human *pistis*. Thus he says that the divine *pistis* cannot be repealed by the fact that some are not faithful *(apisteo, apistia)*. This concept of Paul is underscored by the fact that he illustrates this definition of faith in detail, citing the OT example of Abraham (Rom 4) or even, with respect to *pistis*, when he cites Hab 2:4 (Rom 1:17; Gal 3:11: "the righteous one will live by *pistis*").

that is the love that you have for all the saints. In v 5, the key concept is tied only to "love." The word *pistis* does not occur again in the following presentation. Even in v 8, where reference is made to the occasion when Paul and Timothy have heard the good news about the community at Colossae (v 3), the discussion centers on the "love of Colossians." Therefore the "and" between the two expressions "faith" and "love" is to be understood as an "interpretive *and*," meaning *"and* that is, namely, specifically." Faith and love designate one and the same thing; here we have a case of hendiadys.[13]

Love for *"all* saints," which distinguishes the Colossians, is the love which excludes no one. In this, they do not have in mind so much the *large number* of saints all over the world. Col 3:10–14 clarifies that this love for *all* saints is characterized by the fact that social and ethnic differences become meaningless (see the discussion there). Of all the Pauline epistles, only 1 Thess 3:12 seems to indicate that Paul also recognizes love for an anonymous mass of people. There, he refers to an "overflowing of love for one another and for *all people.*" But even here we have to ask whether Paul intends the Christians in the community (= in 1 Thess: love for one another) as well as the people who do not belong to the local community, but who are known to the Christians, (see also Gal 6:10, "Do good for *everyone,* but most for the comrades in faith!").

5 *because of the hope that is securely stored up for you in heaven.* This remark, which seems to be connected very loosely with the preceding, contains a thought that is quite unusual: only here does Paul say expressly that *hope* is the basis for *faithfulness* and *love*. Most notable is the departure from the

---

13. *pistis* in this sense is used in the shorter version of Eph 1:15, which is rendered by almost all the important text evidence ("your *pistis* for the Lord Jesus and for all the saints. . . ."). Compare also the statements in which *pistis* is cited *next to* love, seemingly in order to avoid the misinterpretation that one can have the former without the latter: Gal 5:6; compare Gal 5:13–15; 1 Cor 13:2; 13:13; Eph 1:15 (longer reading); Phlm 5; 1 Thess 1:3; 3:6; 5:8; 2 Thess 1:3; compare 1 Tim 1:5; 2:15; 4:12; 6:11; 2 Tim 1:13; 2:22; Titus 2:2.

declaration in 1 Cor 13:13 which expresses that love is the greatest of the three: faith, love, and hope.[14]

The difference is perhaps best explained by the fact that, in Col, Paul does not mean the "act of hoping" by "hope," but rather the *object* of hope. According to 1:27, this is Jesus, the Messiah (not only of Jews but also) of non-Jews. On this basis, it is understandable that hope is the foundation for the faithfulness and love of the Colossians. Because if the Messiah were not also the Messiah of the gentile-Christians in Colossae, then their love and faithfulness would be without foundation in the truest sense of the word. Further, this love and faithfulness would not exist at all among the Colossians since they are perceived as the fruit of the gospel, which was only available to them because Jesus is also the Messiah of the gentiles, as the following verses will show.[15] Such hope is not dependent on the ups and downs of human emotions and opinions. It is guaranteed by the resurrected Messiah, because the resurrected Messiah himself is this hope. (See Comment III.)

Serious consideration has been given to the question whether "because of hope" refers to *eucharistoumen* (we thank). If so, then the hope which is stored up in heaven would be the cause for thanksgiving. The counterargument is that Paul refers to the conditions of the communities or specifically to those addressed in all his expressions of thanksgiving. In addition, it seems forced to consider v 4 as an insert which does not indicate the cause for thanksgiving. Here, Paul is describing a state of the community which gives opportunity for thanksgiving, and this is emphasized in this "love for all saints" which has such central significance for Paul (see above).[16]

---

14. We find the triad "faith-love-hope," in addition to references in Paul, also in 1 Thess 1:3; 5:8; compare Rom 5:1–15; Gal 5:5+6. R. Reitzenstein, *Nachrichten von der Gesellschaft der Wissenschaft zu Göttingen*, 1916, pp. 367–411, esp. p. 393, thinks that the triad "faith-love-hope" is a shortened concept used by Paul of an original gnostic formula comprising four parts: "faith-*cognizance*-love-hope." This has been countered by the argument that the abbreviated version previously existed for Paul before he encountered the "gnosis" (1 Thess 1:3; 5:8). For a discussion, see W. Schmithals: *Die Gnosis in Korinth, Eine Untersuchung zu den Korintherbriefen*, 3d ed., FRLANT.NF 48 (Göttingen: Vandenhoeck & Ruprecht, 1969), pp. 135–37, esp. p. 136. To summarize. W. Schmithals points out, that we find the formula supposed by Reitzenstein in verse 115 of the Coptic Philippian Gospel.

15. It is not unusual in Paul that *elpis* (hope) is used in an objective sense and thus designates the object of hope: see Rom 8:24; Gal 5:5; 2 Cor 3:12 (?). Paul also emphasizes the special meaning of "hope" elsewhere: see Rom 4:18; 8:24–25; 15:13; Gal 5:5–6; 1 Cor 13:7. In Col, however, "hope" signifies the synthesis of the gospel in general. As E. Lohmeyer notes (p. 23), each of the three words, "faith," "love," "hope," can summarize the richness of the prototype of the Christian life in itself: "faith" in Rom and Gal, "love" in 1 Cor 13, "hope" in Col.

16. Thus T. K. Abbott (p. 196); P. Ewald (p. 295). The implication is not to subvert Paul's idea with the "unevangelical" thought that love should be motivated by "reward."

The verb *apokeimai* (to store up, to lie in readiness) occurs only three other times in the NT besides the instance here in Col.[17] The assuredness with which something comes to pass or is actualized plays a central role everywhere. In Luke 19:20, the concern is for the money which is (safely) put away in a linen cloth in fear of the "harsh Lord." In 2 Tim 4:8, it centers on the victory wreath that is kept for the best runner. In Hebr 9:27, a comparison is made with the inescapability of mortality.

The background for the statement in Col 1:15 may be the Jewish-apocalyptic conception of reward, which is securely kept by the one on high for the piously deceased (until the resurrection).[18] The concept of reward itself, however, is not involved in this passage.

Col does not offer a determination for conceptualizing "heaven" as a place in which hope would fulfill itself after death, after the ascension of the person. Rather, it deals with the place where the Messiah "sits at the right hand of God." This is expressed in 3:1, a passage in which "above" *(anō)* is used as a substitute for "heaven"[19] as 4:1 shows (cf. Comment III).

Of this you have heard previously through the word of the truth, (namely) the gospel (literally: the truth of the gospel). Noteworthy is the fact that Epaphras is not mentioned here, and not until v 7. The "word of the truth" is named first, through which the Colossians have heard of hope. This word itself is the primary agent, the subject of all its actions,[20] and is personified by Paul.

In Col 1:25–27, this word is called "word of God" and is described as the mystery which is revealed by God. The relationship between word and revelation is also emphasized when Paul speaks of the "word of *truth*." "Truth" also elsewhere in Paul signifies, as in LXX Ps 118 (119):42 + 43 (cf. 142 + 160), the proclamation of the word as revealed by God. What God has revealed of himself since creation through his deeds (Rom 1:20) is called "truth" (Rom 1:25). "Truth" is presented as the contrast to "injustice" in Rom 1:18; 2:8; 3:7; cf. 1 Cor 13:6, and we are told about the justice (of God), that it alone is *revealed* in Jesus Christ and verified through the law and the prophets (Rom 3:21f.). "Truth" is synonymous here (as also in Rom 3:5–7) with "justice." In other

---

17. For the meaning of the entire expression, compare also 1 Pet 1:4.

18. Compare ApkBar(syr) 14:12; 4 Ezra 7:14, 77; 2 Macc 12:45; and others. E. Pfister, "Zur Wendung *apokeitai moi ho tēs dikaiosynēs stephanos*," ZNW 15 (1914) 94–96, pointed out that the concept that heaven is proffered as a reward for good deeds is based on an institution at the Persian court. According to this, the names and benefactors of the king were entered into the official annals of the state.

19. "Heaven" occurs in Col 1:16, 20, 23 in the combination "heaven and earth," in reference to the saying "all creation under heaven." But these declarations do not contribute anything substantive to the understanding of this passage.—For "heaven," compare also M. Barth, AB 34, pp. 102f.; 236–38.

20. Compare Rom 1:16: The gospel "is a power of God for salvation. . . ." See also 1 Cor 2:4f.; 1 Thess 1:5.

passages (i.e., Gal 5:7; 2 Thess 2:12), Paul even speaks simply of "truth" rather than the "gospel" or rather he expressly emphasizes the identity of "gospel" and "revelation of the mystery of God" (esp. Rom 16:25; 1 Cor 2:1 + 7; Eph 3:3–9; 6:19).

Since "word of truth" and "gospel" are synonymous concepts for Paul (1:23), the genitive "the word of truth *of the gospel*" can be understood as an appositional genitive. Similarly, in Eph 1:13, "gospel" is in apposition to "word of truth."

On the basis of more immediate and larger contexts, the time frame of the verb *proēkousate* (you have heard *previously*) should refer to the composition of the letter and not to the fulfillment of hope. Immediately following, Paul speaks of the effectiveness of the word since its arrival among the Colossians, and he refers to Epaphras in the context as the one who instructed the Colossians (1:6 + 7). Reference is made to this event also in 1:23 and 2:7.

Hearing here signifies more than a noncommittal perception. This is noteworthy in the next verse, in which the same occurrence which is here simply referred to as "hearing" is emphasized there as "hearing and recognizing" (see the elucidation of the next verse). Even the corresponding Hebrew verb sometimes has this expanded meaning in the OT, as for example in the well-known declaration in Deut 6:4 + 5: "Hear, O Israel, Yahweh is our God, Yahweh only. . . ."

6 *This came to you and became at home with you* (literally: which to you). This word is spoken of as though it were a sovereign and acting person.[21] It is not bound to an "apostolic office," or to a "keeper of truth."[22] Correspondingly, 1:27 expressly states that it was God's own will to make known the "mystery" among the non-Jews. From this perspective, it becomes clear why Paul can so naturally address his readers as "saints," as the chosen ones of God (cf. Notes to v 2). The working presence of the word is guarantor to that.

The word *pareimi*, which is used here, means more than the simple "come." John Chrysostom probably explained its meaning best when he elucidated the "word" in this passage, "It did not come and go again; rather it remained and is there" (PG 62, 302). H. A. W. Meyer (p. 6) renders the verb appropriately by noting that the word "became at home with you."

. . . *as it also continuously brings forth fruit and grows in the whole world, as also among you* (literally: "as it also in the whole world is fruitbearing and

---

21. Compare Ps 107:20; Acts 6:7; 1 Cor 14:36; and others.

22. E. Käsemann: "Eine urchristliche Taufliturgie," in FS für R. Bultmann (Stuttgart and Köln: Kohlhammer, 1949), pp. 133–48, (= EVB I, 34–51), in his examination of the Colossian Hymn, has come to the conclusion that the post-apostolic age is speaking in Col: the community is reminded not only of its creed, but also, at the same time, of the apostolic office as protector of truth.—The first verses in Col point in a different direction.

growing"). The repetition of the expression "as also with you" within the comparison looks like an unnecessary doubling. It does not seem logically necessary, and stylistically it is apparently not very pretty.[23]

In a few Greek manuscripts, an "and" has been inserted between the "is" and the participle "fruitbearing." Thus, it is determined in the first comparison that the word "is there" *(parontos)* among the Colossians, as it also "is there" in the world *(estin)*. A second comparison proclaims that the word (in the world) brings forth fruit and grows, as it does also among the Colossians. That would remove the unappealing doubling, unless one were to maintain that in the expression "in the whole world" the Colossians are already included anyway (cf. T. K. Abbott, p. 198). But such an interjection seems all too pointedly argumentative.

The reading, which inserts "and" into the text, is poorly attested and appears to be a later correction. However, we could solve the problem in the same manner without going back to an uncertain text-rendition if we simply insert a comma after "is" rather than an "and," as does Tischendorf. This could render Paul's meaning with some certainty, since the original Greek text has been transmitted without punctuation.

A further possibility is to consider the whole comparison, indicating the second "as also among you," as an insertion. Then, too, the doubling would be removed, since the first comparative particle would not refer to the previous expression. It would not be unusual for the comparative particle to occur twice, especially since we find a similar construction in Rom 1:13 (although without the double *kathōs*).

It is also possible, and more likely, to ascribe the doubling, even if it is poor stylistically, to the author. If he actually added one thought to the next, and did not have the construction of the whole sentence before his eyes (because this was not really necessary), then he only could attach the relative clause ("since the day . . .") if he repeated the "as also among you. . . ." Otherwise, he would have created the curious sense that the word brings forth fruit and grows in the whole world since the day on which the Colossians had first heard it. This "solution" seems to fit best with the stylistic character of the thanksgiving.[24]

Within the framework of the last, and also the one next to last, possible solution, the modal "is" belongs to the participle "bringing fruit" ("is bringing

---

23. J. B. Lightfoot (p. 201) sees a similar irregularity in 1 Thess 4:1 and explains it as evidence of Paul's fear of leaving out praise where it is indicated. T. K. Abbott (p. 198) views Lightfoot's reference to 1 Thess 4:1 as not applicable and contradicts his explanation.

24. Also Calvin, ZB, RSV, leave the unusual doubling. SegB, JB, NEB, NTTEV, however, simply delete the first comparative. In the revised Luther translation of 1975, the second comparative particle *kathōs* is translated by "thus also," as though the Greek rendered *houtos kai*. E. Schweizer moves the second *kathōs* to the subsequent relative clause.

fruit . . .") which follows it. We thus have a periphrastic construction, examples of which occur elsewhere in Greek literature) and it reflects Semitic influence. Since the context emphatically includes the "whole world," we can assume that the chosen construction is emphatic, thus subscribing to *continuous action*, "continuously bringing forth fruit. . . ."[25]

It is noteworthy that the bringing forth of fruit and the growing of the gospel are so simply claimed as taking place in the *whole* world (cf. also 1:23). Are we dealing with mere exaggeration, a popular oriental hyperbole, or did the author indeed evaluate the spreading of the gospel unrealistically and thus create an illusion among the Colossians about the significance of the gospel in the world?

We find assertions of this kind elsewhere in Paul,[26] and don't need to suspect exaggeration. This manner of expression could be intended "representatively." Acts illustrates such an interpretation (cf. Acts 1:8 and 28:31): the gospel has reached the "end of the earth" when it can be proclaimed unhindered in Rome, the capital of the world. The idea of leavened dough[27] is a possible referent, as it is found in the gospels: if this "leaven" is once present in the important centers of the world, then it will bubble up everywhere on the earth. However, Paul uses this image only for an "unhealthy" spreading, namely in relation to erroneous teaching.[28] But the expression is known to him, and also the thought connected with it.

The "fruitbearing" is mentioned before the "growing." This order does not correspond to the process as we observe it in nature, and it seems unusual to us. We find it in the NT in Mark 4:26–29: "bringing fruit" and "growing" are in this sense synonymous concepts because growth is understood as the "carrying of fruit" of the earth.[29] It can be argued that this unusual sequence of "bringing fruit" and "growing" here is an instance of a hendiadys.[30]

The picture here is reminiscent of imagery elsewhere in the OT and in the

---

25. BDR 253.—This construction can certainly be found in 2 Cor 2:17, among others.

26. Rom 1:8 also refers to the "whole world." Rom 1:5 refers to "all gentiles," 1 Thess 1:8 and 1 Cor 1:2 to "every place," and Col 1:28 to "every human being." In 2 Cor 8:18; 11:28, among others, Paul speaks of "all communities." The references in all these passages are rather representative places, persons, communities, as the sum of each individual one. This has become clear also, for example, in Col 1:4, where Paul spoke of the love of the Colossians for "all the saints" (see Notes).

27. Compare J. Gnilka, p. 35.—Compare also the image of "salt" (Matt 5:13, "You are the salt of the earth!").

28. 1 Cor 5:6–8; Gal 5:9; compare also H. Windisch, ThWNT II, 907f.

29. Compare also Gen 1:22 (Hebrew text): "Be fruitful and multiply. . . ."

30. Of a different opinion are, for example, J. B. Lightfoot (p. 201), H. A. W. Meyer (p. 220), and P. Ewald (p. 299), who assert that "bearing fruit" refers to the effect of the word on the inner and outer life, "growing," however, to the general dispersion of the gospel.

later Jewish literature, in which Israel is conceived of as the garden or tree of God[31] and wisdom or the law[32] are understood as the fruit-bearing seed. Now we find in Col 1:5 the "word of truth, the gospel" instead of "wisdom" or "law," and the unbelievers also belong to Israel.

The context shows what is meant by this growth of the word: first of all, because the comparison is drawn from it, that the word has become at home among the Colossians. "Faithfulness and love" (cf. 1:4), "recognition of the will of God" (1:9), and "good works" (cf. 1:10) "sprout forth" among the Colossians.[33]

The verb *karpophoreō* (to bear fruit) in the middle is documented (aside from Col 1:6) in only one Greek inscription.[34] In Col 1:10, the same expression "bringing fruit and growing" occurs once again, but refers not to the "word," but to the Colossians. There, *karpophoreō* is used in the *active* voice. J. B. Lightfoot (p. 201) suspects a difference in meaning, because of the changing verb forms in such a short distance. He explains the difference of the two forms in 1:5 and 1:10 thus, that the middle has "intensive" significance, the *active* form "extensive." The middle describes the energy residing within the word, the active its exertion toward the external. The gospel is described as an organic being with its own reproductive capabilities.

In conclusion, we can agree with E. Lohmeyer (pp. 27f.), "Like a new creation, it (the gospel, H.B.) grows forth from the dying world, and Paul can accompany this empowering occurrence with the gratefully enchanted gaze of an observer." And we have only this one gospel for the whole world, which also came to Colossae, which also became at home among the Colossians, and through which the Colossians became members of a worldwide "ecumenical" church.

since the day when you heard and knew the grace of God. Again we have a hendiadys: hearing and knowing. The same substance which could be described at the beginning of this verse simply with "hearing" is here restated by the combination of both verbs, "hearing" and "knowing."

The thought process of vv 3–8 emanates from appreciation of the faithfulness and love of the Colossians. This faithfulness and love, on the human part, have their basis in the fact that the Christians in Colossae have "heard the word of truth and have known" it. But that indicates that "knowing" is not a rational act, but rather an existential relationship.[35] Expositions in other Pauline epistles confirm this.

---

31. Compare Isa 5:1–7; 60:21; Jer 17:8 (compare Ps 1:3); Ezek 17:3–10; Ps 92:13–15; Jub 1:16; 16:26; 1 Enoch 10:16; 62:8; PsSol 14:2–3; 1 QS VIII:5; XI:8; and others.

32. Compare Ben Sir 24:12–17 (wisdom), 4 Ezra 3:20; 9:31–37 (law).

33. To supplement this listing, we refer esp. to Gal 5:22 + 23.

34. Compare BauerLex.

35. In 1:9, we are dealing with recognition of the will of God, thus with obedience. That points in the same direction.

In the undisputed letters of Paul, there are three important passages in which the apostle uses the passive of "knowing" in order to make clear what it means "to know."[36] They are (1) 1 Cor 8:3, (2) Gal 4:9, and (3) 1 Cor 13:12. The first two examples are especially illuminating in this connection.

1. In 1 Cor 8:3, we read, "He who loves God is known by him." By this determination, Paul turns against a "knowing" which solely "inflates." True knowing, by contrast, like the knowing with which God knows man, is a knowing which *engenders love*, a knowing which, as the context in 1 Cor 8 shows, is not unmindful of the weak brother or sister.

2. We have a similar instance in Gal 4:9. Here it is stated, as in First Corinthians, that the Galatians are known by God. By that, Paul wants to exhort the Colossians to obey. According to the context, "to be known by God" is to have received filiation from God, which signifies for the non-Jewish Galatians that they may also say, "Abba, dear Father."

3. 1 Cor 13:12 explains that the knowledge that emanates from God is complete, but that human knowledge is only "fragmentary." Someday, it also will be complete.

In conclusion, we can say that true knowledge is present for Paul in a relationship that is marked by love. When we are dealing especially with the love for God (Gal 4:9), this love is manifested by obedience.

Paul was undoubtedly influenced by the use of the word "to know" in the OT.[37] There, it often marks an intimate relationship between two persons. Two examples serve to clarify this point. In Gen 4:1, 17, 25; 19:8, "knowing" signifies the sexual union between man and woman. In Jer 31:31–34, "knowing" means the faith of (Bundestreue!) the human covenant partner: the law has now been "written upon the heart."

In Col 1:6, the word used is not *ginōskō* (to know), but rather the compound

---

36. Compare M. Dibelius, "Epignōsis alētheias," in *Botschaft und Geschichte*, Ges. Aufs. II, ed. by G. Bornkamm (Tübingen: Mohr, 1956), pp. 1–13. See also Rom 11:33+34, where (wisdom and) cognizance of God is placed in prior position to recognition, which puts God as object.

37. In Col, there is hardly reference to the fact that Paul has differentiated the concepts "recognition," "recognize" from the gnostic comprehension, or has been influenced by gnosis; by "recognition," which deals thematically with questions like, "Who were we? What have we become? Where were we? To where are we put? To what place are we hurrying? From what have we been freed? What is birth? What is rebirth?" as we find them in a transmitted text of Clement of Alexandria from the Valentine Gnosis (Exc Theod 78, 2; German in H. Jonas: Die Gnosis, vol. 1, *Zeugnisse der Kirchenväter*, pub. by C. Andresen (Zürich and Stuttgart: Artemis, 1969), p. 297.—Also, in Col, "recognition of truth" is not used as a *terminus technicus* to designate recognition of "correct teaching," which has now taken the place of "faith in the gospel." The expression, however, is understood in this sense in the Pastoral Epistles (compare 1 Tim 2:4; 2 Tim 3:7; 1 Tim 4:3; 2 Tim 2:25; Titus 1:1.

form *epi-ginōskō*. Very often in the Greek, the latter replaces the former without there being a difference in meaning.[38] However, in some passages, it is possible to define a difference between the two verb forms (specially between the corresponding substantives). Then, the compound form indicates complete and perfect knowledge as distinct from fragmentary understanding.

J. B. Lightfoot (p. 204) refers not only to Justin Martyr (Dial,3, 221 A = PG 6, 481 B) and to Clement of Alexandria (Strom I 17, 369 = PG 8, 801 B) in this connection, but also to Paul himself.[39] 1 Cor 13:12 chiefly indicates a possible variation in the meaning of the two verb forms: "Now I know in part *(ginōskō)*; then I shall know *(epiginōskō)* just as I also am known *(epiginōskō,* by the complete knowledge, whose subject is God)."

In Col 1:6, it is not clear whether such a difference is intended. Here, the compound form probably has the same force as the simple one. (Cf. 2 Cor 8:9, where Paul uses the simple verb form in order to express the same subject as in Col 1:6, "because you have known the grace of our Lord Jesus Christ.")

While Paul spoke of the "word of *truth*" in 1:5, he now choses as a synonymous concept the word "grace." But he still speaks of truth once more by attaching the formulaic "in truth."

The "word," of which he speaks, does not only tell of "grace," but also brings it. For the Colossians, it brings the message that the Messiah is also the Messiah of the gentiles. This illuminates the special meaning which the concept *charis* (grace) has for Paul. It is the overflowing grace of God which now also includes the gentiles.[40] In this, the grace of God does not stand in tension to his justice. For Paul the revelation of the justice of God is the message of God's grace (cf. Rom 1:16f.; 3:21–31).[41]

as truth (literally: in truth). For the first time in Col, the preposition *en* (in) appears here with an abstract substantive.[42] "In truth" can just as readily belong to the predicate, "you have heard and known," as to the substantive "grace."

The formula can mean that the Colossians have known the word as that

38. In the LXX, for example, Hab 3:2; in the NT, Mark 2:8/8:17; Luke 24:31/24:35. Further examples in R. Bultmann, ThWNT I, 703.

39. Also in the LXX, R. Bultmann (ibid.) views *epi-ginōskō* as intentionally positioned in some places, such as in Gen 27:23; 31:32; Judg 18:3.

40. Compare Rom 5:12, 15; 6:14; and others. Esp. also Eph 2:7f.

41. There is also no tension for the writer of the second part of Isa (Deut-Isa) between the grace of God and his justice: God's justice consists of a gracious, saving intervention into the history of his people; it demonstrates itself in that God remains true to the terms of his covenant (compare esp. Isa 45:1–8, 23–25).

42. See Col 1:8, 9, 12, 29; 2:4, 15; 3:4; compare Eph 2:22; 3:5; 4:2, 19, 24; 5:21, 26; 6:18, 24. Compare E. Percy, PKE, pp. 27–33; also BDR 272. E. Percy (p. 60) points out that the prepositional attributes are also incomparatively more frequent in the Homologumena than they are in the remaining Christian literature and in Greek literature in general.

which it really is, namely as truth.[43] It makes no essential difference whether "in truth" is understood as an attribute or a predicate. True knowing would be founded in that which the formulaic expression voiced in its attributive meaning: to know the word as truth. This interpretation is preferable because there is an evident connection to the assertion in v 5. While we have an ontic expression there which keeps in mind what the word is, v 6 contains the corresponding noetic affirmation.

We should discuss two further possible interpretations.

1. "In truth" can be intended predicatively in order to differentiate false from true knowledge: a false knowing, which only inflates, from the knowing which is God-pleasing and which shows itself in the fact that it founds a relationship whose outstanding mark is love (cf. Notes to "knowing").

2. "In truth," however, can also be meant attributively in order to differentiate the "true word" from a false one. This does not imply that already at this place Paul intends to make polemics against the so-called "Colossian false teaching." In 1:6, Paul speaks of the origins of the community of Colossae and consequently also of the fact that when the word came to them, the Colossians turned from wrong to true "knowledge." Such an assertion can certainly be intended hortatively, as for example in Gal 3:1ff. However, here in the prayer of thanksgiving, and curiously also elsewhere in Col, this is not really the case.[44] This observation cautions us against searching for hidden or openly polemic assertions in the thanksgiving prayer.

The time phrase "since the day" underscores the strength and power of the word. In connection with the hendiadys "to hear and know," the following sense emerges: that which can easily fall apart, hearing and knowing, was a unit for the Colossians from the beginning. From the onset and immediately, since the day on which the Colossians perceived the word of truth, it forged ahead mightily, bore fruit, and grew.

7 *As you (certainly) learned it from Epaphras, our beloved fellow servant.* The sovereign effect of the word does not exclude a human herald, but it does determine the approach to his task. Indeed, a human being is proclaimer of this word, but it is sovereignly effective of its own power and thus human force cannot make it bear "fruit and grow." The proclaimer does not have the task of pushing the word through the world. Rather, in this regard, he is only the thankful observer.

In Colossae, Epaphras proclaimed the gospel. The references to him here in

---

43. Compare 1 Thess 2:13: ". . . for you have received the word of God which was proclaimed through us not as the word of human beings, but rather as it also truly is, as the word of God. . . ."

44. Additionally, this is also the case in Col 3:9, but here also it is not the decisive argument. We do not find this form of argument where we are dealing with the so-called "false teaching."

Col may seem to interrupt the prayer,[45] in contrast to the expression of thanksgiving in other Pauline epistles (cf. 1 Thess 1:2f, 1 Cor 1:4–7; Phil 1:3–6; Phlm 4–7). Still, they do not disturb the context, but rather they contain a theologically important statement: the sovereignly effective gospel does not relegate the human proclaimer to the sideline where he might remain unnoticed. What is evident here in Col is briefly summarized in 1 Thess 2:13, "we thank God unceasingly, because you have the *word of God,* which *has been preached by us*" (literally: the word of the sermon through us of God). The grammatical compartmentalization of both proclamations in the Greek text of 1 Thess expressly underscores this connection.

Epaphras proclaimed the gospel to the Colossians as that which it truly is: the word of truth. The weight of this lies in the proclamation in 1:7. Even he proclaimed in the knowledge that he was bringing the sovereignly working word to the Colossians. The characterization of the gospel in the previous verses makes it unlikely that the verb *manthanō* (to learn) indicates a post-apostolic time or a Deutero-Pauline composition.[46] In Col, the instruction in right teaching or acceptance of the message does not receive greater emphasis than "hearing," "obeying" or "believing."[47] It is certainly correct that concepts such as "to learn," "to teach," and "teaching" occur relatively seldom in the Pauline epistles of undisputed authorship, but that is also true for Col (and Eph).[48] We should observe further that Paul can summarily characterize his proclamation in 1 Cor 4:17 as "teaching" (didaskō). And in Rom 16:17 (cf. Phil 4:9), the gospel can be termed *didachē* (teaching). Beyond that, the language used is of significance in the synoptic gospels. Thus, to use a pregnant example, in Matt 7:29, we read about Jesus, "he *taught* with authority, and not as the scribes." Further, Jesus is called *didaskalos* ("teacher") and the disciples *mathētai* ("students"). The use of the verbs and the corresponding substantives which deal with teaching and learning do not necessarily need to originate from "early Catholicism" and be molded by traditionalism, institutionalism, and intellectualism.

Epaphras is mentioned in the NT not only in Col 1:7, but also in Col 4:12 and in Phlm 23. His name is probably a short form of Epaphroditus.[49]

---

45. Compare H. Hegermann, *Die Vorstellung vom Schöpfungsmittler im hellenistischen Judentum and Urchristentum,* TU 82 (Berlin: Akademie Verlag, 1961), p. 167.

46. H. Merklein, *Das kirchliche Amt nach dem Epheserbrief,* StANT 33, (München: Kösel, 1973), p. 338, sees in the use of the verb the intention of ascertaining that the gospel should have the quality of revelation and that Ephaphras should be viewed as the "guarantor" for this.

47. Compare, among others, E. Lohse, p. 53.

48. Only for *didaskalia* (teaching), which occurs twenty-one times in the NT, can we determine a noticeable frequency in the Pastoral Epistles (fifteen times).

49. MMLex, p. 230.—There are, however, no clues for equating Epaphras with Epaphroditus, a Christian from Philippi (Phil 2:25; 4:18).

Information about him is sparse. Since Paul specially lists his Jewish co-workers in Col 4:10f, Epaphras was presumably of non-Jewish origin. He belonged to the community in Colossae (4:12) and he had delivered the good news about the Christians of Colossae to Paul. While Aristarchus was the fellow prisoner with Paul during the composition of Col, Epaphras occupied this position during the composition of Phlm. Epaphras not only proclaimed the gospel in Colossae, but also was responsible for the communities in Laodicea and Hierapolis, the neighboring communities of Colossae (4:13). He can well be considered the missionary of the Lykos Valley. The less reliable textual reading does not necessarily change this viewpoint, ". . . as you *also (kai)* have learned from Epaphras . . . ," since this text variant does not necessarily mean that Epaphras was a teacher in the community *among others*. The word "also" *(kai)* in the text variant could also refer to the verb (which it precedes!) and exalt the art of learning, ". . . as you have also learned (not differently) from Epaphras. . . ."[50]

The designation "our fellow servant" places Epaphras on the same level with Paul and Timothy, in analogy to the description of the relationship between Paul and his co-workers in 1:1 + 2. "Servants," in the OT, are people whom God puts into his service so that his will may be made known and carried out through them, as, for example: Abraham, Isaac, and Jacob (Ps 105:42; Ex 32:13; Deut 9:27); Moses (Ex 14:31; Josh 1:2, 7; Ps 105:26, etc.); Joshua (Josh 24:29); David (2 Sam 7:5; Ps 89:4, 21); the Prophets (Amos 3:7); and also the heathen emperor Nebuchadnezzar (Jer 25:9). In Rom 1:1 and Gal 1:10 (cf. Titus 1:1), Paul uses the title "servant" for himself, and in addition to Timothy (Phil 1:1) and Epaphras, only Tychicus is called so (Col 4:7).

He is a faithful servant of the Messiah in our place (literally: who is a . . .). In his service, Epaphras stands on an equal level with Paul, who calls himself "servant of the gospel" (1:23), which is in fact the same. Epaphras is not a servant of Paul, and there is no reference to the fact that only as his deputy is he bearer of apostolic authority. This also cannot be concluded from the expression "in our place." The designation of Epaphras as "fellow servant" and "servant of Christ" lets him appear quite clearly as commissioned directly by God/by the Messiah; also the earlier description of the sovereignty of the gospel points decidedly in another direction. "In our place" rather circumscribes the relationship which Paul has to the community at Colossae, which he does not personally know. The fact that he was not in Colossae himself does not imply indifference on his part toward the Christians there. Quite the contrary! They are decidedly brothers, co-workers in the service of the same Lord (cf. 1:1 + 2 and Notes as well as Comment I to 1:24–2:5). Thus, Paul thanks for them,

---

50. H. A. W. Meyer, p. 228.—Thus also W. M. L. de Wette (p. 20), who interprets *kai* (and) as support for the comparison which refers to truth, and which he translates with "real."

implores God for them, and lets them know what a battle he has for them. Thus, as though he himself had founded the community, he also feels responsible for them.

Next to the very good transmission of "in our place," we find the variant "in *your* place," which is, however, to judge from the value of its text evidence, probably not original. Still, we could support its originality by supposing that the *hēmon* precedes it, and a *hēmin* (our, dative) follows:

1. With *hyper hymōn* (in your place), the representative service can be defined, which Epaphras gives Paul in place of the community. Epaphras would then serve as designate to the community in Colossae for Paul during his imprisonment, just as Epaphroditus served in this capacity when he was sent to the community in Philippi.[51] However, this interpretation is not likely, since contextually we are dealing with the proclamation of Epaphras in Colossae and thus with his service *to the Colossians*.

2. *hyper hymōn* can also mean exactly this service to the Colossians. The idea in 4:12 would then have been anticipated here: there it says, "Epaphras greets you, who is one of yours, a servant of the Messiah (Jesus), who fights *for you (hyper hymōn)* at all times in (his) prayers, so that you may stand there in perfection. . . ."

8 *and he has also reported to us of your love which is a gift of the Spirit* (literally: who also reported to us of your love in the spirit). In the preliminary portion of the thanksgiving address, Paul takes up the starting point again and returns to the "love" of the Colossians. As also in 1 Cor 1:11, *dēloō* (to report) means the transmission of news.[52]

Is the reference here to the love of the Colossians for Paul, for Epaphras, or as in 1:4, for all the saints?[53] The last is probably the case.

1. The occasion for thanksgiving was specifically this love for all the saints, and it is probable that Paul also means this love when he points to the co-worker within the framework of his thanksgiving, the one who brought him the news of the love of the Colossians which gave rise to the thanksgiving.

2. Even the emphatic *hymōn* (your), placed in preliminary position, points to "the love for all the saints," because it is exactly that which is *especially* gratifying among the *Colossians* and caused the apostle to give thanks.

---

51. Compare Phil 2:25 ("Epaphroditus . . . your messenger . . .") and Phil 2:30 ". . . because for the sake of the work of Christ he has come near death . . . , so that he might complete what is still lacking in your service to me."

52. J. Gnilka (p. 38) thinks we are dealing with a report to the apostle, who has the final responsibility for the missionary work. Clues for this interpretation are given within the context.

53. Thus, for example, P. Ewald (p. 302) is of the opinion that the emphatic *hymon* (your) requires the opposite, which he finds in 1:7 "in *our* place," meaning that only love for the apostle could be meant. H. A. W. Meyer (p. 228), who reads *hyper hymōn* (in your place), argues the same way and is of the opinion that love for Epaphras is meant.

3. We might have expected that Paul would speak expressly of the love *for him* or to *Epaphras* in the prior reference, if he had intended to refer to that. Even more so than in the other letters that he wrote to a community unknown to him (Rom and Eph), he does not refer to love for himself.

This love is more closely characterized as a "love in the Spirit." The article in front of "in spirit" is not found in the Greek, which is common "when several attributes are combined with a substantive, specifically with one with verbal force" (BDR 269,1a).

If it is correct that the reference in 1:8 is to the same love as in 1:4, the phrase "in spirit" circumscribes that which was said previously about this love; a love is meant, which does not exclude anyone and which has its foundation in the fact that Jesus is the Messiah also for the gentiles. We are dealing with the love which arises solely through the *sovereign* working of the gospel. In short, we are dealing with the love that alone is a "gift," or expressed differently, with the "love of God that has been *poured* into our hearts through the Holy Spirit who has been *given* to us" (Rom 5:5).[54] This encompassing sense of *en pneumati* (in the spirit) is preferable to an interpretation which translates *en pneumati* with "spiritually" in order to differentiate the love named here from a "worldly," "sensual" love. Such expressions can also be found in Col (1:9; 3:16), but in these cases, the adjective *pneumatikos* is used. The translation "spiritual love" does not fit the meaning that *en pneumati* possesses from the context; neither does it correspond (from all appearances) to the sum total of the preceding verses.[55]

COMMENTS I–III TO COL 1:3–8

I. The "Literary Plural" in Col

To whom is Paul referring when he uses the plural in Col 1:3ff. and writes, "*we* thank . . ."? Is he referring to himself *and* Timothy, so that the use of the

---

54. Love is the fulfillment of the law (compare Gal 5:14), even the embodiment of the law. Paul sees the final revelation obviously fulfilled because God wants to write the law into our hearts (compare Jer 31:33), for he says that the gentiles (that is, the gentile Christians) do naturally what the law says (Rom 2:14, 15). That sheds light on the statement that love is a gift of the spirit. For this love demonstrates that God has redeemed his promise to renew the covenant.

55. E. Schweizer: "Christus und Geist im Kolosserbrief," in *Neues Testament und Christologie im Werden; Aufsätze* (Göttingen: Vandenhoeck & Ruprecht, 1982), pp. 179–93 (first published in *FS for C. F. D. Moule*, Cambridge, 1973, pp. 297–313); compare also *Kol-Kommentar*, p. 38, esp. fn. 64, which indicates that in Col, "exclusively the Lord Christ" has stepped into the place of the spirit (p. 186). On the one hand, we cannot find anything which is impossible in Paul, but the tone has become a different one.—Col 1:8 does not justify this declaration in its exclusivity. Here we have an example

singular forms (see 1:23, 24, 25, 29; 2:1, 4, 5; 4:4, 7, 8, 10, 11, 13, 18) is to be explained objectively,[1] or do we have a so-called "literary plural" here? Then Paul would mean himself by the "we," perhaps to emphasize that only and very especially his voice should be audible. Or perhaps he uses the plural to indicate that he and his readers want to combine their thanksgiving; or perhaps also to choose the median between the impersonal passive and the personal "I" in addressing a community unknown to him.[2]

Among the Pauline epistles in which several people are named among the co-signers, the first-person singular is used in some (1 Cor, Phil, Phlm) and the corresponding plural in others (1 + 2 Thess). But we have no evidence that, when Paul is named alone at the beginning of the letter, he then continues with the plural form, "we thank. . . ." That would be unequivocal proof of the "literary plural" in a thanksgiving. In Rom 1:5, we have the contextual contrast to the singular form, "through whom *we* have received grace, and (namely the) apostleship," but even here it is not certain that Paul means himself alone."[3] Possibly he wished to include his co-workers in the service entrusted to him among the gentiles (cf. Rom 16:21f.). In Col, however, indications are that the plural "we" implies the sense of the literary plural in these passages (1:3–9, 28; 4:3).

Paul changes from the plural to the singular for the first time in 1:24, after he has referred to himself in v 23. The singular is thematically required here, because Paul addresses his special situation, the special form of his service, namely his imprisonment. Thus we cannot argue with certainty that Paul in v 24 uses the "we" in 1:3 in the singular sense. The contrary is more probably the case. In 1:28, the plural surfaces in a context in which the "I" predominates, "*we* proclaim him, . . . that we . . . every man. . . ." It is noticeable that here also, as in Rom 1:5 (see above), the plural form appears when we are dealing with the command to preach. It points to the fact that Paul perceives himself to be among the other co-workers in a universal commission to preach, which is expressed through the numeric change. At the same time, it seems probable that the plural form in 1:3 indicates Paul and his co-workers. Just as he works together with the others on the gospel, so he also will give thanks together with them for the fruit of their joint efforts.

---

as to how the same thing can be expressed "christologically" and "pneumatically." An impressive example for this context is also the synonymity of the statements "in the spirit," "the spirit of God lives in you," "to have the spirit of Christ," "Christ in you" in Rom 8:9 + 10.

1. Compare, for example, H. A. W. Meyer (p. 222); also BDR 280.

2. Compare, among others, E. Lohse (pp. 42f.); R. P. Martin, NCC 47; A. Lindemann (p. 18); E. Lohmeyer (p. 21).

3. Also the change from plural to singular in 1 Thess 3:1f./3:5 does not unequivocally document the use of the "writer-editor-redactor's plural." We might find the closest approximation of such an example in 2 Cor 10:11ff.

The change from the plural in 1:28 to the singular in 1:29 is also explicable from the content, because Paul here refers to his special share in the universal commission, namely his suffering (cf. Notes to 1:29). So Paul also in Col 2:1 uses the I-form, where he again speaks of his special situation, of *his* battle. And because *his* suffering is to serve the community (cf. 1:24, 29) and especially its consolidation in view of (possible) external threats, so he also chooses the singular and not the plural in 2:4. If the author of Col had used the literary plural, we would have expected that use especially in 2:4, at the beginning of the elucidation of the so-called "false doctrine," in order to emphasize the "apostolic authority" with this stylistic device.

In Col 4:3 we again find a change to the plural. Characteristically, we are dealing here again with a commission to preach. In 4:4, we have the singular again, because Paul writes about the fact that he partakes in this commission in a special way: he is bound because of the secret which has to be communicated further. Even the plural used in 4:8 ("so that you may know, how *we* are") is not necessarily synonymous with the corresponding singular form in 4:7 (Tychikus will report to you all about "how I am"). There is a conscious differentiation between the singular and the plural forms here in order to convey to the Colossians news about the other prisoner with Paul, Aristarchus (4:10), as well as news of the other companions who send greetings to the Colossians.

II. "God the Father"

While Paul spoke of God "our Father" in the benediction in 1:2, the prayer which begins with 1:3 is addressed to God "the Father of our Lord Jesus (Christ)." This difference in the description of God shows that God only can be designated as "our Father" because he is "the Father of our Lord Jesus."

In Col, the designation of God "the Father" occurs only twice more and confirms this supposition. In 1:12, we read "thanks to the Father, who has qualified us to take part in the inheritance of the saints in the light." This is further elucidated by pointing to the Son, "in whom we have the redemption, the forgiveness of sin." Likewise, this context is addressed in 3:17, where we read, ". . . give thanks to God the Father, *through him* (the Lord Jesus)." This thought is more fully amplified in Eph 2:18, "For in him (in the Messiah Jesus) we two (i.e., Jews and gentiles) have *access to the Father* in one Spirit." Noticeable is the fact that in the Pauline Corpus God is repeatedly designated "Father" without use of any amendment when the reference is to access of Jews *and* gentiles to God. This usage is illustrated especially graphically in Gal 4:6 (see below).

This designation of God and the acknowledgment of God as Father[4] is not something original to Christianity. Both have wide dissemination in the ancient

---

4. Compare esp. E. Lohmeyer: *Das Vater-unser*, 2d ed. (Göttingen: Vandenhoeck & Ruprecht, 1947), pp. 18–40. See also J. Jeremias: "Abba," in *Abba. Studien zur*

Orient since archaic times. The concept of absolute authority, as well as the concept of absolute mercy, were closely intertwined with this name of God in the lands surrounding Israel.[5]

In the OT, "father" (in relation to God) was not understood mythologically, but was rather viewed in the context of Israel as the chosen people. Since ancient times, Israel claimed to be the "first-born son" of God (Ex 4:22; cf. Deut 32:6; Jer 31:9). The covenant of God with his people, his faithfulness to the covenant, and his fatherliness are always allied to each other, and they create an ever greater contrast to the faithlessness of the people. In consequence, the designation of God as Father finds a firm place in Israel's cry for mercy from God.[6] At the same time, an eschatologically significant component focusing on the completion of the history of God and his people becomes recognizable. Even when God, as we read in Ps 89, is angry, when he has concealed himself, when he has "now" repudiated his anointed, Israel, which has "now" broken the covenant, he still, despite everything, has not renounced his covenant, has not broken his faithfulness. It will remain steadfast. God smites the transgressors of his people, but he will establish in Israel his (messianic) king in the "first-born son," the greatest of the kings upon the earth (Ps 89:27). And it will then be true, "He will call me: you are my Father, my God and my strength, (the source) of my salvation" (Ps 89:27).[7]

Similar thinking is also evident in Paul. He also does not believe that the father relationship of God and Israel has been rescinded.[8] Israel was an heir not yet come of age, so that there was no difference between it and a servant (Gal 4:1–7). But God sent His Son and redeemed Israel (Gal 4:5, "those under the law," namely the Jews). Israel thus became the heir that had come of age. It was given the distinction of being called son, which signified that it now called God "Abba, (dear) Father" (Gal 4:6; Rom 8:15). Not only Israel, but with it also the gentiles, attained this adoption as sons. In Gal 4:5, this idea is further developed, after speaking of the redemption of Israel, "that *we* (meaning Paul and the Galatians, thus Jews and gentiles) might receive adoption as sons." God's steadfastness to his people, which he has confirmed in Jesus, is so wonderfully munificent that it overflows also to non-Jews. This is the essence of the message

---

neutestamentlichen Theologie und Zeitgeschichte (Göttingen: Vandenhoeck & Ruprecht, 1966), pp. 16–67; Jeremias: *Neutestamentliche Theologie, Teil I, Die Verkündigung Jesu* (Gütersloh: Mohn, 1971), pp. 67–73; E. De Witt Burton: *The Epistle to the Galatians*, ICC [Edinburgh: Clark, 1921 (reprinted 1950)], pp. 384–92.

5. J. Jeremias, "Abba," op. cit., p. 15; E. Lohmeyer, *Vater- unser*, op. cit., p. 22.

6. Isa 63:16; 64:7; Jer 3:4,19; 31:9; Mal 2:10, compare Mal 1:6; Ps 89:27.

7. Just as much as "the faithfulness of God" and the ability to "call him father" belong together for Jeremiah (Jer 3:19).

8. Even according to the statements in rabbinic literature, God has always remained the father of Israel: compare St.-B. I, pp. 371ff.; E. Lohmeyer, *Vater- unser*, op. cit., p. 26.

of Paul.[9] It is also the predominant theme in Rom, Gal, and Eph. In Col, Paul focuses on this central theme which is summarized in the fact that Jews *and* gentiles may call God their Father (cf. esp. Notes to 1:26f. and Comment V to 1:9–23).

The fulfillment of the hope of Israel, once restricted to Jews, now also the hope of the gentiles,[10] that is what Paul means when he calls God "Father."

III. Temporal and/or Spatial Hope

According to G. Bornkamm,[11] "a new, unreflected and self-evident use of the concept *elpis* (hope, H.B.) in 1:5" becomes a case in point for the entire epistle to the Colossians, which gives expression to a new and basically different structure in theological thinking, compared to the other undisputed Pauline epistles. The author of Colossians is thought to be still using the language of the Jewish, apocalyptic original Christian tradition, but it is employed under a different view. He is perceived to be oriented not from a temporal but rather from a spatial perspective, as is the case in the Gnostic texts. According to G. Bornkamm, completely new (especially also in comparison to all related statements in the late Jewish texts) is that the thinking in spatial terms becomes predominant and the temporal-eschatological statements are relieved of their significance; "hope" has lost its temporal meaning; it has become "the encompassing designation of even this very completed, in the hereafter 'prepared' reality of salvation (Heilswirklichkeit) of the faithful.[12] Decisive for G. Bornkamm is that in Col (as also in Eph), the eschatological thought patterns, such as Parousia (Second Coming), resurrection of the dead, Last Judgment, are not discussed, which is not accidental; just as noticeable is the complete absence of the *verbs* designating hope, which are otherwise characteristic of Paul.

E. Grässer[13] has expanded and refined this perception. Like G. Bornkamm, he does not fail to notice that there are eschatological prophetic expressions in Col, which are inherent in the Jewish apocalyptic tradition, and would seem-

9. Rom 16:25f.; Gal 1:16; 3:13f.; Eph 3:1–9; compare 1 Tim 2:7; Acts 9:15; 15:12.

10. Paul even bases this hope on the OT: see esp. Rom 4; Gal 3:1–18. J. Jeremias, "Abba," op. cit., esp. p. 63, has arrived at a contrary conclusion, ". . . it would have been disrespectful for Judaic sensibility, and therefore unthinkable, to address God with this familiar word. It was new and impertinent that Jesus dared to take this step. He spoke with God the way a child does with his father, so simply, so intimately, so securely."

11. G. Bornkamm, "Die Hoffnung im Kolosserbrief. Zugleich ein Beitrag zur Frage der Echtheit des Briefes," in *Geschichte und Glaube II*, Ges. Aufs. IV, BEvTh 53 (München: Kaiser, 1971), p. 206–13.

12. Ibid., p. 211.

13. E. Grässer: "Kol 3:1–4 als Beispiel einer Interpretation secundum homines recipientes," ZThK 64 (1967) 139–68.

ingly point to a seemingly temporal perception of eschatology. But while Bornkamm focused attention only on the language of this tradition in Col, which, however, did not make any claims about temporal eschatological assumptions, E. Grässer does interpret temporal eschatological *contents*. According to his interpretation, the author of Col assimilated the Hellenistic viewpoint of his readers about the world and salvation, that is "the longing of Hellenistic man to participate in the upper world, which would actualize deliverance from the evil world, its precepts, and its demonic rulers."[14] But for E. Grässer in this assimilation, the author of Col dares only to touch the edge of the Gnostic Christian heresy. He carefully returns "to the orthodox line of normalcy" (p. 153) by adding an anti-Gnostic correction. Following E. Grässer, we can outline the argument for the eschatological concept as follows: in the face of the terrifying fear ("Weltangst") of his (Hellenistic) readers (which the Judeo-Christian Gnostics encounter in the cult), it would have been inadequate to speak only of a *futuristic hope, only of a futuristic resurrection*. The resurrection was thus proclaimed as having occurred already in baptism; and baptism was understood as an ascension, as deliverance from cosmic powers and forces, both astral and demonic in character. But the author of Col avoided the danger of taking salvation into unhistoric mystical depths by clinging to a central part of the original Christian futuristic expectation, the act of the Second Coming, the return of Christ. This futuristic expectation contained a different quality than it does in the genuine epistles of Paul. Ideas, such as judgment and the resurrection of the dead, would evaporate. Individual perfection was perceived in terms of the model of the Hellenistic apotheosis (deification). However, the most constant idea of the NT, the moment of belonging to Christ, was affirmed and not surrendered.

The concept of "hope" in Col occurs, in fact, only in chap. 1 (vv 5, 23, 27), and not in chap. 3, where Paul refers to the final futuristic revelation of Christ at the end of time. We can hardly conclude from that, that the concept of hope had been emptied of its temporal significance or had only or especially been understood in its spatial sense within the context of a Hellenistic perception of salvation and the world. Such an opposition of "space" and "time" is hardly fair to the message in Col. As Col 1:27 demonstrates, "hope" designates Christ in that unique way, as Christ is lauded in 1:12–20(23).[15] Hope designates the Jewish Messiah who *has* begun his dominion not just over Israel but also over all of creation, and he therefore is the Messiah also of non-Jews, and thus their hope. Based on the OT Judaic background, hope as a designation of Christ is combined with temporal concepts, because the beginning of the reign of the

---

14. Ibid., pp. 155f.
15. Compare Notes and especially Comments II, 3 and V to 1:9–23, as well as Comment II to 1:24–2:3.

Messiah is perceived as the fulfillment of OT prophecies.[16] In addition, the significance and effect of this hope, specifically as the fulfillment of prophecies, can be circumscribed with spatial perceptions. In doing so, however, we are not referring to the Gnostics, but rather to the OT messianic concept of king. Thus we read in Col 1:13, "He has transferred us to the kingdom of his beloved Son" (cf. Notes to 1:13).

Hope, in this sense, is the Messiah, who has already *now* begun his reign, he, who *has* already fulfilled the hope of Israel, he, who *has* reconciled all things (1:20). It is thus a *present* hope. The message in 1:5, however, points to a futuristic meaning of hope. Here also, *hope* means not *the act of hoping* for something futuristic or otherworldly, but rather the object of hope, the Messiah, who sits in heaven, that means "at the right hand of God" (see Notes). The concept "to be well kept, to lie in readiness" (*apokeimai*) contains an implicitly temporal component: it indicates a point in time in which something "safely deposited will be received." By that is meant the described event of the revelation of the Messiah in 3:4, the coming again of the one who ascended to heaven.

The juxtaposition of the messages in Col which emphasize the fulfillment of events at the end of time and indicate *future* eschatological occurrences, bring up new problems and questions. They are dealt with in the framework of the Notes to 3:1–4.

2. The Intercession (1:9–14)

9 Therefore we also do not cease, since the (first) day when we heard (the good news about you), to pray for you. We ask that God may fill you with the knowledge of his will, by the gift of all spiritual wisdom and all spiritual understanding, 10 so that you will live a life worthy of the Lord, pleasing in all things. He who lives thus brings forth fruit and grows in every good work, through the knowledge of God! 11 He lets himself be made powerful with all power, according to his glorious strength, for all endurance and patience with joy! 12 He thanks the Father, who has qualified you to take part in the inheritance of the saints, (which is) in the light. 13 He has delivered us from the dominion of darkness and transferred us into the kingdom of his beloved Son. 14 In him freedom belongs to us, forgiveness of sins.

NOTES

The thanksgiving (1:3–8) is now followed by the intercession. The two are separated from each other, as at Phil 1:9 and 2 Thess 1:11 (cf. Rom 1:10; Eph 1:16). But it becomes clear in Col how closely aligned these parts are.[1] On the

---

16. 1:13 probably alludes to David's calling in 2 Sam 7. See Notes.

1. The intercession for the thanksgiving has also been interwoven in Phlm 4 and 1 Thess 1:2.

one hand, reference is made repeatedly to the thanksgiving (1:3–8) by incorporating words and phrases from the latter.[2] On the other hand, the intercession in vv 9–14 leads into the larger theme, the thanksgiving, which is taken up again in v 12 and continues to v 20.

Grammatically, we have a very long sentence, which extends from v 9 to v 16. The *main clause* stands at the beginning, and deals with the unceasing prayer of supplication of Paul and his co-workers for the Colossians. It is followed by a *final clause* that specifies the content and purpose of the prayer, ". . . that you may be filled with the knowledge of his will. . . ." An *infinitive clause* follows and spells out the practical purpose of being filled with the knowledge of God's will, "walking worthy for the Lord." Three participial clauses ("to bear fruit and to grow" probably form a hendiadys) are attached and give information about Paul's concept of walking in a worthy way. In an appended *relative clause*, the purpose of the thanksgiving, which is to be offered to the Father, is finally explained: "who saved us from and transferred us into the kingdom of his beloved Son."

9 *Therefore we also do not cease, since the (first) day when we heard (the good news about you), to pray for you. We ask* (literally: to pray and to ask). Thanks and intercession are two aspects of one and the same thing, because in both phrases, the verb *proseuchomai* (to pray) is used.[3] Paul uses *proseuchomai* also in the special sense of "to ask,"[4] but that is probably not the case here. In a synonymous usage of the verbs *proseuchomai* and *aiteomai*, one could recognize the special force with which the prayer is brought before God.[5] But that is hardly applicable here, since the emphasis is not so much on the request but rather on the thanks to which the former connects. The use of synonyms in pairs is a stylistic peculiarity of the liturgical style, which can also be observed in these verses. But analogously to v 3, *proseuchomai* should be understood in its general meaning of "to pray" and *eucharisteō* (to thank) as an explanatory addition. *Kai* (and) then has an explanatory function. We need to consider that the origin of the intercession is not caused by worrisome circumstances in the community of the Colossians, but rather by the good news that Epaphras has delivered. The verb form "we have heard" in v 9 has no object. This can only be supplemented from 1:8.

Once again Paul refers to the thanksgiving by taking up almost literally an expression from 1:6. There he wrote: ". . . since the day when you heard . . ."

---

2. "Since the day, when we/you have heard" (1:9/6); "pray" (1:9,10/3); "recognition"/"recognize" (1:9/6); "bring fruit and grow" (1:10/6).

3. In Phil 1:9; 2 Thess 1:11 (compare Rom 1:10; Eph 1:16), the intercession has been set off from the thanksgiving.

4. Compare Phil 1:9; 2 Thess 1:11; 3:1; Col 4:3. In 1 Cor 11:4, 5, *proseuchomai* is used to describe prophecy, in 1 Cor 14:14 to describe speaking in tongues.

5. Compare E. Lohse (p. 56).

Here he formulates: ". . . since the day when we heard . . ." Hereby the corresponding expression of the thanksgiving is recalled to the readers' consciousness and the following thought-combination is intimated to them: just as the word "bears fruit and grows" among the Colossians since the (first) day on which they heard it, so also Paul and his co-workers do not cease to pray since the (first) day on which they received news of the "fruit bearing and growing." The petition is directed at the sovereign working of the word among the Colossians in the present as well as in the future. If it seems that Paul is praying for something here that already exists, then Phil 1:9 may offer a further explanation, where Paul prays that love may overflow more and more.[6] If Paul here prays that fruit bearing and growing may overflow, it is impossible to become lazy and satisfied with the things obtained and achieved in the past; then rather a prayer as it is formulated in Col 1:9–10 becomes significant and necessary.

In front of "we do not cease" stands *kai* (also/and). As in 1 Thess 2:13, it most likely modifies the verb, not the following personal pronoun[7]; it means, "we also do not cease. . . ." An emphatic "we *too*," as though, in addition to Paul and his co-workers others too perform this intercession, does not make sense in this context.[8]

that God may fill you with the knowledge of his will (literally: that you may be filled). The possessive pronoun *autou* (his) is used, although the pertinent noun is not expressly named. We can conclude that the passive form "to be filled" is a so-called *passivum divinum*, which in the Jewish tradition circumscribes the name of God.[9] This "knowledge" stems not from human capability, but is a gift from God. In 1:6, this same "knowledge" was called "knowing the grace of God," because there also "knowing" designates something practical, the love for all the saints. There is no contrast between 1:6 and 1:9, no difference between theory and praxis, between dogmatics and ethics.

Israel also understood the law in the OT not as opposition to the grace of God, but rather as the sign of divine election.[10] According to OT witness, God revealed himself not by abstract truths from a distance; rather he put the witness

---

6. In Col 2:7, Paul invites "to overflow in thanksgiving."

7. Compare, among others, E. Lohse (p. 56).

8. The pronominal placement of "and" would be sensible and possible if Paul wanted to produce the following thought sequence: "The word is effective with you in Colossae, and we, here, pray for its effectiveness." The "and we" could then be rendered with "we, for our part." We could see this relationship established through the literal citation "since the day." This translation was still not chosen, however, because the expression "therefore we also . . ." can also be found in Paul without our being able to establish a similar relationship as here in Col 1:3/9.

9. In Rom 15:13–14, however, Paul writes expressly, "May the God of hope fill you with . . ."

10. Compare esp. M. Noth, "Die Gesetze im Pentateuch. (Ihre Voraussetzungen

into his service. He revealed what was *to be done* as a blessing to many. "To know God" means to do his will, in the OT much as for Paul.[11] Based on this, it is comprehensible that Paul can simply speak of the knowledge of God rather than of the knowledge of the will of God in the next verse. The reverse, the synonymous use of the two expressions in vv 9 and 10, confirms the background cited for the concept of "knowledge."

Instead of the common genitive, we have an accusative here after a verb of "to fill," as in LXX Ex 31:3; 35:31 (cf. LXX 2 Chr 5:14; Phil 1:11).

by the gift of all spiritual wisdom and all spiritual understanding (literally: in all spiritual).

Since "wisdom and understanding" *(sophia kai synesis)* is a firmly established and well-known figure of speech from the OT (LXX), the preceding *pas* (each/ all) and the following *pneumatikē* (spiritual) modify both substantives. The adjective *pneumatikē* gives primary emphasis to the Greek phrase, since it is placed at the end of the sentence. The knowledge meant here is differentiated from one that inflates the ego, for example, or that is inconsiderate of the weak brother and does not build him up (cf. 1 Cor 8:1ff.). It arises from the idea that God fills man "with all spiritual wisdom and all spiritual understanding." Thus, it is not knowledge that is the predecessor and that only later or eventually carries the fruit of wisdom and understanding. The order rather is reversed. Knowledge originates only from conferred wisdom and conferred understanding. That corresponds to the concept, based on the OT, in which the expression *"sophia kai synesis"* occurs repeatedly (in the LXX).[12] Here, we are dealing with attributes of God. With *sophia* or with *synesis* God created the world (LXX Prov 3:19; Ps 135[136]:5). God bestows gifts on those whom he calls into his service, and he equips them for this ministry.[13] More than once and so also in Col 1,

---

und ihr Sinn)," in *Ges. Aufsätze aum AT*, ThB AT 6 (München: Kaiser, 1957), pp. 9–141. M. Noth convincingly works out the idea that the laws in the Pentateuch are conditioned by the bond between God and his people, which constitutes the original ordering of their basic premise.—See also G. v. Rad, Theol.d.AT I, pp. 192–202; on p. 193, he writes, "Und da kann nun kein Zweifel sein, dass sich mit der Ausrufung des Dekalogs über Israel die Erwählung Israels verwirklicht." Based on this, compare Paul's positive statements concerning the law: Rom 3:1–3; compare 2:17f.; 7:12, 14; 9:4.

11. E. Lohse (p. 156) refers especially to examples from Qumran, which make the Jewish prerequisites for this concept "cognizance" very clear (1 QS III:15; XI:17f.; and others).

12. See, among others, Ex 31:3; 35:31, 35; Deut 4:6; 1 Chr 22:12; 2 Chr 1:10ff.; 2:12; Isa 11:2; 29:14; Dan 2:21.

13. God calls the artisans for the building of the tabernacle and empowers them for their handiwork by giving them (and others) the "spirit of wisdom and understanding" (Ex 31:2f.). Solomon pleads with God for "wisdom and understanding," so that he may be capable of judging his people Israel. While the false prophets speak lies, Micah is equipped to fulfill his prophetic office: he is filled with strength in the spirit of the Lord (Micah 3:5–8).

"wisdom" and "understanding" denote not intellectual abilities but rather manual skills and craftsmanship.[14] The extent to which we are dealing with God-given gifts and also with the practicalities of "wisdom" and "understanding" becomes especially clear in Deut 4:6: the keeping of the commandments is Israel's "wisdom" and "understanding." When the other nations hear those commandments, they will say: What "wise" and "understanding" people![15]

The two concepts "wisdom" and "understanding" can hardly be separated.[16] We are doubtless dealing with synonyms.[17] Their use in LXX Ex 31:3–6 illustrates this fact. "God's spirit of wisdom and understanding and skill (epistēmē)" is reduced to "understanding" (synesis). There, the Hebrew word ḥokmâ, which LXX Ex 31:3 translates by sophia, is rendered three verses later by synesis in v 6.[18]

The parallel expressions in Eph 1:17–18 show that the plea for "wisdom and understanding" is comparable in meaning to the plea for the Holy Spirit.[19] The adjective pneumatikē (spiritual) in Col 1:9 is probably closest in meaning to the genitive compound "spirit of wisdom" in Eph 1:17.[20]

The expression "wisdom and understanding" is also more closely determined by pas (each/all), in addition to the adjective "spiritual." Bo Reicke[21] divides the variation of meaning of pas into four groups: (1) if a unity or aggregate is meant independently, then a summarizing sense prevails; (2) if we are dealing with an "inclusion of all the individual parts or representatives of a concept," we have an implicit meaning; (3) if the concept extends "to relatively independent particulars," we have an example of a distributive meaning; (4) if we are dealing with the attainment of greatest depths or expansion of a concept, then we are dealing with an elative (or amplificative) sense.

---

14. See esp. Ex 31:3ff.; 35:31ff.; 1 Kgs 7:14; 2 Chr 2:12(13).

15. Also in the Qumran, "wisdom and understanding" are perceived as gifts from God. Compare E. Lohse (p. 57), who refers esp. to 1 QS IV:3; 1 QH XII:11f.

16. Differently in Aristotle (and in his followers among the Stoics), for whom sophia is the "most complete form of knowledge," and to which knowledge of the primary origins, synesis, is subordinated (Nic Eth VI 2–13, 1139b–1145a). Probably following this differentiation, J. B. Lightfoot (p. 204), for example, and many others before and after him, have explained synesis (and phronesis ⟨comp. Eph 1:8⟩) as "applications of sophia to details" and have differentiated synesis from phronēsis in that the former concept is assigned to a "critical" and the latter to a "practical" sense.

17. As also sophia and phronēsis in Eph 1:8; compare M. Barth, AB 34, pp. 84f., 119–23; compare 162f.

18. Compare also LXX Ex 35:35; Deut 34:9.

19. We have the same situation in statements in the LXX. "Wisdom" and "understanding" are also characteristic attributes of the "divine spirit" there (comp. Ex 31:3ff.; Isa 11:2).

20. Compare E. Lohmeyer (p. 33).

21. ThWNT V, pp. 885–89.

We most likely have the *elative* meaning in Col 1:9. In the NT, this occurs only in connection with abstractions.[22] Here, we are dealing with unparalleled wisdom, which is the one *true* wisdom. The multiple use of *pas*, as we observe it in 1:9ff, is certainly a characteristic of the liturgical style, but it is difficult to imagine that we should therefore regard the *pas* only as a stylistic device without deeper theological significance.[23] A relationship to assertions that Christ is creator and propitiator of *all* things (1:15–18), that in him lives the total fullness of God (1:19; 2:9), and that in him are kept all riches of wisdom and understanding, lead us to expect God to bestow not less than "all" wisdom and "all" understanding.

10 *so that you will have a life worthy of the Lord, pleasing in all things* (literally: walking worthy in the Lord). The possibility of misunderstanding Paul in what he means by "knowledge" is now further decreased. "Knowledge . . . *in order to walk*" is the intended meaning. Paul makes the closest association possible by choosing the Greek infinitive *peripatein* (to walk), thus connecting this expression with the preceding verb. The verb "to walk," which occurs more than thirty times in the Pauline corpus, means the total conduct of life. The application of the word corresponds to the usage of the Hebrew verb *halak* ("to walk"). Parallels in the Classical Greek are not extant (cf. H. Seesemann, ThWNT V, 941, 6).[24] What is understood by this conduct is outlined in three ways: (1) to bring forth fruit and to grow, (2) to be made powerful with all strength, and (3) above all, to give thanks, because Paul puts most emphasis on this, and he repeatedly invites the Colossians to do so.

It is not clear, whether *kyrios* (Lord) indicates God in harmony with the LXX use of this title. In 1 Thess 2:12, we have almost the same expression, but there it says clearly: to walk worthy of *God*. The statements in the epistle to the Ephesians also point in the direction of such an interpretation when they deal with becoming "God's imitators" (Eph 5:1), with the appointment "to the praise of his (God's) glorious grace" (Eph 1:12; cf. Eph 1:14). However, "Lord" in Col occurs elsewhere only as a designation for Jesus. Thus, in chap. 1 (cf. 1:3, 3:17) Paul refers expressly to "God the *Father*" and "our *Lord* Jesus Christ." In chap. 2 (2:6), we read, "As you have now received the Messiah Jesus, the Lord" (with emphasis on the designation "Lord") and in chap. 3, after reference is made several times to the "Lord" without a closer determination (3:13, 18, 20, 22, 23, 24; cf. 4:7, 17), this declaration in 3:24 becomes unequivocally clear: "you serve the *Lord* Christ."

22. B. Reicke, op. cit. (p. 886), points out that, outside the NT, this meaning occurs in material objects, for example: *pan agyrion*, all kinds of silver.

23. Compare E. Schweizer (pp. 23, 40), who is of the opinion that *pas* (all) has a purely plerophoric meaning.

24. The expression "walking in a way worthy of the Lord" can be found in the NT only in Col 1:10. In 1 Thess 2:12, Paul summons, "walking worthy of God;" in Eph 4:1, "walking worthy of the calling;" and in Eph 5:9, "walking as children of light."

The statement "pleasing in all things" also has multiple meanings. Paul will not have meant his own pleasure, as though his own conduct in life were gaining its true destiny thereby. It is characteristic of him to point toward Jesus and away from himself.[25] Also, the Colossians should hardly have been called upon to determine their lives according to opinions and concepts of human beings in order to please them.[26]

This does not exclude a different sense, which prevails in passages such as Matt 5:16. The intended meaning,[27] can still be the pleasure of people: "Let your light so shine before men that they see your good works and praise your Father in heaven."[28] Specifically, because a closer determination is missing and also because *pas* is used, divine pleasing is not excluded.

Areskeia (well pleasing) occurs in the LXX only once, in Prov 31:30, and then in a different context. But frequently, the formula with the same meaning, "to do that which is well pleasing *(to areston, ta aresta) before God*," is used.[29] This can have influenced the formulation in Col 1:10. Paul does speak expressly of something well-pleasing before God in other places.[30] We may say, along with E. Lohmeyer (p. 34), that both are meant here, the pleasing of men and of God, according to the Jewish pattern of thought.

He who lives thus brings forth fruit and grows (literally: bringing forth fruit and growing). Notably, the participles are not in the accusative, as we might have expected in the Greek after the infinitive "to walk," but rather in the nominative.[31] This grammatical problem can be solved if one understands the

---

25. Rom 3:27; 4:2; 1 Cor 1:29, 31; and others.

26. Not only Gal 1:10 ("If I were also pleasing to human beings, then I would not be the servant of Christ"), but also Col 3:22 speak against this.

27. In the Classic Greek, *areskeia/areskō*, and others, occur frequently in a negative sense (ingratiate, cringe) when a human demeanor is intended; compare also J. B. Lightfoot (p. 205); E. Lohse (p. 59); E. Lohmeyer (p. 34); and others. See also 1 Thess 2:4; Gal 1:10; but different in 1 Cor 10:33.

28. Expressed somewhat more irresolutely, this thought is also in Phil 2:14f., "Do all things without grumbling and without questioning, so that you may be without blame and innocent, children of God without blemish in the midst of a perverse generation, *among whom you shine as lights in the world*."—Compare also the already cited statement, Deut 4:6. 1 Cor 10:33 should also be understood in this sense, where Paul writes that he (tries) "to please everyone in every respect."

29. See in the LXX, among others, Ex 15:26; compare Lev 10:19; Deut 6:18; 12:25, 28; 2 Ezra 10:11; Tob 4:3; Prov 21:3; Isa 38:3; Dan 4:37a.

30. Compare 1 Cor 7:32; 2 Cor 5:9; *1 Thess 4:1*.—Also in Qumran, reference is made to being well pleasing *to* God (i.e., 1 QS VIII:6). In Philo, *eureskeia*, of being pleasing to God, occurs without additional comment whenever the context is unambiguous (Spec Leg I 300).

31. Some have attempted to explain this by determining that the logical grammatical sentence construction has now been left behind (E. Schweizer, p. 41), some have perceived here an abruptly broken sentence construction (so-called "anacoluth"), or

participles imperatively. Such participial imperatives do not determine legalistic regulations. Rather, they appeal to the status of the addressee. Paul addresses the Colossians as those who are already filled with the knowledge of God, and he suggests that which should be further self-evident.[32] Here, the intercession clearly fulfills a parenetic function, as P. Schubert has assumed for all Pauline expressions of thanksgiving, and especially for those in Col.[33]

"To bring forth fruit and to grow" is a citation from 1:6. Here, as there, we have a *hendiadys*, as was earlier observed, so that both closer determinants, "in every good work" *and* "through the knowledge of God," modify both verbs and are thereby also closely tied to each other.[34] An intellectualistic misunderstanding of "knowledge" is thus again avoided.

Both elucidations designate the means or specifically the medium through which the fruit bearing and growing occur. The goal and purpose of this growing, however, are not mentioned. This problem has found its expression in a variety of textual renderings. The majority of texts and a correction of Codex Claramontanus (sixth century) have "for *(eis)* the knowledge of God" in place of the dative "through the knowledge of God." This variant, however, is not only poorly attested, but must also be suspected as a later assimilation of the two following imperative participles which are connected to statements introduced by *eis*.

Since the participles are close contextually to the declaration in v 10a, the same indication of purpose is applicable to all of them: "pleasing in all things." This will help clarify the aim of the first invitation (1:10b), since another indicator is missing here. The idea of things being well-pleasing before God and *men* (see above) is at least a part of that which Paul intends by "bringing forth fruit and growing." Thus the reference to 1:6 means not only that the dynamic, which is particular to the gospel, is also inherent in the Colossians. Rather, Paul

---

some even determined "schematic errors" or "stylistic incapability" (compare BDR 468, fn. 4).

32. We encounter such imperative participials frequently in Paul. Compare esp. Rom 12:9–15; Eph 4:1–3; and in Col, 3:9–10, 12–17, esp. 16; 4:2–5. Compare also D. Daube, "Participle and Imperative in 1 Peter," in E. G. Selwyn, *The First Epistle of St. Peter* (London: Macmillan, 1947), pp. 467–88; H. G. Meecham, "The Use of the Participle for the Imperative in the New Testament," ET 58 (1946/47) 207–8; M. Barth, AB 34, p. 372, par. 23.

33. P. Schubert, *Form and Function*, op. cit., p. 89, "All Pauline thanksgivings have either explicitly or implicitly paraenetic function. This is definitely true of the *hina*-clauses of the *eucharistō* periods. Col 1:9–12 is, structurally speaking, the *hina*- clause of the Colossian thanksgiving and is very explicitly paraenetical."

34. K. G. Eckart, "Exegetische Beobachtungen zu Col 1:9–20," ThViat 7 (1959/60) 87–106:93; "Urchristliche Tauf- und Ordinationsliturgie (Col 1:9–20; Acts 26:18)," ThViat 8 (1961/62) 23–37:26f. separates both participles and refers "bringing fruit" only to "in every good work," and "grow" to "cognizance of God."

intended to intimate to his readers that their fruit bearing and growing is a form of the same fruit bearing and growing described in 1:4–8.

in every good work. As also in LXX Ex 35:5, the particle *pas* signifies that the equipment which God gives is sufficient to do all that should be done according to his will.[35]

Agathon/kalon ergon (good work) also elsewhere has positive significance for Paul. In Rom 13:3, Paul speaks of "the good work" in contrast to "the bad," and Paul offers the invitation to do "the good." The context of Rom 13:1–7 (12:9–21; 13:8–10) determines this good work more precisely through love. Only a few things that are listed in this connection will be given here: in addition to the invitation, they are to burn in the Spirit, to serve the Lord, to be patient in trouble, and to pray continuously. Paul admonishes his parishioners to take up the needs of the saints, to give refuge gladly, to bless those who "curse you," to rejoice with the joyful, to weep with the weeping, to give food and drink to the hungering enemy, etc. In 2 Cor 9:8, the collection for the community of Jerusalem is meant by "every good work."[36] In the rabbinic literature, the corresponding Hebraic expression is a set concept that does not contradict the Pauline one. It designates "works of compassion," such as visits to the sick, refuge for strangers, comfort for the grief-stricken, dowry for the newly married poor.[37] This tradition forms the background for the Pauline usage of "good work."

through the knowledge of God! See Notes to "the knowledge of his will" in 1:9.

11 *He lets himself be made powerful with all power according to his glorious strength* (literally: in all power made powerful according to the strength of his glory). For the translation of the middle voice of this imperative participle, cf. BDR 317.

Here words which are related in meaning and are equal in significance occur in more cumulative fashion than in the previous line. The liturgical stylistic elements become more and more compact, to the point that we have a hymn worked into the epistle with the unfolding of the third participle (thanking . . .). This gradation of liturgical language attests to the contextual weightiness of this verse: the thanksgiving is of special concern in this letter.

The substantive *dynamis* (power) and the verb *dynamō* (to make powerful)[38]

---

35. Here in v 6 is the explanation "so that they can do everything that I have ordained for you."

36. Compare further: Rom 2:7; Eph 2:10; 2 Thess 2:17. In Phil 1:6, the working of God among the Philippians is described as "good works." The expression occurs frequently in the Pastoral Epistles—1 Tim 2:10; 3:1; 5:10, 25; 6:18; 2 Tim 2:21; 3:17; Titus 1:16; 2:7, 14; 3:1, 8, 14—with the meaning which hardly corresponds with that in the uncontested Pauline Epistles.

37. St. B. IV, 536.

38. The verb *dynamoō* occurs otherwise in the NT only in Heb 11:34. In other

are joined through the related meaning of the stem, which adds emphasis to the statement.[39] Here also, the passive circumscribes the name of God (see above). The contrasting idea of the weakness of the Christian, who is mighty only *through God,* is brought to the forefront.

"According to his glorious strength" is probably a Semitism, because in the Hebrew the genitive construction is preferred to the adjective.[40] Through this locution, the compounding of related concepts for "strength" becomes especially noticeable. Not only the quantity, the overly great *abundance* of strength, which is to be imparted to the Colossians, is to be indicated, but also the *quality* of the strength that is to be conferred.[41]

Kratos (strength) occurs twelve times in the NT. Among the epistles which name Paul as author, it occurs in Col 1:11, in Eph 1:19; 6:10, and in 1 Tim 6:16. It is noticeable that the word is used mostly in liturgical hymnic contexts.[42] Usually, it designates the strength of God.[43] In the LXX, it occurs more frequently, but most of the instances are found in writings which do not belong to the canon of the Hebrew Bible. When the discussion concerns the strength of God, the reference, in most cases, is not to an irrational, arbitrary force for which everything is possible.[44] Rather, in most cases, the concern is with the strength that comes to the aid of weak, miserable Israel in a struggle against its enemies, or even to the individual who finds himself in a similar situation.[45] *Kratos* comes close to the concept of godly compassion. The quintessence of the saving action of God toward his people can also be found in Eph 1:19, where "strength" is expressed in connection with the power of God: God's power triumphs when God raises the messiah from the dead and elevates him to his right hand.

for all endurance and patience. The conferred strength enables one to withstand life situations that require endurance and patience, and thus does not

---

places, Paul uses *endynamoō:* Rom 4:20; Eph 6:10; Phil 4:13; compare 1 Tim 1:12; 2 Tim 2:1; 4:17; Acts 9:22.

39. Compare BDR 153; for the Hebrew GK 117, 2.

40. Compare GK 135n.

41. Compare also E. Lohse (p. 63), who interprets *kata* (corresponding to his power) that God remains true to himself, that he acts in accordance with the evidence which he has already demonstrated.

42. Compare—aside from Eph and Col—1 Tim 6:16; 1 Pet 4:11; 5:11; Jude 25; Rev 1:6; 5:13. Luke 1:51 (the song in praise of Mary) focuses on the power of God which nobody can defy.

43. In Heb 2:14, *kratos* is used of the power of death and thus of the devil.

44. Only in Job 12:16 can we recognize statements with such an orientation.

45. Compare in the LXX, 2 Ezra 8:22; Jude 9:11, 14; 11:7; 13:11; Ps 58⟨59⟩:10; 61⟨62⟩:13; 85⟨86⟩:16; Wis 15:2f.; Sir 18:5; 47:5; Isa 40:26; 2 Macc 3:34; 7:17; 9:17; 11:4; 12:28; and others. Ps 89(90):11 concerns the force of divine wrath, Wis 11:21 divine force in general which human beings cannot resist.

free man from such situations.[46] Here also, the particle *pas* (all/each) certifies that God equips those who are called by him to a life that is sufficient according to their appointment.

In *Paul*, we can recognize a trend in the use of the two concepts that enables us to differentiate (1) *hypomonē* (endurance) from (2) *makrothymia* (patience):

1. Paul views *hypomonē* in close connection with "hope" and "suffering/sadness," and similar things. Because the children of God have not yet been *revealed* as such, because creation is still subject to futility, because the redemption of our body is still to come, in brief, because our salvation is based on "hope," *hypomonē* is necessary. Hope and *hypomonē* belong together,[47] because "to hope" means to wait in *hypomonē* (Rom 8:24f.). Because the redemption of the body is still to come, because all of creation is still "groaning," "the present" time is characterized by groans and sufferings (Rom 8:18). Thus hope and thereby *hypomonē* have great significance. The statements in 2 Cor 1:6ff. may illustrate this point: hope in the God who awakens the dead (cf. Eph 1:19f.) makes suffering in *hypomonē* possible especially when the suffering exceeds purely human abilities,[48] and makes Paul ponder despair. Because "perseverance" or "patient endurance" plays a significant part in the use of this Greek concept, it has been translated as "endurance."[49]

2. We can then consider the meaning of *makrothymia*. In contrast to "endurance," where we are dealing with demeanor in suffering, despair, etc., in the human condition, *makrothymia* characterizes a certain relationship with one's fellow man, or God's with mankind.[50] That is specifically demonstrated in Rom 9:22, where *makrothymia* describes the circumstance in which God holds back his anger.[51] In lists, this concept is often paired with words like "gentleness," "friendliness," "goodness," and it thus receives a special coloring.[52]

---

46. Compare esp. also 2 Cor 1:6ff.; 12:1–10; Phil 4:13. God proves his power in this weakness, so that all glory will accrue to him.

47. Compare also the statements in 1 Thess 1:3; compare 4:13; 2 Thess 3:5.

48. Compare Rom 5:3f.; 2 Cor 6:4; 2 Thess 1:4. Also Rom 15:4 belongs among these. Bearing the powerlessness of the weak means here bearing their invectives or abuse, and thus suffering tribulation. When God is called "the God of perseverance" in Rom 15:5, it is not so much because this is one of his attributes, but rather because he bestows this attribute.

49. In Luke 8:15, the concept of "bearing fruit" is used. There also the question is a rational component of constancy. In Luke 21:19, we are dealing with perseverance. Compare also Heb 10:36; 12:1; Jas 1:3, 4; 5:11; Rev 1:9; 2:2f., 19; 3:10; 13:10; 14:12.

50. But that does not mean that the *hypomonē* is without reference to human beings. Thus, for example, in 2 Cor 1:6ff., suffering in *hypomonē* serves to express comfort to the Corinthians.

51. Thus in the LXX, the Hebrew expression "to be slow to express anger" is translated as *makrothymia*.—See also F. Horst, ThWNT IV, pp. 377–90.

52. See also Rom 2:4; 2 Cor 6:6; Gal 5:22; Eph 4:2; Col 3:12; comp. 2 Tim 3:10. The corresponding verb occurs in the Pauline corpus also in 1 Thess 5:14, "be patient

Beyond the Pauline corpus, the range of meaning of these two words becomes fluid. In Jas 5:10f., the two concepts are used synonymously. In Heb 6:12, *makrothymia* is used where *hypomonē* would be expected, according to the differentiation above. In view of the liturgical context of the text before us, both concepts may well have the same meaning.

with joy! Disagreement reigns among the commentators as to whether "with joy" belongs to v 11 or to the following verse, which would relate it to "thanksgiving."[53] In favor of the latter interpretation is the fact that a prepositional phrase precedes the first two participles ("in . . ."). For reasons of symmetry one could presume that the third prepositional phrase (with joy) belongs to the third participle (thanking); in this case, *en* (in) would have been replaced by *meta* (with).

Such strict symmetry does not prevail in vv 9–11 to the point that the argument would be decisive. A phrase beginning with *eis* ("for all endurance . . . [v 11]"; "for the portion . . ." v 12) is added to the second and third participial clauses, but not to the first ("bearing fruit . . ." v 10). The symmetry is further disrupted by the additional phrase "according to his glorious strength." Further, the replacement of *en* with *meta* in v 11 does not argue in favor of a strictly parallel construction of the individual lines of this section.[54]

"With joy" is most likely part of the *preceding* statement, for Paul speaks of joyful suffering or joyful endurance in the face of suffering and sadness also elsewhere.[55] Further, the two other participles are connected to the larger context. "To bear fruit and to grow" is literally attached to 1:3–8, and the "thanksgiving" is elucidated in 1:13–20 in detail. In addition, the key words "strength," "suffering," *and* "joy" all recur in 1:24–29 (1:24) and are closely related to "perseverance and patience"; we therefore conclude that the term "with joy" belongs in v 11. Paul participates in the mission to proclaim the Messiah, through the power which works within him. He fulfills this commission in a special way: through suffering in which he is joyful.

12 He thanks the Father, who has qualified you (literally: thanking the

---

with everyone," and in 1 Cor 13:4, where it is described as an attribute of love. According to 1 Tim 1:16, God's mercy to Paul is a signal expression of divine "patience."

53. This interpretation to v 11 is advocated by, among others, Thomas Aquinas, J. Calvin, J. A. Bengel, J. B. Lightfoot, W. M. L. de Wette, E. Haupt, C. F. D. Moule, E. Schweizer, R. P. Martin, P. T. O'Brien; for the subsequent, among others, John Chrysostom, H. von Soden, E. Lohmeyer, E. Lohse, J. Gnilka, F. F. Bruce.

54. J. Gnilka (p. 43, fn. 34) points out that prepositional figures with *eis* are better suited as conclusion, but that a prepositional figure with *meta* would fit better with the subsequent verb. He does, however, leave room for the idea that "the characteristic connecting participles do not infrequently leave transitions hanging."

55. Rom 5:3; 12:12; 1 Thess 5:16; 1 Pet 1:6; 4:13; compare Acts 5:41; Jas 1:2ff.

Father). The change from the second-person plural (you plural)[56] to first-person plural (we) in v 13 gives these verses special emphasis and demonstrates that Paul thinks and speaks from the Jewish perspective. Those who previously were considered strangers and enemies (1:21), the non-Jews in Colossae (cf. 1:27), are invited to join in thanks with (Christian) Jews within the framework of the prayer of intercession. V 21 is reconnected to v 12 by the address "you" plural, and v 27 testifies that the abundance of the grace of God is revealed in the fact that these previous strangers to Israel may praise the Messiah as their hope. Non-Jews have received a portion of the inheritance which was first promised to Israel—this bequest has qualified them. The Greek verb *hikanoō* and the corresponding adjective *hikanos* mean basically "to make, to be sufficient, ample, abundant, (being) relatively much or relatively large."[57] The adjective occurs frequently in the NT as an indicator of quantity, time, or quality.[58]

The verb is found only in one other place in the NT besides the one mentioned above, namely in 2 Cor 3:6, together with the corresponding adjective and substantive. The word group there designates the "capability" tendered by God to be servants of the New Covenant.[59]

In Col 1:12, the verb is used in connection with the concept of inheritance, a connection for which there is no parallel in the LXX. The translation "qualify" comes close to the sense of the Greek word, since it is used in a legal comparison.[60]

The aorist might signify that we are dealing with an already completed event. All the subsequent verbs that refer to "qualifying" agree with that sense.

In the Pauline Corpus, the address "Father" for God is used in this absolute

---

56. For the change of person of the personal pronoun, see esp. Gal 4:4–6; compare also Rom 6:14f.; 12:1–6; 1 Thess 5:5. Further, see Comment II to 1:3–8.—Reliable text readings (i.e., Codex Alexandrinus) here read "we" as in v 13. This reading, however, is probably an assimilation of just this personal pronoun in v 13.

57. Compare K. H. Rengstorf, ThWNT III, p. 294.

58. Compare Matt 28:12; Luke 7:12; 8:27; and others—Luke 8:27; 20:9; 23:8; and others—Matt 3:11; Luke 3:16; 7:6. The adjective is found a total of three times in Matt, three times in Mark, six times in the Pauline Corpus. All other instances (twenty-seven times) are in the Lukan writings.

59. Compare also 1 Cor 15:9,10, "For I am the least of the apostles, who am not worthy *(hikanos)* of being called apostle, because I persecuted the church of God. But by the grace of God I am what I am. . . ." In this context, compare also Matt 3:11 par.; 8:8 par.

60. Thus, T. K. Abbott translates (pp. 205f.), "given you a title." E. Lohse (p. 70), E. Schweizer (p. 46) translate "empower/authorize."—In place of *hikanōsanti*, some mss render *kalesanti* (call). This rendering is hardly reliable. In Codex Vaticanus (fourth century), we find both readings: *kalesanti kai hikanōsanti*. Possibly, the rarely used expression *hikanoo* was replaced by the more usual *kaleō*.—The verb *kaleō* (to call) in this context is reminiscent of Hos 11:1, "Out of Egypt I called my son."

sense only in Rom 6:4; Eph 2:18; 3:14; and in the vocative in Rom 8:15 and Gal 4:6.[61] The parallel use between this passage and Rom 8:15ff. as well as Gal 4:6f. is noteworthy: it is a sign and privilege of the children (of God), who are *now also* (his) heirs, that they may call him Abba, Father.

E. Käsemann[62] interpreted only the participial form "thanking" (referring to G. Bornkamm[63]) as an imperative and as terminus technicus to introduce the homology of the community. According to him, vv 12–20 are a declaration of faith by the community and they were thus incorporated by the author of Col. However, such a technical use of this verb cannot be documented in the NT[64] (cf. Comment II.1).

to take part in the inheritance of the saints, (which is) in the light (literally: for the portion of the inheritance of the saints in the light). Parallels to vv 12 + 13 exist in the writings of Qumran. The expression "inheritance/lot of the saints" does not occur in the OT, but it does occur in several places in the Qumran texts. We refer specifically to the *Rule of the Sect* (1 QS XI:5ff., esp. 7f.), in which the discussion concerns the chosen ones to whom God "has given the portion of the *lot (Hebr. goral) of the saints* and has united their assembly with the sons of heaven. . . ."[65] On the basis of the cited Qumran parallel, are "saints" also conceived of as angels in Col 1:12?[66] We may find a reference point

---

61. Otherwise in the NT also: Matt 11:27; 24:36; Mark 13:22; Luke 9:26; 10:22; Acts 1:4, 7; 2:33; in the vocative: Matt 11:26; Mark 14:36; Luke 10:21; 11:2; 22:42; 23:34,46; and very frequently in the Johannine Gospel and the Johannine Epistle: John 1:14,18; 3:35; 4:21, 23, and others.—In Col, the infrequency of the absolute usage in different manuscripts was noted and "God" or "God and" was given priority over the concept "father."—Compare also Comment II to 1:3–8.

62. E. Käsemann, *Taufliturgie*, op. cit., p. 136. H. Löwe, "Bekenntnis, Apostelamt und Kirche im Kolosserbrief," in FS für G. Bornkamm, *Kirche*, ed. D. Lührmann and G. Strecker (Tübingen: Mohr, 1980), pp. 299–314, attempted to solidify and to extend E. Käsemann's position.

63. G. Bornkamm, "Das Bekenntnis im Hebräerbrief," in *Studien zu Antike und Urchristentum*, Ges. Aufsätze II, BevTheol 28 (München: Kaiser, 1959), pp. 188–203:196.

64. Compare R. Deichgräber, "Gotteshymnus und Christushymnus in der frühen Christenheit," StUnt 5 (Göttingen: Vandenhoeck & Ruprecht, 1967), p. 145.

65. Compare 1 QH XI:11f., where being united in "destiny with one's saints" is the issue. For the interpretation of "saints" as angels, see, among others, 1 QM XII:1; 1 QH III:22; IV:25; 1 QSb III:25f.—However, we also find in the Qumran writings the designation "saints" for those belonging to the covenant people, of whom it is said that they see the holy angels (1 QM X:9ff.).

66. Compare, among others, E. Lohse (p. 71); J. Gnilka (p. 47); R. P. Martin (NCC, 54); F. F. Bruce (p. 49); A. Lindemann (p. 22). Also, E. Käsemann, *Taufliturgie*, op. cit., p. 140, interpreted "saints" as angels; however, not from the Qumran sources.—H.-W. Kuhn, "Enderwartung und gegenwärtiges Heil. Untersuchungen zu den Gemeindeliedern von Qumran," StUNT 4 (Göttingen: Vandenhoeck & Ruprecht),

in 1 Thess 3:13 for this, where "his saints," with whom Christ will appear at the Second Coming, also means angels.

However, the following arguments counter such an interpretation[67]: (1) in Col, "saints" is never used to designate angels, but rather always human persons chosen by God (cf. 1:2, 4, 22, 26; 3:12). (2) There is such a close terminological and contextual relationship between Acts 26:18, where Paul's ministry is described concisely, and Col 1:12–14, that this needs to be considered in the explication. There also, the discussion concerns a change from *darkness* to *light*, in which darkness is interpreted as the domain of the power (*exousia* cf. Col 1:13) of Satan. The citation also deals with *forgiveness of sins* and with *inheritance*, although not of *saints* but rather of those *sanctified (hagiosmenoi)*. These, however, are unequivocally the believers in Christ. (3) In the further course of the epistle, the angels do not gain such significance and the salvation of God is not represented in such a way that it seems justified to perceive the hope of the recipients of the epistle as taking part in the "lot of the angels."

On the basis of the differentiation between "you" plural and "we" (see above), "saints" in this context has a more circumscribed meaning than in 1:2 + 4. As in the OT, the word is used to designate the covenant people Israel,[68] in whose inheritance the "former outsiders" are now entitled participants. This idea is significantly formulated in Rom 15:8–13.[69]

Klēros has the basic meaning "lot." The word is used frequently in this sense in the LXX.[70] It gains special significance in connection with the partition of land. In addition to the original meaning (cf. Josh 18:10), a different set of circumstances becomes the determining factor: *klēros* changes places with

---

1966, pp. 73–75, documents that "destiny" in the late-Jewish literature is a characteristic concept to describe eschatological redemption/condemnation.

67. P. Benoit, "*Hagioi* en Colossiens 1:12: Hommes ou Anges?" in FS für C. K. Barrett, *Paul und Paulinism*, ed. M. D. Hooker and J. G. Wilson (London: SPCK, 1982, pp. 83–101), sees no mutually exclusive alternatives, but would rather see both interpretations validated. The same for F. Zeilinger, *Der Erstgeborene der Schöpfung. Untersuchungen zur Formalstruktur und Theologie des Kolosserbriefes* (Wien: Herder, 1974), pp. 138f. (cited in: ESpg).

68. Compare Ex 19:6; Deut 7:6; Dan 7:18, 21ff.; and others. In Deut, not only the concept "saints" to designate chosen people, but also "inheritance" or "inherit," plays a central role (Deut 9:26; 12:9; 19:14; 32:9; and others).

69. "Christ has become a servant of the *Jews* for the sake of the truth of God, in order to confirm the promises which were made to our fathers. The gentiles, however, are to praise God for the sake of mercy. Be happy, you gentiles, with his people."— Compare Rom 1:16 (the Jews *principally* . . .); Gal 4:4; Eph 2:1ff. See also Comments II.3 and V to 1:9–23.

70. For example, for the throwing of the lot in the division of booty (Ps 21⟨22⟩:19); or within the realm of the cult for determining the two goats: one for JHWH, one for Azazel (Lev 16:10).

klēronomia (inheritance) and largely takes on this meaning in relation to the allotted land, which emphasizes the constancy and permanence of the apportionment.[71] Even the combination of the two terms *klēros* and *meris* (part) has a fixed place in the OT context of partition of the land. It signifies "portion of inheritance,"[72] but without the connotation that *meris* designates the portion of the whole *(klēros);* for *Klēros* is also used to designate a portion (cf. among others Gen 48:6; Josh 17:14; Deut 19:14). The genitive *tou klērou* after *meris* is appositional and interprets the preceding noun without reducing or increasing its weight. We agree with T. K. Abbott when he states, "What a *meris* is in relation to the whole a *kleros* is in relation to the possessor" (p. 206).

The "place" of this inherited portion is indicated by "in the light." Having a portion in the inheritance of the saints means being transposed into the kingdom *(basileia)* of the beloved who is placed in opposition to the realm of darkness (cf. v 13). The parallelism of the opposition of these pairs of concepts suggests connecting "light" with the entire phrase "inheritance of the saints" and not only with "the saints"[73] (cf. Comment I). To 1:12–14 cf. also Comment V.

He has delivered us from . . . and transferred us into (literally: who has . . .) The aoristic forms indicate that we are dealing with things which have already occurred. We cannot determine the time frame more closely until v 14 (cf. v 14). Paul is using the first person ("us") again, because the mentioned darkness concerned both gentiles and Jews (cf. Comment I).

Ryomai (to deliver) is a word frequently used in the LXX (141 times). It denotes deliverance from every kind of circumstance[74]; and Yahweh is the subject in the great majority of instances.[75] Redemption is a distinctive feature

---

71. See esp. Num 18:23f.: Josh 19 passim. Compare also Num 33:53f. with Josh 12:6.—See also W. Foerster, ThWNT III, p. 759, "*Klēros* hebt an diesem einen Tatbestand das Zugeteiltsein, *klēronomia* die Dauer und Sicherheit des Besitzes hervor."

72. In the sense of the portion which the Levites, or rather Aaron, should not receive, Num 18:20; Deut 10:9; 12:12; 14:27, 29; 18:1; Josh 19:9.—In the transmitted sense concerning punishment or salvation, we encounter the concepts in the LXX: Isa 57:6; Jer 13:25; Ps 15(16):5; compare Acts 8:21. In Deut 32:9, the people Israel are designated as "inheritors of JHWH."

73. The expression "saints in the light" is, as far as we know, otherwise not attested. It is thus not a terminus technicus for "angel." If we understand "saints" here formally from the Judeo-(Christians) and we then reference "light" only to this concept, then this results in a shift in emphasis which is not just to the text: the declaration of both verses aims toward the "son of love," who is then praised in vv 15–20; *he* comprises the distinctive quality of the inheritance, not the saints who are already a part of it.

74. Thus, for example, the deliverance from persecution (Ps 7:2); from evil neighbors (Ps 33(34):5); from murder (LXX Ps 17:30); from hunger (32(33):19); etc.

75. Even human beings are, in rare cases, designated as "saviors": thus Gidion or the king (Judg 9:17; 2 Kgs 19:10). In Ps 81(82):4, the judges are summoned to save the poor and needy from the hand of the godless people. Compare also Ex 2:17,19; Prov 6:31; Sir 40:24; 3 Macc 2:32.

of the God of Israel; it differentiates him from other gods (cf. 2 Kgs 18:33). He is even called "redeemer" by name (Isa 63:16; cf. also Ps 78[79]:9).

The verb has a fixed place in the tradition of the Exodus,[76] and it is here that it receives its decisive contextual stamp. The "ancient declaration" which is associated with the deliverance of the Israelites out of Egypt is found "at all times" in the OT and in the "most diverse connections." "In the deliverance from Egypt Israel saw its reassurance for all future times in Yahweh's unwavering willingness to save, something like a guarantee on which its faith could rely in times of danger."[77]

The circumlocution of the event of salvation in local categories and with help from the verb *metestēsen* (he has transferred) and the prepositions "from" as well as "in" is probably founded in the perception of the deliverance from Egypt or from exile, as the "new exodus." In the LXX, this word does not occur in the context of the exodus, but it is used by *Josephus* for the "deportation" of a people.[78] The geographical, spatial sense of the term is significant in the context of Col. The concepts in v 13 can be elucidated on the basis of its OT background. There is no need to refer to, or to rely on, thought patterns of Gnostic mythology (cf. Comment III to 1:3–8).

from the dominion of darkness . . . into the kingdom of his beloved Son (literally: the Son of his love). The term *basileia* (kingdom/kingly realm) should not be used to imagine a restricted location and sphere of rule of the Son, be it the earth in contrast to heaven, or the church in contrast to the world. Vv 15–20 clearly affirm that the Messiah is Lord over *all* things and thereby also Lord and king everywhere. *Basileia* consequently means the kingly *realm* of the Messiah. Analogously, *exousia* means the *dominion* of darkness.

Exousia does not mean "tyranny" in itself, nor only "conferred reign," just as *basileia* does not in itself designate a realm which would not require legitimation and could be characterized by freedom. Both concepts can be used

---

76. Ex 5:23; 6:6; 14:30; compare 12:27; Judg 6:9; Isa 51:10. Compare J. J. Stamm: "Erlösen und Vergeben im Alten Testament. Eine begriffsgeschichtliche Untersuchung" (Bern: Francke, 1940), p. 18; C. Barth: "Die Errettung vom Tode in den individuellen Klage- und Dankliedern des Alten Testamentes" (Zollikon: Evang. Verlag, 1947), p. 125. We cannot, however, speak of a terminus technicus for the deliverance from Egypt on the basis of the broad usage of this concept (compare U. Bergmann, THAT II, p. 98).

77. Compare G. von Rad, Theol.d.AT I, pp. 177, 178.

78. *methistēmi* designates a change of location even in the LXX and the NT: i.e., giving way to the left (1 Sam 6:12), the removal of idol images (Judg 10:16; 2 Kgs 3:2; 12:4), the moving of mountains (1 Cor 13:2). More frequently, we encounter it in the transmitted sense (i.e. Deut 17:17; Josh 14:8; Acts 19:26). It also means "take down, remove from office" (compare Dan 2:21; Luke 16:4; Acts 13:22).—For the meaning in Col 1:13, J. B. Lightfoot (p. 207) refers to Josephus (Ant IX, 235). He reports of Tiglath Pileser, who "deported the inhabitants as prisoners of war into his kingdom" (*metestēsen eis tēn autou basileian*).

synonymously (cf. Rev 12:10) as also when *basileia* denotes the rule or realm of Satan (Matt 12:26 par; Luke 11:18; cf. Matt 4:8 par; Luke 4:5; Rev 17:12,17). Both expressions receive their specific meaning only from the context in Col 1:13 through the attributes of "darkness" and "beloved Son."[79]

In the NT, especially in Mark 11:10 and Acts 1:16, *basileia* receives and possesses meaning on the basis of the Davidic proclamation in 2 Sam 7:12ff.: at the entrance of Jesus into Jerusalem, the people cry, "Praised is the kingdom *(basileia)* of our father David, which is imminent." And the apostles ask the risen one, who proclaims to them the outpouring of the Spirit, "Lord, will you raise up again the kingdom of Israel 'at' this time?" The closer characterization of *basileia* in Col 1:13 through the addition of "beloved *Son*"[80] gives impetus to interpret the proclamation of this verse also in light of the OT reference, since here as there, both concepts are closely connected in characteristic fashion.[81] In 2 Sam 7:12f. it is proclaimed that the (Davidic) kingdom (LXX, *basileia*) shall last forever. We find in this passage the affirmation of Yahweh concerning the inheritor of the throne, "I will be his Father, and he shall be my *Son*." The legitimization of the king as son of God was of particular significance for the Israelite kingdom, as Ps 2:7 and Ps 89:27f.[82] make clear. Thus the king was

---

79. The Hebrew equivalent for *"basileia"* occurs also in Qumran: thus in 1 QM VI:6; XII:7 refer to the *"basileia"* of God; in 4 Qpatr 4 to the "anointed of justice," to the "offspring of David," to whom was given the *"basileia"* over his people for "eternal generations." In 1 QSb V:21, God is asked "to resurrect the *'basileia'* of his people" (compare 1 QM XIX:8). Even the Hebrew equivalent of *exousia* in connection with "sacrilege" (1 QS IV:19) or with "Belial" (1 QS I:18), among others, occurs in the Qumran literature. E. Lohse (p. 73) points out that the concept occurs in connection with "darkness" (1 QH XII:6), but not in the transmitted sense (as in Col).

80. The clumsily constructed expression "son of his love" is probably a Hebrewism. See Notes to "power of his glory" in 1:11.

81. Compare Rom 1:3.—Whether the Colossians were able to comprehend this type of terminology, which was specific to the OT, depends on how determinate Paul's and his co-workers' Jewish self-consciousness was for his proclamations.—Otherwise, Paul speaks primarily of the *basileia* of God (Rom 14:17; 1 Cor 4:20; 6:9–10; 15:50; Gal 5:21; 1 Thess 2:12; 2 Thess 1:5); in 1 Cor 15:24 of the *basileia* of Christ (compare 2 Tim 4:1,18). There is no contradiction here, however. The title of son already demonstrates that we are dealing not with a contradiction but rather with a component of the power of God. In Col 4:11, this same *basileia* is called the *"basileia* of God" (comp. Eph 5:5). Even in 1 Cor 15, we are not dealing with a separation, but with a retroversion to him from whom it was received. Besides that, there is no contradiction here to the other Pauline Epistles, where the kingdom of God is spoken of as a mutual power (compare E. Lohse, pp. 73f.): see Rom 14:17; 1 Cor 4:20; 15:24.

82. ". . . he said to me: You are my son; today I have begotten you" (Ps 2:7); "He shall cry to me: You are my father, my God and the rock of my salvation!—Thus I will also make him the first-born, the highest among the kings of the earth" (Ps 89:26f.).

certified by God as the legitimate ruler over God's people and his power was part of the sovereign right of God over his chosen people.[83]

Col 1:13 refers to the confirmation of this proclamation in 2 Sam 7 and thus to the *dawn* of the kingdom of Jesus who has been legitimized by God and who is thus the true Messiah. The addition of "beloved" gives prominence to the concept that *this one* is the one who has been "chosen" by God. In the LXX, the term "beloved" designates the chosen one of God[84] and serves equally in the translation of the Hebrew *yaḥid* [only (son)],[85] which clarifies its meaning as the "first-born son." In PsSol 13:9, "beloved" and "first-born" masculine are used synonymously (cf. Notes to 1:15).

The two halves of 1:13, which are distinguished by designations of place, "from the realm" and "into the kingdom," are presuppositions of the freedom mentioned in the next verse. "Freedom *from*" is just as important as "freedom *to.*" Without the latter, the former would be an empty freedom or one without a master. What this might lead to can be ascertained from the misery of some of the freed slaves from the time of Paul, as well as also in American history of the emancipation of the slaves in the Southern States at and after the time of the Civil War. Redemption is the transfer from the dominion of a bad overlord into the dominion of a good one. This concept of freedom corresponds exactly to the OT reports of the redemption of Israel out of Egypt. God demands of Pharaoh through Moses, "Israel is my first-born son; and I demand of you to let my son go, *so that he can serve me.* . . ." (Ex 4:22–23; cf. also Rom 6:18–20; 8:21–23).

14 *In him, freedom belongs to us* (literally: we have the deliverance). In this phrase, we also have echoes of the exodus terminology. The word *apolytrōsis* (deliverance) occurs only in LXX Dan 4:34, and the simplex *(lytrōsis)* also is not found very frequently,[86] but the verb *lytroō* (to deliver) plays an important role in the Greek rendition of the OT. It is not only a special terminus for the

---

83. G. Fohrer (ThWNT VIII, p. 350:25ff.) notes regarding the father-son relationship, "Wie ein Vater oder dessen Hauptfrau das Kind einer Nebenfrau oder Sklavin als legitim anerkennen konnte, so legitimiert Jahwe ausser dem dynastischen Grundsatz den jeweiligen einzelnen König, indem er ihn als seinen Sohn bezeichnet, und räumt ihm einen Anteil an seinem als des Vaters Herrschaftsrecht ein." Compare also the voice from heaven in Mark 1:11, "You are my beloved son, in you I am well-pleased." This stands within the context of the proclaimed kingdom of God. "It is a question regarding the person of the *king*, which is answered by the heavenly voice." (M. Barth, "Die Taufe—ein Sakrament?," Zollikon-Zürich: Ev. Verlag, 1951), p. 86. Compare E. Schweizer, ThWNT VIII, pp. 369f.

84. Compare LXX Deut 32:15; 33:5,26; Isa 44:2.

85. Gen 22:2, 12; Jer 38:20; and others; Judg 11:34.

86. Lev 25:29, 48; Num 18:16; Judg 1:15; Ps 48(49):9; 110(111):9; 129(130):7; Isa 63:4. The composite *apo-lytroō* occurs only in LXX Ex 21:8 and Zeph 3:1.

designation of deliverance of the first-born, of slaves and alienated property,[87] it is also a firm designation for the release of the people out of Egypt.[88] It is used almost exclusively for this event in Deuteronomy, so that we can speak of a terminus technicus here. In the prophetic literature, its use by Deutero-Isaiah should receive special mention. He specifically alludes to the release of bondage from Egypt (Isa 44:24; 52:3ff.) and God receives the surname "Redeemer" (Isa 41:14; 43:14; 44:24; and others). Redemption, deliverance of the exiles, their departure from Babylon and return into the homeland, accompanied by Yahweh himself, this theme has eschatological overtones in Deutero-Isaiah, and it promises that the time will come for a conclusive, worldwide revelation of the glory of Yahweh.[89] According to Col 1:14, this proclamation has been fulfilled, because the redemption has occurred.[90] Such an assertion demands "legitimization,"[91] which is not given in a theological treatise but rather through a doxology (1:15–20).

We need to consider that redemption here, as well as in the Deuteronomic text, as also in Isa, is not tied to the concept of payment of ransom. Deut-Isa, in fact, expressly excludes the concept of ransom from the idea of redemption.[92] We have in the place of ransom the sacrifice of the servant of God (Isa 53:10).

---

87. Ex 13:13; 34:20; and others; Lev 19:20; 25:25, 30; and others.

88. Ex 6:6; 15:13, 16; Deut 7:8; 9:26; 13:6; 15:15; 21:8; 24:18; 2 Sam 7:23; 1 Chr 17:21; Neh 1:10; Esth 4:17g; Ps 73(74):2; Ps 76(77):16; and others.

89. Compare G. von Rad, Theol.d.AT II, p. 258; see also the description of salvation in Isa 35.—*lytroō* (and its derivatives) in the LXX designates, in addition, the salvation from all kinds of distress and affliction (2 Sam 4:9; 1 Kgs 1:29; Ps 7:3; 25⟨26⟩:11; 30⟨31⟩:6; and others). Only once, Ps 129(130):8, does the discussion concern redemption from sin.—"Redemption" in the NT is used in the Lukan Gospel as an eschatological concept in reference to the hope of Israel (see 1:68; 2:38; 21:28; 24:21).

90. *apolytrōsis* occurs rarely in Paul: in Rom 3:24, "redemption" is designated as an *occurrence* through Jesus Christ (that is, according to v 22, through his faithfulness or his faith). Thereby are all the faithful, Jews and gentiles, justified. This declaration is tied to the concept of sacrifice. The last goal of this divine action is God's justice as demonstrated through his works.—Rom 8:23 speaks of the yet futuristic "redemption of the body" as freedom from servitude in this transitory life to the wonderful freedom of the children of God—According to 1 Cor 1:30, Christ was given to us for redemption. In Eph 1:7, "redemption through his blood" and "forgiveness from sin" are placed on an equal par, and in 1:14, the goal of redemption is called "his possession." Eph 4:30 speaks of the prospective day of redemption.—Compare Luke 21:28; Heb 9:15; 11:35. The verb *lytroō* occurs in the NT only in Luke 24:21; Titus 2:14, 1 Pet 1:18, the simplex *lytrōsis* in Luke 1:68; 2:38; Heb 9:12.

91. Compare esp. E. Lohmeyer (p. 52).

92. Compare Isa 45:13; 52:3. We can hardly determine a difference in meaning between the simplex *lytr-* and the compositum *apolytr-*. The usage of the latter can be explained by a preference for the koine for composita (see BDR 116).—The documented citations in the previous notation demonstrate that, in Paul, as also otherwise in the NT,

This is perceived as an intercessory prayer, but not as payment, which would obligate the recipient to respond with a reciprocal action.[93]

The verb *echomen* (we have) in the present tense[94] does not refer to the act of redemption; reference was made to that in the aorist forms in the previous verses. Rather, it means its result, *freedom*. To translate with "have" is too colorless in view of the written context in which we are concerned with the sharing of an inheritance. "Freedom belongs to us" would be more appropriate in the context of the declaration.

The subjective moment has not been mentioned so far in the description of the act of redemption. Redemption has occurred through God in Christ, which means, according to the declaration in 1:20(22) (cf. Notes there), that it resulted as a consequence of the beginning of the reign of the Messiah with his death on the cross.[95]

forgiveness of sins. This more particular explanation of "deliverance" or "freedom," which originates from the realm of the cultic, seems to fit poorly with the concept of "redemption." In the LXX, the Greek word for "to redeem" does not reflect the Hebrew *kippēr* (to propitiate), which is so significant in the cultic realm. As previously mentioned, in the OT mention is made only once of the deliverance from sins (Ps 129[130]:8), but even so, the two concepts cannot be separated from each other. The expositions of the deliverance of Israel from Egypt do not make the point as strongly as do the proclamations of Deut-Isa about the deliverance of the people from Babylon. The Egyptian "exile" is treated differently from the one in Babylon, which is regarded as a direct result of the sins of the people, a transgression of the covenant code (cf. Isa 43:24; 48:1–11, 18; 50:1). Consequently, for Deut-Isa, the forgiveness of sins signifies the end of captivity; also its reverse is true: redemption means the

---

the conceptualization of redemption is not necessarily tied to the concept of ransom money. A. Deissmann (*Licht vom Osten*, 4th ed., Tübingen: Mohr, 1923, pp. 273–78) wanted to explain the concept "redemption" as a derivative of the so-called "hierodoulism," according to which a slave in the temple of the divinity could sell *himself* in order to become free. His master then received the money from the temple. For a critique of this, see W. Elert: "Redemptio ab hostibus," ThLZ 72 (1947) 269–70. Compare also D. Hill: *Greek Words and Hebrew Meanings: Studies in the Semantics of Soteriological Terms*, SNTS.MS 5 (Cambridge: University Press, 1967), esp. pp. 58–62, 73f.

93. Some less-reliable manuscripts render the expression "by his blood" after the word *apolytrōsis* (redemption). We are obviously dealing with an insertion from Eph 1:7 into the original text. For an explanation of the resultant sense, see M. Barth, AB 34, pp. 300ff.

94. Codex Vaticanus (fourth century) transmits here also the aorist form. It can hardly be original, but is rather a later correction to accommodate the tense to the time frame used in 1:12 + 13.

95. E. Käsemann, among others, sees a reference to baptism in vv 12–14. For that, see Comment II.1.

beneficial and healing presence of God which brings with it forgiveness of sins. In Isa 40:2, Jerusalem is comforted that "its servitude has ended, its iniquity has been forgiven," and in Isa 44:22 we are told, "I have blotted out your transgressions like a cloud and your sins like the mist. Return to me, because I redeem you!" Viewed from these perspectives, the proclamation of the fulfillment of the hopes of Israel, of the dawn of the kingdom of the Messiah, is unthinkable without the expression of the forgiveness of sins.[96]

The discussion concerns *sins* in the plural.[97] Sin is not dealt with here in the specific sense of a force over mankind, and so the concept is also not used synonymously with the expressions in 1:13 "dominion of darkness." Individual sins that arouse the anger of God are implied (cf. Col 3:5).[98]

3. The Hymn (1:15[12]–20)

15a	He is the image of God, who is not seen.
b	First-born over all creation
16a	For in Him all things were created,
b	in the heavens and upon earth
c	what is seen, and what is not seen
d	be they thrones or dominions
e	be they principalities or powers
f	all things were created through Him and to Him.

* * *

17a	And it is He who reigns over all things,
b	and all things exist in Him.
18a	And it is He who is the head—
b	of the body: of the church.

* * *

c	He is ruler
d	first-born, raised from the dead,

---

96. Compare E. Lohmeyer (pp. 52f.), who sees the basis for this statement in v 14b in the need for visible proof on the part of the Jewish person of faith, who had the urgent prayer for forgiveness of sins on his lips. He is said to have had a double focus in his doubting questions: the eschatological day, and the day of reconciliation, but he had been warned about too much trust in the latter. For Paul, the eschatological day had already arrived.

97. Compare in the uncontested Pauline Epistles, esp. Rom 4:7 (citation from Ps 32:1f.; 7:5; 1 Cor 15:3, 17; 2 Cor 5:19; Gal 1:4; 1 Thess 2:16.

98. See Notes to 2:13.

e	so that among all things He should be the first;
19	For it was the will of God to let in Him dwell all the fullness,
20a	and to reconcile through Him with Him all things
20b	by creating peace through His blood of the cross,
20c	through Him, be it that, which is on earth, be it that, which is in the heavens.

NOTES

Vv 15–20 form a hymnic piece, which is introduced in 1:12–14. It can be subdivided into two main stanzas (1:15 + 16; 1:18c–20) and a middle stanza (1:17 + 18a + b). In Comment II.1, the questions of hymnic character, demarcation, division, unity and symmetry, as well as those of origin of the Colossian Hymn, are discussed in more detail.

The hymnic glorification in 1:15(12)–20 is the high point of Col. It celebrates in song the Jewish Messiah as creator and reconciler of the universe, who has now acceded to his reign not only over Israel, but over all of creation. These thoughts form the basis for the principal affirmations of Col. The fact that the Jewish Messiah is king of all of creation means that the non-Jews (and therefore also the Colossians) have been transferred into his kingdom and are thus given a portion of the inheritance of the Jews (1:12–14). Paul's universal mission charge is grounded in this, as well as his service to the Colossians (1:24–29). Because the Messiah is lord over all things, the religious viewpoints and prescriptions that are cited in chap. 2 can be refuted as "empty deception"; the orientation toward the glorified Messiah who is celebrated in 1:15–20 determines also the ethical appeals in chaps. 3 + 4 (cf. especially 3:15).

15 *He is the image of God, who is not seen. First-born over all creation* (literally: first-born of all creation). He is praised, into whose kingdom the Colossians have been transferred, he in whom they have redemption and forgiveness of sins, accomplished through the cross. When the "pre-existing one" is glorified in the following verses, that is done in the knowledge that he is the one who "became a human being." In reverse, the one who "became human" is referred to as the "pre-existing one."

Both titles, "image" and "first-born Son" are closely associated with each other; they are grounded and explained by the causative clause in v 16: the "image and son of God" are in a direct relationship to all of creation.

Prōtótokos (first-born) occurs in extra-biblical Greek only rarely, in contrast to its active form *prōtotókos* (bearing for the first time). In the LXX, however, the word occurs frequently (ca. 130 times). "These latter references are still older than the earliest references for extra-biblical examples of *prōtótokos.*"[1]

---

1. W. Michaelis, ThWNT VI, pp. 873, l. 22.

There, it is used in reference to humans and animals (Ex 13:2 and elsewhere). While in statements such as Ex 13:2; Num 8:16; 18:17; Deut 15:19, the components of "first" and "to bear" are inherent in the concept of "first-born," in other instances they recede almost completely (cf. for example LXX Ex 4:22; Ps 88[89]; 28; Sir 36:11). Neither the notion of procreation, nor birth, nor temporal priority is present; rather, "first-born" designates a position of preference or predominance. The concept then carries the meaning of "chosen" or "beloved." This use corresponds to the frequently used extra-biblical word *prōtogonos*, which also means "first-born" and can also designate the first one in priority.[2] Cf. Comment III.

Eikōn in common Greek terminology means "image" in different perspectives. For one, in the sense of a true pictorial representation, it means a painting, a statue, a mirror image, or a representation impressed upon a coin.[3] *Eikōn* also carries the meaning not of a figurative representation, in which we are dealing with the exterior form of a person or thing, but rather with the "depiction" of its being or essence. Thus we can translate the word as "manifestation," "embodiment," or "representation." However, more can be intended by *eikōn* than only a medium which brings the essence of a person or thing into cognizance. In fact, the concept incorporates a "radiance, a visible revelation of the being with substantial participation *(metochē)* of the object."[4] We can find this concept of "image" in the Platonic cosmology, for example, in which the cosmos is described as the visible image of an intelligible god.[5] We could recognize a remote parallel to Col 1:15 here, in which it is not the cosmos, but rather Christ who is the image. The proclamation would be that Christ reveals the invisible God and that he himself has a part in his being.[6] This explanation, however, does not suffice for the statement in Col 1:15. Christ is not called an "image" because he reveals God or has a part in his being; rather, he bears this title as the "first-born over all of creation" (cf. Comments III and IV). This indicates that *eikōn* does not primarily express his relationship to God but rather to all of creation. Cf. Comment IV.

Aoratos is usually translated as "invisible." But the verbal adjective in the biblical Greek not only designates a possibility or impossibility, but is also used in a factual and pragmatic sense: the *agnostos theos* in Acts 17:23 is the

---

2. See ibid., p. 872.

3. See the references in BauerLex and LSLex. In the NT, compare Matt 22:20 par; Rev 13:14f.; 14:9, 11; and others.—*eikōn* is used in transmission as a connection to this meaning, in the sense of "imaginative conception" (comp. Plato, Ti. 29b) or "parable" (comp. Plato, R. VI 487 E).

4. H. M. Kleinknecht, ThWNT II, pp. 386 l. 31.

5. Plato, Ti. 92 C.

6. H. M. Kleinknecht, ThWNT II, pp. 386f.; comp. also E. Lohse, "*Imago Dei* bei Paulus," in FS für F. Delkat zum 65. Geburtstag, *Libertas Christiana*, BEvTh 26 (München: Kaiser, 1957), pp. 122–35:126.

"unknown God," not the "unrecognizable" one; as also the *aniptoi cheires* (Matt 15:20) are the "unwashed hands," not the "unwashable" ones.[7]

It is recommendable in Col 1:15 to translate *aoratos* in this pragmatic sense.[8] This corresponds to the OT usage because there is no Hebrew equivalent of *aoratos* with the meaning of "invisible." According to the proclamation of the OT, God is not invi*sible*[9]; it is simply not within the capacity of human beings to see Yahweh. And without his protection, sight of Yahweh is feared to result in the imminent death of the human who had dared to see him.[10] We find this same anxiety in the rabbinic literature; where the inability of man to see God is compared to his inability to look at the sun, for example.[11] It is unlikely that Paul fostered different notions and cannot be demonstrated. In 1 Cor 13:12, he speaks of a "time" when we will no longer look as though through a mirror, but rather "from face to face." Obviously, he does not presuppose an "invisible God." He also speaks of an "eschatological" vision of God at the end of time, although only in a few places.[12]

The attribute *pasēs ktiseōs* is added to the designation of "first-born son." In the Greek, *ktisis* means in one sense "the act of accomplishing or creating,"[13] in another the result of this action, that which was "created." It is used predominantly in this latter, passive sense in the LXX, although both for the sum of all creation (cf. Jude 16:14), as also for the individual acts of creation (cf. Tob 8:5). This passive use also prevails in the NT.[14] The burden rests either upon mankind (cf. Mark 16:15; Col 1:23) or upon all of creation, including uninhabited nature (cf. Rom 1:25; 8:19–22). A specific application of *ktisis*

---

7. Compare also *klētos*, "called" (Rom 1:1 and others); *agapētos*, "beloved" (Rom 11:28 and others); etc.

8. Comp. John 1:18; "No one has ever seen God." Comp. also 1 John 4:12, 20.

9. Ex 3:6; 24:9–11; Isa 6:5; com. Judg 6:22f.; 13:22; and others.—Comp. esp. R. Bultmann, "*Theon oudeis eoraken popote* (John 1:18)," in *Exegetica, Aufsätze zur Erforschung des Nts*, ed. E. Dinkler (Tübingen: Mohr, 1967), pp. 174–97 [first in: ZNW 29 (1930) 169–93].

10. Ex 33:18ff.; comp. Gen 16:13; 32:30f.; Ex 19:21, 24; Lev 16:2; Num 4:20; Judg 6:22f.; 13:22.

11. In a declaration by R. Jehoshua b. Chananja (about 90 c.e.), St.-B. III, pp. 31f.

12. 1 John 3:2; Heb 12:14; Rev 22:4; comp. Matt 5:8.

13. *ktisis* is used for "creation of the world" (comp. Josephus, Bell 6, 437), for "founding of cities" and also for installing an authority or magistracy (see the references in LSLex and BauerLex). LSLex also cites a single reference, in which *ktisis* simply means "doing, activity."

14. For the meaning of creation as a whole, comp. Heb 9:11, Rev 3:14. For the meaning of "creature," "created being," comp., among others, Rom 8:39; Heb 4:13.—The active meaning of "the act of creation" occurs in the NT only in Rom 1:20. (In Mark 10:6; 13:19; 2 Pet 3:4, we are probably dealing with the passive usage.)—In 1 Pet 2:13, *ktisis* means "authority." Comp. for this the corresponding active meaning cited in fn. 13, which does not occur in the NT, however.

occurs in Gal 6:15 and 2 Cor 5:17, in which the reference is to the "new creation or creature."[15]

In Col 1:15, *ktisis* is used in the passive sense and means that which has been created. Because the article in front of *ktisis* has been left out in the Greek, the "correct" translation of the attribute *pasēs ktiseōs* is "every creature." Since, however, we have the addition of *ta panta* (all things) in the next verse, which substantiates the declaration in 1:15, we would recommend the translation "all creation." This can be justified from Eph 2:21, where the undefined expression *pasa oikodomē* (the whole construction) is used without a difference in meaning, in place of a defined one.

16 *For in Him . . . were created . . . through Him and to Him.* V 16 is purposely joined to the previous verse, which justifies the declaration that the glorified one is the "image of God."

The prepositional word play "in-through-to" in the cosmological context is similar to the formulaic style of stoic doxologies.[16] An often-cited example is a gloria from the "Self-Contemplations" (IV, 23) of the philosopher Marcus Aurelius (Roman emperor from 161 to 180 C.E.), in which the peaceful harmony of nature is praised, "Oh nature, from (ek) you (are) all things, in (en) you (are) all things, for (eis) you (are) all things." Similar expressions, which permit speculation as to their common origin, can be found in different variations and are not limited to the philosophy of the Stoics. We do find differences, especially in choice of prepositions.[17] Seneca describes their meaning (Ep 65, 8; referring to Plato) when he recites and explains "out of," "from," "in," "to," "because"; still his elucidations help us little in analyzing Col 1:16. Thus, he determines the pattern or model by "in," and the likeness by "to" (Lat. *ad*; Gr. *eis*), or the product that the artist forms by replicating the model.[18] In Philo we find a similar catalog (Cher 125): God is called the origin, so that

15. F. Zeilinger, ESpg, p. 188, foremost among other exegetes, interpreted *ktisis* as "new creation." For this word usage in the apocryphal, pseudoepigraphic, and rabbinic literature, as well as in the writings of Qumran, comp. esp. H. W. Kuhn, *Enderwartung*, op. cit., pp. 75–77. When *ktisis* is used in this sense in the NT, the active adjective *kainē* (new) is also always used (2 Cor 5:17; Gal 6:15). Since the context for translating "new creation" is not necessarily requisite, and since the original meaning "creation" in the hymn makes sense and is, in addition, explainable in view of the OT background (comp. Comment II.3), then this usage is preferred.

16. See esp. E. Norden: *Agnostos Theos. Untersuchungen zur Formengeschichte religiöser Rede* (Leipzig: Teubner, 1913), pp. 240–50, who allots an entire chapter to this so-called "Stoic 'Allmachtsformel.'"

17. References in E. Norden, op. cit., pp. 240–50; Dibelius-Greeven (p. 13f.); J. M. Robinson, "A Formal Analysis of Colossians," 1:15–20, JBL 76 (1957) 270–87: 276, fn. 11; R. M. Grant, "Causation and 'the Ancient World View,'" JBL 83 (1964) 34–40:35.

18. While Seneca uses "from" *(ex)* for the material, out of which something is produced, Paul uses it to designate the creator (comp. Rom 11:36; 1 Cor 8:6).

something can develop; this is brought to expression by *hypo* (from); as in Seneca, the substance from which something develops is designated by *ex* (from); by *dia* and the genitive ("through") is expressed the tool namely the "logos," and by *dia* and the accusative the reason for which something came into being. The few instances of agreement between these statements and Col 1:16 probably rest only in the fact that both contain the idea of the "mediatorship of creation."[19]

In the verse under consideration, this "stoic formula" is employed very freely. By utilizing three different prepositions, the author has not aligned three different statements, but has rather explained "in" by means of "through" and "to," which is indicated by the stylistic form of an inclusio. The preceding phrase (v 16a) is thus repeated in v 16f., although not exactly, but rather with interpretative differences.

1. The expression "in him" is dissected by "through him," into an instrumental[20] component of meaning, and by the words "to him" into a final component. While the instrumental use also occurs in Jewish wisdom literature (Wis 9:1), the corresponding usage of *eis* (to . . .) is absent there.[21] A Hebrew equivalent of this preposition *(le)* does occur in rabbinic declarations and might facilitate clarification of its use in Col 1:16. In testimonies, though they date only from the third century, David, Moses, or even the Messiah is understood as the purpose and aim of creation when it is explained that everything was created *for* the cited person respectively. However, the statements in Col 1:16 exceed such assertions, as the second interpretative instance in Line f of v 16 clearly demonstrates.

2. In place of the aorist form *ektisthē* (it has been created) in v 16a, the perfect *ektistai* was selected in the last line of v 16. Both times, the so-called *passivum divinum* is used which omits the name of God.[22] This Jewish peculiarity also presupposes the OT idea of creation as background to the declarations of 1:16, which conceptualizes the creation not mythically, not as a "timeless revelation which occurs in the course of nature," but rather as a historic work of Yahweh which is part of the story of God with his people.[23] The aorist thus describes this unique occurrence at and as the beginning of history.

---

19. If we want to interpret "in him" from Philo, then there are primarily two possibilities: (1) The idea of logos as formative image and seal of the cosmos is the basic idea here, and "in him" is used instrumentally in this sense (Leg All III, 96; H. Hegermann, *Schöpfungsmittler*, op. cit., p. 96). (2) The idea is that logos is a "band of the all" which encompasses this (comp. Fug 112; Rer Div Her 23), and "in him" has local meaning (comp. E. Schweizer, p. 60).

20. Compare BDR 219, 1.

21. Comp. J. B. Lightfoot (p. 220); E. Lohse (p. 91, fn. 8); E. Lohmeyer (p. 61); among others.

22. Comp. BDR 130, 1.

23. Comp. esp. G. von Rad, Theol.d.AT I, pp. 140–44, esp. p. 143.

The perfect *ektistai* does not change anything in this concept, but does not permit this unique creative act of God to be concluded in the far-distant past; rather it allows it to continue, and thus it includes the work of the Messiah who has become man. He and his work become a part of, and the real purpose for, the act of the creation by God.[24]

all things. *Ta panta* (all things) in v 16 serves as a synonym of "all creation" in v 15. As such, it gains special significance, while it is also used in a general sense in Paul.[25] This use corresponds to a peculiarity in the Hebrew Bible which has no expression for "universe," "cosmos," etc., and which thus designates the entire creation by Hebrew *kol*,[26] which in turn might be rendered by the Greek *(to) pan* (all). In the Col Hymn, as elsewhere in the OT and NT,[27] the concept *ta panta* serves to praise the universal might of the Son, or that of God. In Col 1:15ff., God's "omnipotence" is attributed to the fact that he, as creator, is set off from all created things. This is quite opposite to the "stoic formula of omnipotence" and its related assertions that are directed at identifying the deity within the universe. In the viewpoint of Col, *everything* that is not creator is represented as having been created. But the more striking contrast to the Hellenistic statements is the idea that the omnipotence of God has been placed into the hands of one man, the Jewish Messiah, who dominates all of creation as Lord.[28] M. Barth has noted that "the connection with Israel's hope and call which was thus established had much more than an apologetic value. It was an

---

24. In Col 1:16, statements are transferred to the son, which are otherwise made by God. Thus in Rom 11:36 and in 1 Cor 8:6, it is said of God that all things are "to him"; and while in Rom 11:36, the statement, all things are "through him" is made by God, in 1 Cor 8:6, as also in Col, this is connected to Christ. The same is also true of the reawakening, resurrection, and last judgment declarations (comp. 1 Cor 4:5; 2 Cor 5:10; Phil 3:21–Rom 2:16; 8:11; 14:10; 1 Cor 6:14; 2 Cor 4:14; comp. also 1 Thess 4:14,16). We cannot draw further conclusions given the paucity of comparative material to say that, in Col 1:16, the preposition *ex* (comp. Rom 11:36; 1 Cor 8:6) was replaced by *en*, because the former is reserved for God's creative actions (comp. E. Lohse, p. 89; E. Lohmeyer, p. 56; among others). Paul was hardly concerned with such dogmatic differentiations. He wanted to determine that Christ's and God's actions were not two things which could be played against each other.

25. 1 Cor 2:15; 9:22; 2 Cor 4:15; and others.

26. Comp. Gen 1:31; Isa 44:24; 45:7; Jer 10:16; and others.—In the LXX, *panta* (all things) usually serves to translate these passages, which is used more frequently without the article than with it. Either with or without, *panta* in the NT can mean the same thing, as is made clear in 1 Cor 15:27f. and also in Heb 2:8, where *panta* is assimilated contextually from *ta panta* from OT citations.—In the NT, the Greek concepts for "world" are used, and synonymously also the OT circumscriptions (comp. Eph 1:4/10; Rom 8:19–20/Eph 3:9).

27. Comp. esp. 1 Cor 8:6; 12:6; 12:24ff.; Eph 1:11; Heb 1:3; 2:8; Rev 4:11.

28. Comp. AB 34, p. 78f. M. Barth refers to the preparation for this idea in the so-called Royal Psalms.

apt instrument to counteract pantheistic notions, to proclaim the historic manifestation of God's omnipotence in one man . . . to ridicule magic ways of perceiving and manipulating God's power, and to introduce statements on the ethical responsibility of Christians."[29]

The concept of "all things." is elaborated in the following enumeration in the Col Hymn.

in the heavens and upon the earth. In the LXX, "heaven and earth" is a combination for that which can be expressed by "cosmos" in Greek and it is used more frequently than *(ta) panta* (all things).[30] At the same time, this locution is a means of expressing the universal dominion of God, which becomes especially clear in Isa 66:1f. (cf. Matt 5:34; Acts 7:49f.), where in the LXX "all things" and "heaven and earth" are interchangeable: "thus says the Lord, '*heaven* is my throne and the *earth* is the footstool for my feet! . . . My hand has made all *these things* and all these things are mine' says the Lord." This dominion of God, thoroughly familiar from the OT, is carried out by the Son according to the declaration of the Colossian Hymn.

what is seen, and what is not seen. It is not likely that these expressions, along with v 16b, form a chiasm,[31] meaning "what is seen" and "upon the earth" (v 15), as well as "what is not seen" and "in the heavens," would correspond to each other. These impressions probably originated from Gen 1, in which heaven is the place of the heavenly bodies, and thus something visible.

The terminology may be reminiscent of the Platonic notion that the world is divided between visible and invisible areas, that is, between the realm of appearance and the realm of ideas (Phaed 79A). Even if proclaiming the Messiah as Lord of both realms of a Platonic conception of the world were to correspond to the intent of the hymn, a worldview of this nature is hardly presupposed in the Colossian Hymn. Preferable is the interpretation of the verbal adjectives *horata* and *aorata* (analogous to *aoratos* in 1:15) in their pragmatic and factual meaning, and to translate them with "what is seen" in reference to "what is not seen." The verbal adjectives do not pertain to the previous references, but they also introduce the subsequent list, which includes the powers of angels. According to OT as well as NT perceptions, it is not justifiable to characterize angels as "invisible."[32]

29. Ibid, p. 179.

30. Comp., among others, LXX Gen 1:1; Ps 120(121):2; 123(124):8; 133(134):3; Isa 37:16; 42:5; Jer 39:17; of the new creation, Isa 65:17; 6:22; in addition to heaven and earth, the "sea" is also named in a few places, such as in Ex 20:11; Ps 68(69):35; 145(146):5f.

31. Comp. E. Bammel, "Versuch Col 1:15–20," ZNW 52 (1961) 88–95:89, 95.

32. The reference is only to angelic phenomena, which are described, for example, in Gen 18:2; Josh 5:13; Judg 6:11ff.; 13:3ff.; 2 Sam 14:17, 20; 2 Kgs 19:35; and others; Matt 25:31; Luke 1:11–20, 26–38; 2:9ff.; 24:4ff.; Acts 10:30; 12:7; 27:23; 2 Thess 1:7; and others.

be they thrones or dominions, be they principalities or powers. Whether the above enumeration means powers of angels or earthly powers or both is an open question. E. Bammel has come to the conclusion that *thronos* (throne) sometimes, *exousia* (power) frequently, *archē* (principality) predominantly have angelogic significance, and *kyriotēs* (dominion) is used almost exclusively in a metaphoric sense.[33] The angelogic significance of "throne" and "power" is at the least uncertain. His attempt to turn this uncertainty into clarity and unambiguousness on the basis of stylistic observations breaks down because a chiastic construction, as E. Bammel postulates it, cannot be documented in vv 15 + 16.[34] Neither "upon the earth," "what is seen," "thrones," and "powers" necessarily correspond, nor "in the heavens," "what is not seen," "dominions," and "principalities."

All the Greek titles listed can initially be understood as *political titles,* whose bearers control and exert relationships of dominion.[35] At the same time, they also designate attributes of God, or Christ: "throne" is the image of the reigning majesty of Yahweh (cf. Ps 47:9; 93:2; Jer 17:12). Yahweh is the "Lord" (*kyrios*). Christ is designated by the title *archē* (principality) in v 18. And the *exousia* (power) is suitable to God in a very special way (cf. Luke 12:5; Acts 1:7; Rom 9:21), as well as to the Messiah (Matt 28:18).

The relationship between God/Christ and other rulers becomes clear if one considers the relationship between God and the kings of Israel. Each of the latter is commissioned to represent God's kingdom (cf. 1 Chr 29:23; 1 Kgs 22:10, 19; Ps 72); he can use the power invested in him by God justly, or he can misuse it. In the end, however, God remains the supreme Lord, as is acknowledged by Israel throughout the history of its kings. The relationship between God and the "gods" (of other nations) is understood in a very similar fashion (cf. Ps 82; 1 Cor 8:5f.).

A sociopolitical interpretation of the titles would also be possible, if *principalities of angels* were intended in the preceding passage [cf. Eph 3:10; 6:12; 1 Cor 15:24; 1 Pet 3:22(?)]. The conception of national guardian angels (as in

---

33. Ibid., p. 92.

34. E. Bammel views v 16 constructed as follows:

a	in the heavens	b	be they thrones
b	and upon the earth	a	be they dominions
b	that which is visible	a	be they principalities
a	that which is invisible	b	be they powers

35. "Throne" is used as a metaphor for the ruling powers of gods and kings in extrabiblical Greek; see, for example, Aeschylus, Eum 229; Sophocles Oed Col 425. In the OT (LXX), see, among others, 2 Sam 3:10; Isa 14:13; compare 2 Sam 7:16; Jer 13:13; 17:25; Ps 88(89):5, 30, 37. "Dominion" is rarely attested. In later times, it is a terminus for legitimate authority. "Might and power," in this connection, occurs in the NT as designation of wordly and spiritual authorities: Luke 12:11; 20:20; Titus 3:1.

Dan 10:13 + 20), who stand behind the earthly political rulers, could form the background for this idea.[36]

Any attempt to limit the scope of the titles will not do justice to the intention of the hymn in Col 1, where the first strophe emphasizes the universality of the dominion of the Messiah. This enumeration is intended to be as universal as possible, which is confirmed in the parallel statement to Col 1:16, namely Eph 1:21. There, a general statement is added to the various titles after the enumeration "and whatever title might also otherwise still be bestowed." Everything is apparently kept in mind which could appear (legitimately or illegitimately) as some kind of principality, which could possibly be a religious *Weltanschauung* with proscriptions of servile cultic attitudes and actions, founded on human teaching (Col 2:8), or a state of being "dead in sins" (Col 2:13), or racial, religious, or social groups (Col 3:11).[37] These are all structures which determine human lives and to which men are subjected, seemingly regardless of their own wishes. By circumscribing these forces with titles, the author of Col has in mind (personal) principalities of angels which influence the destiny of creatures, but are subject to God.[38] In this connection, speculation about certain hierarchies of angels is not encouraged as is demonstrated by a comparison between Eph 1:21 and Col 1:16, or by extra-canonical and extra-biblical lists of several classes of angels.[39]

M. Barth is probably quite justified in interpreting the listing of these principalities as "an outdated expression for what modern man calls the structures, laws, institutions, and constants of nature, evolution, history, society, the psyche, the mind."[40]

36. For the conceptualization of otherworldly powers which exert influence over earthly occurrences, comp. Rom 8:38f.; Eph 6:12; Col 2:15.—See G. Delling, ThWNT I, 481f.

37. We find a similar listing also in Rom 8:38f. In addition to designations which also occur in Eph 1:21 and Col 1:16, here named are: death–life, things present–things future, heights–depths, angels–every other kind of creature.

38. The idea that powers of angels as a whole are conceived of as bad or evil in themselves is improbable and cannot be attested conclusively. [Despite H. Schlier, "Mächte und Gewalten nach dem Neuen Testament," in *Besinnung auf das Neue Testament, Exegetische Aufätze und Vorträge II*, (Freiburg: Herder, 1964), pp. 146–59; for a debate regarding his viewpoint, see also M. Barth, AB 34, p. 180]. Their inclusion in redemption, which the hymn maintains, exhorts to caution in such assertions. A pessimistic worldview would be reconcilable neither with the positive statements of the hymn, nor with creation in other expositions, such as in Rom 13:1ff.

39. Compare indicated as well as cited sources of the time in J. B. Lightfoot (pp. 219f.); H. Bietenhard, *Die himmlische Welt im Urchristentum und Spätjudentum*, WUNT 2 (Tübingen: Mohr, 1951), pp. 101–42, esp. pp. 104ff.; St.-B. III, p. 583.

40. M. Barth, AB 34, pp. 170–76, esp. p. 175. Similarly also G. H. C. MacGregor, "Principalities and Powers: The Cosmic Background of Paul's Thought," NTS 1 (1954/55) 17–28.

Among many other interpreters,[41] E. Schweizer (p. 54) viewed the listing "be they thrones or . . ." as an insertion into an earlier shorter hymn, by which the author of the epistle intended to create a connection between the hymn and the concrete situation in Colossae. Even if Paul composed the hymn himself in its present form, only a forced interpretation would discover a polemic tendency in or between its lines. Two reasons speak against the assumption of "implicit" polemics: First, in the "polemic" part of Col, in chap. 2, the terms "throne" and "dominions" are not reintroduced. And second, enfolding enumerations, as those found in Col 1:16, can be explained as a typical element of the hymnic plerophoric style. They need not be seen as polemical. They also have their function in an "unpolemic" hymn.[42] Even if hymnic elements are employed polemically in other circumstances, that does not automatically demonstrate the occasion, intention, or uniformity of the Col Hymn itself.

17 *And it is He who reigns over all things* (literally: And he is before all things). Vv 17 and 18a are distinguished from the context with an emphatic "and He"[43] (cf. Comment II.1). The expression "before all things" may be interpreted as an indication of priority in time or rank; they are not mutually exclusive alternatives. When vv 15 and 16 distinguish the rank of the Messiah, the idea of preexistence is a necessary ingredient, since the text deals with the agent of creation. His temporal existence before created things thus signifies, within the context of the Colossian Hymn, his active involvement in creation, which in turn gives expression to the ranking of the Messiah above all things.

Pro (before) occurs frequently in the NT as well as in the LXX, chiefly in a temporal sense. The colloquial meaning of this preposition has been replaced in the Hellenistic Greek and in the LXX by nonliteral prepositions such as "in front of, vis-à-vis, facing"—always in a spatial sense (cf. BDR 214). The

---

41. See the overview in P. Benoit, "L'Hymne Christologique de Col 1:15–20. Jugement critique sur l'état des recherches." In FS for Morton Smith at Sixty, *Christianity, Judaism and Other Greco-Roman Cults*, ed. J. Neusner, Part I, *New Testament* (Leiden: Brill, 1975), pp. 226–63:238, or in C. Burger, "Schöpfung und Versöhnung. Studien zum liturgischen Gut im Kolosser- und Epheserbrief," WMANT 46 (neukirchen-Vluyn: Neukirchener Verlag, 1975), p. 10.

42. W. Pöhlmann, "Die hymnischen All-Prädikationen in Kol 1:15–20," ZNW 64 (1973) 53–74, points out that v 16 in this transmission corresponds to the form of the predicate as it is also otherwise rendered in Greek and Judaic hymns (esp. pp. 57ff.).—In the reference to angels, see L. R. Helyer, "Colossians 1:15–20: Pre-Pauline or Pauline?," JETS 26 (1983) 167–79; 178, argues that there is no compelling reason to explain these from the circumstances of the recipients of the letter (thus as a later addition to an adopted hymn), and refers to OT parallels such as Ps 89:6–7; 103:20–21; 148:2–5; Job 38:7; Isa 34:4.

43. W. Pöhlmann, op. cit., p. 61, fn. 33, sees also in the *kai* . . . (and . . .) a distinctive characteristic of the hymnic style. He refers to K. Deichgräber, "Hymnische Elemente in der philosophischen Prosa der Vorsokratiker," 88 (1933) 347–61:352.

temporal meaning of *pro* cannot be excluded in Col 1:17a, since *pro* is also used in contexts that suggest the idea of pre-existence.[44] In Prov 8:23–27, "before" is used in the temporal sense in a listing of works of creation *before* which wisdom was born. On the other hand, *pro* does not occur in the important expositions concerning the pre-existence of Christ in John 1 and Phil 2:6ff. Hardly ever in the NT and the LXX or in extra-biblical Greek texts does *pro* appear to point out only a rank. We might be able to demonstrate such an application in Acts 14:13, most clearly in the transmission of the Codex Bezae Cantabrigiensis.[45] Uncertainty in the attestation of this meaning makes it advisable to interpret "before" in a temporal sense as the reflection of the sublimity of Christ (cf. Ps 90, where, on the contrary, the statement of preexistence [v 2] is elucidated by examples of the sublimity and majesty of God). In the sense that *pro* in Col 1:17 is used as a means to describe the sublimity of the Messiah, the translation of the entire prepositional phrase comes closest to the sense of the Greek expression "rule over."[46] The present tense "He *is*" supports the assumption that Christ's eternal rank is emphasized here—or else a form of the past tense would have been chosen.[47]

Since the Greek text was originally rendered unaccentuated, there are two possibilities of translating the present tense of *estin* (He is): in the enclitic form, it is the copula which connects the personal pronoun "he" with "before all things"; in the substantive form, however, it has its own status with the meaning, "to exist, to be." If we consider *pro* to be a direct designation of rank, then we could best interpret *estin* as the copula. C. F. D. Moule suggests (p. 67; cf. J. B. Lightfoot, p. 222) that, in a temporal interpretation, the preposition "to exist" would be the more logical translation. However, that is not obligatory, especially when we consider the meaning of the statement of preexistence in vv 15 + 16. In any case, the Messiah's unique power, glory, and domination are praised in vv 15–17.

and all things exist in Him. In the intransitive sense of "to consist to exist," the verb *synhistēmi* is used only rarely in the cosmic context in the biblical tradition. We can only cite 2 Pet 3:5 (cf. below) as a direct parallel.[48] In Philo, however, we encounter the word more frequently and we can understand it on

---

44. 1 Cor 2:7; Eph 1:4; 2 Tim 1:9; Titus 1:2; 1 Pet 1:20.

45. Here, *pro* probably describes not the location of the temple of Zeus as situated in front of the city, but rather Zeus as protective deity of the city (comp. B. Reicke, ThWNT VI, 684).

46. The omission of the article is frequent in prepositional phrases, esp. in expressions such as *kosmos*, *gēs* (earth), *ouranos* (heaven), and others; comp. BDR 253.

47. Comp. John 1:1, "In the beginning *was* the word. . . ." This observation, however, does not exclude a temporal component in interpretation, as John 8:58 demonstrates, ". . . *before* Abraham was, I *am*."

48. In addition to the parallel cited in par. 19 in Philo (Rer Div Her, 23), see also Pseudo-Aristeus, Mund 6, 397b, "Everything exists from god and through god."

the basis of the influence of Stoicism upon his thought and diction (cf. *Die Darstellung and Kritik des Lösungsversuches* by H. Hegermann in Comment II.2). Philo argues that the world is a combined whole, and the logos (or sometimes also the "divinity" or simply "god" [cf. Rer Div Her 23]) is described as a band" surrounding the universe, "which binds together all its individual parts and holds them together, and prevents them from dissolving and separating from each other" (*Fug* 112; cf. *Rer Div Her* 23). In this connection, however, the verb *synhistēmi* is not used. Rather, we find this verb describing the organism as a mass, filled with blood, which "dissolves itself from within but is *held together* through the providence of God *(synestēke),"* (Rer Div Her 58). Accordingly, the verb is hardly a terminus technicus of the Stoic Alexandrian worldview, and its use in Col 1:17b does not assume these Stoic ideas.[49] That is also true for 2 Pet 3:5, where the verb seems to mean simply the preservation of creation through God's word, because it is used in parallel construction to *thēsaurizō* (to keep, v 7). In connection with the preposition "in," which is used in the same sense here as in v 16, Col 1:17b says that the creation is maintained "through him and to him." As a summary of vv 15 + 16, v 17 stresses the two previous verses, which proclaim that Christ is the goal of creation. V 17b contains the *entire* proclamation of v 16 and deals with the act of creation as well as with the "maintenance of creation to Christ." These two components of meaning are included by translating *synhistēmi* as "to exist," a sense which often occurs in extra-biblical texts.[50]

And it is He who is the head of the body: of the church (literally: And He is the head of the body of the church). The image of head and body was also used by Paul in 1 Cor 12, but the exclusive relationship of head to body is unfolded only in Eph and Col although 1 Cor 2:3 prepares the way to these allegedly Deutero-Pauline letters. In the LXX (and in the Hebrew Bible) the images of head and body are not juxtaposed. We do find there, next to a common expression,[51] the superior of a community referred to as its head (*kephalē*; cf. Deut 28:13; Judg 10:18), but the metaphor is not extended to the concept of head-body. The same is true of the apocryphal Jewish literature.

---

49. Rather preferable for observation are parallels in Wis 1:7 and Sir 43:26, which circumscribe the preservation of creation through God in similar imagery of coherence (of all things). Comp. also R. B. Y. Scott, "Wisdom in Creation: The ʾĀmōn of Proverbs VIII, 30," VT 10 (1960) 213–23, who translates the description for wisdom as *amon,* "a living link," "a vital bond" ("between the creator and his creation").

50. See LSLex; W. Kasch, ThWNT VII, 895f.

51. Comp. H. Schlier, ThWNT III, pp. 673f.: (1) the "uppermost, highest," that which is at the beginning or at the end; (2) the "most prominent, most convincing, most determinate"; (3) as designation of the entire human being.—In Isa 43:4, the Hebrew *nephesh* is translated into Greek *kephalē* (head). For the history of this concept, see also J. Ernst: "Pleroma und Pleroma Christi, Geschichte und Deutung eines Begriffs der paulinischen Antilegomena," BU 5 (Regensburg: Pustet 1970), pp. 154–56.

While the Gnostic original man myth does not come under consideration in this discussion (cf. Comment II.2), the concept of "Zeus" or specifically of "heaven" as the head of the universe (which is in turn conceptualized as the world *body*) can be documented in Philo and the Orphic fragments for the time before Col (and Eph) were written. But we do not find this juxtaposition of "head" and "body" in a cosmic context.[52] The documented examples do not suffice to support the technical use of the idea of body as designation for world body, which would be presupposed if "body" were used in Col 1:18a without the explanatory addition of "church." A preparatory remark or subsequent explanation would be necessary for such a cosmic application. It is unlikely that 1:18a never existed without the genitive "of the church" (cf. Comment II.1).

What does it mean according to Col that Christ is related to the church as the head of the body? Col 2:19 gives distinct answers:

1. The head protects the body from dissolution.
2. It provides for the body.
3. It grants the growth that God imparts (cf. Notes to 2:19 and Introduction, Section IX.A.3).

V 18a confesses by means of the imagery of body and head that he who fully cares for the existence and life of the church is the same Messiah who also has called the cosmos into being and who sustains it.[53]

---

52. E. Schweizer cites as unambiguous proofs: "Zur neueren Forschung am Kolosserbrief seit 1970" in *Neues Testament und Christologie im Werden*, (Göttingen: Vandenhoeck & Ruprecht, 1982), pp. 122–49:144; Philo, Som I, 144, and Orph Frag 21a. In Som I, 144ff., the soul of the human being, whose "foot" is "earthiness, sensuousness," and whose "head, on the contrary, is its equal in heavenliness: of pure spirit," is compared to the air: "The air is imagined very rightly with the image of a ladder which is supported upon the earth; thus the vapors which rise from the earth become thinner and thinner, and finally become air, so that the foot and root of the air is the earth, but its head is heaven." In Orph Frag 21a, Zeus is called "head" and "middle," "from whom all things come forth," but there is no express discussion of "(world)body."—See also E. Schweizer, ThWNT VIII, 1036, 1ff.; 1051, 36ff.; *Kol Kommentar*, p. 53, fn. 113. Besides that, we read in Philo (Quaest in Ex 2, 117), "The head of all things is the eternal logos of the eternal father, under whom lies the entire world as though it were his feet or limbs." This passage is suspected of having been edited under Christian influence. (see E. Schweizer, ThWNT VII, p. 1051, fn. 340.)

53. Comp. Eph 1:22b in the translation by M. Barth, AB 34, ". . . and appointed him, the head over all, to be head of the church." The explanation of this concept by F. Mussner, "Christus, das All und die Kirche," TThSt 5, 2d ed. (Trier: Paulinus, 1968), does not suffice from a stoic/sociological perspective. He cites an individual reference from *Curtius Rufus*, Hist 10.9.4 (pp. 155f.), "Without their head, the dispersed members scatter." This is said of the empire of Alexander the Great, which was threatening to fall apart after his death.

The difference in the use of the imagery in 1 Cor 12, especially v 21 (cf. Rom 12:3ff.), and Col 1:18; 2:19 is caused by the different themes that are treated in their respective contexts. Paul deals with the unity of the community and condemns divisions within it in 1 Cor 12. The corresponding discussion in Col does not deal with the relationship of the community members to each other, but rather with the relationship of the church to Christ. It is inappropriate to speak of a contradiction in this case. It is more reasonable to presume that Paul himself employed the same imagery in different contexts. The Pauline origin of Col need not be put into question for this reason.[54] (Cf. Comment II.1, for the grammatically surprising construction "of the body of the church.")

He is ruler, first-born, raised from the dead (literally: He is the beginning, first-born out of the dead). Both titles belong together and augment each other, as in v 15. The subsequent final sentence shows that both predicates are understood to be a designation of rank, which is defined by the explication of "first-born" in 1:15. It is unlikely that the same title is used within the hymn in a different sense.

---

54. Concerning the origin of image as it is used in Col (and Eph), we can supply only suppositions. We are hardly dealing with spontaneous creation, which would be imaginable on the part of any favorite writer (differently than in 1 Cor 12). In contrast to its derivation from gnosis, stoa, orphic, and others, see P. Benoit, "Leib, Haupt und Pleroma in den Gefangenschaftsbriefen," in *Exegese und Theologie, Ges. Aufsätze,* (Düsseldorf: Patmos, 1965), pp. 246–79 (= *Exegese et Theologie,* Paris: Cerf, 1964; = RB 63 1956 5–44), that the body-Christ idea originated from Paul's own original thinking. He derives it from a physically realistic conceptualization of sacrament and from the designation of Christ as "head" as the highest authority over angels. Paul is said to have avoided the subsequent misunderstanding of too strong a separation between Christ and the community by using the comparison of head for the community through the physiological interpretation of head *and* body. We have a similar consideration in the medical sphere, for example in Hypocrates, where "head" is understood as life giver, and thus we have an expression not only for unity, but also for differentiation between Christ and the community. Also J. Ernst, *Pleroma,* op. cit., esp. p. 159, relies on the aid of the supposedly Pauline physical-realistic conceptualization of sacrament in his explanation. In addition, he cites the Hebrew conception of the "corporate personality" (p. 157: in Adam was seen the sum of all his progeny). For this concept, see esp. H. W. Robinson: "The Hebrew Conception of Corporate Personality," BZAW 66, pp. 49–62; J. W. Rogerson: "The Hebrew Conception of Corporate Personality: A Re-Examination," JThS 21 (1970) 1–16. M. Barth, AB 34, pp. 183–99, refers (like P. Benoit) to medical parallels in Hippocrates (460–380 B.C.E.) and Galen (130–200 C.E.); however, he emphasizes also the differences to this conceptualization in Eph and Col. In his explanation, he gives preference to orphic, stoic, or Gnostic sources, but without using them as *passe partout* to all the secrets of the head-body conceptualization. "They provide a background to those elements in Paul's teaching which cannot be explained on the ground of OT and Jewish conceptions" (p. 191).

Archē in common Greek can mean primate in time as well as rank.[55] The same is true of the LXX. Very often, the word designates the temporal beginning, but it is also occasionally used in the spatial sense, for example, for the tops of the cedars of Lebanon (cf. Ezek 31:3). Often it also signifies "dominion, might," and the derivative thereof, "supreme head."[56] In Isa 9:14, the word designates the "superiors" (of the people), after *kephale* (head) was used for them in v 13. A close connection exists between the two concepts in the OT biblical Greek, because both are used for the translation of the Hebrew *rō'š* (head, beginning, etc.)[57]

In view of 1 Cor 15:20, 23, and especially Acts 26:23, passages which emphasize the temporal superiority of Christ at the resurrection as a standard element of the original prophetic proclamation regarding Christ, the decision in Col 1:18 seems necessarily to be in favor of the temporal meaning. Still, the construction "first-born" *out of* the dead" is unusual.[58] It can be explained by the fact that "to be raised, to rise, etc., from the dead" and its corresponding derivative nouns are construed prevailingly with "out of" *(ek)*. The expression "out of the dead" could be the result of this custom.[59] It appears to be without reference to rank, since "first-born over the dead" in Col 1:18 as well as in the similar locution in Rev 1:15 would be a nonsensical expression.

There is, however, an alternative to this explanation, suggested by Rev 1:5, where the expression "first-born of the dead" occurs. There, it is used in close connection with "the ruler *(archōn,* which in turn is related to *archē)* over the kings of the earth." The dependence on LXX Ps 88(89):28 (cf. Notes to 1:15) makes the temporal component of "first-born" disappear into the background, if it does not vanish entirely.

Ek (out of) is frequently used to designate origin in the NT.[60] To describe

---

55. A concept which is expressed in cosmological statements is meaningful in Greek philosophic language-usage, and it chiefly designates the "original materials" and the basic cosmic laws. In the stoa, this is used for God and for matter, neither of which are considered opposites. Philo names the four elements of which the cosmos is composed; *archai* uses this concept, but in the larger sense of "principal," and also to designate the logos, and most frequently, to designate God (citations in G. Delling, ThWNT I, 478f.).

56. LXX 1 Chr 12:33(32); 2 Ezra 19:17 (= Neh 9:17; Hos 2:2; Mic 3:1; Jer 13:21); as designation of "first-born," Gen 49:3; Deut 21:17.

57. Comp. S. Bedale, "The Meaning of *kephale* in the Pauline Epistles," JThS 5 (1954) 211–15:213.

58. The more poorly attested v 1 reads in the genitive: first-born of the dead. In Rev 1:5, the reverse is the case in that the genitive construction is better attested than the prepositional expression "first-born from the dead."

59. Since we have the unaugmented genitive construction in the substantive formulation here (Acts 17:32; compare 17:3; 23:6; 1 Cor 15:12; and others), this would explain also v 1 and the modulation in Rev 1:5.

60. Paul is descended *from* the ancestry of Israel (Phil 3:5); Jesus *from* the seed of David (Rom 1:3); in Gal 2:15, the discussion concerns sinners *from* the gentiles. In John

this, as well as lineage, we often find the substantial construction in the NT, "those out of Israel" (Rom 9:6); "those out of the law" (Rom 4:14); "those out of the faith" (Rom 3:26, etc.); "those out of circumcision" (Rom 4:12, etc.); "those out of the synagogue" (Acts 6:9); etc. "First-born out of the dead" can be interpreted as a parallel to these expressions; what is meant is He who has come out of the dead, that is, He who has risen.[61] "Out of the dead," then, is the description of a special distinguishing attribute of the "first-born," and "first-born," as in 1:15, is a designation of rank and thus a (Messianic) royal title. Compare Acts 2:27, where it is a distinguishing feature of the "Holy One of God," that he will not see decay, and Rom 1:4, where the resurrection is the "installation of the son of God into power." Because Jesus has risen, he can be confessed and glorified by the church as "first-born of all creation." The second stanza of the hymn contains convincing reasons for declarations of the first.[62]

so that among all things He should be the First (literally: so that in all things he become the first). *Ta Panta*, (all things), here used in the dative and without article, is here as elsewhere in the hymn an expression for "cosmos," "creation," etc. (cf. Notes to 1:15 + 16). Other translations or interpretations of *panta*, as for example "without exception of any kind of relationship" (H. A. W. Meyer, p. 256), "in every conceivable relationship" (E. Haupt, p. 36), "in all pieces" (P. Ewald, p. 332), "not in the universe only but in the church also" (J. B. Lightfoot, p. 224, cf. p. 222) may well all be included but look, if taken individually, somewhat arbitrary. A reference to the pre-existence of Christ before the creation does not fit into the context of the second stanza of the hymn; therefore, *proteuōn* (to be the first) is to be interpreted here as a designation of rank. The verb is used only here in the NT: a hapax legomenon. In the LXX (Esth 5:11; 2 Macc 6:18; 13:15; cf. Zech 4:7) as also in secular Greek, the verb is never used in a temporal sense.

The preposition *en* (in) designates the forum, before which, as well as the size, in comparison with which Christ became the first.[63] No fundamental

---

4:22, it says that "salvation is *from* the Jews," etc. Frequently, the adjunct verb *einai* (to be) is absent in these expressions; compare John 10:32; 2 Cor 5:1; and others.

61. In the examples cited, the designation of origin is almost completely obscured by that of membership or affiliation. It is obvious that this cannot be the case in "from the dead," but the sense is rather that origin denies membership here.—A parallel for this interpretation can perhaps be found in Luke 16:30. In the parable of the rich man and the poor man Lazarus, the reference is to "someone from the dead" who is to go to the family members of the rich man, and here we are dealing with someone risen from the dead, according to Luke 16:31.

62. This interpretation is equally fitting for v 1, as also for Rev 1:5, since origin is not only "from," but can also be expressed in the genitive. Compare fn. 59.

63. *Prōteuein en* with the meaning of "to be the first one among" cannot be attested—as far as we can determine. Nonetheless, we should compare Matt 20:27, "Whoever would be the first one among you" (*en hymin einai prōtos*).

declaration is made about the superiority of Christ over creation; it is intended to demonstrate his dominion over creation. The final sentence "so that . . . He should be the first" is related to "from the dead": the proof of his precedence before creation has occurred in his resurrection. Christ is the Lord of creation, because the universe was created through him. He has *begun* this reign in his death on the cross. (This will be explained in the exegesis of 1:20, 22 and 2:14.) *God* has proclaimed and certified this ascendancy before the forum of creation in the resurrection of Jesus from the dead. Thus, because the crucified one was raised up by God, Paul and the church can glorify and proclaim him in the manner of the Colossian Hymn. [64]

19 *For it was the will of God to let in Him dwell all the fullness* (literally: For it pleased God). The verse is problematic in grammatical as well as lexical considerations. Above all, it is unclear what is to be considered as the subject of *eudokeō* (to please, to select). There are three possibilities.

1. "God" could be the subject, without being explicitly named. [65] But we can counter that "God" has not been named explicitly as subject since v 13. In addition, we cannot document an "accusative with infinitive" (ACI)[66] dependent on *eudokeō* in the NT, in which *eudokeō* has a subject other than the infinitive. [67]

2. Similarly, it is grammatically possible that "the Son" is the subject of the main verb. [68] In that case, the personal pronouns "in him, through him, for him," are to be understood reflexively, which in principle is possible without conjectures. The Greek text was originally rendered unaccentuated and a reflexive form can be indicated only by an accent. [69]

3. "All the fullness" could also be the subject. [70] In that case, it would be disturbing that the neuter *pan to plēroma* (all the fullness) in v 20 is joined with

---

64. There is no tension in this interpretation between v 1, according to which Christ is already placed above creation, and v 2, according to which Christ is yet to be placed above creation. It is therefore also not necessary to delete the final sentence, as do, among others, E. Schweizer, E. Bammel, H. J. Gabathuler, J. Lähnemann, and W. Pöhlmann.

65. See, among others, J. Calvin (p. 87); J. A. Bengel (p. 784); J. B. Lightfoot (p. 224); H. A. W. Meyer (p. 258); J. Ernst, *Pleroma*, op. cit., p. 87 (for the Hymn reconstructed by him).

66. This is a frequent grammatic construction in Greek, in which the accusative object of the first verb is simultaneously the subject of a second verb which is in the infinitive.

67. Compare C. Burger, *Creation*, op. cit., pp. 19f.

68. Tertullian, Marc V, 19.

69. It is not entirely certain whether this also applies to the genitive form (see BDR 64). We could have attestations in Matt 6:34 v 1 or 2 Cor 3:5 v 1.—Compare C. F. D. Moule (170).

70. Among others, T. K. Abbott (p. 219); G. Münderlein: "Die Erwählung durch das Pleroma," NTS 8 (1961/62) 264–76; E. Lohse (p. 98); E. Schweizer, (pp. 65f.).

a masculine participle. However, that could be a construction in accordance with its meaning, a *constructio ad sensum.*

Since God is finally presumed to be the agent through the Son in stanza 1, which is indicated by the *passivum divinum* in v 16, we can hardly suppose that stanza 2 would emphasize that Christ should be the sole agent. The second of the three possibilities is therefore too tenuous to be upheld. If we supply "God" as the subject, because he is presumed by the verb *eudokeō* and can remain unnamed,[71] a stylistic parallel would exist between stanzas 1 and 2. In both stanzas, the substantiation phrase introduced by *hoti* (because) would imply "God" as the agent through Christ, by means of the special verb form, without naming him explicitly.

But such a stylistic supposition alone cannot be sufficient to make a determination between alternatives 1 and 3. The possibility that "all the fullness" is subject and is surrogate for God[72] must be considered. In this connection, the examination by G. Münderlein of Col 1:19 (cf. fn. 70) is significant. It is his opinion that the construction of v 19 suggests that "all the fullness" is the subject of *eudokeō.* He points to the connectedness of *en autō* (in him) and *eudokeō*, since *eudokein en* is a special phrase for the designation of divine selection.[73] Münderlein explains two problematic facts by pointing to possible Semitisms: (1) the words "in him" can modify the main verb (to select) as well as the dependent infinitive (to dwell),[74] and (2) unequivocal parallels for the word connection *en autō eudokein (to select him)* with a subsequent infinitive are lacking in Greek literature. But if 1:19 is an expression concerning the selection of Christ, and subsequently even an allusion to his baptism, Münderlein's argument can hardly be refuted, that "all the fullness" must be understood as a "personal designation of God," or specifically as a "remarkable designation of the Holy Ghost."

The difficulties of this solution lie in the fact that the Greek construction here can be explained as a Semitism, but the presence of the latter is demonstrated by Münderlein. By contrast, *eudokeō* is used without an object (cf. LXX Ps 76 [77]:8; 1 Chr 29:23; Sir 45:19; Rom 15:27): a usage of *eudokeō* is possible when God is presupposed as subject, and the Greek active infinitive with various subjects for *eudokeō* and the infinitive is also an attested variant (2 Macc 14:35).

---

71. The usage of this verb is possible, based on the substantive in the stated absolute manner; compare Luke 2:14; Phil 2:13.

72. This expression *as subject* can hardly mean something different, since, according to v 20, there it is also the subject of "reconcile."

73. In addition to OT parallels such as LXX Ps 34:4 (LXX Ps 43:4 is probably meant), G. Münderlein, "Erwählung," op. cit., pp. 266f., cites especially the "heavenly voice" at the baptism and denial of Jesus, *"en hō/en soi* (him/you) *eudokēsa* (have I chosen)" (Matt 3:17; 17:5; Mark 1:11; Luke 3:22).

74. Such a construction is otherwise only attested whenever two verbs are constructed the same way and refer to the same thing.

Therefore, it seems more reasonable to take God as the subject and to connect *en* (in) with *katoikeō* (to dwell)[75] than to accept G. Münderlein's thesis. However, his theory about the phrase "all the fullness" as deriving from the OT background remains unaffected by the above argument. To understand this phrase in this sense as subject in 1:19, it is as probable to assume that "God" is the presupposed but not expressed subject. But then we should translate: "For it was the will of all the fullness to dwell in him."

Katoikeō (to dwell), when used in reference to God, has a special echo from the LXX: it is used to describe the presence of God upon the earth, in the temple, on Mt. Zion, etc.[76] We have especially close parallels to Col 1:19 in Ps 67 [68]:17; Targ Ps 68:17; and Targ 1 Kgs 8:27,[77] where the declaration about the dwelling place of God, specifically about his *shekinah*, is tied in with the use of the verb *eudokeō*.

What is true of the verb "to dwell" is also true of the concepts of "fullness" (*plēroō*, to fill; *plērēs*, full; *pimplēmi*, to fill) as OT descriptions of the presence of God.[78] Even though *plērōma* (fullness) in this sense occurs neither in the LXX, nor in the NT,[79] it still seems more appropriate to interpret the substantive from the LXX because of the contextual OT terminology and conceptualization rather than from Gnostic or stoic expressions.[80]

Plērōma (fullness) in this context, then, much as in Col 2:9, is the fullness

---

75. The placement of words does not counter this, as G. Münderlein, "Erwählung," op. cit. p. 266, argues, since, especially in poetic texts, this is determined by emphasis and rhythm.

76. Esp. LXX 2 Sam 7:6; 1 Kgs 8:27; 2 Chr 6:18; Ps 21(22):4; 67(68):17; 131(132):14; 134(135):21; Isa 8:18. The LXX uses *(kata)skēnoun* in the same context, esp. for translation of Heb *skn*. The basis for this is probably the vocal similarity between the Hebrew verb and the Greek stem *sken-*.

77. "It was well-pleasing to the word of Jahweh to let his shekina dwell on it (Sinai)" (Targ Ps 68:17). "Who can imagine that it was actually well-pleasing to Jahweh to let his shekina dwell among men?" (Targ 1 Kgs 8:27).

78. Esp. LXX Ex 40:34f.; Num 14:21; 1 Kgs 8:10f.; 2 Chr 7:1f.; Isa 6:1, 3; Jer 23:24; Ezek 43:5; 44:4; Ps 32(33):5; 118(119):64; Sir 42:16; Wis 1:7.

79. In the profane language usage, *plēroma* has (1) active meaning: that, which fills; and (2) passive meaning: that, which is filled. Connected with 1 are variants in meaning: "quantity, full measure, totality, sum" and others. In addition, *plēroma* can also mean (3) the activity of filling. In the LXX, the substantive is used only in the active sense to designate that which fills the seas, the earth, the land, or also a hand: 1 Chr 16:32; Ps 95(96):11—Ps 23(24):1; 49(50):12; 88(89):12—Jer 8:16; 29(47):2; Ezek 12:19; 19:7; 30:12—Eccl 4:6.—Only in HL 5:12, there is possibly a differing meaning: "His eyes are like doves at the fullness of water. . . ."—A similar usage of the concept as it is used in Eph and Col to designate the fullness of God, Christ, and the church cannot be found in the NT [compare Mark 2:21; 6:43; 8:20; Rom 11:12, 25; 13:10; 15:29; 1 Cor 10:26; Gal 4:4, with the exception in John 1:16 (see fn. 81)].

80. A Gnostic derivative, as it was suggested, for example, by E. Käsemann,

of God (in the active sense), filling Jesus, and is thus the depiction of the presence of God in his Son and thereby in the world. In contrast to statements which speak of God "dwelling" on Mt. Sinai, Mt. Zion, etc., or more specifically of the fact that God or his magnificence "fills" these places, Col 1:19 proclaims that the presence of God exists now, and now only in Christ (therefore *pan to plērōma; all* the fullness).[81]

20 *and to reconcile through Him* (literally: to reconcile to him). The basic meaning of *allassō* is to "make different." The verb occurs six times in the NT

Taufliturgie, op. cit., p. 139, and H. Schlier, *Der Brief an die Epheser. Ein Kommentar* (Düsseldorf: Patmos 1957), pp. 96–99, already miscarries in the sense that this concept cannot be proven in a technical sense before the 2d century. Beside that, it is not frequent in the Gnostic literature and it has special meaning only in the system of the Valentinians. The dualistic idea that is connected there with *plēroma* is, however, distant from that in the Colossian Hymn. Compare for that M. Barth, AB 34, pp. 201f.; P. Benoit, "Leib," op. cit., Pp. 270f.; N. Kehl, "Der Christushymnus im Kolosserbrief: Eine motivgeschichtliche Untersuchung zu Kol 1:12–20," SBM 1 (Stuttgart: Katholisches Bibelwerk, 1967), p. 111; J. Ernst, *Pleroma*, op. cit., p. 14; P. D. Overfield, "A Study in Content and Context," NTS 25 (1979) 384–96; G. Delling, ThWNT VI, 299f. The interpretation that this expression is used to circumscribe the universe as "filled by God" which derives from a stoic background (esp. P. Benoit, "Leib," op. cit., Pp. 272ff.; H. Langkammer: "Die Einwohnung der 'absoluten Seinsfülle' in Christus. Bemerkungen zu Kol 1:19," BZ.NF 12 1968 258–63) pays too little heed to the OT Jewish character of 1:19. J. Ernst, *Pleroma*, op. cit., points out, "dass sich zwar die allgemeine Vorstellung eines erfüllten Raumes bei den Stoikern findet, dass aber an keiner Stelle dieser Gedanke mit dem Wort *pleroma* wiedergegeben wird." He therefore warns of putting too much emphasis on stoic assumptions in determining this concept (p. 11)—In Philo, *plēroma* does not occur in a cosmic sense. Compare also N. Kehl, *Christushymnus*, op. cit., pp. 112ff.—The assumption that we are dealing with an expression concerning "false teachers in Colossae" adopted by Paul (i.e., *Dibelius-Greeven* 18) can hardly be substantiated.

81. Compare Heb 1:1f.; Matt 12:6, "But I say unto you, something greater than the temple is here." In observing the OT Jewish derivatices, we should regard esp. John 1:14–16: the glory which is visible in the incarnate logos is derived from the father and is designated as "full *(plērēs)* of grace and truth." In v 16, it says, "From his *fullness* we have received grace upon grace." Here, fullness is a concept which describes God's grace and truth and which is to be perceived in the life of the incarnate son.—It is uncertain whether we have a conscious circumscription for the shekina of God or for the Holy Ghost here. G. Münderlein, "Erwählung," op. cit. p. 272, observed this, and A. J. Bandstra, "Pleroma as Pneuma in Colossians," in FS for R. Schippers, *Ad Interim*, (Kampen, Kok, 1975), pp. 96–102, attempted to document this interpretation and to clarify the usage of the concept of false teaching in place of "ghost," which is attacked in Col. It is worth noting the theses by G. Münderlein and A. J. Bandstra as alternatives to E. Schweizer (*Christus und Geist*, op. cit.) which contest any kind of meaning of Holy Ghost in Col.

with the meaning of "to change," "to transform," or "to exchange."[82] The composite *kat-allassō* occurs as often, but, only in Paul's letters and always in the sense of "to reconcile."[83] With one exception,[84] it describes an act or relationship between God and mankind/creation. In these, God is always presented as the agent: he reconciles men/creation to himself, or mankind is reconciled to him, never the reverse.

The double composite *apo-kat-allassō* occurs only in Eph 2:16 and Col 1:20, 22. It has not yet been documented in non-Christian literature. The contexts of the Eph and Col passages do not compel to give special meaning to the prefix *apo*. Some critics have done so and have interpreted the verb to mean "reversion" to an original state."[85] Others have attributed an emphatic function to *apo* and have rendered the verb in the sense "to fully reconcile."[86] However, it seems more probable that no difference in meaning underlies the two verb forms, *kat-allassō* and *apo-kat-allassō*, but rather that the true explanation of the unusual form lies in the Hellenistic propensity for replacing simpler forms with composites (e.g., the modern American preference for a longer form like "interpretative" for the simpler "interpretive" with no change in meaning).[87]

As in Rom 5:10 and in 2 Cor 5:18–20, so in Col also, God is the agent of reconciliation, and here as well as there, the act of reconciliation is referred to in the aorist tense. It is conceptualized as something that God has carried out before the conversion of man.[88] In Col, as opposed to the corresponding references in Rom and 2 Cor, the reference is to reconciliation with Christ rather than with God. Attempts to harmonize this difference, and to interpret *eis auton* (to him) by changing the accentuation to the reflexive and referencing it back to "God,"[89] are hardly convincing. It seems arbitrary to translate *eis*

82. Acts 6:14; Rom 1:23; 1 Cor 15:51f.; Gal 4:20; Heb 1:12.

83. Rom 5:10; 1 Cor 7:11; 2 Cor 5:18–20.—In the LXX, only Jer 31:39 ("to change oneself") and 2 Macc 1:5; 7:33; 8:29.

84. 1 Cor 7:11: concerning the reconciliation of the divorced wife to her former husband.

85. Compare, for example, J. B. Lightfoot (p. 126); H. v. Soden (p. 29); P. Ewald (pp. 336f.); E. Lohse (p. 101).

86. Compare, for example, T. K. Abbott (p. 220) (who, however, also considers the first possibility); F. F. Bruce (74, fn. 164); John Chrysostom, PG 62, pp. 320f.

87. See BDR 116; compare the Notes to *epiginōskō* (to recognize) in 1:6.

88. In 2 Cor 5:18–20, the answer is given "to allow to be reconciled" for people whose reconciliation has already occurred, which is thus perceived as belonging to the occurrence of reconciliation, however without the idea that something can be changed in the reconciliation which has already occurred from God. Compare Rom 5:10: those who were reconciled when they were yet enemies have now "seized" reconciliation, meaning that they have become such who *glorify* God.

89. Compare J. A. Bengel (p. 785); J. B. Lightfoot (p. 126); H. A. W. Meyer (p. 267); F. F. Bruce (p. 74).

auton differently than in stanza 1, especially since the parallel use of "in-through-to" is a markedly characteristic formula (cf. Comment II.1).

Eis auton (to him) here does not indicate the completion of "imminent" reconciliation, and thus does not indicate a futuristic occurrence. The expression, which is construed in the aorist tense, "all things are reconciled *with him,*" is to be interpreted as a parallel construction to the expression in stanza 1, "all things were created in him" (cf. Notes there), and its special significance derives from there. It signifies, as the use of the aorist shows, the fulfillment of the corresponding expression in 1:16. Accordingly, reconciliation has its foundation in the creation and is now arriving at its completion in the dominion of the Son over all things (cf. Comment II.3).

. . . *all things . . . in the heavens (and) on earth* (cf. Notes to 1:16). The following questions[90] are misleading and superfluous: does the text speak the reconciliation between heavenly things and those on the earth, but not with God? Or its intention to describe the reconciliation of the earth to God and heavenly things with earthly things? Or is the reconciliation of angelic and human spheres with God in mind, which raise the problem to what extent angels must be reconciled? These questions presume a concept of reconciliation which is not applicable to the hymn, and they ignore the close connection between stanzas 1 and 2, as well as the concept of the unity of creation and redemption represented in the hymn (cf. Comment II.3).

by creating peace (literally: creating peace). The participle "creating peace" is an explanatory expression for the work of reconciliation, so that it seems best to translate it with a model (by . . .).

eirēnopoieō (creating peace) occurs in the NT only in Col 1:20 and in the LXX at Prov 10:10, but there it is not used relative to God. In other later Greek translations of the OT, it is used to render the Hebr. *ʿaśāh shālōm* (to create peace),[91] for which we find *eirēnēn poiein* (to create peace) in the LXX. Both Greek expressions probably have the same meaning.

The praise of reconciliation is continued in Col 1:21–22 and is amplified to include former strangers and enemies. Analogously, in Rom 5:10, reconciliation is mentioned in a context which speaks of enmity, and in 2 Cor 5:18, the context deals with sin. Likewise, in Eph 2:16ff.—there, *eirēnēn poiein* is the wording—the concern is with conquering enmity, especially between Jews and gentiles, even though an echo of Isa 57:19 regarding "peace" seems to have larger implications.

---

90. Compare the listing by E. Haupt (pp. 40ff.).—For the reconciliation of angels, see, among others, B. N. Wambacq, "Per eum reconciliare . . . quae in caelis sunt (Col 1:20)," RB 55 (1948) 35–42; E. Percy, PKE, pp. 95ff.; ibid.: "Zu den Problemen des Kolosser- und Epheser-briefes," SNW 43 (1950/51) 178–94: 185f.

91. Compare the translation of Isa 27:5 through Aquila (ca. 130 C.E.), Symmachus (ca. 170 C.E.), and Theodotion (end of second century).

In contrast to all the contexts of Rom 5:10; 2 Cor 5:18; and Eph 2:16ff.; the hymn in Col mentions neither discord nor hostility among the different parts of creation or between God's creatures and God, nor concern about the depravity of creation. It is possible that the estrangement and fall of creation away from God, including the result of mutual enmity among the creatures are presupposed as a matter of course[92]; references cited above might support this assumption. But there is an alternative interpretation that measures up better to the immediate affirmations of the hymn.

The predication of "establishing peace" may well be connected in two ways with the hymn as a whole: (1) it is derived from the central theme of the hymn, namely the sole domination of God over creation through his Son; and (2) it proclaims the presence of the end of time by presupposing that the purpose of creation has already been attained.

There are OT parallels for both connections, in which the key word "peace" plays a significant role and which are therefore important for the understanding of Col 1:20:

Concerning 1. In the LXX, "peace" is used mainly as the translation of the Hebr shālōms, and does not serve primarily or even nominally as a counterpoint to "war" or "conflict." The meaning of this word extends much farther (cf. Notes to 1:2). A poignant example is the blessing formula for the dwelling place of the people Israel in the promised land (Lev 26:6ff.): "peace" is a gift from Yahweh which protects the life of the people by the providence of its God. This is characterized by the fact that the people will know no care, want, fear, or defeat but will rather experience fruitfulness of the people and the earth, as well as confirmation of the covenant with God, and they will know his *dwelling place among his people* (cf. Col 1:19).

The political and social circumstances make it comprehensible that "peace" carried a special significance in the prophetic canon.[93] Yahweh is proclaimed by Deut-Isa as the deliverer of his people, the sole and single powerful God (whom even the mighty Cyrus must obey), and "peace" is perceived as the act of salvation in contrast to "calamity" (LXX Isa 45:5ff.); ". . . I am the Lord, and there is no other! I *create peace* and *create calamity*. I, the Lord, am he, who creates all these things."

Concerning 2. Although the word "peace" does not occur often in this connection, the expectation of peace still plays an important part in eschatological contexts. The statements in Isa 9:5 and Mic 5:1–4 are of special significance for the elucidation of Col 1:20. Both references point to the awaited

---

92. Compare, among others, E. Lohse (p. 101); P. T. O'Brien (p. 53).
93. Compare esp. Jer 14:19; 15:5; 23:17; 36(29):7; 37:5; 40(33):6, 9, etc; Isa 14:30; 26:3,12; 32:17f.; 48:18; 53:5; 54:10; 57:19; 66:12; etc.

Davidic king, in whom the promise about the throne of David in 2 Sam 7:14ff. will be fulfilled (cf. Notes to 1:13), and they characterize his kingdom as a "kingdom of peace." Especially in Micah 5 it is clear that the concept of peace elaborated in 1 is intended.

The Col Hymn has close parallels to the abovementioned proclamations which acknowledge "creating peace" as a characteristic of the universal power of God, and which expect peace as an eschatologically messianic gift. This urges consideration of *eirēnopoiein* in this wider sense in Col 1:20 as well,[94] because the gift of *this kind* of peace cannot be received in discord and enmity. The treatment of these themes cannot be separated from the coming and revelation of the Messiah who alone makes, brings, and is peace (cf. Eph 2:14; Luke 2:14). But concepts such as "enmity, discord, sin," etc., do not suffice as criteria of and keys to the essence of peace.

through his blood of the cross (literally: through the blood of his cross). The Messiah brought the gift of eschatological peace with his "blood of the cross." This expression is unusual and unique in the NT. It most closely resembles expressions like "blood of the covenant" (Heb 9:20; 10:29) or "blood of sprinkling" (Heb 12:24).[95] The central significance of blood in the OT sacrificial cult leads us to ask whether we have a reference to OT sacrificial imagery in Col 1:20, and whether the designation "blood of the cross" was formulated in association with similar utterances from the cultic language. Should the death of Jesus on the cross be perceived as a sacrifice?

In favor of such an interpretation would be the fact that mention is made of blood even though crucifixion itself is not an especially bloody form of execution. On the other hand, "blood" is universally used to denote a violent death whether blood actually flowed or not (cf. Matt 27:25; Luke 11:50f.; Rev 6:10; 19:2, etc.). In addition, the death of Jesus is mentioned again in 1:22 in the expression "in the body of his flesh through death." There, as elsewhere in Col, the imagery of sacrifice is less prominent and significant than the emphasis on the incarnation and death of Jesus on the cross. Both themes are explicitly and repeatedly treated in the course of the epistle (cf. 2:9; 2:14, 20; 3:3). The idea that the theme of sacrifice should be totally

94. E. Schweizer (p. 68) interprets the declaration of peace differently on the basis, in his opinion, of the feeling common in the Hellenistic world that mankind was living in a fractured world in which the human being was like a prisoner who was in a battle with the nature within himself. Compare also, ibid.: "Das hellenistische Weltbild als Produkt der Weltangst," in *Neotestamentica, deutsche und englische Aufsätze 1951–1963* (Zürich-Stuttgart: Zwingli Verlag), 1963, pp. 15–27.
95. Compare E. Lohmeyer (p. 67), who refers to rabbinic parallels. See St.-B. I, p. 991.

excluded for this reason cannot be demonstrated,[96] but it does not rise to the forefront in Col.[97]

4. The Conclusion of the Prayer of Thanksgiving and Intercession (1:21–23)

21 You also, who formerly were excluded and enemies, with a mind that evokes evil works, 22 but now he has reconciled (you) in the flesh of his body through the death, in order to place you holy, blameless and irreproachable before him. 23 If only you (continue to) remain faithful, firmly grounded, and do not let yourselves be moved away from the hope, that you know through the gospel that you have heard (and) that is proclaimed in all of creation under heaven. I, Paul, have become its servant.

NOTES

V 21 relates the reconciliation proclamation of the hymn to the recipients of the epistle. The proclamation is formally differentiated from the preceding hymnic piece through direct address. In addition, vv 21 + 22 are tied together through the comparison schema characterized by "formerly" and "now," which occurs frequently in the NT.[1] Thus, it is not justifiable to treat v 21 as an appendix of the hymn in order to solve syntactic difficulties in vv 21 + 22. By its terminology and its substance, v 23 resumes the beginning of the prayer of thanksgiving and intercession (1:3ff.).[2] This indicates that v 23 forms the conclusion of that prayer.[3]

---

96. M. Barth in AB 34, pp. 291–305, attempted to answer the question as to how a sacrifice can create peace. He refers to Isa 53, where the suffering servant of God is the only one who really pays with his life for his intercession. His death is understood to be an offering for sin (Isa 53:10). "Thus Second Isaiah understands sacrifice as an intercessory prayer" (p. 301). "The method of unification, pacification, and reconciliation is in this case the prayer of Jesus Christ . . . but a prayer, a cry magnified by the voice of 'his blood' (Heb 12:24). Peace was made at the price of the Messiah who prayed himself to death" (pp. 301f.).

97. The use of the concept "blood of the cross" can probably be explained by the fact that, in Col 1:20, we have a contraction of elements from Eph 1:10 and Eph 2:11–18. Compare M. Barth, "Introduction."

1. Compare the investigation of P. Tachau, " 'Einst' und 'Jetzt' im Neuen Testament. Beobachtungen zu einem urchristlichen Predigtschema in der neutestamentlichen Briefliteratur und zu seiner Vorgeschichte," FRLANT 105 (Göttingen: Vandenhoeck & Ruprecht, 1972).

2. Compare F. Zeilinger, ESpg, p. 43; note the recurrence of the following key words: "faithfulness" (pistis); "hope" (elpis); "the gospel which you have heard"; "on the entire world/under all of creation."

3. See fn. 96 above.

21 *You also.* Stylistically, here the beginning proclamation is differentiated from vv 15–20, but their contents are closely connected. If "all things" are reconciled, then the Colossians are *also.*

who formerly. Pote (formerly) does not mean the time before the gospel reached Colossae, nor the span of time before the Colossians' baptism or conversion, but rather it means the time when the gentile Colossians had no part in the inheritance of Israel (cf. 1:12). The difference between Israel and the gentiles in vv 12–14 is directly resumed again.

were excluded and enemies (literally: were estranged). The perfect participle *ontas apēllotriōmenous,* if translated literally, describes a condition which is caused by becoming estranged. It is not stated, however, whether there was a time before the "exclusion" in which there was a time, a history, or a consciousness of an earlier inclusion of the gentiles in God's covenant. Only in God's love, in his beloved Son, were they already included in this love from eternity.[4] The condition which was changed through the reconciliation is such that the verb is best translated by "being excluded."[5] According to 1:13, the exclusion from a life under the promised dominion of the Messiah is equivalent to "enmity" in Pauline conception, because being excluded means not to know the will of God. Consequently, the "justice of the law" cannot be fulfilled. This becomes apparent in a "carnal mind," which is "enmity with God" (cf. Rom 8:7f.).[6]

with a mind that evokes evil works (literally: in evil works). *Dianoia* does not mean only intellectual capacities. In the LXX, the word is most frequently used to translate the Hebrew *lēb* (heart), a concept that incorporates "all the dimensions of human existence."[7] In the NT, this concept becomes especially clear through the parallel use of *dianoia* and *kardia* (heart) in Hebr 8:10 and 10:16 in quoting Jer 31:33. We encounter the substantion only here and in Eph 2:3, 4:18 in the Pauline corpus. The additive "in evil works" underscores the idea that the orientation is not only a spiritual affair, but is also associated with the corresponding actions.[8] They are enumerated in lists, such as Rom 1:29ff. or Gal 5:20f.

---

4. This is implied in the statement of the Messiah being Lord over the entire cosmos since creation. Compare further Rom 4 and Gal 3–4:7, as well as Eph 2:11–19; 1:4.

5. We have the same situation in Eph 2:12; 4:18, the only other passages in the NT where the verb *apallotrioō* also occurs.

6. Rom 2:14ff. does not contradict this argument, because there, we are probably dealing with "gentile Christians." Compare the usage of the concept *ethnē* (gentiles/peoples) in Rom 1:13.

7. Compare F. Stolz, THAT I, 861–67:863.—Comp. esp. Ex 36:1; Lev 19:17; Deut 29:17; Josh 14:8(A); Isa 35:4; and others.

8. As also, for example, the summons in Phil 2:5 to be in a *frame of mind* like Christ, which refers not only to a spiritual orientation, but rather also to the actions of Christ.

The dative *dianoia* does not indicate the reason for the enmity, because this reason lies in the idea of being excluded from God's covenant mentioned above. The dative specifies the kind of enmity (dativus modi). For the syntax, cf. Notes on the next verse.

22 but now he has reconciled (you). Three different variants in which the verb *apokatallassō* (to reconcile) has been transmitted all point out the contextual and syntactic problems of vv 21 and 22.[9]

1. Codex Vaticanus and Papyrus 46 choose the second-person aorist passive, "you have been reconciled." In this construction, v 21 becomes an anacoluthon, since the participial forms and personal pronouns are construed in the accusative, and not in the nominative which the principal verb in v 22 would require. While such a syntactic form is not unusual, we have a further problem in the fact that the infinitive *active* "to place" in v 22b follows immediately. In order to circumvent this grammatical difficulty, the proclamation "but now . . . through the death" could be interpreted parenthetically. V 21 and the infinitive in v 22 could then be presumed to be dependent on the infinitive "to reconcile" in v 20.[10] Such a parenthetical insert, however, would appear to be a curious doubling of the reconciliation proclamation. Other suggestions for the resolution of the syntactic puzzle exist, however without being convincing.[11]

2. Other texts, among them Codex Claramontanus (sixth century), also render the verb in the aorist passive form of the verb "reconcile," but with the participle in contrast to 1 above. Then there are two possibilities which were already mentioned in 1 above, along with the difficulties above.

3. Well-attested is the aorist active form, "he has reconciled." If v 21 is interpreted as the description of the reconciling action characterized in v 22, then most of the grammatical and syntactical difficulties disappear. Indeed, a certain break between vv 21 and 22 continues to exist: the particle *de* is to be interpreted adversatively rather than copulatively because of the contrast indicated by *pote* (previously, v 21) and *nyni* (now, v 22). Then the supposedly harsh anakoluthon disappears almost completely and the "break" fulfills an emphatic function. In this case, the text is to be translated "you *also*, who were previously . . . *but* now he has reconciled you. . . ."

Even if all the grammatical difficulties were resolved by this rendering, it would still hardly be regarded as the original reading, because the presence of

---

9. A fourth and less-attested variant reads the corresponding perfect form rather than the aorist active (see variant 3). We are probably there dealing with a correction which attempts to be fair or attuned to the *nyni* (now).

10. A dependency of *eudokēsen* (v 19) is even more improbable. At the reading of the epistle, the listener would hardly be able to make this connection.

11. For example, J. C. O'Neil, "The Source of the Christology in Colossians," NTS 26 (1980) 87–100:94 reads the infinitive in v 22b as an imperative, and he interprets the anacoluth by assuming the beginning of a "vision report" here in v 21, and he thus supplements "I saw . . ." at the beginning of the verse.

the variant readings could not be explained. It is, however, possible and probable that the dogmatic problems arising from reading no. 3 would be circumvented in variant nos. 1 and 2; thus it was thought that it was more important to avoid dogmatic difficulties than to resolve the possible grammatic and stylistic irregularities or peculiarities. Because if we use the active verb form in v 22, analogously to the proclamation in the hymn, it becomes possible to supply God as subject, so that the reference would be to the "corporal body of God" in the following sequence. The active verb form in v 22 might well take up the subject of the hymn, which is God. Consequently in v 22, reference would be to God's "flesh of his body" (but see below).

In v 22, as also in the hymn, the discussion concerns reconciliation which has already been achieved on the cross. *Nyni* (now) designates time, not as it began with baptism or conversion, but rather the beginning of the period of time which commenced with the accession of the Messiah and the beginning of his reign. The "all-encompassing" objectivity of this work is emphasized.[12]

In the hymn, God was perceived as the final agent of creation and reconciliation which was indicated by using the divine passive, or by the verb *eudokeō*. Such explicit indications are absent in v 22, so that the author most probably refers to Christ here, who is praised in the preceding hymn. Such a change of subject does not signify a contradiction to the proclamations in the hymn in regard to the reconciliation (cf. fn. 81 to 1:9–14; fn. 24 to 1:15–20).

in the flesh of his body through the death. The reference to the death of Jesus, which is perhaps reminiscent of the sacrifice terminology in v 20, is not taken up again. The central focus is elsewhere, though, without excluding all sacrificial ideas. The existing phrasing probably contains a Hebraism for describing the manner of human existence.[13] Unlike Col 2:11, "flesh" does not mean the "sinful flesh," but has a positive sense. The "location" of the divine action (cf. 1:19), the Messiah Jesus who has become human, is essential in these proclamations and this becomes the starting point for the argument in chap. 2.

The addition, "through the death"[14] takes up an element of the second stanza of the hymn and will also be the starting point of subsequent elucidations.

---

12. Comp. E. Lohmeyer (p. 70).—Compare the related statement in 2 Cor 5:17, in which the determination "new creation" refers to the death of everyone, something which occurred at the crucifixion.

13. Compare 1 Enoch 102:5; Sir 23:17; 1 QpHab IX:2. In Col 2:11, this expression is also used to describe death.—See also J. Jeremias, "Beobachtungen zu neutestamentlichen Stellen an Hand des neugefundenen griechischen Henoch-Textes," ZNW 38 (1939) 115–24:132f.

14. A few text transmissions, among them important texts, such as Codex Sinaiticus, Codex Alexandrinus, and Minuscule 2464, add a personal pronoun after "death." This is probably a subsequent correction, since a deletion of this in the original text is unlikely. F. Zeilinger's interpretation (ESpg, p. 141), that what is meant in the reading without the personal pronoun is the *death in baptism* of believers, can be established neither

Christ's death is a key for comprehending the Messiah, as well as for the essence and form of Paul's apostolate (cf. 1:24ff.).

in order to place you holy, blameless and irreproachable before him. Just as in Eph 5:27, so also here, Christ is not only the agent but also the target of this action: he puts those who have been reconciled *before himself.* The verb *parhistēmi* (to present, to show, to offer, to place at one's disposal) is used in the NT as background for various perceptions. For example, it is used in the *cultic* linguistic sense in Luke 2:22–23 (the first-born male is dedicated to God), in Luke 17:14 (the presentation before the priests for the decision about cleanness and uncleanness), or in Rom 12:1 (regarding sacrifice); in a *judicial* sense in Acts 27:24 or Rom 14:10 (presentation before the judge); 2 Cor 4:14 (1 Cor 8:8[?]) is probably reminiscent of the *court tradition* (standing before the throne of the ruler), and in 2 Cor 11:2 and Eph 5:27 of *Jewish wedding customs.*[15] It is difficult to decide whether such a specific background forms the basis of Col 1:22 (+ 28), since the context hardly offers unequivocal reference points. Least likely is a reference to sacrifice or to wedding customs. While *amōmos* (blameless) describes the corporal perfection of the sacrificial animal as well as that of the priest in the cultic language of the LXX,[16] and *hagios* (holy) is also of significance in the sacrificial terminology,[17] *anenklētos* (irreproachable) does not belong in this context. The two other concepts, likewise, may also be used in noncultic contexts.[18]

In Col 1:22, the adjectives "holy, blameless and irreproachable" are placed in noticeable contrast to the designation of the "previous status" of the Colossians (1:21). "Holy" can be understood in contrast to "excluded" (cf. Notes to 1:2); the designations "blameless" and "irreproachable" show that the sentiment toward God is not hostile, and so in the absence of bad works there is no occasion for divine reproach or recrimination. Man is striving for a "state" which has not existed since the reconciliation, even if the mind and works of those who are reconciled do not give evidence of that fact. To place the reconciled ones "holy, blameless and irreproachable" before Christ does not mean that the reconciliation which has already been achieved on the cross must be revealed or that its truth or validity must be proven by a certain state of mind or works. All this will be the work of Christ, when the reconciled ones are revealed with him in glory at the parousia (cf. Notes to 3:1–4). But reconciliation has the aim of allowing those reconciled to *live* as such, not far from Christ, but

---

from the undisputed Pauline letters nor from the other statements in Col (see also Comment II.1 and Comment II to 2:6–23).

15. Compare M. Barth, AB 34A, pp. 678ff.

16. For example, Ex 29:1; Lev 1:3; 4:3; 5:15; 1 Macc 4:42 (of the priest).

17. For example Ex 30:10; Lev 2:3,10; 6:18, 22; 7:1; 7:6.

18. For "holy," see Notes to 1:2; for *amōmos* (without fault), compare 2 Sam 22:31; Ps 17(18):31; 18(19):8; in the NT, esp. Eph 5:27.

rather "before him," in his presence, namely in his service, under his care and for his pleasure.[19]

23 *If only you (continue to) remain faithful* (literally: retain the faith). The conditional sentence introduced with *ei ge* expresses a justified assumption. The cited condition can only refer to the proclamation in 1:22b, in view of what was said about reconciliation, "in order to put you before himself. . . ." Although reconciliation has occurred independently of any kind of action on the part of those concerned, they are still not objects without will. It is the will of him who reconciled them that they should live in this state of reconciliation *willingly*.[20] For the Colossians, that means remaining faithful in the manner in which Paul has lauded them (cf. 1:4).

The dative *pistei* (faith, faithfulness; cf. Notes to 1:4) is not a dative of instrument but rather a dative of location, a construction we also encounter elsewhere in Paul (cf. Rom 6:1; 11:22f.; Phil 1:24; cf. 1 Tim 4:16).

firmly grounded, and do not let yourselves be moved away from the hope, that you know through the gospel, that you have heard (literally: grounded and firm . . . hope of the gospel). Two participles (founded, not moved away) and one adjective (firm) enfold the concept of remaining in faithfulness.[21] Once again, this time indirectly, the delightful situation in Colossae is praised. The image of a building erected on a firm foundation is in the background.[22] The literal meaning of *themelioō* is "to be supplied with a foundation, to lay a foundation."[23] In classical Greek, *hedraios* means primarily "established, residing," and secondarily "steadfast, unshakable." In the NT, the word occurs only three times, in the LXX not at all.[24] In this verse, it describes the stability of a

---

19. Compare Gen 6:11; 48:15; 24:40; 1 Sam 26:20; 1 Kgs 17:1; 2 Chr 27:6; Ps 56:14; Jonah 1:3, 10; and others, where "before his face" is used in the Heb. In the LXX, however, we do not find *katenōpion* in translation. In the NT, comp. Rom 14:22; 1 Cor 1:29; 2 Cor 4:2; 7:12; Eph 1:4; and others.

20. Compare fn. 88 to 1:20.

21. It is improbable that *te pistei* (in faithfulness) belongs with *tethemeliōmenoi* (founded). Then we would expect the preposition *en/epi*. Only with LXX 3 Kgdms (Eng 1 Kgs) 7:47 could the cited alternative possibly be justified.

22. Compare esp. Matt 7:24ff.; 16:17ff.; 1 Cor 3:10f. Also in Qumran, we encounter this comparison. See O. Betz, "Felsenmann und Felsengemeinde. Eine Parallele zu Matt 16:17–19 in den Qumranpsalmen," SNW 48 (1957) 49–77.

23. Thus in Matt 7:25, compare Luke 6:48f. For the transmitted meaning, see esp. 1 Cor 3:10f.—In the LXX, the verb occurs frequently, with God as subject, in order to describe his works in the creation of the world: Job 38:4; Ps 23(24):2; 77(78):69; 88(89)12; 101(102):26; 103(104):5; and others. Behind that, we have the concept of the earth, set up on pillars as its sure foundation over the waters. We have a possible allusion of the creative work of God in the passive in Col 1:23.

24. 1 Cor 7:37; 15:58; Col 1:23. It is used in the Greek translation of Symmachus (170 C.E.). See E. Stauffer, ThWNT II, pp. 360f.

building with a good foundation.[25] The participle form *mē metakinoumenos* (unmoving) fits the image. For *elpis* (hope) cf. Comment III to 1:3–8. The genitive "hope *of the gospel*" means, according to the statements in 1:5, the hope that was made known by the gospel.

that is proclaimed in all of creation under heaven. The passive form *kerychthentos* (which is proclaimed) is reminiscent of the affirmation made in 1:3–8; there, the gospel was described in its personified form. Only secondarily, reference is made to the proclaimers (cf. Notes to 1:5f.). The aorist here designates the present state.[26]

While the place of the proclamation in 1:6 is indicated by "in the whole world" (cf. Notes to 1:6), here *en pasē ktisei* (in all of creation) is chosen as a synonymous expression, probably in association with 1:15. The missing article can be explained by recourse to v 15 (cf. Notes there), so that we can hardly speak of a proclamation to "any kind of creature" here, whether they are angels, animals, plants, mountains, or other creatures.[27]

The addition "under heaven" is an old Hebrew expression and describes the global significance or outcome of an action or an occurrence (cf. Gen 1:9; 6:17; 7:19; Exod 17:14; Deut 2:25; 4:19; 9:14; 25:19; etc.). This formula tries to describe the term *kosmos*, for which the Hebrew has no equivalent (cf. Notes 1:15).

I, Paul, have become its servant (literally: whose). The designation "servant of the gospel" occurs only here and in Eph 3:7.[28] Paul names himself, but only after the general discussion of the proclamation (cf. Notes to 1:5); the spreading of the gospel is not dependent on Paul's person. He places himself on a par with Epaphras (cf. 1:7) and Tychikus (cf. 4:7), by also calling himself "servant"—and not "apostle." The emphatic "I" in this verse emphasizes this equalization. Col 1:23 does not mention anything concerning a special consciousness of office or of a "basic function of the apostolic office for the church"[29] (cf. Notes to 1:1 and 1:7).

---

25. The use of the adjective in this connection is probable from the use of the corresponding substantive (compare 1 Tim 3:15).

26. See BDR 333, 2.

27. In this case, *en* would stand as a dative marker for the normal dative (compare the reference in BauerLex, pp. 517f.). However, because of the obvious reference to Col 1:3–8 in v 23, this interpretation is improbable.

28. "Servant" is elsewhere used with the greatest variety of attributes: of God (2 Cor 6:4), of Christ (2 Cor 11:23); of circumcision (i.e., of Jews) (Rom 15:8); of the community (Rom 16:1); of the New Covenant (2 Cor 3:6); of justification (2 Cor 11:15); of sin (Gal 2:17).

29. Compare E. Lohse (pp. 110f.), in connection with E. Käsemann, *Taufliturgie*, op. cit., esp. p. 144.

COMMENTS I–V TO COL 1:9–23

I. Light and Darkness

"Light" in Col designates the "realm" in which the Messiah exercises his redeeming royal dominion (cf. Notes to "beloved Son" in 1:13). Darkness refers to the opposite, the absence of this dominion. Here, darkness does not formally refer to gentiles in order to characterize their earlier lives, prior to their conversion to God, unlike, for example, the references in Luke 2:32; Acts 26:18; Eph 5:8; cf. 4:17. For Paul includes himself, and thus the Jews, as formerly belonging to this realm. Even more, through the differentiation of "you (pl)" and "us" in vv 12–13, and through the discussion of the Colossian *(gentile)* Christians having a part in the inheritance, it becomes clear that redemption occurred primarily to free the Jews, even though the redemption of the formerly pagan Colossians is the focal point in the further course of this epistle.

The contrast between light and darkness is much emphasized in the Qumran manuscripts, and we suspect their influence especially in Col 1:12 + 13.[1] But we also cannot underestimate the evidence concerning light and darkness in the OT in examining this passage. Thus we also find this connection of "light for Israel"—"light for the gentiles" in Deut-Isa. In the first as well as the second part of the book of Isaiah, these two contrasting concepts, light and darkness, are used to describe the will, the power, and the work of God to save his people in the face of weakness, fear, need, and woe (cf. Isa 8:20–9:2; 42:16; 58:8–10; etc.).[2] In Isa 51, salvation is proclaimed for Israel, and the people are urged to pay attention, because God will make his justice as a light for the people (51:4). If Col 1:12 + 13 makes reference to the Exodus, then Ps 44:3 is an especially significant parallel, because there, "light" is connected with the description of the winning of the land for Israel: not by the sword has the land been won, but by the justice of God, by his arm, and by the *light* of his countenance.

For the gentiles, "darkness" is of radically new significance. While Israel

---

1. For dualism in Qumran, compare, among others, 1 QS I:*9f.*; II:7, 16; XI:7ff.; 1 QM I:1, 7ff., 11; XII:5; XIII:2; 1 QH XI:11; 1 Qpatr 4; 1 QSb V:21. See also fn. 5. Qumran influence is also suspected in related passages in 2 Cor 6:14–17:1 and in Acts 26:18; see esp. J. Gnilka, "II Cor 6:14–7:1 im Lichte der Qumranschriften und der 12-Patriarchen-Testamente," in *Neutestamentliche Aufsätze für J. Schmid*, ed. J. Blinzler, O. Kuss, and F. Mussner (Regensburg, Pustet, 1963), pp. 86–99. In all similarities and with all the influences, we need to observe that the statements about light and darkness in Col 1:12f. have "inclusive" character, and not, as in Qumran, "exclusive" character. The idea that gentiles belong to the chosen people is far distant from the Qumran community. Only in CD XIV:4–6 are proselytes (?) mentioned.

2. Just as in Matt 4:16 (cited from Isa 8:23–9:1); Luke 1:79.

hoped for the light, and was permitted to hope (cf. Eph 2:12), this was not true for the gentiles. Both, however, were subject to the power of darkness. It required the intercession of the one who is lord over "all things" (1:15–20), in order to free them from this power. He alone simultaneously reveals the limitation of darkness. The difference of the biblical "dualism" of light and darkness with respect to a worldview, such as we find in the Gnostic systems, becomes recognizable here. Although both realms are radically exclusive even in the Bible,[3] they do not simply stand side by side. The Messiah is also the victor over the powers of darkness and he subordinates them to his rulership. But dualism of the sort in which two realms could exist independently, each with its own power, is impossible. Impossible also is a pessimistic worldview by setting heaven against earth and spiritual against material things.[4]

Related to this "ontic" meaning of "light" and "darkness" and the relationship each to the other, there is also an ethical meaning. To be in the realm of darkness means not passively to be delivered up to darkness; rather, such a life reveals itself in enmity to the dominion of the Messiah, which becomes evident in evil deeds (cf. 1:21; 2:11; 3:5ff.). Just as much is being placed into the dominion of light inextricably tied to an ethical appeal (cf. 1:23; 2:6; 3:1ff.). It is not a destiny which, having once occurred, frees the individual from responsibility; rather, it is appended to an action that is to correspond to a new status.[5]

---

3. Just as, for example, life and death are mutually exclusive, comp. Col 2:13.—In 2 Cor 6:14, it says, "or what does light have in common with darkness?"

4. Also in OT statements, God is Lord over light *and* darkness: he creates light and limits the darkness (Gen 1:3–5). In Isa 45:7, it says that God forms the light and creates darkness. Light and darkness are mutually exclusive—as also in NT statements (see fn. 3), and thus the contrast life-death is arranged according to both concepts (compare Job 33:28, 30).—"Light" determines the appearance of God in the OT (comp. Isa 60:1ff.; in NT 1 Tim 6:16; 1 John 1:7; Rev 21:24), but it does not determine his essence (comp. M. Saebo, THAT I, p. 90). However, in the NT, God is also identified with "light" (comp. 1 John 1:5; in Eph 5:14, Christ is presented as the light personified. See for that also John 1:4, 5, 7, 9; 3:19 . . . 8:12; 9:15; and others).

5. "Dualism" is understood in a similar way in the Qumran writings: compare 1 QS I:9ff.; II:16; III:3, 13, 19–25; 1 QM I:8–11; XV:9; and others. K. G. Kuhn, "Der Epheserbrief im Lichte der Qumrantexte," NTS 7 (1960/61) 334–46:340, emphasizes that in the Qumrantexts (as also in Eph), " 'Licht—Finsternis' *nicht* die physische *Natur* von Himmelswelt einerseits und Kosmos andererseits und damit auch die Doppelnatur des Menschen als Leib—Materie einerseits und als Licht—Seele andererseits bezeichnen, wie durchweg in der Gnosis, sondern dass 'Licht' und 'Finsternis' die zwei konträren Existenzweisen *der Menschen* meinen." For rabbinic statements, compare St.-B. I, pp. 236–40. For Paul, comp. Rom 2:19; 13:12; 2 Cor 4:6; 6:14; 11:14; 1 Thess 5:5; (1 Tim 6:16). For Eph 5:18ff. see M. Barth, AB 34A, pp. 598–603.

II. The Hymn

1. Structure, Literary Problems, and Authorship

Vv 15–20 can be subdivided into two sections: 15–18b and 18c–20. Each of these parts begins with the words "he is"); *(hos estin)*.[6] Beyond that, they show further structural and terminological parallels: the previously mentioned "he is" both times introduces a predicate which is then followed by the second one, "first-born son." Next follows a *causative phrase* (even if not immediately in both sections), which begins with "for in him" *(hoti en autō)*, and in which the subject both times is "God," although he is not expressly named (cf. Notes to 1:16 + 19). The declarations introduced by this causative sentence are articulated by the so-called stoic omnipotence formula (cf. Notes to 1:16), expressed by well-known elements of "in him *(en autō)* . . . through him *(di autou)* . . . for him *(eis auton)*." In addition, we find in both sections a special stylistic pattern, an "inclusio": one affirmation is included here, a slightly varied repetition of the previous sentence. In v 16, this is the case for the enumerated listing of *ta panta* (all things), in v 20 for the participial expression which explains the verb *apokatallassō* (to reconcile) in more detail, "creating peace through the blood of his cross."[7] Included in this parallelism of vv 15–18b // 18c–20 is also an enumeration, whose parts are connected by the conjunctions "whether . . . whether." In spite of the similarity in the sequence, nevertheless there is an important difference in the positioning (either in the included portion of inclusio, or in the including portion).

The following schema forms the basis of both sections and separates vv 15–20 as a unity from the surrounding context

    he is . . . ,
    first-born . . . ,
        for in him . . .

---

6. The parallelism of these sections has already been observed by J. A. Bengel (784) and by F. E. D. Schleiermacher, "Uber Kolosser 1:15–20," ThStKr 5 (1832) 497–537 (Sek.). E. Norden, *Agnostos Theos*, op. cit., pp. 250–54, documented this on the basis of its arrangement in the Colossian Hymn; G. Harder, *Paulus und das Gebet* (Gütersloh: Mohn, 1936), pp. 46–51, furthered the argument; E. Lohmeyer did not heed this in his commentary. He sees a hymn in vv 13–20 which consists of 2 seven-line verses (15–16e; 18–20), of which a three-line pattern serves as transition. In a differing opinion, E. Käsemann, *Taufliturgie*, op. cit., then received wide acknowledgment in his subdivision of the two strophes 1:15–18a and 18b–20.

7. Since the inclusive statement in v 20 is much shorter in relation to that in v 16, only "through him" is repeated from the previous sentence, and not the entire declaration, as in v 16. If the formal structure of v 16 were copied exactly, then the imposed parallelism would have caused a stylistically distorted declaration.

through him . . .
to him . . . ,

and the stylistic form of the inclusio. Not included in this parallel structure are vv 17 and 18b. They have their own parallel construction and differentiate themselves with respect to form through doubling and emphasis, "And it is he . . ." *(kai autos estin . . .)*, which occurs twice. C. Maurer justly compared this locution to the Johannine "I am" sayings and he contained this assertion with the observation that, here, the article is inserted in front of the predicate ("head") as it is in the corresponding expression in the Johannine Gospel (and in contrast to the other predicates in Col 1:15–20).[8] Vv 17 + 18a are probably to be interpreted as an intermediate or middle stanza, in agreement with Maurer.[9] Details concerning their meaning and function will be discussed later.

Aside from the cited parallelisms, the text 1:15–20 exhibits the typical distinguishing features of the (oriental) hymnic style, which E. Norden has carefully elaborated.[10] Characteristic is the participial as well as relative sentence style of the several predicates, and the description of the praised person in the third person. Therefore vv 15–20 must be designated as a hymnic piece and the two cited parallel sections are properly called stanzas. However, to some extent parallelism and symmetry are not carried through, but are obfuscated: the first Christ predicate of the first stanza, *eikōn* (image), does not correspond to the first one of the second stanza, *archē* (beginning), although the second predicate, "first-born," is the same. The attribute in v 15 "of the God who is not seen" has no corresponding parallel in the second stanza, as is true also of the reverse, where we do not find a counterpoint to the final phrase in stanza two (v 16) in stanza one. Even the long enumeration in v 16 has no parallel in vv 18c–20. We have already pointed to the differences of the two enumerations. In general, v 20 is of a much more complex construction than the grammatically clearer assertions in vv 15 and 16.

---

8. C. Maurer, "Die Begründung der Herrschaft Christi über die Mächte nach Kolosser 1:15–20," WuD.NF 4 (1955) 79–93:84.

9. C. Maurer, ibid., interprets vv 17 + 18a as parenthetical, which holds both parallel pieces v 15 + 16; 18b–20 together, "wobei Vers 17 nach rückwärts und Vers 18a nach vorwärts greift" (p. 83). He views this parenthetical device functionally to emphasize, "dass Er als das Haupt der Kirche *identisch* ist mit dem des Kosmos," which is such a determinative statement for the hymn that vv 15–20 are a torso without the insertion of a strophe (p. 84).—H. J. Gabathuler, "Jesus Christus, Haupt der Kirche-Haupt der Welt, AthANT 45 (Zürich/Stuttgart: Zwingli 1965), pp. 128f., also wants to connect v 16f. with the middle strophe because it thus creates a synthetically parallel four-line verse pattern. But that is already not convincing because this solution ignores the inclusio and thus sunders the summarizing declarations through the "Allmachtsformel." His argument would possibly have more weight if v 16f., as v 17 and v 18a, were introduced also by *kai* (and).

10. E. Norden, *Agnostos Theos*, op. cit., pp. 141–276; 380–87.

These stylistic and grammatical inconsistencies and irregularities have given rise to speculation as to whether an original, stylistically and grammatically "intact" hymn was adopted and then adapted and edited, so that all the "disturbing" elements could be considered as intrusive interpolations and secondary material, in other words to be considered and treated as foreign, if not contradictory to the original poem.[11]

J. M. Robinson[12] attempted to (re)construct a perfectly structured hymn composed after a strict parallel pattern by deleting and transposing the material. But the result which he proposes makes it difficult to explain convincingly why the original parallelism was destroyed to the extent of the present wording of Col 1:15–20. Besides that, it seems very questionable to raise parallelism and symmetry to the level of a mandatory standard. To impose such a rigid structure on the material is quite arbitrary, as can be seen in comparing this poem with early Christian hymns.[13] Hesitation and caution are especially commendable when parts need to be deleted which are characterized by a pleurophorous style. Plerophory, as obviously present in 1:16, is rather typical of early Christian hymns and is documented also in the extra-biblical literature.[14] N. Kehls' attempt to reconstruct an original hymn from speech rhythm, in which the cola in the first and second stanzas each have the same syllable count, is to be viewed with considerable reserve.[15] In order to arrive at this result, we would have to consider portions of the enumeration in 1:16 as not original.

The arguments of E. Käsemann,[16] in which he justifies his reconstruction, seem to be of more significance for the interpretation of the hymn within the context of Col, and more firmly documented than numerous other attempts[17]

---

11. Good overviews of expurgations in the attempted reconstruction of the original hymn, including their interlacings, are offered by P. Benoit, *Hymne,* op. cit., esp. p. 238; C. Burger, *Schöpfung,* op. cit., pp. 9ff.; J. Gnilka (pp. 51–57).

12. J. M. Robinson, *Analysis,* op. cit.

13. R. Deichgräber, Gotteshymnus, op. cit., p. 147, "unser Wissen über das Stilempfinden, das die frühchristliche Dichtung bestimmt hat, ist zu gering, als dass ein einigermassen sicheres Urteil möglich wäre." See also A. Debrunner, "Grundsätzliches zur Kolometrie im Neuen Testament," ThBL 5 (1926) 120–25; 231–33; E. Lohse (p. 82); op. cit., "Christologie und Ethik im Kolosserbrief," in *Die Einheit des Neuen Testaments. Exegetische Studien Zur Theologie des Neuen Testaments* (Göttingen: Vandenhoeck & Ruprecht, 1973), pp. 249–61:254; E. Schweizer (p. 52); W. G. Kümmel, *Einleitung in das Neue Testament,* 8th ed. (Heidelberg: Quelle & Meyer, 1973), pp. 301f.; K. Wengst, "Christologische Formeln und Lieder des Urchristentums," StNT 7 (Gütersloh: Mohn, 1972), p. 175; and others.

14. Compare esp. W. Pöhlmann, *All-Prädikationen,* op. cit., pp. 53–74 (there are also references there).

15. N. Kehl, *Christushymnus,* op. cit., pp. 34–37.

16. E. Käsemann, *Taufliturgie,* op. cit.

17. As far as we can tell, only vv 15aa + b, 16a, 18b, and 19 (with the exception of the verb *eudokēsen*) have remained undisputed.—Compare esp. P. Benoit, *Hymne,* op.

to establish the basis for our extant text. Käsemann's position has found widespread acceptance.

1. He considers the genitive in 1:18b "of the church" as an addition to the original hymn. The decisive reason for this supposition is the fact that in the present version of the hymnus (Col 1:15–20) the formal and contextual beginning of the second stanza would disintegrate.[18] He argues that while the first stanza (1:15–18b) speaks otherwise exclusively of creation, and the second (18b–20), whose beginning is marked with the identical "he is . . ." in v 15 and v 18d, speaks of redemption, stanza 1 unexpectedly deals with soteriology by naming the church. The discrepancy, however, is resolved if one considers "of the church" as an addition and the word "body" as cosmological, as a designation of the world body. Through the genitive "of the church," "a certain clumsiness has been inserted into the formulation of v 18" (p. 134).

Moreover, E. Schweizer (p. 53) has cited a series of improbabilities which speak against the assumption that the genitive attribute originally belonged to the statement in v 18b, to the effect that: (a) the composer of the hymn executes a systematic new formation of the Pauline assertions when he speaks of head and body in this manner; (b) he does not refer expressly to the body of *Christ*, as Paul customarily does elsewhere; (c) the poet of the hymn writes in the style of the author of the epistle, with loosely appended explanations.

2. In Käsemann's opinion,[19] the expression "through his blood of the cross" in v 20 is also an addition. While elsewhere in the hymn, Christ is presented as the agent of creation and the risen/elevated one, and while the hymn elsewhere deals with creation and eschatological new creation, "this relationship is sensibly disturbed when the connection of creation and eschatological new creation is broken by the reference to the event of the Cross—a reference for which the way is totally unprepared and which has immediately an anachronistic effect" (p. 135). If one were to bracket the phrase, the statement would best fit into the other statements of the portions of the hymn which are acknowledged to be original (thus without the "addition" "of the church" in 18b). The cosmic peace cited in stanza 2 would then be "fruit and goal" of the reconciliation of all things to him and would look back to the beginning of the hymn. In its original form it therefore would have attained the idea of a cosmic peace that meant the restitution of the original creation. This peace would in turn be perceived as

cit., pp. 237–50. P. Benoit's assertion (p. 238) that only 15–16a and 19–20a (the fact that v 18b was not cited is probably an oversight) have not been suspect in research does not apply anymore today. C. Burger, *Schöpfung*, op. cit., excluded also vv 15ab and 20a, as well as the verb *eudokēsen* in v 19 for a proto-hymn (compare footnote 48).

18. Ibid., p. 134. H. A. W. Meyer already noted the discrepancy in his commentary (in the 4th edition, which appeared in 1874), if we would allow Strophe II to begin with 18b, with F. E. D. Schleiermacher and J. A. Bengel on the basis of the repeated "He is . . ." He therefore declined the division.

19. E. Käsemann, *Taufliturgie*, op. cit., p. 135.

"characteristic of the new age [as] a sign and result that the world savior has begun his reign" (p. 135).

E. Schweizer (p. 54) also listed further improbabilities for this "addition," which shall counter attributing this declaration of the blood of the cross to the composer of the hymn: one would otherwise have to assume (a) that the hymn writer had been of the "Pauline" tradition like the author of the epistle; (b) that he allowed the cross to remain as an afterthought in contrast to the resurrection; (c) that he did not mention man, who appears everywhere as an object of the reconciliation; (d) that he repeated the "through him" in v 20 in an almost impossible grammatical construction.

Nevertheless, neither of these eliminations seems compelling.

1. H. J. Gabathuler[20] justifiably pointed to an unsolved problem in the middle stanza (1:17 + 18b). On the one hand, it stands out from the rest of the context, and it seems sensible to consider it a connecting link between vv 15–16 and 18v–20. On the other hand, it cannot fulfill this function in an original hymn without the "addition" "of the church," because it does not even mention reconciliation.[21] Attempting to solve the difficulties by considering "the church" as an interpolation and the intermediate stanza as a portion of the first stanza[22] is not satisfying. Such a solution does not do justice to the formal character of vv 17 + 18a (see above), since their corresponding features with regard to the contents are then lacking. We find these in the supposed addition "of the church," through which the verses receive their formal contextual peculiarity and independence. The person who prays the hymn acknowledges in this middle stanza that no lesser being than the one who is praised in vv 15 + 16 is the head of the church, and thus the reason why the church praises him in this manner and how it came to be thankful for this "already accomplished redemption." The deletion of the phrase "of the church" does not resolve anything; rather, it creates larger difficulties than those already present.[23]

The following stylistic consideration may also contribute to considering the words "of the church" in the middle stanza as genuine: the emphatically

---

20. *Jesus Christus*, op. cit., pp. 128f.

21. E. Schweizer, "Die Kirche als Leib Christ in den paulinischen Antilegomena," in *Neotestamentica* (Zürich/Stuttgart: Zwingli Verlag, 1963), pp. 293–316: 295, who, like C. Maurer, views the intermediary strophe as connecting strophe, points to this circumstance in a subsequent addition to fn. 4.

22. Compare H. J. Gabathuler, *Jesus Christus*, op. cit., p. 129.

23. N. Kehl, *Christushymnus*, op. cit., p. 98, defended the originality of this expression, because otherwise the rhythmic pattern is disturbed. Besides that, a larger difficulty is introduced into the text if we understand v 18a cosmically, because then (more so than before) it becomes unclear why a salvation is necessary. Also C. Maurer, *Herrschaft Christi*, op. cit., interprets the "community" as original, because otherwise the middle strophe cannot fulfill its function as connecting strophe. Compare also W. G. Kümmel, *Einleitung*, op. cit., pp. 301f.

formulated "And it is He who" points to the parallelism in v 17a, "And it is He who reigns over all things," along with v 18a, "And it is He who is the head." The two genitives in v 18b ("of the body: of the church") are probably constructed as parallels to v 17a, so that the middle stanza consists of two lines with two cola per line:

And it is He who reigns over all things,
            and all things exist in Him.
And it is He who is the head—
            of the body: of the church.

This parallel construction is lost with the deletion of the phrase "of the church."

The problems pointed out by E. Schweizer are not so weighty as would appear initially. The new formulation of the image of head and body is not so far removed from Paul factually that he could not have used it (cf. Notes to 1:18a). Further, the significance of "head" becomes so graphic through the addition "of the church," that the insertion of "Christ" is contextually superfluous. For Paul, a formulaic use of the body imagery is at least plausible. Besides that, the result is a perhaps intentional shift in emphasis, when it says, "of the body: of the church," and not "of the body of Christ: of the church." Because the figurative sense is elucidated by the following explanatory genitive "of the church" (cf. for example, Rom 5:18; 2 Cor 1:22), the anatomical/medical comparison in the image of head and body moves farther into the foreground. This is of significance, as 2:19 will show. Because we find typical stylistic features of the author also in the hymn, we can infer that we are dealing with the same author (see below).

2. Above all, a stylistic observation is the foremost argument against the deletion of "by the blood of the cross." The absence of the expression in a hypothetical original hymn has as its consequence that a parallel element (the "inclusio," cf. above) of stanzas 1–2 is eliminated. If it is true that the stylistic device of the inclusio is present also in v 20, then one will not declare the repetition of the "through him" in a grammatically almost inaccessible style, as Schweizer does, but rather as a hallmark of a typical stylistic form. Schweizer's argument that the theology of the cross "limps after" the declarations of resurrection is not correct in regard to the Colossian Hymn (Gal 1:1+4). Besides, in the brief summary of his mission at the beginning of Rom (1:1–7), Paul describes his Lord with the two designations "David's Son" and "Son of God in strength through the resurrection," without mentioning the cross and death.[24]

In addition, the originality of the expression "through the blood of his cross"

---

24. We are dealing with the same "designations" in the context of vv 15–20. Compare Notes to 1:12–14.

is supported by an observation of K. Wengst.[25] He points to the hymnic expression in Heb 1:3, for which, as in Col 1:20, "the same contrast of the pre-existing agent of creation on the one hand, and the elevated one who previously effected expiation on the other," is characteristic. Since in Heb 1:3 the expiation statement can hardly be excised, the claim to originality can also be raised to Col 1:20, according to Wengst.

In addition to the genitive attribute "of the church" (v 18a) and the expression "through his blood of the cross" (v 20b), the catalog-type listing in 1:16b–e (and usually also v 20c[26]) has been viewed in toto or in part as an interpolation. E. Norden (*Agnostos Theos*, pp. 261f.) described vv 1:16c–e as "decorative trimming." He opined that these verses seem foreign to the Semitic Oriental Psalmstyle which is characteristic of the rest of the hymn, but that there are parallels in Paul. H. Hegermann (*Schöpfungsmittler*, pp. 91f.) joined this viewpoint and went even beyond E. Norden in interpreting v 16b in this sense. The whole listing 1:16b–e is, in his view, a limiting specification of *ta panta* (all things) and a free hymnic enlargement. H. Hegermann further argues, "through such a contrast, not only the character of the *ta panta* predication becomes visible in a purer vein, but also the relationship in size of both stanzas and the related problem of the actual distribution of emphasis to which it is hinged are regularized" (p. 92). K. G. Eckart[27] also views 1:16b–e as an interpolation and he substantiates his decision by the fact that the listing in v 16 breaks up "a very closely reasoned formulation," which is demonstrated by a thoughtfully expressed climax: he, the image of God (v 15), is not only the pre-existing one ("first-born," v 15), he is also the "agent of creation" ("in him all things were created," v 16a), "in fact (he is) the all-encompassing end, basis, and aim of the cosmos" ("all things were created through him and to him," vv 16f.).

W. Pöhlmann[28] is probably right to reject the view that the enumeration in v 16 is an interpolation, if only for stylistic reasons. He mentions parallels which demonstrate that unfolding enumerations (additionally as the included portion of an inclusio) are a stylistic element of hymns. But even the cited arguments used by H. Hegermann and K. G. Eckart are hardly persuasive enough to us. (1) It is not compelling to interpret 1:16b–e necessarily as a *restricted* elucidation. On the contrary, the enumeration rather serves to emphasize the *universality* of the Messiah's dominion (cf. Notes to 1:16). (2) The problem of the actual emphatic distribution, which is indicated by the relationship of the different

---

25. *Formeln*, op. cit., p. 173.
26. R. Deichgräber, *Gotteshymnus*, op. cit., p. 150, sees 1:16e–f as interpretament, but not 20c. Similarly, K. G. Eckart, *Beobachtungen*, op. cit., p. 106, views 1:16b–e as an interpolation, but not v 20c.
27. K. G. Eckart, ibid., pp. 104f.
28. W. Pöhlmann, *All- Prädikationen*, op. cit., esp. pp. 57f.

lengths of the two stanzas, is not a serious problem, since creation and redemption are considered as a complementary "unity" in the hymn (cf. Comment II.3). The different sizes of the two stanzas in regard to length are less disturbing when one considers 1:17 + 18ab as the middle stanza. (3) If we interpret 1:16b–e as an interpolation along with K. G. Eckart's viewpoint, but not the last line of v 16, then the (slightly varied) repetition of 16a at the end of v 16 seems curious, even though it makes sense as an *inclusio*. K. G. Eckart sees in the concluding line the highpoint of a climax, but his opinion would be more persuasive if either *di autou* (*by him* all things were created) were left out entirely, or if we read *di auton* (because of him). In the "original" hymn that Eckart reconstructed, *di autou* merely repeats the "in him" from v 16b, and the real climax is reached only in the statement "to him" in vv 16f. H. Hegermann (*Schöpfungsmittler*, p. 92) is more consistent when he interprets vv 16f. as an addition by the author of an adapted hymn. But in so doing, he destroys the existing parallelism which is created in stanzas 1–2 by the adoption of the so-called Stoic omnipotence formula of the "in-through-for."

The difficulties cited under 3 are generally circumvented if we, along with E. Schweizer (p. 54),[29] consider only 16d + e as an insertion by the author into a hymnic prototype. But the reasoning that the typically Judaic listing of powers only enumerates the invisible and therefore contradicts the Hellenistic summarization of the entire cosmos into "visible and invisible" is not convincing. It is possible, and in our view probable, that *ta horata kai ta aorata* should be translated in the (Judaic) pragmatic sense, "That, which one sees, and that, which one does not see" (cf. Notes to v 16c). As observed earlier, the listing should not be understood to be limiting (see above).[30]

If we cannot ascertain decisively commentary or corrective additions to Col 1:15–20, and therefore also cannot reconstruct a prototype hymn which would have been adapted by the author of the Colossian epistle, the question becomes a practical one as to whether the author of the hymn and the writer of the epistle are one and the same person. This would be improbable if we could unequivocally prove a "Sitz im Leben" for the hymn; this would increase the probability that a generally familiar and often utilized hymn had been taken over by the author of the epistle. E. Käsemann is of the opinion that this is possible, and he interprets Col 1:12–20 as a baptismal confession which was cited by the author of the epistle.[31] He justifies his opinion by referring to Col

29. Compare also H. J. Gabathuler, *Jesus Christus*, op. cit., p. 131; J. M. Robinson, *Analysis*, op. cit., p. 286; H. M. Schenke: "Der Widerstreit gnostischer und kirchlicher Christologie im Spiegel des Kolosserbriefes," ZthK 61 (1964) 391–403:401, who view 16c–e as an interpolation.

30. For a polemical interpretation of the listing, see Notes.—V 20c is to be viewed as an interpolation even less than parts of 1:16. This is even more true if it is the case that we have an inclusio in v 20.

31. *Taufliturgie*, op. cit.; H. Löwe, *Bekenntnis*, op. cit., attempted to develop the

1:12–14, a passage whose terminology, so he believes, points unequivocally to baptism: "deliverance from darkness and translation into the kingdom of God's Son are unquestionably thought of as following from baptism" (p. 140). This assertion, however, contradicts the proclamation of the hymn, according to which the transfer into the realm of the Son is due to the fact that the Messiah acceded to his reign over all things by his death on the cross (cf. Notes to 1:18b–20, Comment II, 3, and mainly Notes to 2:14f.). It also has no support in the "explanation" of baptism in Col 2:12ff. (Comment II to 2:6–23). Since there is no point of reference in the context, we agree with R. Deichgräber that in the hymn a "Sitz im Leben" of the Christian community can no longer be determined.[32]

In addition, the vocabulary of the hymn[33] does not necessarily speak in favor of the hypothesis that we are dealing with a traditional piece. The special stylistic form that designates a hymn also indicates a special vocabulary pattern. Paul, or any other author of the epistle, can be excluded as the poet of the hymn with a certain assurance only if either the hymnic style and the "hymnic vocabulary" of the author of the epistle are known and are not associated with the Colossian hymn or if the author has excluded himself as the original author of the poem. Neither is the case.[34]

If 1:15–20 contains elements of an adapted hymn, then an original introit

hypothesis that this is certainly a declaration. He wants to prove that *eucharisteō* (to thank) used again and again in Col is a terminus technicus and thus a key word for remembrance of the Hymn as an acknowledgment of baptism. Besides that, the letter in general refers to this acknowledgment as the basis for the argument. The assumption of a technical usage of *eucharisteō* is hypothetical (in connection with G. Bornkamm, *Hoffnung*, op. cit.) and cannot be ascertained (see Notes to 1:12). It is more probable that the repeated summons to the Colossians to thank is also a summons to become imitators of the writers of the epistle, who give the primary example of giving thanks in 1:3–23. Certainly no technical usage is the precedent for the verb in 1:3, as H. Löwe himself determines (p. 303).

32. *Gotteshymnus*, op. cit., pp. 154f. G. Bornkamm wants to group the liturgy of the Christ Hymns in the NT to the celebration of the eucharist on the basis of the later history of the liturgy, but he does point out that this cannot be ascertained from the NT (*Bekenntnis*, op. cit., p. 196).

33. Compare E. Lohse (pp. 78f.): "image of God" can be found "formulaically" as Christian predicate also only in 2 Cor 4:4; *horatos* (visible/that which one sees) only here; *aoratos* as contrast to *horatos* only here; "throne" only here; "authority" (*kyriotēs*) also only in Eph 1:21; the intransitive *synestekenai* only here in Paul; *archē* (beginning) in Paul otherwise never as Christological title; *prōteuein* (to be the first one) and *eirenopoiein* (to create peace) are hapax lemomena; *katoikein* (to dwell within) also occurs only in Col 2:9 and Eph 3:17; *apokatallassein* (to reconcile) also only in Col 1:22 and Eph 2:16. "Blood of the cross" is without parallel in the NT.

34. The debate concerning the religiohistorical background of the hymn is a wide-ranging one, but attempts to reconstruct the history of the transmission of an adapted

must have been deleted and an introit or a theological transition (1:12–14) composed by the author (or before him by another redactor) must have been substituted as replacement. If we assume, however, that the author of the epistle is himself the author of the hymn, the demarcation of beginning and end of the hymn is less problematic or complicated.[35] Then it seems obvious to consider vv 12–14 not only as an element of the intercession, but also as genuinely being a part of the hymn. As, for example, in Ps 105 the praise of God (vv 7ff.) is preceded by an invitation to glorify and laud the deities (vv 1–6), Col 1:12–14 is most likely an introit to the hymn contained in 1:15–20.[36] The intertwining of intercession and hymn indicates that the hymn was formulated *ad hoc* when the epistle was composed. (For the strophic arrangement of the hymn, refer to the translation.)

2. Discussion of the Religiohistorical Background

By deleting the two additions, "of the church" and "through his blood of the cross" (cf. Comment II.1), from the hymn, E. Käsemann intended also to "blot out any kind of specifically Christian character" (p. 136). The result of his reconstruction is a pre-Christian hymn in which he assumes us to recognize "the contours of the gnostic myth of the Archetypal Man who is also the Redeemer. Indeed, the myth is present in a form characteristic of Hellenistic Judaism." ["Precursor and sophia specifically logos speculation are related to one another" (p. 137).] According to Käsemann, the mythological character

---

hymn are of no consequence when we cannot reconstruct a primary hymn and when the composer of the epistle is himself the poet of the hymn.—E. Käsemann, *Taufliturgie*, op. cit., esp. pp. 136–39, reconstructed three levels: a Gnostic hymn (level 1) was reworked with a Christian orientation; (level 2) was equipped with additions and a liturgical introduction; (level 3) this reworked hymn was cited by the composer of Col. This thesis, that a pre-Christian hymn was reworked with a Christian orientation, was criticized by, among others, H. Hegermann, E. Lohse, and E. Schweizer and could not be substantiated (compare Comment II.2). Thus, for the genesis of the hymn, only two stages have been accepted: a Christian original hymn which was reworked by the composer of Col. C. Burger, *Schöpfung*, op. cit., again attempted to work out three phases: a Christian original hymn which was reworked by the composer of Col and after that yet again by an editor.

35. Differing opinions exist esp. regarding the beginning of the song: K. G. Eckart (*Beobachtungen*, op. cit.; *Taufliturgie*, op. cit.) establishes it at v 9, E. Käsemann, (*Tauf- und Ordinations-liturgie*, op. cit.) at v 12. E. Lohmeyer at v 13, F. Mussner at v 14, E. Lohse at v 15.

36. If this attempted interpretation of the hymn hits its mark, then vv 15–20 refer directly to the statements in vv 12–14, also as far as their suppositions and terminology are concerned. E. Lohse's objections (p. 77, fn. 1) against a cohesive unit (differing conceptuality, differing assumptions, changing form of speech) are then no longer compelling.

appears in the first stanza, especially in the declaration "All things are held together in him" (v 17). Here, one is reminded of the "cosmic extent of thinking of the Archetypal Man."[37] The world is conceptualized as the cosmic body, the Archetypal Man as its soul or its head, and consequently the first stanza ends with the prediction "He is the head of the body." In the second stanza, the myth culminates in the words "It was pleasing that all the fullness (*plēroma*) should dwell in him." Only in a Gnostic text is this expression really comprehensible (p. 139). God is no longer being spoken of. Rather, the subject is *plēroma*, the all-embracing, all-uniting fullness of the new aeon. The *plēroma* makes itself present and manifest in the redeemer according to the proclamations of the original Gnostic hymn; thus the universe was reconciled and its conflicting elements pacified. He himself, the redeemer and cosmocrat, is the "redeemed redeemer" in so far as the restituted creation now forms his body (p. 139).

This interpretation is problematic because it lacks the support from source documentation. Research by C. Colpe and H. M. Schenke[38] have shown that a prototype redeemer myth is not demonstrable in the first century. It can be documented with certainty only in Mani, who was executed as a heretical Christian presumably in 273 C.E. In addition, some outstanding elements in the text of the hymn make their derivation from Gnosticism improbable. E. Käsemann's assertion, that the proto-hymn reconstructed by him demonstrates no specifically Christian elements, is not borne out. Foremost in countering this theory is the expression "first-born from the dead," and the curious word *apokatallassō* (to redeem), which is probably Christian in origin[39] (cf. Notes to 1:19). H. Hegermann[40] disputes a connection between Gnosis and the Colossian Hymn. His main argument is the total absence of dualistic thinking from the substance of the hymn. "Even if one tried to detect a cosmic fall in the hymn, one would not reach a dualistic view, because it is the fallen universe which as a whole would be renewed in redemption" (p. 154). Thus, he justifiably asks,

---

37. The cosmic soteriological conceptualization of the original human being was reconstructed especially from Manichaean and Mandaeian texts. According to these, the appearance of the heavenly messenger corresponds "to the appearance of the heavenly original man, who came down from the heavenly world into the material world in ancient pre-historic times and was overpowered and taken captive by it. Since the form of the messenger was now compared to that of the original man, the messenger also seemed captured and overwhelmed in his earthly appearance, and his arising is also his own salvation; he is the saved savior." (R. Bultmann, "Die Bedeutung der neu erschlossenen mandäischen und manichäischen Quellen für das Verständnis des Johannesevangeliums," in *Exegetica*, op. cit., pp. 55–104:59; compare Dibelius-Greeven, p. 16.

38. H. M. Schenke, *Der Gott "Mensch" in der Gnosis* (Göttingen: Vandenhoeck & Ruprecht, 1962); C. Colpe, "Die religionsgeschichtliche Schule," FRLANT 78, (Göttingen: Vandenhoeck & Ruprecht, 1961).

39. Compare R. Deichgräber, *Gotteshymns,* op. cit., pp. 153f.

40. *Schöpfungsmittler,* op. cit.

"If the Christ–Archetypal Man really contains the universe within himself, . . . namely if he is identical with the universe, where then is the hell into which he could fall in order to arise from it again as the redeemed redeemer?" (p. 101). Also, the designation "first-born from the dead" is not compatible with the redeemer in Gnostic thinking since the redeemer is here basically associated with the "dead" (p. 101). According to R. Deichgräber,[41] the title "first-born from the dead" (prōtókos ek tōn nekrōn) does not seem to occur at all in the Gnostic writings. Also, the Gnostic-technical sense of plērōma (fullness) cannot be applied to the Colossian Hymn, or specifically, it cannot be found there. In the Gnostic context, "an indwelling of the aeons in the redeemer is not a matter of discussion. The Gnostic redeemer leaves the pleroma in his descent and returns to it again."[42]

Unlike E. Käsemann, C. F. Burney[43] attempts to elucidate the religiohistorical background of the Colossian Hymn entirely from the OT. This attempt has the undisputed advantage of reaching back only to sources that were known to the author with certainty. Burney interprets the hymn as an exegesis of the rabbinic tradition of Gen 1:1 in connection with the Hebrew text of Prov 8:22.[44] The same word (beginning; Hebrew rēʾšît; Gr. archē), which in Prov 8 is used to designate wisdom, and is a Christ title in the Colossian Hymn, occurs also in Gen 1:1, together with the Hebrew preposition (bĕ before) and is usually translated by "in the beginning. . . ." In light of Prov 8:22, it has now been interpreted as the title of wisdom, specifically of Christ, "In wisdom/Christ, God created. . . ." The hymn is then simply a collection of related words from Gen 1:1, interpreted in the sense just mentioned. First, the Hebrew preposition is unfolded in its possible meanings.

in—in him were all things created (1:16)
by—through him were all things created (1:16)
for—into him (as their goal) were all things created (1:16)

Then, the dimensions of meaning of rēʾšît are sorted out:

as beginning—he is before all things (1:17a)
as sum total—all things are summed up in him (1:17b)
as head—he is the head of the body (1:18a)
as first one—he is the first-born, the first-begotten of the dead (1:18c)

---

41. Gotteshymnus, op. cit., p. 153.

42. Schöpfungsmittler, op. cit., p. 105.

43. C. F. Burney, "Christ as the ARXH of Creation," JThS 27 (1925) 160–77. In his following is, among others, W. D. Davies, Paul and Rabbinic Judaism. Some Rabbinic Elements in Pauline Theology (London: SPCK, 1948), pp. 150–52.

44. C. F. Burney translates, "The Lord begat me as the beginning of His way, the antecedent of His works, of old" (op.p. 168).

This attempt expressly demonstrates that important ideas of the hymn can be explained from the OT Jewish background, even where they are expressed in typically Hellenistic terminology (cf. the so-called Stoic omnipotence formula). Thus, caution is advised in drawing conclusions about the religiohistorical/philosophical background directly from the terminology. It is still rather unlikely that the Colossian Hymn originated through the rabbinic exegesis proposed by Burney. Foremost, a weakness of Burney's argument is the fact that in the first stanza of the hymn the designation of Christ as *archē* (beginning), which one would expect within the framework of this theory, is missing and is replaced by *eikōn* (image).

Similarly, E. Lohmeyer (pp. 43–47) has attempted to interpret the hymn from the OT background. He proceeds from the concept of reconciliation and emphasizes its significance for the Jewish faith, in which one pillar is the law and the other the cult. The cultic sense, however, has its center in the "great day of atonement," which for the Jews is "simply 'the day,'" The yearly atonement before the sacrificial worship of God on this day confirms for Israel the idea of its selection from among the nations—its relationship to all the nations thus achieves special significance on this day. At the heart of the celebration is the reading from the Prophet Jonah, "the book that expresses the transmission of the Jewish faith to the world and the acknowledgment of sin and the forgiveness of sin among all nations." This relationship to the world becomes uniquely clear in the connection of the idea of atonement with that of creation.[45] This connection is proclaimed in the cult in the fact that the celebration of atonement and the festival of creation on the day of the new year are temporarily separated from each other by the "ten principal days of penitence," and yet both, atonement and creation, together form a cohesive celebration cycle. Lohmeyer is convinced that the hymn has this Jewish cultic practice as its basis. In it, in place of a divine institution which is characterized by repetition, a unique and eternal divine figure has taken this place, namely "Christ as the essence and fulfillment of the Jewish cult of penitence."

The idea of finality and uniqueness, however, cannot be explained only from the Jewish institutions. Lohmeyer reaches back to the Archetypal Man myth here, yet he emphasizes that the myth did not constitute the substantial base of the praise of Christ; it determined its special form only, not its content.

Even though it is difficult to trace the concept of atonement in the hymn (cf. Comment II.3) directly back to the OT statements about the great day of atonement, and even though Lohmeyer does not succeed in documenting convincingly that the assumed unity of the day of atonement and the feast of the new year in a festival cycle manifests itself in the celebration of this festival, two considerations are still relevant:

---

45. E. Lohmeyer (p. 44) points out that according to Gen 2:3, God separated light

1. Lohmeyer points to the central significance of the concept of redemption for both the hymn and the OT (and Jewish) tradition and cult. This remains a consideration and is an admonishment for caution in involving other religio-historical parallels too quickly in the explanation of the hymn.

2. Lohmeyer also dealt with the idea of considering "creation and atonement" not as opposites, but founded in the concept of Israel as the chosen people. If this attempt in relation to the cult was not really convincing, it is still worthy of consideration before other explanations are brought forth, especially when they rely on sources whose knowledge remains hypothetical for Paul and for other NT authors.

H. Hegermann[46] criticized E. Lohmeyer's attempt to derive the entire hymn from the Jewish background and to view Hellenistic influences only as an "external addition." He is disturbed not only by the fact that this interpretation cannot be carried out "without forcing the issue," but above all by not "seriously considering the qualified importance of the Hellenistic Synagogue as a far-reaching independent entity, which was, however, in no way equally heretical" (p. 93). Hegermann is oriented toward the conceptualization of the hymn in his investigation, namely by the "central message" of the first stanza in v 17, which he translates, "The universe has its existence in him." He links up with Dibelius (Dibelius-Greeven), who made use of the statement in the sense of the Gnostic Archetypal Man myth, but he disputes the Gnostic influences (see above: the criticism of E. Käsemann). He argues that we are not dealing with the Archetypal Man myth, but with the underlying conception of this myth, that is the so-called "aeon conception," in the stoically modified form which was familiar to Philo (a representative of the Alexandrian synagogue) and which was further modified by him (p. 94). The "aeon conception" in its Stoic form claimed not only that "the universe" was made "by Zeus," and that "Zeus was the universe," but also that Zeus was the "world-soul." This worldview was modified by Philo to the extent that "as the stern immanence of the world dynamic is broken, the logos as the head stands opposite to the universe which it suffuses, analogously to the anthropological localization of the soul in the head" (p. 94). Like the central conception of the first stanza, so the other decisive concepts of vv 15–18b fit in with the philosophical ideas of Philo, according to Hegermann.

This derivation of the hymn would certainly be supported from the Alexandrian synagogue, if it could be demonstrated that "body" in v 18b had exclusive cosmological meaning in the original hymn; but that is not the case. A further difficulty, which Hegermann himself points out, makes his attempt

---

and darkness, etc., on the day of creation in order to combine them again on the day of reconciliation.
46. *Schöpfungsmittler*, op. cit.

problematic.[47] The presumably Philonically influenced ideas of the first half of the hymn are not compatible with the statements of the second half. In a cosmic view, stamped by the Stoics and Philo, in which the agent of creation is the head of the world-body, the ideas of a redemption and a redeemer are superfluous. Everything that could be effected by a redemption has already been put into effect at the creation (cf. p. 108). Hegermann explains this "irresolvable difficulty" (p. 106)[48] by the co-joining of the Palestinian kerygma (which marks the second half) with the Hellenistic worldview (reflected in the first half), which is reflected in the hymn. The Palestinian proto-kerygma contains the "announcement of the immediately imminent ascension to power of the Messiah Jesus as the Son of man, and of the judgment associated therewith" (p. 124). "In that, the proto-Christian conception of the Son of man was joined to the corresponding Jewish one, in which the old messianic expectation had been topped in an apocalyptic-cosmic manner" (p. 124). Cosmic dominion was synonymous with the power of creation in the orientation of the Alexandrian worldview, so that the analogy of the Alexandrian speculation regarding the agency of creation must have been appropriate for the proto-Christian mission, in order for its message to be passed on to the type of people who "heard it with Hellenistic Jewish ears" (p. 125).

This explanation is hardly persuasive. The point of the hymn is precisely to praise the incomparable importance and might of Christ, which are evident precisely in the work of redemption. This purpose would definitely not be realized if the hymn's statements about Christ "the" redeemer would demonstrate no more than that such a redeemer is superfluous. Indeed, it is possible in a syncretistic environment that important thoughts and words are borrowed by one religious group from another and are alienated from their original meaning in order to be used with a new meaning.[49] Synonymous terminology is no evidence for synonymous concepts. Sometimes, so it appears, difficulties have

---

47. For those, as well as the attempts of those who understand the religious background of the hymn as he does, for example E. Lohse and E. Schweizer.

48. C. Burger, *Schöpfung*, op. cit., did remove these, for Hegermann, "insolvable difficulties" in his reconstruction of the hymn. He deems all formal and logical difficulties in vv 19 + 20 solved by removing the causative element, namely the verb *eudokēsen* (it was pleasing to him), and with it the problematic parts of the two verses which are attached to it. Then the original vv 19 + 20 would read, "In him resides all the fullness, be it that which (is) in the heavens" (see esp. pp. 25f.). The original hymn thus did not deal with salvation at all, and thus did not recognize *Hegermann's* problem.—*Burger's* reconstruction, however, invades the hymn without giving due consideration to the stylistic structures which point to its originality.

49. Compare B. Vawter, "The Colossian Hymn and the Principle of Redaction," CBQ 33(1971) 62–81:73.

been introduced into the hymn by Hegermann, rather than solved in favor of its interpretation.[50]

3. Creation—Reconciliation—Reconciliation of All Things

The relative or personal pronoun occurs fourteen times in the hymn; six times a form of *ta panta* (all things) is used, in which "all of creation" occurs once for this concept. This expression is developed in v 16b–e, as well as in v 20. These data show that the central concern of the hymn is Christ and creation. In addition, through the stylized forms of the *inclusio* in stanzas 1–2, two focal expressions are emphasized which expose the theme of the hymn: in stanza 1, the development of "all things," in stanza 2 the statement "He created peace through his blood of the cross."

The assumed religiohistorical background is decisive for the interpretation of the author's concept of the connection between creation and reconciliation expressed in the hymn. As important as the assumed religiohistorical background is, we must question the assumption or rejection of the hypothesis that an originally non-Christian hymn was adapted, commentated, or corrected by the author of Col, if not by earlier hands. The range of the results attained can be illustrated by the position chosen by E. Schweizer.[51] According to him, the Colossian Hymn is based on an ancient composition which reflected the "feeling which was disseminated in the Hellenistic world that [mankind] was living in a fragile world in which the battle of all against all determined all nature" (p. 68). Therefore, according to Schweizer, the first stanza takes up the problem of the existence of the world, which is otherwise unknown in the NT. The cosmos is held together in Christ and it is his body according to the claim of the original hymn. In Christ alone God's works in creation became recognizable as the gesture of his love for mankind. Thus, the world is purposeful from its origin, but also from its aim. The second stanza (vv 18–20) praises the already final pacification of the world through Christ. This pacification happened by the

---

50. F. B. Craddock, "All Things in Him": A Critical Note on Col 1:15–20," NTS 12 (1966) 78–80, reproached H. Hegermann that he misunderstood "in him" in Col 1:16f., 19. He maintains that in Col it does not say, as it does in the Stoa, "he is in all things," but rather, "all things are in him," as a pre-existent being. But "pre-existence reflects a need to move outside existence to find life's meaning. . . ." Craddock suspects the myth of the Urmensch, who also occurs in Philo, behind the declarations of the hymn, whether one associates that with Gnosis or not (p. 80, fn. 5). Hegermann's retrogression to Philo is supposedly correct in itself, but he has chosen the incorrect suppositions therein.

51. See E. Schweizer, "The Church as the Missionary Body of Christ," NTS 8 (1961/62) 1–11; (= *Neotestamentica*, op. cit., pp. 317ff.). *Leib Christi*, op. cit., (pp. 44–80); compare also "Versöhnung des Alls," in op. cit.; *Neuer Kol-Kommentar, Testament und Christologie im Werden, Aufsätze* (Göttingen: Vandenhoeck & Ruprecht, 1982), pp. 164–78.

inhabitation of the fullness of God, namely through the fullness of the strength of God in Christ to raise the dead, that is, in the resurrection. The core of these assertions is cosmic, not anthropological. First and foremost the elements are reconciled, and then also mankind.

Such declarations are not heretical in the least for E. Schweizer.[52] Rather, they are an expression of liturgical enthusiasm when they are sung in a hymn that is used in the worship service. In such a situation, the goodness of God might be praised by viewing the world in light of God's creation in the beginning ("everything was very good") and at the end of time ("a new heaven and a new earth"). But the author of the epistle was forced to reinterpret the statements of the intermediate hymn, since he removed them from the situation of the worship service to a completely different level of speech, to one of encouragement and admonition. In the worship service, the actual orientation is connected to God through the act of singing, so that in place of the laudation, a pre-election is rendered about him, which could actually control the praised divinity "without the need to repeat the wonder of the encounter with Christ and of the immersion in his love" (p. 72). In the epistle, written *words* had to take the place of the functions of the orientation toward God which occurs in the singing. These are still recognizable as commentary additions to the hymn in Col. By the additions, the hymn becomes an address, a summons for a continuously renewed act of faith. The world is not perceived as the body of Christ, but the church, because the central question of divine action is no longer one concerning *creation.* The emphasis is on the statement that Christ can only be acknowledged as head, "where the church turns toward him in faith and it thus becomes his body and is filled with life through him" (p. 70). Thus, along with the corresponding declaration of worldwide reconciliation through the establishment of divine power in the resurrected Christ, we also have the expression of "peace through his blood of the cross," because the author of the epistle is concerned with the suffering of Christ, which awakens faith. Schweizer rejects the misunderstanding that reconciliation by God through Christ is comparable to a physical or metaphysical occurrence which falls upon mankind like a natural disaster and degrades men and women to the status of simple objects. In its place, we have a category of faith in its ethical expression. The cosmic significance of Christ is not denied, but the "cosmic penetration occurs historically, in the mission to the nations," as the application of the declarations in the hymn in Col would show.[53]

---

52. *Schöpfungsmittler,* op. cit., esp. pp. 72–74. In contrast to the opinion of E. Käsemann, (*Taufliturgie,* op. cit.), who regards the hymn without the additions "of the community" in v 18 and "through his blood of the cross" in v 20 as a pre-Christian hymn which contains the post-historical and metaphysical drama of the Gnostic redeemer (pp. 136f.). According to E. Lohse (p. 102), a "theologia gloriae" was corrected by a "theologia crucis."

53. *Leib Christi,* op. cit., p. 300.

Two objections may be raised, one psychological, the other rhetorical: (1) Was the author of Col really so foolish as to attempt to build a case for his theology on statements that he considered to be heretical?[54] (2) Were there practical concerns that would make it possible for an author simply to correct false theology with such scant additions to make it more likely for him simply to strike wrong statements?[55] Objections such as these do not really touch upon E. Schweizer's position presented in his commentary. According to him, the original hymn was not heretical at all. A dispute about the idea whether such enthusiasm in the early Christian worship service as E. Schweizer supposes would have been approved of by Paul or by any other author of Col is not helpful, since we cannot make that kind of determination from the extant source material.

It is questionable, however, whether Paul viewed reconciliation in such exclusively existential categories as Schweizer is doing. It is also questionable whether extrahuman creation in Pauline theology is of such secondary interest as the explanations of E. Schweizer would make it appear. The statements in Rom 5 and 2 Cor 5 in regard to reconciliation point in a different direction.[56] According to these, reconciliation has occurred independently of faith and of the "miracle of the encounter with Christ," where man is, in fact, first "only" an object but does not remain so. This "event" is guided by the idea that mankind should break out into praise of God, but that is exactly the intention of this "event." In addition, creation for Paul is not only the stage on which the reconciliation of mankind is consummated, because according to Rom 8:20ff., all of creation is transitory and is subject to servitude and longs for redemption. And the glorious freedom of the children of God is proclaimed for all of creation. Thus, it may be justified to ask about an alternative understanding of the hymn.

As we have tried to show in considering the structure of the hymn (cf. Comment II.1), we cannot prove definitively that the Colossian Hymn was reworked by the addition of corrections or comments. On the basis of exegetical observations, as they are carried out more precisely in the Notes, the hymn is linked directly to 1:14 and extols the Davidic Messiah as king of the universe. The whole world has not only its origin in him, but also the purpose of its existence. Creation is not understood "statically," as though in the beginning of all time, origin and purpose had once been identical. Also, there is no evidence in the hymn to view the world's development and history as becoming "dynamic" only because of creation and after the fall from God. The "dynamic" of the cosmos is rather founded in the creator himself. Indeed, a grave theological alternative must be mentioned at this point. There is the school of

---

54. Compare B. Vawter, *Colossian Hymn*, op. cit., p. 74.
55. Ibid., and P. T. O'Brien (35).
56. See the Notes to 1:20, and there esp. fn. 88.

the followers of Thomas Aquinas, according to which the *logos* was incarnated only because of Adam's fall, and the school of Duns Scotus, according to which the incarnation was the essence and the purpose of creation itself. Certainly the Colossian Hymn aligns itself more with the side of Scotus. However, this points up problematical aspects of the alternative mentioned not on "Christmas," but rather on "Good Friday," the event on which creation achieved its purpose.

This event is called reconciliation. Reconciliation, in turn, is synonymous with the idea that the Messiah has become Lord and ruler over all things through his death on the cross. The question here becomes inescapable as to how one can consider the kingship of Christ since creation and simultaneously through his death on the cross. It would be wrong to interpret the tension that exists between these two statements as the tension between stanzas 1–2, and to attempt then to explain it with the assumption of differing religiohistorical concepts in the two stanzas. Also, the puzzle is not solved through the assertion that the fall was presumed at the creation.[57] The tension is already signaled in the first stanza in the fact that we are dealing with one purpose of creation whose fulfillment lies in the future. It can best be explained by OT statements about the kingdom of Yahweh which point up similar seeming contradictions: while some passages simply refer to the kingdom of Yahweh of their time,[58] there are others that rather emphasize the future and the expectation of things to come[59] without contradicting the idea that Yahweh is also the king of the present time. It is the *manifestation* of the status of Yahweh as king that is awaited.[60] *This* is the future, according to the declarations of the hymn, that has become real in the crucifixion, for which in turn the resurrection is the proof even more than the creation.

We also find a special cohesiveness between creation and redemption in the OT, which is exhibited especially in Isa 51:9ff. and in Ps 74. For Deut-Isa, creation and redemption are not two separate things,[61] and the poet of Ps 74 perceives creation as a divine "state of salvation" (vv 12–17). It is noteworthy that in Ps 74, as well as also in Deut-Isa, the perceptions of God as creator, redeemer, and king are parallel. In all these statements, as also in the priestly and Yahwistic accounts of creation, the central theme is not one of creation for its own sake, not even of creation as a state of salvation. Rather, the theme deals

---

57. Compare Comment II.2, the representation of the salvation attempt of H. Hegermann. The concept of a case of creation is presupposed by, among others, J. B. Lightfoot (p. 226); E. Lohse (p. 101); P. Ewald (pp. 336f.).

58. Ex 15:18; Num 12:21; Deut 33:5; 1 Sam 12:12; 1 Kgs 22:19; Ps 145:11ff.; 146:10; Isa 6:5; 33:22; compare also the so-called Royal Enthronement Psalms: 47; 93; 96–99.

59. Isa 24:23; 41:21; 43:15; 44:6; Zeph 3:15; Obad 1:21; Zech 14:16f.

60. See esp. Isa 52:7, which is best translated by, "Jahweh has begun his royal reign" with the redemption of Jerusalem.

61. Compare also the statements which speak of Jahweh's "creative works": Isa 41:14–20; 43:1, 15; 44:24; 46:4–13; 48:12ff.; 54:5; and others.

with creation because that belongs to the etiology of Israel (cf. Isa 51:9–16).[62] As in Col so here also we have the perception of creation oriented toward a purpose. The close relationship of the explanations in Col is still more deliberate if we consider that the selection of Israel comes to a focal point in the eschatological Yahwistic act of salvation (specifically also, according to Deut-Isa), and consequently also with it in creation.

The Colossian Hymn does not, however, explicitly speak of the manifestation of the divine dominion over Israel, but praises God's and Christ's rule over "all things" (without attempting to dispute the special role of Israel, since the Messiah of Israel is the one who is lauded).

The extension of concern for all creatures is also prepared for in the prophetic literature, especially in Isa and in Jer. The proof of the commitment of God to his people concerns not only Israel, but the entire assembly of nations.[63] And Jeremiah, along with the other voices of the exilic and post-exilic times, speaks of Yahweh as the king of the *world*,[64] whose royal reign is evident especially also in its power over the forces of nature (Jer 10:10ff.).

When we consider the middle stanza of the Colossian Hymn, which refers to Christ as the head of the body, the church, we can hardly justify an anthropological correlation of the message of the hymn in this statement. The church is not the medium of the cosmic dominion of Christ, but rather the medium of the proclamation of this cosmic dominion which has existed since creation but was made manifest in the cross. Col is primarily interested in this cosmic dominion of Christ, since it is the basis for contesting any kind of claim, justification, or actualization in the orientation of "created things" (cf. Comment IV to 2:6–23). While the statements of the hymn in NT times can be applied to contradict a religious misuse of creation, this hymnic praise of Christ can have vital relevance for today's discussion, preservation and integrity of creation. It is a basis for thoughtful reflection in the face of threats, exploitation, and destruction of creation by man, who seems to recognize no superior being besides himself. The hymn of Col is instructive in theology and in the church, for it shows that this reflection on the origin, the coherence, and the purpose of all creation does not belong among the adiaphora but is a most serious task, since it has to occur as a result of reflection about reconciliation.[65]

III. "The First-born"

The choice of the title *prōtótokos* (first-born), and not *protoktistos* (first-created) appears to stand in tension with the designation of all things as *ktisis*

---

62. See G. von Rad, Theol.d.AT I, p. 143.

63. See Isa 2:2–4; 45:14f.; 49:22f.; 60; compare 42:6, 10ff.; 43:9; 49:1, 6. In addition, see Hag 2:6ff.; Zech 14:10f., 16, 20.

64. Compare Jer 10:7, 10ff.; Zech 14:9, 16f.; Mal 1:14; Ps 22:29; 47:18.

65. For the problem of eschatology, see Comments I to 3:1–4:6.

(that which is created). Does the hymn, by using this term, describe Christ as so eternal and uncreated as only God is, and therefore as the opposite of all creatures? A negative answer is suggested by the designation "first-born," and is buttressed by the statements about wisdom in Prov 8:22f., where we read (v 22), "Yahweh *created* me, first-fruits of his way, before the oldest of his works. From everlasting, I was firmly set."[66] For an interpretation in this vein we could also cite a Pauline text: Rom 8:29.[67] There, "first-born" seems to designate the chronological first in a long series, whose members appear to exhibit a certain "sameness."[68]

Still, we cannot justify the concept "first-born" in Col 1:15 as a basis for building up a dogma about the "creatureliness" of the pre-existent Christ; neither can we endorse the opposite interpretation.[69] Because in vv 15–20 we are dealing with the problem of createdness of the beloved son of God, through whom the world was created, nor primarily with his pre-existence. In order to maintain the latter, it would have been sufficient, as in Prov 8:22ff., where no mention is made of the cooperation of wisdom in creation,[70] simply to state the begetting of Christ by the divinity before his activity of creation. The hymn in its further statements does not deal with the theme of Christ's pre-existence; rather, it emphasizes the superiority of the Messiah, the creator over all creatures. Thus, the concept "first-born" is most likely a designation of rank. Of special significance also are vv 12–14, which introduce the hymnic statements of vv 15–20. They point in the same direction because they address the *princely dominion* of the Son.

The aspect of pre-existence in this interpretation is only of secondary

---

66. Compare the careful analysis of the Heb text by C. F. Burney, APXH, op. cit., pp. 160–73.—See also Wis 7:25f., 29–30; Sir 24:3f.

67. "For those whom he foreknew he also predestined to be conformed to the image of his Son, in order that he might be the first-born among many brothers" (Rom 8:29).

68. But even here we cannot exclude the idea that the designation "first-born" is conditioned by the concept of the oriental family (brothers!), which is possibly the basis of this concept. Then "first-born" could mean a special rank among the brothers (comp. Gen 27:29).

69. For the followers of Arius (died 336 c.e.), the Arians, Col 1:15 played an important role in supporting their teaching of the creation-concept of Christ. They represented the viewpoint that the pre-existent Christ was not equally eternal with God, but that he was rather God's first and highest creation.—For the patristic text-historical criticism, see esp. A. Hockel, *Christus der Erstgeborene. Zur Geschichte der Exegese von Kol 1:15* (Düsseldorf: Patmos, 1965). Compare also J. B. Lightfoot (214ff.); N. Kehl, *Christushymnus*, op. cit., pp. 11–27.

70. The rabbinic interpretation of the Heb ʾāmōn (beloved, favorite child) as "work master" was probably distant from the original text. It can be found in the later literature, as in Wis 7:21; 8:6; and others. See G. von Rad, Theol.d.AT I, p. 446; G. Fohrer, ThWNT VII, p. 491; U. Wilckens, ibid., p. 507, fn. 291.

importance, and is inseparably connected to the Son's role as mediator of creation. [71]

Not only OT but also NT parallels support such an exposition.

1. In the OT, the designation "first-born" exists as a precedent not only in the literal sense. In the transmitted sense, the Israelite people are called the "first-born" of God (Ex 4:22; Sir 36:11, v 1) in which the component that these people are the *"first*-born," foremost among the other "brothers," is not an important factor anymore. [72] The special relationship of this people to Yahweh as the beloved and chosen one is expressed and explicit in this terminology. Especially illuminating for this purpose is LXX Ps 88(89):28. This passage is of interest in the exegesis of Col 1:15 because there the subject deals with the Davidic king; "first-born" designates the ideal king "David" in his predominant position over the kings of the earth.

2. In the NT, "first-born" is used in Heb 1:5–6 in a similar fashion as in LXX Ps 88(89). There are also significant similarities to the statements in Col 1:13ff. Hebr 1:5 speaks of the *Son* and refers to the proclamation in 2 Sam 7 (cf. Notes to Col 1:13). Heb 1:5–6 reveals that "Son" and "first-born" can be used as parallel or even synonymous titles of Christ. Essential in both designations is, as the reference of Heb 1:6b to Ps 97:7 shows, the pre-eminence of Christ among and over all powers or supposed deities ["and all the angels (Heb. *ĕlōhîm*) shall worship him"].

IV. The Image of God

The close relationship of the two honorifics, "first-born" and "image," leads to the question as to how the designation of Christ as "image" aligns itself with the interpretation of "first-born" suggested in Comment III.

Unlike Plato, [73] for example, who comprehends the cosmos as the perceptible image of an intelligible god, in Col 1:15 the same person is called the "image of God" who stands in opposition to the cosmos because the world has been created by him. This interpretation, along with the usage of the designation "image" in the cosmological context, can be reminiscent of the thought of

---

71. As is also the case in the creation concept of wisdom and her role as agent in creation, these functions are not mutually exclusive.—Just so, we also need to observe that, in the OT, the judicial functions are connected with the chronological fact of the first-born, which determines the dominance of the first-born over his brothers (comp. esp. the blessing for the first-born in Gen 27:28f.). The rights of the first-born were not necessarily tied to the one who was born first, as Gen 25:31–33 demonstrates (compare Deut 21:17; 1 Chr 5:1).

72. Compare W. Michaelis, ThWNT VI, p. 874, fn. 5.

73. Tim 92c. In the Hermetic Writings, the world is the first image of God, the human being the second; in Plutarch, the sun appears as the image of God; see the references in G. Kittel, ThWNT II, 386f.

Philo. In his view, the *logos* is the immediate image of God, and transmitted by the logos, the cosmos is the image of God. This way, the difference between creator and creation is retained rather than factually denied.

While "first-born" as a designation of *logos* does not occur in Philo, the philosopher calls the Logos "image" *(eikōn)* in the context of his pedagogy on creation.[74] The meaning of logos as "image" is based on the idea that he who represents the *spiritual* cosmos is the proto-image which is the pattern of the visible cosmos and has also played a certain active role at creation, "as with a stamp has the creator shaped the unshaped essence of the universe through him, has fashioned the unformed, has completed the entire cosmos."[75]

H. Hegermann especially drew on this Philonic interpretation to elucidate the statements of the Colossian Hymn (cf. Comment II.2). Quite justifiably, he wanted to offer an alternative to the widely disseminated derivations from the Gnostic myth regarding Prime Man.[76]

There is still another possibility for interpretation without having to introduce the Platonic tradition by way of Philo into the hymn and without having to speculate about the essence and meaning of the term "image" when it is used as a title of Christ. It is possible, and made probable by the context, that "image" as in Gen 1:26–28 denotes a *function*, namely the divine mandate to dominate the earth.[77] This interpretation is supported in 2 Cor 4:4f., which together with Col 1:15 is the only place in the Pauline corpus which discusses the divine image of Christ: the gospel of the glory of Christ who is the image of God preaches Jesus Christ "that *he is Lord,* but that we are your servants for Jesus' sake." It thus becomes probable that "image" as well as "first-born" both proclaim the supreme position of the Son in the cosmos.[78]

---

74. "Der Logos ist (das) Bild Gottes, durch den der gesammte Kosmos gebildet wurde" (Spec Leg I 81).

75. H. Hegermann, *Schöpfungsmittler,* op. cit., p. 97; Philo, Som II 45: Op Mund 25.

76. *Eikon* is then a designation of the Urmensch. Further, see Comment II.2 (to E. Käsemann's thesis). Compare also J. Jervell, "Imago Dei. Gen 1:26 f im Spätjudentum, in der Gnosis und in den paulinischen Briefen," FRLANT.NF 58 (Göttingen: Vandenhoeck & Ruprecht, 1960), p. 169.

77. When, in Gen 1:27—after it said in v 26, "Let us make mankind in our image, after our likeness, let them have dominion . . ."—the repeated statement of the likeness of God is explicated to say that God created mankind as man and woman, then we hardly have a statement concerning the essence of likeness. As v 28 indicates (". . . be fruitful and multiply, and fill the earth and subdue it . . .") the Priestly creation account (different from the Jahwist) interprets creation of humans *as man and woman* as a closer elucidation and facilitation of the command to subdue the earth. Being fruitful and *filling* the earth are prerequisite to subduing it.

78. Also H. Wildberger, "Das Abbild Gottes," ThZ 21 (1965) 245–59; 481–501, directs us to the context and views *eikōn* (image) as interpreted from 1:13, where the discussion concerns the "beloved Son" and the "reign of the king" (p. 500).—He directs

The attribute "image of God *who is not seen*" does not contradict the above statement. At first glimpse, the combination of the Christ designation as "image" with the fact that God is not seen by human eyes *(aoratos)* seems to demand that in v 15a Christ means primarily agent or paragon of God's revelation.[79] But aside from the fact that such an interpretation would fit into the context only with great difficulty,[80] this inference is not compelling. If we consider the expression "of God who is not seen" in light of the OT, then it becomes clear that we are not dealing primarily with the "invisibility" of God and therefore not with the attempt to make him visible. Rather, the emphasis lies on the glory including the power of God which no human eye and no living person could withstand unless God himself provided special protection. Col 1:15 proclaims the greatness of God's glory and power, as well as his inaccessibility and sovereignty (cf. Notes to "of God who is not seen").

When we interpret "image" as title for a royal ruler, then the infinitive "of God" in Col 1:15 refers to God who has enthroned his Son as Lord over all things (cf. Phil 2:10–11). The addition of "who is not seen" indicates the glory and power not only of God but also of him who is installed by the Father. Jesus is legitimatized by God as "image" and "first-born," namely as ruler and king of all creation.

V. The Church in the History of Israel

As in the epistle to the Ephesians, so also in the epistle to the Colossians, the gospel is distinguished by the message that, through the Messiah, non-Jews have attained access to the God of Israel and to a share in the Jewish inheritance. But while in Eph the ecclesiological significance of this act of salvation, namely the church as the unity of Jews and gentiles, is unfolded on a broad scale, in Col *cosmological* proclamations have the position of prominence. But in so

---

the "image" statement back to the OT to the ancient Egyptian conceptualization of king as image of the godhead. Compare also J. Jervell, *Imago Dei*, op. cit., p. 333, "Durch *eikōn* (. . .) wird die einzigartige Stellung Christi als Schöpfungsmittler und Kosmokrator geschildert." "Christus ist nicht Stellvertreter Gottes in der Welt in dem Sinne, dass Gott selbst nicht hervortreten kann; sondern Gott selbst ist in Christus für die Welt als Schöpfer und Regierer anwesend."

79. The following, among others, interpret the verse in this sense: J. Calvin (p. 85); H. A. W. Meyer (p. 240); E. Haupt (p. 25); M. Dibelius–H. Greeven (p. 12); E. Lohmeyer (p. 54); E. Lohse (p. 85); A. Lindemann (p. 26); R. P. Martin (p. 44); N. Kehl, *Christushymnus*, op. cit., pp. 65f., 72–76, 98; F.-J. Steinmetz: "Protologische Heilszuversicht. Die Strukturen des soteriologischen und christologischen Denkens im Kolosser- und Epheserbrief," FTS 2 (Frankfurt: Knecht, 1969), p. 70 (cited in PHZ).

80. The statement "He is the revealed (image) of God, who is not seen, because God has created everything through him and for him" would make sense in itself. However, it seems strange within the context, which describes the relationship of Christ to all creation, but not that of Christ to God (see Comment II.3).

doing, there is no aspiration to actualize or translate the Christian message (which grew out of Judaism) for Hellenistically oriented people (cf. Comment II.2). On the contrary, the author of Col appears to have two central concerns: the interpretation of the cosmos as the work and object of grace of God and Christ, and the redemption of the world by its participation in Israel's history. First, all the cosmological statements in 1:15ff. are related to the Hebrew Messiah, who has now begun the dominion that was announced in the OT (cf. Notes to 1:13). Second, the commencement of his reign over the cosmos, which is also the focus in 1:13 but in special application to the gentiles, is described by allusions to events from the OT history of Israel (cf. Notes to 1:12–14). It is connected to the "exodus tradition" ("he has delivered us"), to the "tradition of the monarchy" ("he has transferred us into the monarchic dominion of his Son"), and to the consummate hope of Israel (as well as of the intimate tradition of the cult) ("the redemption, the forgiveness of sins"). The entire history of Israel from its beginning to its "end" is succinctly summarized in these characteristic themes. And non-Jews are now participants in this history of Israel through the Messiah. Together with Israel, the gentiles can now acknowledge and praise the mighty acts of God for his people to which they now also belong. He has led them out of the "realm of darkness" and they now also belong to the dominion of the proclaimed king established on the throne of David; for them also God has fulfilled his promises for the end of time by redeeming them and forgiving them their sins. The origin of the "Christian" church was therefore not intended as a new beginning of divine action in the world, just as the church's theology was never intended to be "specifically Christian." The history of the church is *participation* in the OT Judaic history, just as the theology of the church is participation in the OT Jewish theology. The community and unity of Jews and gentiles is to glorify the magnitude of God's love for his people. This love reaches deeper and farther than the men and women in the accounts of the Hebrew Bible ever expected (cf. Col 1:26).

III. PAUL, SERVANT OF THE COLOSSIANS
(1:24–2:5)

24 Thus I rejoice in my sufferings, which I suffer for you. Indeed, I repay for His body (i.e. the church), what is still lacking of Christ's affliction in my flesh. 25 Because I have become servant of the church according to the will of God who gave me my commission, with the purpose to fulfill specifically for you his word; 26 (i.e.) the secret, which has been hidden since far-distant ages. Now, however, it has been revealed to his saints! 27 To them God wanted to make known what are the glorious riches of this secret among the gentiles: this

is the Messiah among you, the glorious hope. 28 Him we proclaim, by admonishing each person and teaching each person in all wisdom, because we want to present each person perfect in Christ. 29 And for this I struggle and strive, because his power works mightily in me. 2:1 For I want you to know what a struggle I have for you and for the (brothers) in Laodicea, even for all those who (also) do not know me personally. 2 So that all your hearts will be comforted, held together in love, in order to gain all the abounding fullness of understanding, namely the knowledge of the secret of God, that is the Messiah. 3 In him all the treasures of wisdom and knowledge are stored, (specifically) hidden. 4 All this I say, so that no one may delude you with specious arguments. 5 For even if I am absent in body, I am still with you in spirit, as someone who rejoices and who sees your orderly discipline and the constancy of your faith in the Messiah.

NOTES

After the previous statements, the change to Paul as subject of the sentence which begins here is noticeable and demonstrates the beginning of a new section. Vv 1:24–2:5 concern the service of Paul. However, instead of the general fundamental and essential rendering of Paul's apostolate, his specific service to the community at Colossae is being discussed. The frequent expressions which define his relationship to the community at Colossae demonstrate this point. Paul rejoices in his suffering *"for you"* (pl; 1:24); "with the purpose . . . *for you*" (pl) he is to fulfill the word of God (1:25); he makes known the glorious riches of the secret, which is Christ *"among you"* (pl; 1:27); he refers to his "struggle . . . *for you*" (pl; 2:1). No reason exists to assume that Paul has to justify his authority among the Colossians; on the contrary, he emphasizes and praises the order and stability of this community (2:5). This indicates that Paul intends to underline his specific concern for the Colossians which already became manifest in the thanksgiving, his intercession, and in Col 1:23, his first admonition. He, the servant entrusted with a universal mission, elaborates how important this out-of-the-way community of Colossae is to him, that congregation which he had neither founded himself nor had ever visited.

He does this in two patterns of thinking. In the first (1:24–27), he affirms to the Colossians that his suffering for the (universal) church is also suffering specifically for the Colossians, as also the riches of the secret proclaimed among the gentiles consist exactly in the message that Christ is the Messiah among the Colossians. In a second train of thought (1:28–2:5), the goal of the Pauline service is summarized (v 28): "because we want to present *each person* perfect in Christ." Here also, the worldwide commission is also aimed specifically at the community in Colossae (and Laodicea; 2:1f.). In the elucidations in 2:6–23, this point becomes concrete. Chap. 2:4 + 5 summarizes the concern of the declarations in 1:24ff. once again and simultaneously form a connecting link to the following section.

24 *Thus I rejoice* (literally: Now). In its temporal significance, the adverbial determinant *nyn* (now) appears abruptly and without a direct connection after 1:21–23. It is therefore not probable that any kind of time frame is intended.[1] Rather, the Greek *nyn* here marks the beginning of a paragraph to define and elaborate on one of the earlier statements. The designation at the close of v 23, which describes Paul as "servant of the gospel," is elucidated in 1:24ff. in its special relationship to the community in Colossae. In this function and meaning, the *nyn* here can be paraphrased as: "this now is the situation (that here I am the servant of the gospel). . . ."[2]

in my sufferings, which I suffer for you (literally: the sufferings for you). The possessive pronoun "my (sufferings)" occurs in only a few less significant manuscripts. While "my" is probably a later addition to the original text, it fits in with the intention of the author. Col 1:24ff. emphasizes the close relationship of Paul to the Colossians (see above), even though he was never there, and consequently also his deliberate suffering for them. Unlike our English version, in the Greek original the words "suffering" and "for you" immediately follow each other and build a unit. The suffering of a servant of the gospel cannot be separated from the people for whose sake it is endured: apostolic suffering is a social suffering. This interpretation is not dependent on the translation of *hyper* (for) either by "for (your) benefit" or "in place of (you)"; the former possibility is included in the latter.

Like *hyper*, the preposition *en* also offers two possibilities for translation. It can be rendered not only in the sense of place, "*in* my sufferings," but also with the meaning of "I rejoice *about* my sufferings." Usually, to indicate the latter meaning, the Greek *epi* is used (cf. Rom 16:19; 1 Cor 13:6; 16:17; 2 Cor 7:13),

---

1. J. B. Lightfoot (p. 230) interprets, "now when I see all the glory of bearing a part in this magnificent work . . . ," but in this he does not presume—without any kind of frame of reference in Col—that Paul had experienced his suffering as too difficult, but *now* he could be glad again. H. von Soden (p. 35) applies "now" to the receipt of the good news about the Colossians (1:3–7), but in our opinion, he takes too little note of the immediate connection between suffering and joy in Paul. E. Lohse (p. 112) suggests, "Jetzt, wo von dem universalen Heilswerk der Versöhnung die Rede ist . . . ," without, in our opinion, also being just to the cited connection between suffering and joy. R. P. Martin (NCC, p. 69) wants to create a relationship to the present situation in Kolossae, according to which false teachers infer that his demand to leadership is false. This is true for 2 Cor, but in Col it is a supposition which cannot be substantiated. F. Zeilinger (ESpg, p. 88) interprets "now" as "eschatological now" (compare G. Stählin, ThWNT IV, pp. 1112f.).

2. We find a similar usage of "now" also in 1 Cor 12:20 which demonstrates a concretization or illustration of a previously expressed idea. Compare also 1 Cor 5:11 ("now" in a form of the past !) and 2 Cor 7:9.

but the use of *en* in place of *epi* also occurs in the NT (Luke 10:20; Phil 1:18). We are dealing with a borrowing from the Hebrew. Both variants hardly make a difference in the meaning of this context, which deals with a very specific understanding of suffering (cf. Comment 1).

I repay . . . what is still lacking . . . of Christ's afflictions (literally: and repay the lack of the afflictions of Christ). This statement is full of exegetical difficulties, which are multiplied because of the double genitive and the resultant variety of possible interpretations.

1. In the genitive "lack of afflictions," we can have (a) a subjective genitive, so that "lack" denotes the afflictions of Christ as being less than complete. Or the genitive may be (b) partitive; then we would be dealing with a lack of afflictions without a commentary on quality.[3]

2. The genitive "afflictions of Christ" can be translated as (a) subjective genitive and can thus designate the sufferings that Christ suffers or suffered, or both. The number of possibilities for this expression is even increased by the fact that we can interpret "Christ" as the "earthly" or the "elevated" Lord, or both, or even as the so-called "mystical Christ," namely either the church[4] or, in an individualistic sense,[5] as Christ residing in the saints and as the saints' being in Christ. (b) If we are dealing with a genitive *auctoris*, then the sufferings

---

3. Still a third possibility can be named: the genitive can be understood as a genitive of the object of concern in an absolute sense (comp. for that LXX Judg 18:10; 19:19). It would then say that no "suffering of Christ" had existed and that Paul was only now filling this absolute deficit. The suffering of Christ could then mean only the suffering of Christians. This interpretation can hardly be taken seriously, for the statement in 1:11 alone already presumes suffering also of the Colossians (comp. 4:8).

4. The differentiation of "head" and "body" characteristic of the representation of body in Col puts the equivalent of "suffering of Christ" to "suffering of the church" into question. Precisely when we use this to interpret the concept "suffering of Christ," it would primarily mean the suffering of the head. Compare also B. N. Wambacq: "Adimpleo ea quae desunt passionum Christi in carne mea . . . ," VD 27 (1949) 17–22:22.

5. As a representative example of this concept, A. Deissmann, *Paulus. Eine kultur- und religionsgeschichtliche Skizze* (Tübingen: Mohr, 1911), p. 107, quotes, "Nicht der alte Paulus leidet, sondern der neue Paulus, der ein Glied am Leibe Christi ist, und der darum alles mystisch miterlebt, was der Leib erlebt hat und erlebt: er 'leidet mit Christus,' ist 'mit Christus gekreuzigt,' 'mit Christus gestorben,' 'begraben,' 'auferweckt,' und er 'lebt mit Christus.' " Compare also J. Schmid, "Kol 1, 24," BZ 21 (1933) 330–44.—Since suffering according to this concept does not mean an act accomplished after the suffering of Christ, but means rather a union in suffering with Christ which no longer justifies "my suffering" and "suffering of Christ," the argument of E. Lohmeyer (p. 77) makes this interpretation improbable, namely that the expression "insufficiency of suffering" remains incomprehensible in the context of the suffering mystique, "Denn in dem 'mystischen Nachleiden' ist entweder das ganze Leiden Christi gegenwärtig und 'Mangel' in keinem Augenblicke spürbar, oder es bleibt das eigene Leiden des Glaubens

that are endured "for the sake of Christ" are intended. (c) If we have a qualitative genitive, the reference is to sufferings as Christ has endured them or endures them.

In the combination of the variously enumerated possibilities under 1 and 2, we theoretically have at least fourteen different variants. For discussion of the question as to what 1:24 can mean, cf. Comment 1.

A help in limiting the number of possible interpretations could be provided by the verb *antanapléroō*, the Greek verb *pléroō* (to make full, to fill completely, to finish, to complete), supplied with the two prefixes *ant-* and *-ana-*. This double composite occurs only in this passage in the NT; it is not in the LXX and is also rarely used in the extra-biblical Greek texts. Particularly decisive in this context is the prefix *ant-* in comprehending the meaning of the passage. J. B. Lightfoot (p. 231) sees in it the idea "that the supply comes *from an opposite quarter* to the deficiency." J. Kremer concurs on the basis that the extra-biblical occurrences of the word, six in number, lead to the conclusion that in the prefix *ant-* in *antanapléroō* we are dealing with the replacement of something missing with *something else.*[6] This explanation leads J. Kremer to his interpretation of the phrase "afflictions of Christ" on the basis of the determination of this concept, since his interpretation of the prefix *ant-* demands that the "afflictions of Christ," whose lack is admitted, and the suffering of Paul, must be the sufferings of two different parties. Consequently, the genitive expression

---

von jenem vorbildlichen Leiden Christi geschieden, bleibt aus sich heraus mangelhaft, solange bis der Tod oder die Parusie alle diese irdischen Mängel nachsichtig ausgleicht. Dann kann auch niemals von einem 'Erfüllen' gesprochen werden." For criticism, see also the detailed explication of the suffering mystique in E. Güttgemann, "Der leidende Apostel und sein Herr. Studien zur paulinischen Christologie," FRLANT 90 (Göttingen: Vandenhoeck & Ruprecht, 1966), pp. 102–12, and the criticism in J. Kremer, "Was an den Leiden Christi noch mangelt. Eine interpretationsgeschichtliche und exegetische Untersuchung zu Kol 1.24b," BBB 12 (Bonn: Hanstein, 1956), pp. 183–87.

6. J. Kremer, op. cit., p. 160. He found E. Käsemann's agreement in this conceptual determination [Rez., J. Kremer, op. cit., ThLZ 82 (1957) 614f.]. T. K. Abbott (p. 229f.) countered this interpretation in response to J. B. Lightfoot, with the response, among others, that the idea, to which the latter attributed the prefix *anti*, was not specifically tied to this prefix and could also be expressed simply by *anapléroō* (compare 1 Cor 16:17; Phil 2:30). T. K. Abbott refers the prefix to the attributed lack which is indicated by *antanapléroō*, in connection with J. J. Wettstein (*Novum Testamentum Graecum*, Vol. II, Amsterdam, 1752, z. St.), *in which place* we have *(anti)* a fullness (thus also, among others, H. A. W. Meyer, E. Haupt, H. von Soden). However, with the observation that *anapléroō* can have the same meaning as *antanapléroō*, it is not yet proven that *antanapléroō* is also equivalent to *anapléroō*. W. R. G. Moir, "Colossians 1,24," ET 42 (1930/31) 479–80:480, interpreted the prefix *anti* as an emphatic of the composite *anapléroō*, "He (Paul, H.B.) implied that his afflictions were following one another in quick succession; in other words, that he was much afflicted and that he was nearing the full sum of them—in other words, that the time of his departure was at hand."

"afflictions of Christ" can be understood only as a subjective genitive to designate the suffering of the earthly or elevated Christ. The sufferings of the church cannot be intended, since it is of the same kind as the sufferings of Paul.[7]

But the basis for this argumentation is weak, (1) because there are only few occurrences of the verb *antanapléroō* to support J. Kremer's reasoning, and (2) because we need to remember that the Koine, and thus the NT Greek, has a preference for using composites in places where the classical language uses the simple form. In Col also, this tendency to use composites has been observed without enabling us to determine a difference in meaning from the simpler forms elsewhere in the NT.[8] (3) It is noticeable that among the ancient Greek textual exegetes of Col, no one except Photius[9] pointed to a special meaning of the prefix. (4) Of significance is also the observation that *ant-* was placed before composites "since classical times to an increasing extent."[10]

On the basis of these indications, we should not attribute special significance to the prefix or make it decisive for the interpretation of the entire verse. We further deem it likely that the prefix did not change the meaning of the simplex. In short: *antanapléroō* and *antapléroō* have the same sense. *Anapléroō*, literally translated, means "to fill to the top."[11] In addition, in every occurrence in the NT and in the LXX, it is presupposed that we are dealing with a complete filling up, fulfilling, completion.

The expression "to fill the lack" seems to be a set phrase.[12] It occurs in the NT also in 1 Cor 16:17 and Phil 2:30. However, in both instances, the word "lack" is used in the singular, whereas in Col it is used in the pl, without a difference in meaning (cf. 2 Cor 8:14/9:12). In both cases, we are dealing with the concept of *removing* a lack.

As in Col 1:24, in Phil 2:30 the expression "to fill the lack" is also construed in the genitive. There, it designates the "thing" that is lacking (cf. Comment I).

in my flesh. If this phrase refers to the verb "repay," then it indicates the location where the repayment has to take place. It is just as possible grammatically that the formula serves to interpret the expression "afflictions of Christ" by saying that very special "afflictions of Christ" are meant, i.e. the "afflictions of

---

7. According to J. Kremer, *Leiden Christi*, op. cit., p. 189, the genitive "suffering *of Christ*" in connection with the declaration in 1:24 determines "the *thlipseis* (tribulation, H.B.) foremost as the affliction suffered by the historical Jesus, but beyond that also the affliction of those who stand in place of Christ." He thus marks the connection to *John Chrysostom*'s explication.

8. Compare *epi-ginōskō* (recognize) in 1:6; *apo-kat-allassō* (reconcile) in 1:20; *epimenō* (remain) in 1:23.

9. Photius, in "Quaestiones Amphilochii," rendered *anti* together with "in place of (Christ)" (see J. Kremer, op. cit., p. 32).

10. E. Schwyzer, *Grammatik II*, p. 442.

11. Compare G. Delling, ThWNT VI, p. 304.

12. U. Wilckens, ThWNT VIII, pp. 597, 591.

Christ in my flesh." A third possibility is to combine "in my flesh" with "lack;" in this case, a still existing vacuum in Paul is meant, and the genitive "afflictions of Christ" would be the missing element.[13] For the discussion of these possibilities, cf. Comment I.

for His body (i.e. the church). The community is identified by the same imagery as in 1:18. There and here, the image of the body is a corollary to the Messiah who is the head (see Notes to 1:18 and esp. also Notes to 2:19).

As already in the expression "for you," we also have two possibilities here for translating "for" *(hyper):* the preposition means either "for the benefit of," or "in place of" (cf. Comment I).

The parallel structure of "for you" and "for the church," which we encounter in similar form again later in this context, is noteworthy. As a servant of the church, Paul has to fulfill the word of God specifically *for the Colossians* (v 25). The riches of the secret *among the gentiles* is Christ *"among you"* (v 27). Paul thus gives expression to the idea that it is a significant feature of the universality of his office that specifically he serves this single and unpretentious community.

25 Because I have become servant of the church (literally: whose servant). As servant of the gospel (1:23), Paul is servant of the church. This latter designation, together with the description of the Pauline mandate "to admonish and to instruct" in 1:28, has given rise to the idea in v 25 that a post-Pauline era becomes apparent at this place (cf. Comment III to 1:3–8). Thus, for example, F. Hahn[14] pointed out that unlike Rom (16:25–27) it is no longer the *mission* to the gentiles, but to the church, as whose servant Paul is presented, which is the focal point here. According to Hahn's understanding of this passage, God's divine redemptive will is fulfilled no longer in the mission to the gentiles but now by the existence of the church, which was chosen from among the gentiles. It is the church, he argues, that must be protected in its position of grace; *it* must grow and must be guided toward perfection. Though the mission to the gentiles is still a function of the church, the church's main commission lies in its foundation as the legitimate church(!) and its primary service in the world consists of its existence(!) and its growth toward the head.

However, we should not forget that Paul also in Romans describes his activities as missionary to the gentiles as a "priestly service."[15] He emphasizes that he perceives his service in and to the existing communities as a substantial

---

13. Compare LXX Judg 18:10, which also reads *hysterēma* (lack) with the genitive of the "thing" that is lacking which belongs with it, and which adds an indication of place; however not with *en* (in), but rather with *hou . . . ekei* (where . . . there).

14. F. Hahn, *Das Verständnis der Mission im Neuen Testament,* WMANT 13, (Neukirchen-Vluyn: Neukirchener Verlag, 1963), esp. pp. 129f.

15. Rom 15:16, "that I will be a servant of Christ for the gentiles and that I will perform the ministerial service of the gospel, so that the gentiles will be a well-pleasing offering for God. . . ."

component of his apostolate.[16] In fact, all preserved Pauline writings are the result of this aspect of his apostolate among the gentiles. Since Col 1:25 was not written to carefully elucidate every side and aspect of the Pauline apostolate (cf. the introductory remarks to 1:24ff.), and since the captivity of Paul is viewed in Col as one aspect of his "pioneering *mission*" (cf. 4:3), the statements in this passage are hardly sufficient to support F. Hahn's viewpoint (cf. Notes to 1:28).

For the meaning of the emphatic "I" (*egō*), compare Eph 3:8[17] and Notes to 1:1 ("apostle"). In view of the statement in Col 2:5, a polemic meaning is most improbable.

according to the will of God, who gave me my commission. (literally: in accordance with the administrative office given to me by God). The Greek word *oikonomia* occurs nine times in the NT, three times in Luke where it designates the office of *oikonomos* (administrator, manager) (Luke 16:3).[18] The statements in Luke indicate that the *oikonomos* is put in charge of the servants and all the goods of his lord. Sometimes he had risen from the rank of slaves (note the parallel usage of *oikonomos* and "slave" in Luke 12:42–43).[19] Though even as a chief administrator, unless he was manumitted, or even after his emancipation, he remained a slave. But not only useful and trustworthy slaves, but also free administrators could still be called *doulos* (either in the sense of slave or servant). *Oikonomos* also occurs as the title of a city official (Rom 16:23). The most important attribute of an *oikonomos* was his loyalty (Luke 12:42; 16:10f.; Matt 25:21, 23), a reason for Paul to adopt this official title for describing himself and his service.[20]

The concept of *oikonomia* also has a second meaning.[21] It designates official occasions and decrees,[22] and also indicates "order" or "arrangement," "tactic," "plan," as well as the execution of an undertaking.[23] In the religious realm, magical practices are described by this concept. The Church Fathers use this in

---

16. Compare also 1 Cor 4:14f.; 2 Cor 11:2.

17. "To me, the least of all the saints, has been given this grace of bringing the gospel of the inexhaustible richness of the Messiah to the gentiles."

18. In the LXX, *oikonomia* occurs only in Isa 22:19, 21, both times in reference to an "office."

19. According to Gal 4:2, he was also responsible for the upbringing of the heir.

20. 1 Cor 4:1f.—in this sense possibly also in 1 Tim 1:4. O. Michel (ThWNT V, 155, 18), however, translates with "Heilserziehung," in association with the patristic usage of the word.

21. Compare the references in LSLex and BauerLex.

22. This concept is attested in the second century C.E. as a designation in the testament of a private person. See J. Reumann, "OIKONOMIA = 'Covenant'; Terms for Heilsgeschichte in Early Christian Usage," NT 3 (1959) 282–92:284.

23. Compare Josephus, Ant. 2, 89, according to which Pharaoh accorded the "execution" (*oikonomia*) of his counsel to Joseph.

the sense of a "(divine redeeming) plan."[24] The interpretation of *oikonomia* in this latter sense is suggested by several exegetes of Eph (1:10; 3:2, 9).[25] In Col also, a number of interpreters translate *oikonomia* in the second sense, namely "(redeeming) plan, counsel, decision, etc."[26]

Such an interpretation could be supported by the genitive *tou theou* (of God) which is aligned with *oikonomia* and fits the meaning "plan/redeeming plan" seemingly without difficulty. (But see fn. 25.) Still, the translation "office" is possible as well, since we could be dealing with a genitive *auctoris*, which elevates God as the one who gave Paul his office. We can justify this explanation in reference to 1 Cor 3:10, where the genitive *tou theou* is used in this sense in connection with the concept of "grace" (*charis*: cf. Rom 1:5; 12:3; Gal 2:9),[27] which is also used to describe the Pauline sense of service. Neither interpretation can be confirmed with certainty. Also the phrase "to give God's plan (of redemption)" makes sense; it means "to give insight into God's plan (of redemption)" using the translation: "plan."[28] But since the meaning "plan of redemption/decision" for *oikonomia* is documented chiefly in late references, and is neither in the OT nor definitely in the NT and since the translation "office" for *oikonomia* is meaningful, we prefer the translation "office" as the most applicable and likely here.

The preposition *kata* (according to) then defines Paul's servanthood more closely from two perspectives, first as an office from God and not from men (cf. Gal 1:1), and second as an office among the gentiles and thus also among the Colossians (cf. Rom 1:5; 15:16).

with the purpose . . . for you. Do these words refer to the preceding or the

---

24. For that, compare J. Reumann, op. cit. (fn. 23), 282f.

25. M. Barth, however, refutes this interpretation for important reasons (AB 34, esp. pp. 86ff.; 329; 342f.).

26. Among others, J. Reumann, "OIKONOMIA—Terms in Paul in Comparison with Lucan Heilsgeschichte," NTS 13 (1966/67) 147–67:162ff. E. Lohmeyer (p. 80); F. F. Bruce (p. 84); P. T. O'Brien (p. 81; he considers the concept in both meanings in 1:24 as intentional); W. Bieder (p. 92); C. F. D. Moule (p. 80); O. Cullmann, *Christus und die Zeit. Die urchristliche Zeit- und Geschichtsauffassung*, 2d ed. (Zollikon-Zürich: Evang. Verlag, 1948), pp. 27, 67.

27. E. Lohmeyer (p. 80) thinks that the preposition *kata* (in accordance with) excludes the translation "office." The argument is not convincing, since the concept "servant of the church" can be elucidated further. J. Reumann, op. cit. (fn. 26), p. 163, considers the translation "office" impossible, "because of the general sense which *oikonomia tou theou* had in the Hellenistic world," in addition to the reasons already mentioned. We can still argue, however, that the known usage by Paul (as well as by Luke and the LXX) favors the translation "office." And even the genitive "of God" can be explained in this context as well.

28. Compare Matt 13:11, "To you it has been given *to know* the secrets of the kingdom of heaven," with the parallel and synonymous passage in Mark 4:11, "To you has been given the secret of the kingdom of God."

following statement? Both alternatives are possible grammatically. The use of the preposition *eis* in comparable references[29] and above all the parallel statement in Eph 3:2 ("surely you have heard that I was given God's grace in order to administer it to [*eis*] you") seem to recommend that *eis hymas* should refer to "office."[30] However, in contrast to Eph 3:2, the corresponding statement in Col 1:25 is introduced by "according . . ." and is thus a closer definition of a previous utterance. It serves to elucidate the assertion that Paul has become servant of the church.[31] A translation similar to Eph 3:2 in this context would seem to be less appropriate here, because the use of the aorist form *egenomēn* "I have become (servant of the church)" would imply that Paul has been installed by God as servant of the *Colossians* and *because of this* has become servant of the church. Therefore *eis hymas* probably belongs to the subsequent statement, "with the purpose to fulfill the word of God."

with the purpose to fulfill specifically his word for you (literally: the word of God). Paul here maintains that he became the servant of the church specifically to fulfill God's word in Colossae.[32] He thus emphasizes once more that, not only for him but also within the framework of his office, his endeavors for the Colossians are not of secondary interest.

In Rom 15:19 (7–19), we have a similar choice of words in a context similar to Col 1:25. The word used is the simple verb form *plēroō* (to make full, to fulfill, to complete, to finish); in Rom 15:19 that which is "filled" is the "gospel." But "gospel" and "word of God" are interchangeable concepts for Paul (cf. for example 1 Cor 14:36; 2 Cor 2:17). In addition, in both passages, the context deals with Paul's service among the gentiles. In Rom 15, however, the expression "to fulfill the gospel" is coined in the context of OT promises regarding the calling of the gentiles, and its meaning is colored by these references. But Col 1:25 is different. E. Haupt (pp. 58f.) justifiably pointed out that we are dealing with a completely unknown quantity here,[33] which means

---

29. See 2 Cor 8:4, in which the discussion is focused on the offertory for the Jerusalem community as one of "service (*diakonia*) to (*eis*) the saints." Compare also Rom 15:16, "servants (*leitourgos*) of Jesus Christ to (*eis*) the gentiles."

30. Thus, among others, J. B. Lightfoot (p. 233); T. K. Abbott (p. 233); E. Lohse (p. 118).

31. In view of this function, we would rather use Eph 3:7 for comparison, where *eis hymas* is noticeably absent: "whose servants (of the gospel, H.B.) I have become according to the gift of the grace of God. . . ."

32. We can probably also explain the aorist form *plērosai* (in order to fulfill) from this limitation of his service to the community in Colossae, instead of the present or perfect (comp. Rom 15:19). The aim does not have to be an accomplished goal, perhaps the conclusion of the missionary effort to the gentile people, specifically in the Mediterranean basin of its day (comp. E. Schweizer, pp. 86f.).

33. According to E. Haupt (p. 59), the focus is on the actualization of the word of

the *plēroō* can hardly indicate the fulfillment of concrete expectations (based on OT promises).

The concept of "God's word" in Col 1:25 is identified with the term "secret" in v 26 just as (Christ's) body and the "church" in 1:18. This "secret" is the role of the Jewish Messiah as creator, reconciler, and king of all of creation. The revelation of this secret calls for the commission to preach to the gentiles (cf. Comment II). Consequently, "to fulfill God's word (specifically the revealed secret)" means to proclaim its riches among the gentiles in the way described in 1:28 (cf. Notes).

26 . . . *the secret. Mystērion*, used in the pl *(mystēria)*, is a widespread religious concept in the extra-biblical Greek documents and is used to designate not only the numerous ancient mystery cults but also the characteristic holy activities and rites of these cults. The latter represented the actual mystery events. Through them, the participants were granted a share in the fate of their respective deities and in the divine life force. Only consecrated individuals could be participants and were subject to stringent injunctions to guard the secrets and maintain silence about them. Probably for this reason, the cults came to be known as *mystēria*.[34] However, in the NT this is not used in this sense. "As a whole, *mystērion* is an infrequent concept in the NT, which does not permit us to acquire specific knowledge of the relationship to any mystery cults."[35]

Aside from that, the profane use of the word is attested in the extra-biblical Greek texts as well as in the LXX,[36] and its employment in Col 1:26 is derived from this profane use (cf. Comment II). In the ancient church, the word *mystēria*, or rather its Latin equivalent *sacramenta*, again assumed a more

---

God, specifically its content, namely that the gentiles also belong. Compare among the numerous interpretations also E. Lohse (p. 118), "Das Wort Gottes wird erfüllt, wenn es an allen Orten ausgerufen und aller Kreatur unter dem Himmel verkündigt wird." J. H. Schutz, *Paul and the Anatomy of Apostolic Authority*, SNTS.MS 26 (Cambridge: University Press, 1975), p. 47, "fully in word and deed, with signs and wonders." P. T. O'Brien (p. 83), ". . . when it is dynamically and effectively proclaimed in the power of the Spirit . . . throughout the world, and accepted by men in faith (. . .)."

34. The concept is probably derived from *"myein"* (to close: the eyes, the lips, the mouth). Compare H. Kramer, "Zur Wortbedeutung 'Mysteria,'" WuD.NF 6 (1959) 121–25. According to G. Bornkamm, the etymology of the word is itself a puzzle. It leads "only to the somewhat certain determination that *mysterion* is something which mandates silence" (ThWNT IV, p. 810).

35. G. Bornkamm, ThWNT IV, p. 831.

36. Compare LSLex.—In the LXX, compare, among others, Tob 12:7, 11 (secret of a king); 2 Macc 13:21 (military secrets); Sir 27:16 (secret of a friend).—Dan 2:28 uses *mystēria* in a specialized sense of the impending occurrences of the last days. Compare G. Bornkamm, ThWNT IV, p. 821; E. Lohse, p. 119.

general meaning[37] alongside a resumption of its specialized significance for the ecclesiastical sacraments.[38]

which has been hidden since far-distant ages (literally: since the ages and the generations before the aeons and the generations). For the compound *apo-kekrymenon* (which was hidden), cf. Notes to 1:24 (*antanapleroō*, I complement).[39]

The preposition *apo*, which we have translated by "since," allows two different interpretations, which in turn necessitate different variants of the pertinent substantives:

1. The temporal meaning "since" is one possibility. When *apo* precedes *aiōn* in the LXX, the meaning is "since far-distant ages or past" and it is to be interpreted from the Hebrew *ʿôlām*, the equivalent of *aiōn*.[40] The usage of the pl *aiōnes* (times) can be traced to the Hebrew *ʿôlāmîm*, which then has an intensifying force.[41]

The second term "generations" *(genea)* can be understood in a similar manner. In the Hebrew Bible its equivalent is *dōr*. The primary meaning of this word is also temporal and designates a length of time. "But a temporal extension is not merely an abstraction in the corresponding Hebraic comprehension of time. It must always be realized within its context (. . .). The length of time, which is designated by *dōr*, is only comprehensible as the continuity of time of the people living within that time-span."[42] Both concepts, "ages" and "generations," can thus stand in an almost synonymous relationship to each other, as is already the case in the LXX (cf. Exod 40:15; Lev 3:17).

2. In association with Hebrew usage, *apo* can also introduce the person from whom something is concealed (cf. LXX 4 Kgdms (Eng 2 Kgs) 4:27; Ps 118[119]:19; Matt 11; 25; Rev 6:16; BDR 155.3). This interpretation would imply a personal understanding of *aiōnes*. We can document this usage already from the third/second century B.C.E. The veneration of a god *Aion* in Alexandria is attested from this period.[43] The expression *aiōnes* in Col 1:26 could be related

---

37. It stands for different components of Christian teaching, esp. for the virgin birth and the death of Jesus. See Ignatius, Eph 19; Justinius, Apol I.13; Dial 74; 91.

38. Compare G. Bornkamm, ThWNT IV, 831–33.

39. J. Chrysostom (PG 62, 331) attributed intensive meaning to the prefix *apo*, and translated: "totally hidden."

40. For this usage, compare, among others, LXX Ps 40 (41):14; 105 (106):48. For the meaning of the Heb *ʿolam*, see E. Jenni, THAT II, p. 230.

41. Compare E. Jenni, THAT II, p. 231.

42. G. Gerlemann, THAT I, p. 444.

43. Compare H. Sasse, ThWNT I, p. 198.—See also Epictetus (died 138 C.E.), "For I am no aion, but am rather a human being. . . ." (2, 5, 13) The continuation of this statement demonstrates that *aion* meant a heavenly being.—Perhaps in an equally personal sense, *aion* was used in a glorification of God in 1 Enoch 9:4, "Lord of Lords, God of Gods, King of Aions."

in a similar sense and could serve to identify heavenly powers.[44] Such an interpretation might be supported by the assertion in Eph 3:10 (cf. 1 Pet 1:12), according to which the church is to proclaim the wisdom of God to the heavenly powers and forces, a wisdom which is made known through the revelation of God's secret. We should also cite Eph 2:2 in this connection, "you followed the *aiōn* of this world, the ruler of the atmosphere . . . ," where *aiōn* is a description of a deity. But one can just as easily translate Eph 2:2 as "this world-age."[45]

In Col 1:26, there are at least five reasons that favor a temporal meaning:

a. Paul (as also elsewhere in the NT and in the LXX) never uses the pl form *aiōnes* to designate (heavenly) powers and forces. This usage only comes into its own with the Gnostics in the second century.[46]

b. It would also be difficult to ascertain why the usual sense of a nontemporal meaning would be intended in this connection for "generation" *(genea)* where other designations for powers are introduced and used in Eph as well as in Col.

c. The synonymous application of *aiones* and *genea* is familiar in its temporal meaning and is therefore suggested in this context (cf. for example Eph 3:21). A synonymous connection of "generations" to the word *aiōnes*[47] in the sense of persons or powers can only be attested from Gnostic sources which belong to a later time than the composition of Col.[48]

d. The following "but now . . ." points rather to a temporal contrast although there is also another contrast to the ages: the saints.

e. A similar expression in Rom 16:25, "concealed since eternal *ages*, but now revealed" (cf. Eph 3:5), also speaks for a temporal interpretation.

44. Compare R. Reitzenstein, *Das iranische Erlösungsmysterium* (Bonn: Marcus, 1921), pp. 86, fn. 3; 171ff., 214f.—E. Lohmeyer (p. 82) understood the expression "since ages and generations" in a temporal sense, but he reached the same conclusion. For with this expression we reach back beyond the limits of this aion "into the unmeasured expanses of time before all creation," in comparison with those in which the world and its history is only an episode. He claims that the discussion concerns a concealment of the secret from the "spirits and angels."

45. For Eph 2:2, compare M. Barth, AB 34, pp. 214f.

46. The concept of the thirty "Aions" is typical for the systems of the Valentinian Gnosis (second century C.E.). These are beings which stand in the rank between the highest god and the material beings. They form the "realm of fulfillment," the so-called "pleroma." (Compare Irenaeus, Haer I, pp. 1–8. See also the schematic representation in PG VII, pp. 435f). Further, see H. Sasse, RAC I, 192–204:201f.

47. Compare H. Jonas, *The Gnostic Religion. The Message of the Alien God and the Beginnings of Christianity* (Beacon Hill/Boston: Beacon Press, 1958), pp. 53f.; and H. Jonas, *Gnosis und spätantiker Geist*, vol. I, 3d ed., FRLANT 5 (Göttingen: Vandenhoeck & Ruprecht, 1964), p. 100.

48. The possibility has also been weighed that *aiōnes* means (heavenly) powers and *genea* means human beings (thus J. A. Bengel, p. 786). But then the resultant statement is equal to a purely temporal meaning and is less hypothetical.

In this decision, we need to consider that the two possibilities, 1 and 2, are not mutually exclusive. True, it is not likely that the concealment of the secret is to be limited to the heavenly powers, but these are included in the circle of those from whom the secret was concealed (cf. Eph 3:10). The aim of v 26 is to emphasize the previous total concealment of the secret, which is now contrasted with the unlimited revelation of this same secret (cf. Comment II).

Now, however, it has been revealed. The revelation of the secret has made a profound intrusion into the history of the people of Israel and surrounding nations, which is mirrored also in the syntax of this sentence. The previous sentence dealing with the concealment of the secret is not continued with participial verb forms, which is what we would expect. Rather, it ends abruptly. A new insertion follows, introduced by "now, however," which contains the passive finite verb "it has been revealed."

Once again, we are dealing with a so-called "divine passive" (cf. Notes to 1:9), which describes God as the agent. In the following verse he is expressly referred to as the one by whose will the revelation of the secret is decided.

The aorist points to a unique occurrence that precedes the revelation by means of "the saints." This latter revelation, however, is indicated as a continuous process ("we proclaim," present; v 28). The reference is to the revelation of the Messiah as he is praised in 1:12–20.[49]

to his saints! The parallel expression in Eph 3:5 is more specific and cites the recipients of the revelation "his holy apostles and prophets." The difference is probably connected with a peculiarity of Col, which we observed earlier in 1:2. There, Paul addresses the Colossians as his "brothers," a term which includes their status as *co-workers* (cf. Comment II to 1:1–2). The dignity and rank of all Christians in Colossae is also a factor in Col 1:26. In this connection, we would also like to point out the notable parallel between 1:28 and 3:16. The description of the Pauline office as "admonishing and teaching in all wisdom" is repeated almost verbatim in his summons to the Colossians, "in all wisdom, teach and admonish each other."

Less likely is the assumption that angels are intended by "saints."[50] The customary Pauline manner of expression does not argue in favor of this interpretation in Col (cf. Notes to 1:12), as does also the idiosyncrasy of such an assertion in this context, which is unpolemical. We would expect an explanation of veneration of angels in Colossae in a different place and also in a more detailed form.

27 *To them God wanted to make known.* The verb *gnōrizō* (to make known) has the same stem as *(epi-)ginōskō* (to know, to recognize), which is used in 1:6

49. If Paul designates his proclamation of the secret with the same verb in Col 4:4, then he means the revelation which occurred through him of the secret which was earlier revealed by God.
50. Compare E. Lohmeyer (p. 82); W. Bieder (p. 94).

in reference to the hearing of the gospel. Analogously with "to know or recognize" (cf. Notes to 1:6) *gnōrizō* means an imparting of knowledge that connotes a simultaneous charge and mission, and not merely a simple manner of communicating which fades into noncommittal attitudes (cf. Comment II).

what are the glorious riches of this secret among the gentiles (literally: the riches of the glory . . . in the gentiles). We are presumably dealing with a Semitism here in the genitive attribute "of the glory," which represents the adjective "glorious" (cf. Notes to 1:11).

en (in) should here be translated with "among (the gentiles)," analogously to the statement in 1:6, where we are told of the gospel that it bears fruit and grows "in *(en)* the whole world," "as also among *(en)* you (pl)." But we are hardly concerned with a "pneumatic inhabitation," or specifically the "inhabitation of Christ in each believer" in this instance[51] (cf. Comment II).

this is the Messiah among you, the glorious hope (literally: in you, the hope of glory). For the translation of the preposition "in" and the genitive attribute "of glory," please refer to the preceding Note.

The relative pronoun at the beginning of this proclamation, which was rendered in the translation as the beginning of a new sentence with "this," is masculine in some Greek manuscripts and neuter in others. The prevailing argument, as documented in the reliable manuscripts, favors the neuter form as the original one. The "internal criteria" would support this preference, esp. since we cannot be certain that the masculine relative pronoun represents the more difficult and therefore the more original reading.[52] It is also possible that the original grammatically "correct" neuter form was absentmindedly changed into the masculine by a scribe habitually modifying the relative pronoun with the gender of the predicate noun (cf. BDR 132, 2). Neither alternative poses significant problems to the exposition of the context.

The attached relative clause rendered by "this is" refers to the entire substance of vv 26–27, not only to the "secret." The construction as indirect question ("what . . . the *riches*") focuses our attention even more on the "*riches* . . . among the gentiles" than the conceptual differentiation between "secret" and "*riches* of the secret" already does (cf. Comment II, as well as Comment III to 1:3–8).

28 *Him we proclaim, by admonishing . . . and teaching* (cf. Comments I to 1:3–8 for the change in number). The verb *kataggellō*,[53] which is used elsewhere in Paul for proclaiming the gospel, is further illustrated by the two participles "to admonish" *(noutheteō)* and "to teach" *(didaskō)*. F. Hahn (cf. Notes to

---

51. Compare Dibelius-Greeven (p. 25).

52. Thus, among others, E. Lohse (p. 121); J. Gnilka (p. 102, fn. 57); Dibelius-Greeven (p. 25).

53. 1 Cor 2:1; 9:14; 11:26; Phil 1:17, 18. In the profane Greek, it is used, among others, for official proclamations. Compare SIG, 364, 5 (37 C.E.).

1:25), as among others also E. Schweizer (p. 89),[54] observed a certain tendency in this construction, which was later fully developed in the Pastoral Epistles, and points to a discrepancy in relation to the genuine Pauline epistles. The weight was shifted according to Hahn and Schweizer from the apostolic message aimed at founding churches to an advisory function which Paul usually entrusted to the church members.

The usage of the two verbs, "to admonish" and "to teach," hardly supports this thesis. True, in the Pastoral Epistles we observe a preponderant use of the substantive "teaching" which bears upon the corresponding verb form although this occurs less frequently. But Paul uses the verb "to teach" also elsewhere to summarize his apostolic function (1 Cor 4:17; also Notes to 1:7). The verb "to admonish" (noutheteō), on the other hand, does not occur at all in the Pastoral Epistles.[55] Aside from that and more important than these observations is the idea that service among the gentiles in this passage in Col should be considered from the perspective of the reconciliation accomplished through Christ discussed in 1:22. Just as reconciliation is not the end itself, but calls for acceptance, faith, and obedience by those hearing of their redemption, so also has the missionary service of Paul and his co-workers its purpose not only in the establishment of congregations and specified ecclesiastical traditions, offices, and activities but it also focuses directly on the *life* of every listener of the gospel. Even though Paul did not found the community at Colossae himself (and even after it had been founded already), his considerable efforts are concerned with this community and are assigned to him by God. Paul presents a similar viewpoint in Rom. There it is his mission to convey the gospel to those who previously had not heard the message of Christ (Rom 15:20, 21). But Paul emphasizes simultaneously that he is "servant of Jesus Christ for the gentiles" (Rom 15:14–16) by reminding (anamimneskō) the Christians in Rome (Rom 15:15) by "cautioning" (noutheteō) them (cf. Notes to 1:25). The verb *epanamimnesko* is used there in a related sense to *noutheteō* (to admonish) in Rom 15:14.

noutheteō can best be rendered literally by "to lay at one's heart." In its extra-biblical usage, it describes an influence upon the "will and feelings" of an individual and means predominantly "to caution, to warn, to soothe, to remind, to admonish."[56] In the NT, it occurs only in the Pauline corpus, with the exception of Acts 20:31 (and there also from the mouth of Paul).[57] It describes a "pastoral" activity, and to judge from its usage in the NT, it is not an element of the "pioneer mission."[58] It does not only mean "to admonish," where a

---

54. Compare also E. Lohse (p. 123); J. Gnilka (p. 103).

55. There, we should really expect it, according to F. Hahn's and E. Schweizer's thesis.

56. Compare J. Behm, ThWNT IV, p. 1013.

57. Rom 15:14; 1 Cor 4:14; Col 1:28; 3:16; 1 Thess 5:12, 14; 2 Thess 3:15.

58. H. A. W. Meyer (p. 291) wanted to align *noutheteō* (to admonish) with the

wrongdoing is presupposed (cf. 1 Cor 4:14; 2 Thess 3:15), but also includes a larger sense, as Acts 20:31 indicates, where the three-year service of Paul in Ephesus is described by *noutheteō*. But this general usage becomes even more clear in Rom 15:14f., where "to remind" in connection with the description of the Pauline service among the gentiles is put on an equal par with "to admonish." Intended is a (mutual) pastoral service which calls the received message to active remembrance (and thus also to action). The word is probably also used in this way in Col 1:28. Admonition is not dependent on deplorable grievances; neither does it respond to them. But it is rather embedded in praise over the gratifying situation in Colossae (1:4; 2:5). "To admonish" in the sense of "to remind" also occurs in Col 3:16, where it is further supplemented by "psalms, hymns, and spiritual songs." Those are the instruments of "remembrance" that are best suited to remind the listener of that which was spoken.

each person. This expression, repeated two more times in this verse, therefore possesses special emphasis. Contextually, it is determined by the preceding elucidations concerning the participation of the gentiles in the hope that is incorporated for Israel and the nations in the Messiah. The proclamation of the gospel breaks through religious and social barriers and excludes no one.[59]

in all wisdom. What Paul requests for the Colossians in 1:9 is also what he received as a divine gift and which now enables him to perform his service (cf. Notes to 1:9).

because we want to present each person (literally: so that we). What has been cited as the purpose for the act of redemption of Christ and also as *his* work in 1:22 becomes the focal point for the activity of Paul and his co-workers.[60] The change of subject and the replacement of the preposition *"before* Christ" by *"(en)* in Christ" makes the suggested meaning in v 22 evident: it is not the "last judgment" which is in focus, but rather the evident daily conduct of the believer.

perfect in Christ. Because this final phrase is closely related to the context in 1:22f., we have to understand the essence of perfection by relying on those earlier statements. "To be perfect" then means to cling to the promise of the gospel with unshakable trust in Christ. Because the promise is incorporated in the Messiah and is identical with him (cf. Comment III to 1:3–8). There is no perfection except in firm unshakable trust in the Messiah and in faithfulness to him. The parallelism between the affirmations of vv 21f. and 28 further makes

related concept *metanoia* (penance, conversion) and *didasko* (to teach) to the concept *pistis* (faith). Then the two verbs would describe the apostolic proclamation which "founds churches" and which "continues on." Such a ranking cannot be attested in the NT. Compare, however, Test Benj 4, "he admonishes *(noutheton)* and converts *(epistrephei)* him who is contemptuous of the highest one."

59. This explanation seems to be closer to the context that an interpretation which discerns a polemic against the false teachers who presumably represented an exclusive teaching (comp. T. K. Abbott, p. 235).

60. Comp. 2 Cor 5:20, "We beseech on behalf of Christ. . . ."

clear that perfection is not attained through striving for an ideal in a *process* of teaching, so that perfection would be attained by progressing on a ladder step-by-step. Since v 23 refers to a *steadfastness* in trust, v 28 means that "being perfect" is a *remaining* of perfection. The key to understanding this concept of perfection probably lies in the meaning of *teleios* (perfect) in the LXX and which occurs there as the equivalent of the Hebrew *tāmîm* or *shālēm* (esp. in connection with "heart"). Undivided obedience to *one* God, the God of Israel, is intended, the God who stands in opposition to the heathen idols including the cultic and magical practices and customs by which they are served.[61] This concept of perfection knows no graduated steps of attachment and obedience, only the alternative obedience *or* disobedience, holiness *or* profanity through idol worship. This understanding of perfection is thoroughly suited to Col, because here also the admonition is to trust in one Lord, Jesus Christ, the Lord over all powers and forces.

There are, however, elsewhere in the NT, some passages which express the unequivocal OT concept of perfection in typical Greek fashion: they mention a progression.[62] Paul mentions it, for example, in 1 Cor 3:1, although without using the term *teleios*, when he writes, "and I . . . could not speak to you as to spiritual men, but rather as to men of the flesh, as to *children* in Christ who have *not come of age.*" Luke 2:40, 52 speaks of a growth or progress in wisdom and grace; the epistle to the Hebrews 5:11–6:12 makes use of technical terms of Greek pedagogies; and in Gal 3:23–4:7, Paul's argument is unfolded by the image of the contrast between childhood and adulthood. And yet the decisive Greek concept of hopeful development toward maturity and perfection—the term *ephibos* (adolescent), which describes the stage of transition—is not found in the NT.

29 *And for this I struggle and strive* (literally: for that I struggle striving). *Kopiaō* (here translated "I struggle") in the extra-biblical sources designates hard physical and mental exertion or also its consequence, exhaustion. Paul uses the concept frequently to describe his own service and that of other workers of the

---

61. See esp. Deut 18:13; 1 Kgs 8:61; 11:4, 10; 15:3, 14; 1 Chr 28:9; comp. Gen 6:9.

62. Thus, for example, when, according to Aristotle (and also Plato), a higher technical ability (i.e., that of a physician or musician) were meant by *teleios* beyond which a degree of comparison is no longer possible (Metaph V, 16, 1021 b; Plato, Leg I 643 D). In addition to this, however, *teleios* also designates the highest ethical status (comp. Aristotle, Eth M II 3, 13, 1200 a). The reference goes back to the Stoa when someone is described as a "complete human being" who possesses all cultural abilities, and an act is referred to as a "complete act" when all the virtues are joined together therein (Plutarch, Stoic Rep 27). See also G. Delling, ThWNT VIII, pp. 70ff. For further literature, see M. Barth, AB 34A, p. 492, fn. 301. We cannot document, at least not to the time of the writing of Col, whether *teleios* was a typical concept in reference to initiation into the mystery cults (comp. E. Schweizer, p. 90; G. Delling, ThWNT VIII, p. 70, ll. 11ff.).

gospel. Whenever Paul displays the meaning of this verb more fully, he speaks of hard labor and/or experiencing great hardships in using this verb,[63] and was less oriented toward the efforts of athletes, as for example J. B. Lightfoot (p. 237) suggested. Only the verb *agōnizomai*, which, in its participial form, elucidates the verb *kopiaō* more fully, is a special term to denote athletic competition. The corresponding substantive *agōn* describes the place of competition, the gathering of spectators at a sports arena, or even the competition itself. In the transmitted sense, it is also used in oral competitions or debates. Thus *agōn*, when used in a context describing court procedures, can mean a trial process as well as the argumentation before the court. It further generally means "fight" (i.e., of the fights of Hercules) and can also indicate the "inner fight" as well in the sense of worry, fear, and similar emotions.[64] The verb *agōnizomai* corresponds to the substantive and generally means "to fight for the prize of victory." In addition, it can have the various or metaphorical connotations of *agōn*.

In the NT in 1 Cor 9:25, 2 Tim 4:7, and Heb 12:1, *agōnizomai* directly refers to athletic competition. In other passages however,[65] as also in Col (1:29; 2:1; 4:12), such a reference is not expressed and seems not to be of primary interest in Col. First, two different forms are chosen for the two verbs in 1:29. The ruling verb *kopiaō* is used in the indicative; the participle *agōnizomenos* is appended and of lesser weight.[66] Second, both verbs are chosen for describing the suffering of Paul, because they resume and elaborate on the content of 1:24. This connection is indicated through the repetition of "for you" (*hyper hymōn*) in 2:1 ("the struggle [*agōn*] which I have *for you*"; compare 1:24, "I rejoice in my sufferings *for you*").[67]

The use of the verb *agōnizomai* does not, however, completely exclude the picture of athletic competition, for instance, the loneliness and breathlessness of the long-distance runner. V. C. Pfitzner (*Agon*, op. cit., p. 127) was surely correct when he warned against an overinterpretation. His statement deserves

---

63. Comp. 1 Cor 4:12; 2 Cor 11:23; 1 Thess 2:9; 2 Thess 3:8; see also Matt 6:28; Luke 5:5; John 4:38; Acts 20:35; 2 Tim 2:6. See also A. v. Harnack, "Kopos (Kopian, Hoi Kopiontes) im frühchristlichen Sprachgebrauch," SNW 27 (1928) 1–10:5, "thus it is probable that in using *kopian*, the Greek primarily had in mind rough earth work."—The meaning "to become weary" (comp. John 4:6; Rev 2:3) can hardly be considered in Col 1:29, where we are dealing with divine power working in Paul.

64. See the references in LSLex. Compare also E. Stauffer, ThWNT I, pp. 134–40.

65. Luke 13:24; Rom 15:30; Phil 1:30; 1 Thess 2:2; 1 Tim 4:10; 6:12. In John 18:36, *agōnizomai* is used in the military sense. Compare for these passages also V. C. Pfitzner, "Paul and the Agon Motif: Traditional Athletic Imagery in the Pauline Literature," NT.S 16, 109–29.

66. That means, "I am wearying myself, wrestling . . . ," not "I am wrestling (*agonizomai*), wearying myself (*kopion*)." Compare A. v. Harnack, op. cit. (fn. 63), p. 5, fn. 1; V. C. Pfitzner, "Agon," op. cit., pp. 109f.

67. *Agōn* is used in connection with the suffering of Paul also in Phil 1:30.

serious consideration: "to what extent Paul's readers perceived an image behind his word cannot be conclusively determined by our non-Greek ears." But perhaps the significance of suffering in the course of the service of the proclaimer explains best the choice of words in Col. Just as the athlete is *totally* challenged if he or she wishes to attain victory (cf. 1 Cor 9:25), so does the proclamation of the gospel demand total action on the part of the proclaimer. For proclamation is not only a matter of words, but in the course of this service to Christ and humankind, physical suffering is also as essential (cf. Comment I).[68]

because his power works mightily in me (literally: according to his power of working, which works in me in power). Here again a parallel to the prayer of intercession is recognizable. As Paul has asked for wisdom for the Colossians (1:9) and has himself received this gift (1:28), so he also asks for power for the Colossians (1:11) and he himself has received this power in order to be able to endure the suffering concerning which he can rejoice.

The same word that occurs in v 29 *(energeia)* is used in 2:12. There it describes the power of God to raise the dead, and probably the same is anticipated here. Paul's special understanding and joyful acceptance of suffering is founded upon his conviction that the power of God has and will overcome death (cf. Comment I).

The social relevance of the power wielded by God is very pronounced in this verse. God's power sustains God's servants to present every person perfect in Christ, as the preceding verse has averred.

2:1 *For I want you to know.* Paul frequently uses this expression and also its corresponding negative formulation, "I do not want you to know." It often serves to introduce a new theme (see 1 Cor 11:3; 12:1; and 1 Cor 10:1; 1 Thess 4:13), but along with it he expounds previous statements and adds concrete details (cf. Rom 11:25, and Rom 1:13; 2 Cor 1:8).[69] In Col 2:1, it is used in this fashion to expound the preceding remarks. What Paul wants the Colossians to know is his *agōn* (struggle), his continuous engagement in fighting in 1:29 [*agōnizomenos* (fighting)] and thus also his suffering, which according to 1:24 is a service for the church (see below). The use of the formula "I want you to know" in 2:1 stands in harmony with the results which T. Y. Mullins found in examining the

68. E. Lohmeyer (p. 89) designated *agōnizomai/agōn* as "a firmly technical word for the concept and act of martyrdom" and referred to Sir 4:28; 2 Macc 8:16; 13:14. Such an interpretation can also be supported from 4 Macc 17:14. ". . . the comparison is all the more applicable when the torture and execution of the martyrs frequently took place in the same arena and before the same audience as the *gymnikoi agōnes* (gymnastic competition, H.B.)." (E. Stauffer, ThWNT I, 136, 9ff.). But we cannot attest this technical meaning in the NT. In Col, there is no clue that Paul had martyrdom in mind. If Col was written at the same time as Phlm, then E. Lohmeyer's conceptualization for the two letters is probably impossible (comp. Phlm 22, "prepare a guest room for me.")

69. It is thus not necessary to begin a new section here for purely stylistic reasons (comp. E. Lohmeyer, p. 92; J. Gnilka, p. 107).

papyri letters. He identified this formula specifically as "a rhetorical stereotype for the presentation of specific information" and termed it "disclosure."[70]

what a struggle I have for you. The reference is neither specifically to an "inner struggle," be it a struggle in prayer (cf. J. B. Lightfoot, p. 238) or concern for the Colossians, or both (cf. T. K. Abbott, p. 237), nor specifically to the martyrdom of the apostle (cf. E. Lohmeyer, p. 92). *Agōn* (struggle) rather means the suffering described in 1:24 (cf. Notes above and Comment I).[71]

Helikos (here translated "what a") occurs only twice more in the NT: in Jas 3:5 and in a text variant to Gal 6:11. In the LXX and in the OT Apocrypha, the word is absent. The Jas citation illustrates this expression beautifully. Depending on its context, it can mean "how large" or "how small": "In this way also the tongue is a *small* member and accomplishes *large* things. See *what a small (hēlikon)* fire sets a *large (hēlikon)* forest ablaze!" In the extra-biblical Greek sources the precise meaning of *hēlikos* is determined from its context.[72]

In Col 2:1–2, it is hardly the quantity of Paul's suffering that is emphasized, because, according to 1:24ff., the sheer number of tribulations and pains does not have the ability to comfort. Rather, the apostle intends to point to the special "quality" of his suffering: it reveals God's comforting power and verifies the Gospel proclaimed by the apostle (cf. Comment I).

for you and for the (brothers) in Laodicea. The textual evidence of the reading *hyper* (for) is so clearly superior to that for the reading *peri* (for) that the suggestion that *peri* was originally connected to *hyper* in 1:24 and 4:12 can hardly be valid.[73]

It is noteworthy that in Col 2:1 the neighboring city of Laodicea is mentioned, but not the neighboring city of Hierapolis.[74] We can hardly suppose

---

70. T. Y. Mullins, "Disclosure: A Literary Form in the New Testament," NT 7 (1964/65) 44–50:46. Four elements are said to be constituent for this form: (1) the verb *thelō* (I want); (2) a noetic verb in the infinitive; (3) the addressed person(s); (4) the information. A fifth element, an address in the vocative, can be absent (p. 46). In the papyri, the sequence of these elements was usually 2/3/1/4 (pp. 47f.). Yet this order was not constituent, as P Oslo 50 demonstrates, where the sequence 1/3/2/4 occurs, which corresponds to that in the NT (p. 48). Compare also Dibelius-Greeven, p. 25.

71. For the substantive *agōn*, see Notes to 1:29.

72. In comparatives, it is: as large as . . . ; as small as . . . ; as old as . . . ; in indirect questions, it is: how large; how small. In addition, this also occurs in exclamations. (See the references in LSLex, BauerLex, and MMLex.)

73. H. A. W. Meyer, p. 294. *Hyper* is frequently replaced in Greek by *peri*, as we also frequently find the reverse in the Attic Hellenistic usage of *hyper* for *peri* in the NT, especially in Paul (comp. BDR 229, 4; 231).

74. "Hierapolis" can be found in a few minuscules (from the eleventh century), in one manuscript of the Vulgate, and in one Syriac translation from the seventh century, the Harklensis, in which the translator made it noticeable that "Hierapolis" was an addition in (one of) his text original(s). We cannot say with certainty that "Hierapolis" was in the original Colossian text.

an oversight by the author, because in 4:16 there is reference to the fact that the epistle to the Colossians should be read also in Laodicea (and an epistle to the Laodiceans in Colossae). Hierapolis is not mentioned there either, even after this city was expressly named just previously (4:13). The reason for this omission in both passages lies probably in the fact that the ties between the two communities in Colossae and Laodicea were closer and those between Colossae and Hierapolis more distant (cf. J. B. Lightfoot, p. 238; T. K. Abbott, p. 237). The concern and care of Epaphras, who came from Colossae and was probably the missionary of the whole Lykos valley (cf. Notes to 1:7), were equally cordial and deep for all three cities (4:12 + 13). In addition, since the steadfastness and love of the Colossians for *all* the saints in 1:4 is expressly emphasized, it is not probable that coolness or tension existed between Colossae and Hierapolis. The supposition that Hierapolis was less threatened by false teaching than Colossae and Laodicea (cf. J. B. Lightfoot, p. 238; T. K. Abbott, p. 237) is also doubtful because of the close proximity of the three cities.[75] P. Ewald (p. 13) was of the opinion that the Christians in Hierapolis had not formed an independent community and therefore participated in the worship services in Laodicea, which would account for their not being mentioned separately. But his solution is also not convincing. Why should the supposed participants from Hierapolis not be addressed directly in the worship service in Laodicea? Or why should the Christians of one city participate in the worship service of a neighboring one but not be able to celebrate their own worship service? It is perhaps most likely that Paul did not intend the Colossian epistle as a lecture for the Christians in Hierapolis because the positive description of the situation in the community in Col did not apply to them and would require a separate letter which is no longer extant, like the Laodicean epistle.

Laodicea occurs in the NT, besides the citations in Col, only in Rev 1:11 and 3:14, as well as in the postscripts to 1 and 2 Tim (among others, in the Codex Alexandrinus from the fifth century), but more often in the ancient Greek writers.[76] The location was originally called *Diospolis* ("city of Zeus") later *Rhoas* (Pliny, Hist Nat V, 105) and was renamed *Laodicea* at its refounding by the Seleucid ruler Antiochus II, Theos (261–246 B.C.E.) in honor of his first wife, Laodice. Compared with Colossae and Hierapolis, it was more important not only economically but also politically. It was the center of the sheep trade

---

75. Laodicea and Hierapolis were situated opposite each other, and each was on the hills of the upper Lykostales. The distance between the two cities was approximately 9.5 km (6 miles). Kolossae was in the middle of the valley, about 16 km (10 miles) distance.

76. Among others, in Strabo, Geogr XII, 8, 13; Tacitus, Ann XIV, 27, 1; Pliny, Hist Nat V, 105. Further references can be found in B. Reicke, "The Historical Setting of Colossians," RExp 70 (1973) 429–38:430–32; J. B. Lightfoot, pp. 5–9; Pauly-W., s.v. Compare for the following expositions esp. J. B. Lightfoot, pp. 5–9; J. Gnilka, p. 109; A. H. M. Jones, *The Cities of the Eastern Roman Provinces*, 2d ed. (Oxford: Clarendon, 1971), p. 74.

and wool industry in Lykostal, as well as the capital city of a "diokesis"[77] to which not fewer than twenty-five cities belonged. According to a reference by Tacitus (*Ann* XIV, 27, 1), Laodicea was destroyed by an earthquake in the seventh year of the reign of Nero, thus in 60/61 C.E., but was rebuilt without Roman assistance. Little is known about the religious life in the city. In a city document from the first century we read that the Jews were not hindered from freely practicing their religion.[78] The earlier name, Diospolis, refers to Zeus, the patron deity of this city. But we can presume with some certainty that, in a commercial center like Laodicea, which lay along the trade route leading from Ephesus/Milet to Syria by way of Apamea and on into the area of the Euphrates and Tigris, the religious syncretism which characterized the religious life of Phrygia would have been found in ample measure here also.[79]

even for all those who (also) . . . *me* (literally: and all). The word combination *pantes hosoi/panta hosa* (all those/all which) occurs frequently in the NT (i.e., Matt 21:22; Mark 6:30; Luke 18:22; John 10:8). But *hosos* in its absolute sense (without *pas*, "all") has the same meaning (for example in Matt 14:36; Mark 3:10; Rom 2:12; 3:19; 6:3; 8:14; 15:4; Gal 3:10, 27).

The use of the word *hosos* in Col 2:1 allows for two basically different meanings here which can only be verified or contradicted from the context: (1) *Hosoi* may denote group which includes the previously cited persons.[80] In that case, the Christians in Colossae and Laodicea are among those whom Paul did not personally know. (2) *Hosoi* can also designate a group which should be differentiated from the persons mentioned earlier.[81] Then the Christians in Laodicea and Colossae, or rather a portion of the communities in these cities,[82] would be known personally to Paul.

For a decision on this exegetical intricacy in Col 2:1, we should observe two points:

1. *Hosos* is in the nominative, and not in the genitive construction *(hosōn)* like "you" and "those in Laodicea." This incongruent grammatical construction could be an indication of the fact that the three groups are not simply to be placed side-by-side on an equal basis, namely the Christians in Colossae, the Christians in Laodicea, and the Christians who do not know Paul personally.

---

77. That is the sectional area of a province. From this word is derived the ecclesial concept "diocese."

78. E. Schürer, *Geschichte des jüdischen Volkes im Zeitalter Jesu Christi*, vol. III (Leipzig, Hinrichs, 1902).

79. Compare esp. F. Cumont, *The Oriental Religions in Roman Paganism* (Chicago, Open House, 1911), pp. 46–51; N. Nilsson, *Geschichte der griechischen Religion*, vol. II, 3d ed. (München: Beck, 1974), pp. 622–701; J. Lähnemann, pp. 82–89.

80. That is the case in Acts 4:6 and Rev 18:17.

81. See Herodotus, VII, 185. (J. B. Lightfoot, p. 238, points this reference out.)

82. Compare E. Lohse (p. 127, fn. 1): Not just generally all, but rather "all who are with you and who do not yet know me personally." Also E. Lohmeyer, p. 92, fn. 1.

The incongruence of case[83] would then be more than a meaningless grammatical anomaly. A comment or rather an afterthought in reference to the two groups of persons enumerated above should be added, to the effect that Paul either emphatically counted the Colossians and Laodiceans together as one group that did not personally know him, or that he entertained the idea that his directives were pertinent also for those in *Colossae and Laodicea* who did not know him personally.

2. A second observation is more decisive. In v 2, reference to the content of v 1 is made, but the possessive pronoun is used in the third person (*autōn*) instead of the second person (*hymōn*): "so that their instead of 'your' hearts will be comforted." This ties in grammatically with the third person in the phrase "and all who do not know me personally." Paul's comfort which is an outgrowth of his battle applies to them. If in v 1 a different or special group in the communities of Christians in Laodicea and Colossae was intended by "all those, who" that would mean that Paul's struggle would pertain to only this special group but not to the remaining Christians in the two cities. That would contradict the explanations given in 1:24ff. in which there is no clue to the effect that the repeated "you" (cf. Notes to 1:24) should pertain only to one group in the community of Colossae or even to no community at all. The only real possibility is the one mentioned above for the Greek *hosoi*, according to which the Christians in Colossae and Laodicea are included in a general sense among those whom Paul did not know personally.[84]

Thus Col 2:1 offers an explanation of Paul's effort to emphasize in 1:24ff. the fact that his service pertains *also to the Colossians*. He wants to dissipate doubts that the Colossians (and Laodiceans) might be less important to him because he neither personally visited nor testified at these communities before this time.[85]

do not know me personally (literally: have not seen my face in the flesh). The aorist ending *-an*, as we have it here appended to the perfect stem *heorak-* (they have seen) in place of the perfect ending *-asin*, occurs repeatedly in the NT as well as in inscriptions and papyri.[86]

Prosōpon is used in the Greek[87] to refer not only to the face (presumably of humans) or generally to the front side, but it is also used in reference to the total person.[88] Thus the association *kata prosōpon* (literally: according to the

---

83. Comp. for that also BDR 136, p. 1; 137, p. 3.

84. Comp. also J. B. Lightfoot, pp. 28f., fn. 4; 238; H. A. W. Meyer, pp. 296f.

85. In our opinion, it is not convincing when A. Lindemann (p. 36) recognizes a reference to the pseudonymity of Col here, since Paul involves himself differently in the disputes of the churches not founded by him in his attested letters. In the end, Epaphras traveled to Paul and involved him in the occurrences in Colossae.

86. Compare Luke 9:36; John 17:6; and others. See BDR 83, p. 1.

87. Compare the references in LSLex and E. Lohse, ThWNT VI, pp. 769–71.

88. In theater language, *prosōpon* means "mask" and also "role."

countenance or face to face) serves to designate the personal presence. It occurs also in the dative *(to) prosōpo* in this sense. This usage is especially clear in 1 Thess 2:17, "But since we were separated from each other for a while, dear brother, face to face *(prosōpo)*, not in heart, . . ."

The expression in 2:1 of "seeing someone face to face" follows Biblical Hebrew linguistic usage and occurs frequently in the LXX. Next to its specialized meaning of "seeing the face of a king (or another personage of high rank)," it indicates "to be given audience,"[89] and means the personal encounter (cf. among others Gen 32:20; 33:10; 46:30; 48:11). The literal meaning of *prosōpon* has faded by this time so much that it seems simply to serve as a surrogate for the personal pronoun.[90]

Unlike the case in Acts 20:38, Gal 1:22, and 1 Thess 2:17, *prosōpon* is here supplemented by *en sarki* (in the flesh).[91] This wording emphasizes the fact that a *personal* acquaintance does not exist between Paul and the Colossians (and the Laodiceans). Perhaps Paul wanted to distinguish between a personal acquaintance and an acquaintance of a different nature, analogously to 2:5 where he contrasts his physical absence in Colossae to his presence in spirit.[92] Such an acquaintance surely exists, as Col 4:7 demonstrates. But the expression "to see someone's countenance" in this sense cannot be documented, as far as we are aware.

2 *So that . . . will be comforted.* *Parakaleō* really means "to call together, to call over to someone." In addition to this basic meaning, it has an extended sense in extra-biblical Greek: "to summon, to call to a hearing, to call on the gods (to summon the gods[!]), to petition, to admonish, to encourage."[93] Only occasionally can the verb be rendered by "to comfort," although it is used frequently in this sense in the LXX. In the Pauline corpus, *parakaleō* occurs 54 times (out of a total of 109 times in the NT).[94] In the context of Col 2:2, the special association in which *parakalein* is understood as a fruit of suffering, this

---

89. See Ex 10:28; 2 Sam 3:13; 14:24, 28, 32; comp. Gen 43:3, 5; 44:23, 26.—2 Kgs 25:19 and Jer 52:25 also belong in this context (comp. in the NT: Matt 18:10), where the expression is used as a title for court officials.

90. See LXX Gen 45:28/46:30; Ex 10:28f.; comp. Gen 48:11.—in Rom 1:11, it says simply, "For I long to see you."

91. "In the flesh" is not to be connected to the verb. The resultant meaning (comp. 2 Cor 12:2f.) would then be a reference to the fact that the Colossians had possibly seen Paul in a vision. This hardly makes sense from the context.

92. Comp. T. K. Abbott, p. 238; E. Haupt, p. 64.

93. Comp. O. Schmitz, ThWNT V, pp. 772–77. *Preisigkelex* cites as meanings in the papyri: (1) to call for aid, to plead, petition, seek, request; (2) to summon (before a court); (3) to address, comfort, encourage.

94. For its usage and meaning, see esp. H. Schlier, "Vom Wesen der apostolischen Ermahnung," in *Die Zeit der Kirche, Exegetische Aufsätze und Vorträge* (Freiburg: Herder, 1956), pp. 74–89; comp. also C. J. Bjerkelund, *Parakalo. Form, Funktion und*

verb receives special meaning. While Paul uses *noutheteō* to describe his service in 1:28, he now uses *parakaleō* to specify the intention of the preceding verses. As in 1:28, he does not intend to administer a disciplinary reproach which would impose a burden upon the community, because the community is exemplary in its gratifying submission to and steadfast faith in the Messiah (2:5). We also find a connection between *parakaleō/paraklōsis* and "suffering/ tribulation" in the explanations in 2 Cor 1, which provide a key to the understanding of the perception of suffering in Col 1:24ff. In 2 Cor 1:6, *paraklēsis* is an outgrowth of tribulation and is conducive to perseverance in the face of suffering, and to endurance with patience (2 Cor 1:6), which can best be translated by "invigoration, fortification" and therefore perhaps also by "comfort." *Parakaleō* is used in a similar way along with *stēr* (to strengthen, make firm).[95] The context indicates that the verb in question in Col 2:2 is to be understood in this same sense. The basis for the detailed explanations in 2:1f. (and thus also in 1:24ff.) is the *potential* threat to the community (from the outside; cf. 1:4)[96]; in the face of looming danger, Paul wishes to see the community "firmly rooted . . . and anchored" (2:7).

your hearts (literally: their hearts). The third-person plural pronoun ("their") refers to those not personally acquainted with Paul who are mentioned in 2:1. Since the Colossians belong to this group, Paul emphasizes that they are of very special concern to him (cf. the earlier notes). The translation "all your" (instead of "their") intends to avoid the misunderstanding that Paul may have in mind another group in addition to the Christians in Colossae and Laodicea (or a special circle among them).

Sinn der parakalo- Sätze in den paulinischen Briefen, BTN 1 (Oslo, Bergen, Tromsö: Universitetsforlaget, 1967); A. Grabner-Haider, *Paraklese und Eschatologie bei Paulus. Mensch und Welt im Anspruch der Zukunft Gottes*, NTA.NF 4 (Münster: Aschendorff 1968), pp. 4–55.—H. Schlier works out that in the apostolic paraclesis, it is not the voice of a bare summons which is heard, but it is rather the demand for a summons which is hidden in an address (p. 76). As designation of the proffering of the gospel or instruction, *parakaleō/paraklēsis* designates neither the argumentative nor the truly pedagogical manner of proclamation, but rather an insistent petitionary form of sermon (p. 77). "Als eine besondere Form der Verkündigung, als jenes andringende, beschwörende Ermahnen, das der Bekümmernis um den Ermahnten entspringt, ihn fast mehr bittet als fordert, richtet sie sich, nicht Stimme des anfahrenden und beschämenden Gesetzes, sondern Träger eines verborgenen Trostes an die Brüder, die Glieder der Familie Gottes auf dem Grunde genenseitiger Liebe sind" (p. 78).—The apostle is named as the subject of admonishment, but the primary subject is said to be God, or rather the mercy or grace of God (p. 79).

95. See 1 Thess 3:2–3, "We sent Timothy . . . to you to establish *(stērizō)* and strengthen *(parakaleō)* you in your faith, so that no one be moved. . . ." Comp. also 2 Thess 2:17. In Rom 1:11f., both verbs are used synonymously.

96. Which have not yet led to insecurities in the community. But they will yet lead to "afflictions" in the Pauline conceptualization (comp. 1 Thess 3:3).

Heart in the OT as well as in the NT signifies more than it does in our language. The Hebrew *lēb* (heart) encompasses "all the dimensions of human existence,"[97] the spiritual as well as the physical. The heart is the center of man's physical life force (cf. Gen 18:5; Judg 19:5, 8; Ps 104:15), his feelings and perceptions (Deut 28:47; Isa 65:14), his will (1 Kgs 8:17; 2 Sam 7:3) as well as his reasoning (Ex 7:23; Josh 14:7). In addition, it can also designate the inner concealed human being (1 Sam 16:7), without implying the formal meaning of "heart."

Paul is in accord with the farreaching OT meaning.[98] This is illustrated by the statement following Col 2:2: where hearts are comforted, people are held together in *love* and they shall *recognize* the secret of God. Even though the *will* is not expressly cited in v 2, it is still called upon in vv 6ff.

held together in love. The participial phrase is added as a further elucidation. The grammatically correct form would be either the feminine nominative plural (to modify *kardiai*, "heart") or the masculine genitive plural (to modify *autōn*, "their").[99] But since "heart" is a label for the entire person, the author of Col chose the masculine nominative plural participle in a construction that follows the sense or intent.

The meaning of *symbibazō*, as well as the syntactic connection of the clause "held together in love" is in dispute.

1. *Symbibazō* can mean not only "to hold together" (cf. Eph 4:16; Col 2:19) but also "to teach, to instruct." This is the exclusive meaning in the LXX. In the NT we find this meaning in 1 Cor 2:16, where the LXX cites Isa 40:13, and in Acts 19:33. *Symbibazō* also means "to prove, to demonstrate" (Acts 9:22), and also signifies the attitude that results from such activity: "to be convinced, to be assured" (Acts 16:10).

In Col 2:2 we might pick up the theme from 1:28, in which Paul describes his services as admonishing *(noutheteō)* and teaching *(didaskō)*," and translate *symbibazō* by "to teach." This is reinforced in 2:2 by the fact that *noutheteō*, which is contextually related to the verb *parakaleō*, appears as well. An added reason for such a translation would be that the substantives in the second half of the verse "understanding" *(synesis)* and "recognition" *(epignōsis)* seem to fit well together. Underscoring this is the fact that in the context we are not dealing with cohesion in the community but rather with its enlightenment in the face of false teaching and practice.[100]

---

97. F. Stolz, THAT I, 861–67:863.—Comp. also esp. W. Eichrodt, *Theologie des Alten Testaments*, vol. II, 4th ed. (Stuttgart: Klotz; Göttingen: Vandenhoeck & Ruprecht, 1961), pp. 93–95.

98. Comp., for example, Rom 9:2, 2 Cor 2:4 (feelings and sensibilities); Rom 10:1, 1 Cor 4:5, 2 Cor 9:7 (will); 2 Cor 4:6, Eph 1:18 (reason); Rom 8:27, 1 Cor 4:5, 14:25 (the hidden inner self). The heart as the seat of life force is not attested in Paul.

99. Corresponding corrections are transmitted in a few text variants.

100. Compare for this interpretation esp. Dibelius-Greeven, pp. 15f., and P. T. O'Brien, p. 93. The Vulgate also translates with "instructi" (taught, instructed).

On the other hand, the determinant "in love" speaks for a translation "to hold together." Col 3:11 refers expressly to the "bond of love" that holds the community together in unity.[101] The recognition of the secret of God also includes the idea of unity, esp. that of Jews and Gentiles (cf. Comment II). Beyond that, the remark concerning the manner of being instructed or about those who instruct is less fitting here, since 2:2 deals with the purpose of Paul's battle and thus with those to whom this battle should be of benefit. In general, according to the declarations under consideration here, reinforcement grows not from an instructive activity but rather from suffering. Thus the translation "*held together* in love" seems more fitting in light of the statement in 2:1f.

2. There is also some disagreement about how the expression relates to the remaining statements of the verse. Should it be: (a) connected to the appended "and all the treasure" or is it intended (b) as parenthetic? If we proceed from the viewpoint that *symbibazō* means "to hold together," we have two resultant nuances of meaning:

a. In this case the assertion would be made that reinforcement consists in the fact that Paul's suffering should be the causative factor in binding the Colossians more closely. This cohesion would have as its goal obtaining the riches of all learning.

b. If the phrase is understood parenthetically, *kai eis* would mean "and namely to" and, dependent on *parakaleō*, would name the direct purpose of the reinforcement.[102] "Held together in love" would then be an inserted idea that would not specify the immediate purpose of reinforcement but would be indissolubly connected with it.

Regardless of how one decides, in both variations of meaning the firm connection between love and knowledge is emphasized. Solution b would probably render the intention of the author of the verses more closely. Love is not a prerequisite of knowledge. Rather, it is because of the revealed mystery of the *unity already created by the work of the Messiah* between Jews and Gentiles that the recognition of this mystery can be expressed and realized in the love among each other. Just as in 1:26–28 Paul's service is in the proclamation of God's revealed mystery, so also the service of Paul has its specific purpose in his suffering so that this mystery should be discovered. "Held together in love" only makes explicit whatever is implicit when the focus is the revelation of God's mystery.

in order to gain all the abounding fullness of understanding (literally: and for the entire riches of the fullness of understanding). The declaration that begins

---

101. The explanation of Dibelius-Greeven (p. 26), that "in love" is a softening of *symbibazein* ("not rules for teaching, but rather friendly admonishment") seems less convincing, since the meaning of *didaskein* or *symbibazein* is unfounded in Col 1:24ff. in the sense of "rules for teaching."

102. *Eis* (unto) is used in this sense also in 2 Cor 1:4 in connection with *parakaleō*.

here is directly dependent on the verb *parakaleō*. This syntactic connection is made possible by *kai* (and), which has an explanatory function here ("and that is"). If *kai* had not been inserted here, this statement would be directly attached to "held together in love." *Kai* also has an emphatic function. The phrase "and namely" in front of the remaining expressions, which refers to 1:26, adds an emphasis that urges the reader to infer that the purpose of the battle of the apostle for the Colossians is identical with his basic mission to proclaim the revealed mystery.

The string of genitive attributes (compare 1:5f.; 1:27) and of the (almost) synonymous concepts later on (cf. esp. 1:9–11) renders the meaning of this passage more difficult. In addition, the concept *plērophoria* is attested only occasionally and our knowledge of its spectrum of meaning is correspondingly uncertain. Its literal meaning is "greatest fullness." In extra-Christian literature it is found only with the meaning "certainty."[103] It does not occur at all in the LXX, and in the NT besides Col 2:2 only in 1 Thess 1:5, Heb 6:11, and 10:22.[104] Even in these three passages the meaning of *plērophoria* is not unequivocal. We can translate "certainty" there, but also "fullness."[105] Is *plērophoria* in Col 2:2 now a tautological concept for "all riches" or does the strengthening that is the topic of this verse extend to mean an exceedingly great certainty?

The context gives some clues to the solution to this problem. In 2:3, the object of understanding is described more closely. In it are hidden *all* (!) the treasures of wisdom and understanding. It is obvious that this description of the object of understanding is supposed to correspond to the description of its understanding. We need to observe also that the contextual connection of the concepts "all treasures" and "all riches" points toward the fact that *ploutos* (riches) is the determining concept of the expression in 2:2. Accordingly, *plērophoria* should probably be translated by "fullness."

namely the knowledge of the secret of God, that is the Messiah (literally: for the knowledge of the secret of God of the Messiah). This statement is parallel to the previous one, which is also introduced by *eis* (for). The abounding fullness of the understanding is exactly the knowledge of the secret of God.

If we refer this passage only to *synesis* (understanding), then the last part of v 2 makes no sense. For if this knowledge of the secret of God were the result of a previous understanding *(synesis)*, then it would still be unclear as to what this

---

103. Comp. G. Delling, ThWNT VI, p. 309.

104. Aside from this, also in a text variant to Rom 15:29, where (with fairly good certainty) the original text transmits *plērōma* (for this concept, see Notes to 1:19).

105. G. Delling, ThWNT VI, 309, points out that this is also possible in 1 Thess 1:5 ("for our sermon of the gospel came to you not alone in word, but also in power and in the Holy Spirit and in *plērophoria*"). *Plērophoria* here is not on the same level as "power" and "Holy Spirit," "nicht im blossen Wort, sondern in grosser *Fülle göttlichen Wirkens* geschah das Ausrichten der Frohbotschaft durch den Apostel."

abounding fullness in the discussion refers. *Synesis* in v 2 would be curiously without reference and would demand an object. An understanding that refers to something else besides the secret of God would generally contradict the concern of the entire section of 1:24ff., if not the whole of Col. If *plērophoria* is translated as certainty, then the argument that an object for "understanding" is lacking would not apply. Still, the fact that a certainty of the knowledge of the mystery of God should be presupposed would hardly be in accordance with the declarations of Col in regard to the effect of the gospel (cf. for example Notes to 1:6).

According to our proposed interpretation, *synesis* (understanding) and *epignosis* (knowledge) are synonymous concepts. What is elucidated in 1:6 in reference to *epiginōskō* (to know) is confirmed by the participle "held together in love" (see above). Understanding is not only an intellectual process.

The question remains as to why the flow of thought in v 2 is interrupted by a second *eis* (for) and the concern is not simply the overabundant fullness of the understanding of the mystery of God. One explanation evolves from vv 3 + 4, according to which *all* the treasures of wisdom and of knowledge in Christ lie hidden, and in the face of the fact that "such" exist (2:4) which offer an ostensible wisdom next to Christ (cf. 2:23). Paul emphasizes that he also is concerned (as are also surely the representatives of the ostensible wisdom) that his readers should obtain an abundant fullness of understanding. One may recognize many things that have the sheen of wisdom, but the entire overabundant fullness of understanding is the knowledge of the Messiah alone.

The genitive attribute *christou* can hardly be misunderstood because of the close-knit connection between 2:2 and 1:26f. and here it replaces the relative clause chosen in 1:27 "which is the Messiah. . . ."[106] Even so, there are a confusing number of text variants for this particular passage (2:2). Altogether, fifteen different textual readings have been preserved. These are listed and discussed in B. M. Metzger.[107] All the variants can be explained as paraphrases

106. Thus, among others, J. B. Lightfoot (p. 239); W. M. L. de Wette (p. 39); E. Haupt (p. 67); P. Ewald (p. 358); E. Lohse (p. 1299); E. Schweizer (p. 94); J. Gnilka (p. 110). T. K. Abbott (p. 240) interprets it from Eph 1:17 ("God, the Father of our Lord Jesus Christ"). H. v. Soden (p. 40) explains it similarly, as does H. A. W. Meyer (pp. 300f., "Whoever knows God as the *God of Christ*, for him, the divine *mystērion* is thus fulfilled"). E. Lohmeyer (p. 93) viewed *christou* as a "later, in itself not incorrect interpretation," so that, in his opinion, the fullness of the substantive could be ranked "without force into three lines with three components each" according to the original text. Before him, E. Haupt (p. 69) already interpreted *christou* as a marginal gloss (derived from 1:27), which later slipped into the text.—This supposition cannot be supported by any text transmission.

107. B. M. Metzger, *The Text of the New Testament. Its Transmission, Corruption, and Restoration* (Oxford: Clarendon, 1964), pp. 236–38. Comp. also P. Benoit, "Colossiens 2:2–3," in FS für Bo Reicke, *The New Testament Age*, pp. 41–51.

or modifications of the most reliable text tradition: *mystērion tou theou Christou.* The number of the variants is probably conditioned by the fact that two interpretations are possible from the original transmission, whose form or specifically whose expression is without parallel in Paul: (1) the mystery of the God of Christ (gen: Christi); (2) the mystery of God, Christ (nom: Christus).[108]

3 *In him . . . are . . . (specifically) hidden.* Since we interpret the Messiah by the mystery that is revealed by God (1:27; 2:2), it is without contextual significance whether the relative pronoun *nō* (in *whom*) refers to "Messiah" or to "mystery."[109] Both are possible in Greek since the masculine and the neuter forms of the relative pronoun are identical in the dative.

The adjective *apokryphos* (hidden) is used without the article. It can therefore be understood only predicatively,[110] and not as an attribute of "treasures." We need to consider that this adjective is not placed between the verb ("are") and the subject ("all treasures"), but is rather in a posterior position. The statement in v 3 should therefore rather be interpreted as, "all treasures of wisdom and knowledge that are in him are hidden (treasures)" (cf. BDR 270, 3), but not as, "in whom all the treasures of wisdom and knowledge are hidden." *Apokryphos* thus gives information about the kind and manner of existence of the treasures of the Messiah.[111] *Eisin* (they are) then contains the sense of "existing" and is not merely a copula. The shift in emphasis, which is mandated by the placement of the adjective "hidden," also corresponds to the other statements of Col, according to which the Messiah is not the "place of hiding" but, on the contrary, he is the "place of the revelation" of the mystery of God (cf. 1:27).

Still, the paradox remains that the statement is used in connection with the now finally revealed secret of "that which is hidden."

J. B. Lightfoot (p. 240) attempted to solve this by the supposition that "hidden" was a favorite term of the misguided Gnostic teachers. Paul is said to have appropriated this term in order to refute their teaching.[112] In order to underpin this thesis, J. B. Lightfoot cites examples from the writings of the Church Fathers in which secret writings or teachings are enumerated (see above).[113]

Aside from the question as to whether we can assume a reference to *gnostic*

---

108. Comp. Hilarius, *De trinitate*, PL X, 331 A, "Deus Christus sacramentum est" (God Christ is the secret).

109. V 3 should, at any rate, not convey the concept "secret" through the adjective *apokryphon* (hidden). The reason why a secret is discussed becomes clear from 1:26 (see Notes and Comment II).

110. See BDR 269, 3; 270, 3.

111. Comp., among others, E. Haupt (p. 68); H. von Soden (p. 40); E. Lohmeyer (p. 94, fn. 1); E. Lohse (p. 130, fn. 1).

112. Comp. also C. F. D. Moule (p. 86); J. Gnilka (p. 112).

113. The criticism by E. Haupt (p. 68) of J. B. Lightfoot, that the sources which he cites only speak of "books" and could therefore not explain the use of the word

viewpoints in Col 2, we cannot even determine with certainty whether Paul had some (religious) groups in mind who assigned a place of honor to secret text transmissions. Since the usage of the word *apokryphos* occurs both in the LXX and in Paul in connections that are comparable to Col 2:2, we prefer to draw on an interpretation from these passages.

In the LXX Sir 43:32 "hidden things" *(apokrypha)* occurs at the end of a long passage of glorification that praises God in light of his works. The concept there describes the inexhaustible riches of God's works, which this small excerpt illustrates, in which God is praised in light of his creation:

Who has seen him, and could tell of it?
Who can praise him as he is?
There are many *hidden things* which are larger than that
(which we have seen)!
Only a little have we seen of his works.
For the Lord has made everything,
And he has given wisdom to the faithful.

What is intended here by *apokrypha* (hidden things) corresponds to that which Paul has in mind when he exclaims in Rom 11:33–36,[114] "How unsearchable are the judgments of God, how inscrutable his ways!" Paul reminds his readers "expressly that despite everything which God has already made known through revelation, there are still treasures, dimensions, connections, heights, and depths which even he and other learned ones of God have not yet understood, or fully investigated, or fully fathomed."[115] This interpretation would apply best to Col 2:3, where *apokryphos* is the attribute of "treasures," and thus revealed as the place of "hidden (until now not revealed) treasures."

A further application of *apokryphos* which should be considered for the interpretation of Col 2:3 can be found in 1 Cor 2:6ff. There also the discussion concerns the mystery (1 Cor 2:7), and its "presently" occurring revelation (1 Cor

---

apokryphos, does not suffice. For according to J. B. Lightfoot, Paul appropriated a catchword from the "Gnostics" with *polemic* intent, with somewhat the following sense: Not in your secret transmissions, but rather in Christ are all treasures of wisdom . . . hidden.

114. Also in Rom 22:33–36 do we encounter the three substantives "riches—knowledge—wisdom," but the discussion concerns the knowledge which God has, and his wisdom. For the relationship between divine and human knowledge, see Notes on "know" in Col 1:6.

115. M. Barth, "Theologie—ein Gebet (Rom 11:33–36)," ThZ 41 (1985) 330–48:337. The translation of the citation from Rom 11:33 also originates from M. Barth (ibid.).

2:10), and there also the central issue is the *hidden aspect*[116] of this secret. The latter is elucidated by the fact that the secretive hidden wisdom of God can be recognized only through the Spirit that is bestowed by God. However, it remains hidden from the "natural human being" on whom this Spirit is not bestowed (1 Cor 1:14).

The use of *apokryphos* in Col 2:3 is probably also to be interpreted in a similar sense, except that here a more eschatological orientation predominates. This explanation suggests itself in the elucidation in 3:1–3. There we read that the Colossians have died with Christ, but have also risen. Their life, however, is said to have been "hidden in God" with the (risen) Christ. When Christ is revealed, they also are to be revealed with him in splendor. The same idea also seems to be the basis for Col 2:3, namely this secret that all the treasures of wisdom and knowledge reside *in the Messiah* but that now (still) a part of creation is hidden; however, the Messiah himself will reveal all of creation worldwide at his revelation in majesty (cf. 3:4).[117]

all the treasures of wisdom and knowledge. Thēscuros (treasure) is used also in extra-biblical Greek[118] with the same sense in connection with the concept of "wisdom." In Col 2:3 the word implies more than simply an invitation to *hunt for* knowledge and wisdom (like a treasure hunter).[119] The declaration that *all* treasures reside in the Messiah is expounded in connection with a warning about "those" who offer only illusory wisdom (2:4, 23). This tie-in is reminiscent of the speech about the treasure in Matt 13:44: he who finds a treasure finds everything else worthless; he will sell everything in order to obtain the treasure.[120]

The terms "wisdom" *(sophia)* and "knowledge" *(gnōsis)* occur in combination in Paul also in Rom 11:33 and 1 Cor 12:8.[121] Cf. the Notes on Col 1:6 and 1:9 (28) for their meaning.

4 *All this I say.* The demonstrative pronoun *touto* (this) anticipates that

---

116. It is not the adjective *apokryphos* that is used, but rather a participial form of the corresponding verb *apokryptō*.

117. Comp. G. Bornkamm, ThWNT IV, 828, 26, "Das offenbarte Mysterium verhüllt also zugleich die endliche Vollendung; das eschatologische Geschehen eröffnet sich vorerst nur im Wort, die Vollendung des Alls erscheint vorerst nur durch die Kirche, die *doxa* ("Herrlichkeit," H.B.) kommt in der Verhüllung der *thlipseis* ("Trübsale," H.B.) (Kol 1,24f.; Eph 3,13)."

118. Plato, *Phileb* 15e; Xenophon, *Mem* I, 6, 14; IV, 2, 9.

119. See Prov 2:4; comp. J. Gnilka (p. 111).

120. Comp. also Sir 40:18. The opinion of F. Hauck (ThWNT III, p. 138), that the declaration of the treasures in Col 2:3 is at least instigated by the concepts current among the "gnostics," according to which "treasure" designated "the land of light" from which the soul also originated and to which it would return, is without support in the text.

121. In the LXX, see Eccl 1:16–18; 2:26; 7:12; 9:10. Comp. Prov 21:11. There, the concepts are not continuously used with a positive valuation, however. See Eccl 1:18,

which is expressed in the following sequence, as also in 1 Cor 1:12 (cf. 7:29; 15:50); Gal 3:17; and Eph 4:17. Except in Eph 4:17, a direct connection is made in elaborating that which has preceded and the expression signifies as much as, "I want to say the following by. . . ." In Eph 4:17 we also have a contextual connection with the preceding statement, but there the formula introduces a new sequence.

The same expression is used in 1 Cor 7:6 and 7:35, but there *touto* merely refers to the preceding statement. Distinct from all the citations mentioned above, in Col 2:4 a conjunction such as *gar, de,* or *oun* is probably missing from the original manuscript reading. But whether this is an indication that something new begins in v 4 needs to be determined by closer examination of this verse.

Whether *touto* aims at the subsequent statement cannot be determined in a final or consecutive sense from the *hina* (actually: so that) in the attached sentence. In this case, *hina* is connected with an imperative (cf. BDR 387, 3; Moulton-Turner, p. 102). We find this use in Paul also in 1 Cor 7:29; 16:16; 2 Cor 8:7; and Eph 5:33. In 1 Cor 7:29, this imperative association occurs in statements that earlier were characterized as personal opinions of Paul, not as the "command of the Lord" (v 25). Similarly in 2 Cor 8:7 the invitation that follows the *hina* construction emphasizes spending generous amounts of money for the community in Jerusalem, "I say this not as a command!" M. Barth deduced from the passage cited that this imperative defined by *hina* cannot simply be translated in the imperative. Rather, Paul wanted to say something like, "I hope confidently that . . ." ("I hope and trust . . . ;" AB 24A, p. 648). However, if *hina* also qualifies the imperative in Col 2:4, this interpretation of M. Barth would hardly apply, since here the false teachers are formally addressed and such a mild form of the imperative hardly makes sense (cf. 2:16).

The interpretation of *touto* as a preceding pronoun can be challenged primarily for the following reasons:

1. This would then necessitate an imperative translation of the sentence that is introduced by *hina* and v 5 could be joined to this construction only with difficulty. We would then need to paraphrase, along with C. F. D. Moule (p. 88), somewhat as follows: ". . . and you need not succumb, for I am helping. . . ." Even then, the logical connection to the adjoining participle (lit.) "rejoicing and observing the order and steadfastness of your loyalty to the Messiah" would be difficult to discern.

2. V 5 ("For even if I am absent in body, I am still with you in spirit") is closely linked with 2:1 ("who have not seen me in body") and seems to bind 2:1–5 as a unit.[122]

"For in much wisdom is also much vexation, and he who increases knowledge also increases sorrow."

122. Comp. for that also H. A. W. Meyer (p. 302) and P. T. O'Brien (p. 97).

touto probably refers directly to the preceding passage and not only to v 3,[123] owing to the close contextual connection of the previous verses to 2:1–3 and thus also to 1:24 ff., since 2:1 refers back to 1:24 (cf. Comments). The conjunction *hina* is then understood to be final. At the end of the section which began with 1:24, we have a clear formulation of what Paul's concern was in the previous exposition (cf. the frequent use of "you" plural). The Colossians are close to his heart, even if he does not know them personally, nor they him. This affectionate relationship does not remain abstract and theoretical; no one is to "deceive" the Colossians and thus endanger the orderliness and steadfastness of their faithfulness to the Messiah (cf. also the Notes to *chairōn* [rejoicing] in v 5).

so that no one may delude you with specious arguments. Parologizerthas literally means "to miscalculate." It is frequently used in Greek, although not exclusively, of deceitful and misleading actions.[124] In the LXX, however, the verb always has this negative connotation. The sense of deception is described rather graphically in the OT accounts, as when Laban substitutes the wrong daughter as the bride to his unwitting future son-in-law and thus detains him for further years of service (Gen 29:25), or when the Gibeonites disguise themselves as travelers from afar and thus seal a friendship agreement with Joshua (Josh 9:22).[125] In the Pauline corpus, the verb is used only here, and elsewhere in the NT only in Jas 1:22.

pithanologia occurs in the entire NT only in Col 2:4 and it also does not occur in the LXX. In classical Greek it often designates a judgment based on probabilities as opposed to an irrefutable (mathematical) proof which is designated by *apodeixis*.[126] *Pithanologia*, which has the root meaning of "reasons of probability," is used in the papyri in the negative sense of "probable reasons."[127] This meaning probably also applies to Col 2:4.

5 *For even if I am absent in body, I am still with you in spirit* (literally: but in spirit I am with you). For the logical connection of v 5 to v 4, cf. the earlier Notes.[128]

The corporal absence of Paul from the communities of Lykos valley is

---

123. Comp. E. Haupt (p. 69).

124. See LSLex 1317. Compare also the references cited by E. Lohse (p. 131). PreisigkeLex suggests the following translations: to charge sums unjustly, to defraud someone, to fleece, to cheat.

125. Comp. also LXX Gen 31:41; Judg 16:10, 13, 15; 1 Sam 19:17; 1 Sam 28:12; 2 Sam 19:27. For other usages, comp. 2 Sam 21:15; Esth 8:12f.; Lam 1:19; Dan 7.

126. See, for example, Plato, *Theaet* 162e; 163a; comp. also 1 Cor 2:4.

127. P Lips I, 40 col III, 7 (cited in PreisigkeLex). Dibelius-Greeven (p. 26) translate the word in this papyrus reference with "verbal ability," " 'durch Redekunst suchen sie das Geraubte zu behalten.' "

128. The substance with which one could attempt to "deceive" the Colossians (comp. P. Ewald, pp. 59f.) is not indicated here. That is not discussed until v 6ff. and esp. after v 16.

countered by the use of the strongly emphatic conjunction *alla* (but, however): "in spirit, however, I am with you." The Greek *syn* ("together with"), instead of *en* ("among" you) points to the importance to Paul of the emphasis of the connectedness between him and the recipients of the letter. Among interpreters there is much dispute as to what the author of Col 2:5 meant by a "presence in spirit." The question is whether *pneuma* ("spirit") is used here principally for the human spirit and therefore signifies a participatory intention, or whether "spirit" here has a more specific meaning and stands for the "Holy Spirit."

According to Dibelius-Greeven (p. 26), Col 2:5 has the sense, "just as Paul, who is someone unknown to the Colossians, an absent person, can express such warnings (as in v 4, H.B.), he is connected to them through the Holy Spirit as though he were with them. . . ." E. Lohse (p. 131) and R. P. Martin (NCC, p. 76) also interpret in a similar vein. P. T. O'Brien (p. 98) agrees that the reference here is to the Holy Spirit, but holds that Paul is present with them in spirit not because he grants authority, but rather because the Spirit has closely united *both* the Colossians and Paul in Christ. It is surely to the point that the authority of the apostle is an authority granted through the Holy Spirit. And it is also to the point that the communion between Paul and the Colossians is effected through the Holy Spirit. But in this passage it is not evident that the term *pneuma*, which is sharply differentiated from physical absence, refers especially or solely to the Holy Spirit. Further, the expression "to be with you in spirit" is probably used in the same way as the formula "separated from sight, but not from the heart" in 1 Thess 2:17.[129] Col does not offer any leads for deliberation by Paul or the recipients of the epistle as to whether the apostolic authority or the communion created by Christ was undermined by spatial distance.[130] We have no further indication whether the physical distance separating the apostle from the Colossian church was effectively overcome by the transmission of apostolic authority to the latter or by the communion in Christ effected by the Holy Spirit, or vice versa.

as someone who rejoices and who sees (literally: rejoicing and seeing). The placement of the participle "rejoicing" in a prior position seems to represent a reversal of the logical sequence of the two events "to see" and "to rejoice."[131]

---

129. Comp. also R. Bultmann, *Theologie*, p. 209, fn. 1, and E. Schweizer, p. 96, who corrects the supposition expressed in ThWNT VI, 434, 11ff., that the gift of the Holy Spirit was meant.—G. Karlsson, "Formelhaftes in Paulusbriefen," Er 54 (1956) 138–41:140, here sees a formula which is a technique characteristic of letters and is expressed by the author in a letter through the replaced present tense. The elucidations in the context (see esp. 1:24) demonstrate that, in this passage, more is intended.

130. The Colossians hardly questioned the authority of Paul. The contrary is rather the case: the elucidations in 1:14–2:5 indicate that the Colossians thought themselves "taken no notice of, or overlooked."

131. Differently, for example, LXX 1 Sam 19:5; Matt 2:10; John 8:56; Acts 11:23, where seeing is cited first, and then the joy resulting therefrom.

But we need to consider whether a different sequence of participles would not be fitting in retaining the sentence structure as we have it. That would have led to an unusual grammatical construction in the Greek, since the verb *chairō* (to rejoice) seldom occurs with only an accusative object.[132] Therefore, it would be better to assume that the explanatory element in the first participle "rejoicing" is joined by means of the "and" *(kai)* and serves to define the content of the latter, or specifically the reason for joy.[133] But it is also possible, and here perhaps more probable, that both participles are equal in order of priority and are not logically dependent upon one another. In favor of this argument is the fact that joy has a special significance in the previous passage (1:24ff.) in relation to the suffering of Paul. The recurrence of this key word from 1:24 would be a further confirmation of the idea that 2:5 concludes the section that began with 1:24. The second participle, "seeing," would then focus the intent of this passage on the concept that Paul personally "oversees" this community that is not known to him, with the intention of dispelling their doubts (cf. also Notes on the previous verse).

your orderly discipline and the steadfastness of your faith in the Messiah. Both substantives are rare in the NT: *taxis* (nine times) is used again by Paul only in 1 Cor 14:40; *stereōma* only in this passage in the entire NT. Both words occur in nonbiblical Greek as technical military terms, although they may be used with a broader sense, or their usage is not restricted to this sense; rather, each case depends on context.

Taxis in military terms means primarily[134] the order of an army in rank and file, or the battle formation. The substantive also designates the army when drawn up for battle formation. In addition, the substantive designates the standing army itself, a troop unit (such as a company), the battle front, or even the military encampment. Further, the position of the individual in the battle row is called *taxis*.

Stereōma is used to denote the central corps of the military (cf. 1 Macc 9:14). We could probably include in this military terminology those passages in which *stereōma* is translated in the LXX from the Hebrew word for "rock" which is a designation for a place of refuge from foes (cf. LXX Ps 17⟨18⟩:3; 70 ⟨71⟩:3).

Some commentators have supposed that the author purposely chose military

---

132. Comp. LSLex; in the NT, this construction occurs in a text variant for Rom 16:19.

133. See BDR 442, 9 b. The context/reason for joy is frequently indicated by a participle.—The *kai* could also be conditioned by the fact that the verb "to be joyful" is constructed in Greek also as a participle, "Steht auch *charein* (to be joyful, H.B.) im Partizip, so tritt zwischen beide Partizipien ein *kai*" (BauerLex, p. 1727).

134. See the references given in LSLex.—Compare also LXX Num 1:52; 2 Macc 8:22; 10:36; 13:21.

imagery in Col 2:5.[135] This usage would then describe the threat to the community, as though prepared for battle, positioned in rank and order. *Stereōma* in this interpretation is usually translated as "rampart, bulwark," and the genitive *pisteōs* should be viewed as a *genitivus exepegeticus*: faith is the rampart that offers secure refuge before the charge of the enemy.

This interpretation is problematic, however, in view of the corresponding expressions in the Psalms (see above) from which the expression of *stereōma* is derived. There it is Yahweh who is the refuge, not one's own faith. Further argument against such a militaristic interpretation is the fact that this is not close to the meaning of the context. What we know of the community situation from the earlier details of the epistle, about which Epaphras informed Paul (cf. 1:7), is not evocative of a community in the throes of battle. Even the following elucidations, in which the imperative verb forms are to be especially observed, do not hinge on military images. *Taxis* as well as *stereōma* are to be interpreted in Col 2:5 according to their general meaning.[136]

Taxis (order) does not refer to generally acceptable norms of behavior, even outside the Christian community. What is meant can be sensibly explained in Col 2:5 from the use of the corresponding adverb in 2 Thess 3:6, where "disordered" *(ataktos)* is in parallel construction with "and not according to the tradition which you have received from us." For one, this would correspond to the declaration in Col 1:7, in which reference is made to the preceding verse (with the verb "to see"): the situation of the community at Colossae corresponds entirely to how the Christians there were "taught" by Epaphras. For another, this meaning is intimated in 2:7 (see below on *stereōma*).

Whether the genitive attribute *pisteōs* (of faith) also refers to "order," thus of the "order of your faith," or whether "order" is rather to be understood as a more carefully explained object and thus as the "order of the community"[137] are two not mutually exclusive possibilities. For *pistis* (faith) is a social concept that describes the relationship of the community members among themselves (cf. Notes to 1:4).

What is meant by *stereōma pisteōs* (steadfastness of faith) has already been described in the previous verses in different words. Thus it says in 1:23 "if you will only (further) remain *faithful* to him, *firmly founded*, and *not let* yourselves *be led astray*. . . ." Of greater significance for the exposition of this citation, however, is the connection between 2:5 and 2:7. In 2:7, Paul challenges the Colossians: "It is incumbent upon you to be firmly *rooted* and *to be built up* through him . . . *to be made firm* in *faith* as you have been *taught*." A

---

135. See J. B. Lightfoot (p. 242); E. Haupt (p. 70); H. von Soden (p. 41); K. Staab (p. 89); W. Bieder (p. 118); comp. E. Lohmeyer (p. 95); R. P. Martin (pp. 76f.).

136. Comp. T. K. Abbott (p. 243); H. A. W. Meyer (p. 304).

137. Compare for this in the extra-biblical Greek for example Plato, *Crit* 109 D, where *taxis* is used for the subordinate condition of the state.

contextual connection with 2:5 can hardly be overlooked. It is to the point, also here, as in 1:9 (see Notes there), to recognize a challenge to that which has already been ascertained in previous expressions. *Stereōma*[138] then corresponds to "rooted—built up—made firm" and *taxis* is interpreted by "as you have been taught," in correspondence with 2 Thess 3:6 (see above).

COMMENTS I–II TO COL 1:24–2:5

I. What Is Still Lacking in the Sufferings of Christ

Is it valid to argue that in Col 1:24 Paul or whoever writes in his name assigns himself a uniquely important role, through which he, and only he, is viewed as the one who completes the work of salvation which was begun by Christ? Or along the same lines, is it valid to say that Paul, and only Paul, should suffer the afflictions that were imposed upon the church and were to be fulfilled only at the parousia? If both, or even one, of these questions are to be answered in the affirmative, then it would be conclusive that Col comes from a different and later age than the "apostolic" one. But then the message which Col wants to convey to its audience is also to be considered from a different perspective than would be the case in a genuine Pauline epistle. That would be from the perspective of an official authority which necessarily disguises the truth of the formulated utterances and commands obedience (which was foreign to Paul). H. Löwe would be right to speak of a new view of the relationship among Christ, apostle, and church. And there would be important reasons to agree with him when he asserts, "Probably in retrospect on Paul who is no longer alive, his position as apostle should be highlighted in its fundamental and lasting significance for the later church: the apostle belongs actively in the midst of the work of salvation itself. This determines his primary position above all the authorities in the future church and the church as *ecclesia apostolica*."[1]

A decision is dependent on the answer to the following four key questions:

1. What is meant by the "afflictions of Christ"?
2. Does the discussion concern a suffering that is imposed only on Paul and thus on him in a privileged way?
3. What is meant by the word "lack," and what concept underlies it?
4. How should the double occurrence of *hyper* (for) be translated?

Since philogical and grammatic criteria are of little further aid in the exegesis of Col 1:24, the context of the verses and the statements of Col are of special

---

138. For *stereōma*, used in the predominant sense for a firm secure position, see LXX Ezek 13:5; comp. also Acts 3:16; 16:5; 1 Pet 5:9.

1. H. Löwe, "Bekenntnis," op. cit., p. 313. Comp. E. Käsemann, *Taufliturgie*, op. cit., FS für R. Bultmann (Stuttgart and Köln: Kohlhammer, 1949), pp. 133–48:144.

importance. But it is important for our purpose to ask still more of the text. The point of departure of the verse is a declaration concerning the suffering of Paul, but this theme is not formally explored in the epistle. Thus we shall attempt initially to ascertain Paul's concept of suffering from his undisputed epistles in order to determine then whether this understanding can also be applied to Col. It is a question of whether this is possible, whether this concept of suffering can also be assumed for Col 1:24, and whether all other solutions are problematic which might be possible grammatically but appear to stretch to the limit or contradict other Pauline statements.

The best statement concerning Paul's suffering and afflictions is in 2 Cor 4:7ff. To elucidate this theme, we should also draw on the statements from 2 Cor 1:3ff., from which we conclude that the terms for "suffering" and "afflictions" are used to convey the same meaning.[2]

Thlipsis (affliction) is a concept used often in the LXX and is familiar from that work "for the most varied kinds of need and suffering."[3] It designates distress that comes upon humanity from without (i.e., through enemies and warfare, Judg 10:14; Deut 28:53ff.) as well as from within (i.e., in the form of fear, Gen 42:21). Paul uses this concept (which occurs forty-five times in the NT) frequently (twenty-four times),[4] and analogously to the LXX, as a designation for internal and external needs (cf. esp. 2 Cor 7:5). Concretely there are references, among others, to persecution (2 Thess 1:4), captivity (Eph 3:13/1), poverty (2 Cor 8:13), and sadness or fear (2 Cor 2:4; 7:5).[5] These afflictions are also called "suffering"[6] and specifically the special "suffering of Christ" (2 Cor 1:5). This conceptual closeness to Col 1:24, where the reference to Paul's suffering is made in connection with the "affliction of Christ," makes the statement of 2 Cor concerning the suffering of the apostle especially interesting for the exposition of this verse.

2 Cor 4:7ff. deals with the suffering of the servant of the new covenant. Paul wants to put special emphasis on two things:

1. Suffering occurs so that God, not his servants, is granted honor.

---

2. "Affliction" *(thlipsis)*, v 4, is called "suffering of Christ" *(pathēmata)* in v 5. In v 6, the verb "to suffer affliction" *(thlibomai)* is used synonymously with "to suffer suffering" *(pathēmata paschō)*. Compare 2 Thess 1:5–7: "suffering" *(paschō)* and "suffer affliction" *(thlibomai)* are equated.

3. H. Schlier, ThWNT III, p. 141.

4. The one-time occurrence in Eph and Col is counted in. In the Pastoral Epistles, *thlipsis* is not used.

5. Compare also the listings in Rom 8:35 and 2 Cor 11:23ff.

6. The substantive *pathēma* (suffering) is not as frequent in the NT as is *thlipsis* (affliction): it occurs 16 times in the NT, of which 9 times are in the Pauline Corpus, however only 7 times in the sense of "suffering." In reverse, the verb *paschō* (suffer) occurs 42 times in the NT, and *thlibō* (oppress; pass. to suffer affliction) 10 times. In Paul, they occur in almost equal numbers: *thlibō* 6 times, *paschō* 7 times.

2. It is in the suffering of his servants that God reveals his message which is entrusted to them, so that they themselves—and not their words—become the medium for this proclamation, and finally so that God reveals himself as the proclaimer (cf. 2 Cor 5:20). Both are closely linked.

To 1. The thematic and conceptual connection of 2 Cor 4:7 (ff.) with 2 Cor 1:8 is notable. In the latter passage (1:8), the discussion concerns affliction in such *excess (hyperbolē)* that it threatened to overwhelm the *ability/strength (dynamis)* of Paul and his co-workers. Then, in 2 Cor 4:7, in a context that stresses affliction and suffering, the *excess (hyperbolē)* of *strength (dynamis)* which is meted out to Paul and his co-workers is emphasized. This excess—thus a measure of strength that surpasses human faculties (cf. 2 Cor 1:8)—becomes visible in suffering (2 Cor 4:8ff.) and it is revealed to the *community* that it is God who is at work in Paul and his co-workers, thus that they are God's servants.

To 2. This strength, which originates from God, is further revealing: through the fact that the servants of God are not delivered unto death in their suffering, "the life of Jesus" is revealed through their body, namely that he lives and has thus overcome death.[7] The strength of God that works within them and does not permit defeat or suffering to the point of death confirms their message that death was not victorious over Jesus and that God will also raise "us with Jesus." Therefore the suffering of Paul and his co-workers is called the "death of Jesus" (2 Cor 4:10) or the "suffering of Christ" (2 Cor 1:5). The meaning of this expression is not to be elucidated or comprehended by the normal interpretation of the genitive construction. When the subject deals with the "suffering of Christ" in 2 Cor 1:5, we are concerned not with the suffering of an earthly or resurrected Jesus, not with suffering in place of Jesus or in substitution for Jesus, but rather with a suffering in which God allows the sufferer to persevere through divine strength in order thus to reveal that God does not allow Jesus to continue in his suffering, that is, he does not allow death to be victorious.[8]

Does this perception of suffering now apply to Col? Before we explore this question, we will recall some observations that are applicable to the context of Col 1:24:

1. The statements of 1:24 follow immediately on the heels of the expositions about the redemption that has already occurred through the Messiah Jesus and his place of predominance over all of creation. A desire to supplement his works

---

7. The Greek word for "life," *zōē*, originally meant "being alive." See R. Bultmann, ThWNT II, 833.

8. That does not mean that the martyr's death of the apostle would be detrimental to the message. For the patient and joyful ability to persist in suffering precisely affirms hope, so that death by martyrdom cannot be the final word but is rather the resurrection of the dead.—For background to the statements in 2 Cor 4, we can also understand Phil 1:29, "For it is given to you, for the sake of Christ, not only to believe in him, but also to suffer for his sake." And it becomes clear why suffering is viewed as a necessary component of Christlike existence (comp. John 16:33; Acts 14:22; 1 Thess 3:2f.).

here thus seems unnecessary, or at least it contradicts that which was stated earlier (cf. also 2:8–15).

2. Section 1:24ff. does not emphasize, justify, or vindicate the authority of the Pauline apostolate; the status of the apostle does not even arise. Rather, the core question concerns the close relationship Paul has to the Colossians, who are personally unknown to him (cf. the introductory remarks to 1:24ff. and Comment II to 1:1–2).

3. Where the discussion concerned the proclamation of the gospel in the previous verses, the dynamics of this process were emphasized and the proclaimer was mentioned only in a secondary way (cf. Notes to 1:6f.). The same situation occurs in the statements in 1:25–2:3. The statement in v 23, in which the same commissioned activity of the Messiah is spelled out, precedes the description of the service of Paul and his co-workers in v 28. If in 1:24 the Pauline apostolate were included in the work of redemption or the important role of a Christlike agent or surrogate were attributed to Paul, then that would not only contradict the Pauline statement, "I am the least among the apostles" (1 Cor 15:9), but it would also create tension in the statements of Col itself.

Now the expression "lack of Christ-suffering" is introduced with the article and is thus treated as a known quantity, but without being explained to the reader of Col. Alongside that concept, the discussion concerns the joy in suffering and the God-given strength of endurance in suffering (cf. 1:13–29). These components indicate that the same suppositions relevant for comprehending Paul's use of suffering as it is developed in 2 Cor also apply to Col 1:24. We hesitate, nonetheless, as regards the absolute use of the first person singular and to the general manner in which the "Christ-suffering" is mentioned without indicating a limitation, such as the possessive pronoun "my." In so doing, the Pauline apostolate seems to be evaluated in an unknown manner which is very unusual in Paul. The following becomes clear in connection with two important possibilities of understanding the word "lack" and the ideas associated with it.

1. Some exegetes see behind the word *hysterēma* (lack) the eschatological apocalyptic concept of a fixed amount of suffering which the church must fulfill before the parousia, the reappearance of Christ, is possible.[9] This perception goes back to the Judaic idea of the "woes of the Messiah," according to which mankind must suffer a certain measure of woes before the arrival of the Messiah.[10] The linguistic connection of *thlipsis* (misery/suffering) and "woes"

---

9. See, among others, E. Lohse (pp. 113f.); the same: "Christusherrschaft und Kirche im Kolosserbrief," NTS 11 (1964) 203–16:211ff. (= the same, *Einheit*, op. cit., pp. 262–75; E. Lohmeyer (p. 78); J. Zeilinger (ESpg, pp. 89f.).—We can view Thomas Aquinas as a precursor of this viewpoint, who interpreted the phrase from his concept of predestination. According to him, the measure of suffering of the church was predetermined, and even Paul had to subjoin the measure determined for him (p. 61).

10. We find a wealth of documentation in St.-B. IV, 977–85.

(cf. John 16:21, where the travail of a woman is called *thlipsis*) could argue in favor of this viewpoint.

However, a certain difficulty with this interpretation lies in the fact that in the original concept we are dealing with suffering before the coming of the Messiah, whereas in the NT application the concern is with suffering after his arrival. Such a sequence might be explained by the fact that, according to the proclamation in Rom 11:25ff., the parousia of the Messiah signifies a messianic coming for Israel.

More difficult, in our opinion, are the questions connected with the evaluation of the suffering of Paul in this exegesis. It is said that with his suffering the measure of suffering has been fulfilled that God has decreed for the church until the parousia. The result is necessarily a reassessment of the Pauline apostolate which is otherwise unknown in the Pauline epistles.[11] We must express an admonition to use restraint in this interpretation. A further difficulty exists, namely the presupposition in the NT that God has predetermined events and their sequence (in the OT see, for example, Gen 15:16; in Paul: Rom 11:25f.; Gal 4:4; 2 Thess 2:1–12). There are also indications that, according to divine decree, a measure of suffering must occur before the parousia [cf. Matt 24:3ff.; Mark 13:3ff.; Luke 21:7ff.; Rev 6:10f.(?)]. But nowhere do we find the idea of a measure of suffering until the parousia which is predetermined for the church and which can be realized by substituting the suffering of an individual.[12]

---

11. The combination of a fixed measure of suffering and its substitution was only advocated after the Reformation, first by J. A. Bengel (p. 785) (comp. J. Kremer, *Leiden Christi*, op. cit., p. 196). Among the more recent exegetes, comp. among others, E. Lohse (pp. 77f.); the same, "Christusherrschaft," op. cit. (fn. 9), pp. 211ff.; E. Lohmeyer (p. 78); P. T. O'Brien (pp. 79f.); A. Lindemann (p. 33); F. Zeilinger (ESpg, pp. 69f.); F. Mussner, *Christus, das All und die Kirche*, 2d ed., TThST 5 (Trier: Patmos, 1968), p. 142.—K. Staab (p. 84) views the statement in 1:24 as not limited to Paul. He sees a "we" included in the "I" and traces the usage of the first-person singular back to the "stirring speech." J. Kremer, *Leiden Christi*, op. cit., pp. 161–63, represents a similar opinion. He also wants the statement of these verses to pertain not only to Paul, and he views the use of the first-person singular in the sense that Paul affirms a position against his opponents. But the statements in 1:24ff. represent no polemic character, and there is in Col no reference point for the idea that the authority of the apostle was undermined.—Since the meaning of the verb *antaplēroō* does not permit any expansion of the statement of the verse to another person (see Notes), such an idea could be stated only by an express limitation of the "I." But this does not occur. If we wanted to place a period after "for you" and interpret the subsequent *kai* in a limiting function (also I), then there would probably have to be an emphatic *ego* (I). Comp. also J. Schmid, Kol 1,24, BZ 21 (1933) 330–44:337, "Will man dem Verbum (*antaplēroō*, H.B.) seinen vollen Inhalt lassen, dann hätte der Apostel mit dem Satz, seine eigenen Leiden würden das der Gesamtkirche von Gott bestimmte Leidensmass *ausfüllen*, in einer Hyperbel ohnegleichen gesprochen."

12. Comp. J. Kremer, *Leiden Christi*, op. cit., p. 199; E. Schweizer (p. 85, fn. 242).

2. E. Percy[13] excludes the idea of a measure of suffering *entirely*. According to him, the term *hysterēma* (lack) does not mean "remainder" and therefore does not include the concept of an ideal whole. Rather, it designates the lack that one discerns in something that has been accomplished. In regard to the suffering of Christ, this consists in the idea that the purpose for which Jesus suffered has not been accomplished through his suffering. Paul is said to be suffering now for the same purpose as Christ, which is indicated by *hyper* (for), namely in the execution of his commission and thus for the external and internal growth of the community.

The idea of measure can hardly be excluded in determining the exact meaning of *hysterēma* (lack),[14] although the interpretation by E. Percy offers an alternative to the eschatological apocalyptic view represented above. In this, E. Percy aligns himself with the interpretation represented by J. B. Lightfoot (pp. 232f.) and P. Haupt (p. 56), among others.[15] Even if we differentiate, as do these critics, between a "satisfactory suffering of Christ," which brings about the forgiveness of sins and is in no way deficient, and an "edificatory suffering of Christ," which serves to build up the church and needs to be supplemented,[16] even so the statement of the lack in Christ's suffering remains a problem, esp. in Col. Above all, though, in this interpretation Paul becomes a Christlike agent, because only through his suffering does the work of Christ attain its goal. The search for an alternate solution is still open.[17]

---

13. E. Percy, PKE, pp. 129–32; the same, "Zu den Problemen des Kolosser- und Epheserbriefes," ZNW 43 (1950/51) 178–94:190 fn. 43.

14. The use of *hysterēma* (lack) with a genitive, which designates the thing that is lacking and not the lack itself (see Notes), speaks against this. For the statement that a thing (or yet an action) is lacking presumes a concept of measure (in the quantitative sense). See further: M. Carrez, "Souffrance et gloire dans les épîtres pauliennes (Contribution à l' exégèse de Col 1,24–27)," RHPhR 31 (1951) 343–53; J. Kremer, *Leiden Christi*, op. cit., pp. 166–69.

15. Among the exegetes of today, see esp. J. Gnilka (p. 98).

16. The use of *thlipsis* in place of *pathēmata* as exegetical foundation for this differentiation seems insufficient to us. It is correct that *thlipsis* (and also the corresponding verb) is never used to designate the "satisfactory" suffering of Christ, but it is also not used for a so-called "aedificatorical" suffering of Christ.—We need to observe also that, in 2 Cor 1:5, within a context in which *thlipsis* and *pathēma* cannot be differentiated in their meaning, the suffering of Paul and his co-workers is also called *pathēma* of Christ. The editors or translators of the Luther Bible 84 and the GNANT are correct when they chose *an* equivalent for both Greek concepts in Col 1:24.

17. J. B. Lightfoot's reference to the present form of the verb does not resolve the problem. He interpreted this as inchohative time form (that which thus only designates the point of origin of an action) with the observation, "These *hysterēmata* will never be fully supplemented, until the struggle of the Church with sin and unbelief is brought to a close" (p. 232).—However, the present tense can only affirm that Paul—but he—is still attempting to do away with the lack.

A way out could be found by referencing the expression "lack in the suffering of Christ" to a measure of suffering determined by Paul. The argument that the possessive pronoun "mine" is not used seems to counter that.[18] Still, the expression "in my flesh" could fulfill this function by connecting these words not with the verb, *antanapleroō* (to fill out, to restore), but rather, to interpret them as an explanation of the phrase "suffering of Christ."[19] Then the emphatic location of "sufferings of Christ" in this interpretation would most likely point to a suffering of the exalted Christ in Paul. Such a statement would be without analogy in Paul, at least in such transparent form.

A different solution seems more probable to me, one that would permit the concept of suffering which forms the basis of the statements in 2 Cor and which includes the concept of measuring the "suffering of Christ" as it is expressed in 2 Cor 1:5; this should apply to Col 1:24 as well. There, "in my flesh" refers to "lack." Since suffering is an essential and substantial component of the concept of Pauline service, the fulfillment of one of the measures of suffering apportioned to Paul confirms the fulfillment of the commission given to him by God/Christ.[20] From this perspective, it seems to us less problematic to interpret this as a predetermined measure of Paul's suffering, as E. Schweizer views it (p. 85, fn. 241).

The double *hyper* (for) in this reading does not mean a substitution. Rather, it means "for the benefit of, for the good of." Intended is not the suffering in itself, but rather the suffering endured with joy to reveal the strength of God, because in this God verifies the gospel proclaimed through his saints. Because of it, they can be of help to the community, as is elucidated in Col 2:2.

The suffering referred to by Paul in 1:24 signifies more for this reading than simply the concern for the Colossians.[21] The imprisonment of Paul is presumably the chief point of reference. The thoughts of the Colossians will have been directed to this fact when they heard v 24, even though Paul mentions his captivity only in 4:3. Still, Epaphras traveled from Colossae to Paul, and Paul begins with the supposition that the Colossians are saddened by his present situation (4:8). In addition, Paul refers in 4:3 to the "secret of Christ" as the reason for his imprisonment, and in 1:24ff. his suffering and specifically this secret that is entrusted to him to proclaim are mentioned in the same context.

---

18. This is also absent in *pathēmata* (suffering), but there it is more articulate that Paul's suffering is meant (see the Notes).

19. The expression "the lack of suffering of Christ in my body" would not be especially unusual in Col: comp. 1:12, "part of the inheritance of the saints in the light," or 1:27, "the riches of the glory of this secret among the gentiles."

20. The present designates an action, without taking into consideration the conclusion of the same. Thus it is not necessarily said here that Paul is fulfilling his obligation in his suffering for the Colossians in a manner indicating that he is immediately mindful of death. A tension to Phlm 22 is not present.

21. Comp. 2 Cor 2:4, where *thlipsis* means "inner needs."

COLOSSIANS

II. The Revealed Secret

Col refers to the secret (1:26; 2:2; 4:3), as well as to a special aspect of this secret, namely to its *riches among the gentiles* (1:27). This participation of the secret raises the question as to just what this secret is that is called "Christ" in 2:2 and 4:3 and that is implemented in its significance only for the gentiles in 1:27. One answer is given in vv 12–20 and their relationship to the statements in 1:21–23.

It seems fair to assume that the "riches of this secret among the gentiles" in this terminus gives concrete form to the secret, just as the reconciliation of the Colossians is a consequence of the reconciliation of the cosmos according to 1:21–23, of which they certainly are a part. Then the "revealed secret" means Christ as he is praised in 1:12–20: the Jewish Messiah as creator, reconciler, and thus king of *all of creation*. This interpretation is also confirmed in the explanations of Eph 1:9f., where it is expressly stated, "He has made known to us the secret of his decision . . . : All things are to be comprehended under one head, the Messiah, those in heaven and upon earth—under him."

This secret, however, has not been revealed for its own sake, as an object of contemplation so to speak, but rather to apportion the richness among the gentiles, who are also included, in addition to the Jews. The revelation is of equal significance with the mandate of the mission to the gentiles, as it is also revealed *to those* who are to proclaim it to the gentiles: "God has revealed this secret to his saints, (namely) he wanted to let them know what the glorious richness of this secret among the gentiles is: the glorious hope" (v 27).[22]

As distinct from the mystery religions (see Notes to 1:26), in Paul the name "secret" does not rest on the fact that the knowledge of the proclaimed word is to be accessible only to a certain exclusive circle of people and is to be a secret from all others.[23] On the contrary, in Col, as also elsewhere in Paul, the

22. The insoluble connection between the revelation of the cosmic dominion of the Messiah and the mission to the gentiles makes it comprehensible that, in Eph, which has a main theme different from Col in the calling of the gentiles, the gentiles also have a portion of the Jewish heritage which can be designated as the secret revealed by God (3:4). In Eph 3:4ff., this is not conceptually differentiated as it is in Col, where the point of emphasis is more on the cosmic dominion of the Messiah.

23. Such an exclusivity is characteristic also for the Apocalyptic literature and for Qumran. It differentiates the perception of "secret" in Col also from the writings of Qumran in a fundamental way, even when we can determine a stronger similarity to other parallels in the study of history of religions. For that, see further M. Barth, AB 34, pp. 18–21; comp. also K. G. Kuhn, "Der Epheserbrief im Lichte der Qumrantexte," NTS 7 (1960/61) 334–46:336; G. Gnilka (pp. 100f.); the same, "Die Verstockung Israels. Isaias 6:9–10 in der Theologie der Synoptiker," StANT 3 (München: Kosel, 1961), pp. 177–83; J. Coppens, " 'Mystery' in the Theology of Saint Paul and its Parallels at Qumran," in *Paul and Qumran. Studies in New Testament Exegesis*, ed. J. Murphy-O'Connor (London: Chapman, 1968), pp. 132–58.

emphasis is specifically on the universal proclamation of the secret to all people, without differentiation (cf. 1:6, 23, 28). Additionally, the secret does not rely on the idea that God will reveal the "reason" for or the "significance" of the proclaimed word by Paul only sometime in the future.[24] According to the proclamations of 1 Cor 2:6ff., the designation "secret" is rather founded on the fact that we are dealing with that which is revealed here as something from the deepest, innermost part of God, which is accessible to no one except Paul and which only he himself can therefore proclaim. This concept seems to be the basic idea also in Col 1:26f.: God is named as the subject of the act of revelation, and the revelation of the secret is directly attributable to the divine will (v 27: God *wanted* to make known). To the same extent, the contrasting position of "since eternal times" and "now" in v 26 seems to emphasize this meaning. "Now" points to a moment in time that is determined by God's will alone, since he proclaims his decision and executes it.[25] This is closely related to the expression in Gal 4:4, "when the time was fulfilled."

If one interprets the expression "since far-distant ages" in a temporal sense, and not in a personal sense as the designation of exclusively heavenly powers, then we have tension, if not contradiction, between the statements of Col and the thinking of Paul in the other epistles.[26] While Paul emphasizes elsewhere the idea that the calling of gentiles was promised to the OT saints (cf. Rom 15:8ff.), certainly, even while this *promised* participation of the gentiles in the inheritance of Israel plays a predominant role elsewhere in the theological argumentation and serves as the justification of Paul's missionary activity (cf.

---

24. As perhaps, when it says in the rabbinic literature that God will only reveal at a future time why pork may not be eaten. (see St.-B., I, 660)

25. For the antithetical parallelism, which is characterized by the contrary sentence "since far-distant times—but now revealed," N. A. Dahl introduced the designation "Revelation schema," in "Formgeschichtliche Beobachtungen zur Christusverkündigung in der Gemeindepredigt," in *Neutestamentliche Studien fur R. Bultmann*, BZNW 21 (Berlin: Topelmann, 1954), pp. 3–9:4f. D. Lührmann, "Das Offenbarungsverständnis bei Paulus und in den paulinischen Gemeinden," WMANT 16 (Neukirchen-Vluyn: Neukirchener Verlag, 1965), pp. 124–33, preoccupied himself more with this schema. He designates the sermon as the "Sitz im Leben" and comes to the conclusion that the "schema" is not Christological, but is rather in special relationship to the proclamation which is soteriologically determined. The *mysterion* is not Christ; rather, since Christ, ("now") the revelation (= proclamation) of the mysterium is possible as the mysterium of the meaning of salvation of the Christ-occurrence (p. 132).—In case such a sermon schema did exist with such a function, decisive changes occurred with the changes of a *Sitz im Leben*, that is with interpretation of Col: (1) Christ is named explicitly as the essence of the mysterium. (2) God himself is subject of the revelation, in a primary and foremost way. (3) No soteriological function is attributed to the proclamation; it does not "redeem" (Col 1:13f.), but rather it proclaims the revelation which has occurred and the reconciliation which has occurred.

26. The same is true for Eph. Comp. M. Barth, AB 34, p. 334.

esp. Rom 4 and Gal 3), this participation of gentiles seems to be something totally new and is presented as something revealed only now in Col (and Eph).

We need to keep in mind, however, that more than the mere fact of the participation of gentiles in the inheritance of Israel is described as "the (only) now revealed secret." This participation is designated as a consequence of the fact that the Jewish Messiah has begun his reign not only over Israel but over the entire cosmos, and thus he is the Messiah for the Jews as well as for the gentiles. The latter do not need to fulfill any preconditions (such as circumcision, cf. Col 2:11) in order to be able to participate in life under the dominion of the Messiah. Possibly because the participation of the gentiles in the inheritance of Israel is emphasized in Col as the sole work of the Messiah, which has occurred now at the beginning of his reign (cf. 1:13)—thus before any initiative by the gentiles—the author of Col has not yet referred to the OT proclamations. Whether this "peculiarity" is sufficient, however, to deny the Pauline authorship of this letter seems to me doubtful (see Comment I to 1:1 and 2).

IV. THE THREAT TO THE COMMUNITY (2:6–23)

1. The Messiah and "The Deceitful Religion" (2:6–15)

6 As you have now received the Messiah Jesus, the Lord, so lead your lives in obedience to him: 7 it is suited to you to be firmly rooted and to be built up in him, namely to be made firm in faith, as you have been taught; but above all, overflow with thanksgiving! 8 Beware that no one may appear, who would carry you away as prey, by "philosophy," and (namely) by empty deception accomplished by the betrayal of people according to the elements of the world and not according to the Messiah. 9 For in him resides all the fullness of the deity in corporal form. 10 And you have (also) been fulfilled in him who is the head of every rule and power. 11 In him you are also circumcised with a circumcision not performed by human hands, because the human body was cast off in the circumcision of the Messiah. 12—With him (also) you have been buried in baptism. In him you have also been resurrected through the powerful working of the faith of God who raised him from the dead. 13 You also who were dead in your sins namely because of the uncircumcision of your flesh, (even) you he made alive with him by having forgiven us all our sins. 14 Thus he has also canceled a bill of indictment against us which indicted us with legal charges. He specifically removed this by nailing it to the cross. 15 By disarming the powers and forces, he has publicly exposed them as they truly are. In him he has revealed them.

NOTES

In 2:6 we have a challenge to a way of life that is obedient to the Messiah Jesus. The foundation and manner of this way of life are more closely described in 2:7. Both verses indicate the theme of these practices, which continue to 4:6. In a large opening section, 2:6–23, Paul warns the recipients of the epistle insistently and openly of threats to their community. That occurs in the first subparagraph, 2:8–15, in the form of principles, and in a second, 2:16–23, with concrete examples.

The warning expressed in v 8 to beware of a deceitful religion that is not focused on the Messiah is justified in vv 9–15. The fact that the Messiah is the central focus of the discussion for Paul is already evident in that the entire section is filled with prepositional phrases that refer to the Messiah. The central proclamation of the message is expressed in vv 9 + 10, which is formulated almost verbatim from 1:19 ("in him lives the total fulness" [of the Godhead]) and the proclamation that the Christians in Colossae participate in this event of the indwelling of God. What the latter signifies is unfolded in vv 11–15. The basis for this revelation is Paul's declaration of dying with Christ, being buried with Christ, and being raised with Christ. These refer especially to non-Jews—among whom the recipients of the epistle are counted—and they are understood to be participants in the forgiveness of sins that is given to Israel (2:11–13). In vv 14 + 15, Paul concludes that since forgiveness of sins has occurred, any legal demands that are based on religious principles (which include the valuation in v 8), and with this also any legal rights in exercising dominion, have been removed from contention as well.

6 *As you have now received the Messiah Jesus, the Lord.* The verb *paralambanō* used here has a general meaning in the NT: "to take with oneself/to oneself" (i.e., Matt 1:20; 2:20; 4:5) or "to take up" (i.e., John 1:11). It also has another meaning along with the verb usually associated with it *paradidōmi* ("to give up, to hand over"), in the specialized terminology of tradition and teaching. They correspond to the hebraic-rabbinic *qibēl* and *māsar* as technical expressions for the receiving and handing on of tradition, specifically the Torah and its interpretation.[1] In classical Greek there is a similar usage of both verbs. Thus,

---

1. Compare Ab 1, 1, "Moses received the Torah from Sinai and delivered it to Joshua, Joshua to the elders, the elders to the prophets and the prophets delivered it to the men of the great synagogue" (see St.-B. IV, p. 444).—Pea 2, 6, "Nahum the scribe said, I have received a tradition from Rabbi Meascha. He received it from his father, he received it from the Zugoth, these received it from the prophets as Halakah: given by Moses in Sinai" (cited by J. Gnilka, p. 115, fn. 14).—In NT, see esp. Mark 7:4. Of the pharisees and Jews, it says there, "And there is much that they *have observed* (i.e., received), in order to keep it: the washing of drinking vessels and jars and pots and benches."

Plato (Theaet 198b) defines the relationship between teacher and student by citing these two verbs: *paradidōmi* and *paralambanō*.

Except in Col 4:17, where *paralambanō* designates the receiving of a "service," the word occurs in the Pauline corpus only in the technical meaning above, or in association with it.[2] Nowhere does it mean "to take/to accept." The latter action is expressly defined by a different verb in 1 Thess 2:13, namely *dechomai* (to take), which is to be distinguished sharply from the meaning associated with *paralambanō*. In Col 2:6 there is no reason to interpret the verb differently from the other instances in Paul. On the contrary, the words in the context point to the same meaning as elsewhere in the Pauline epistles: in the next verse, which explains v 6 more clearly, we read, "as you may have been taught." And in the connecting sentence, v 8, the warning is of a "philosophy" that supports itself on the "handing over of people" *(paradosis)*.

We must, however, observe that, according to Col 2:6, the recipients of the epistle are not to be regulated by any traditional norms, so that no dogma or ecclesiastical teaching or confessional tradition is transmitted to them.[3] Different from 2 Tim 4:3, here we do not have "healthy teaching" contrasted to a false one. Rather, it is a person, the Messiah Jesus himself, who is the alternative to the delivery of people cited in v 8.[4]

Paul does cite precedents and traditions in his letters (cf. 1 Cor 11:23 and 15:1),[5] but it is improbable that we have a *verbatim citation* of an assumed

<hr>

2. 1 Cor 11:23; 15:1, 3; Gal 1:9, 12; Phil 4:9; 1 Thess 2:13; 4:1; 2 Thess 3:6.

3. Comp. also J. Lähnemann, *Kolosserbrief,* op. cit., p. 112; L. Goppelt, "Tradition nach Paulus," KuD 4 (1958), 213–33:214, 216f.; E. Schweizer, p. 98f.

4. H. Löwe, "Bekenntnis," op. cit., p. 308, however, thinks that due to the references to human transmissions (2:8) and because it falls back on the Hymn in 2:6ff., that the transmission is to be identified with Christians by whom the Colossians had been taught and the baptismal creed which is characteristic of being a Christian. Comp. among others also J. Gnilka (p. 116) and R. P. Martin (NCC, p. 78). K. Wegenast, "Das Verständnis der Tradition bei Paulus und in den Deuteropaulinen," WMANT 8 (Neukirchen: Neukirchener Verlag, 1962), pp. 128ff., thinks that *paralambanō* (to receive) is a concept taken over by the opposition, which was used by these for the initiation "into the secrets of the elements." Paul then transferred it to baptism. Here as there, the reference is to the transmission into the art of the mysteries or the gnosis. The difference is that here we are dealing with the real revelation, there with the false one (for the usage of *paralambanō* in the mysteries and the gnosis, see ibid., pp. 123–26).—Now, however, we can neither prove from the statements in Col that *paralambanō* was used by the "opponents" in the sense suspected by K. Wegenast, nor even whether there is any reference to mysteries at all (see Comment V). Since Paul used the verb "receive" also elsewhere in a similar connection (comp. esp. 1 Thess 2:13; 4:1; 2 Thess 3:6), it makes most sense to interpret the usage of the word in Col 2:6 also from there.

5. Comp. J. Jeremias, *Die Abendmahlsworte Jesu,* 3d ed. (Göttingen: Vandenhoeck & Ruprecht, 1960), pp. 95–97.

tradition in Col 2:6 (the confessional formula: Christ Jesus, the Lord).[6] Aside from the fact that an introductory *hoti* (to designate a citation, as we also have it in 1 Cor 11:23 and 15:3) would have demonstrated this unmistakably, the argument against such an assumption is the subsequent "thus walk *in him*,"[7] which designates a person and can refer to the Messiah. The phrase *"in him"* in the preceding section (2:6–15), which recurs frequently, is used consistently in this sense (cf. 2:8) and thus presumably does not pertain to confession. The assertion by G. Conzelmann (p. 189)[8] that "Christ, namely the one who was taught in the confession of faith (and who thus) adopted ecclesiastical teaching tradition," which according to Col 2:6 is the behavioral norm, does not seem convincing to us. *Christos* was put on an equal plane earlier, in 2:3 as well as in 1:27, with the "revealed secret," which was called the glorious *hope* also for non-Jews. In turn, *hope* in Col is considered the content of the *gospel* (cf. 1:23 and Comment III to 1:3–8). The *gospel* is introduced as the personified, sovereignly effective magnificat in 1:6ff.—even before its proclaimer is named. But this in itself does not indicate that the reference here is to Christ in the ecclesiastical teaching tradition.

It is more probable in this passage that the verb *paralambanō* has leanings closer to the rabbinic concepts in that it designates the receiving of the law from God as well as the faithful transmission of the same. The word in Col 2:6 expresses the intention that the gospel is not something that was created by human beings but is rather an entrusted and unfalsified possession which is to be passed on (cf. 1:6ff.; 1:26f.). The personal object, however ("the Messiah . . ."), indicates that the reception and proclamation of the gospel are not the transmission of a "tradition" but rather signifies the coming of the Messiah himself.

The form of the expression *ton christon iēsoun ton kyrion*, "the Messiah Jesus, the Lord," is unusual. We do encounter the formula containing all three designations "Christ," "Jesus," "the Lord" more than 60 times, but the sequence "Lord—Jesus—Christ" predominates (approx. 48 times).[9] The order "Christ—Jesus—Lord" occurs otherwise only in Rom 6:23; 8:39; 1 Cor 15:31; Eph 3:11; Phil 3:8; 1 Tim 1:2, 12 (cf. 14); 2 Tim 1:2. In these references, *christos* is cited

---

6. Comp. J. Gnilka (p. 116), who sees in v 6 "das auf eine Bekenntnisformel reduzierte Evangelium [the gospel reduced to a confession formula]."

7. "in him" *(en auto)*: vv 6, 7, 9, 10, 14; "in him" *(en hō)*: vv 11 + 12; "with him" *(syn autō)*: v 13.

8. Comp. also O. Cullmann, *Die Tradition als exegetisches, historisches und theologisches Problem* (Zürich: Zwingli Verlag, 1954), p. 19, who is of the opinion that we are dealing with instructions whose connection and source of origin is Christ, and according to which the believers should walk.

9. In this, we frequently have the article before *kyrios* (Lord) and/or a possessive pronoun added. This formula occurs primarily in blessings without any kind of addition: Rom 1:7; 1 Cor 1:3; 2 Cor 1:2; Gal 1:3; Eph 1:2; 6:23; and others.

with an article only in Col 2:6 and Eph 3:11.[10] The article before *christos* cannot alone indicate decisively whether the substantive is titular (as in Luke 18:5, 28) or whether it is used as a proper name (cf. Notes to 1:2). However, since this form is rarely used and since in the deliverance non-Jews are recognized as participants in the inheritance of Israel in these passages (cf. 1:12–14, 27), we proceed with fairly good assurance that *christos* can be understood as a title in this passage and should be translated as "Messiah."[11]

Ton kyrion (the Lord) is probably not a predicate accusative and thus does not mean: "to receive the Messiah as *the Lord*." This interpretation would be probable if the possessive pronoun ("your/our") were used (cf. Eph 3:11). It is significant that this expression occurs specifically in Col, which emphasizes cosmological pronouncements, while Eph places more emphasis on the church. The elucidations in Col 1:12–20 that praise the Messiah as the king over all creation suggest that, even at the beginning of the paragraph, which refers back to Col 1:12ff. from a different vantage point, the Messiah is intended as the Lord with regard to everything that has been created. This position of predominance is the basis for the argument about things that threaten the Colossians. In accordance with this datum, v 6a summarizes everything that has been said before: *paralambanō* (to receive) the proclamations concerning the working of the gospel with the Colossians (1:3ff.), *kyrios* (Lord) the praiseworthy proclamations about the son in 1:12ff., *christos* (Messiah) the expositions in 1:24ff. according to which the son is to be proclaimed Messiah even for non-Jews. The particle *oun* (now) points to this function which is one of referring back and summarizing in the passage before us.[12]

(so) lead your lives in obedience to him (literally: walk in him). After this verse was introduced by the comparative particle *hōs* (how), we would expect a *houtōs* (so) here in the sequence. But it is left out, here as often elsewhere in contemporary Greek.[13] The gospel is not proclaimed to be received in a nonobligatory sense. Rather, its reception is aimed at an acceptance which corresponds to that of the Messiah, namely that he is recognized as Lord over all things, he who leads both Jews and gentiles on a good road as Yahweh once led his people from captivity into the promised land. The two words "in him" which refer back to v 6a express precisely this point.

The presumption is expressed by the practical and ethical verb *peripateō*

---

10. The same case applies in some other text variants to Phil 3:8. The determining preceding *christos*, connected only with the name "Jesus" and without "Lord," is also rare: it occurs only in Gal 5:14; Eph 3:1; and in a text variant to Gal 6:12 (comp. C. F. D. Moule, p. 89).

11. The following interpret it as a proper name, among others, E. Lohse (p. 142, fn. 3) and J. Gnilka (p. 116).

12. Compare for example H. A. W. Meyer (p. 306); J. A. Bengel (p. 787); P. Ewald (p. 363).

13. Compare the cited examples in BauerLex.

(actually: to go about, to walk). The word was used already in 1:10 and applies to the conduct of one's entire life (see Notes to 1:10).

7 *It is suitable for you to be firmly rooted and to be built up in him . . . !* (literally: to have been being rooted and to be being built up in him). The imperative invitation from v 6 (literally: to walk in him) is elucidated in more detail by the four participles. In this connection, as well as in the corresponding forms in 1:10, they are imperative in character. We are dealing less with a summons and more with expressions of encouragement in order to remind the Colossians about what is fitting for them.[14] The *passive* form of the first three participles, as well as their imagery, point toward the idea that one's conduct in life alluded to here is not in the realm of human possibility. Only the affirmation of a person concerning what *has* already *happened* and concerning what *is* still *to happen* are decisive.[15]

The recipients of Col will hardly have noticed an unevenness or even a break in the imagery of the language of this verse. With *rizoō* (literally: to sink roots), we have an image from the botanical realm, specifically from the realm of agriculture, and *oikodomeō* (to build [up]) draws a comparison with a building, but this configuration is not unusual. We find it not only with Paul (cf. 1 Cor 3:9; Eph 3:17), but also in other writings. *Odes Sol 3:16f. (Hennecke-Schneemelcher,* II, 619) is an especially attractive example: "I, however, was made firm and lived and was redeemed, and my foundation was laid by the Lord, because he planted me. For he set the root and watered it and gave it strength and caused it to prosper, and its fruit is eternal."[16] The concept of the root as the (secure) foundation of a plant explains the blending of the two images. *Rizoō* and the composites of this verb are used generally of cities and buildings.[17]

The first participle *errizōmenos* (to be rooted) is used in the perfect tense, contrary to the other verb forms of the verse, and thus expresses the persistence of something fulfilled (cf. BDR 340). This corresponds to the chosen image,[18]

---

14. For that, see Notes to 1:10, esp. fn. 32.

15. E. Lohmeyer (p. 97) even goes as far as to remark, "Wenn es in den bisherigen Sätzen noch scheinen konnte, als sei alles Ubernehmen und alles Handeln an Willen und Wohl des Einzelnen geknüpft, so erläutern die beiden folgenden Partizipien, dass gerade diese Freiheit nur der Widerschein schlechthinniger Abhängigkeit ist; denn sie sind beide passivisch und schliessen in ihrem bildlichen Sinn jeden Gedanken an eigenes Wollen aus."

16. This reference from the second century is later than the Colossian Epistle, yet the connection to images is older, as for example 1 QS VIII:5 demonstrates.

17. See Epigr. Gr., 1078, 7 (of an entry with earthen steps made long ago and now overgrown with roots); Sophocles, Oed Col 1591 (of a bridge); Plutarch, Mor 321 d (of a city). Compare also the usage of *ekrizoō* ("to uproot") in 1 Macc 5:51 (of the destruction of a city) and Sir 3:9 (of the tearing down of foundations).

18. P. Vielhauer, *Oikodome. Das Bild vom Bau in der christlichen Literatur vom*

because the foundation that is laid *once* has to lend continuous support to the structure which is erected thereon.

Both the composite[19] *ep-oikodomeō*, as well as the simplex *oikodomeō*, are used by Paul for the building up of the individual[20] as also with the image of the building of the community (see Eph 2:20; 1 Cor 3:10ff.). Even though the metaphoric language in this verse uses the *firmness* of a well-founded construction as the point of comparison and does not compare the community with a building, there is still no reason to exclude the latter concept in the verses under consideration. We can hardly justify the idea that a certain individualization of the concept of building up can be determined in the sense that the eye on the neighbor as "the primary movement of the Pauline view" has disappeared.[21] The use of *pistis* (faithfulness) in this verse counters such a thesis (see below). Also, the concept of the building of the community is not excluded in this passage (as W. M. L. de Wette [42] argues), because the preterite tense was not used. Certainly we read in Eph 2:20: "Build upon (aorist!) the foundation of the apostles and the prophets," but the community is not described as an already completed structure. In Eph 2:22 we read, "through him also you are 'built together.'" The verb here is in the present.

The words *en autō* (in him) probably do not indicate the foundation "in which the structure is rooted" and "on which it is erected." As opposed to 1 Cor 3:11, this linkage is not affirmed explicitly here, as the subsequent phrase *en autō* (in him) after the verbs "to be rooted" and "to be built up" can hardly be interpreted in this sense. In order to make such a statement, the preposition *en* (in) attached to *errizōmenos* (to be rooted) would be fitting, but *epoikodomeō* (to build up) with *en* instead of *epi* (on) is unusual and, as far as is known to us, without parallel. Since "in him" is placed after both participles, it cannot refer back only to the first one. Thus, in our interpretation, the preposition would seem to be strictly instrumental.[22]

With this chosen image, the Messiah is represented as the *master of construction* who erects a firmly grounded structure (compare also Matt 16:18).

In 1 Cor 3:10, laying of a foundation and constructing a building are

---

Neuen Testament bis Clemens Alexandrinus, Diss. (Karlsruhe, 1940), pp. 102f., thinks that plasticity had completely disappeared, since "to be ingrown (or overgrown with roots)" and to be "built up" do not fit with "walk," but this is not persuasive. There is a contrast between the dynamic verb *peripatein* (really, to walk about) in v 6 and the static verbs that describe a firmly standing structure, yet because of the technical meaning of *peripatein* used to describe a way of life, both concepts are reconcilable with each other.

19. If the composite in contrast to the simplex even has a special significance in this passage (comp. BDR 119), then the prefix *ep-* emphasizes the concept of a structure which is raised *on (epi)* a firm foundation.

20. Comp. *oikodomeō* in 1 Cor 14:4a, 17; 1 Thess 5:11; and *epoikodomeō* in Jude 20.

21. P. Vielhauer, *Oikodome*, op. cit., p. 105.

22. In 1:16, the words "in him" are explained on the basis of "through him" and

described as activities of the apostle. If the Messiah himself is named in their place in Col 2, this stands in agreement with the explanation in 1:6ff. about the sovereign working of the gospel in the world.

namely to be made firm in faith (literally: and being made firm). If all three verb forms, "to be founded," "to be built up," and "to be made firm," were equally ranked, then we would expect "in him" after the third and not after the second verb form. It is improbable that the "being made firm" was consciously excepted from the working of the Messiah. The *kai* (and) should therefore be interpreted as an "explanatory and" ("namely"). While *bebaioo*[23] takes up the participle *errizōmenos* (to be founded) again, *pistis* (faith) refers to *epoikodomoumenos* (being built up). *Pistis* in v 6 hardly has a different meaning from that of the same term in the preceding verse, which refers back to 1:4–8. It means the faith in the Messiah which represents itself in "the love of everything holy" (1:4). Thus the concept of "building up" (or edification; see above) bears its typical Pauline social reference also in the Colossian epistle.

As in 1:9ff., so also in 2:6, the Colossians are urged to do something which was described earlier as something which already exists with them. Here, as there, this state of affairs can be explained by the idea of overflowing, as it can be found in Phil 1:9 and as it occurs also at the end of Col 2:7 (see Notes to 1:9).[24]

"toward him." Perhaps this second component in meaning, next to the instrumental one, is also contained here.—J. B. Lightfoot (p. 243) thinks that *en* (in) was chosen because "Christ is represented rather as the binding element than as the foundation of the building" (comp. also H. A. W. Meyer, p. 307). This interpretation would fit with *epoikodomeō* (to build upon), but it would seem forced in connection with *rizoomai* (to be rooted). The latter would also be the case if one wanted to refer the second verb only to "in him." Because more so than this one, the former would demand a closer determination, esp. since the idea of connection in v 19 is described more clearly, explicitly, and unmistakably in a different image.

23. *bebaioō* means "to make firm, to give something a firm hold." In the NT, the verb occurs above all in the transmitted meaning "to confirm, strengthen" (Mark 16:20; Rom 15:8; 1 Cor 1:6; Phil 1:7). In 1 Cor 1:8 and 2 Cor 1:21, the verb is used in a similar sense as in Col 2:7.—The substantive *bebaiōsis* and the verb *bebaioō* had special significance in legal terminology: the *bebaiosis* was the obligation of a seller in which he took over the guaranty of defending the legal right of a sale in opposition to the demands of a third party (see A. Deissmann, *Bibelstudien. Beiträge zumeist aus den Papyri und Inschriften, zur Geschichte der Sprache, des Schrifttums und der Religion des hellenistischen Judentums und des Urchristentums* [Marburg: Elwert, 1895], pp. 100–5; comp. H. Schlier, ThWNT I, pp. 602f.). This use of the language found its way into the LXX, as esp. Lev 25:23 demonstrates, "The land may not *eis bebaiosin* ("legally guaranteed;" in Heb, it says here "completely, forever") be sold." It is, however, uncertain whether there is precedent for this in the NT. A. Deissmann suspected it in Phil 1:7 and 2 Cor 1:21f. (ibid., pp. 104f.).

24. The dative *tē pistei*, which is rendered with "in faithfulness," has been translated in the instrumental by some exegetes (among others J. B. Lightfoot, p. 243; H. A. W.

as you have been taught. The contextual relationship that exists between *pistis* (faith) in 2:7 and 2:5 (and also in 1:4ff.; see above) does not permit the proclamation in vv 6+7 to be interpreted to mean the Colossians are urged to maintain traditional acts of faith that are offered as teaching,[25] and does not even specifically refer to baptismal instructions (R. P. Martin, p. 73). The expression "as you have been taught" corresponds rather to the phrase "as you have been taught by Epaphras" in 1:7, which there refers to the proclamation of the sovereignly working word. In 2:7 it is used in a parallel construction to "as you have received the Messiah Jesus!" (see Notes to v 6). In that sense, *didaskō* (to teach) does not designate an activity which transmits only a teaching tradition instead of a proclamation by the strength of God and thus points to Deutero-Pauline authorship of this epistle in the so-called post-apostolic age (see Notes to 1:7).

But above all, overflow with thanksgiving! (literally: overflowing in thanks). Asyndetically, a last participle has been attached without a connecting *kai* (and). In different manuscript traditions, a connection with that which precedes immediately is made explicit. Thus, a very important manuscript like Codex Vaticanus (fourth century) adds "in thanks" *en autē* (in it) and thus establishes a relationship to *pistis* (faith) made earlier: the Colossians shall overflow in faith, which in turn should demonstrate itself in thanks.[26] It is documented in important manuscripts that this reading, "overflowing in thanks," is more original: in the Codex Sinaiticus (fourth century), and in the minuscules 33 and 1739, which offer a very reliable text. In addition, the insertion of *en autō* (in it) seems to smooth over the stylistically harsh effect of the asyndetic connecting link.[27]

If "overflowing" does not refer to *pistis* and if it is set off from the preceding participles, then it emphatically refers to the entire proclamation in v 6.

Meyer, p. 107; P. Ewald, p. 364; J. Gnilka, p. 117) (compare Heb 13:9). The connection between 2:5 (where we are dealing with the "steadfastness of faithfulness") and 2:6 does not approximate this interpretation.—Differing text variants have inserted the preposition *en* in place of the bare dative (and thus left off the article, in part) or have inserted also "in him" next to the *en* before "faithfulness." These variants are hardly original, for either their textual value is small or they are perhaps to be understood as supplemental explication of the bare dative, or both.

25. Comp. E. Lohse (p. 143); P. T. O'Brien (p. 108); A. Lindemann (p. 39).

26. The variants, which render "in it" (i.e., in faithfulness) in place of "in thanks," or which read "(overflow) in him (i.e., in the Messiah) in thanks," are already eliminated as original readings because of their minimal text value.

27. E. Haupt (p. 72) considers the reading "in it in thanks" original (attested, among others, from Codex Vaticanus), and he explains the deletion of the words "in it" in a few manuscripts by the fact that the tired eyes of the scribe skipped from the first "in" (before "it") to the second one (before "thanks").—Be that as it may, it results only in a shift in emphasis, not in an engraved contextual change.

Overflowing thanks is the distinguishing mark of a way of life as it is described by the first three participial expressions in v 7 (cf. also 1:12; 3:17; and 4:2).

This image of overflowing does not fit well with the thesis put forward by H. Löwe, among others,[28] who maintains that *eucharisteō* is a technical liturgical concept and means the specific expression of faith in a characteristic confession.

8 *Beware that no one may appear, who would carry you away as prey.* (literally: not someone may be who would rob you). Paul often uses the warning expression *blepein mē* (to beware, that not; cf. among others 1 Cor 8:9; 10:12; Gal 5:15), but differently than it is generally used, and differentiated from the classic rule, it is here constructed with the indicative future but not with the conjunctive (usually that of the aorist). This difference from the Classical Greek which can also be observed in connection with the conjunctions *hina mē* (so that not) and *hina* (so that) is not a grammatical mistake but is rather a peculiarity of Koine Greek, the common language in Hellenistic times, which is also the language of the NT.[29] We cannot determine a difference in meaning between the two usages.[30]

It is also noticeable that the object "you," which should go with the participle *sylagōgōn* (robbing), is separated from it in a fashion similar to the construction discussed above. The sequence of words in the Greek reads, "that not someone you (obj) be the robbing (one)." But even this construction is grammatically permissible. We find similar constructions also elsewhere in the NT, and even in Classical Greek the participle can be separated from its modifier.[31]

The definite participle *ho sylagōgōn* (the robbing one) represents a relative clause here.[32] The verb "to be" attains an independent status as *verbum*

---

28. H. Löwe, "Bekenntnis," op. cit., p. 303.—Further, see Notes to "thanksgiving" in 1:12.

29. Comp. esp. Heb 3:12; Mark 14:2; but see also Matt 26:5.—See for that BDR 369,2. There is a listing of further references in fn. 5.

30. E. Haupt (p. 74) concluded from the usage of the future that the "temptation" had not yet taken place. The tense is not itself sufficient to make such a deduction: in Rev 9:20, we have such a construction with *hina mē* (so that not) in the future which alludes to a *continuation* of idol worship. Also nonsupportable is the thesis that the indicative itself describes real danger (J. B. Lightfoot, p. 244; T. K. Abbott, p. 246), because the subjunctive, for example, in Gal 5:15 or 1 Cor 8:9 refers to a not less real danger.

31. In the NT, comp. esp. Heb 12:25. Further, see BDR 474, 5c, and Kühner-Blass-Gerth II.2, pp. 616f., 623f. The change in position of "you" and the verb *estai* (he will be) in a few text variants is probably a correction of the unusual word order.

32. See BDR 412, 4, "it is evident that the equation of the relative clause and the attributive clause justifies this construction. . . ." Comp. also BDR 353, 2 b. The supposition of Th. Zahn, Einl. I, p. 333, that it is perhaps only a single person of some significance, from whom the entire movement emanated, is therefore hardly applicable.

existentiae ("to be present, to exist") because of the article; thus we do not have a predicate construction ("he is robbing"). The expressed warning is radicalized in this manner.

The verb *sylagōgeō* occurs in the NT only in Col 2:8 and in the LXX not at all. We seem not to be able to document it before Paul.[33] It can mean "to rob something" and also "to rob someone."[34] The meanings hardly come under consideration here because in the context the indication of what should be taken away from the Colossians is missing. We could assume this would be self-evident and therefore not mentioned. Then in the parallel expression to 1:23 we could only think of hope as the something being stolen or to be stolen. But according to our understanding of Col (compare 1:5 and Comment III to 1:3–8), hope has been "securely kept" and can therefore not be robbed. The description that the Colossians themselves should be robbed fits well with other images in the letter to the Colossians, just as does the idea that the recipients of the letter are to be transported into the kingdom of the Son (1:13). Therefore, they should be wary of a deportation, of being taken away as booty. This image fits in well with the wealth of traditional references in the OT, as does also 1:13.[35] But we should observe a further parallel that arises from this translation: the image of being led away as booty, and thus out of slavery, is reminiscent of Gal 4:3 in connection with Col 2:8 (and 2:20) in the cited *stoicheia tou kosmou* (elements of the world). Only in Gal 4 and Col 2 in the Pauline corpus do we encounter "elements of the world" of which it is said that "we were enslaved" by them (cf. Comment IV).

by "philosophy" (literally: by the philosophy). The article before *philosophia* could allow us to presume that Paul is using the concept here for Greek philosophy as a known phenomenon and wishes to condemn this as "the parent of all deception."[36] But when Paul uses *philosophia* in this context, an expression that occurs in the NT only here, then he is probably thinking "neither generally of Greek philosophy as a spiritual phenomenon nor of one of the classical school orientations."[37] The other expositions in Col 2 which cite circumcision, baptism, food laws, festivals, etc., indicate rather that "philosophy" here means that which for us expresses the idea of "religion." The Greek word *philosophia* is also used in this sense of the surrounding world of the NT. Thus, in the LXX,

---

33. Comp. LSLex; BauerLex; MMLex; J. B. Lightfoot, p. 244.

34. For the former meaning, see Heliodorus, Aeth 10, 35 (third century c.e.), "he is the one who took my daughter by force." For the second meaning, see Aristaenetus, Epistola II, 22. (Both references are cited in MMLex.)

35. For this usage of the OT, comp. esp. 1 Cor 10:1–13.

36. Then Tertullian was right, "the apostle already then saw philosophy as the shattering of truth" (de Anim 3). Comp. ibid., *Apol* 46, 18, "What do philosophy and Christ have in common?!"

37. O. Michel, ThWNT IX, 182, 33.

in 4 Macc,[38] where the word is used to designate the "Jewish religion" (exclusively and with emphasis on the cultic laws), it is to represent "true philosophy" in agreement with Stoic principles (cf. among others 4 Macc 1:1; 5:22–26).

Philo of Alexandria speaks of the "philosophy of the fathers" or of the "philosophy according to Moses" or even of the "Jewish philosophy," and he even calls the Mosaic law "the commands . . . of holy philosophy."[39] In the same vein, Josephus (Ap 2, 47) characterizes perhaps the whole Torah (= the Pentateuch) by this expression "philosophy." He describes the Jewish religious groups of Essenes, Sadducees, and Pharisees as "three philosophies which have existed since oldest times."[40]

Even in a religious interpretation of *philosophia* in Col 2:8, the article can hardly be understood generically, as though religion in itself were intended and Christianity (as also Judaism) were differentiated from it. Since we have no comparative material to the Pauline usage of this concept, or even to pre-Christian usage, and since we also do not find this usage in the writers cited above in this sense, we need to defer such an interpretation of the statement in Col as long as other possibilities in this context are likely and more probable.

Many critics view the term *philosophia* as one cited by Paul and therefore as a definitive self-designation of the so-called teacher of falsehood.[41] But when this expression is to be understood as a collective designation of religious viewpoints, it hardly makes sense that Paul should have cited it since nothing is said about the special characteristics of "false teaching" nor how a characteristic self-designation appears. The fact that *philosophia* is a hapax legomenon does not prove anything, because *sylagōgeō* (to rob) occurs only here in the NT and is surely no terminus for the "teacher of falsehood."

The article has probably been inserted because the following substantive is

---

38. Compare esp. the event which is related in 4 Macc 5: there, *philosophia* is related in vv 11 and 22. Comp. also 4 Macc 1:1; 5:7, 35; 7:7, 9, 21; 8:1; LXX Dan 1:20.

39. Comp. Leg Gaj 156; 245; Som II, 127; Mut Nom 223; Vit Cont 26.

40. Ant 18, 11. Comp. also 18, 9.23; Ap 1, 54; comp. Ant 15, 371; Vit 12. —*Philosophia* is also used in connection with the induction into the mysteries. But there "appears a direct equation first in Theon in the 2nd Century and Stobaeus in the 5th Century C.E." (E. Schweizer, p. 106, fn. 322; comp. E. Lohse, p. 144).—For the meanings of *philosophia*, see also C. Spicq, *Theologie Morale du Nouveau Testament*, vol. I (Paris: Gabalda, 1965), p. 385, fn. 1.

41. Comp. among others, J. B. Lightfoot (p. 245); T. K. Abbott (p. 246); H. A. W. Meyer (p. 310); H. von Soden (p. 43); Dibelius-Greeven (p. 27); E. Lohmeyer (p. 103); E. Lohse (p. 144); E. Schweizer (p. 107); J. Gnilka (p. 122); A. Lindemann (p. 39); G. Bornkamm, "Die Häresie des Kolosserbriefes," in op. cit., *Das Ende des Gesetzes. Paulusstudien. Gesammelte Aufsätze I*, BEvTh 16 (München: Kaiser, 1952), pp. 139–56:143.

elaborated and is thus limited in its meaning[42]: as empty deception, aimed at traditions of people, at the elements of the world, but not at the Messiah. In our translation we would therefore choose an undefined form because no predeterminable shape is introduced.

and (namely) by empty deception (literally: and empty deception). The definite substantive *philosophia* which follows *kai* (and) is best understood as an "explanatory and" *(kai exepegeticum;* cf. BDR 442, 6a).

That the two substantives that are connected by this conjunction are closely related as already indicated by the fact that the preposition *dia* (through) as well as the article in front of the second substantive ([empty] deception) are not repeated. We do, however, need to observe what F. Pfister called to our attention, namely that this alone does not prove that "philosophy" is designated by Paul as deception.[43] The idea that Paul means two different things is not evident from the context. F. Pfister's explanation, that Paul, by using *apatē* (deception), is pointing at some kind of (!) manipulation which is not more closely defined (!) by him but is still perceived as deceptive manipulation is not very convincing, in our opinion.

Eph 5:6 illustrates what is meant by the shortened expression "empty deception": a deception with empty words. Both concepts, "empty" and "deception," are noticeable as express contrasts to that which was said previously about the gospel:

1. While the gospel and its discernment are described in terms of "overflowing fullness" (2:2) or "all the treasures of wisdom" (2:3), *philosophia* addressed here is described as deception through *empty* words—empty, including its content along with its effect.[44] For in the Messiah lie *all* the treasures of discernment, so that all discernment which passes by him must be empty and of no consequence.

2. "Deception" stands in opposition to the gospel which is called "word of *truth"* in 1:5. We find this antithesis also in 2 Thess 2:10. Truth is that which God has revealed (compare Notes to 1:5). Deception, however, is that which relies only on "that which is transmitted by people." This deception misleads its listeners (and "actors") about its effects. It leads back to slavery (compare *sylagōgeō,* to "lead away as prey"), while with the gospel comes the one who leads people out of slavery (cf. 1:13f. and 2:6).

---

42. Comp. for that, for example, the use of the article in Col 3:5 before "greed."— According to P. Ewald (p. 366), the article represents a possessive pronoun dependent on "someone." This is possible (comp. the citations in BauerLex, Sp 1089), where the relationship is clear and self-evident, which, however, is not the case in Col 2:8.

43. F. Pfister, "Die *stoicheia tou kosmou* in den Briefen des Apostels Paulus," Ph 69 (1910) 411–27:414 (esp. also fn. 20).—He refers, among others, to Luke 15:9, where, in the Greek, an expression is repeated by two substantives from Luke 15:6 connected by "and," wherein the repetition of the second substantive is undetermined.

44. Thus also in the transmitted usage of the extra-biblical Greek. Comp. LSLex.

accomplished by the betrayal of people . . . and not . . . the Messiah. (literally: according to . . . not according to . . .) The verb *paralambanō* (to receive) in 2:6 corresponds to the substantive *paradosis* (transmission), which is a technical term for the receiving of tradition (cf. Notes). Here also, a deliberate contrast between statements in v 6 and v 8 is intended. Paul warns of people whose words and actions are supported only by the traditions of people, who can also render only that which is human with human authority (cf. 2:22 + 23), not, however, that which is revealed by God. The gospel, however, "transmits" the Messiah himself. The emphasis lies more on the content and the origin of that which is transmitted rather than on the process of transmitting itself. It goes beyond the text to conclude that Paul might have in mind a "false teaching" of a religious group, which would be highly valued within its tradition or even within the secret tradition.[45]

The contrasting position of the proclamation in v 6 rendered by the key word "transmission" is not sufficiently recognized if one refers the explanations that are introduced by *kata* (according to) not to *philosophia* but rather to the verb "to rob."[46] Then it would be stated that the robbing intended here is according to the manner of "human transmission" and the "elements of the world," not according to the Messiah. Since it is self-evident that the Messiah neither enslaves nor deals in deception, this interpretation of v 8 could be understood only as a sharp polemic. Its content, however, would hardly require further justification, which is provided in v 9. Contextually, the statement of v 9 does not fit with v 8 if such an interpretation were accepted.

according to the elements of the world. For this expression, see Comment IV.

9 *For in him resides all the fullness of the deity.* Attempts to interpret v 9 as the beginning of a hymn[47] are not convincing, if only because in 2:9 (cf. also v 10) the subject matter of the hymn in Col 1:12–20 is taken up by way of a commentary. The Greek *hoti* is also here a substantiatory conjunction, but not the so-called *hoti recitativum* which indicates the beginning of a citation (see also Comment VI).

The proclamation in 1:19 is taken up almost verbatim in this verse. There, it stated, "That in him should reside all the fullness was the will of God." Chap. 2:9 is stated in the present, in contrast to the other formulation in which the aoristic time frame was chosen. For here the action is kept in mind, which was carried out through the divine will cited in 1:19: only in the Messiah does God allow himself to be "recognized." J. B. Lightfoot's translation (p. 247) of this verb form with "has its fixed abode" fits exactly this sense.

45. Comp. among others J. B. Lightfoot (p. 246); Dibelius-Greeven (p. 27); E. Lohmeyer (p. 103); E. Lohse (p. 145); J. Gnilka (p. 122); R. P. Martin (NCC, p. 79); G. Conzelmann (p. 189).

46. H. A. W. Meyer (p. 311) interprets it that way.

47. See above all G. Schille, *Frühchristliche Hymnen* (Berlin: Evang. Verlagsanstalt, 1965), pp. 31–37; comp. also K. Staab, p. 92.

Vv 1:19 and 2:9 are also differentiated in the sense that in 2:9 the expression "it was the will of God" does not occur. Instead, the concept "all the fullness" is elucidated by the genitive attribute *tēs theotēs* (of the deity). This gives the author of the epistle the occasion and opportunity to explain the expression in 1:19. "All the fullness" does not accordingly describe something that is differentiated from God, perhaps the world. Rather, it means the "God who is present" (cf. Notes to 1:19). Chap. 1:19–20 intend to demonstrate that God is present in the Messiah through his actions. By emphasizing that *all the fullness* resides in the Messiah, prominence is given to the idea that God does not act except through him.

In the sense that "fullness" *(plērōma)* in 1:19 already appears unusual as a designation for God, it is equally notable that in 2:9 the impersonal word *theotēs*, which occurs only here in the NT, is used, and not simply *theos* (God) as in Eph 3:19. The explanation is widely acknowledged that the "true divine presence" of Christ in the sense of the old ecclesiastical creed is proclaimed here: *theotēs* designates the substance of the divine, the being of God, and is to be distinguished from *theiotēs*, which signifies the *attribute* of the divine.[48] However, the difference in the meaning of both concepts probably belongs to a much later time and is determined by assumptions and presuppositions quite foreign to Paul's thinking. At the time of the composition of the NT, as also of Paul's epistles, both substantives had nearly the same meaning.[49] (For a more exact justification, see Comment I.)

in corporal form (literally: bodily). Just like *theotēs* (deity), the adverb *sōmatikōs* (corporally) is a word used only once in the NT. It does not occur at all in the LXX. Its meaning is equally disputed. We suggest seven possible interpretations here:[50]

1. According to J. B. Lightfoot (p. 248), the adverb is indicative of Christ becoming human: "*sōmatikōs* is added to show that the Word in whom the pleroma thus had its abode from all eternity crowned His work by the Incarnation."[51]

2. Closely related to this solution is the concept that *sōmatikōs* asserts that

---

48. Among the Classics, in Thomas Aquinas (p. 96); ibid., *Ad Romanos*, p. 117; comp. also J. B. Lightfoot (p. 247); T. K. Abbott (pp. 248f.); J. A. Bengel (p. 788); E. Haupt, (p. 80, fn. 1); H. von Soden (p. 105); E. Lohse (pp. 150f.); J. Gnilka (p. 128).

49. The fact that *theotes* in the NT is a hapex legomenon is not sufficient here in order to adequately justify that Paul took over a concept from the "false teachers." Also, *theiotēs* occurs only once in the NT, in Rom 1:20, and there certainly not in a citation.

50. The suggestions are not necessarily mutually exclusive, but could rather be partly combined with each other.

51. Comp. also Oecumenius of Trikka (cit. in K. Staab, *Katenenhandschriften*, p. 454); R. P. Martin (NCC, p. 80); F. F. Bruce (p. 101); J. Lähnemann, *Kolosserbrief*, op. cit., p. 118, who emphasizes that the polemic was not against the concept that Christ had only an apparitional body, but rather against asceticism (Col 2:23).

312

even the *elevated one* is placed into a body. This interpretation takes more cognizance of the present verb form (all the fullness of the deity *resides*) than is done in solution 1, which represents the viewpoint that the aorist is to be expected.[52]

3. E. Haupt (pp. 31–33) sees no sense in the meaning of the adverb "bodily" within the context. He therefore falls back on the meaning of *sōma* (body) preserved in Classical Greek (i.e., in Plato, Tim 31 b) in which the substantive designates something that forms an enclosed organism, like a body. Thus, Col criticizes "false teachers" who would obtain full recognition by means of other media and not solely through the Messiah.[53]

4. In the ancient church and even in the Middle Ages, *sōmatikōs* was often interpreted as "something of substance" or "something of essence." Among others, Oecumenius of Trikka (sixth century; PG 119, 32), John Damascenus (eighth century; PG 95, 893) and Theophylakt (tenth century; PG 124, 1240), as well as J. Calvin (p. 104) represent this interpretation.

5. *Sōma* (properly "body") can also be used in contrast to "shadow."[54] Col 2:16 offers support for such an idea. Correspondingly, *sōmatikōs* can then mean "real."[55] In this connection, we can point out that the "real dwelling of the divinity" is contrasted with the divine presence (in its graphic representation) in the Solomonic Temple; that is, the "real" presence of God was mediated symbolically by his "name" and his "glory."

6. E. Lohmeyer (p. 106) has argued that the Christ who became man lived in poverty and that the "fullness" by contrast is the sign of the Risen One (therefore also the present tense). This fullness can dwell in him bodily, because he is the head of the body, namely of the reconciled universe.[56]

7. *Sōmā*, esp. in Col, is an expression that designates the community. With the corresponding adverb it could proclaim the idea that the deity lives bodily in Christ because he has a body, the church.[57]

---

52. Comp. H. A. W. Meyer (p. 314); W. M. L. de Wette (p. 44); E. Schweizer (p. 108); F. Zeilinger, ESpg, p. 164.

53. J. B. Lightfoot (p. 248) refers to Hieronymus, *Comentarii in Isaiam Prophetam*, IV, p. 156.

54. Comp. Philo, Conf Ling 190; Decal 82; Migr Abr 12; and others; Josephus, Bell 2, 28.

55. Comp. Thomas Aquinas (p. 97); Dibelius-Greeven (p. 29); E. Lohse (p. 151); E. Schweizer (p. 107); F. F. Bruce (p. 101); A. Lindemann (p. 40). J. Jervell, *Imago Dei*, op. cit., p. 224, interprets similarly that *somatikōs* means as much as *eikonikōs* ("figuratively," derived from the designation of Christ "image" in 1:15) and that it designates the highest level of reality. J. Jervell justifies this meaning with Heb 10:1, where "shadow" and "image" are set opposite each other.

56. Comp. P. Benoit, "Leib," op. cit., p. 275; C. Burger, *Schöpfung*, op. cit., p. 87.

57. Comp. E. Lohse (p. 151); E. Schweizer (p. 169); J. Gnilka (p. 80); J. Ernst, *Pleroma*, op. cit., p. 103; J. Zeilinger, ESpg, p. 164.

Least likely of all these propositions is solution 4. It mirrors a problem in Christology and reflects disputes of later centuries, not that of Pauline thinking. It is surely not in agreement with the concerns of the Epistle to the Colossians that the recognition of the deity should be divided among "several different media" (solution 3). This thought is expressed through the emphatic "in him" and through the expression *"all* the fullness." But the idea that *sōmatikōs* should only summarize this position is dubious in view of the deep theological significance of the body concept and in view of a declaration like the one in 1:19f. concerning the living God who died on the cross and has thus reconciled the world as Messiah. This objection is true also for the suggested meaning in 5. Beyond that, the contrary idea of *skia* (shadow) is absent in the immediate context. It is used in v 16, but only for (Jewish) food and festival regulations. The contrast, "shadow/representation-body," is unsuitable for the statement in 2:9, because that would imply that God is shadowlike and would be representative of a "religion" which is disqualified as deception and which leads into slavery.

It seems problematic as well to interpret "corporal/bodily" as "world body," thus from creation. This interpretation requires the intermediary idea: because he is the head of the world body. We do have reference in 2:10 to the primary position of Christ over any kind of might and power with the imagery of the head, but noticeably the word "body" is not used here or elsewhere in Col in reference to creation. Textual evidence is therefore too meager to justify this interpretation of the adverb *sōmatikōs*.

The suggestion that *sōmatikōs* refers to the church as the body of the Messiah (solution 7) belongs in a different setting. This idea is emphasized in Col (1:18, 24; 2:17/19; 3:15). This conclusion is also suggested on the basis of the statement in 2:10 that the Colossians have a part in the abundance of God which dwells in the Messiah, that the abundance of the deity dwells in the body of Christ, namely in the church. Still, the bare adverb "bodily" seems too brief and multifaceted to justify an important combination of ideas of this sort: because Christ is the head of a body, namely the church, the deity living in him lives also in his body, thus in the church.

Sōmatikōs describes the corporality of Christ during his earthly existence as well as his elevation, according to the Pauline conception (cf. 1 Cor 15:35–44). The emphasis in this matter, however, does need to be placed on the corporal existence, not on the denial of God's attainment of true human form or on ascetic tendencies. We have no clues for the first point elsewhere in Col, and the emphasis on the corporality of the elevated one is only conditionally supported in the second point.[58] When Paul discusses the body of Christ in the untransmitted sense, he always intends the body of Christ "which has been given for us." This is formulated in an impressionistic sense in the tradition of

---

58. Comp. for example Matt 22:30 and also 1 Cor 15:42–49.

the Lord's Supper (cf. 1 Cor 11:24). The corporality of the Messiah which is qualified in this sense is also a characteristic of the risen one and the elevated one (see above). Thus, when the dwelling place of God in the Messiah is described as a corporal dwelling, then this aims pointedly at God's acting presence *for the well-being of all creation* (see Comments for the concept of "all the fullness" in 1:19). Similarly, in 1:19f. the discussion concerned the fullness in connection with the reconciliatory actions of God through the "blood on the cross," and correspondingly in 2:10ff. we are dealing with the "effects" of divine action in the Messiah for the recipients of the epistle.

10 *And in him you have (also) been fulfilled.* The reference is to the "fulness *(plērōma)* of the deity" cited in the previous verse which is reiterated through the verb form "to be fulfilled" *(peplērōmenoi)*. For this reason, and since the verb *plēroō* (to fill) is used without an indication of circumstance,[59] it seems probable that in v 10 a being fulfilled by the deity is also intended. As the emphatic "in him" indicates, this is understood as participation in "all the fulness of the deity" which resides in the Messiah.[60] "You have been fulfilled *in him*" means, accordingly, that the Colossians are participants in the presence of God in the Messiah, whose purpose, according to 1:20, is to reconcile the world.[61] What that means is detailed in the subsequent verses: the Colossians have died with the Messiah, have been buried with him, have been made alive with him (2:11–13), and are "revealed in glory" with the Messiah (3:1).

A shift in emphasis occurs when the *first* (you are) is not drawn in as the complement to the participle (fulfilled), but is rather understood as an independent verb form. The resulting proclamation, whose chief weight would rest on the participle, could be paraphrased as follows: you are in him, and therefore you are already people who "have been fulfilled." However, the oft-repeated and thus emphatic "in him" in vv 6–15 allows us to presume that the emphasis

---

59. It is improbable that what should be said is that Christ is the "element" with which the Colossians are filled. Grammatically this translation would be possible, as for example Eph 5:18 demonstrates.

60. This meaning would lead to difficulties, if *theotēs* were to be interpreted as "substance of the divine" (comp. Comment I). A different exposition would then be required. Comp. for example E. Haupt (p. 83), "they are used to full measure;" P. Ewald (p. 373), "to be full in the sense of 'to be brought to one's goal.'" These interpretations could perhaps be supported from Eph 3:19, where the verb "to fill" is also used in an absolute sense. M. Barth translates there (AB 34, p. 373), "May you become so perfect as to attain to the full perfection of God." In the Colossian Epistle, this interpretation is hardly applicable, since it makes little sense in 1:19 + 20.—G. Delling, ThWNT VI, 291, 15 translates, "Ihr seid *schlechthin erfüllt* durch ihn als den Gebenden." Originally, C. Burger, *Schöpfung*, op. cit., pp. 89, 90, interpreted, "In ihm seid ihr eingefüllt," which means "und ihr seid in ihm integriert."

61. ". . . and through him to reconcile all things with him, so that he would create salvation through his blood on the cross, . . ."

in v 10 rests also on this prepositional phrase: the Colossians are fulfilled *in him* because the fullness of God dwells *in him.*

who is the head of every rule and power. Some ancient manuscripts, among others Papyrus 46 (ca. 200 C.E.) and Codex Vaticanus (fourth century) preserve the neuter form of the relative pronoun[62] instead of the masculine. That causes the relative clause to modify "all the fullness of the deity." However, the idea that Paul wanted to convey that the "fullness of the deity" is the head of every rule and power is very improbable in view of the statements in 1:12–20. Most likely we are dealing with a scribal error in this variant reading which occurred in the course of copying. The declaration introduced by the relative pronoun was perceived as a later explanation, as in 1:24 and 27 (as well as also 3:14), and the words *hos estin* (who is) were read falsely as *ho estin* meaning "that is/ namely" (literally: which is). The latter makes no sense in the statement before us.

Even here the reference is back to the hymn in chap. 1. The two substantives *archē* (rule/might) and *exousia* (power) have already been discussed in the elucidation of 1:16. Just as in 1:19 they were used to give an example of the development of the concept "all things," so they are here representative of everything that has been created. The fact that they are cited, and perhaps not the proclamation itself, "that which one sees and that which one does not see," indicates that Paul wants to make allusion to creation in detail insofar as the rule exerts power in competition with the real power, the Messiah.[63] In order to express this, it is not necessary to elucidate the "thrones and dominions" cited in 1:16 (cf. also Comment IV and v 3).

We should observe that the discussion concerns the head in the sense of "superior,"[64] but that creation as such is not designated as "body." This image is reserved for the relationship between the Messiah and the church. But we can hardly conclude from that, as H. J. Gabathuler[65] maintains, that Christ is not the *common* head of two different realms, of the world and of the church but that he is "the imperious lord" of one and the head which determines growth of the other. As we tried to explain in Comment II.3 to 1:9–23, this view cannot be reconciled with the declarations of 1:12–20. O. Cullmann,[66] by contrast, renders the intent of the Epistle to the Colossians quite appropriately: no

62. Transmitted, among others, in Papyrus 46 (about 200), from Codex Sinaiticus (fourth century) and Codex Alexandrinus (fifth century).

63. Comp. the expression "to lead away as booty" in v 8.

64. Compare, among others, LXX Deut 28:13; Judg 10:18 (A); 11:8, 9 (A). See also the Notes to 1:18.

65. H. J. Gabathuler, *Jesus Christus*, op. cit., p. 171; comp. also E. Lohse (pp. 152f., fn. 9); E. Schweizer (pp. 109; 69f.); J. Gnilka (p. 131).

66. O. Cullmann, *Die Christologie des Neuen Testaments* (Tübingen: Mohr, 1957), pp. 229–39; comp. also ibid., *Königsherrschaft Christi und Kirche im Neuen Testament*, ThSt 10 (Zollikon-Zürich: Evang. Verlag, 1941).

element of creation has been utterly excluded from the dominion of Christ. Further, that his dominion is much larger than the realm of the church, is not limited only to the visible sky and the visible earth, but rather that Christ reigns also over the invisible forces that stand behind empirical occurrences (p. 234). Thus, he maintains that the church is a part of the entire dominion of Christ, on the one hand, but it is also in a special way present in this limited part, on the other, differently than in all other parts (p. 236). The difference between the more far-reaching and the closer area of dominion consists in the fact that the members of the church know about the dominion of Christ, but the other members are unaware of this (p. 237).

We also need to look at the reasons for this special relationship between Christ and the church and the reasons why the "body-head imagery" is directed by Paul only at the church (cf. also Notes to 2:19).

11 *In him you are also circumcised.* The subject of circumcision is taken up without a direct challenge expressly to the Colossians. It is noticeable that any such challenge is absent from the "catalog" of proscriptions (2:16ff.) to which the Colossians should not subject themselves. However, the express warning in 2:8 to protect themselves from the deception of certain religious practices sets the overriding tone also for the proclamation in v 11ff. It could therefore be perfectly justified to view the problem of circumcision as having been dealt with through the "religion" cited in 2:8. We need to consider, however, that there is a reference in v 13 to the noncircumcision of the recipients of the epistle. It could therefore also be possible that Paul has chosen a subject in this proclamation that was not imposed, or rather not simply imposed, by some opponents. For further elucidation cf. Comment II.

with a circumcision not performed by human hands. The adjective *acheiropoiētos* (not done by human hands) indicates that Paul does not mean circumcision performed by man, and thus not the removal of a portion of skin from the penis. This could simply be a reference to the Jewish rite of circumcision to mean that the Colossians also count as having been circumcised and that circumcision is no longer a mark that separates the chosen from the nonchosen. However, the adjective could also have a more far-reaching meaning:

1. In the LXX, *cheiropoiētos* (done by hands) is used in reference to images of idols (Isa 2:18; 10:11 etc.) and specifically once for a heathen sanctuary (Isa 16:12). If this is an allusion to these passages, then a circumcision in the service of idol worship should be separated from a God-pleasing circumcision.

2. *acheiropoiētos* (not done by hands) in the NT differentiates the work of God from that of human beings, where the latter is qualified as something temporary and incomplete, and which stands for and symbolizes and foreshadows the final and finished work, which is accomplished by God (cf. Comment II).[67]

---

67. Comp. Heb 9:11, 24 and also Acts 7:48; 17:24; 2 Cor 5:1.

because the human body was cast off (literally: in the laying down of the body of the flesh). Petrus Lombardus[68] as well as Thomas Aquinas (p. 104) both discuss the possibility that this expression is to be understood as a closer approximation of the circumcision performed by human hands referred to earlier in Col. Then *sōma* in its general meaning would be used as designation of a favorite material fabric, and *"sōma* of the flesh" would mean the piece of flesh, specifically the piece of skin which is removed in the circumcision performed by hands. Aside from linguistic difficulties,[69] this meaning is already inappropriate, since the words "body of the flesh" very probably represent a familiar expression which is preceded here by 1:22 and which serves to represent the earthly human manner of existence (cf. Notes to 1:22).

Since a possessive pronoun is lacking, it must be explained whose "body of the flesh" is meant. Various interpretations are possible:

1. If the discussion concerns the Messiah, then the death of Jesus on the cross is being referred to.

2. However, the expression can also refer to the Colossians. Then we are dealing not with a physical death but rather with a turning away from life in disobedience to God. The "laying down of the body of the flesh" would be similar in meaning to Col 3:9 and Eph 4:22, where it is termed "taking off the old human being." In this case, *sarx* (flesh) would formally designate the sinfulness of the human beings and their enmity with God (cf. Rom 8:7). The whole concept "body of the flesh" would equal Paul's other concept of "body of sin" (cf. Rom 6:6). The time frame of this concept of "laying down of the body of the flesh" could be fairly well established from the context as the time of baptism.

3. A further possibility of interpretation to consider is that the possessive pronoun could have been left out because both "bodies" are intended: "his and your (pl) body of the flesh." Accordingly, in the death of Jesus on the cross, the "body of the flesh" which controls the human being would have been disempowered if the "redemption from this body of death" (cf. Rom 7:24) had occurred. As M. Barth[70] explains, the dethroning of the corporal body and the completion of his right upon the human being occur only when the person takes off the "old human being." The taking off of the old human being is the legitimate and sensible manner of justifying the new relationship of power and justice (cf. Comment II).

in the circumcision of the Messiah. Since the term "circumcision" is qualified

---

68. Petrus Lombardus (PL 192, 273f.).

69. The phrase connects with the adjective *acheiropoiētos* (not made by hands), but *cheiropoiētos* (made by hands) does not occur. We would thus have to supplement a negation.

70. M. Barth, *Taufe*, op. cit., p. 249.

by a *genitive* attribute, several possibilities are possible grammatically, according to the force of the genitive here:

1. In a *genitivus objectivus*, a circumcision performed on the Messiah would be intended. Here, however, the intention would hardly be the event described in Luke 2:21 of the circumcision rite of the eight-day-old infant Jesus, but rather the "circumcision of Christ" would be a reference of the death of Jesus.[71]

2. If we have a *genitivus subjectivus*, then the Messiah is the one who performed the circumcision cited above.

3. The genitive could also be interpreted as a *genitivus qualitatis*. Then we would be dealing with a "Christian" circumcision—as opposed to any other (cf. Comment II).

12 *With him (also) you have been buried in baptism* (literally: having been buried). This proclamation constructed with a participial phrase could provide an elucidation of the previous verse. It is grammatically possible to translate the participle in the following ways:

1. temporal (when/after)
2. modal (by being)
3. causal (because)
4. final (so that)

However, it is just as possible that none of these analyses is correct and that instead we have

5. a parenthetical remark outside the context of the sentence:
   "—you have been buried with him in baptism—"

If we see in v 11 *no* allusion to the death of Jesus on the cross, then solutions 4 and 5 make little sense. It would then remain unexplained what is meant by circumcision in v 11. Solutions 1 and 3 would either (a) identify circumcision performed not by hands; or if one translates in a temporal sense "after"; (b) baptism is to be understood as a prerequisite for the "laying down of the body of the flesh." In case a, baptism would be the means for the laying down of the "flesh," namely the "body of sin" which is cleansed in the process of baptism. In case b, "circumcision" would be designated for the taking off of the "old human being" in 3:9. In 2:11, a "circumcision of the heart" would be meant which was already required in the OT (Deut 10:16; 30:6; Jer 4:4; 9:25) and to which Paul refers in Rom 2:28f.

---

71. A similarly transmitted usage is in Mark 10:38, where Jesus' death is called a baptism.

If, however, the death of Jesus on the cross is implied in 2:11, then the possibilities of solutions 1 and 4 described above are least applicable.[72] Essentially, the following possible interpretations regarding baptism remain:

a. Baptism is understood as an act through which the baptized person then fundamentally *takes part in* the "taking off of the body of the flesh" in Christ (solutions 2 and 3).

b. If the proclamation on baptism is interpreted as parenthetical (solution 5), then this seems to be a conscious differentiation from a circumcision that has already occurred in the Messiah and that has already been credited to the Colossians. Baptism could then be only the proclamation, the thanks, the praise of that which has already occurred[73] (cf. Comment II).

For "baptism" the less common *baptismos* (in the NT used only four times, in the Pauline Corpus only here) is used instead of the more frequently used *baptisma* (nineteen times in the NT). Whether *baptismos* designates (only) the act of baptism in itself, while *baptisma* means the "act with inclusion of the result and thus the institution"[74] cannot definitely be proven because of the limited number of opportunities for comparison in the NT. The parallel proclamation in Rom 6:4 where *baptisma* is used leads rather to the inference that *baptismos* is synonymous here with *baptisma*. On the basis of occurrences in the NT we can say only that *baptisma* is used only for baptism (including the baptism of John) and *baptismos* is used also for (cultic) washing (cf. Mark 7:4; Hebr 6:2; 9:10).[75]

In him you have also been resurrected (literally: in whom/who). Since the concept *baptismos* (baptism) is masculine in gender, the relative pronoun can refer either (1) to "baptism" or (2) to "him," thus the Messiah.

For the first interpretation,[76] primarily the following arguments are offered:

a. The substantive "baptism" immediately precedes the relative pronoun.

b. The identical prefix *syn-* (with) associated with the two verbs "to be buried with" and "to be resurrected with" demonstrates a close association with both proclamations.

c. If we relate the relative pronoun to Christ, then the nearby association of

---

72. A temporal meaning of the participle is eliminated, since the time frame of circumcision is fixed in this interpretation with the death on the cross of Jesus.

73. If we translate final, then interpretation a or even b could be meant, according to which the (not cited) concept of baptism was presupposed by the author.

74. A. Oepke, ThWNT I, 543, 14f.

75. While in Col 2:12, Codex Sinaiticus (fourth century) and Codex Alexandrinus (fifth century) transmit *baptisma*, we find *baptismos* in Papyrus 46 (about 200) and in Codex Vaticanus (fourth century), among others. The original *baptismos* was probably replaced by the more customary *baptisma*.

76. Compare, among others, D. G. Estius (p. 694); J. B. Lightfoot (p. 251); T. K. Abbott (p. 251); W. M. L. de Wette (p. 45); H. von Soden (p. 47); E. Schweizer (p. 112); R. P. Martin (p. 78); A. Oepke, ThWNT I, 543, 34.

en (*in* Christ) and *syn* (*with* Christ) is difficult to comprehend (E. Schweizer, p. 113). But the argument against this interpretation and for the fact that the reference is to the Messiah instead of to baptism[77] is more convincing in the sense that paragraph 2:6–15 is characterized by references back to the "Messiah" on the basis of prepositional phrases *en autō* (in him, vv 6, 7, 9, 10, 15), *en hō* (in him, v 11), *syn autō* (with him, vv 12, 13). It is therefore very improbable to view *en hō* in v 12 differently from the other corresponding expressions in this paragraph and above all differently from *en hō* in v 11. Beyond that, it would be equally "highly improbable, that since Paul attributes all the effects of salvation, reality of salvation, and fulfillment of salvation only to Christ from the beginning to the end of the Epistle to the Colossians, that he would now casually bestow the role of baptism to a domain in whose rule and power the resurrection of the Colossians is placed, has been placed and where it remains."[78]

The common prefix of both verbs "to be buried" and "to rise up" can hardly be cited as a basis for the assumption that the resurrection has occurred in baptism. The common *syn-* (with) has its basis in the fact that both "to be buried" and "to rise up" are involved in the burial and the resurrection of one and the same person, the Messiah.[79] Also the concern, that since *en* and *syn* adjoin, if they are not both related to baptism they are difficult to understand, is not well founded. In Eph 2:6 we find just these two terms together.[80]

Except in Eph and Col, nowhere in the Pauline corpus do we see the idea explicitly represented that the resurrection has already occurred. On the contrary, we are repeatedly told about its future occurrence, and still in 2 Tim 2:18 it is designated an aberration from the truth to claim that the resurrection has already occurred. Now, however, in Col, as 3:1ff. demonstrate, the future occurrence of the corporal resurrection is not denied. Consequently, we also do not find in Col the fanatical enthusiasm regarding the word, as it is rebutted in 2 Tim (cf. also 1 Cor 4:8ff.). Above all, however, we need to consider that Paul, after discussing dying with Christ in Rom 6:8, can call upon his listeners in Rom 6:11, "(to) consider yourselves dead in regard to sin, but *alive* for God in

---

77. Comp. among others, H. A. W. Meyer (p. 321); P. Ewald (p. 377); E. Lohmeyer (p. 111); E. Lohse (p. 156, fn. 4); P. T. O'Brien (p. 119); A. Lindemann (p. 43); J. Gnilka (p. 134), who thinks that "*in* him" here could point to the place where the change of dominion took place, thus to the church as the body of Christ, different from the subsequent "risen *along* (*with*) him."

78. M. Barth, *Taufe*, op. cit., p. 259.

79. Compare for that P. D. Gardner, "Circumcised in Baptism—Raised Through Faith," A Note on Col 2:11–12, WThJ 45 (1983) 172–77:175, "And this may well be an additional pointer to Christ, rather than baptism, being the referent of *synēgerthēte*."

80. "And he has raised us in the Messiah Jesus *with* him and placed us into the heavens *with* him."—The idea that an adjoining of *en* (in) and *syn* (with), referring to Christ, could occur in Col only once, hardly means, as E. Schweizer (p. 113, fn. 349) suggests, that this relationship is not possible in Col.

Christ."[81] And even more significant for understanding this passage in Col are the elucidations in 2 Cor 5:14–15 "If one has died for all, then all have died. And he died for all, so that all *those living* (!) might not live for themselves, but for him who died for them and *rose up* for them." The following logic seems to determine these proclamations: One who has died for all means that all have died. One who has arisen means that they are now all living (and they should therefore no longer live for themselves). A few verses later, in 2 Cor 5:17, Paul even speaks of a "new creation" (in the present tense).

While Paul does not say in any of these verses "you have arisen," based on the background of this context, greatest care must be exercised if one is to assert that this formulation in Col 2:12 is impossible for Paul.

However, what conditioned this remarkable formulation? E. Schweizer (p. 112) has tried to explain it based on his reconstruction of the situation of the community of the Colossians. According to him, in Col 2 the concern is to counter the fear of the community that it may not someday be able to get to Christ because of the "elements" which bar the way to heaven. Therefore the need arises to emphasize the fact that all decisive measures have already been taken so that no "element" could block the way of access to the one who was raised from the dead.

However, another explanation is also possible from v 12, one which has the advantage that it does not have to rely on a more or less hypothetical reconstruction of the worldview which threatened the Colossians. According to this explanation, neither the subject of circumcision nor the "unusual" remark about resurrection had been ascribed to Paul as a "false teaching." Rather, both resulted from the development of the intrinsically Pauline theme concerning the relationship of Jews to non-Jews[82] (cf. Comment II).

through the powerful working of the faith of God, who resurrected him from the dead (literally: through the faith/the steadfastness of the power of God). As in 1:5f., 1:27, and 2:2, we have here also a multiple genitive construction, seemingly typical of Col, which can assert various things according to the interpretation of the genitive.

Especially if we interpret *synēgerthēte* (you have been resurrected) to refer to the corporal resurrection, we could then see in this expression the necessary Pauline limitation of this proclamation of a resurrection having already occurred: not yet actually, physically, but rather in faith have the Colossians risen with Christ.[83] There is a striking similarity to the declaration in 1 Thess 4:14

81. Comp. also Gal 2:19f., "I was crucified with Christ; I thus do not live, but Christ lives in me. . . ."

82. A development of the idea of Paul concerning this theme can be determined from 1 Thess 2:14–16 to Rom 9–11. It has advanced even further in Col (and Eph). This progression in the thinking of Paul could also have conditioned the "new" meaning for the interpretation of the resurrection.

83. Comp. J. B. Lightfoot (p. 251); T. K. Abbott (p. 252); H. A. W. Meyer (p. 322);

("for if we believe that Jesus died and rose again, then (even so) God will also lead those who have fallen asleep with him through Jesus" (cf. also 1 Cor 6:14).

Still, the instrumental formulation "through faith . . ." allows faith to appear altogether too much a condition of the participation in the resurrection and thus places this declaration in tension with the intention of the whole section 2:6–15. This becomes especially clear[84] if it is correct that in the resurrection the participation of non-Jews in the inheritance of Israel is here no longer denied or restricted (cf. Comment II). Just that situation is described and emphasized in Col as fact accomplished by (and attributed to) the Messiah.[85] If it were conditioned by faith in 2:12, then such a presentation would stand in open opposition to other declarations. The entire manner of argumentation in 2:6–15 would be overthrown if that which occurred "in him (the Messiah)" were dependent for its validity on the existence or the stability of human faith. In place of this "in him," there should rather have been *en pistei* (in faith).

Martin Luther seems to have discerned this problem and he translated: "through the faith *which God works.*"[86] Grammatically, this is possible. This would provide a ligature to the misunderstanding that faith is a human accomplishment and as such also requires resurrection. The concept used here, however, of *energeia* is that it is the power of God, as Eph 2:19ff. demonstrates, which is characterized by the fact that thereby Christ awakened from the dead and has been positioned as Lord over all things. Now we could say concerning *this* power that *it* affects the faith intended here for the Colossians. But in an expression which designates God as the one who raised the Messiah from the dead, it is more probable that *energeia* is also a referent to the power of God that directly awakens the dead, and not to be the "awakening of the faith."

We should thus not interpret the genitive *tēs energeias* (the power) as a

---

E. Haupt (p. 91); H. von Soden (p. 47); E. Lohse (p. 158); E. Schweizer (p. 112); A. Lindemann, "Die Aufhebung der Zeit. Geschichtsverständnis und Eschatologie im Epheserbrief," StNT 12 (Gütersloh: Mohn, 1975), p. 41; W. G. Kümmel, *Intro.*, p. 303.

84. If the reference is to the bodily resurrection in the statement "you are resurrected," then we could interpret with M. Barth (*Taufe*, op. cit., p. 260), who interprets the words "by faith" in no case as a weakening or conditioning of the declaration about the reality and validity of the resurrection with Christ, "Der Glaube ist bei Paulus die Wirkung desselben Geistes, der die Erweckung der Menschen vollzieht. Dem Glauben gegenüber steht in Kol. 2,12 nicht der Unglaube, sondern (wie in 2. Kor 5,7 u.o.) das Schauen in der Vollendung. Die Kolosser sind demnach noch nicht sichtbar und greifbar, aber schon im Glauben auferstanden." However, in this interpretation we would have to assume that in this passage about the resurrection, the emphasis is placed on a nonverbalized (!) *"already now* (resurrected by faith)."

85. Comp. esp. Notes to 1:13, 22, 27 and 2:6, as well as Comments III to 1:3–8, II, 3 and V to 1:9–23 and II to 1:24–2:5.

86. Comp. for the H. H. Buls, "Luther's Translation of Colossians 2:12," CTQ 45 (1981) 13–16.

genitivus objectivus[87] which names the object of faith. Rather, this is in imitation of the practice in Biblical Hebrew of indicating a qualification or specification of an attribute with the genitive *tēs energeias* (cf. 1:27 and 2:2) and *pistis . . . tou theou* as *genitivus subjectivus*, "the faith . . . of God" as in Rom 3:3.[88] Intended is the powerful working, namely the faith of God which awakens the dead. In the fact that God has awakened the Messiah from the dead he has revealed that his faith for his people Israel is not an empty word. It is valid for this reason: in him he has also awakened you[89] (cf. Comment II).

13 *You also who were dead in your sins namely because of the uncircumcision of your flesh* (literally: And you, who . . . and the uncircumcision). We have here, as also in 1:21, an emphatic "you also" which refers to the non-Jewish heritage of the Colossians. The themes of circumcision and resurrection are resumed again in this connection, and specifically it becomes clear here why and how Paul would address a circumcision not accomplished by hands and a resurrection that has already occurred (v 12) (cf. Comment II).

In Notes to 1:21 we referred to the causal connection between the state of being excluded from the bond of God and "God works." This connection is possibly given voice in this passage. In the probable original text rendition, the preposition *en* (in) has been inserted before the dative ("sins")[90] but it is

---

87. In Phil 1:27, *pistis* is connected with the genitivus objectivus (comp. also Mark 11:22; Acts 3:16; 2 Thess 2:13; Rev 14:12). In this sense, R. Bultmann (ThWNT VI, 204, fn. 230) interprets also Rom 3:22, 26; Gal 2:16; 3:22; Phil 3:9; Eph 3:12. But in our opinion, in these passages we are dealing with genitivi subjectivi.—H. H. Buls, op. cit., p. 15, points out that Col 2:12 is the only place in the NT where the genitive after *pistis* designates an attribute of God. He thus sees evidence in this that we do not simply have a genitivus objectivus here.—W. Kramer, "Christos, Kyrios, Gottessohn. Untersuchungen zu Gebrauch und Bedeutung der christologischen Bezeichnungen bei Paulus und in den vorpaulinischen Gemeinden," AThANT 44 (Zürich/Stuttgart: Zwingli Verlag, 1963), p. 19, sees a typical shift in accent toward the statement in the Pauline Corpus. The resurrection, he says, is not as strict anymore as the content of faith in Paul; rather it is the characterization of the power of the working of God.

88. Comp. LXX Num 28:6; Ps 22(23):2; Isa 28:4; and others. See GK 128p.

89. Comp. also Gal 1:1; 1 Cor 6:14; Rom 4:24; 8:11.

90. Attested, among others, by Papyrus 46 (ca. 200), by the Codex Alexandrinus (fifth century), and also by the very reliable Minuscule 1739.—Codex Sinaiticus and Codex Vaticanus (both fourth century) do not render any preposition.—A text-critical decision is difficult. The idea that the preposition "though highly supported is doubtless an interpretation for the sake of grammatical clearness" (J. B. Lightfoot, p. 252), does not seem self-evident to us. It would be imaginable that a misunderstanding of an interpretation in the sense of Rom 6:11 ("so you must consider yourselves dead in sin") should be warded off. But such a misunderstanding is distant in this passage. It would be possible that the original *en* with the dative was interpreted as a causal in this context (comp. BDR 219, 2) and was then replaced by the simpler grammatical construction, the plain *dativus causae*.

missing from the dative "uncircumcision." It is possible that a repetition of the preposition was omitted in the Greek (BDR 479, 1), but it is just as grammatically valid to interpret the dative "uncircumcision" as *dativus causae* (causative dative). Whichever it is, we will have to interpret the conjunctive "and" between the two substantives "sins" and "uncircumcision" as *kai exepegeticum* (cf. BDR 442, 6a) in any case, which carries the connotation "and namely."

The designation *nekros* (dead) for an existence in disobedience to God occurs not only in Col, but also elsewhere in the NT literature, as well as in such sources as the Rabbinic literature, the Dead Sea Scrolls, and Philo.[91] The roots of this expression come from the OT, "The dead were absolutely outside the cultural domain of Yahweh, and Israel was permitted to know no domain other than this. The dead were separated from Yahweh and his community because they were placed outside the cult of Yahweh (Ps 88:11–13). Herein lies the primary bitterness of death, and this is addressed very movingly in the death-experience in the lament of the Psalms."[92] On the basis of this viewpoint, the characterization of the condition of death concerning physical death or the reverse, physical life, which could be applicable to being called "dead" (cf. esp. Eph 2:11ff.), is easy to understand.

In place of *hamartiai* (sins) as in 1:14 we have here *paraptomata* (sins). This, however, does not signify any mitigation of the seriousness of the charge as the radical designation of the description of the state of death already demonstrates. Since the "sins" cited here point to the exclusion from the covenant of God with Israel (cf. Comment II), it is also improbable that *paraptōma* is used in contrast to *hamartia* in order to emphasize purposely a willfully sinful appearance (cf. E. Lohmeyer, p. 113, fn. 1; P. O'Brien, p. 122). The two singular forms *paratōma* and *hamartia* are used synonymously in Rom 5:20, and accordingly they will also be synonymous in Col in the plural forms.

(even) you he made alive with him (literally: with him made alive). For the formulaic "with him" see Notes following.

"God" will need to be added as subject of the verb; there would be some serious problems in the analysis of v 15 if "Messiah" were subject.[93] Because

---

91. For the rabbinic literature, comp. St.-B. I, p. 489; III, p. 652. For Qumran, comp. K. G. Kuhn, "Epheserbrief," op. cit., pp. 343f. For Philo of Alexandria, see Fug 56. In the NT, see esp. Luke 15:24: in the parable of the prodigal son, the father exclaims, ". . . this my son was dead and has become alive again; he was lost and is found." Comp. also John 5:24f.; Rom 7:9ff.; Eph 5:14; Jas 2:26; Rev 3:1.

92. G. von Rad, Theol.d.AT. I, p. 276; comp. also ibid., pp. 275f.; 367; 385–87. See also Ps 6:6; 30:10; 115:17; Isa 38:18f.; Sir 17:27f.

93. It is not possible to come to a decision on the personal pronoun "him," since here, this is not proven in the Greek by an accent as reflexive or nonreflexive and the original Greek text was transmitted unaccented. Further, see Notes to 1:19.

according to v 12 it is *God* who has awakened Christ from the dead, a different subject for the verb "to make alive" in v 13 would hardly be acceptable.[94]

As is readily observable in Greek, the preposition of the object phrase (*with him*) is repeated as the prefix before the verb (to make alive).[95]

The textual tradition concerning the personal pronoun is uncertain, as is also the case in 1:7, 12; 3:4. "You," as well as "us," is well documented.[96] The manuscripts which read "us" require a new sentence with the verb form *synezpoiēsen* (he has made alive) and thus draw v 13a to v 12: "God, who awakened him and you from the dead, who were dead." The argument against this apportionment in the sentence is that v 12b destroys this line of reasoning. That "you" are awakened should, according to all the evidence, be underpinned by the reference that the power of God to overcome death has proven itself in the resurrection of the Messiah.[97] We will thus need to consider "you" as the original rendering and "us" as an assimilation to the "us" in the latter part of v 13. For further elucidation, cf. Comment II.

by having forgiven us all our sins (literally: having forgiven). The change of personal pronoun from "you" to "us" is noteworthy.[98] It was on this basis that E. Lohse conjectured to have found the beginning of the citation for a "tradition piece" (cf. Comment V), so that the "'we' of the confessing community" is speaking (p. 159).[99] But on the one hand, tradition would need to be worked through, as E. Lohse himself determined for the Hymn in chap. 1, and on the other hand, there is not much evidence in terms of argumentation for a purely formal and stylistic explanation. Further, Paul the Jew seems to include himself expressly in the proclamation concerning the forgiveness of sins. He thus says expressly that there is no forgiveness of sins for gentiles without forgiveness for Jews. The former is a shareholder with the latter. The share which non-Jews have in the inheritance of Jews finds expression in the change in the personal pronoun, as also in 1:12f. (further cf. Comment II). The formula "(made alive) with him" is thus given an emphatic *social* emphasis in the context of v 13: the

---

94. Compare also the parallel declaration in Eph 2:4f. There, God is named explicitly as the subject.

95. Comp. Matt 2:21; 5:20; 6:6; 7:21; 8:5; and others. (Without prefix: Matt 2:11; 2:23; 4:13; and others.)

96. "Us" is transmitted, among others, in Papyrus 46 (ca 200), Codex Vaticanus (fourth century) and Minuscule 33. "You" is transmitted, among others, by Codex Sinaiticus (fourth century), by Codex Alexandrinus (fifth century), and by the Minuscule 1739. A few less-reliable text variants transmit no personal pronoun, probably because it was viewed as an unnecessary repetition of the "you" from v 13a.

97. Comp. 1 Cor 15:20ff.; Eph 1:18ff.; 1 Thess 4:13.

98. The text variant "you" is so poorly attested that it can remain disregarded.

99. Compare also E. Lohmeyer (p. 114).

resurrection with Christ forms the basis for the togetherness of Jews and gentiles, who are now one single chosen people of God.[100]

The verb used here *charizomai* really means "to exemplify something joyful/ a favor/a benefit." In the LXX, it occurs almost exclusively with the meaning of "to give (as a present)" and it is used also in this sense by Paul in Rom 8:32; 1 Cor 2:12; Gal 3:18; Phil 1:29; 2:9. The use here forms the basis of the meaning which is to be understood as "to forgive, to pardon," which can also be found in the uncontested epistles of Paul (2 Cor 2:7, 10; 12:13).

14 *Thus he has also canceled a bill of indictment against us* (literally: having wiped off . . . the handwriting). The participle "having wiped off" is subordinated to the participle "having forgiven" in v 13, but not, however, to the main clause "he has taken it away and. . . ." This main clause is set off by *kai* (and) and is thus an elucidation of the previous declaration (see below).

As is explained in more detail in Comment III, this verse does not deal with an indictment that proceeds from God, so that we also do not have a qualification of the process of forgiving sins mentioned in the previous verse. It is possible that indictments, even if they are raised by a "deceitful religion" (cf. 2:8), can be perceived subjectively as guilt, but to this Paul would surely not have responded that this "guilt" has been forgiven by God. It would not be guilt before God, but only a basis for evaluation, and therefore irrelevant. Thus, the participle in v 14a describes a "circumstance of accomplishment" of forgiveness cited in v 13 (cf. BDR 418, 5a): in the sense that God has forgiven "us" all *true*

---

100. E. Lohmeyer, "Syn Christo," in FS für A. Deissmann zum 60. Geburtstag (Tübingen: Mohr, 1927), pp. 218–57, placed greater emphasis on the eschatological and sacramental character of the "with-Christ-statements." The content of the "with-Christ-formulas," he says, were determined from the Jewish Apocalyptic, in which two worlds stood opposite each other. The individual justified person was led over to the place of God and his angels in death, the people at a future time (p. 244). On the basis of this perception, all "with-Christ-formulas" would not affirm anything different than being the eschatological hope "with Christ" (p. 248). That death and burial and being made alive *with Christ* had taken place once and for all in baptism, in a sacramental act. "Sakrament und Eschatologie, beide gegründet auf die 'Heilstatsachen' von Tod, Auferstehung und Leben Christi, bestimmen also das 'mit Christus Sein'" (p. 221).—Comp. also E. Schweizer, "Die 'Mystik' des Sterbens und Auferstehens mit Christus bei Paulus," in ibid., *Beiträge zur Theologie des Neuen Testaments. Neutestamentliche Aufsätze (1955–1970)* (Zürich: Zwingli Verlag, 1970), pp. 183–203 [English in NTS 14 (1967/68) 1–14], who works out the ethical content of the "with-Christ-formulas" in addition. For the mystical-psychological interpretation of this formula, see esp. A. Deissmann, *Paulus. Eine kultur- und religionsgeschichtliche Skizze* (Tübingen: Mohr, 1911), p. 147.—For the history of religion derivative, comp. esp. the excursus to Rom 6:3 in H. Lietzmann, *Der Brief des Apostels Paulus an die Römer*, HNT 8, 4th ed. (Tübingen: Mohr, 1933). Comp. also M. Barth, AB 34, p. 220 (there also the literature citations in fn. 61).

transgressions, then every further far-reaching assignment of guilt or indictment is declared void beforehand.[101]

The verb *exaleiphō* occurs only in Col 2:14, among the letters which cite Paul as author. In addition to its basic meaning "to wipe off, to wipe away"[102] it is frequently used in transmission. Often it means "to root out, to destroy," in reference to people or to animals.[103] It is thus also used for the rooting out of sin (cf. LXX Ps 50 [51]: 11; 108 [109]; 14; Isa 43:25; Jer 18:23; 2 Macc 12:42; Acts 3:19) and for the striking out of an entry in a book (LXX Ex 32:32f.; Ps 68 [69]: 29; Rev 3:5).[104] The suggested translation in Col 2:17 results from the association with the word *cheirographon* (actually "manuscript"). The latter occurs in the NT only in this passage. For its meaning, cf. Comment III.

The article before "manuscript" does not necessarily signify that in this verse a specific "manuscript" is meant, which was "prepared" by the representatives of a religion that threatened the Colossian community. The article can also be placed there because the concept is limited in meaning by the statements that elucidate it.[105] *Cheirographon* would in this case be determined because one "manuscript" of the kind described in v 14 is meant. (Further cf. Comment III).

which indicted us with legal charges (literally: the legal demands). The grammar of the Greek language permits several possibilities in interpreting the dative *tois dogmasin* ([on the basis of] the legal demands).

Perhaps the best grammatical solution is supported by most of the Greek Church Fathers.[106] They read *tois dogmasin* as instrumental dative belonging with the verb "to wipe away." Accordingly, the Mosaic Law has been invalidated and replaced by "the new regulations," namely through the gospel.

This interpretation is grammatically without problems, but it incorporates a number of contextual difficulties that make it improbable:

1. Paul calls the OT law *nomos* more than one hundred times in his letters, never, however, *dogmata*. But *nomos* does not occur at all in Col. Thus we urge caution before presuming all too readily that the reference is to the OT law.

2. In Paul, as also elsewhere in the NT, the gospel is never called a "new law," a "nova lex."

3. According to the Pauline view, the law is not oriented against human

---

101. Comp. for this argumentation, Rom 8:33f.

102. Rev. 7:17; 21:4. Comp. in the LXX Num 5:23.

103. LXX Gen 7:4, 23; 9:15; Ex 17:14; Judg 15:16; 21:17; and others. A circumscription for "root out completely" is the expression "root out the name of someone" (comp. Num 27:4; Deut 9:14; 25:6, 19; and others).

104. Comp. also Tob 4:19 ("struck from the heart"). In the LXX Lev 14:42f., 48, it is used in the framework of the cultic ordinances for the removal of "leprosy" from a house for the new coating of the same with plaster.

105. See BauerLex, pp. 1088f. Compare also Notes to *philosophia* in 2:8.

106. Compare for that J. B. Lightfoot (p. 254). It was represented, among others, also by H. Grotius (927, 50) and J. A. Bengel (p. 789) and in more recent times by O. A.

beings, but on the contrary, the sinful human being orients himself against the law. The law is holy, just, and good (Rom 7:12), even though it is "weakened by (sinful) flesh" (Rom 8:3). The law did not bring about death for human beings; rather, sin brought death through that which is good, namely through the law (Rom 7:13).

4. In addition, in this solution, which is suggested by most of the Greek church fathers, the relative clause "(the bill), which stood against us" in 2:14 appears as an empty repetition of that which was already stated.[107]

This last argument (4) also places in question the suggestions for resolution which deal with the dative *tois dogmasin* (the demands) in the following ways:

a. They interpret the phrase as *dativus instrumentalis*[108] or *dativus causae* and refer to the "bill" so that its content (or more specifically its justification) is indicated.

b. They refer to *kath hēmōn* (against us), so that the content, or more specifically the reason for which the bill is against us, is given.

c. They understand it as a dative object, so that "our" acquiescence to the demands is meant.[109]

If we connect *tois dogmasin* to the relative clause, however, the clause achieves an independent meaning, "(namely) which stood against us *on the*

Blanchette, "Does the Cheirographon of Col 2:14 Represent Christ Himself?" CBQ 23 (1961) 306–12:310f.
107. It is less convincing to interpret *kath hēmōn* in a more general sense, "that which pertains to us," (H. von Soden, p. 48; comp. P. Ewald, p. 384). For the idea that the author of Col used the *kata* (with the genitive) in the sense of "against" in order to emphasize a difference to *hypenantios* (with enmity against) is difficult to see. The suggestion that it should differentiate "the validity of the bond" (J. B. Lightfoot, p. 254) or rather "brute fact of indebtedness" (P. T. O'Brien, p. 126) from "active hostility" seems more likely a solution in response to a dilemma.
108. For example, J. B. Lightfoot (p. 253) and H. A. W. Meyer (p. 329) interpreted the dative as instrumental dative, which can be explained from *cheirographon* (manuscript) belonging to *gegrammenon* ("written [with instructions]") and thus indicates the content of the manuscript. Since "manuscript" should probably not emphasize primarily that we are dealing with something that is written, E. Percy (PKE, p. 88, fn. 43) is probably correct when he contests the explanation.—This problem could be circumvented if we interpreted the dative "for the instructions" as a causal dative (dativus causae), which indicates the (legal) basis for the exhibition of the manuscript.
109. J. A. T. Robinson, *The Body. A Study in Pauline Theology*, SBT 5 (London: SCM, 1952 [repr. 1957]), p. 43, fn. 1, advocates this interpretation. C. F. D. Moule (p. 98) followed suit. According to them, "manuscript" means "our subscription to the ordinances," namely "our written agreement to keep the law, our certificate of debt to it." J. A. T. Robinson refers to Ex 24:3; Deut 27:14–26, but difficulties arise with this interpretation, since in Col 2:14, also non-Jews were included in the declaration. See also Comment III.

basis of the demands."[110] The unusual proleptic positioning rendered by this ordering of words can be comprehensible from the proclamations in vv 16–20. In v 20, the concept *dogmata* (demands) is resumed again even expressly through the verb *dogmatizo* (to make demands). Thus in v 14, the basis for the refusal of the demands attached to vv 16ff. is given through which one would like to, or could, obligate the Colossians. Also, the article before "demands" does not necessarily mean that only those cited in vv 16ff. are intended. It could also simply be placed there because in v 14 the subject concerns (religious) demands for which *examples* are then given in vv 16ff. (cf. further in Comment III).[111]

Hypenantios (against) can be found only here and in Heb 10:27 in the NT. In the LXX the word is used exclusively to designate national or personal enemies or adversaries. While the simplex *enantios* is used frequently in a parochial sense,[112] the composite *hyp-enantios* is the more commonly used word to designate a relationship of enmity. J. B. Lightfoot's thesis (p. 255), that the prefix *hypo-* (in *hyp-enantios*) has strong emphatic significance beyond that, and that the adjective is to be translated "*directly* opposite," should at best be regarded with caution in view of its use in the LXX (cf. esp. Gen 22:17; Ex 23:27).

He specifically removed this by nailing it to the cross (literally: removed from the center). Since the subject concerned only the "bill" that was nailed to the cross, we cannot translate *kai auto* with "*also* this (= the bill)." *Kai* can thus only have the meaning "and specifically" and it introduces an elucidation to that which was said immediately before. Consequently, this elucidation, which is constructed with a finite verb, cannot be interpreted as a main clause to which the previous participial pronouncement is subordinated as a dependent clause. The change from participle to finite verb has emphatic significance. Paul stresses on the cross as the place where the annulment of the "bill" occurred.

The perfect form *hērken* (he has removed) emphasizes the *continuing validity* of the event that once took place on the cross and is now a totally accomplished occurrence.[113]

Prosēloō (to nail fast)[114] occurs in the NT only here. The expression "to nail

110. Compare also E. Percy, PKE, p. 88; J. Gnilka (p. 139, fn. 107).

111. E. Percy, ibid., fn. 43, refers to the comparison of the following references, among others: John 4:18; Rom 11:2; 1 Cor 15:36; 14:9; 2 Cor 2:4.

112. Compare esp. its use in the LXX. In the NT, see Matt 14:24; Mark 6:48; Acts 27:4.

113. It is not sensible that we also have a change in subject (now "Christ") with the change of the participle to the finite verb and with the replacement of the aorist through the perfect, as J. B. Lightfoot (p. 255) suggests.

114. In the Papyrus Tebt II, 332.15 (176 c.e.; cited in MMLex, p. 548), the phrase *tas thyras exēlōsantes* occurs with the meaning "to pull nails from the doors." Since, according to early Christian conception, Jesus was nailed to the cross (John 20:25; Luke

fast to the cross"—a description of the manner of the execution on the cross—is, however, also attested elsewhere.[115] The imagery used is reminiscent of Gal 6:14, where Paul writes, "far be it from me to glorify myself, except alone the cross of our Lord Jesus Christ by which the cosmos was crucified for me and I for the cosmos." It is clear that the "bill" with its function aimed "against us" has been disposed of with the "death of Jesus on the cross." Whether, beyond that, another practice from the surroundings of Paul comparable to the crucifixion should be associated with the allusion to the nailing cannot be precisely determined on the basis of the terse formulation in this verse.[116] We can most easily assume with E. Percy (PKE, 91) that Paul invented the image ad hoc.

The Greek expression *ek tou mesou* means "away, gone," without necessarily implying a disturbing hindrance.[117] C. Burger overinterprets this proclamation, in our opinion. He thinks the law has been understood as an impediment in the middle of the large reconciling elements.[118]

24:39 [?]), we may also assume the meaning "to nail" here, and not the more general sense "to fasten."

115. Josephus, Bell 2, 308, reports that the Roman procurator Florus took men in Jerusalem from the rank of soldiers, who were of Jewish heritage but were dressed according to Roman rank, had them scourged before his judgment seat and then "nailed to the cross" (*tō staurō prosēlosai*).

116. Dibelius-Greeven (p. 31), E. Lohse (p. 165, fn. 7), and F. Mussner (p. 69) have in mind the custom cited in Mark 15:26 of fastening a tablet to the cross indicating the guilt of the delinquent. In Col 2:14, however, what is meant are the proscriptions to the "opponents" and thus this interpretation is hardly fitting for Col. W. Carr, "Two Notes on Colossians," JThS 24 (1973) 492–500 has in mind a custom which he documents for the second century C.E. (which, however, in his opinion, is older), of publishing acknowledgments of sin on stelae.—F. J. Dolger, "Die Sonne der Gerechtigkeit und der Schwarze. Eine religionsgeschichtliche Studie zum Taufgelöbnis," LF 2 (Münster: Aschendorff, 1918), pp. 129–41, points out a military custom of hanging the weapons of the conquered opponents on a triumphal insignia in the form of a cross, the so-called tropaion.—A. Deissmann, *Licht vom Osten*, op. cit., p. 283, also suspects an ancient custom as the basis for Col 2:14, when he writes, "es möge ihm erlaubt sein, solange die *Schuldhandschrift auf dem Kreuz* noch nicht nachgewiesen werden könne, wenigstens nebenbei das *Kreuz auf der Schuldhandschrift* zu erwähnen, wonach mit dem griechischen Kreuzbuchstaben Chi (X) Schuldhandschriften durchkreuzt und so annuliert wurden."

117. See LXX Isa 57:2; 2 Thess 2:7.—In Acts 17:33; 23:10; 1 Cor 5:2; 2 Cor 6:17, the expression is used without the article but with a possessive pronoun. The article can be placed or can be lacking in such prepositional clauses without indicating a difference in meaning (comp. BDR 255), but it may possibly have been placed in Col 2:14 as a replacement for the self-evident possessive pronoun "our" (comp. BauerLex, p. 1088).

118. C. Burger's argument (*Schöpfung*, op. cit., pp. 110f.), that the statement before us only gains in profile in such a literal translation in contrast to the first half of v 14, is not apt. It already gains in profile by the fact that the statement in v 14a is elucidated by the reference to the cross.

If we insist on translating *ek tou mesou* literally, then we should consider an interesting observation by E. Lohse (p. 140), especially because "bill" is probably a judicial term. E. Lohse refers to the fact that, in the Greek judicial trial, the plaintiff stood *in the middle* (cf. Mark 14:60).

15 *By disarming the powers and forces, he has publicly exposed them.* The reference to the rulers and powers in 2:10 is taken up again here (cf. the Notes here and Comment V).

The compound verb *ap-ek-dyomai* (actually to fully disrobe or to make a full disclosure in one's own interest) occurs in the NT only in Col 3:9, and the corresponding substantive *ap-ek-dysis* only in Col 2:11. Even outside the NT, this verb occurs very rarely.[119]

If the middle voice is to be understood in its classic function, in other words if it makes a statement concerning the affective active subject, then we have two possibilities for interpretation in this verse:

a. *Apekdysamenos* can be used absolutely: "in having 'unclothed' himself, he has . . . the rulers and powers." Judging by the statement in 2:11, it would be easiest to have in mind the unclothing of the body.[120] In this interpretation, we would have to assume that, in contrast to the previous statements, Christ is now the subject, but without being named. For this interpretation, it would further be necessary to read "in him" reflexively at the end of the verse. That is a possibility (cf. Notes to 1:19), but if Christ is the subject anyway, then these words would really be superfluous.[121] The resulting sense would fit well within the context, but aside from the problem of the change in subject which is not made explicit, the question would remain why Paul does not speak expressly here about the "clothing *of the body.*"

b. Equally possible is the translation "He has stripped himself of rulers and powers."[122] This view is represented and justified in detail by J. B. Lightfoot (p. 256), "Christ took upon Himself our human nature with all its temptations (Heb 4:15). The powers of evil gathered about Him. Again and again they assailed Him; . . . The final act in the conflict began with the agony of Gethsemane; it ended with the cross of Calvary. The victory was complete. . . . The powers of evil, which had clung like a Nessus robe about His humanity, were torn off and

---

119. See A. Oepke, ThWNT II, 319, 16; comp. J. B. Lightfoot, p. 225. LSLex indicates as references only the corresponding statements from Col.

120. Comp. J. Lähnemann, *Kolosserbrief*, op. cit., p. 131. This interpretation is represented by a majority of the Latin patristics (comp. for that J. B. Lightfoot, p. 256).

121. "In him" can hardly be a referent for "cross" (2:14) (thus J. Calvin, p. 109; J. B. Lightfoot, p. 258; E. Haupt, p. 100; H. A. W. Meyer, p. 336; R. P. Martin, NCC, p. 88; C. F. D. Moule, p. 100). It is improbable that the personal pronoun, whose stereotypic repetition characterizes section 2:6–15, can refer to other than the usual, namely to "Christ."

122. This is the interpretation to the majority of the Greek patristics (comp. for that J. B. Lightfoot, p. 256).

cast aside for ever."[123] This solution, however, creates more problems than it solves. Its representatives must also presume a change of subject which was not made explicit between v 15 and the previous statements, and they must interpret "in him" reflexively.[124] In addition, the image of a garment consisting of evil powers is without parallel in the OT and the NT.[125] Above all however, Col 1:16 indicates that the phrase "rulers and powers" does not signify evil powers. And the implied picture of a battle between the rulers and powers on the one hand and Christ on the other is unexpected and stands rather in tension with the declarations in 1:15–20, according to which the rulers and powers have been reconciled as parts of the creation. We need also to observe that there is no reference to a "fall (from sin)" of the rulers in 1:15–20.

In the NT Greek we have various instances where the middle voice is used in the active sense.[126] Since a change in subject between vv 11–14 and v 15 does not explicitly occur, we should take it for granted that the middle voice is to be understood in its classic sense or on the basis of "other usage" of *apekdyomai*, which says little anyway for a word which is used so sparsely. Furthermore, Col 2:15 should be interpreted as evidence for the active use of the middle voice of *apekdyomai*. We would then translate, "Because God has unclothed the rulers and powers . . ."

Some interpreters have translated this verb by "to disarm" or "to plunder."[127] Such a translation is possible, as the use of the simple composite *ek-dyein* in LXX 1 Chr 10:9 demonstrates, but in this verse it would only be defensible, if

---

123. Comp. also J. Rutherfurd, "Note on Colossians 2:15," ET 18 (1906/1907) 565–66.—R. P. Martin (NCC, pp. 87f.) suggests a combination of these solutions a and b, ". . . that Christ (who is the subject of the participle) stripped off from himself the evil forces which attacked him and that he did so by stripping off his flesh, since it was his flesh (i.e. the frail humanity) which the evil powers assaulted."

124. T. K. Abbott (p. 258) wants to hold firm to "God" as subject regardless. In his opinion, what is stated is that God had revealed himself to the order of the angels who deliver the laws, who were meant here by "powers and authorities." That God reveals himself continuously "without a veil in the exalted person of Jesus." But since the "ordinances" in the preceding verse are not intended as OT law, this meaning is improbable.

125. J. B. Lightfoot cites as references, Isa 64:5 and above all Zech 3:1ff. In both passages, the imagery of a cloak is used to describe sin or iniquity, but it does not say that "evil powers" form this cloak. The "satan" who is mentioned in Zech 3:1 (and by whom is meant not the "devil" but rather the accusing angels) is precisely not the "unclean garment" that the high priest is to take off. Also the reference from Ps 40:12 (13) cited as a parallel statement by J. Rutherfurd, op. cit., p. 566, does not speak of a garment, among other things. The word for this used in the LXX *(periechō)* does not point to such a comparison; it means simply "to encircle."

126. BDR, p. 316; comp. A. Oepke, ThWNT II, pp. 319, 28ff.

127. H. A. W. Meyer (pp. 333f.); H. von Soden (p. 50); Dibelius-Greeven (p. 32); A. Oepke, ThWNT II, 319.

at all, on the basis of a military comparison. The verb *thriambeuō* has often been cited as a parallel in the argument for a military analogy. In the Roman tradition, it would be used to designate a victorious general in a triumphal procession. But since this comparison is not necessarily appropriate with the verb cited, and since it also does not apply in the passage in Col (see above), *apekdyomai* should be translated simply as "to unclothe."[128]

Deigmatizō here means "to bring into the open; to present publicly." If there is no analogy at hand here, to the effect that the rulers and powers have been paraded in a triumphal procession, then there is no occasion to translate the verb by "to place in view publicly, to subject to public scandal."[129] Such an interpretation, which would necessarily suggest a triumphal procession, would stand in sharp contrast to the declarations in 1:15–20 regarding the reconciliation of the rulers and powers effected by Christ. Serious consideration of this representation should be given only if no other possible interpretation can be justified.

Even the allusion to nakedness need not necessarily be understood as a sign of shame. "Naked" can also mean something unveiled, something that can be seen as it actually is.[130] This view is supported by the words *en parrēsia* in the previous verse.

as they truly are (literally: *en parrēsia*). The basic meaning of *parrēsia*, according to E. Peterson,[131] comes from the political realm and originally meant *freedom of speech* in the Attic Democracy. Three main connotations are associated with this concept in its semantic history:

1. the *right* to something (especially to speak one's opinions).
2. the relationship to *truth*, especially to call things the way they are.

---

128. The double composite perhaps wants to emphasize that a complete undressing is meant (comp. A. Oepke, ibid.). But this interpretation is uncertain, since too little comparative material exists in order to support it. The Koine likes to use composita, without there being a difference in meaning from the simplex (comp. BDR, 166; see also fn. 91 to the Notes to Col 1:15–20).

129. The common word for "give over to public shame" is the composite *paradeigmatizō*. The simplex *deigmatizō* can come very close to this meaning, as Matt 1:19 demonstrates, because the limit between the meanings "bring into the open" and "expose" is fluid depending on who or what is brought into the open. Comp. for both verbs H. Schlier, ThWNT II, pp. 31f. and R. B. Egan, "Lexical Evidence on Two Pauline Passages," NT 19 (1977) 34–62:53 (esp. also fn. 48).

130. Comp. esp. Heb 4:13. After the discussion in v 12 that the "word of God" is judge of the thoughts and sense of the heart, it says in v 13 that no being is hidden from him, but that all are *"naked"* and revealed in his eyes. Comp. also Philo, *Migr Abr* 192; Diodorus Siculus (first century B.C.E.), *Historische Bibliothek*, I, 76, 3; Marcus Aurelius, *Selbstbetrachtungen*, 12, 2.

131. E. Peterson, "Zur Bedeutungsgeschichte von *Parrēsia*," in FS für R. Seeberg

3. the *courage* or the *candor* to then use the freedom of speech even when the uncovering of truth is associated with danger.

From the fact that freedom of speech can also be misused, we can explain the associated rendering of "impudence." The LXX documents a special case in Hellenistic semantics, which refers to a *parrēsia* toward God, and even of a *parrēsia* of God (cf. Ps 93[94]:1). The word occurs frequently in the Johannine Gospel to designate the public works of Jesus (7:4, 13, 26; 10:24; 11:54; 18:20). The letters which name Paul as author never use *parrēsia* to designate the work of God or Christ except here in Col 2:15. In this verse, which corresponds to the use cited in the Fourth Gospel, the translation "publicly" seems to fit well. Yet this component is already emphasized in the *deigmatizō*. Combined with the verb "to unclothe," the phrase *en parrēsia* brings out its full force.[132] Similar to the usage in John 11:14; 16:25, 29,[133] Col 2:15 states that the rulers and powers have been presented publicly by God, "unveiled," as that which they really are.

In him he has revealed them. As in v 14, so here also, the "location" is named in a subsequent remark where the previously described action took place: in the Messiah. The remark is, however, constructed with a participle, unlike the previous verse. Three possibilities have been suggested for the translation of the verb *thriambeuō*[134] here:

1. to triumph over the rulers and powers, i.e. to gain a victory over them.

2. to parade the rulers and powers like prisoners-of-war (or fallen rulers) in a triumphal procession.

3. to make known, to reveal, etc.

L. Williamson comments on no. 1.: This meaning "is not documented any earlier than the eighteenth century in the lexical works consulted."[135] No. 2: This second meaning is common, however, and designated the ceremony

---

1929, Bd. I (Leipzig: Deichert, 1929), pp. 283–97; comp. also H. Schlier, ThWNT V, 869–84.

132. J. B. Lightfoot (p. 257) and H. A. W. Meyer (p. 335) suggested the meaning "audacious" (comp. also H. von Soden, p. 50). But it is difficult to see where the audacity in God's act described here should lie.

133. After it was reported that Jesus said about the dead Lazarus that he is sleeping and the disciples responded, if he is sleeping, it will be better with him, it says in John 11:14, "Then Jesus told them 'plainly' *(parrēsia)*: Lazarus is dead."

134. In the NT, it occurs only again in 2 Cor 2:14, in the LXX it is absent.

135. L. Williamson, "Led in Triumph. Paul's Use of *Thriambeuō*," Interp. 22 (1968) 317–32:322. R. B. Egan, *Lexical Evidence*, op. cit., p. 37, fn. 13, confirms this result.

practiced in the Roman Empire of preparing a triumphal reception for a successful general in Rome.[136] This meaning has been widely accepted by scholars in the interpretation of Col 2:15. Still, however, this image presents difficulties if the declarations in this verse are placed alongside the elucidations of Col 1:15–20. On the one hand, in Eph 1:20–22 we read that even the powers and dominions have been "put under his feet," and possibly "captives" in Eph 4:8 is applied to the rulers and powers. Nevertheless, that rulers and powers should be subjected to *public shame* in a triumphal procession is something different and an assertion that would be difficult to defend in the context of Col.[137]

R. B. Egan[138] questioned whether it was necessary to consider a triumphal procession. He suggested for this verb, which occurs elsewhere in the NT only in 2 Cor 2:14, a translation with the sense of to "manifest, publicize, display, divulge, noise abroad, etc." While L. Williamson maintains that such a meaning cannot be proven prior to *Athanasius* (p. 321), R. B. Egan elaborates that not only is *thriambeuō* used in this sense in a papyrus from the year 14 B.C.E., but also that the preponderance of early translations and explanations of 2 Cor 2:14 support this meaning. Besides that, he offers a series of contextual reasons that make an allusion to a triumphal procession in 2 Cor 2:14 improbable.[139]

If the verb thus does not necessarily postulate a triumphal procession in which the rulers and powers are placed on display, then this meaning should not be introduced into Col. The statement means that God has revealed in toto publicly what these rulers and powers are by the fact that he has reconciled them in the Messiah (cf. 1:20), specifically that they are works of creation whose Lord is the Messiah. This concept corresponds better to the other statements in Col about the powers and forces than any other interpretation.

2. The Opponents (2:16–23)

16 Therefore do not let anyone judge you concerning food and drink or that which concerns feast days or new moon or sabbath, 17 things that are only shadows of what is to come, because the body belongs to the Messiah! 18 Let

---

136. Compare for that Plutarch, *Aemilius Paulus*, pp. 32–34 (cited in part in L. Williamson, op. cit., pp. 322f., fn. 22).

137. Among others, J. B. Lightfoot (p. 258); E. Lohse (p. 167, fn. 8); E. Schweizer (p. 117); J. Gnilka (p. 142); R. P. Martin (NCC, p. 88); P. T. O'Brien (p. 128); C. F. D. Moule (p. 100); G. Conzelmann (p. 145); J. Lähnemann, *Kolosserbrief*, op. cit., p. 132.—Also E. Lohmeyer (p. 120) thinks of a triumphal entry, however on the occasion of a royal ascension to the throne where the king leads the deposed rulers in his retinue.

138. *Lexical Evidence*, op. cit.

139. R. B. Egan cites BGU, 1061.

not those condemn you, who find pleasure in self-abasement and worship of angels, who are (only) concerned with justifying what they have envisioned; who are puffed up by their sensuous orientation without basis, 19 and who do not hold fast to the head, from which the entire body, as it is provided and joined together with ligaments and sinews, grows in the manner as God ordains it. 20 When you (thus) have died with Christ to the elements of the world, what regulations will (then) be made for you, as though you were still living under the dominion of the world. 21 Do not handle! Do not taste! Do not touch! 22 All that leads to corruption if it is used according to the commands and teachings of human beings. 23 These—even though they have an appearance of wisdom, through willing piety and humility and severe treatment of the body, not however through deference toward someone—these lead (only) to gratification of the flesh.

NOTES

After more general remarks about a doctrine contradictory to the gospel, Paul now turns his attention to their representatives and to the separate perceptions of these people. He refutes their aims and the demands which they make in three units: (1) in vv 16 + 17, he describes their action basically as pretentiousness; (2) in vv 18 + 19, he unmasks the "illegitimacy" of their claim of winning influence in the church on the basis of their life-style; and (3) in vv 20–22, their demands are exposed as worthless and unjustified. V 23 then summarizes the preceding argumentation in the concluding judgment.

16 *Therefore do not let anyone judge you.* In Rom 14, Paul forbids judging a brother because of "food and drink," or because he holds certain days in more esteem than others. He justifies this "prohibition" by the fact that Christ is the master of this brother (Rom 14:4, 10–12), so that no one has the right of proclaiming himself judge. This line of argumentation also lies at the basis of Col 2:16 + 17. The fact that Paul is mainly concerned with "judgment" in these two verses becomes clear in that *tis* (anyone) is used instead of *mēdeis* (no one). The verb *krinō* (to judge) is negated and thereby emphasized in the direct address to "you." This repudiation of the act of judging is defended in the next verse (cf. Notes there).

concerning food and drink. Both terms, *brōsis* and *posis*, can designate not only food and drink but also the act of eating and drinking.[1] They are distinguished from the substantives *brōma* and *poma*[2] in this respect.

---

1. Comp. John 4:32; 6:27, 55; Rom 14:17; 1 Cor 8:4; 2 Cor 9:10.

2. "Eating *and* drinking" seems to be a formulaic expression (comp. next to Rom 14:17 also Matt 24:49; Luke 5:30, 33; 7:34; 10:7; 12:29; 22:30; 1 Cor 9:4; 10:7; 11:22, 29; 15:32. From these, we can explain the choice of the conjunction "and" (attested, among others, by Papyrus 46, Codex Vaticanus, and the Minuscule 1739). The conjunction

As will be shown in the exposition of v 17, this verse should very likely be understood as an allusion to OT Laws. That does not imply, however, that Paul is turning against Judeo-(Christians, cf. Comment V). The fact that there are only a few regulations regarding beverages in the OT[3] does not justify the inference that we are concerned with the laws of "false teachers" in 2:16, who go beyond the OT Law.[4] Rather, the same background should be assumed for this declaration as for 1 Cor 8 + 10:23ff. and for Rom 14, where Paul also refers to the food laws. There, the question is whether meat that was obtained from the marketplace could be served by an "unbeliever" as host (1 Cor 10:27), and could be consumed, since it could be a meat offering for idols (and indeed usually was). In 1 Cor 10:31 and Rom 14:17 the subject also concerns drinking associated with idols, and in Rom 14:21 specifically wine. In these passages, the reference is probably to libation wine, since in heathen surroundings one could count on the fact that the wine which was a libation offering, and not only the meat, was offered to idols.[5] Both were considered "unclean" (cf. Rom 14:20), because according to OT concepts, everything was "unclean" that had to do with heathen cults.[6] Possibly because no specific foods and beverages to be avoided are listed the Greek concepts *brōsis* and *posis* were chosen, rather than *brōma* and *poma* (see above).

or that which concerns feast day or new moon or sabbath. En merei is an improper preposition and means "respectively, because of, concerning."[7] The

---

"or," which is transmitted, among others, by Codex Sinaiticus and Codex Alexandrinus, is probably an assimilation of the triad "or" in the second portion of this verse.

3. Comp. Lev 11:34, 36 and also the ordinances about fasting in Lev 16:29ff.; 23:27ff.; Num 29:7, which also concern "eating and drinking."

4. J. B. Lightfoot (p. 259) is thinking of a general prohibition of wine and meat and draws a comparison with the Essenes. (J. Behm, ThWNT IV, 930, 44, however, points out that we do not hear about the Essenes that fasting belonged to their devotional exercises, nor can we deduce with certainty from the sources that they disallowed meat and wine.) H. A. W. Meyer (p. 337) suspects that the "false teachers" in Colossae extended the prohibition of wine for the Nazirites (comp. Num 6:3) and for the time of the priestly service also to the Christians generally (comp. also P. T. O'Brien, p. 138). E. Schweizer, "Christianity of the Circumcised and Judaism of the Uncircumcised. The Background of Matthew and Colossians," in FS for W. D. Davies, *Jews, Greeks and Christians: Religious Cultures in Late Antiquity*, ed. R. Hamerton-Kelly and R. Scroggs (Leiden: Brill, 1976), pp. 245–60:258, cites Greek, Jewish, and Christian examples for the abstention from wine and meat.

5. Comp. L. Goppelt, ThWNT VI, pp. 136–38.—See also Dan 1:8, where it says of Daniel that he did not wish to make himself unclean from the food and wine of the Babylonian king.

6. Comp. esp. Lev 18:24–28; Num 35:34; Jer 2:7; 7:30; 32:34; Ezek 20:7, 18, 30f., 43; 22:3f.; 23:7; and others.

7. Comp. the references in BauerLex, p. 1001.—*en merei* can also mean "partially" (comp. LXX Job 30:1). John Chrysostom (PG 62, 343) interprets in this sense: It is given

definite article is often omitted in prepositional expressions in Greek, so that the indeterminate use of "feast day" *(heortē)*, "new moon" *(neomēnia)*, and "sabbath" is without contextual significance (cf. BDR 255 and also 259, 3).

The enumeration of "feast days, new moons, sabbaths" can also be found in the LXX of Ezek 45:17 and Hos 2:13 (cf. 1 QM II:4) and in a different order in the LXX 1 Chr 23:31; 2 Chr 2:3; 31:3. It serves as a summary of all feasts that Israel was to celebrate according to the prescriptions of the law.[8] *Heortē* thus designates the yearly feasts, *neomēnia*, as the name already indicates, the feast at the beginning of the month and *sabbata* the weekly holy day. Ezekiel especially emphasizes the significance of the feast for Israel and places their ritual requirements next to warnings not to pollute itself through worship of idols (cf. Ezek 20:18–20; 22:8, 9, 26; 23:3, ff.). These feasts, according to this exilic prophet, preserve the identity of this nation in a special way as the people of God and they demonstrate that Yahweh is the God of this nation.

In Col 2:16 also we have a statement that refers to pollution through offerings to idols next to a listing of feasts. Thus it is probable that Paul here addresses the observance of food and feast regulations in its sociological function. After the theme of unity of Jews and gentiles had been addressed in its fundamental sense in v 13, he now turns against the "teachers," who seek to differentiate the nonchosen from the chosen and who seek to make visible the exclusivity of the latter (cf. also Comment V).

17 *things that are only shadows of what is to come.* (literally: which (things) . . . is) In Greek, it is not unusual to have a neuter plural as subject with a finite verb in the singular as predicate, as here. This is especially the case with abstracts and pronomina.[9]

Skia literally means "shadow."[10] Frequently this word is used in the figura-

---

to understand that most things had already been abandoned. For if the Colossians kept the sabbath, this would not occur with precise exactitude.—However, *en merei* refers to "set up" and not to keeping of holy days.

8. While we find the plural in the cited passages, in Col 2:16, the "general singular" is used. The plural form *sabbata* is probably to be understood in the singular (comp. for that among others LXX Ex 20:10; Josephus, Ant 3, 143). We are probably dealing with the appropriation of the Aramaic singular form *sabata*, which is similar to a Greek form in the neuter plural and its declination (comp. J. B. Lightfoot, p. 260; comp. also E. Lohse, ThWNT VII, 7, esp. fn. 39).

9. See BDR 133, "Diese Konstruktion ist im Att. besonders fest. Seit hellenistischer Zeit wird statt des Sgl. des Verbs in zunehmender Weise der Pl. gesetzt, der im Ngr. allein gilt. Im NT zeigt sich wie in LXX und in den Pap. starkes Schwanken, oft auch in den Einzelfällen Schwanken der HS." The latter is also the case in this passage. Codex Vaticanus (fourth century) and a few other important texts render the relative pronoun in the singular.

10. Comp. among others, LXX Judg 9:36; 4 Kgdms (Eng 2 Kgs) 20:9–11; Jonah 4:5; and others, as well as in the NT Mark 4:32; Acts 5:15.

tive sense to represent inconstancy or worthlessness or futility of things or persons, or to designate the "appearance" as opposed to "reality."[11] The word occurs frequently in the LXX to describe transitoriness.[12] In Philo, *skia* takes its place in his *Urbild/Abbild* (archetypical image/image, likeness) speculation and becomes a parallel to *eikōn* (image) to designate logos as the image of God.[13]

In contrast with Philo and to Platonic ideas, in Col 2:17 *skia* is interpreted eschatologically through the addition of *tōn mellontōn* (literally: of future things). The question is not directly answered, whether we are here referred back to the rabbinic-apocalyptic concept of *"future aeon"* (*ʿōlām habāʾ*) as the aeon of absolute fulfillment of salvation (cf. St.-B IV/2, pp. 816–44), or whether as in Heb 10:1, we have an allusion to the final apocalyptic redemption through the sacrificial death of Jesus which has already occurred. First we should say that the food and feast regulations cited in v 16 are preliminary and preparatory and prefigure or signify that which is "primary." That this "primary" idea for the author of Col can only be the Messiah Jesus and his work is self-evident. Thus in 17a the writer is not primarily trying to demonstrate the invalidity of food and feast regulations, but rather Paul the *Jew* stresses the positive significance of the OT regulations and seeks to avoid a possible misunderstanding—as also in Rom 7:7, 12–14 or Gal 3:21; he refutes the OT law as invalid in itself and irreconcilable with the gospel.[14] The reference in v 16 can hardly be to something other than the OT, because it is not thinkable that some sort of regulations of a deceitful religion are attributable to a work (i.e., book) which points to the Messiah. The role of the OT law, however, becomes clear, as for example in Gal 3:19ff., according to the Pauline view of the fulfillment of God's promises: namely that "we" were "kept" under the law until the faithfulness of Jesus Christ was revealed, through which the promises of God were fulfilled.

because the body belongs to the Messiah! (literally: the body however/but of Christ). Two completely different interpretations of this terse expression are possible.

1. Instead of the concept-pair *skia-eikōn* (cf. Heb 10:1), the extra-biblical Greek words *skia-sōma* are also used in Col 2:17, in order to characterize the contrast of "shadow-body," "image-the thing itself," "appearance-reality," and others.[15] If in this verse also *skia* and *sōma* were contrasted to each other in this

---

11. See the references in S. Schulz, ThWNT VII, 397.

12. LXX Ps 87(88):7; 101(102):12; 106(107):10; 108(109):23; Job 3:5; 28:3.—It is also used in the positive sense: comp. among others LXX Ps 56(57):2; Isa 4:6; Lam 4:20; Ezek 17:23; 31:6.

13. Thus in Leg All III, 96. See for that also Comment IV to 1:9–23.

14. Compare also statements such as Rom 3:31; 7:22; 13:8–10.

15. Comp. the statements in Philo, according to which the "shadow" pertains to the "body" as does the "name" to the "thing" (Decal 82; comp. Rer Div Her 72), or as the "sound" of a statement to its real "meaning" (Conf Ling 190) or as "appearance" to "being" (Migr Abr 12).

sense, that would say, that the "thing itself," to which the food and feast day ordinances refer, is the Messiah himself.

You may notice that it is not the nominative *ho christos* ["the body"/which (really is) *the* Messiah] that has been chosen, but rather the genitive (. . . [is] of Christ), so that what is said is: the "body" belongs to Christ.[16] The statement in Heb 10:1 can explain this choice of case. There the same content as in Col 2:17 (according to the stated interpretation) is given expression, "The law *has* the shadow of good things to come, but not, however, the essence/real form *(eikōn)* of the things themselves."[17] It can be assumed that the declarations "the 'real thing' is the Messiah" and "the 'real thing' is of the Messiah" are interchangeable.

Doubts arise, however, since *sōma* (body) is used repeatedly in Col to designate the church as the body of the Messiah (1:18, 24; 2:19; 3:15). It is difficult to imagine that "body," with the added genitive attribute "of the Messiah," is used in a nontheological sense as counterpoint to "shadow," especially with the argument that begins at the end of v 16, when the word "body" in its ecclesiological meaning occurs in v 19. Dibelius-Greeven (p. 34) have recommended a solution to this problem, in connection with E. Lohmeyer (p. 123), to accept "a kind of brachiology" (cf. also F. Zeilinger, ES, p. 161). They suggest that a word, namely *sōma* (with the meaning: "reality"), has been omitted, and that the statement really means, "The reality *(sōma)* is the body *(sōma)* of Christ."[18] Yet this solution does not satisfy, since an omitted *sōma* is not obviously and automatically supplemented in reading the text and could therefore also hardly be left out in writing the text.[19]

A different solution is therefore preferable.

2. The possibility exists that in v 17 the words "shadow" and "body" are not placed opposite each other as contrasting concepts. Even the particle *de* used here does not necessarily need to indicate a contrast (cf. BDR 447). V 17b can be viewed as an independent statement that justifies the prohibition expressed in v 16 of judging the recipients of the epistle. It is asserted tersely and categorically in a prominent place (cf. 1 Cor 3:23), "the body (namely the church) belongs to the Messiah!" This reasoning corresponds to that in Rom 14:4 and also in 1 Cor

16. For this construction, comp. 1 Cor 3:23.

17. P. Ewald's interpretation (p. 393, esp. fn. 1), ". . . die Realisierung, das Wesen selbst, auf das der Schatten vorbereitete, ist Sache des Christus," is probably hardly applicable.—E. Schweizer's assumption (p. 121), that the nominative form was original and by changing a letter, it had changed to the common expression "the body of Christ," is not supported by any text transmission.

18. At least an allusion to the church is also noted by: E. Lohse (p. 173, fn. 1); G. Conzelmann (p. 193); A. Lindemann (p. 47); J. Gnilka (p. 148); C. F. D. Moule (p. 103); F. F. Bruce (p. 117).

19. John Chrysostom (PG 62, 343) cites the possibility of connecting v 17b to v 18. But the resultant statement makes little sense (comp. also E. Schweizer, pp. 121f.).

4:1 + 5, where the right to judge a brother is contested on the ground that the brother has only Jesus as master and judge.[20]

18 *Let not those condemn you.* Paul is now focusing on those persons who would dare claim the right to judge, and he characterizes them more precisely.

The verb "to judge" *(krinō)* which is used in v 16 is taken up again through *katabrabeuō.* The latter verb occurs only here in the NT, does not occur in the LXX, and is also extremely rare in extra-biblical Greek. The simplex *brabeuō,* which is also used in the NT only in Col (3:15), is a technical term used in sports contests, and designates the activity of the referee. It is also, however, used in the more general sense of "to judge, to decide" and in addition bears the meaning "to lead, to rule."[21] Since Paul chooses the comparison with a sporting match in 1 Cor 9:24ff. and in Phil 3:14 in order to express theological matters, and since he speaks in both passages also of the "prize of victory," the *brabeion,* perhaps in Col 2:18 such a comparison is equally intended. *Katabrabeuō* should then best be translated by "to disqualify" (cf. E. Schweizer, p. 122). But since such an allusion is not demanded by the context, the word can be understood as synonymous to *katakrinō* and simply be translated as "to condemn." However one decides, the sense of the statement is not changed. In any case, we are concerned with a condemnation whose main point is to reject the choice of the Colossians.

who find pleasure in (literally: having pleasure/willing, like). The expression *thelōn en* reflects the Hebrew *ḥapaṣ bĕ,* used several times in the LXX, and it means, "to find pleasure in."[22] This Hebrew usage is probably a precedent for this passage also. It is grammatically possible to interpret *telon* (happily, eagerly) as an adverb modifying to "condemn,"[23] but the argument for such a closer

---

20. J. Lähnemann's interpretation (*Kolosserbrief,* op. cit., p. 137), that the corporality of Christ should be cited as argument against ascetic demands, is improbable, since in v 16 and certainly in v 16b, we are not dealing with asceticism. Also, C. F. D. Moule's supposition (p. 103), that there is probably reference to Ps 39(40):7 in the transmitted edition of the LXX from Codex Sinaiticus, Vaticanus, and Alexandrinus, which is also cited in Heb 10:5 ("sacrifices and offerings you did not desire, but a body I did prepare for myself"), is improbable, since vv 16 + 17 do not discuss offerings.

21. See the references in LSLex. MMLex cites an inscription from the second century B.C.E. (Syll 929, 32) in which *brabeuo* is used in a juristic context, not in an athletic one.

22. LXX 1 Kgs 18:22; 2 Kgs 15:26; 3 Kgdms (Eng 1 Kgs) 10:9; 2 Chr 9:8 v 1; Ps 111(112):1; Ps 146(147):10.

23. See among others, A. Fridrichsen, "THELŌN Col 2:18," ZNW 21 (1922) 135–37. He cites references for this interpretation. Fridrichsen himself chiefly relies upon Epictetus, Diss II. 19, 16 (in his translation: "Wir schweben in der höchsten Gefahr, und bei dieser furchtbaren Lage machst du Scherze mit *kaltem Blut* [*thelōn,* H.B.])" (p. 136). He translates Col 2:18, "Es darf nicht vorkommen, das jemand euch das Heil abspreche—so wie es tatsächlich bei euch geschieht, und zwar mit kalter Überlegung—. . ." (p. 137).

connection is not compelling. Vv 16 + 17 do not specify a certain manner of judging, but rather that judging in its basic manner should be prohibited. Also, the two participles, "who are puffed up" (at the end of v 18) and "who do not hold fast" (at the beginning of v 19), which refer back to *"let no one* condemn*,"* indicate that the two other participles in this verse equally describe the activities of the "teachers" against whom Paul has turned.[24]

self-abasement and worship of angels (literally: service of angels). The Greek word *tapeinophrosynē*, which is here translated by "self-abasement," is verified outside the NT in Epictetus (ca. 50–130 C.E.), Diss III, 24, 56. There, the entire word group which belongs with *tapeinophrosynē*,[25] according to its usage in common Greek, is used in a negative sense and means a low slavish orientation.[26] The foundation for the positive use of the term in the NT (cf. Acts 20:19; Eph 4:2; Phil 2:3; Col 3:12; 1 Pet 5:5) is to be found in OT usage. Its meaning emerges in the action of God who chooses the lowly and the weak, and saves and elevates them (cf. among others Deut 7:7f.; 1 Sam 2:8; 2 Sam 22:5; Ps 51:19; Ps 113:7; Isa 25:4ff.; 49:13). Correspondingly also, self-abasement becomes the correct demeanor toward this God, and this becomes especially evident in the book of Isaiah (cf. among others Isa 2:11f.; 10:12ff.; 14:32; 25:11f.; 26:5; 66:2). Paul speaks of "self-abasement" in a positive sense, especially as a submissive attitude toward one's fellow human being (cf. Col 3:12). Jesus himself is described as an example of this "self-abasement" in impressive detail in Phil 2:3ff.

In Col 2:18, "self-abasement" is used in connection with the "worship of angels." The affinity of these two things is indicated grammatically by the fact that in Greek the preposition *en* is not repeated before "worship of angels." An explanation has been suggested that the "self-abasement" is expressed in the sense that this highly elevated God was considered unreachable and therefore the worshippers considered themselves dependent on intermediary beings, namely the angels.[27] E. Lohse (p. 174) interprets *tapeinophrosynē* to convey a readiness to be of service with which one fulfills the cultic requirements (among one's adversaries), and according to J. Gnilka (p. 149), the "basic tone of the

---

24. M. Luther, in his Bible translation, referred *thelōn* to *embateuōn* (see below) and translated, "der nach eigener Wahl einhergehet." This meaning is already improbable because of the distance between both words in the sentence.

25. *Tapeinoō* (to degrade, debase, suppress, weaken); *tapeinos* (low, weak): *tapeinōsis* (degradation, weakening, discouragement); *tapeinophroō* (to be oriented toward the lower element).

26. Compare (also for the following elucidations), esp. W. Grundmann, ThWNT VIII, 1–27; J. Gnilka, *Der Philipperbrief*, HThK, X.3 (Freiburg: Herder, 1968), pp. 105f.; N. Kehl, "Erniedrigung und Erhöhung in Qumran und Kolossa," ZKTh 91 (1969) 364–94:367f.

27. J. B. Lightfoot (p. 262); E. Haupt (p. 105). Comp. H. von Soden (p. 53) and W. Grundmann, ThWNT VIII, 23ff.

servile, the dependent, the belligerent, which the Greek associates with 'self-abasement'" comes to the surface again here. He says what is meant is the submissions to cosmic forces.

Tapeinophrosynē has also been translated as "fasting" and has been associated with a part of the cult in which angels are worshipped.[28] One could argue for this translation on the basis of v 23 in the sense that *apheidia sōmatos* used there means "asceticism." On the one hand, in the LXX *tapeinoō* is used as a parallel to *nēsteuō* (to fast cf. LXX Ps 34 [35]:13; Isa 58:3; 2 Ezra 8:21 [= Ezra 8:21]), and this verb can also denote fasting on the great day of Atonement (LXX Lev 16:29, 31; 23:27, 29). Still, in the LXX the word can hardly be explained as a terminus technicus for "to fast," because in fasting penance and abasement before God are given expression in a special way.[29] Even when examples of such technical usage can be observed in the extra-biblical literature (which is later than Col),[30] there are still no compelling reasons to limit *tapeinophrosynē* in Col 2:18 to mean "fasting." At most, "fasting" could be viewed as a part of this "self-abasement," but even that is questionable, since neither 2:16 nor 2:23 (see below) speak of "fasting."

It is possible, at least grammatically, that neither a worship of angels through "false teachers" nor their own self-abasement is meant. The phrase "service of angels" can be construed as a *genitivus subjectivus*, which designates the worship which the angels themselves render. Then we could say that the topic in this verse addresses the "self-abasement of angels."

Thrēskeia[31] is used in the NT, besides Col 2:18, only in Acts 26:5 and in Jas 1:26f. In Acts, the term designates the "Jewish religion" (as also in 4 Macc 5:7, 13 and in Josephus for example: Ant 19, 284). In the Letter of James, *thrēskeia* describes the correct way of serving God (cf. Josephus, Ant 1, 222). However, the word is also used very generally to mean the "practice of religion."[32] In Wis, 14:18, 27 it designates the worship service. It is clear that the word does not

---

28. Comp. Dibelius-Greeven (p. 35); C. F. D. Moule (p. 104); K. Staab (p. 94), and also E. Schweizer (p. 122), as well as W. Grundmann, ThWNT VIII, 23, 21f. See also F. O. Francis, "Humility and Angelic Worship in Col 2:18," in *Conflict at Colossae: A Problem in the Interpretation of Early Christianity Illustrated by Selected Studies*, ed. and trans. by F. O. Francis and W. A. Meeks, Sources of Biblical Study 4 (Missoula, Mont.: Society of Biblical Literature, 1973), pp. 163–95: 168–70, who interprets "service of angels" as the service which the angels render and which is seen in a vision, and who refers primarily to Jewish texts in which *tapeinophrosynē* is understood as fasting in preparation for visions and revelations.

29. Comp. also N. Kehl, "Erniedrigung," op. cit., pp. 368–71.

30. *Herm. Vis.* III, 10, 6 (18, 6f.); *Herm. Man.* IV, 2, 2 (30, 2); *Herm. Sim.* V, 3, 7 (56, 7).

31. For this concept, see F. O. Francis, "Humility," op. cit., p. 180, and K. L. Schmidt, ThWNT III, 155–59.

32. Comp. K. L. Schmidt, ibid., p. 156.

automatically have a negative connotation, as the citations above demonstrate. The object to which religious honor, or rather religious service, is rendered is frequently rendered in the genitive. A genitive linked with *thrēskeia* can also indicate the persons who practice this reverence (cf. 4 Macc 5:7, 13).[33] In Col 2:18f. it is to be noted that a remark about a provisionary function of the head for the body, the church, is contrasted with the declaration about the "worship of angels."[34] Paul does not use this occurrence of "worship of angels," which characterizes the piety of his "adversaries," to point out that only God is to be revered (cf. Rev 19:10; 22:8f.). If veneration of angels were meant, it would be very astonishing that such worship would escape comment from Paul. A reverence for angels would raise questions concerning the supremacy of Christ over all things, which is so broadly detailed in Col. Thus it is more likely that we have a *genitivus subjectivus* in this verse. F. O. Francis gathered together extensive source materials which indicate that the motif of participation in the heavenly worship service of angels was widely distributed in the Jewish apocalyptic literature.[35] Even the interpretation that by "self-abasement," the abasement of angels was meant can be supported from Jewish sources.[36] In contrast to F. O. Francis' suggestion of interpreting "worship of angels" as a *genitivus subjectivus*, E. Lohse (p. 175, fn. 2) countered that this interpretation is not possible, since the element *thrēskeia* in v 23 is picked up again with the word *ethelothrēskia* (according to E. Lohse: "self-chosen cult"), so that a cult practiced by human beings would have to be intended. But this rebuttal can be disarmed with one argument, which F. O. Francis himself presented in his response to

---

33. F. O. Francis, "Humility," op. cit., p. 180, refers to Josephus, who uses *thrēskeia* with a genitivus subjectivus (Ant XII, 253) and a genitivus objectivus (Ant XII, 271) in close succession.

34. For the problem of angel worship among the Jews, see primarily A. L. Williams, "The Cult of the Angels at Colossae," JThS 10 (1909) 413–38; comp. also W. Bousset, *Die Religion des Judentums im späthellenistischen Zeitalter*, 3d ed., ed. H. Gressmann, HNT 21 (Tübingen: Mohr, 1926), pp. 320–31.—How close the danger of angel worship was, however, is demonstrated, for example, in Rev 22:8f.—For this question, see also Comment IV.

35. F. O. Francis, "Humility," op. cit., pp. 177–79; comp. also C. Rowland, "Apocalyptic Visions and the Exaltation of Christ in the Letter to the Colossians," JSNT 19 (1983) 73–83, and G. Scholem, *Jewish Gnosticism, Merkabah Mysticism and Talmudic Tradition* (New York: The Jewish Theological Seminary of America, 1965), pp. 20–30. For Qumran, see N. Kehl, *Erniedrigung*, op. cit.

36. See St.-B. III, p. 629, where AbRNat (an extra-canonical Talmudic tractate) is cited, "From where can we prove that they (the angels) show reverence to each other and honor each other, and that they are more humble than are the children of men? Namely in the hour when they open their mouths in order to sing a song (to God), the one says to the other: you begin, for you are greater than I! and the other responds: you begin, for you are greater than I!"—C. Rowland, *Visions*, op. cit., p. 75, fn. 15, refers to related concepts in 3 Enoch 18; 35:1; 39; *Apoc. Ab.* 17; 4 Q Serek Sirot.

E. Lohse's critique.[37] Even if we accept E. Lohse's translation of *ethelothrēskia*, there is no problem with interpreting the expression "worship of angels" in v 18 as a *genitivus subjectivus*. Then v 23 would say, that the envisioned worship of angels has been taken over as a self-chosen cult or has been copied.[38]

who are (only) concerned with justifying what they have envisioned (literally: which things he has been espousing). The statement "he has seen" has been interpreted by many commentators as visionary perception.[39] This interpretation is likely, since the text earlier dealt with self-abasement and the worship of angels. Even if we do not consider the question whether visions were meant or not, the fact alone that Paul acknowledges that his adversaries "have seen something" has caused problems. These are already mirrored in the textual transmission of the verse. Thus we find inserted in some manuscripts a negation of the statement as an emendation. There are also some text variants which only preserve the reading "he has not seen." Yet the text with the nonnegated statement is so well attested that its originality can hardly be placed under suspicion.[40] P. Ewald (p. 400) objected that a negation using the Greek participle *me* is poorly attested, but that this can also not be understood as a subsequent correction, because a corrector could only have inserted the Greek *ou*. Thus the text is in error and requires a conjectural emendation, he maintains. He suspects that the original text may have read: *ametrokenembateuōn* (making air strides into the unmeasured, to stab recklessly into the void), from which was then derived the Greek (unaccented) *a mē eoraken embateuōn*. But we need to observe that the negation of a relative clause with *mē* cannot be fully precluded (cf. BDR 428, 4), and therefore P. Ewald's rejection of the preserved text is not

---

37. F. O. Francis, "Humility," op. cit., pp. 181f. (Ergänzung vom Frühjahr 1973 zum ursprünglichen Aufsatz). Comp. also C. Rowland, Visions, op. cit., pp. 76f.

38. Compare the "angel-liturgy" which was found at Qumran in this connection (4QSirSabb; see J. Strugnell, *The Angelic Liturgy at Qumran—4Q Serek Sirot ʿolat haššabbat*, Congress Volume Oxford 1959, VT.S 7 [1960] 318–45). We are probably dealing with a liturgy of the earthly worship of God, but for which the divine is the prototype. Comp. N. Kehl, *Erniedrigung*, op. cit., p. 389; F. F. Bruce, p. 119, and also E. Schweizer, p. 122.

39. Compare among others, T. K. Abbott (p. 269); H. von Soden (p. 54); E. Schweizer (p. 124); C. F. D. Moule (p. 104); M. Dibelius, "Die Isisweihe bei Apuleius und verwandte Initiations-Riten," in ibid., *Botschaft und Geschichte*, Ges. Aufsätze II, ed. G. Bornkamm (Tübingen: Mohr, 1956), pp. 30–79:63.

40. This is transmitted, among others, in Papyrus 46 (ca. 200), Codex Sinaiticus (fourth century), Codex Alexandrinus (fifth century), Codex Vaticanus (fourth century), and also by the important Minuscules 33 and 1739.—It is also objectively hardly necessary to deny the "opponents" the possibility that they saw visions. Thus Paul also does not resort to this in 2 Cor 12; rather, he reports his own visions in order to demonstrate that he is also nothing less than "the super apostels" in this regard (2 Cor 12:11).

as justified as he claims, or his emendation. J. B. Lightfoot (p. 263) had already previously thought it not possible that Paul wrote this passage in its existing form, and he suspected "some corruption in the text prior to all existing authorities." According to his interpretation, Paul possibly wrote,[41] "*eōrakenembateuōn* or *aiōrakenembateuōn eōra kenembateuōn* or *aiōra kenembateuōn.*" By *eōra/aiōra* had been meant "balancing in the air," by *kenembateuein* "treading the void." However, as J. B. Lightfoot himself points out, in the Greek only the verb *kenembatein* is attested, not the verb *kenembateuein*.

The interpretation suggested by M. Dibelius was and is of great significance for the exegesis of this puzzling declaration.[42] For his elucidation he draws on inscriptions from the Temple Apollo at Claros, which date to the second century C.E. There the verb *embateuein* (really: to enter) which also occurs in Col 2:18, is used in the inscriptions that deal with queries addressed to the oracular god. From these we can deduce that a mystery cult was practiced in Claros. In comparing the inscriptions, M. Dibelius concludes that "*embateuōn* was used in a technical sense in at least one mystery cult in Asia Minor in the 2nd century C.E." (p. 62) and that it means "to be consecrated" (p. 63).[43] Based on this usage, M. Dibelius interpreted *embateuōn* in Col 2:18 to mean: "he enters (at the initiation) what he has seen." What is meant is that the initiate in his ecstasy first sees the sacred chambers which his feet may later enter. In a later commentary, M. Dibelius refined his interpretation (Dibelius-Greeven, pp. 34–36) so that he connects the relative clause, "what he has seen . . ." to "self-abasement and worship of angels"; ". . . in that he appealed to self-abasement and worship of angels (gen. obj., H.B.), as he saw them at his initiation."

This exegesis has been severely questioned by F. O. Francis.[44] He places

---

41. The Greek text was originally unaccented and transmitted without spaces between words.

42. M. Dibelius, "Isisweihe," op. cit.

43. In the inscriptions, *embateuein* (to enter) is used with *myēthentes* or with *paralabōn ta mystēria*. The expression *epetelein kai mystēria* ("to perform the mysteries") also occurs without the previously cited concepts. M. Dibelius concluded from this that "perform the mysteries" summarized what was meant by *myēthentes/paralabōn ta mystēria* and *embateuein*. *Myēthentes* and *paralabōn ta mysteria*, he says, are equivalent concepts and designate the first component to initiation, after which the second component follows. This is designated by *embateuein*, the "entering" of the inner sanctum and thus means the actual mysterium (pp. 59–61). M. Dibelius supported this interpretation of the inscriptions from Claros with the outcome of his study of Apuleius, Met XI, 23, which is also elucidated in the article previously cited. For a critique of this study, see H. Krämer, "Die Isisformel bei Apuleius (Met. XI 23, 7)—eine Anmerkung zur Methode der Mysterienforschung," WuD 12 (1973) 91–104.

44. F. O. Francis, "The Background of Embateuein (Col 2:18) in Legal Papyri and Oracle Inscriptions," in ibid., and W. A. Meeks (ed.), *Conflict*, op. cit., pp. 197–207; compare ibid., "Humility," op. cit., p. 172.

emphasis on the fact that the Temple in Claros was renowned as an abode for oracles and not as a site for mystery cults. Consequently, the mystery cult mentioned in the inscriptions would have been celebrated only as a complement to the oracle. F. O. Francis then worked out that the inscriptions do not suffice to establish *embateuein* (to enter) as a technical term for "to consecrate," but rather "that *embateuein* has the simple meaning that one is led to expect from a study of verbs of "entering" in oracle literature: one may have been enabled to *enter* an exceptional chamber at the oracle shrine by exceptional preparation, namely initiation."[45] A visit to the oracle in Claros was probably subdivided into three activities, "preparation, entrance into the sacristy of the oracle, and questioning." The initiation into the mystery cult of Claros was a certain kind of "preparation" (*Background*, ibid., p. 202).

F. O. Francis now suggests an interpretation of this passage in Col on the basis of known Jewish traditions. He refers to sources in which visionary *entry* into heaven is discussed,[46] and he reads *embateuein* in Col 2:18 in that sense. However, it cannot be demonstrated that *embateuein* is used as a technical expression for the entry into heaven (as it occurs in visions). From the context, which points to visionary experiences, we could deduce that "naturally" heaven was meant where the worship of angels was observed. But still we need to ask why *embateuein* was even put here when it cannot explain the context, but rather must be explained from within it. On the one hand, we could count on the fact that catchwords for "false teachers" could be cited here, which only hint at but do not explicate what was familiar to the addressees. Still, an explanation of the verb *embateuein*, which is acceptable without such a hypothesis, should be noted. This was presented by T. K. Abbott (p. 269) and E. Lohmeyer (p. 124, v 2), among others. In addition to the meaning "enter (into a sacristy)" as well as "to enter into (to succeed to) an estate,"[47] *embateuein* can also mean "to absorb oneself intensively in, to thoroughly immerse oneself in, to scrutinize something thoroughly" (2 Macc 2:30; Philo, Plant 80 [H]). This translation fits into the context of Col 2:18 in a meaningful way, and beyond that it explains better the present tense of the participle *embateuōn* than do the other solutions suggested above, "who continuously (only) search through what they have seen" (namely the self-abasement and the worship that the angels perform). For this,

---

45. F. O. Francis, "Background," op. cit., p. 202. F. O. Francis demonstrates that the allying of the individual concepts in the inscriptions, as M. Dibelius undertakes them (see above, fn. 43), does not necessarily arise from the texts. It could easily be as likely that *epeteilein ta mystēria* (to perform the mysteries) is equivalent to *myēthentes/ paralambanōn ta mystēria*, and thus that *embateuein* is not necessarily the technical designation of the actual mysterium ("Humility," op. cit., p. 172).

46. "Humility," op. cit., p. 174. Comp. C. Rowland, "Visions," op. cit., p. 76. In the NT, comp. for example, Rev 4:1–2; 2 Cor 12:3–4.

47. For the meanings of this verb, comp. F. O. Francis, "Background," op. cit., esp. pp. 197, 199.

the declaration in v 19 is an appropriate contrast. It as much as says that the "opponents" of Paul are preoccupied with their own religious experiences, but who do not follow the example of the Messiah to be concerned with the church. The fact alone, that someone has visions and finds pleasure in self-abasement(!) of the angels and their worship is not analogous to a "puffed up" fleshly orientation.[48] Thus the criticism of being continuously preoccupied with these visions is significant for the inner logic of the statements in vv 18 + 19.

who are puffed up . . . without basis. The verb *physioo* occurs elsewhere in the NT only in 1 Cor (4:6, 18, 19; 5:2; 8:1; 13:4) and means an arrogant attitude and arrogant conduct. It describes a quality that is incompatible with love (1 Cor 13:4). According to the statement in 1 Cor 8:1, the antithesis of "to be puffed up" is "to build up." Just this opposition is also found in Col 2:18 + 19.

The Greek *eikē* in the NT means either "without basis" (in a text variant to Matt 5:22) or "to no purpose" in regard to its effect. In this verse, only the first meaning is applicable, because otherwise Paul would not have needed to utter the warnings in Col 2.

by their fleshly orientation (literally: from the orientation of his [their] flesh). The preposition *hypo* indicates the cause. The expression *ho nous tēs sarkos* only occurs here in the NT. However, the expression in Rom 8:7 *phronēma tēs sarkos* has the same meaning. A dualism of spirit and substance does not form the basis for the negative use of the term "flesh" *(sarx)*. Already the statements in Col 1:15–20, where the Messiah is praised as creator and reconciler of all creation, preclude such concepts as gnosis, neo-platonism, and Manicheism. A fleshly orientation means, as is elucidated in Rom 8:7ff., "enmity against God," that is, against his commandments, so that one is not subjected to his will. The reason for that is that the flesh is not "strong enough" *(oude gar dynatai)*, to obey the command of God (Rom 8:7). This idea is central in the OT, in which it is strongly asserted that human beings can accomplish nothing if they rely on their own resources rather than on the help of God (2 Chr 32:8; Jer 17:5; cf. Ps 118:8, 14; 146:3ff.). Similarly, in Col 2:18f. the statement concerning the "fleshly orientation" expounds that those whose lives are shaped in this way live a piety which does not consider the example and thus the will of Christ (cf. 2:8).[49]

19 *and who do not hold fast to the head* (literally: not holding fast the head). *Krateō* (with accusative) in the NT usually means "to grasp someone/something, to hold fast, to hold (with hands)."[50] In addition, the verb has some specialized

---

48. Comp., for example, Acts 10:3, 10–16; 16:9; 18:9f.; Rev 1:10ff. Comp. also 2 Cor 12.

49. For the concept "flesh," see further E. Schweizer, F. Baumgärtel, R. Meyer, ThWNT VIII, pp. 98–151, and R. Bultmann, *Theologie*, op. cit., pp. 232–46. Comp. also M. Barth, AB 34, pp. 229f.

50. "To seize someone by force" (Matt 14:3; 18:28; 21:46; and others; "to seize the

meanings of which the following are of interest for this text: in Acts 3:11, the verb should be translated "to cling to someone."[51] And in Mark 7:3, 4, 8, *krateō* means "to keep to the statutes/ordinances" (cf. also 2 Thess 2:15; Rev 2:14f.). This last possibility for translation also comes into consideration in Col 2:19. Just as in 2:6 a "textual term" is employed for the transmission of traditions about the Messiah (to which commandments also pertain; cf. Notes to 2:6, 8), thus the verb *krateō* here can include the meaning "to keep, to observe" in obedience to the Messiah. Whichever translation is chosen for this verse, the sense remains the same as long as one observes that head-body image here does not reflect a primarily hierarchical order. The function of the "head" consists in providing for the "body," to join it together, to allow it to grow and, according to Eph 5:23–30, to foster it through love and self-devotion. We will recognize in this closer characterization of the "head" the actual reprimand that is directed against the "adversaries." Consequently, the declaration hardly justifies the conclusion that Paul is speaking of persons who regard themselves as non-Christians or persons who are no longer Christians.[52] Rather, Paul reprimands Christians whose conduct cannot be recognized as belonging to those whose primary concern is the welfare of the church. If he were referring to non-Christians, then this closer characterization of the Messiah would not be significant.[53]

from which the entire body. The following describes the importance of the head for the body and thus the term "head" is contextually fleshed out inasmuch as it employs the head-body image. In doing so, Paul falls back on ancient psychological concepts, yet the idea that the body is provided for by the *head* and receives growth therefrom is a distinctive one for which there are no exact parallels.[54]

The form of the relative pronoun used in the Greek can be masculine as well as neuter, whereas the grammatically correct form here should be feminine.

---

hand" (i.e., Matt 9:25; "to hold firm (what one has)" (i.e., Rev 2:25); "to hold (in the hand)" (i.e., Rev 2:1).

51. The translation "he held Peter and John firmly" is improbable (comp. Acts 4:14).

52. F. Foerster, "Die Irrlehre des Kolosserbriefes," in FS für T. C. Vriezen, *Studia biblica et semitica* (Wageningen: Veenman E. Zonen, 1966), pp. 71–80:72, translates *krateō* with "to seize something" and means (unjustly, in our opinion) that in this sense, the statement fits the opponents exactly when they are not to be looked for in the community at all and when their teaching does not contain Christian elements.

53. Instead of the expected Greek negation *me*, the participle is negated by *ou*. For that, see BDR 430.

54. In the opinion of Hippocrates and Galen, the brain, not the head, is of major significance for the body. See for this esp. M. Barth, AB 34, pp. 186–92.—For the origin of image, comp. also Notes to 1:18, there esp. fn. 54.

Since "head," however, is a "title" for Christ, this grammatical "irregularity" can be explained as a *constructio ad sensum.*[55]

M. Dibelius has interpreted "body" as "world body."[56] However, this interpretation is improbable. In Col 1:18 + 24, the church is expressly designated as "body," not however the creation, which is especially remarkable in light of the cosmological exposition in 1:15–20. It is also noticeable that Christ is called "head" "of every ruler and power" (2:10), but that especially in this connection the word "body" does not surface. Also in 2:17 and 3:15, where "body" next to 1:18 is also used in the transmitted sense, the church is intended.[57] As confirmation of his exposition, M. Dibelius (Dibelius-Greeven, p. 36) has observed that in the previous verse the discussion revolves around the *"entire body."* There is no problem in confronting the worshippers of angels with the truth that the All is subject to Christ as its "head" without exception. Hence, the worship of angels is superfluous, erroneous, blasphemous for those who are "in Christ." However, in reference to the church, the emphasis on the *whole* body in this context is significant. Because being preoccupied with their own piety and being puffed up in addition, as is mentioned in the previous verse, indicate a separatist attitude on the part of the "adversaries," it is countered with the argument that the Messiah is concerned with the whole church and thus with its unity.[58]

as it is provided and joined together with ligaments and sinews. Syndesmos, as a "physiological" term, means "band, sinew."[59] The verb *symbibazō* is associated with it and means "joined together" in this context. The wording does not indicate that the primary focus is the cohesion between head and body.[60] Rather, the text addresses the coherence of the body, thus generally its

---

55. In the parallel statement in Eph 4:16, "namely the Messiah" is inserted after "head," so that the masculine form of the relative pronoun is completely correct there. In Col, such an insertion is transmitted in Codex Claramontanus (sixth century) and the Harclensis (seventh century). For the question of the mutual dependency of Eph 2:18 and Eph 4:16, consult M. Barth, Introduction.

56. Dibelius-Greeven, p. 36; comp. C. Burger, *Schöpfung,* op. cit., p. 77. See for that also Notes to 1:18.

57. The meaning of "body" in 2:17 is contested. The sense of "world body," however, is certainly not meant there.

58. E. Schweizer's explanation (p. 125) is not comprehensible to us. He means, the indication that the *entire* body of Christ was provided for results from the sense that the Colossians were afraid of being held fast when the souls ascended to the elements and that they would thus not be able to pass on to the risen Christ, which demonstrates that they did not trust everything to his power after all (comp. also Comment V, 2).—Then, should it not have said that the body will be provided for "in every respect"?

59. Comp. Galen, I, 236; II, 268, 739; III, 149; IV, 2, 369 (in J. B. Lightfoot, p. 265).

60. Comp. J. B. Lightfoot, (p. 266); P. T. O'Brien (p. 147); G. H. Whitaker, "Synarmologoumenon kai symbibazomenon," JThS 31 (1929/30) 48f.; M. Barth, AB 34A, p. 447.

limbs subjoined to or interacting with each other, and thus subordinated and under warranty to the head.

The verb *epichoregeō* (to provide) is frequently attested outside the biblical text in the papyri, e.g., in marriage contracts and means "to provide with what is necessary for life," for which the husband obligates himself to the wife.[61] This word in this context is probably associated with the term *haphē*,[62] whose meaning is disputed. J. B. Lightfoot (p. 265) refers to Hippocrates, the founder of the science of Greek medicine (born about 460 B.C.E.), who denoted the "muscle fibers" by *haphai* as those to which the same function as "bands" is attributed. Lightfoot, however, considered this meaning "quite exceptional." Yet this determination says little since it also serves for the use of *haphē* in Col 2:19, since exact parallels are absent in this verse for this usage.

It seems that in Col 2:19 two almost synonymous technical expressions derived from the physiology of antiquity are used, whose exact difference in meaning cannot be determined. What is clear to a nonspecialist in medicine could only be underscored here, namely that the "joining together" and thus the unity of the body is of decisive significance for its care and its growth. It is, however, also possible that *haphē* is used here in a special sense to convey a theological meaning that is significant for the church.

Aristotle (Metaph V, 4, 1014b, 20–26) also uses the term *haphē* with the meaning of "contact" in his discussion about growth. By means of a force that is inherent in two limbs that come into contact, a "growing together" results from this "simple contact."[63] We also find *haphē* as a physiological term in the plural (as in Col 2:18), in Aristotle *Gen Corr* I, 8, 326b; I, 9, 327a.[64] There the word designates the points of contact or connecting points of parts that touch each other. In this connection, the plural *haphai* in Col 2:19 could mean the "connecting points" of the individual limbs (and organs) in the body through which the provision for all the parts of the body and thus for the whole body is made possible.[65] Accordingly, Paul could be pointing out that the individual

---

61. Comp. also Galen, III, 617 (in J. B. Lightfoot, p. 266), where the corresponding substantive of the simplex *chorēgia* is used in reference to functions of corporal organs.

62. This is also similarly the case in Eph 4:16. Comp. for that M. Barth, AB 34A, pp. 447f.

63. M. Barth, AB 34A, pp. 447f., also interpreted *haphe* as "contact" from this statement.

64. See in J. B. Lightfoot, pp. 264f.

65. The meaning "joints" (comp. J. B. Lightfoot, p. 265; H. von Soden, p. 54; K. Staab, p. 89; J. Gnilka, p. 152) is not documented at this time. Comp. also M. Barth, AB 34A, p. 448. If this meaning existed for Col, then one could perhaps think "joints" (or even also "bands") made special reference to official carriers (E. Schweizer, p. 126, fn. 419, refers to representatives of this viewpoint). But Col gives no clue for interpretation of such an image. Not even a special apostolic self-consciousness is developed in Col. (Comp. Comments I to 1:24–2:5 and II to 1:1 + 2, as well as the Notes to 1:6.)

members of the church are dependent on each other in order "to be able to live" as such, and that therefore the connection between them is of decisive importance for the growth of the church. A similar thought is vocalized in 1 Cor 12:24f.: "But God has joined the body together, and has given higher honor to the lesser member, so that there may be no division in the body, but rather that the members may provide for one another in the same manner."

grows in the manner as God ordains it (literally: grows [with] a growth of God). The substantive *auxēsis* (growth) is adjoined to the verb *auxanō* (to grow) as an internal object, which is related in its root form.[66] The reason for this is the genitive attribute "of God," which thus emphasizes God as "the (sole) bestower of growth."[67] The two participles, "being provided" and "being joined together," point to the fact that less emphasis is placed on the numerical growth of the church than its growing together into a unit.

The statement seems to refer to the "fleshly orientation" mentioned in the previous verse, which consists in relying on one's own resources rather than on God (cf. Notes to v 18).

20 *When you (thus) have died with Christ to the elements of the world* (literally: away from the elements of the world). The premise of this conditional clause is an actually existing reality. Col 2:11 elucidated the fact that participation in the death of the Messiah is to be understood as "circumcision" for non-Jews. There, however, due to the specialized interpretation of resurrection that followed immediately, the affirmation "to die along with him" was avoided.[68] Here it is utilized. To the statement that even non-Jews are accepted into the covenant of God with Israel is closely linked the assertion that they are thus removed from the realm of power to which they belonged earlier (cf. 1:13, 21; 2:13). This other realm of power is defined in 2:20 by the expression "elements of the world" (for this phrase, see Comment IV).

Unusual in Paul, the verb *apothnēskō* (to die) is not constructed with the dative here,[69] but rather with the preposition *apo*, which designates separation or turning away. The use of this preposition in this fashion is not unusual in

---

66. Comp. Matt 2:10; Mark 4:41; John 7:24; and others. See BDR 153 for this construction.

67. Compare the similar idea in 1 Cor 3:7, according to which Paul and Apollo are "servants of God" who have been "planted" and "watered," but God alone provides for growth.

68. See for that esp. Comment II. Because of this interpretation, which is peculiar to Col, the question as to whether and to what extent Christ himself died for the "elements of the world" (comp. for example H. A. W. Meyer, p. 353; H. von Soden, p. 55) goes past the intention of the statement in the text, as this would be the case in v 11 if one asked there whether his death on the cross is a circumcision also for Christ himself.

69. Comp. Rom 6:2 ("died for sin"); Gal 2:19 ("died for the law"). See BDR 188, 3.

Pauline writing. We also find it in Rom 9:3; 2 Cor 11:3; and 2 Thess 2:2 (cf. BDR 211, 2).

what regulations will (then) be made for you. The verb *dogmatizō* occurs many times in the LXX, where it means "to proclaim an edict" or "to give an order."[70] In the NT, this word is used only here. It evokes or echoes 1:14 (*dogmata*, regulations) and is used intransitively to mean "to make demands of or to impose (regulations) on someone." The Greek form here can be either a middle or a passive, where we should note that even a passive can have middle force: "to make demands on oneself."[71] If we translate the verse in this way, then in 2:19 the quarrel with the adversaries, or rather the false teachers, would be concluded and Paul would now turn his attention to the false behavior of the Colossian community. With v 20, then, a new section, the paraenesis would begin.[72]

The translation as a middle verb, however, has inherent difficulties. We cannot reconcile the two ideas that in Col 1:4(+8), the faithfulness of the Colossians to the Messiah and their love for all that is sacred is given praiseworthy prominence, and that in 2:20 this same community is reprimanded because it obeys false teaching that is characterized by faithlessness to the Messiah and indifference toward the church (thus through lack of love for all that is sacred). If v 20 is a reprimand to the community, then it is hard to see how Paul in 2:5, which is regarded as an introduction to the elaborations that culminate in this reprimand, can declare his joy in the order of the Colossians and in their firm faithfulness to the Messiah. We cannot resolve the contradiction with the argument that there is in these praiseworthy declarations a *captatio benevolentiae.* Paul would not win the favor of his readers thereby. Rather, they would regard the applicable statements as bitter irony. This, in turn, would not be in accord with the description of his relationship to the recipients of the epistle in 1:24–2:5 (cf. esp. Comment I to 1:24–2:5).

Therefore, *dogmatizesthe* should be interpreted as passive. It is used here as an intransitive verb, which in the active mood would be connected to a dative object. In Greek, such verbs can form a *personal passive* (cf. BDR 312, 1). Then this passage is to be translated, "What regulations are made for you. . . ." Thus, it is not the Colossians who are being reprimanded, but rather, analogously to 1:16+17, the false teachers.[73]

---

70. 1 Esdr 6:33; Esth 3:9; LXX Dan 2:13, 15; 2 Macc 10:8; 15:36; 3 Macc 4:11. In profane Greek, it means "to set up an opinion/a tenet, and to validate it" (comp. G. Kittel, ThWNT II, 234, 18ff.).

71. BDR 314. E. Lohse, p. 180, fn. 4; E. Schweizer, p. 127; J. Gnilka, p. 157; R. P. Martin, NCC, p. 96; and others, translate in this sense.

72. Comp. among others, E. Lohmeyer, p. 126; A. Lindemann, p. 50; E. Kamlah, "Die Form der katalogischen Paränese im Neuen Testament," WUNT 7 (Tübingen: Mohr, 1964), p. 31.

73. Compare for that, among others, J. B. Lightfoot (p. 268); E. Haupt (p. 110); H. A. W. Meyer (p. 353); P. Ewald (p. 403).

as though you were still living under the dominion of the world (literally: in the world). *En kosmō* is not a bare indicator of place meaning "in the world" because, according to the declarations in Col the world is neither something inherently evil nor is it in conflict with God. As the elucidations in 1:15–20 demonstrate, "all things"[74] have been created by God, and they are reconciled through the death of the Messiah. The Hymn in chap. 1 proclaims this in order to make clear that the Messiah is king and master of all creation. The negative connotation attached to "world" can be explained from this perspective. What is meant is the creation insofar as it exerts dominion in concurrence with its creator, and demands obedience. But the Colossians are removed from such a "specious dominion," because they belong to him who is master of all creation without competitors.[75]

21 *Do not handle! Do not taste! Do not touch!* Three prohibitions are listed as examples of the cited regulations, without, however, expressly saying what they refer to. Today's readers, however, are dependent on suspicions and informed guesses.

The second verb, *gueomai* (to taste), surely refers to the food prohibitions expressed in 2:16. The first and third verbs are difficult to differentiate from each other in their specific application. *Haptomai*, here translated by "to handle," is used frequently in the LXX in cultic contexts in reference to the handling of sacred or specifically unclean things.[76] *Thigganō*, here rendered with "to touch," is less frequent than *haptomai* in the biblical writings. In the LXX it occurs only in Ex 19:13, where it is used synonymously with *haptomai*. This passage is cited in Heb 12:20, or rather it is paraphrased. It then also occurs in the NT in Heb 11:28 in the sense of "to touch, to feel." In the LXX, the verb *haptomai* also has this connotation (cf. LXX Gen 26:11; Isa 9:19; Ruth 2:9; among others), which indicates also that the words are synonyms. It has been suggested that *haptomai* is used here in the same sense as in 1 Cor 7:1, to characterize sexual relations with a woman.[77] If in v 22 reference is made to "destruction through consumption" (see above), then a sexual interpretation is improbable.[78] The charge of disdain for women should not then be leveled at Paul on the basis of this dubious reading of a disputed text (or another unknown author of the epistle to the Colossians if it is not Paul). Since v 22 can also be interpreted in a variety of ways (see above), we cannot exclude with certainty

---

74. For the concepts *kosmos* and "all things," comp. Notes to 1:16.

75. For *kosmos*, see also H. Sasse, ThWNT III, 867–98, esp. 892–94, and R. Bultmann, *Theologie*, 26, pp. 254–60.

76. For example, LXX Ex 29:37; 30:29; Lev 12:4; Num 4:15. Lev 5:2f.; 7:19, 21; 11:8, 24, 26, 27, 31, 36, 39; 15:5, 7, 10, 11, 12, etc.

77. See also Gen 20:4 + 6; Prov 6:29; Josephus, Ant 1, 163. Comp. for that esp. also J. Gnilka, p. 158.

78. *haptomai* is not differentiated in this special meaning from *thigganō*, which is a synonym to *haptomai* also in this application. (See the references in LSLex.)

that *haptomai* or *thigganō* are intended in a sexual sense. But if we consider the context, we note that there is no reference to sexual matters, and the inference is much more likely that all three commands refer to food and the three verbs all relate to the same procedures.[79] Perhaps they reflect the rulings of the false teachers, but it is also possible that Paul himself is summarizing and mimicking them. In any case, by repeating these key words, Paul expresses his vexation and anger over these regulations.

22 *All that leads to corruption* (literally: which [things] all is for corruption/ for destruction through use/consumption). For the construction of the subject in the neuter plural with a verb in the singular, cf. Notes to 2:17.

Many interpreters have viewed v 22a as a rebuttal of the food prohibition by the author of Col. Accordingly, the relative pronoun reflects or points to the objects of the prohibitions cited in v 21 that remain unnamed, and it is stated analogously with the ideas in 1 Cor 6:13, yet in totally different wording, that foods are there in order to be consumed through use.[80] The argument for this interpretation seems to be, above all, the fact that instead of the simplex *chrēsis* (use) the composite *apo-chrēsis* is used, which seems to point to the idea that the author is not referring only to simple use, but rather to "using up" or consumption. But in Koine Greek, we often find composite verbs with a preposition as the first component without any difference in meaning with the corresponding simplex.[81] Whether there is a difference in meaning can only be proven by a comparison of the usage of the two terms. *Apochrēsis*, however, is a very infrequent word. In the NT it occurs only in Col 2:22, in the LXX not at all, and even in extra-biblical Greek it is so rare that a determination of meaning through comparison with the simplex does not lead to any useful result. The corresponding verb *apochraomai* helps a little. We can find evidence which shows that the prefix in this verb has an intensification function. The composite then means "to use up" or even "to misuse."[82] But it can have the same meaning as the simplex, as Aristotle demonstrates in Dec II, 2.20, 1349b, 17.

---

79. *haptomai*, as well as also *thigganō*, are used in the extra-biblical literature in the sense of "eating."—According to J. B. Lightfoot (p. 269), *haptomai* is differentiated from *thigganō* in the sense that it is often, even when not necessarily, a conscious or willful effort. The same is true, however, also for *thigganō*, as the meaning "have sexual intercourse" already demonstrates (see fn. 78). We can therefore document no climax in this passage ("do not take hold—do not even touch").

80. Comp. also 1 Cor 10:23, 26, 30f.; Rom 14:17, 20; 1 Tim 4:4f., as well as Matt 15:17; Mark 7:19.—For this meaning, comp. among others, E. Schweizer (p. 128); J. Gnilka (p. 158); R. P. Martin (NCC, p. 97); P. L. Hedley, "Ad Colossenses 2.20–3.4," ZNW 27 (1928) 211–16:213f.—The substantive *phthora*, which then means "destruction," is used in a similar sense in 2 Pet 2:12.

81. See BDR 116 and also fn. 91 to Notes to 1:15–20.

82. See, among others, MMLex (p. 228), where the following references are cited: P Hib I, 52, 7 ("consume"), OGIS 665, 16 ("abuse").

Thus we cannot exclude the idea here, that *apochrēsis* simply means "use." If this meaning is accepted, then the possibility should be considered of referring the relative clause in v 20 to the cited regulations for which three examples are given in v 21. An argument for this view is that the syntactic connection to the second half of the verse can most easily be explained (see above). The word *phthora* should then be translated by "corruption," similar to Gal 6:8, where it is a counterexpression to "eternal life." Even the idea that *apochrēsis* (use) occurs in connection with legal regulations is not without parallels in the NT. In 1 Tim 1:8 the verb *chraomai* is used in reference to the law.

if it is used according to the commands and teachings of human beings. F. Zeilinger (ES, p. 59) interpreted not only v 21 but also this clause as a citation of a formulaic expression of the false teachers to which Paul then responded critically in v 23a. But this formulation imitates LXX of Isa 29:13[83] and seems rather to be an evaluation by Paul in which he exposes the "making of regulations" by false teachers to public ridicule as not authorized by God.[84] If we want to sustain the thesis that v 22a argues that all foodstuffs are ordained for consumption, then we would either have to interpret vv 21 + 22a as parenthetical and v 22b as a continuation of v 20b, or we would have to see the beginning of a new idea in v 22b, which, however, causes problems because a predicate is lacking. The first thesis is problematic, because the presumed parenthetical expression is an independent and self-contained refutation of the food laws, so that a reference back to the statement in v 20b would have an unnatural effect and would not be helpful for the reader. And more likely than the supposition that v 22b introduces a new idea for which the predicate is lacking, because a declaration forms its basis, or because we are now beginning a parenthetical expression here (again),[85] is, in our opinion, the idea that the statement introduced by *kata* (according) refers to *apochrēsis*. If *apochrēsis* simply means "use" (see above), and if the relative clause in v 22a relates to the regulations addressed in v 20, this would be possible and sensible. The resultant statement confirms that the regulations cited lead to corruption if they are used according to the commands and teachings of human beings. Paul then acknowledges here also, as in v 17, that the OT food laws in question in v 20, as also in v 16 (cf.

---

83. LXX Isa 29:13, (lit.) ". . . their heart, however, is distant from me, they honor me in vain, teaching precepts *(entalmata)* of men and doctrines *(didaskalias)*."

84. E. Lohmeyer (p. 127) thinks that "almost always has a drop of polemic irony" flowed into the citations. Here, however, a hypothesis ("it is cited") is underpinned by another one ("polemic has been instilled").

85. See P. L. Hedley, "Ad Colossenses," op. cit., p. 214. He suggests that v 22b should be translated either as exclamation ("according to human praecepts, indeed"), or (his preferred) as a parenthesis, "setting Paul's view categorically in opposition to the opinion of the 'false teachers.'" In this, he translates *kata* with the accusative, which usually means "according," like *kata* with the genitive: in opposition to. This meaning is in the least unusual.

Notes to 2:17), are not condemned in themselves, but their misuse is, if they are imposed on gentile Christians in opposition to their designation—according to the "laws and teachings of human beings," not however according to the will of God.

23 *These—even though they have an appearance of wisdom, through willing piety and humility and severe treatment of the body, not however through deference toward someone—these lead (only) to gratification of the flesh* (literally: they have a reputation of wisdom in willing worship service . . . severe treatment of the body, not in any kind of honor [honor toward someone] for the satiation of the flesh). Since earliest times, this verse has caused difficulty for the interpreters, especially as concerns the syntax. Theodor of Mopsuestia (died 428)[86] considered it incomprehensible; Westcott and Hart suspected "some primitive error."[87] Yet the transmitted text lends no support for such a thesis. There are no text variants which testify to problems of scribes with the syntax of this passage.

The basic meaning of *logos* is "collecting, reading." In transmission, the concept means "counting, calculating, explicating." For this usage, the meaning "enumeration, narration, recitation," among others, is also pertinent, and derived from that, "that which is narrated or recited about a person or thing" as well as their "reputation" (cf. H. M. Kleinknecht, ThWNT IV, 76f.). The polemic of Paul in Col 2:23 demonstrates that he wishes to unmask as unjustified the "reputation of wisdom" that his "opponents" have. Thus "reputation" here is used as a counterconcept to "reality," and means "semblance." E. Schweizer (p. 128, fn. 436) refers to Diodorus Siculus, who wrote a popular world history at the time of Caesar Augustus and who used *logos* (= "story") as counterconcept to *alētheia* (truth) (XIII, 4, 1; XIV, 1, 2).

The real difficulty is in the last part of the verse, "not through deference for

---

86. In "Epistulam Pauli ad Colossenses," PG 66, p. 931.

87. *The New Testament in Original Greek*, I, 1881, p. 578. Among others, A. Schlatter (p. 291) and E. Haupt (p. 117) aligned themselves with this. Compare also the suggested conjectures in P. L. Hedley, "Ad Colossenses," op. cit., and E. Clapton, "A Suggested New Reading in Col II,23," ET 36 (1924/25) 382.—G. Bornkamm, "Häresie," op. cit., pp. 151f., sees *five* key words of "Colossian heresy" cited in v 23 ("voluntary service," "humility," "asceticism toward the body," "honor," "satiation of the flesh"), of which the last was turned into its opposite by Paul with an ironic edge. In G. Bornkamm's opinion, the number five cited here proves what can be suspected, that the penta schema familiar from the Iranian Gnostic speculation concerning the elements stands behind this, which we also encounter in 3:5, 8, 12. But why does he not add "wisdom" to this? See also Dibelius-Greeven (p. 37), "The hypothesis is burdened 1. by the double assumption a. of a pedantic formula at its base, b. its ironization through 'plurals;' 2. because key words of a dogma, even though not on the same plane, hardly have the same inclination to formulaic sequentiation, we have the generally valid concepts of virtues and vices."

the gratification of the flesh." Johnannes Chrysostomos (PG 62, 345) saw in these words of Paul the reprimand of ascetic regulations of the false teachers, who would not give proper respect to the body, which God honors as part of his creation. Yet v 23 takes up key words or themes from vv 16ff. and is, to all appearances, a concluding summarizing judgment. Thus it is hardly justified to interpret the term "flesh" differently from the way it is understood in v 18: the laws and teachings of human beings "gratify" the "fleshly orientation."[88] *Plēsmonē* (satiation) occurs in the NT only in this passage, but in the LXX more than twenty-five times. There it is used frequently in reference to food stuffs (cf. LXX Gen 41:30; Ex 16:3, 8; Lev 25:19 and others), but it is also used in the conventional sense (cf. LXX Deut 33:23; Sir 1:16; Hag 1:6; Isa 1:14).

J. B. Lightfoot (pp. 272f.) has suggested the following translation, "yet not really of any value to remedy indulgence of the flesh." Lightfoot attributes the meaning "check, prevent, cure" to the Greek preposition *pros*, which really describes a movement toward something. He refers to sources that concern medicines which are to help *against (pros)* a certain illness. This interpretation has been rejected, unjustly, by the argument that *pros* has no such inherent meaning, but is given this specialized connotation from its context (cf. among others, Abbott, p. 277). But that is just what Lightfoot is trying to show; in his opinion the context of Col 2:23 suggests just this meaning for *pros*.

However, Lightfoot's translation of *timē* as "not of any value" is problematic. *Timē* can mean "purchase price" (cf. Acts 19:19) or even the "collected money" itself (cf. for example LXX Gen 44:2; Acts 5:2, 3), or even "costliness, treasure" (cf. LXX Ezek 22:25), but *en timē* in the sense of "valuable," or rather *ouk en timē* in the sense of "worthless" is not attested, as far as is known to us. The expression *en timē einai* does occur in extra-biblical Greek, but there it means as much as "to be held in esteem, to stand in high regard."[89]

If we interpret *ouk en timē* as "not to stand in high repute," then J. B. Lightfoot's interpretation of the preposition is no longer applicable. R. Leaney pointed out that *pros* in Rom 8:18 reads "compared with" and suggested the

---

88. There is disunity about whether the relative pronoun in v 23 refers to "laws and teachings of men" (v 22), or whether, as in v 22, reference is to the special "ordinances" of the false teachers. This alternative does not result in much. If the "laws and teachings of men" is meant, then the observed OT food and festival ordinances are also intended indirectly. If reference is to the cited ordinances in v 16 and 21, then this would be insofar as they are observed by the "laws and teachings of men."

89. J. B. Lightfoot (p. 272) justifies his translation by the usage of *en timē* in Lucian, De Mercede Conductis 17, and in Homer, Iliad IX, 319. T. K. Abbott (p. 277), however, points out that in the passages cited by J. B. Lightfoot, the meaning "to be in esteem" prevails, not "to be of value."—Compare also Xenophon, An 2, 5, 38; Arrian, Anabasis 4, 21, 10, where *en timē einai* means "stand in honor."

translation for Col 2:23,[90] "but not of any value compared with actual indulgence of the flesh." In his opinion, Paul argues "in the spirit of Isa 29:13 that this man-made asceticism, . . . is of no more service to God than living the life of the flesh." If this were so, then *pros* could be understood in this sense in J. B. Lightfoot's translation; but his interpretation of *en timē* would have to be corrected, as we have indicated. R. Leaney's argument for Paul's meaning makes sense if *pros* were used causally (on account of), but if it is the comparative particle as in Rom 8:18, it would result in a different sense. It would state that the teachings of the false teachers, specifically their regulations, are of no value (or without repute) in comparison with indulgence of the flesh, which means that indulgence of the flesh is more worthwhile.

The list of attempts at interpretation can be lengthened. The following seems of special significance: Bo Reicke seized on a suggestion by P. Ewald (p. 407)[91] and suggested that the concluding words "to the gratification of the flesh" are to be understood at the beginning of the verse as the *copula* belonging to it.[92] The material that stands between is a detailed opposition to the subject. This hypothesis[93] opens up the question why the *copula* and the predicate are torn apart through an interpolation and why the latter is not appended as a concluding sentence. Still, it explains the syntax of this verse best, in our opinion. Open or unsatisfactorily explained questions about the "essential necessity" of stylistic peculiarities of an author will always remain, since the spontaneity of thoughts in dictation of a letter is not calculable.

The interpolation suspected by Bo Reicke and us, which interrupts the main

90. R. Leaney, "Colossian II.21–23. (The use of *pros*)," ET 64 (1952/53) 92. Compare also B. Hanssler, "Zu Satzkonstruktion und Aussage in Kol 2,23," in FS für K. H. Schelke zum 65. Geburtstag, ed. H. Feld and J. Nolte (Düsseldorf: Patmos, 1973), pp. 143–48:144. For this usage of *pros*, see also Sir 25:19, "Any iniquity is insignificant compared to (*pros*) the iniquity of a wife."

91. Bo Reicke, "Zum sprachlichen Verständnis von Kol 2,23," StTh 6 (1952) 39–53.

92. Comp. John 11:4, where the expression *einai pros* also occurs in the sense of "lead to."

93. B. Hollenbach, "Col II.23: Which Things Lead to the Fulfilment of the Flesh," NTS 25 (1979) 254–61, attempted to dislodge it with the argument that in Paul, the *men* (namely) used in Col 2:23 always stands behind the first word of the unity to which the particle belongs, unless a conjunction such as *hoti*, *alla*, or *hoste*, or a vocative precedes it. 2 Cor 10:10 is an exception, but *men* never stands in fourth place, which would be the case in Greek, and thus in the statement in Col 2:23, "having the appearance of wisdom," would not be an insertion. But if this statement were an insertion, *men* would stand as usual behind the first word.—This argument, however, is problematic. We need to ask whether the "regularity" observed by B. Hollenbach is also valid if the unusual construction of a conjugatio periphrastica is present ("which *are having* the appearance of wisdom"). Acts 3:21 does not confirm B. Hollenbach's investigative results. There we also have a relative clause whose predicate consists of two components: *dei* (it is necessary) and an infinitive. There also, the particle *men* is used—in fourth place in the sentence,

clause, allows that the teachings of the false teachers have an *appearance* of wisdom.[94] Where this appearance originates is indicated by three short clues: "willing piety" *(ethelothres kia)*, "humility" *(tapeinophrosynē)*, and "severe treatment of the body" *(apheidia sōmatos)*. All three terms refer to the preceding elucidations. The idea of "severe treatment of the body" probably is in reference to the food laws in vv 16 + 21. The expression *apheidein tou sōmatos* occurs occasionally in extra-biblical Greek, i.e., to describe a military virtue,[95] but it is not a technical term for ascetic accomplishments. It does not designate anything reprehensible, and even Paul did not evaluate severe treatment toward the body negatively, as 1 Cor 9:25, 27 demonstrate (cf. Rom 13:14). "Humility" occurs in 2:18 and is only cited here.[96] The word *ethelo-threskia* is joined to these works; it harks back to *threskeia* (worship of God [as practiced by the angels]). This word is otherwise not attested. Composites with *ethelo-*, however, occur frequently in Koine Greek, even when they are lacking in the LXX as well as in the NT, except in Col 1:23. *Ethelo-* means "either 1. 'by free choice,' usually in the sense of willing service, not of self-chosen action; 2. 'gladly,' 'seeking after;' or 3. 'ostensibly,' 'quasi.'"[97] Next to the terms "humility" and "severe treatment toward the body," which in themselves do not mean anything corrupt, we should surely not translate *ethelthreskia* as "quasi-piety/quasi-worship-service," but rather as "willing/gladly-rendered worship-service."

Why all this would only generate an appearance of wisdom, but would not be wisdom in itself, is explained by the expression "not in deference toward someone." The expected adversative particle *de*, which should follow the chosen *men* ("namely [the appearance . . .]") is absent. The omission is common in

---

before the infinitive, thus in the place which would correspond to *men* in Col 2:23, in case a conjugatio periphrastica existed there.

94. For this concept, see Notes to 1:9, comp. 1:28 + 23; 3:16 + 4:5.

95. Comp. Josephus, Bell III, 7, 18, "if they (the Jews, H.B.) were successful, however, in reaching the proximity of the Roman divisions, because these were shooting at a distance, then they stormed these and pressed them hard, for they fought *without sparing their bodies or their lives.*" Further, see the references in J. B. Lightfoot, p. 272.

96. A few important manuscripts, such as Papyrus 46, Codex Vaticanus, and Minuscule 1739, transmit no "and" before "severity toward the body," and thus do not perceive this expression as an independent portion of the listing, but rather as an explanation of the concept "humility" ("humility through severity"). It is not certain that this reading is the more problematic one, and that therefore the equally well-attested text transmissions (among others, Codex Sinaiticus and Codex Alexandrinus), which contain the conjunction "and," should be preferred. Possibly, with the deletion of the conjunction, a dogmatic correction was undertaken, which was to avoid the impression that Paul attributed uncommented "humility" to his opponents.

97. Bo Reicke, "Kol 2:23," op. cit., p. 45. There, we also have examples and references.

Greek (cf. BDR 447, 2) and is excusable in this passage, since the antithesis is indicated anyway through the negation *ouk* (not).[98]

Timē, meaning deference, is used in different ways by Paul to describe a relationship that he requires of all Christians toward fellow Christians (Rom 12:10); it, however, is especially proffered to the seemingly not honorable, lowest members of the community (1 Cor 12:23, 24) and is in general to be rendered to everyone to whom "deference" is owing (Rom 13:7). *Timē* interpreted in this sense would appropriate Paul's criticism of the false teachers, which he expresses in 2:18, and it thus interposes itself well into this context.[99]

The indeterminate personal pronoun *tini* can be read as feminine (any kind of deference), but a better rendering can be achieved if we read it as masculine: deference toward someone (cf. P. Ewald, p. 408).

COMMENTS I–VI TO COL 2:6–23

I. Nature and Grace

The use of the terms *theotēs* in Col 2:9 and *theiotēs* in Rom 1:20 possibly already addresses the difference between the nature of God and the attributes of God in Paul. If *theiotēs* is understood to designate the attributes of God, then this concept seems to fit well into the context in Rom 1:20: It would state that the gentiles could obtain a knowledge of divine attributes from the "works of creation." In Col 2:9, however, the use of *theotēs* gives expression to the idea that recognition of the divine being is revealed solely in Christ. The problem which arises through this differing conceptualization has intensely preoccupied theory in later times, esp. in the nineteenth and twentieth centuries under the

---

98. Bo Reicke, ibid., p. 43, suggests that the particle *men* should be understood as *men-* solitarium, which has the purely internal assignment of emphasizing the pregnant meaning of the word to which it is attached, without any kind of external relationship to the context. B. Hollenbach, "Col II.23," op. cit., p. 260, offers a very complicated solution. He determines the main sentence as does Bo Reicke, but then he sees an indication of a concessive relationship of the inserted clause to the main clause through the particle *men*. The *de* corresponding to the *men* would have to be after the relative pronoun "which," but was left out because both first words in v 23 had already been written when the author made the decision to insert a clause.

99. G. Bornkamm, "Häresie," op. cit., p. 151, explains *timē* from the use of this word in the mysteries. There it means the selection and deification which the mystics experience from the deity [comp. for that R. Reitzenstein, "Die hellenistischen Mysterienreligionen," Nachdruck der 3. Aufl. von 1927 (Darmstadt, Wiss. Buchgesellschaft, 1980), pp. 252–54]. Thus, "Paul" seems to dismiss the opinion of the heretics, so that "honor" would accrue to them from the cult of the *stoicheia* and the keeping of the *dogmata* of the faithful.—But it is doubtful that there is even reference to the mysteries in Col (see Notes to 2:18).

headings "General and Specific Revelation of God," "Nature and Grace," Natural Theology and Theology of Revelation," "Theology from below and Theology from above."

However, in the face of such interpretations of both passages, the following should be considered:

1. The proposed analysis cannot finally be verified through Paul's use of language, since the two words, *theotēs* and *theiotēs*, each occur only once. Whether Paul could not have used *theotēs* in Rom 1:20 and *theiotēs* in Col 2:9 cannot be determined with certainty.

2. It is doubtful that Rom 1:20 concerns a precedent recognition of God from the works of creation. Because with the works (poiēmata) which are referred to in Rom 1:20, the divine states of grace in and among his chosen people could also be intended.[1] Such a reading would more readily correspond to Pauline thinking, according to which the Jews are not chosen for their own sake, but rather as a "light for the gentiles."[2] The differentiation between the "essence" and the "attributes" is foreign to this kind of thinking. The precondition is, "that exactly in his workings God himself is in the plan, he is not only a force undifferentiated from his own self. . . . God *is* specifically God in his action."[3] This orientation, imprinted in the OT, is also the model in Col 1:19, when "living in the entire fullness of God in the Messiah" is elucidated with a final statement concerning the *action* of God, "in order to reconcile all things through him. . . ."

3. Of great significance is an investigation by H. S. Nash[4] of the two expressions *theotēs* and *theiotēs*. He put together a rich variety of sources which demonstrate that both substantives were used almost synonymously until far beyond Paul's time. H. S. Nash (p. 16) summarizes, "The history of the interpretation, roughly divided, falls into two periods: the Patristic period, and what may be called, by a stretch of terms, the Greek renaissance of the ninth to the twelfth centuries. In the first period, I have not found a single exegetical support for the tradition" (that is the conventional exegetical differentiation between the two concepts, H.B.).[5]

II. Circumcision—Baptism—Resurrection

One of the most detailed and dogmatically most interesting statements about the significance and purpose of baptism seems to be present in Col 2:11–13.

---

1. See, among others, LXX Ps 63(64):10; 91(92):5; 142(143):5; comp. Deut 11:7. In the LXX, *erga* is frequently used in place of *poiēmata*. Both concepts are synonymous, as we can see from the cited passages. They both serve in the LXX to translate the Heb *ma⁽ᵃ⁾seh*.

2. Comp. Rom 2:19; 4; Isa 42:6; 49:6.

3. E. Schweizer (p. 108).

4. H. S. Nash, "*Theiotēs—Theotēs*. Rom I.20; Col II.9," JBL 18 (1899) 1–34.

5. The oft-cited passage in Plutarch (Def Orac 10) also points to this, where the

Even when it is not explicitly stated that "opponents" of Paul demanded circumcision of the Colossians, Paul seems opposed to such a demand. Perhaps also, though, because of his Jewish background, a comparison between circumcision and baptism was obvious to him. Thus it is conceivable that the expression "in the laying down of the body of the flesh" as well as the assertion "in the circumcision of Christ" can be taken as a further reference to baptism: in contrast to circumcision which is accomplished by hands, *the whole body* of the flesh, thus the whole sinful body, is laid down in baptism (cf. the Notes).[6] Only *this* "circumcision," namely baptism, is suitable for the Christian; it is the circumcision of Christ, namely the circumcision which belongs to Christ, or specifically the Christian circumcision.[7] This "dogma of baptism" supposedly stands in marked contrast to the assertion in 1 Pet 3:21, according to which baptism is not to be understood as a "laying down of the dirt of the flesh." But can we claim such an interesting diversity of opinion about baptism within the NT on the basis of the assertions in Col?

It is more probable that v 11 alludes to the death of Jesus. Otherwise the subsequent words concerning his burial and resurrection would stand curiously

---

discussion concerns the idea that the outstanding souls are awarded the metamorphosis from human beings to heroes, and from heroes to demons, from which a few in turn finally participate in the *theiotēs* (sic!). J. B. Lightfoot (p. 247) here cites *theotēs* (!) and remarks that in this passage, "*theiotētos* would be quite out of place, because all *daimones* without exception were *theioi* (beings with divine attributes, H.B.), though they only became *theoi* (gods, H.B.) in rare instances and after long probation and discipline." Def Orac 10 thus documents the opposite of that which J. B. Lightfoot wants to prove. And even if he had cited correctly, his argument would not stand the test. H. S. Nash (who also proceeds from the idea that Plutarch chose the word *theotēs* in the cited passage), does not refer to Def Orac 10, but rather to Def Orac 5 (where *theiotēs* is used without differentiation in meaning from *theotēs*, "for the prior reputation of the divinity there was great"). With that, he would have probably made the point that both words, *theotēs* and *theiotēs*, were practically synonymous, "In both contexts, he (Plutarch, H.B.) is speaking of the same phenomenon,—the inspiration of the oracles; and he is explaining it by the agency of the demons or intermediate spirits, to whom he ascribes *theiotēs* in the one context and *theotēs* in the other" (p. 12).

6. Compare, among others, P. Ewald (p. 376); Dibelius-Greeven (p. 30). Even the bi-composita *ap-ek-dysis* could support this interpretation, in so far as one assumes with J. B. Lightfoot (pp. 249f.) that putting aside *in its entirety* should be emphasized. But a prefix alone is not sufficient to justify such a translation, since the Koine has a predilection for prefixes without there being a difference in meaning to the simpler form (see BDR 116 and fn. 91 to Notes to 1:15–20).

7. Comp., among others, T. K. Abbott (p. 250f.); E. Haupt (p. 88); P. Ewald (p. 376); E. Lohse (p. 155); E. Schweizer (p. 111, fn. 341); J. Gnilka (p. 132); R. Schnackenburg, "Das Heilsgeschehen bei der Taufe nach dem Apostel Paulus. Eine Studie zur paulinischen Theologie," MThS.H 1 (München: Zink, 1950), p. 63; F. Zeilinger, ESpg, p. 144.

without a reference point. Besides, we can best explain the absence of the possessive pronoun in the expression "in the laying down of the body of the flesh" in the light of the emphatic "in him" not only in v 11, but also in the whole paragraph; the pronoun was viewed as self-evident and therefore was left out.[8] The phrase "body of the flesh" is also best interpreted as in 1:22 (cf. Notes there) to define the earthly/human existence of *Jesus*, where the entire expression "in the laying down of the body of the flesh" is the description of *his* death. If, accordingly, the circumcision of the Colossians has occurred in the death of Christ, then this circumstance does not simultaneously preclude that circumcision may *also* occur in baptism. The central role of baptism in Paul's argument here cannot be denied. E. Lohmeyer (pp. 109–11) expressly demonstrated this. He refers to the formula "in him," which is to say that the circumcision of Christ has occurred, that he has put off his carnal body, that his death is thus the determinate sign from God and the reality determined by God of the invisible circumcision. This death was accomplished uniquely in Christ, but exactly in this uniqueness lies the perpetuity of its validity for all; that which occurred in him originates from God for the world and from the world for God. Both are contained in the formula "in him," in which also every possibility of stepping out of the circle of this occurrence by one's own action is precluded. The chief event is now in baptism, which is only a peripheral event in the occurrences in Christ. While v 11 speaks of what God accomplished in Christ, it only dimly hints at how this act is meaningful to the believer. This latter motif is predominant in the declaration about being buried in baptism: " 'In Christ,' all life and thought, action and activity, of the believer stands firm, but above all this temporal state of the believing life stands the eternal wonder of sacramental grace, which alone is possible 'with Christ.' The believer experiences the divine act in Christ in baptism as though it occurred in him; it is God who places him into this eternal divine history" (p. 111).[9]

If the divine act in Christ is equivalent to baptism in this relationship, then the meaning that in v 12 the sacramentally occurring resurrection is meant would be the logical result. That would then also be true if the relative clause in v 12 does not refer to baptism, but rather to Christ. Then v 11 would

---

8. In Greek, a simple determination can be made by using the article instead of the possessive pronoun in a case like this. Comp. the references in BauerLex, pp. 1088f.

9. See also E. Lohmeyer, "Syn Christou," op. cit., pp. 249ff.—For this evaluation of baptism, see also H. A. W. Meyer (p. 320); H. von Soden (p. 46); E. Lohse (p. 155); E. Schweizer (p. 111); J. Gnilka (p. 134); A. Lindemann (p. 42); J. A. T. Robinson, "The One Baptism," in *Thelfe New Testament Studies*, SBT 34 (London, SCM, 1962), pp. 158–75:168f.; R. C. Tannehill, *Dying and Rising with Christ. A Study in Pauline Theology*, BZNW 32 (Berlin: Töpelmann, 1967), p. 42; H. Frankemölle, *Das Taufverständnis des Paulus. Taufe, Tod und Auferstehung nach Röm 6*, SBS 47 (Stuttgart: Kath. Bibelwerk, 1970); pp. 123f.; G. Delling, *Die Taufe im Neuen Testament* (Berlin: Evang. Verlagsanstalt, O.J.), p. 123; A. Oepke, ThWNT I; 539, 13ff.

have just demonstrated that Paul's concern is to emphasize the *sacramental appropriation* of the event in Christ. A contradiction in these elucidations would hardly arise, since baptism would not enter into competition with the occurrences in Christ. It would remain as the appropriation of that which was fundamentally accomplished in Christ and therefore its value and significance are derivative.

But does baptism in fact play the central role in the argument in Col 2:11–13 that is attributed to it in the interpretation outlined just now? Or do we have indications in this text that point in a different direction?

The contextual connection between v 11 and v 13 is noteworthy. While v 11 speaks of a circumcision not accomplished by human hands, v 13 talks of an uncircumcision of the flesh. The genitive attribute *tēs sarkos* (of the flesh) seems to be a striking contrast to *acheiropoiētos* (not made by hands). It emphasizes that what is meant here is not the uncircumcision of the heart (cf. Rom 2:25–29), but rather the uncircumcision in the literal sense. Likewise, in Rom 2:28 the discussion concerns the "circumcision in the flesh," which is elucidated by a further addition as "eternally visible" *(en tō phanerō)* circumcision. This literal meaning should be preferred to the traditional interpretation[10] in Col 2:12, as long as there are no reasons which necessitate a different conclusion. An additional argument against the traditional view would arise from equating the literally understood uncircumcision with "being dead in transgressions," which would lead to the conclusion that the circumcised one is living a life without sin. This could neither be reconciled with ideas in the uncontested Pauline epistles (cf. esp. Rom 3:9), nor would it be thinkable for a Pauline pupil if such a one was the author of Col. Even the "us" which encompasses both Jews and gentiles in the declaration at the end of Col 2:13[11] demonstrates that sinlessness of Jews is not perceived as one of the differences between Jews and gentiles.

The stated conclusion is, however, not the only possible or necessary consequence of a literal interpretation of "uncircumcision." That becomes clear if we draw on Eph 2:11ff. for an explanation. Based on this background, Col 2:13 could be interpreted as follows: Jews or gentiles, or to refer to current Jewish terminology circumcised or uncircumcised, can be differentiated in that the Jews could trust in God despite their sins, while the gentiles were "without hope and without God in the world" in their sins.

If v 13 is meant this way, then we can discern why the discussion concerns

---

10. In a transmitted meaning of *akrobystia* (uncircumcision), *tes sarkos* (of the flesh) would most likely be an explanatory genitive (genitivus exepegeticus). *Akrobystia* would then be a figurative expression for the idea that the Colossians were condemned "to the power of the flesh," the enmity against God (comp. Rom 8:7). Compare for that, among others, H. von Soden (47f.); E. Schweizer (p. 114); J. Gnilka (p. 136).

11. ". . . in that he has forgiven *us* all transgressions." See the Notes for that.

not only "your failings" and why, at the beginning of the statement in v 13, the phrase "you *also*" is emphasized.

Two things become clear in v 13a, understood thus, in which the previous status of the Colossians is defined as being excluded from the covenant of God with Israel:

1. Now we can understand what is meant by circumcision (v 11) not accomplished by hands: the concept of the OT and of Judaism, that circumcision is a sign of the covenant of God with Israel,[12] is presumed. Paul argues on this basis (cf. Eph 2:11) that the sign that the gentiles are chosen is the death of Jesus, that this death is thus equivalent to their circumcision. Circumcision accomplished by hands as a separating differentiation between chosen and nonchosen is therefore no longer valid (cf. Col 3:11; Gal 6:15), because the previously uncircumcised people were now "circumcised" by God himself.[13]

2. We can also understand what is meant by the resurrection that has already occurred (v 12). This theme is resumed again in v 13 with the verb form "he has made alive," which is immediately attached to the statement about the gentiles being dead in sin. The statement of the resurrection in v 12f. thus does not refer to physical resurrection but rather to resurrection from the "death" of being from the "nonchosen."

In this connection, however, of what significance is the statement "you have been buried with him in baptism"? In v 13 Paul speaks conspicuously of a death of the (previously) uncircumcised in sin, while in v 12 he refers to being buried with Christ. In v 11 he speaks of the death of Christ, in vv 12 + 13 of the resurrection *with* Christ. We could have expected that the exposition of the earlier "death" of the recipients of the epistle would also have referred to the death *with Christ*. But this does not occur.[14] Thus a series of exegetes viewed this as a breach (or a shift) in the usage of the death concept in vv 11–13, and have explained this apparent state of affairs for example by the "versatility of the

---

12. In the OT (Gen 17:11) and in Judaism (comp. St.-B. IV, pp. 31ff.), circumcision served as a sign of belonging to the covenant of Abraham (comp. also Rom 4:11). In addition, other significance was attributed to this, which is listed in AB 34; pp. 279–82 (comp. St.-B., ibid.).—G. Vermes, "Jewish Exegesis: New Light from Ancient Sources," NTS 4 (1958) 309–19, explains the comparison here with circumcision in the Jewish tradition, according to which the blood of circumcision was interpreted as sacrificial blood. Col, however, gives no clues for verification of this interpretation.

13. Thus the objection that Paul could not have referred to circumcision in a literal sense in v 13, since this was not significant to him (comp. J. Lähnemann, *Kolosserbrief*, p. 125, fn. 62; E. Haupt, p. 92; H. von Soden, p. 48; J. Gnilka, p. 136), is without substance.

14. The assumption that baptism was understood as burial for the long-deceased (in their sins) gentiles would not solve this tension. Such an interpretation is very hypothetical anyway, since the connection of the baptismal declaration with the statement concerning being dead in sin is too unclear.

Pauline spirit" (cf. E. Haupt, p. 92), or with a presumed use of traditional goods in v 13,[15] or with the idea that "this unreflected use" demonstrates how concerned the author was in this passage solely with the already accomplished resurrection from death (cf. E. Schweizer, p. 114).

Still, the "traditional" expression "of being dead" in v 13 is not used in such an unreflective manner, because the death of Jesus is to be understood manifestly not as a dying along with him, but rather as a circumcision. The topic is not "dying." That seems to occur consciously on the basis of the statement regarding the status of gentiles in v 13. Thus, vv 11 and 13 give evidence of the continuity of the imagery already used earlier, not of a breach. In this connection, however, the remark concerning baptism as burial along with Christ is striking. Yet this does not seem to have escaped the author, as the participial construction of this statement demonstrates, which distinguishes it from the context. If we do not wish to impute insufficient reflection to the author in the development of his ideas, and if we are not coerced on the basis of dogmatic preconceptions to adhere to baptism as the central argument in vv 11–13, then we are obliged to interpret the participial construction in the statement on baptism in v 12a as parenthetical. In short, it has been set apart by the author from the logical coherence and continuity of the argument.

The fact that Paul even mentions burial here can be comprehended from 1 Cor 15:1ff. The statements about the death, burial, and resurrection of Jesus are a marked characteristic of the gospel, which Paul has received and rendered faithfully.[16] When Paul also cites burial in Col 2, he is clearly alluding to this marked characteristic of the gospel, and he is thus implying that his proclamations are founded on that same gospel that he and the Colossians have received. He is thus imparting to them what they have basically already been told and which they have already accepted.

If this interpretation is correct, then the expression used in v 11, "circumcision of Christ," becomes clear. It cannot be a designation of baptism, but rather only a description of the death of Jesus. It was chosen for the reason that the death of Jesus is understood as "his circumcision" for the gentiles and thus as their circumcision also.

The impression that Col is a detailed source on baptism here is deceptive. It is solely and explicitly stated here concerning baptism, analogously to Rom 6:4, that it is a burial along with Christ. In the sense that it is removed from the context of the argument, we are given an indication that it is not to be understood as a means for the appropriation of the fundamental occurrence in Christ. The exposition under consideration rather argues against the idea that

---

15. J. Gnilka (p. 136); comp. also G. Conzelmann (p. 191), who suspects that the incongruence in the picture can be traced back to the fact that both were firmly entrenched figures of speech in the language of the community.

16. Compare for that J. Jeremias, *Abendmahlsworte*, op. cit., pp. 95–97.

Paul has made a differentiation between that which has fundamentally occurred in Christ and that which is separated from this occurrence by time but which has been appropriated by the individual as a source of power. On the contrary, these statements in Col seem to build on the idea that appropriation and occurrence are one simple, inseparable event. Thus, baptism will be understood only as proclamation, thanks, and praise of that which has already occurred in Christ and was also appropriated—as also a "burial" among Christians is confirmed—and proclaimed in thanks and praise as the already commencing death and certainty of resurrection. Whether this proclamation, this thanks, and this praise are given expression at baptism in the conscious decision-making process, or whether this occurs through the community versed in this praxis, in other words, whether baptism is a conscious step of obedience by the child to be baptized or whether baptizing small children can be justified from the NT, all these questions find no answer in Col. It also gives no answer about how circumcision of Jews is to be practiced after the death and resurrection of the Messiah Jesus. Certainly it becomes clear that gentiles no longer require circumcision accomplished by hands, since they are "circumcised" through the death of Jesus. But to conclude from this that Jews would no longer need to be circumcised (by hands) is not justified. Paul himself did not come to this conclusion, in case the report in Acts 16:1–3 is applicable and the apostle did not change his mind (cf. Comment I to 1:1 + 2).

III. The "Bill of Indictment" Against Us

The expression of the cancellation of a "bill of indictment" against "us" in Col 2:14 seems to have a parallel in the rabbinic conceptualization of the divine list of transgressions. According to the rabbinic formulation, the good as well as the evil deeds of men are listed (by angels) and are used in the arraignment before God.[17] Closely linked to the statement in Col 2:14 seems to be a petition from the prayer *Abinu Malkenu:* "our Father, our King, erase through your great mercy all our letters of transgression/entries of transgression."[18] In the Greek translation of the so-called anonymous Apocalypse, which is of Jewish origin and is also extant in the Coptic language, the word *cheirographon* is used for these divine lists of transgressions, and it also occurs in Col.[19] The question is whether this rabbinic understanding lies at the basis of the statement in Col 2:14?

---

17. See for that the references in St.-B. I, p. 583; II, pp. 170–73; III, pp. 78f., pp. 628, 840.

18. Comp. St.-B. III, p. 628.

19. Anonymous Apocalypse 3:13ff.; 4:3ff. It was edited and translated by G. Steindorff, *Die Apokalypse des Elias, eine unbekannte Apokalypse und Bruchstücke der Sophinias—Apokalypse, TU* 17, 3 (Leipzig, 1899). Comp. also F. J. Dölger, *Sonne der Gerechtigkeit*, op. cit., pp. 138f., and E. Lohse, ThWNT IX, p. 425, fn. 2.

Within the context of Col, which addresses the forgiveness of transgressions, this idea would fit in, but the adjoining more detailed elucidation of the concept through *dogmata* (regulations) leads to difficulties. *Dogmata* could well be understood on such an interpretation as a designation of OT law, because only this—and not any kind of regulation of a "religion" designated as deception—can be the legal basis for the divine lists of transgressions. But it is improbable that *dogmata* is a designation of OT law. The term occurs only five times in the NT, and even then never in this sense. That is probably also true of Eph 2:15, which next to Col 2:14 is the only passage in which *dogmata* is used in a letter which names Paul as its author.[20] The circumstance in the LXX is similar. Only in 3 Macc 1:3 and 4 Macc 10:2 is reference made to the OT law with this expression but these passages do not support the view that *dogmata* in Col has this meaning. Because the corresponding language usage in Maccabees[21] is connected to a "Hellenistic outlook of the Jewish faith as divine philosophy and *dogma* here as a sacred tenet; both however are totally foreign to Paul."[22]

The word *cheirographon* is also documented as a legal technical term. Specifically, it is used to designate a legal instrument of default which was drawn up freely by a debtor himself, without involving a notary, and was signed by him in his own hand. If the debtor himself could not write and therefore contracted a substitute as signatory, this was expressly noted.[23] Paul was certainly familiar with this legal custom, as Phlm 18f. demonstrates.[24] Whether and to what extent this very special sense of "bill of indictment" in Col 2:14 is possible depends to a large extent on the expression *dogmata* (regulations) which also occurs here.

Among others, J. B. Lightfoot, T. K. Abbott, and H. von Soden have used the technical legal sense of "bill of indictment" as the basis of their analysis or exegesis, and have interpreted *dogmata* as a designation of OT law. While H. v. Soden (49) also observed the point of comparison that the document of transgression was issued *by the debtor* (and he observed an allusion to Ex 24:6-8),[25] J. B. Lightfoot (p. 253) and T. K. Abbott (p. 255), among others, rejected such a far-reaching interpretation of this image. It was not possible, in

20. Comp. M. Barth, AB 34, pp. 287-91.—*Nomos* as designation of the Mosaic law occurs in Paul more than 100 times, however.

21. As also in Philo, Leg All I, 54f.; Gig 52; and in Josephus, Ant 15, 136; Ap 1, 42.

22. E. Lohmeyer (p. 117, fn. 1). Comp. also ThWNT II, p. 234.

23. See A. Deissmann, *Licht vom Osten*, op. cit., pp. 281f.; comp. also E. Lohse, ThWNT IX, pp. 424f.; N. Walter, "Die 'Handschrift in Satzungen' Kol 2,14," ZNW 70 (1979) 115-18:115.

24. "If, however, he did damage to you or owes you something, put it on my account. I, Paul, write to you with my own hand: I will pay it." In the LXX, *chenographon* occurs only in Tob 5:3; 9:2, 5, and designates a kind of receipt for money which is put aside.

25. Ex 24:7, "And he (Moses) took the book of the covenant and read it before the

their opinion, since the gentiles were included in the declaration of Col 2:14 and the subject was not limited for Jews. N. Walter,[26] in turn, expressed sharp criticism of such an argument: it is difficult to defend philologically the application of the word *cheirographon* in reference to the described technical usage in only half of its technical sense, and then not in the other half. For in doing so, the scholars emphasize the basic sense of "document of transgression" (which it would not have without its legal-technical character), while deleting the premise or presupposition from which it derives its technical usage, namely that we are dealing with a document of transgression that was drawn up by the transgressor himself. Thus the author of Col would not be referring to an indictment that originated from the deity, and not to the law as the basis of the bill of indictment, but rather he means by *cheirographon* the confession of the sinners who issued these of their own volition in view of these statutes. The scholars maintain that reference is made to the fear of sin on the part of the Colossians. Vv 16–18 indicate what is meant by statutes. The Christians addressed are not certain as to whether the self-sacrifice of Christ on the cross was sufficient in removing everything that stood between them and God, and who therefore thought they would have to observe assiduously strong legal requirements and additionally have to take part in other religious practices.

N. Walter is correct, in our opinion, in his argument that this passage does not refer to OT law and is not based on an indictment from God. Yet this does not necessarily derive from the legal-technical meaning of *cheirographon*, but rather from the term *dogmata* (see above). *Cheirographon* with the meaning of "document of transgression," in other words in the legal-technical usage, is used not only in the *strictly* legal sense presumed by N. Walter, but is also used to designate a document issued by the debtor himself. The use of this concept (specifically its Latin equivalent) in the anonymous Apocalypse and in the Apocalypse of Paul 17[27] demonstrates that the meaning "document of transgression" can be supported without the requirement that the document must be written and issued by the debtor. In both cited sources, angels are the authors.

It would be misleading in general to limit *cheirographon* to the described specific legal interpretation. The sources which Preisigkelex cites confirm P. Ewald's (p. 383, fn. 1) determination that "bill of indictment" means simply "document" in the sense of a binding instrument. Since "bill of indictment" in Col 2:14 is elucidated in some detail, it is not necessary to refer back to specific technical usages of this expression, which the context does not require and which create problems. Col 2:14 results in a plausible statement if *cheirographon*

---

eyes of the people. They said: everything that Jahweh has said we will do and observe." Comp. also Deut 27:11–26.

26. N. Walter, "Handschrift," op. cit.

27. Cit. in E. Lohse, ThWNT IX, p. 425, fn. 2. See also Hennecke/Schneemelcher II, p. 538.

is simply translated by "document." The discussion concerns a document aimed at "us" with hostile intent on the basis of "regulations" (of a deceptive "religion"), so that we are surely dealing with a kind of bill of indictment. The fact that Paul includes himself among those implicated by this indictment is understandable. If the Colossians are indicted, who base themselves on the gospel which also Paul proclaims (cf. 1:5f., 23), then such an indictment pertains also to him, yes very especially to him. In response, Paul explains his position: any kind of indictment against us on the basis of regulations is meaningless right from the start because of the cross of Christ (cf. Notes to 2:14).

We should mention yet another interpretation that explains the figurative use of the language in an interesting way. O. A. Blanchette[28] proceeds from a thesis of J. Daniélou,[29] according to which the Jewish Christians took up the apocalyptic concept of a heavenly book which contained the secret will of God and which could be read in a visionary manner. The early Christians adopted this idea of a heavenly book based on the idea that Christ is the new revelation of the father, and they transferred it to Christ. This use of the apocalyptic conceptualization is reflected in the Odes of Solomon 23 and in the so-called Veritatis Gospel. O. A. Blanchette, however, considers this interpretation inapplicable to Col because the passage talks about a "bill of indictment against us." He therefore suggests a combination of the "classical exegesis," which interprets "bill of indictment" as a document of guilt, and the Jewish-Christian exegesis, which took over the cited apocalyptic conceptualization. "Paul seems to have drawn from both the Jewish tradition and the legal usage of his day, but only to express an idea that was richer than anything in either of his sources" (p. 312). As it is stated in 2 Cor 5:21, for example, that God made Christ to be sin, so also has "the document of guilt against us" become identified with Christ. This "document of guilt against us" is our body and flesh which Christ took up and which is nailed to the cross.

On the one hand, this interpretation reasonably explains the perhaps curious imagery of the crucifixion of a document of guilt, but Col 2:14 lacks the necessary affirmation that God has made Christ into this document of guilt, which would be required for O. A. Blanchette's interpretation. Thus it is still very dubious that the recipients of the Colossian epistle could have understood the statement in 2:14 in the sense proposed by O. A. Blanchette.[30]

---

28. O. A. Blanchette, "Cheirographon," op. cit.

29. J. Daniélou, *Théologie du judéo-christanisme*, *Bibliothèque de Théologie* (Paris: Desclee, 1958), esp. pp. 151–63 (Sec.).

30. Still more hypothetical seems the interpretation that the manuscript in Col 2:14 means a contract with the devil. This reading is only mentioned here peripherally. It was chiefly advocated by G. Megas, "Das *cheirographon* Adams. Ein Beitrag zu Col 2:13–15," ZNW 27 (1928) 308–20, and also by E. Lohmeyer (p. 116), as well as W. Bieder (pp. 150f.).

IV. The "Elements of the World"

The Greek word *stoicheia* occurs in the NT apart from Col 2:8 + 20 only in Gal 4:3, 9, Heb 5:12, and 2 Pet 3:10 + 12. In extra-biblical texts, on the other hand, the word is used frequently. A. Lumpe (RAC I, 1074), as well as G. Delling (ThWNT VII, 672, 6) take "word particle, letter" as its basic meaning. Additionally, up to the time of the composition of Col, the following meanings can be attested[31]:

1. The "length of shadow" from which the time of day was determined.

2. The "foundations" of a science, teaching, art, etc. In Heb 5:12, also, *stoicheia* has this sense, where it is modified by the genitive phrase *tēs archēs* and means "original fundamental principles." The connotation of the unfinished, the unripe, however, is not inherent in the term *stoicheia*.[32]

3. "(Basic) components of the cosmos." The stoa made this meaning popular, and it "had thus become common ground for the average Greek-speaking educated person"[33] by the first century C.E. It is used in this sense in the NT in 2 Pet 3:10 + 12.

In addition, *stoicheia* can designate "constellations, stellar and elementary spirits" such as spirits in general. But as J. Blinzler and G. Delling demonstrate, all sources for these meanings are later than the Colossian epistle.[34]

But precisely the assumption that *stoicheia* designates personal beings determined the exegesis of Col 2:8, 20 for a long period since the end of the last century. The opinion that "Elements of the World" meant spirits of the elements found wide recognition.[35] This interpretation cannot be established philologically; rather, its justification rests mainly on a presumption which is

---

31. See for that esp. J. Blinzler, "Lexikalisches zu dem Terminus *ta stoicheia tou kosmou* bei Paulus," AnBibl 18 (1963) 429–43, and G. Delling, ThWNT VII, pp. 670–87.

32. J. Blinzler, op. cit., p. 431.

33. Ibid., p. 439. J. Blinzler indicates that of 175 references in the known writings before and after Paul, 78.3 percent slip away from this meaning. In Philo alone, he counts 82 examples, of which 67 slip away from this meaning, and of these, 14 to "letters" and one to "basis."

34. See for that the detailed discussion of the references pertinent to the point in J. Blinzler, op. cit., pp. 432–39; G. Delling, ThWNT VII, pp. 676, 37–677, 18; pp. 679, 12–682, 40; pp. 683, 9ff.; and also in E. De Witt Burton, *The Epistle to the Galatians*, ICC [Edinburgh: Clark, 1921 (repr. 1950)], pp. 510–18.

35. T. K. Abbott (pp. 247f.); E. Haupt (pp. 76ff.); H. von Soden (pp. 43f.); K. Staab (pp. 90ff.); W. Bieder (p. 132); P. T. O'Brien (pp. 110, 129–32); F. Pfister, *stoicheia*, op. cit. F. Spitta, *Der zweite Brief des Petrus und der Brief des Judas. Eine geschichtliche Untersuchung* (Halle: Verlag der Buchhandlung des Waisenhauses, 1885), indicated this at the end of the last century in an exegesis of 2 Pet 3:10. (Comp. N. Kehl, *Christushymnus*, op. cit., pp. 141f.). F. Spitta opposes the father exegesis, which is rendered in the *stoicheia* primarily with "heavenly bodies," since then the corresponding Greek expres-

formulated in an exemplary way in Dibelius-Greeven (p. 27), "The Hellenistic syncretism, from which philosophic ideas were given new mythological forms (. . .), *had to* (emphasis H.B.) conceive the philosophic *stoicheion* mythologically, because the 'elements' were represented to it through spirits." It is applicable that in the world of antiquity and even still among Jews and Christians at the time of Paul—despite progress for example in medicine (cf. M. Barth, AB34, p. 187, fn. 205)—the concept was widespread that nature was ruled by spirits or angels.[36] But from this we cannot automatically deduce a change in meaning from "element" to "spirit of the element," as the usage of the term *stoicheion* in the second century C.E. and later demonstrates. J. Blinzler (p. 436) points out rather that the opposite is the case: again and again we can confirm that even then, when the elements are brought in close contact with spiritual beings, there are terminological differences between these and those. The elements are inhabited, ruled, dominated by spiritual beings, but they are not the spiritual beings themselves.

Stoicheia also picks up another meaning as spiritual being, but in this it relies less on the usage of this word in the larger framework of the NT and more on its use as a concept in the epistle to the Galatians. In Gal 3 + 4, the two expressions "under the law" (3:23; 4:4 + 5) and "under the elements of the world" (4:3) are used in parallel fashion. In addition, the "elements of the world" are compared with "guardians and trustees" (4:2), as well as with "gods" (4:8). That is why the *stoicheia* are to be understood as personal beings, which can then mean only the angels referred to in Gal 3:19, through whom the law was given.[37] If this argumentation were unchallengeable, then the letter to the Galatians would be the oldest known source for a personal meaning of *stoicheia*. But a comparison with personal figures still does not require that the objects compared must also be understood on a personal level. Thus for example in Gal 3:24, the law is designated as "educator" *(paidagōgos)*, but we cannot conclude from that that the law is a person. And even the reference to "gods" says little in this regard, as a look at the idol-polemic of the Old and New Testaments demonstrates (cf. for example Ps 115:4–7; Isa 44:9–20; Jer 2:28; 10:5, 14; Hab 2:18f.; 1 Cor 12:2). The statements in Gal 3 + 4 are not sufficient to identify the *stoicheia* as spirits or even angels of the law. By "elements of the world," it seems to us that not even the law is meant in Gal, and thus the language used

sion *ourania* would have to be chosen. In his opinion, the original meaning "elements" should not be ceded overly quickly, due to the closer determination *tou kosmou* (of the world), if we are only trying to "connect the same with the conceptualization of personal beings, which the passage (2 Pet 3:10, H.B.) so decisively indicates" (p. 265).

36. Comp., for example, Jub 2; Ps 104:4; Rev 7:1, 2; 14:8; 16:5; 19:17.

37. See primarily A. Ritschl, *Die christliche Lehre von der Rechtfertigung und Versöhnung*, vol. II, 4th ed. (Bonn: Marcus und Weber, 1900), pp. 252f.; E. Percy, PKE, pp. 136–67; Bo Reicke, "The Law and This World According to Paul: Some Thoughts Concerning Gal 4:1–11," JBL 70 (1951) 259–76.

there can also hardly underpin a corresponding meaning of *stoicheia* in the epistle to the Colossians.[38]

In Gal 3:24, the function of the law is compared with that of a slave in antiquity, to whom is assigned the supervision of minor children. Even if we are also dealing with the same minority status in 4:1ff., the analogy of 3:24 is not taken up again. The reference to "guardians and trustees" is from a different vantage point than that to "educators" in 3:24. In 4:1ff., it is to be determined that the minor heir is *subject* to the "things" over which he should someday be master. This becomes clear in the conjunction *alla* (4:2), which cannot simply mean "but" here, since no contrast exists. It introduces a gradation of the statement and means as much as "not only this, but also . . ." (cf. BDR 448, 6) The train of thought becomes understandable if we consider that the administrators of the household in antiquity could be bondsmen and therefore represented a portion of the future possession of the inheritance.[39] The *stoicheia tou kosmou* thus simply describe this future possession. In Rom 4:13 we read instead that the promise is that the inheritance of Abraham is "the world" *(kosmos)*. It is improbable that the law now also belongs to the things over which the inheritor will be master. For one, the law "kept/protected" the inheritor during the time of minority, in which he himself was slave, until the "redemption" (Gal 4:5), and it would be curious if the "redemption" from the protector were meant. For another, the idea that the inheritor at the age of majority should be master of the law is very unusual. Paul does represent the viewpoint that the law has

---

38. M. Luther (WA 40 I, 553–56), in his *Grosser Galaterkommentar of 1531*, interpreted "elements of the world" as a transitional concept for all things "which refer to this life," and which in Gal refers especially to OT laws. W. Foerster, *Irrlehre*, op. cit., interpreted the expression "elements of the world" in the Colossian Epistle similarly, only that he saw in this an expression by which Paul wanted to characterize man's existence under the law and under gentile statutes *simultaneously* (p. 76), "Was an Raum und Zeit gebunden ist, ist von den 'Elementen der Welt' abhängig. Das kann also Paulus als das Gemeinsame der jüdischen und heidnischen Religiosität bezeichnen; es ist 'Dienst der *stoicheia tou kosmou*,' der Bestandteile dieser Welt." (p. 77)—Comp. also A. J. Bandstra, *The Law and the Elements of the World*, Diss. [Kampen: Kok, 1964 (Sek.)]. According to him, the genitive attribute "of the world" means "that whole sphere of human activity which stands over against Christ and His salvation, not considered first of all as inherently and structurally evil, but . . . which is ineffectual for overcoming sin and . . . for bringing salvation" (p. 57; cit. in P. T. O'Brien, p. 130). Their basic components (p. 57) are designated with the concept *stoicheia*, which A. J. Bandstra determines as "law" and "flesh" on the basis of the statements in Gal 4 and Col 2. (A summarizing presentation of the investigation of A. J. Bandstra can be found in H. Weiss, "The Law in the Epistle to the Colossians," CBQ 434 (1972) 294–314:299–303.

39. Comp. the change in the concepts of "stewart" and "slave" in Luke 12:42, 43, 45f. It is probable that "stewarts" meant a group of persons no different from "guardians," because the former concept should elucidate the latter. See for that St.-B. III, 565, "Vormund u. Verwalter war für das Volksbewusstsein eben ein u. dasselbe."

fulfilled its (protective) function with the coming of age of the heir, but he ties to this the concept that the heir when he reaches the age of majority would then do what the law desires (cf. Gal 5:14/Rom 5:5). Consequently, Paul can even say that he does not wish to suspend the law, but rather to uphold it (Rom 3:31).

In Col, an interpretation relating to OT law would be more hypothetical than in the letter to the Galatians. Even when, according to the indications in Col 2, the false teachers go back to OT law in their regulations, in Col the discussion does not concern the law as such: the term *nomos* (law) or *entolē* (command) does not occur even once.

Another possibility of interpretation is to translate *stoicheia* in Col 2 as in Heb 5:12 by "basic elements."[40] This meaning would not be inapt next to the concepts of "philosophy," and "deliverance of people" (Col 2:8). It would state that "philosophy," the false teacher, their "religion," does not have Christ as its foundation (cf. 1 Cor 3:11), but that it rather builds on the "foundations of this world." The genitive phrase "of the world" would be used in the same manner as also in 1 Cor 1:20, where the subject concerns the "wisdom of the world" in contrast to the wisdom of God.

This interpretation cannot be excluded. But the question remains whether through the genitive phrase "of the world," the most widespread meaning of *stoicheia* at the time of Paul, "basic elements *of the world*" is not simply recommended. J. Blinzler presents the argument that by addition "of the world" every other meaning is excluded as "physical elements." Wherever both concepts stand together, this meaning (= "basic components") is foremost in consideration.[41]

E. Schweizer (p. 101)[42] considers it necessary, based on this finding as well as the implication in Col 2:8 + 20, that in antiquity the common elements were considered to be "earth, water, air, fire (and "aether")." He then reconstructs the "Colossian philosophy" based on the interpreted "elements of the world," in which man has been coerced into the luckless cycle of elements from which he could only escape through the strictest asceticism, which viewpoint, according to him, predominated since Empedocles,[43] and which had considerable impact (cf. Comment V).

---

40. Comp. for that, among others, J. B. Lightfoot, pp. 246f.; C. F. D. Moule, p. 92; E. De Witt Burton, *Galatians*, op. cit., pp. 516–18.

41. J. Blinzler, "*stoicheia*," op. cit., p. 440. He found 11 sources, in which *stoicheia* occurs with the genitive "(of the) world" (p. 441, fn. 1–6), and in addition, 23 further passages in Philo alone, where *stoicheia* and *kosmos* stand in close proximity to each other.

42. Comp. also Blinzler, "Die 'Elemente der Welt.' Gal 4:3.9; Kol 2:8.20." G. Stähelin zum 70. Geburtstag am 28. Febr. 1970, in Blinzler, *Beiträge zur Theologie des Neuen Testaments. Neutestamentliche Aufsätze (1955–1970)* (Zürich: Zwingli Vlg., 1970), pp. 147–63; Blinzler, *Background*, op. cit.

43. The teaching of the four elements is traced back to Empedocles in antiquity.

If on the basis of the philological finding for this expression "elements of the world," also the meaning "components of the world" is close, even if not exact, still the conclusion that it reflects Empedocles' teaching about the elements is not compelling.

N. Kehl[44] tried to determine the "Sitz im Leben" for the expression "elements of the world" in Jewish-Christian apologetics. He proceeds from the "common ground of Christian apology of the first centuries, which accuse [sic!] the gentiles of worshipping the world elements as deities" (p. 145). As the criterion of true veneration of the deity in this context, creator and creation were contrasted with each other, in which, however, creation was not designated as a collective idea but rather in listed series of created categories based on components of the all. The term *stoicheia* also occurred, which meant the four basic elements (earth, water, air, fire) or their corresponding world realms (such as heaven, earth, ocean). In addition, stars, humans and animals, streams, rivers, etc., were added. In this respect, *stoicheia* was differentiated from *eidōla* (images), because the former were created directly by God. This motif and its structure were analyzed by Kehl by way of Jewish apologetics back to the OT, and he refers especially to Deut 4:15–19, where the prohibition against images is elucidated (p. 150). The concept *stoicheia tou kosmou* does not occur there, but a series of listings does which clearly represents an elaboration of the word "creation," because it follows the description of the works of creation from Gen 1:14–26, although in reverse order.[45]

In Wis 7:17, however, in term "elements" occurs within the framework of a series of listings comparable to Deut 4. There the words *stoicheion* and *kosmos* are closely associated. A series of things is listed under the heading "composition of the all *(kosmos)* and the activity of the elements *(stoicheia)*," whose knowledge can give wisdom to the wise one because it has "formed" these things (Wis 7:21). In this listing, an "element" is always listed next to its "activity": the beginning and end and middle of time; the alterations of the solstices and the change of the seasons; the cycles of the year and the constellations of the stars; the nature of living creatures and the driving forces of wild animals; the power of spirits and the thoughts of human beings; the differentiation of plants and the healing qualities of roots. By *stoicheia* are thus meant "created things" and the whole listing is an elaboration of the term *kosmos*.

The translation of *stoicheia tou kosmou* by "elements," or specifically

---

However, he did not use the concept *stoicheion*. The four elements are unfinished and intransient, according to his doctrine. Everything is derived from them by changing their mixture, not only plants, but also animals and even human beings and gods. This change of mixture also causes a change of that which occurred previously: a plant is derived from the human being, an animal from the plant, etc. For sources, see G. Delling, ThWNT VII, 672, 8ff.

44. N. Kehl, *Christushymnus*, op. cit., pp. 138–61.

45. The sequence of creeping things and birds is reversed, however.

"components of the world" in the sense of "created things" does justice to the philologic findings as well as to the specific concerns of the Colossian epistle, namely of giving praise to the Messiah as lord and king of the world (cf. esp. 1:12–20). The criticism of false teaching in 2:8, namely that it is directed at the "elements of the world" but not at the Messiah, then becomes of special concern in Col. Paul reproaches the false teachers in Col, as he also reprimands humanity in general in Rom 1:21: they venerate "created things" rather than the creator (cf. also Comment V).

V. The "Threat" to the Colossian Community

1. The Problem

In Col 2:4, 16–23, Paul expressly warns his readers about a certain religious teaching. He reprimands them with sharp words; yet he does not attempt to give a description of this teaching. He also does not go into detail about opposing concepts and argumentations, but rather he only makes a curt reference to them. He presupposes that the addressees know of what he spoke and would recognize immediately to what he was referring. If the "false teaching" was the occasion and even provocation of the epistle, then one is inclined to find hidden polemics beyond the expressly polemic portions of the letter. In any case, however, the information about persons and concepts toward whom Paul commands vigilance consists of short unconnected remarks. The task is thus for the modern reader of the epistle of placing these "fragments" in relation to one another. It is mostly presumed as self-evident that the "false teachers" must have been members of a certain "sect" with its own doctrinal system. Attempts at reconstructing this doctrinal system have been made again and again. In order to avoid vague combinations and unfounded hypotheses, scholars tried and still try to identify the individual dates and to reconstruct from these the total picture with parallel phenomena drawn from the study of comparative religion and the history of religions.[46]

At first sight, the Colossian epistle seems to offer very good conditions for undertaking such a reconstruction. Of the 34 words that appear in the NT only in Colossians, 17 alone occur in 2:4–23, and of the 28 words which occur in the rest of the NT but not in the uncontested Pauline epistles, 11 are to be found in the same paragraph of Col.[47] The suspicion that Paul is citing key words of his opponents can be presumed. The listing of commands and prohibitions in 2:16 and 21 is most probably derived from such a source. We can hardly assume this, however, for words such as *pithanologia* (phantom arguments, 2:4), *paralogizoma* (to trick, 2:4), *sylagōgeō* (to lead away as booty, 2:8), *exaleiphō* (to annul, 2:14), *skia* (shadow, 2:17) while unusual are not

---

46. Comp. G. Bornkamm, *Häresie*, op. cit., p. 139.
47. For that, see the overviews in E. Lohse, p. 133f.

specifically sectarian or even theological. We must therefore deal with the possibility that the author of the epistle is not citing his opponents, but has rather caricatured with his own words, which (words) are not known from the uncontested letters of Paul. In favor of this is also the sense that not only unusual concepts and comparisons,[48] but other materials that would hardly have been used by false teachers, characterize the paragraph. Because of this circumstance, the possibility of obtaining an even somewhat objective picture of the opponents in the Colossian epistle is very limited.

2. Attempts at Solution

J. B. Lightfoot (pp. 73–113) attempted to explain "heresy" in the Colossian epistle from heterodox Judaism, in particular, from the Essenes. He views the opponents of Paul to whom the apostle refers in Col as characterized by Jewish elements, as well as by "gnostic elements." For him, the characteristics of gnosis are: (a) exclusivity; (b) speculation about creation, according to which the material world is the seat of evil and "certain intermediate spiritual agencies (form) necessary links of communication between heaven and earth" (93); and (c) strict asceticism. These Gnostic elements can also be found among the Essenes in Judaism, so that it can be assumed that Paul is battling not two differing false teachings in Col, one Jewish and one Gnostic, but rather that he is dealing with Gnostic Jews of a type like the Essenes. In his argument, Lightfoot emphasizes, "when I speak of the Judaism in the Colossian Church as Essene, I do not assume a precise identity of origin, but only an essential affinity of the type with the Essenes of the mother country" (94f.).

The discoveries of the scrolls at Qumran have strengthened J. B. Lightfoot's observations to some extent.[49] But against this presumption, that Paul is turning against persons of Essene or Qumran orientation in Col, is above all the fact that the term "law" does not occur in Col and Paul also does not delve more closely into the meaning of OT law as such and with regard to the gentiles. As is well known, the law and its exact compliance played a central role for the Essenes as well as for the people at Qumran.[50]

---

48. The interpretation of circumcision and resurrection (for that, see Comment II): the image of nailing the indictment to the cross (see Comment III): the image of head and body (2:19).

49. Comp. for that S. Lyonnet, "Paul's Adversaries in Colossae," in F. O. Francis; W. A. Meeks, op. cit., 1973, pp. 147–61; E. W. Saunders, "The Colossian Heresy and Qumran Theology," in FS für K. W. Clark: *Studies in the History and Text of the New Testament* (Salt Lake City: University of Utah Press, 1967), pp. 133–45; W. Foerster, *Irrlehre*, op. cit., and also N. Kehl, *Erniedrigung*, op. cit.

50. Comp. also H. Braun, *Qumran und das Neue Testament*, vol. I (Tübingen: Mohr, 1966), pp. 228–30. This argument can also be used against attempts to allow the false teaching addressed in Col to be tied to the rabbinic adherence to the law (comp.

G. Bornkamm[51] locates the false teaching refuted in Col in Judaism. Yet in his interpretation, the criticism of J. B. Lightfoot's position does not apply. According to G. Bornkamm, the "Colossian heresy" is a "degeneration of Jewish gnosis," in which, however, Jewish obedience to the law was of subordinate importance. The point of departure of his attempted reconstruction is the expression "elements of the world." This is a key word for the heresy, according to him, and the teaching of the world elements is its first and most important characteristic. These are perceived as "person-like, angelic beings" because they are also called "rulers and powers," and the false teaching is summarily designated as "angel worship." According to Col 2:16, the observance of certain feast days and times is part of their regimen and thus they would have to observe "at least also the veneration" of the powers of the constellations. We can further conclude from the antithetically formulated expression in Col 2:9, "for in him lives all the fullness," that according to the heretical teaching, the fullness of the deity lives in the world elements. They placed people under certain statutes, demanded obedience in "humility" (2:18, 23) to which the declaration was tied that they were to participate in the elements of reigning deifying forces. The latter proceeds from the antithetical formulation, "in him you are fulfilled" (2:10). Since Bornkamm is starting from the viewpoint that the Colossian heresy was a Christian false teaching, he suspects "that the opponents understood the *stoicheia tou kosmou* (elements of the world, H.B.) themselves as the *sōma* (body, H.B.) of Christ, or as his limbs, and Christ as the embodiment of the world elements" (p. 141).

The Jewish origin of this false teaching demonstrates itself for G. Bornkamm chiefly in the recognition of a function in the story of the life and suffering of Christ, of *stoicheia* and their laws, indicated in 2:17 by the term "shadow." This assessment of the law has only one sense, if the heresy is of Jewish and not of gentile origin. G. Bornkamm then makes the connection of the Colossian teaching of the elements with the "ancient far-reaching and efficacious mythology of Hellenistic syncretism and speculation of oriental Aeon-Theology" (p. 142), whose origin is derived from Indo-Iranian conceptions of cosmology. This cosmic mythos of the body as the world deity and the elements as his limbs

---

E. Percy, PKE, pp. 142f., ". . . dass es sich in der kolossischen Irrlehre um eine spekulativ ausgestaltete Frömmigkeit handelte, die unter Huldigung einer gewissen Art von Christusglauben an jüdische Gesetzesbeobachtung anknüpfte, womit sie Tabuge-bräuche nichtjüdischen Ursprungs sowie direkte Askese verband; . . ."). This also argues against F. F. Bruce's (pp. 17–26) interpretation, which supposes a connection with the Jewish *Merkabah-Mystique*. As he himself works out, the "punctilious observance of the *minutiae* of the law, not least the law of purification, (was) essential" (p. 23). For the Merkabah-Mystique, see esp. G. Scholem, *Jewish Gnosticism, Merkabah-Mysticism and Talmudic Tradition* (New York: The Jewish Theological Seminary of America, 1965).

51. G. Bornkamm, *Häresie*, op. cit.

occurs again in Gnosis in the form of the Urmensch-Mythos[52] and there it attains a cosmic-soteriological status. The *stoicheia* (elements) turned into elements of the world of lights in contrast to the world of darkness in the dualistic worldview of Gnosis. The redemption of the Gnostic meant his metamorphosis into the form of the Urmensch (primitive man) as his heavenly representative, so that his simultaneous rebirth would be generated from the elements of the lower world to which his real self belonged according to his origin. Mystic activities, revelation formulas, and magical prayers were to serve this redemption process which would influence favorably the heavenly elements for the Gnostic and mystic and would thus effect his deification. Gnostic redemption and deification exactly in this sense would characterize the heresy in Col. The fact that the representatives of this false teaching had appeared as mystagogues could be concluded from 2:8, 18: they had appealed to special traditions and had maintained "that they had penetrated the content of their teaching in secretive visions" (143f.).[53] The Colossians seemingly also practiced a rebirth mystery which was termed by them "circumcision" in dependence on Judaism.

In sum, G. Bornkamm characterizes the Colossian heresy as follows: "It originated from a gnosticized Judaism, in which Jewish and Iranian-Persian elements and certainly also influences from Chaldean astrology amalgamated and combined with Christianity" (p. 153). He then also refers to the sect of "Hysistarians" known in Cappadocia in the fourth century, in which the same Jewish gnosis continued from which the Colossian heresy had sprung.

Objections were raised to the derivation from Gnosis of this false teaching in Col. Thus, H. Hegermann[54] countered that the veneration of the elements was exactly not Gnostic. Gnosis warded off the cosmic powers, so that the world elements turned into elements of darkness, while the world of light was sharply separated from it. The idea that the upper world filled the lower world with deified forces is not Gnostic. In reference to the reconstruction attempt by G. Bornkamm, for example, H. M. Schenke[55] considered the objection by H. Hegermann as justified; however, the conclusion is wrong, that the heretics were therefore not Gnostics. More accurate is a "negative conception of their *stoicheia*-cult" (p. 396). "The evil world-creating and world-ruling archons of the real gnosis (are) to be seen" in the "elements of the world," which are to be identified by the "angels" cited in 2:18 and the "rulers and powers" mentioned

---

52. See Comment II to 1:9–23, esp. fn. 37.

53. The investigation of M. Dibelius, *Isisweihe*, op. cit., was a trailblazer for the concept that the "Colossian false teaching" was a mystery cult. See Notes to 2:18.

54. H. Hegermann, *Schöpfungsmittler*, op. cit., p. 163. Compare also E. Percy, PKE, 176–78, and A. Lähnemann, *Kolosserbrief*, op. cit., p. 101.

55. H. M. Schenke, "Der Widerstreit gnostischer und kirchlicher Christologie im Spiegel des Kolosserbriefes," ZThK 61 (1964) 391–403.

in 1:16; 2:10 (p. 396). A cult in contrast to these archons is imaginable in gnosis. The ascent of the Gnostic souls into the realm of light leads through the realm of the archons, and thus preventative measures need to be taken in order to get past them. Two extreme positions were possible toward the archons: opposition or masking, according to whether the "already" or the "not yet" of Gnostic salvation was emphasized more. The cult of the archons in Col is to be understood as such a masking. H. M. Schenke establishes this position by the fact that the Gnostics, according to statements by the Church Father Irenaeus, took part in sacrifices to idols and that they also had no hesitation in "eternally carrying out a cult which actually stood in opposition to their viewpoint under corresponding political pressure" (p. 398).

The problem with this interpretation, however, is that it does not proceed from statements of the text, but rather that it interprets these from the hypothetical presumption that the false teachers were Gnostics. This becomes clear when H. M. Schenke criticizes the research with the challenge that the concept "gnostic," even when it was not misused, was still used in a glaringly misleading sense. Because if one views the angel cult as positive, then the heretics in Col are no Gnostics (p. 395). But then he agrees with the "existing research fully," (p. 396) that the heretics were Gnostics in order to conclude from that, that then the "worship of angels" must be understood negatively. Further this interpretation rests on the philologically uncertain assumption that angel beings were meant by "elements of the world" (cf. Comment IV), and it proceeds self-evidently from there that the "worship of angels" (2:18) is a worship which has angels as its object (cf. Notes). We must add that based on the use of the concepts "rulers and powers" in the Hymn (1:15–20) and also in 2:15 it must be assumed that the author of Col recognized the existence of "Gnostic archons" and thus also shared a Gnostic worldview. Aside from the fact that hypotheses are justified by other hypotheses here, such an interpretation of the statements in 1:15–20 and also in 2:15 can hardly be confirmed (cf. Notes and Comment II, 2 to 1:9–23).

E. Lohse also (pp. 186–91), like G. Bornkamm, interprets the "teaching of *philosophia*" from the vantage of the "elements of the world," which he equally understands as powers of angels. He also designates the teaching assailed in Col as Gnostic, or if one should judge more carefully, as pre-Gnostic, because of "the emphasis on perception as well as its characteristic of disavowing the world" peculiar to it (p. 189). Whether the powers are to be understood as representatives of the fullness of the deity, or as hostile powers, is not clear. In no case, however, is the identification of "elements of the world" made by H. M. Schenke with the archons of Gnosis applicable (p. 187, fn. 2). We can see here that E. Lohse uses the concept "Gnostic" in a much broader sense than does H. M. Schenke,[56] for example. In light of the fact, however, that in our opinion

56. For the problem of the definition of the concept "gnosis," see esp. K. Rudolph, " 'Gnosis' and 'Gnosticism'—The Problems of Their Definition and Their Relation to

not even a disavowing character of the false teaching can be proven with certainty (see above and the Notes to 1:20), it seems to us that a reference to gnosis is not very useful.

E. Lohse, differing from G. Bornkamm, does not stress the Jewish origin of the false teaching. Rather he remarks that even the Jews who settled in Asia Minor made a contribution to the syncretistic *philosophia* (p. 187, fn. 3). For the false teaching, as it is reconstructed by E. Lohse, the designation "gnosticized Judaism" is less applicable, and the characterization as "Judaized gnosis" more so.

Even for E. Schweizer,[57] the expression "elements of the world" is decisive and is a point of departure for his reconstruction of the false teaching. He, however, considers it necessary on the basis of philological findings to proceed from the view that the doctrine of the elements in antiquity which goes back to Empedocles, correspondingly even in Col means *stoicheia tou kosmou* "earth, water, air, fire (aether)" (cf. also Comment IV), and at any rate not spiritual beings. E. Schweizer points out that, since Empedocles, the viewpoint has predominated that man forced into the unspirited revolution of the elements is driven from one to another, and can flee from this predicament only through strict asceticism. We see this motif also in a Pythagorean text from the first century B.C.E.,[58] in which almost all the motifs of the false teaching described in Col 2 can be found. The text deals with the four elements of the world as the physical components of the world. The souls, which as part of the highest elements of the aether are immortal, would need to rise after their death from the lower elements to the highest ones. They would, however, be pushed back into the constantly revolving elements if they were not pure. In order to purify the soul, man would have to abstain from certain meats and other foods (such as eggs and beans)[59] and from sexual contact, as well as to subject himself to purification baths and to venerate the deities as well as the "demons." The latter were the unclean souls, of which the "air," the element between the lower and the upper realms, was full. These demons were identified by Philo as the so-called angels in the Bible.

There is no mention in this text of the rites of the mysteries which, according to E. Schweizer, were possibly alluded to in Col 2:18, and the feast days which

---

the Writings of the New Testament," in FS für A. H. B. Logan and A. J. M. Wedderburn, *The New Testament and Gnosis: Essays,* ed. R. McL. Wilson (Edinburgh: Clark, 1983), pp. 21–32.

57. E. Schweizer, *Background,* op. cit.; Schweizer, *Forschung,* op. cit.; Schweizer, *Elemente,* op. cit.; Schweizer, *Kol-Kommentar,* pp. 100–4.

58. "Alexander Polyhistor in Diogenes Laertius VIII," pp. 24ff.; in H. Diels, *Fragmente der Vorsokratiker, gr.-dt.,* ed. W. Kranz, vol. I, 17th ed., (unauthorized reprinting of the 6th ed. of 1951) (Berlin: Weidmann, 1974), pp. 448, 33ff.

59. The text of Alexander Polyhistor does not deal with abstinance from drink, but this is discussed in other Pythagorian texts (E. Schweizer, *Background,* op. cit., p. 254).

would have to be kept in the false teachings of Col, and whose listing in 2:16 would indicate Jewish origin, are not mentioned. Thus E. Schweizer comes to the conclusion that the movement in Colossae was possibly a kind of Pythagorean philosophy,[60] which was embellished by rituals of Hellenistic mystic religions and with Judaism.

This reconstruction, however, loses some credibility in that the "elements of the world" did not necessarily mean the common elements in antiquity of "earth, water, air, fire" and thus this term also does not necessarily refer to the "un-souled circulation of the elements" (cf. Comment IV).

3. The Opponents in the Epistle to the Colossians

As we attempted to establish in the Notes to 2:20, the opponents who are referred to in Col are not to be found within the community of Colossae. This community does not even seem to be in pressing danger. Rather, Paul is impressed by its steadfastness and faithfulness (1:4; 2:5). Still, Paul warns about actual persons of whom the Colossians must have knowledge. Only in this way are the abbreviated references in 2:16–23 explainable.[61] These people may possibly be found in the community of Hierapolis. The Colossians were surely informed about them and the situation there, since Epaphras dealt with both communities and was probably even its founder (cf. Notes to 1:7). If this supposition is correct, then we could also explain why the community of Hierapolis is mentioned in 4:13, but not in 2:29 and 4:16: the letter to the

---

60. E. Schweizer, *Background*, op. cit., pp. 251f., noticed the fact that three lists with *five* virtues or vices each are to be found in Col 3:5, 8, 12, and can be construed as a possible confirmation of his reconstruction, since the number five plays a significant role in Pythagorism. G. Bornkamm, *Häresie*, op. cit., p. 151, already suspected a connection with the "pentagon-schema familiar from the Iranian Gnostic speculations of the elements." This sequence of fives in chap. 3 could not be more than a *supplementary* confirmation of one of the references in chap. 2 which attempts to justify this connection in the history of religions.—H. Hegermann, *Schöpfungsmittler*, op. cit., p. 163, fn. 3, refers to Gal 5:20, where 5 + 7 + 3 elements of vices are listed, and to 1 Pet 4:3, where one quintuplet of complete vices is to be found, to which idol worship as Kephale is cited, as in Col 3:13f. the "love" to the five cited virtues is added. But foremost, G. Bornkamm did not take into consideration the introductory portions of the paragraph in the older Pauline paraenesis (see, for that, ibid., pp. 198f.).

61. M. D. Hooker, "Were There False Teachers in Colossae?" in FS for C. F. D. Moule: *Christ and Spirit in the New Testament*, ed. B. Lindars and S. S. Smalley (Cambridge: University Press, 1973), pp. 315–31, is correct in our opinion, when she works out that in Col there is no indication of a danger of apostasy. Her analysis seems problematic, however, namely that the admonishments of Paul in Col 2 were only of the general and fundamental kind, conditioned by the surroundings of the gentile Colossian community, in which the existence of powers (next to Christ) was perceived as fact.

Colossians with its laudatory words about its addressees was probably not applicable for the other community.

The warnings in chap. 2 are thus not rooted in a disquieting situation in the Colossian community. Rather, they serve solely as a far-reaching anticipatory precaution. That means, however, that the occasion for the letter is not in some sort of "Colossian false teaching" but rather to share in the glad tidings about the community that Epaphras conveyed. Even if the elaborations of 2:6–23 have indirectly influenced the remaining elucidations in the letter, still the greatest care must be taken to understand these simply as antitheses to a presumed teaching. If we wish to obtain an image of the persons about whom they are warned, we should proceed from the statements that make most direct reference to the persons, namely to vv 2:16–23. From this point of view, the summarizing evaluations in 2:4 + 8 also become comprehensible (see below).

The chief rebuke is raised in 2:19: Paul accuses the opponents of being concerned, not like the Messiah, with the well-being of the entire church, i.e., with their own community, but rather with shifting their preoccupation with their own piety into first place (cf. Notes). He therefore rejects any value in that piety, and thus unmasks their visions and their striving to revere God in connection with the worship seen in their visions, their humility and their austerity toward their own body, as a *sham of wisdom*.

Two things become clear from this manner of argumentation:

1. The opponents whom Paul is reproaching regard themselves as Christians, because only then is the reproach reasonable that they should subordinate their own piety *to the concern for the church*. Since the false teachers are not part of the addressees of this letter and since the Colossians also do not sympathize with them, the expression "sham of wisdom" can be understood to mean that the visions, the veneration by angels as a prototype of themselves, the humility and the austerity toward their own bodies, are not as such signs of heresy. It is presumed that all these are characteristics of a piety that is not sanctioned by Paul. It is, in our opinion, not justified to draw conclusions about asceticism, enmity of the world, veneration of archons, etc., based on these text-indications.

2. From the chief reproach of undercutting the unity of the church, we can also understand the viewpoint of the opponents of maintaining certain food and feast-day laws (cf. Notes to 2:16). They served to allow the opponents to differentiate between "chosen" and "nonchosen" and led to strife within the church about these ordinances, and necessarily to condemnations (2:14, 16, 18) and thus to divisions. The fact that the regulations of the opponents betray a Jewish-OT background does not necessarily signify that Paul is turning against Judeo-Christians. Since the question concerning the meaning and limitation of the OT law plays no part in this letter, we can only conclude that the opponents had emphasized their elitist consciousness by keeping individual OT ordinances,

which simultaneously gave them the possibility of appealing to "divine tradition."

Even in 2:8–14, the subject of overcoming exclusivity plays a central role. With an adapted citation from the Hymn in 1:15–20 that all the fullness of the divinity resides in the Messiah, elucidations are introduced that determine that this residing of the divinity serves the universal whole, which bonds Jews and gentiles.[62] Even the gentiles are members of the chosen people of Israel through the actions of God in the Messiah, so that even circumcision, such an important distinguishing characteristic between the chosen and the nonchosen, no longer has any significance in this function (cf. Comment II). The summarizing evaluation of his opponents in 2:8 (as well as also in 2:4), that they are orienting themselves toward the traditions of men and toward the elements of the world, becomes clear on this basis. Since the Messiah removes every basic differentiation between "chosen" and "nonchosen" and since he has thus removed the basis for every elitist and exclusionary aspiration, since even circumcision is no longer a mark of exclusivity, then especially food and feast-day commands cannot serve such an objective. If they are misused for this purpose anyway and as a basis for condemnations, then, in the opinion of Paul, a "power" is conferred upon them which enters into competition with the Messiah,[63] and veneration is given to them to which they are not entitled. Therefore Paul raises the objection that created things ("elements of the world") are venerated instead of the creator (cf. Comment IV); so he emphasizes that the Messiah is the Lord of every ruler and power. He thus states basically that nothing created can claim any "potency" in competition with the Messiah.

The complaint that the opponents are oriented toward the "tradition of people" is along the same line of reasoning. OT laws removed from their sense of purpose do not lead to obedience of God but are rather nothing but plain "tradition of people." Equally, the term *philosophia*, which is equivalent here to "religion" (cf. the Notes to 2:8), is to be attributed to Paul, who uses it in a polemical sense. His evaluation is so sharp that he accuses his opponents of having erected a new "religion" in conflict with the Jewish-Christian faith.

In conclusion, we can say that Paul is turning against persons in Col who are to be found outside the Colossian community, who perceive themselves as Christians, and who have an exclusive elitist self-concept to which they give expression through food and feast-day ordinances and which they attempt to

62. The statement "in him dwells the total fullness in corporal form" (2:9) is hardly the antithesis to the supposed conception of the false teachers that the fullness dwells in the powers and forces (see above to G. Bornkamm). Rather, it is aimed at the dismissal of the fact that the "dwelling of God in the Messiah" (that is, his action, see Notes to 2:9) is a "dwelling" for the salvation of all human beings, according to the statement in 1:20, for the salvation of all of creation.

63. Jesus already addressed his opposition to such a false belief, in the opinion of the Synoptics (Mark 7:15 par).

make obligatory for the church in general. They have borrowed these laws from the OT (the Bible of the early Christians) in order to thus lend authority to their views.

VI. A Hymn in Col 2?

After the expressly stated warning against a "deceitful religion" in 2:8, there ensues not the immediate concrete examples (2:16ff.), but rather a long, syntactically problematic sentence structure, which seems like an excursus and continues to v 15. According to E. Lohmeyer (pp. 99f.; 101f.; 114ff.), the paragraph 2:8–15 builds in "constant and well-gauged gradation" and can be separated into three paragraphs: (1) v 8, (2) vv 9–12, (3) vv 13–15. In its first part, it proceeds in normal prose. This format continues also into the beginning of the second part, but then elevates itself "to pathetically joined three-membered sentences." The beginning of the third part (v 13a) at first remains within the "rules of the present rhetoric," but then lifts itself (vv 13b–15) "as though to a further higher flight" and then forms itself into three-line strophes. Almost every line begins with a verb and almost each one is made up of three syllables, according to the requirements of Near Eastern Psalms. This is the reason for the "syntactic irregularity," so that the "you" here was replaced by the more-encompassing "us," which sharply delineates the beginning of the hymnic mode of speech.

Going beyond E. Lohmeyer, G. Schille[64] tried to reconstruct a "song of redemption" from 2:8–15. He interprets the conjunction *hoti* as *hoti recitativum*, which introduces a quotation (see Notes to 1:9), and he supports this analysis with the observation that the thread of v 8 is only taken up again in v 16. While the author addresses the reader directly in v 8 + 16ff., the statements in vv 8–15 are in part in a very impersonal third person singular style and in vv 13f the postulated quotation reverts to a confessional style. The differing variations of style used, which E. Lohmeyer already observed, lead G. Schille to suspect that a prior text was reworked more vigorously than usual. The criteria of hymn research up to now (we, participial, and relative clause style) do not help in reconstructing the original song: the "we" appears only in v 13, while the quotation begins as far back as v 9, and the relative and participial styles would miscarry as criteria in the fact "that they also occur in sentences with epistological address." Thus G. Schille attempts to discern "seams" at which annotation and original text divide in order to use these as a point of departure to work out interpretations of the author. He ends up with a "song of redemption," to which originally vv 9, 10b, 11b, 13b–15 are to have belonged (without the relative clause "which indicted us" in v 14):

---

64. G. Schille, *Frühchristliche Hymnen*, op. cit., pp. 31–37.

In him resides all the fullness of the deity bodily,
who is the head of all rule and power
    by the laying down of the human body,
who has released us from all the sins,
who cancelled the indictment against us with the
        paragraphs,
and he took them from the midst,
    nailed them to the cross,
removed the rulers and powers,
    put (them) on display in public
    led them in triumph to him (i.e. the cross).

This thesis of G. Schille of finding the beginning of a quoted hymn already in vv 9–12 cannot be substantiated.[65] Against this argument is chiefly that vv 9f. hardly introduce the wording of a "redemption song"—even though proclamations of the hymn in 1:15–20 are cited and commented upon. On the basis of his warnings of a false teaching, the author of Col then interprets a tradition, which also provides background for the statements in Rom 6:2–8 and originally contained statements about "death, burial, and resurrection with Christ." The expression in v 11 "through the laying down of the human body" belongs to this interpretation. The phrase "body of the flesh" was already used by the author in 1:22 (cf. Notes).

Since vv 9+10b are hardly, as G. Schille suspects, part of a "song of redemption," there is thus no reason to consider the expression "through the laying down of the human body" as part of such a song.

Even v 13a was originally hardly part of an original hymnic text. K. Wengst[66] suspected that: he restructures vv 13–15 after elimination of the additions of the author[67] into three lines (v 13/v 14/v 15). Each line contains a verb, in the first and third as a participle, in the middle one as a finite verb, to each of which belong one or two nominal determinants. The last two 3-line verses would formally dominate, while the participle in the first line does not describe the action of the subject, but rather serves as the closer determinant of the object. This piece was supposedly part of a baptism liturgy, spoken by the baptized

65. Compare, among others, R. Deichgräber, *Gotteshymnus*, op. cit., p. 167; E. Lohse, "Ein hymnisches Bekenntnis in Kolosser 2,13c–15," in *Die Einheit des Neuen Testaments. Exegetische Studien zur Theologie des Neuen Testaments* (Göttingen: Vandenhoeck & Ruprecht, 1973), pp. 276–84:277; K. Wengst, *Formeln*, op. cit., pp. 186f.; C. Burger, *Schöpfung*, op. cit., p. 81.

66. K. Wengst, *Formeln*, op. cit.

67. "through the uncircumcision of your flesh" (v 13); "through ordinances," "which was against us" (v 14). Besides that, the editor of the letter changed the original "we" to a "you" from the original traditional piece (at the beginning of v 13).

person after the baptism. That would explain the insertion of "and" in v 13, because preceding would be the (not cited) address of the baptizer.

Now, however, we find the same construction in 2:13a, "and you who were (previously) . . . ," in 1:21. Here it refers back to the author and directs the statements of the hymn back to the recipients of the letter. Therefore, in our opinion, it is hardly convincing to identify v 13a as the beginning of a baptismal song.[68]

Do we now have a hymnic pre-text for vv 13a–15? Such a supposition, according to E. Lohse,[69] gains "much credibility through the investigation of the language and style of the paragraph": in v 13b, in contrast to v 13a, the "we" of the confessing community is speaking. The accumulation of participles points to coined expressions. The noticeably high number of otherwise uncommon words and expressions supports the presumption. And the speech of forgiveness of sins corresponds to the early Christian theology of community, not however to the Pauline concept of sin, since "sin" represents a cosmic rule which entered the world with the deed of Adam and which has held all men in its power since then. In this "hymnic confession fragment," the relative clause "which indicted us" (v 14) is to be regarded as an interpretation, which, however, was already in the original source of the author of the Colossian epistle, and was given a new accentuation by the short relative clause introduced by the words "in dogmas."[70]

Whether the "we" in v 13b refers to the confessing community is uncertain (cf. Notes). Relative and participial elements of style are a very uncertain basis in Col for determining an original hymnic source, since they pertain to the stylistic devices of the epistle in general. Thus W. Bujard sees in 2:6–15 typical examples of the style of the author of Colossians.[71] In his opinion, a "certain

---

68. Compare also J. Lähnemann, *Kolosserbrief*, op. cit., p. 126.—E. Lohse, "Bekenntnis," op. cit., p. 279, criticized K. Wengst's attempt at a solution, that the "we" would need to be changed to "you" in order to fit the style of a confessional for the beginning of v 13. The first line also falls outside its framework since it does not describe the action of the subject.—But absolute parallelism as criterion for a hymn is problematic (see Comment II, 1 to 1:9–23). And when E. Lohse himself assumes an actualizing of the statements by the editor of a hymnic *Vorlage* in 2:14 (see below), then why should that not also occur in v 13a through a change in the personal pronoun.

69. E. Lohse, "Bekenntnis," op. cit.

70. Like E. Lohse, R. P. Martin, "Reconciliation and Forgiveness in Colossians," in FS für L. L. Morris, *Reconciliation and Hope: New Testament Essays on Atonement and Eschatology*, ed. R. Banks (Exeter: Paternoster, 1974), pp. 104–24 (American ed.: Grand Rapids, Mich., Eerdmans, 1974), also sees a hymnic *Vorlage*, only he lets its citation begin with 14. C. Burger, *Schöpfung*, pp. 79–114, also thinks that a hymnic fragment is at the basis of vv 14 + 15. But in his opinion, all this is much more rigorously worked out than, for example, E. Lohse assumes (see p. 104–8).

71. W. Bujard, *Stilanalytische Untersuchungen*, op. cit., pp. 74–76, 79–86. See also pp. 49, 63, and also pp. 148, 151, 154, 156. Comp. also E. Percy, PKE, 182.

influence of traditional speech-elements" is to be suspected in 2:9–15, but the passage 2:9–20 (as also 1:9–14, 21–23) is clearly to be viewed as fashioned in the style of the author of the Colossian epistle.[72] In general, participial and relative expressions cannot in themselves be viewed as liturgical or hymnic or stylized, but rather only in a certain manner and with a certain content.[73]

Rare words and the adoption of expressions of early Christian community theology alone are not sufficient to permit the conclusion that here we have an older hymnic text.

Yet a further observation argues against this thesis of a hymn fragment[74] as an underlying source of vv 2:13b–15. In such a fragment, the statement "which indicted us with legal demands" would be an interpretation. For it explains the expression "a bill of indictment against us" with a clause (*dogmata*, regulations) that refers to false teaching (cf. 2:20). Then, however, we would have to assume that the author of Col had interpreted the figure of speech of "bill of indictment," which had defined man's degeneration into sin *before* God in the original hymn, in such a way that the transgression before God is measured in the dogma of the false teachers and would then also have to be erased by Christ on the cross. This idea is difficult to carry into effect and is highly improbable (cf. also the Notes to 1:14).

Aside from the Hymn in 1:15–20, if a hymnic pre-text could have been used as a source in 2:9–15, then this would most likely have to be found in 2:13b–15. Yet even for these verses, the thesis of a literally cited hymn fragment is hardly defensible.[75]

V. EXHORTATIONS (3:1–4:6)

1. The Old and the New Self (3:1–17)

3:1 Since you have thus now arisen with the Messiah, seek that which is on high, where the Messiah is, sitting at the right hand of God. 2 Orient yourselves

---

72. Ibid., p. 227. He thinks the thesis is wrong in general, that the first two chapters of Col are imprinted by a liturgic hymnic style, and that the remainder must be conditioned by the polemic goal of the epistle (p. 228, comp. 119f.).

73. Ibid., p. 228. W. Bujard's investigations emphasize R. Deichgräber's facet (*Gotteshymnus*, op. cit., pp. 168f.), that certain proof for a hymnic basis seems impossible.

74. We could only be dealing with this, because a reconstructed hymnic portion would remain "a very fragmented text, which we could in no way address as a unified hymn" in any case (R. Deichgräber, op. cit., p. 167).

75. J. C. O'Neil, *Christology*, op. cit., pp. 95–99, assumes that in Col 2:9–15, traditional material was cited, but that it was not a connected traditional piece, ". . . it seems to me most likely that the author of the epistle has put together a number of

also toward that which is on high, not toward that which is on earth. 3 For you have died, and your life is hidden with the Messiah in God. 4 When the Messiah, your life, is revealed, then you will also be revealed with him in glory.

5 Now put to death the members that are on the earth: fornication, impurity, passion, evil desire, and always wanting to have more, which is idolatry. 6 Through these the wrath of God comes upon the sons of disobedience. 7 You also walked in these (vices) formerly, when you lived in them. 8 But now you also cast off all this: wrath, anger, malice, slander, abusive language from your mouth. 9 Do not lie to one another. It is self-evident for you that you have taken off the old self with its practices 10 and have put on the new (self) which is constantly renewed in knowledge according to the image of the him who has created him. 11 Where we no longer have Greek and Jew, circumcised and uncircumcised, barbarian, Scythian, slave, free person—rather all things and in all (things is) the Messiah. 12 Now put on, as the chosen ones of God, as holy and beloved ones: a heart full of compassion, kindness, humility, meekness, patience. 13 It is fitting for you to bear one another and to forgive one another if someone has a complaint against someone else. As the Lord has also forgiven you, so also you (forgive one another). 14 Beyond all (this), put on love, that is the band of completeness. 15 And let the peace of the Messiah rule in your hearts, for which you also are called in one body. And become thankful: 16 Let the word of the Messiah dwell among you in its (rich-making) richness. For you it is (then only) reasonable to teach each other in all wisdom, and to exhort with psalms, hymns, and songs produced by the spirit, (and) to sing to God from the heart (standing) in grace. 17 And concerning everything, whatever you do in word or deed, (do) everything in the name of the Lord Jesus. Thank God, the Father, through him.

NOTES

The structural similarity of the beginning of verse 2:20 ("when you have died with Christ") and 3:1 ("when you now have arisen with Christ"), as well as the seeming contextual cohesion of these statements, could give occasion to suggest that 3:1–4 still belongs to the previous passage, to a confrontation with the false teaching. Yet we begin a new section here with 3:1. "You have died with Christ" (2:20) refers back to the statements in 2:11ff. in order to employ them as an argument against the concepts of the false teachers. "You have arisen with Christ" (3:1) contextually belongs to 3:3 ("for you have died"), so that the two sections are not linked to one another. The statements in 3:1–4 go

---

extracts from the sacred literature of the community to which he belonged, . . ." (95). Thus he perceives vv 9–15 as seven independent citations (p. 96). But he also names the difficulties tied to his thesis: the evidence for the traditions from which was cited, in his opinion, is lacking (p. 99).

beyond the subject of false teaching. Central statements of the first two chapters are significantly summarized here, in order then to build up the subsequent reminders, the paraenesis, in 3:5: the significance of the Messiah for the addressees of the epistle (2:11–13/:1a–3a); the dominion of the Messiah as creator over all creation (1:15–20/3:1b–2); the certain preservation of hope (1:5/ 3b + 4) (cf. also J. Lähnemann, *Colossian Epistle*, pp. 30f.).

The individual exhortations (3:5–4:6) are subdivided into three parts. In a first part, 3:5–17, a life not suitable to the chosen ones is described by way of two so-called categories of iniquities (3:5–8), and the rejection of these is summarized in vv 9f. with the challenge to "take off the old self" and "to put on the new one." In v 11, the sense and purpose of this putting-on are subsequently determined, so that the two verses 10 + 11 can be viewed as the contextual center of the entire paraenesis. Vv 12–17 then explicate by way of a "catalog of virtues" (analogously to the catalogs in 3:5–8) and by further admonishments, what is understood by "putting on of the new self." 3:16 + 17 summarize the previous statement and simultaneously serve as the heading of the second part of the exhortations, which is carried out in the form of a so-called *"Haustafel"* (3:18–4:1). This connection is then made clear through the oft-repeated substantive "Lord" (3:18, 20, 22, 23, 24 [2 ×]; 4:1), which refers back to 3:17 ("do everything in the name of the *Lord* Jesus"). In the conclusion, in 4:2–6, there is an appeal to intercession and thanks, especially for the missionary work of Paul and his co-workers. Attached to this, the paraenesis is concluded by some invitations specific to the mission charge of the recipients of Col.

3:1 *Since you have thus now arisen with the Messiah.* This conditional clause presumes a factual reality, as does 2:20. The premise, which *establishes* the subsequent imperative, is better expressed if the conjunction *ei* is translated by "since" rather than by "when." The particle *oun* (also, consequently)[1] indicates that reference is made to familiar things that have already been said: e.g., to the details in 2:12f. concerning the resurrection. As we attempted to demonstrate in Comment II to 2:6–23, Paul did not mean a resurrection that occurred in baptism. Therefore 3:1ff. does not determine any ethical consequences from baptism,[2] but rather determines these through the death

---

1. W. Nauck, "Das *oun*-paräneticum," ZNW 49 (1958) 134–35, points out that an *oun* frequently connects a systematic theological debate with a subsequent paraenetic exhortation, in which the consequences are demonstrated from theological considerations. This *oun* paraeneticum allows us to clearly recognize the character of the early Christian ethic, "Sie ist weder eine autonome, noch eine finale, sondern eine konsekutive Ethik; eine Ethik, die aus dem gnädigen Handeln Gottes die Folgerung im Vollzug der Lebensführung zieht. Christliche Ethik ist Ethik der Dankbarkeit" (p. 135).

2. Compare among others, J. B. Lightfoot, p. 274; J. Gnilka, p. 171; R. P. Martin, p. 101. See for that also R. Schnackenburg, *Taufe*, op. cit., p. 68, who points out that

(and the resurrection) of the Messiah and thus the participation of non-Jews in the heritage of Israel.

seek that which is on high. Zēteō (to seek, to strive for) is a technical term in secular Greek for philosophical inquiry. In the NT, the usage of this verb in 1 Cor 1:22 is reminiscent of the language here. However, the intent in this passage is illustrated well by Matt 6:31–33: *zēteō* specifies the idea that life has inherently determining and imprinted concerns which are usually represented as concerns about the elementary necessities such as nourishment and clothing, but after the sacrifice of Jesus these concerns are to be oriented toward the "kingdom of God."[3]

"On high" *(anō)* corresponds to the term "heaven," which is used in 1:5, and is not a geographic spatial category here. As opposed to a Gnostic system, for example, where an "upper World" and a "lower world" are differentiated, "so that a manifoldly divided whole is developed, whose highest pinnacle is God and whose lowest step is matter,"[4] Col hardly represents such a "dual world doctrine." There is no accommodation for the longing of the so-called "Hellenistic Man" who does not know the concept of a continuous, goal-oriented history, but who rather thinks cyclically, and who hopes for participation in an upper, heavenly world and for emancipation from the evil, earthly world and its demonic forces.[5] According to the statements of 1:12–20, the material world is reconciled, and the Messiah has begun his dominion over it! (Cf. Comment II.3 to 1:9–23.) What is to be proclaimed by this "on high" is elucidated more closely in this verse: "on high" is where the Messiah is sitting on the right hand of God. We are not dealing with flight from the world as the determining moment in the life of the Colossians, but rather with the Messiah who is enthroned as king over all creation and thus over *this world*, and who is to determine the life of the Christians in Colossae. The apparently spatial categories are not conditioned by alleged Hellenistic ideas, but rather by Jewish-Messianic conceptualizations.

"On high" in this connection is, on the one hand, a description of the idea that the Messiah has not yet been revealed before the eyes of *everyone* as ruler over all things. That can be concluded from v 3, according to which the "on

---

Paul does not visualize the symbolism of death and resurrection here in the baptismal rite, since death is named after resurrection.

3. This usage of the word goes back to a usage in the LXX. There, the verb can mean "ask, consult God" (comp. Deut 4:29; 2 Sam 21:1; 1 Chr 10:14 and others), as also "let one's actions be entirely determined by God," "rely totally on him," (comp., among others, Ps 23⟨24⟩:6; 26⟨27⟩:8; Isa 31:1).

4. F. Büchsel, ThWNT I, p. 377.

5. For this worldview, comp. E. Schweizer, *Erniedrigung und Erhöhung bei Jesus und seinen Nachfolgern*, AThANT 28 (Zürich: Zwingli Verlag, 1962), 145–55. For such an interpretation of the declarations in Col, see esp. E. Grässer, "Col 3:1–4," op. cit., Comment III to 1:3–8 go into more detail concerning his exposition.

high" is the "location" of concealment from the revelation of the Messiah and his people in resplendence.[6] On the other hand, the concept designates the "point of departure" of the reign of the Messiah over all creation (of which heaven itself is also a part), and further it is also a point of departure for the revelation of this reign in splendor at the end of time. We accept H. Traub's comments regarding the expression "God in heaven": "We will have to look for the meaning of this expression in the direction that heaven is the point of departure of God's act of salvation" (ThWNT V, 520, 3f.). God as the God of heaven rules the earth from heaven and thus, according to H. Traub, we have a precedent for the expression of absolute dominion. "Accordingly, heaven does not mean an inactive place-designation, but rather a dynamic designation for a point of departure" (ThWNT V, 520, 32f.).

Why, however, does it not say, "Seek him who is on high," but rather impersonally, "that which is on high"? An explanation for this may lie in the fact that within the context, the focus in 3:12ff. is on the listed "virtues." Possibly the formulation has deeper significance. Col 1:18 and also 3:1 allow the probability that, for the author of Col, resurrection and elevation/enthroning of the Messiah are a single occurrence: thus Easter and ascent to heaven, differently than in Acts 1:1ff. Then it would be stated that the Colossians, if they have also arisen *with* the Messiah, are also participants in his "sitting at the right hand of God." In Eph 2:6, this idea is clearly expressed (cf. also Matt 19:27ff.). To seek after that which is on high means, then, to be allowed to rule with the Messiah, in correspondence with his worthiness, to live his life, to conduct oneself as a "co-regent." This idea is further developed in vv 5ff., where the concept "to reign" is elaborated anew through the statements of a general prior understanding.

where the Messiah is, sitting at the right hand of God. "On high" is defined more closely with words from a royal psalm, Ps 110. There is probably no *conjugatio periphrastica* here ("is sitting"). It seems to us more sensible to read the participle "sitting" as an emphatic separate verbal noun. In this way, the

---

6. Comp. also Phil 3:20, "Our commonwealth is in heaven, and from it we await a savior, the Lord Jesus Christ."—This imagery does not need to be connected with a Platonic worldview, for it can already be found in Gen 11:5; Ex 19:20; Ps 14:2; 115:3; Isa 57:15; Ezek 1:26, among others. In the NT, comp. esp. John 3:3, 7, 13, 31; 6:62; 8:23; 19:11; 20:17; Acts 2:34; 10:4; Rom 10:6; Gal 4:26; Eph 4:8–10; Phil 3:14; Jas 1:17; 3:15,17; Rev 11:12; see also C. F. D. Moule, " 'The New Life' in Colossians 3:1–17," RExp 70 (1973) 481–93:485.—For the exposition, see also F. Zeilinger, ESpg, 60–63; 147–51, "That 'up above' can thus not be set apart locationally from the 'earth,' since it encompasses also the Christian existence on earth. We are thus dealing with a *qualitative* concept that does not enclose any locational connection within itself. *Ta anō* thus represents a cipher or code which circumscribes the encompassing reality of the heaven and earth of the new aeon" (p. 149).—Comp. also F. Wulf, " 'Suchet, was droben ist, wo Christus ist, sitzend zur Rechten Gottes!' (KolB 3,1)," GuL 41 (1968) 161–64.

emphasis is on the invitation in Ps 110:1 ("Sit at my right hand"), which is perhaps a component of the ritual of the ascent to the throne of the Israelite kings. Subsequently, the Messiah is enthroned and he reigns.[7]

2 *Orient yourselves also toward that which is on high.* The invitation of the previous verse is repeated in order then to counter with an antithesis (cf. also Phil 3:19f.). The verb *zēteō* used in v 1 is replaced by *phroneō*. It hardly applies that these words should be interpreted differently, that *zēteō* should refer to the will and *phroneō* to the intellect (cf. J. Gnilka, p. 173). Rom 8:5ff. confirms such a differentiation, where the orientation that *"phronein* after the spirit," in contrast to *"phronein* after the flesh" has the same meaning of "being subject to the law of God."[8] A translation which gives the impression that *phroneō* means a formal intellectual activity ("to think, to mean, to plan, to ponder, to judge"), an intellectual facility ("to comprehend"), or an inner orientation ("to be of the opinion")[9] neglects the practical relationship that stands here in the foreground at the beginning of the paraenetic part of Col. It is well accounted for if we translate *phroneō* with "orient yourselves toward" on the basis of a suggestion by D. Sölles regarding Phil 2:5.[10]

not toward that which is on earth. Earthly creation is not in itself evaluated negatively, only its possible function as a life-determining power that appears in competition with the creator. This expression corresponds to an evaluation that is designated by the phrase "elements of the world" (2:8, 20). Cf. Comment IV to 2:6–23.

3 *For you have died.* The ethical challenge becomes even more urgent in the sense that vv 3 + 4 explicitly list as distinct reasons that which is implicit in the determination "you have arisen" (v 1). The Colossians are addressed and Paul does not include himself in the statements. In this way, he forms a connecting link with the reference to "dying" and to "living" in the statements in 2:11 + 13: he addresses the acceptance of the non-Jewish Colossians into the covenant of God with Israel and the participation in the forgiveness of sins (cf. Comment II to 2:6–23).

and your life is hidden with the Messiah in God. This life is connected "with

---

7. For the usage of Ps 110 in early Christianity, see esp. W. R. G. Loader, "Christ at the Right Hand: Ps CX.1 in the New Testament," NTS 24 (1977/78) 199–217, and D. M. Hay, *Glory at the Right Hand: Psalm 110 in Early Christianity,* SBL.MS 18 (Nashville and New York: Abingdon, 1973).

8. *Phroneo* occurs twenty-six times in the NT, twenty-three times of these in Paul (incl. Col). For the exegesis and the different usages, see D. Bertram, ThWNT IX, pp. 216–31.

9. There are also reference points for this meaning in the NT. Comp., for example: Matt 16:23 (comprehend); Acts 28:22 (mean); Rom 12:3; Phil 1:7 (judge).

10. D. Sölle, "Gottes Selbstentäusserung. Eine Meditation zu Phil 2:5–11," in *Atheistisch an Gott glauben. Beiträge zur Theologie* (Olten und Freiburg i.B.: Walter, 1968), pp. 9–25.

the Messiah" *(syn christō)*[11] in every respect, because he himself is this life (cf. v 4). Different from the expression *syn christō* is *en tō theō* (in God), which occurs rarely in Paul. It occurs in Rom 5:11 (literally: "we praise ourselves *in God*"), but the preposition *en* (in) indicates the object of *kauchaomai* (to praise oneself, to boast) by the verb, for which one is praising oneself,[12] so that there is no parallel here. Just as in Col, *en tō theō* is also used in Eph 3:9 together with the passive "to be buried," but there we find the composite *apo-kryptō,* instead of the simplex.[13] In both places, the preposition *en* might be interpreted as an instrumental (cf. BDR 219, 1). In the NT, the use of the bare *dativus instrumentalis* is common. It reflects the Hebrew practice in which the preposition *bĕ* (in) is used, which is reflected in Greek *en.* Besides that, in Eph 3:9 as well as also in Col 3:3, the possible interpretation that "living" or specifically the "secret" is hidden from God is out of the question. Paul surely was not limited to such a viewpoint, represented in the second century by *Marcion,*[14] yet the possible misinterpretations arising from use of the bare dative may have persuaded him to use *en.* The preposition is probably used in this manner in Col 1:16 (where there is an added component) as also in 2:7. If *en tō theō* means "through God," it emphasizes (as does 1:26f. already) that concealment and revelation lie within the realm of God alone. This also states implicitly what a local interpretation of this expression would state. Such an interpretation would connect with 1:5 and would assure the Colossians that their life, even when it is still concealed, is still securely preserved, namely in God. Possibly the author of the letter had in mind, in case he used the local *en,* that the location of concealment is God, because he is the one "who is not seen" (cf. 1:15). The evidence is insufficient to make a decision in favor of one of these explanations in preference to the others.

4 *When the Messiah, your life, is revealed, then you will also be revealed with him in glory.* This last statement of the four verses, which begins with the introduction in 3:1, is asyndetic, without a connecting link to the previous statement. What meaning to assign to this verse depends on how we evaluate the so-called "futuristic eschatology" that is given expression in this verse within the context of the Colossian epistle (cf. Comment I).

---

11. For the expression *syn Christō,* see Notes to 1:13, esp. fn. 100.

12. See Rom 2:23; 5:3 (comp. 5:2); 1 Cor 1:31; and others. In Heb, *b·* (in) is the corresponding preposition and has the same function (i.e., Jer 9:22f.).

13. Comp. also 1 + 2 Thess 1:1, where the formula is used, however without the article and with the addition "(our) father" and continuation "and the Lord Jesus Christ."—For its significance in the address of the epistle, see Comment III to 1:1 + 2.—Comp. also 1 Thess 2:2, "we had courage *in our God* to declare. . . ."

14. He represented a doctrine of dual divinities, in which a lower, "lesser" God, who was proclaimed by Moses and the prophets, would be set opposite a high God, who was only revealed through Christ. This lower God was supposedly meant in Eph 3:9 (see Tertullian, Marc V, 18 ⟨CSEL 47, 638ff.⟩).

With almost the same words as here (*krypto* and *phaneroō*), the words in 1:26f. (*apokryptō* and *phaneroō*) announce that the previously long-*hidden* secret is now finally *revealed*. There the secret was identified with the Messiah, here with "your life," which is also equated with the Messiah. It is not likely that in this verse, the statements from 1:26f. are being circumscribed and the fragmentation and incompleteness of the revelation are being emphasized. We could refer to 1 Cor 13:12 ("now I know in part . . ."), but an explication in such a sense could only be reconciled with difficulty with 1:27, where the "wonderful richness" of the revealed secret is praised. In 3:4 we also are not dealing with a basic concealment as in 1:26f. The futuristic being—revealed in the Messiah in *splendor*—which is addressed here and which simultaneously signifies the glorification of his own, can only mean his stated arrival at the end of time, his parousia.[15] As also in 1 Thess 4:14, 17; 5:10 (cf. Rom 6:8; 2 Cor 4:14), this occurrence is characterized by the words "with Christ" (*syn christō*). Paul, however, does not use the term *phaneroomai* (to be revealed) otherwise for this concept[16]; we do find it in this sense in 1 John 2:28; 3:2; and 1 Pet 5:4. In addition to the correspondence in diction with 1 John 3:2, a contextual similarity is also noticeable. According to E. Lohmeyer (p. 134), Paul hardly came as close anywhere else to the Johannine Eschatology as he did in this verse to express the idea that finds all significance of the eschatological day in the revelation of the world.[17] But even Pauline parallels can also be listed. In Rom 8:18ff., reference is made to future splendor, as it is in Col. It is juxtaposed with the present time, which is characterized as the time of suffering. Also in Rom, the "already of salvation" (8:24) is emphasized, and Paul simultaneously points

---

15. *Doxa*, here translated as "glorification," means in extra-biblical Greek, "opinion," "reputation" (that is, the validity of opinion). In the LXX and also in the NT, these meanings are almost entirely suppressed. The content of *doxa* is coined from the Heb *kābod*, this in relation to the human being, and it is something "that makes him esteemed." The concept is used in reference to God "for a determination of the essence of God, for his striking or spectacular aspects" (G. von Rad, ThWNT II, pp. 241–45). M. Barth (AB 34A, p. 681) remarks, "What used to denote a possibly deceptive impression or opinion, was transformed to designate the 'weighty,' awe-inspiring, irresistible appearance of God in clouds of storm or in radiant light, and his self-manifestation in mighty and wonderful acts by which he proved himself the savior of men . . . just as the brilliant sky around the sun reveals the presence and power of the sun, radiates light, creates brightness, and invites admiration, so the glory of God creates glorification and calls for it."

16. For this, he uses the concept *parousia* (which, however, is not a terminus technicus for this event): comp. 1 Cor 1:8; 15:23; 1 Thess 2:19; 3:13; 4:15; 5:23; 2 Thess 2:1,8.

17. We need to observe, however, that according to 1 John 3:2, a new *essence* is also expected, "It is not yet revealed what we will be (not: are!, H.B.) . . . , when it is revealed, we will be like him."

out that this salvation *is not yet seen* because "we are saved upon hope" and we therefore wait for the fulfillment of this hope with patience. With all the similarities of these ideas to those of the Colossian epistle, we need, however, to ask whether the valuation of "this time" is the same in Col and in Rom. Expressed differently, can we claim, based on the background of the strong emphasis on salvation that has already occurred that the author of the Colossian epistle understood himself in the same way as did the author of the Roman epistle, as someone who in the face of "the sighing and the being frightened on the part of creation along with us up to this moment" waits with patience for the parousia (8:25). An attempt at an answer to this question is in Comment I.

The declaration that the Messiah is "our life" cannot be found in a similar formulation in Paul. Very close to this, however, is Phil 1:21 ("for Christ is my life"), where, however, not the substantive "life" (zōē), but the substantiated verb form *to zen* is chosen. The contextually corresponding passage is Gal 2:20, "Not that I live, but rather Christ lives in me."[18]

As can be observed more frequently in Col (cf. 1:7, 12; 2:13; 4:8), the textual transmission of the personal pronoun is uncertain. Very well attested is "your"—among others by Papyrus 46 (about 200), the Codices Sinaiticus (fourth century), Ephraemi Rescriptus (fifth century), Claromontanus (sixth century), and the minuscules 33 and 1881. In favor of the pronoun "our" we have the reading of the Codex Vaticanus (fourth century), the most significant of all the majuscules. We could interpret the version of "your" as an assimilation to the form of the personal pronoun in its immediate context, while we could consider the "our" suspect as a contextual correction, since it was not sensible to the scribe why Paul would exclude himself. On the basis of exterior attestation, we would probably prefer the reading "your." If "our" were original, however, then a shift in emphasis would occur, which, however, would introduce no new ideas into Col: the change of person ("our life—you also") would, as already in 1:12 and 2:13, emphasize that the concern is with participation of non-Jews ("you") in the heritage of Jews ("our").

5 *Now put to death the members*. For the particle *oun* (now, thus) cf. previous Notes.

In Rom 8:13, Paul writes, "For if you *kill* the deeds of the flesh through the spirit, then you will live." There, as here, the imagery of killing is used, and thus the previously expressed idea of "being dead with Christ" is continued. The previous participation in the death of the Messiah is recalled to succession and needs to be manifested in life. The difference in the words used—in Rom *apothnēskō*, in Col *nekroō*—has no contextual significance. Differently from Rom 8, however, Col 3:5 does not employ the concept "deeds." Rather, the invitation is to the killing of "limbs, members." It is not explicitly stated to which body they belong.

---

18. Comp. also Rom 8:2, 10; 2 Cor 4:10; and John 11:25; 14:6.

E. Käsemann ties a Gnostic mythos of the "cosmic anthropoi" with this concept. The limbs, which are described as vices, would belong to the "old human being," whose body was formed from the elements, specifically by the rulers and powers.[19] But this interpretation is hardly applicable because of the late dating of sources that need to be used. C. Masson[20] read *melē* (limbs) as a vocative. According to him, the recipients of the letter are addressed as "limbs" of the body of Christ, thus of the church. But the indispensable reference to the "body of Christ: the church" is lacking in the immediate context to support such an interpretation.

Codex Alexandrinus (fifth century), in addition to other less important manuscripts, reads the personal pronoun "your (limbs)." This variant reading is hardly original because the better manuscripts do not support it, but contra to E. Käsemann and C. Masson, it probably points in the right direction for a correct interpretation. Intended are the "limbs" of the recipients of the letter.

The fact that "limbs, members" are discussed in reminiscent of rabbinic declarations, according to which the number of commandments in the Torah corresponds to the 248 members of humans that are tools either of "evil or good desires."[21] Paul also knew this concept and understood limbs as tools (cf. Rom 6:13, 19; 7:5, 23; cf. Jas 4:1); yet the identification of members with evil deeds, as it is taken up in Col 3:5, is noticeable. The statement in Matt 5:29f. comes closest to it. There, the invitation is, among others, to tear out the eye, should the latter lead to downfall. The allusion is to lustful looking at a woman, which is adultery. The author of Matt is not thinking of self-mutilation (cf. 15:19), so that the member of the body stands in place of the evil deed. That which is given concreteness and is elucidated by examples in Matt 5 is formulated much

---

19. E. Käsemann, *Leib und Leib Cristi. Eine Untersuchung zur paulinischen Begrifflichkeit*, BHTh 9 (Tübingen: Mohr, 1933), esp. pp. 137–59. The "Christus Eikon" stands opposite this " 'old man' and his elements"; "As eikon, the Christ is the Urmensch and Redeemer, who was created before all and yet contains the essence of all beings. As redeemed, he is the 'first-born from the dead,' as redeemer, the 'head of the body.' As 'redeemed redeemer,' however, he is the aeon which encompasses all fullness" (p. 149). The body of the "old man" was a demonic walled boundary which forms the basis of the Gnostic mythos, which held the souls captive without escape from the domain of darkness. According to the Deutero-Pauline doctrine, Christ stripped away the unity of the mantle of the body from the powers and forces on the cross, and thus made possible the ascent to heaven for his adherents. Whatever the cross is for the Urmensch-Redeemer, the same is baptism for the believer.

20. *L'epitre de Saint Paul aux Colossiens. Commentaire du Nouveau Testament*, (Neuchatel/Paris: Delachaux & Niestle, 1950), p. 142.

21. See St.-B., I, p. 901(d); p. 472(b). Further references in E. Schweizer, "Die Sünde in den Gliedern," in FS für O. Michel zum 60. Geburtstag: *Abraham unser Vater. Juden und Christen im Gespräch über die Bibel*, ed. O. Betz, M. Hengel, P. Schmidt, AGSU 5 (Leiden: Brill, 1963), pp. 437–39.

more generally in Col 3, and here we proceed silently from the figurative concept to the explanation of the image.[22]

that are on the earth. This more specific elucidation can be derived from 3:2 and characterizes the "vices" listed subsequently. They are characteristic of a striving that is not oriented toward the Messiah.

If we, however, interpret "on high" and "on the earth" not based on OT Judaic thinking, as E. Schweizer has done (cf. Notes to v 2), but if we rather presume a Platonic Pythagorean worldview, in which the cosmic sense of "on the earth" is contrasted with a world "above," the question arises how the *cosmic ordering* of members or limbs should be explained. E. Schweizer solves this problem by referring to the ideas of Philo, who places the elements of the cosmos on a par with the members of the human body, along with their virtues or vices. Presumed as a basis is the Greek conceptualization of cosmos as a large human body and of the individual human being as a small cosmos, in which human reason within the body corresponds to the deistic logos within the cosmos. Just as the deistic logos as the medium of creation has formulated the five elements as a world, so also does the soul give life to the body, and reason and will give rise to the virtues in a wise person. In this, the virtues, which the logos attracts, are exactly parallel to the parts ("members, limbs") of the world-all or the human body. Wherever the thought pattern was platonic and pythagorean, as it was at the time of Col, the earthly world in a large sense, and the human body in a small sense, became a hindrance which took the deistic logos captive. Therefore, in place of the virtues, in whose rationale or will the wise one lived, the vices took hold, which tempted him/her and threatened him/her. In the view of the Colossians, according to which the soul of the elements has left the world and must press "upwards,"[23] the idea was close to a new individualistically understood separation of the body and its members, and thus its vices, which would retain it upon the earth, although some particulars still remained open.

fornication, impurity, passion, evil desire, and always wanting to have more, which is idolatry. Such listings[24] are called "catalogs of vices" (or "catalogs of virtues") in NT research.

---

22. The supposition that the background in the history of religions (of which the author was unaware) would form Iranian ideas (comp. E. Lohse, p. 198f.) is hardly applicable.

23. See for this the remarks for the exposition of E. Schweizer in Comment V.2 to 2:6–23.

24. Comp. Matt 15:19; Mark 7:21f.; Rom 1:29–31; 1 Cor 6:9–10; Gal 5:19–21; Eph 4:31; 5:3–5; 1 Tim 1:9–10; 6:4–5; 2 Tim 3:2–4; Titus 1:7; 1 Pet 4:3; Rev 21:8; 22:15.—2 Cor 6:6–7; Gal 5:22–23; Eph 6:14–17; Phil 4:8; 1 Tim 3:2–3; 6:11; Titus 1:7–8; Jas 3:17; 2 Pet 1:5–8.—The quintuplet of components in the three catalogs in Col 3 is noticeable. It is, however, not sufficient for retroverted conclusions toward a certain religio-historical background. For that, see Comment V.2 to Col 2:6–23, fn. 60, and E. Schweizer,

We encounter two "catalogs of vices" and one "catalog of virtues" in Col 3 (v 5; v 8; v 12). Similar catalogs also occur in extra-biblical texts as, for example, in Stoic writings,[25] or in the writings of Qumran. B. J. Eastons refers the NT catalogs back to Stoic origins.[26] S. Wibbing contradicts such an explanation. By comparing NT catalogs with a comprehensive catalog of vices in the Qumran writings (in 1 QS IV), he comes to the conclusion that the NT catalogs go back to a late Judaic tradition. The correctness of this conclusion as opposed to all other comparisons until now with historic religious parallels of such catalogs of vices is especially assured in that more than twenty elements are placed together in 1 QS IV, which can be attested in the NT catalogs almost word for word. S. Wibbing points out that the most numerous vices occurring in the NT vice catalogs are exactly the same as those that turn up in the lists from Qumran. It is not surprising that some vices surface in Stoic and Platonic catalogs, because Paul, after all, was a product of the same environment.[27]

Of more importance than formal comparisons with extra-biblical materials

---

pp. 140f., "Contextually, the catalogs are clearly coined from tradition, which can only be proved in this way in Paul. The number five is thus probably accidental, as is probably also the case in Philo."

25. H. D. Betz, *Lukian von Samosata und das Neue Testament. Religionsgeschicht-liche und paränetische Parallelen. Ein Beitrag zum Corpus Hellenisticum Novi Testamenti*, TU 76 (Berlin: Akademie Verlag, 1961), esp. pp. 185–203.

26. B. S. Eastons, "New Testament Ethical Lists," JBL 51 (1932) 1–12. Another attempt to determine original NT catalogs consists in her retroverted analysis back to a Jewish Proselyte-Katechism (comp. W. D. Davies, *Rabbinic Judaism*, op. cit., pp. 123–29), whose former existence, however, can only be supposed. For thematics, see also M. Barth, AB 34A, pp. 550–53.

27. S. Wibbing, *Die Tugend- und Lasterkataloge im Neuen Testament und ihre Traditionsgeschichte unter besonderer Berücksichtigung der Qumran-Texte*, BZNW 25 (Berlin: Töpelmann, 1959), esp. pp. 118–20. For the basic differences in the Stoa, see esp. pp. 118–20.—The antithetical schema, which is well recognizable in 1 QS IV in the contrast between a virtue catalog and the vice catalog, leads S. Wibbing back to the *Iranian cosmology*, and that these ideas were supposedly transmitted to early Christianity through Judaism.—E. Kamlah, *Paränese*, op. cit., basically adheres to this viewpoint, but in modified form. He works out two types of catalogs in the NT: (1) a descriptive catalog which lists the types (or typical manners of behavior) of sinners, with a supplemental threat from the law, which antithetically corresponds to the types (or typical manners of behavior) of the righteous, and with a concluding declaration of salvation; and (2) a directly paranetical catalog, which depicts the sinful old being, with the summons to lay this aside, to which the new one is contrasted with the summons to strive for this. The difference between the second type and the first one, which is supposedly a component of directly adopted Iranian cosmology into Jewish anthropology, can be explained by means of the fact that the form was first interpreted astrologically in Hellenistic syncretism. The resultant syncretistic mythological anthropology can best be understood in Corp Herm XIII (pp. 214f.).

for the exposition of the lists in Col are their function within the framework of the Pauline paraenesis. Paul is not concerned with proving the high moral position of Christianity. He also does not wish to denounce the non-Christians,[28] but just the opposite—he wants to win them. He also does not wish, as is the case in 1 QS IV, to solve the riddle of ethical conflict in which man stands, through a lesson about the two spirits that battle for domination within man until the end of time.[29] Paul is concerned with making manifest the new event that has occurred through the Messiah in the way in which it is outlined in 3:11. The "vices" or "virtues" are thus seen from the standpoint that they are either denied or confirmed through the interaction described in 3:11. Caution is recommended on the basis of this connection not to transfer contextual points of comparison from the surrounding environment of the NT too quickly. Thus, a fundamental difference between the ethics of Paul and Greek philosophy lies in the fact that the listed evil deeds manifest the not being chosen of the doer in such catalogs (cf. esp. Rom 1:24), just as the good deeds only make possible the being chosen in the Messiah. Therefore, the concepts "virtues" and "vices," understood on the basis of the Greek moral philosophy, are not especially happy choices.

Fornication. If "fornication" *(porneia)* is understood as an allusion to the gentiles which marks the difference between them and the Jews, then this term in its specific meaning may refer to the marriage (or sexual unions) between close relatives, which are forbidden to Jews in the Torah. This is the case in Acts 15:20, 29; 21:25; 1 Cor 5:1; and probably also in Matt 19:9.[30] In the context here, the same special meaning may also apply. The "vices" cited in v 5 are held up as indications of the previous life of the Colossians, that is, when these were excluded from the inheritance of Israel (v 7; cf. 1:12, 21; 2:13). The fact that, for the coexistence of Jews and non-Jews, the observance of the OT marriage laws as applicable to relatives was viewed as important also for non-Jews is demonstrated in Acts 15:20, 29 and can be reconciled also with Pauline thinking (cf. Rom 14:13ff.). At the same time, it is unlikely that marriage within prohibited degrees of kinship is meant by *porneia* in this passage.

Paul uses the term in a comprehensive way as a kind of superconcept, as 1 Cor 5:1 demonstrates. Often, especially when the word surfaces in "catalogs," we cannot determine from the context what is meant. Beside the meaning cited above, one can conclude that by the use of the word *porneia* Paul condemns

---

28. Compare for that M. Barth, AB 34A, pp. 526–29.

29. F. Mussner, *Der Galaterbrief*, HThK IX (Freiburg i.B.: Herder, 1974), Excursus 7, pp. 392–95.

30. Comp. H. Baltensweiler, *Die Ehe im Neuen Testament*, AThANT 52 (Zürich and Stuttgart: Zwingli Verlag, 1967), pp. 92–95.—In 1 Cor 5:1, however, a *porneia* is addressed "which does not even exist among the gentiles." There, they probably had adultery with the wife of the father in mind.

commercial/cultic prostitution in any case (1 Cor 6:13, 18; cf. 1 Cor 10:8) and promiscuity (1 Thess 4:3f).[31] B. Malina[32] justly warned against reading moral viewpoints into the concept that cannot be supported within the context of the *porneia* word group in the OT, the NT, or the rabbinic literature: *porneia* means "unlawful (that is forbidden by the Torah, H.B.) sexual conduct, or unlawful conduct in general." We need to consider, in the interpretation of the word group in the NT, that "pre-betrothal, pre-marital, non-commercial sexual intercourse between man and woman is nowhere considered a moral crime in the Torah" (ibid., p. 17). We need to remark, however, in limiting this argument, that B. Malina's conclusion is only valid if the characterized sexual contact involved the bethrothed couple. Otherwise, if it were proven that a woman did not enter marriage as a virgin *and* that she had deceived her husband, she was condemned for "lewdness" (Deut 22:13–21).[33]

Impurity. The "unclean was the most elementary form in which Israel encountered the displeasure of God."[34] Whoever was "unclean" was excluded from the cult and thus from the community of Yahweh. Everything to do with idol worship made a person unclean, and thus we can understand that *uncleanness* had to be a dividing line between non-Jews and Jews.

In this verse, also, we will not go wrong if we identify uncleanness as an activity that is (still) condemned as idol worship. In this connection we refer to Rom 1:23f., where uncleanness is termed the consequence of idol worship. There, homosexuality is given special emphasis. Yet this example gives no reason to limit the meaning of uncleanness to sexual transgressions. They are, however, included by the fact that the spheres of the cultic and sexual are layered in the religions and cults against which Israel and the young Christian church had to define itself.[35]

Passion, evil desire. Pathos (passion) occurs only three times in the NT. In 1 Thess 4:5, we find the word next to *epithymia* (longing, desire), as we do also in this verse, and in Rom 1:24/26, the two terms seem to be used synonymously.

---

31. This observation is also true for the occurrence of the word group *porneia, porneuō, pornē, pornos* in the rest of the NT.

32. B. Malina, "Does *Porneia* Mean Fornication?" NT 14 (1972) 10–17.

33. J. Jensen, "Does *Porneia* Mean Fornication? A Critique of Bruce Malina," NT 20 (1978) 161–84, attempted to prove that *porneia* meant any kind of "extra-marital intercourse." His substantiations from the NT, OT, and the rabbinic literature seem forced, in part, and are not convincing.

34. G. von Rad, Theol.d.AT. I, p. 272.

35. Cultic prostitution was practiced, among others, in the Canaanite cults, in Syria, and in Egypt, as also in Persia, where it was the "custom of the land," "which was practiced also by the daughters of the most respected families without their being subjected to shame for this activity" (F. Hauck/S. Schulz, ThWNT VI, 581, 25). It was generally rejected in the Greek territories, but penetrated into Athens and Corinth (Temple of Aphrodite) (ibid., p. 581, 31ff.).

Epithymia occurs thirty-eight times in the NT (of which nineteen times are in the letters which cite Paul as author). Since this word is also used in a positive sense (Phil 1:23, 1 Thess 2:17), the adjective *kakos* (evil, bad) has been added.[36] *Epythymia* means longing which urges powerfully to action. The sweep of meaning of this substantive becomes more rounded in Rom 13:14 and Gal 5:19 (cf. also Rom 7:7), where it summarizes all the vices in a catalog. On the basis of extra-biblical word usage, we could presume that *pathos*, in contrast to *epithymia*, emphasizes the effect more strongly. Yet this differentiation is blurred by the fact that both words contain the element of compulsion.

and always wanting to have more, which is idolatry. Pleonexia (here translated with the meaning of always wanting to have more) is emphasized in this listing by the fact that it was supplemented with an explanation, which also reflects the fact that the article was inserted where it is usually lacking before abstract nouns (cf. BDR 258, 1). This does not need to mean that *pleonexia* is to be cited as a second chief vice next to *porneia*, and that all the remaining vices only expand on this first one (cf. E. Schweizer, p. 143f.). It seems to us more probable that *pleonexia* is to be viewed as the source of the previously cited evils. We have a series of examples in the rabbinic literature in which one sin is placed on a par with a "notoriously bad sin," in order to mark its importance (cf. St.-B. III, pp. 606f.). But the declaration in Matt 6:24 is closer to Col, where the "Mammon" is called "Lord *(kyrios)* next to God" whom one cannot serve simultaneously with God.[37] In Col, however, *pleonexia* should not be limited to material goods and should consequently also not be translated by "greed" or "avarice." A more encompassing meaning can be found in the extra-biblical Greek as well as in Eph 4:19 in the NT.[38] It was there rendered by the translation "always wanting more."

6 *Through these the wrath of God comes.* (literally: through which). In the Epistle to the Romans, Paul speaks above all of the wrath of God. In the uncontested letters, the word *orgē* (wrath) occurs again only in 1 Thess 1:10; 2:16; 5:9.[39] For one, the concept points to the revelation of the anger of the deity at the final judgment (cf. Rom 2:5; 5:9; 1 Thess 1:10), and for another, the

---

36. Among the most important textual evidence is the transmission in Papyrus 46 (ca. 200).

37. "Subtle" idol worship is the root of all evil. Comp. also Rom 1:23ff.; Eph 4:18–19; and as a very nice example, Wis Sol 14:25ff. Differently, for example in Test Rub 4, where we have a great exposition detailing fornication and the wickedness of a wife, and in which fornication is perceived as the destruction of the soul, which separates the human being from God and leads to idol worship.

38. For example, Aristotle, Eth Nic IX, 8, 1168b, 16–19. Honor and corporal desires are also mentioned here, in addition to money.—For Eph 4:19, see M. Barth, AB 34A, p. 504, who suggests the translation, "and still ask for more."

39. Otherwise in Eph 2:3; 4:31; 5:6; Col 3:6, 8; 1 Tim 2:8. Only still in Rom 1:18, Eph 5:6, and Col 3:6 can we find the aposition *(tou) theou* (of God); otherwise, *orgē* is

present wrath of God is meant, which shows itself already (cf. Rom 13:4; 1 Thess 2:16).[40] Rom 1:18, also, probably addresses the present God, who manifests himself in vv 1:24 + 26 in the expression "being given over."

In Col, the present tense *erchetai* (he comes) is used, but a future meaning of this verb is also possible (cf. Matt 17:11 and BDR 323). Thus we may have a reference to the coming wrath of God/judgment here. J. Gnilka (p. 182) interprets the statement in this way, and he recognizes a scheme in the explications which begin here, which he characterizes by the terms "Imperative—Series of Vices—Threat of Judgement" and which he views as typical of the mission sermon or the instruction of the community.

Whether the wrath of God is intended, which already manifests itself in "being given over" (see above), or whether a reprimand looking toward the final judgment is at its base, we need to consider in any case that we should not see the motivation for the Paráenesis in v 6. We find this in 3:1–4 in the consciousness of the new life which is bestowed through the "resurrection." This present declaration is not a second motivation (in any case) which uses fear as its means; rather, it underscores the former. It describes the condition from which the recipients of the letter have already been delivered (cf. 1:13), and thus it determines how erroneous it would be, to return "there" of their own free will.

upon the sons of disobedience. In Eph 5:6, in a similar context, the same expression is used. The textual evidence is certain there, while in Col the important textual witnesses, Papyrus 46 (about 200) and Codex Vaticanus (fourth century), do not have it. This gives rise to the suspicion that these words were added to the original text in an assimilation to Eph 5:6. However, the *emphatic* "you also" in v 7 seems to refer back to "sons of disobedience," which speaks in favor of the authenticity of the expression. It is not possible to make a certain decision on this text-critical question.

The expression "sons of disobedience" reflects Hebrew language usage.[41] It is connected by the statements introduced with "formerly—now," and the expression is used formally as the designation for the ones who were formerly excluded from the covenant (cf. 1:21f.). But the fact that this designation is also taken further and that it can include the Jews is demonstrated by Eph 2:2f.

7 You also walked in these (vices) formerly, when you lived in them. The meaning in context is very much determined by the "vices," and the relative

---

used absolutely. We cannot derive from that, however, that anger was perceived as a self-evident power *next* to God. Comp. for that G. Stählin, ThWNT V, 424, 9–425, 17.

40. Comp. for that G. H. C. Macgregor, "The Concept of Wrath of God in the New Testament," NTS 7 (1960/61) 101–9.

41. See the examples in G. Fohrer, ThWNT VIII, 347, 3–15. In the NT, comp. among others John 17:12; Rom 9:8; Gal 4:28; 2 Pet 2:14.—A. Deissmann, *Bibelstudien*, op. cit., pp. 163–66, thinks that the declaration could also be perceived as the decorous speech of a Greek. Since, however, we have similar expressions in the LXX which were cited from Paul, we can suffice with the assumption of lexically analogous imagery.

pronoun in v 6 also refers to them. The relative and demonstrative pronouns in v 7 show the same connections.[42]

These vices formed the former "living sphere" of the Colossians, and the consequence was that they could not conduct their life differently, but walked "in these" (for the verb *peripateō*, "to walk, to conduct," cf. Notes to 1:10). Only the change of "living sphere," the transference into the kingdom of the Son (1:13), made a new way of living possible (cf. 2:6; 3:1f.).

The inquiry of A. Lindemann (p. 56) into whether the image which is depicted here of the former life of the Colossians was in fact realistic, and if not, whether there was any sense in sketching such an image, considers the Jewish consciousness too lightly, from which the catalogs of vices were derived. The ethical standard is not a generally recognized code of norms, but it is rather formally for the Jews (and then also for the gentiles) the revealed will of God,[43] which unmasks behavior such as adultery, disobedience, theft, etc., and which cannot be characterized in the same way outside of this revelation.

8 *But now you also cast off all this.* The image of putting to death the members or limbs (cf. v 6) is replaced by casting off (and putting on) (cf. next Notes). The "former" was marked by a life of vices, the "now," however, does not mean a life automatically free of vices, but rather the enabling of such a life to which the recipients of the epistle were called (cf. previous Notes). Man is not a passive entity in "the kingdom of the Son" (1:13) which is merely transferred there. Rather, he is called to action.

ta panta (all) refers back to the previous catalog, on the one hand, and on the other it is made concrete by the subsequent catalog. Through this connecting link, that which is now to be "cast off" is marked as a relic of the past that is not suited to the present.[44]

The repeated "you also" from v 7 can hardly refer to the shining example of other Christians.[45] They are not addressed in the context. It is rather conditioned by the idea that the non-Jews, after "they now also" have received the Messiah as Lord, "now also" have the possibility of following a new way of life (see above).

The "vices," which are enumerated in this verse, are summarized in the next verse by the admonition "do not lie to *one another*" (see below). This, as well as the statement in v 11, makes it clear that the author is not concerned

---

42. W. M. L. de Wette (p. 61) refers the relative pronoun to "sons of disobedience" and the demonstrative pronoun to "vices." Thus also H. von Soden (pp. 59f.).

43. This will of God demonstrates itself for Paul in the Torah (comp. Rom 2:17ff.) and then in the Messiah, who is the fulfillment of the Torah.

44. E. Kamlah, *Paränese*, op. cit., p. 183, points out that the object of taking something off always characterizes something that is complete.—This idea is more detailed in 3:9 in the concept of "taking off the old man."

45. See, for example, E. Haupt, p. 133; H. A. W. Meyer, p. 376.

with the moral impeccability of the individual, but rather with the cohesion of
Christians in their common life.

. . . from your mouth. It is possible to connect this word syntactically to the
verb "to cast off."[46] Then all the vices might be read as "sins of the tongue." But
such a limitation, especially as concerns the two terms *orgē* (wrath) and *thymos*
(anger), which have a more encompassing meaning, would be unusual. As long
as it is not forcibly demanded from the context, this interpretation should not
be attempted. "From your mouth" should be related to the words to which they
naturally and self-evidently belong, thus to *blasphēmia* (slander) and *aischrologia*
(abusive language).

Wrath, anger. These two terms cannot be differentiated from one another
contextually. While the words *orgē* (here translated by "wrath") and *thymos*
(here translated by "anger") incorporate originally etymologically distinct realms
of meaning, namely *orgē* the feelings and *thymos* the exhibition of the same,[47]
this differentiation is obscured in the NT (as also in the LXX).[48]

Paul only rarely addresses the anger of men, but he evaluates it negatively,
as do other NT writings and the rabbinic literature (cf. St.-B. I, pp. 276–78).[49]
Rom 12:19ff. gives some insight into the background. Wrath belongs to God; so
the Christian is to feed his *enemy* when he is hungry, and to give him drink
when he is thirsty. According to Jas 1:20, the wrath of man is not justified before
God. This conviction is expressed in Eph 4:26, where the first reprimand is not
to let the sun set over wrath, because wrath in v 31 is condemned as not befitting
the Christian.

Malice. The Greek word used here, *kakia*, also summarizes the list given in
Eph 4:31.[50] Such a comprehensive meaning becomes clear also from its use in
1 Cor 14:20. In Col (as also in Titus 3:3 and in 1 Pet 2:1), *kakia* is one vice
among the others. In these passages, the comprehensive sense, as well as the
relationship to one's fellow human being, is rendered more closely by the
word "spite."

Slander. Different from the verb *blasphemeo*, the correlating substantive
blasphēmia is not used in the undisputed letters of Paul. Rather, it occurs only

---

46. Thus C. F. D. Moule, p. 118. Compare also W. M. L. de Wette, p. 61;
H. Grotius, p. 931.

47. J. Fichtner/O. Grether, ThWNT V, 410, 29ff. We also find this difference in
stoic writing (see, for example, Diogenes Laertius VII, 114). Further references are
collected in J. B. Lightfoot (p. 280).

48. Both concepts are used for human anger (i.e., Luke 4:28; Gal 5:20/Eph 4:31; Jas
1:19f.), as well as for divine anger (i.e., Rev 14:19/Rom 1:18). They are used in a parallel
sense in Rom 2:8 (comp. also Rev 16:19; 19:15). The idea that *thymos* is used in contrast
to *orgē* to indicate the *demonstration* of anger is refuted in NT declarations such as Rom
1:18; 2:5; 5:9, etc.

49. Exceptions from this "rule" are in NT Rom 10:19 and 2 Cor 7:11.

50. Comp. M. Barth, AB 34A, pp. 522f.

in Eph 4:31, Col 3:8, and in 1 Tim 6:4. More frequently, it is used in reference to God, but here it means one's conduct toward one's fellow human being.[51] Matt 27:39 and Luke 22:65; 23:39 provide graphic examples as to what such a vice looks like. One can translate it by "to deride, to mock." Paul uses the verb in this sense in Rom 3:8.[52] In 1 Cor 10:30, however, it comes close to the meaning: "to damn."

Abusive language. The Greek word *aischrologia* occurs in the NT only in Col 3:8. It is absent from the LXX, but it is attested in the extra-biblical Greek. *Clement of Alexandria* (died 215 C.E.) understood by this word an "obscene, disgraceful manner of speaking" (Paed 2, 6, 52).[53] A second component in the meaning of "abusive language" becomes evident in the language usage from *Polybius* (first century B.C.E.).[54] Eph 5:4 speaks to the former meaning, the express orientation of all the listed vices toward one's fellow human being in Col to the latter. Yet J. B. Lightfoot (p. 280) is probably correct in his refusal to accept two mutually exclusive interpretations: the word can only mean "abusive," when the abuse is "foul-mouthed."

9+10 Do not lie to one another. The list from v 8 is not simply carried further by using the substantive *pseudos* (lie). The command in question is separated from the previous statement by the verb form *pseudomai* (to lie), and it thus seems to be a summation of that which was stated in v 8. If we take the expression contextually, we come to the same conclusion: the reciprocal act of lying to one another is viewed as a sign of the "old self," which is characterized by both catalogs of vices in vv 4+8. The express addition of "one another" and above all the declaration in v 11 demonstrate that "lying" is understood as a social transgression, and its manifestation signifies a denial of the unity created by the Messiah of Jew and gentile, circumcised and uncircumcised, etc.[55]

It is self-evident for you that you have taken off . . . and have put on (literally: having taken off . . . having put on). The image of taking off (or putting on), esp. in an ethical context, occurs also outside the Pauline writings and does not originate with Paul.[56] The double composite *ap-ek-dyomai* (to take off) is unusual. Otherwise in the NT, *ek-dyomai* is used. But we can hardly

---

51. Comp. for that Matt 12:31 par, where *blasphēmia* toward human beings is differentiated from *blasphēmia* toward God.

52. "Somewhat thus, as we are ridiculed *(blasphēmoumetha)*, and specifically as some say that we say, 'Let us do evil, so that good may come'?"

53. Comp. also Diodorus Siculus, 5, 4, 7.

54. 8, 11, 8; 31, 6, 4.

55. E. Lohmeyer (p. 130) remarks, "Even there also, Jewish origin gives itself away, in the sense that lying is not purely a transgression against the concept of truth, but is rather branded as transgression against a certain community."

56. Comp. in the OT, for example, Job 29:14; Ps 132:9; in the NT, Heb 12:1; Jas 1:21; 1 Pet 2:1; 3:21. In the extra-biblical sources, see P. W. van der Horst, "Observations on a Pauline Expression," NTS 19 (1972) 181–87.

attribute any special significance to this distinction (cf. BDR 116 and fn. 91 to Col 1:15–20). More unusual is the object of the taking off and putting on, the "old" and the "new self" (see below).

M. Barth (AB, 34A, p. 540) sees a meaning in the configuration of taking off and putting on, which could otherwise remain hidden, "that the change of 'mind' will be visible and palpable." And thereby he points to a conviction that is diffused in "all cultures and religions," also in the OT and the NT (cf. among others Gen 37:3, 23; Ex 28 esp. v 43; Zech 3:3–5; Matt 22:11f.; Rev 3:4f.; 6:11), which he renders again by "clothes make the man," namely, "A man's power extends to his garb, and the power of the specific robe is communicated to its wearer" (ibid., p. 541).

The two verbs, "to take off" and "to put on," are framed by imperatives and are constructed participially. It is grammatically possible that these participles have imperative force and that they appeal to the "dignity" of those addressed (here characterized by "it is self-evident").[57] But it is also possible that through them an additional motivation and a justification for explicit imperatives are inserted next to 3:1–4. Most interpreters opt for this second possibility,[58] which is justified, above all, by the opinion that robing and disrobing are a part of the rite of baptism. Reference is made especially to Gal 3:27/24 and Rom 6:4 ff., from which it is clear that "taking off of the 'old self' " presupposes the crucifixion of the human body in baptism.[59] We should observe, however, that in Rom 6, baptism as "a burial" is expressly differentiated from "dying." Gal 3:27 demonstrates a close connection between "being baptized" and "putting on Christ," but it does not state how this connection is to be understood. At any rate, there is no causal connection as a precedent to indicate that baptism itself is the "putting on of Christ" in the sense of a dying with him and of a (to be hoped for) rising with him.[60] Above all, Col gives no indication of attributing such significance to baptism, and it does not justify the assumption that the reference here is to baptism (cf. Comment II to 2:6–23). In Rom 13:14, the reference to baptism is also lacking, and there, proceeding from a catalog of vices, the image of taking off is used imperatively. Thus it is also justified by a comparison with an undisputed Pauline epistle, that the participles "having

---

57. See Notes to 1:10; comp. also 1:12 and 2:7.

58. Among others, T. K. Abbott, p. 283; H. A. W. Meyer, p. 377; P. Ewald, p. 418; H. von Soden, p. 60; F. Mussner, p. 81; J. Gnilka, p. 186; R. P. Martin, NCC, p. 106; P. T. O'Brien, p. 189; J. Jervell, *Imago Dei*, op. cit., p. 236; O. Merk, "Handeln aus Glauben. Die Motivierung der paulinischen Ethik," MThST 5 (Marburg: Elwert, 1968), p. 205; H. Seesemann, ThWNT V, p. 716.—Differently, J. B. Lightfoot, p. 281; E. Haupt, p. 135; Dibelius-Greeven, p. 42; E. Lohse, p. 204; E. Larsson, *Christus als Vorbild. Eine Untersuchung zu den paulinischen Tauf- und Eidkontexten*, ASNU 23 (Lund: Gleerup; Kopenhagen: Munksgaard, 1862), p. 198; comp. E. Schweizer, p. 145.

59. J. Jervell, *Imago Dei*, op. cit., p. 234.

60. See esp. M. Barth, *Taufe*, op. cit., pp. 221–46; 352–62.

taken off" and "having put on" are to be understood as imperatives.[61] A completely certain decision is, however, not possible. If the participles are not intended in an imperative sense after all, then there is in Col either a reference to that which occurred in the death of the Messiah and the associated dying with Christ or, more likely, a summarizing statement about the process of laying down the previously cited "vices" and the putting on of "virtues" in the following passage.[62]

the old self with its practices . . . the new (self). In the uncontested Pauline epistles, the expression "old self" (Rom 6:6) occurs, but not the "new self." In this sense, Paul can speak of an already now existing "new creation" in reference to the human person (2 Cor 5:17; Gal 6:15). The omission of the expression "new self" does not necessarily signify that a "clearly anti-enthusiastic realism" has been declared.[63] Above all, this observation should not serve to posit a significant difference between Col and the "genuine Pauline epistles." In Col 3:10, such "realism" is certainly not indicated. This passage already demonstrates that the image of the "new self" is used in an ethical context, within the framework of admonitions to *Christians* (cf. also Notes for "now" in v 8).

In the parallel passage in Eph 4:24, Paul speaks of *kainos anthrōpos*, here of *neos anthrōpos*. The two adjectives *kainos* and *neos*, which in Greek were customarily used for "new" since Classical times, are usually differentiated from one another in meaning as follows: "*neos is new in the sense of time or origin, young* (in some instances, H.B.), with the secondary meaning *youthfully immature, lacking piety toward the old* (. . .). *Kainos is new in manner, different from the traditional*, therefore *making an impression*, probably also *better than the old, superior to it in value and force of attraction*."[64] E. Lohmeyer (p. 142) therefore thought that Paul wanted to say that the believer, as long as he is in the body, remains a child that would first have to grow to full maturity, that is, to the body of glory, and his renewing led not to the newness of the illumined existence but rather to moral "cognizance." Yet the continuation of the idea

---

61. The idea that this would evoke the remembrance of baptism in the readers is only then probable if, according to Pauline or general early Christian teaching, baptism was understood as the dedication to dying with Christ and in this sense as the taking off and putting on of the "old" and "new human being." This is questionable, however (see esp. 1 Pet 3:21). The image of putting on and taking off in connection with baptism is one usage next to others, both the ethical (comp. Rom 13:14) and the eschatological (1 Cor 15:38, 53f.; 2 Cor 5:2–5). Thus we do not need to speak in the imperativistic translation that the religious concept of baptism needs to be twisted (J. Jervell, *Imago Dei*, op. cit., p. 235).

62. Comp. E. Schweizer, p. 146, fn. 508.

63. Comp. E. Stegemann, "Alt und Neu bei Paulus und in den Deuteropaulinen (Kol-Eph)," H. Thyen zum 50. Geburtstag, EvTh 37 (1977) 508–36:520f.

64. J. Behm, ThWNT III, 450, 10ff.

through *ana-kainoō* (to renew) indicates that the distinction in meaning cited above between *kainos* and *neos* is hardly intended here in Col.[65]

There are no parallels in extra-Christian sources for the imagery of taking off the old self and the putting on the new self.[66] It has not been adopted from gnosis. We find in the latter the traditional usage of the expression "human being" (thus "self"), but the conception of an old and a new human being or self does not occur there.[67]

The supposition that we have an original Pauline formulation here seems correct to us. The contrast of "old" and "new" is a frequent one with Paul (cf. 1 Cor 5:7ff.; 2 Cor 3:6/14). Since Paul considers the life of Christians not as an exchange of some vices for certain virtues, but rather as a change of dominion over the entire human being or self (!), then the idea even within an ethical context is close to the familiar image of taking off and putting on of vices or virtues and could be varied from the designation of objects to a more encompassing concept, namely that of "human beings." We could then translate, "take off your old *I* / put on . . ." (GNANT) or ". . . your old/new *self*" (NJB), or ". . . your old/new *nature*" (NEB; RSV). But such a translation possibly shortchanges the full intent of this passage.

---

65. See also R. A. Harrisville, "The Concept of Newness in the New Testament," JBL 74 (1955) 69–79, who arrives at the conclusion "that the terms *kainos* and *neos* are synonymous in the NT. Both terms imply a qualitative as well as temporal significance" (p. 79). Compare also MMLex, p. 314 (to *kainos*), which notes, "Papyrus usage hardly tends to sharpen the distinction between *kainos* and *neos*."

66. Comp. J. Jervell, *Imago Dei*, op. cit., p. 240.—P. van der Horst, "Observations on a Pauline Expression," NTS 19 (1972/73) 181–87, however, sees a literal parallel in a fragment from pre-Christian times, which is transmitted by Eusebius, Praep Ev XIV, 18, 26. There we have an anecdote about the skeptic Pyrrho, who, being pursued by a dog, flees and climbs into a tree, and who excuses the incongruence of this behavior with his philosophic thinking by saying (literally), "It is difficult to take off the human being." P. W. van der Horst superinterprets this declaration when he thinks it means, "The transition from . . . the unenlightened state to the enlightened state." It hardly means more than, "It is difficult to cast off that which is human," and it does not further the argument to belabor the analysis with formal comparable NT statements. Comp. also C. F. D. Moule, " 'The New Life' in Colossians 3:1–17," RExp 70 (1973) 489.

67. See J. Jervell, *Imago Dei*, op. cit., p. 241, "For the inner human being, the Pneuma-Eikon in the human being, is simply the Anthropos. In Gnosis, the first, the one pneumatic 'man' who fell from heaven, thus the old man, must always be the new one. Because otherwise redemption would be impossible in Gnosis. . . . What was to correspond in the Pauline transmission to the old man in Gnosis, would thus be something like the non-pneumatic components of the human being. . . . But the Gnostic sources do not understand the designation *palaios anthropos* (old man, H.B.) from those components of the human being. And Paul, in turn, does not have a concept of the new human being as the renewed old human being." For Gnostic comparative materials, see ibid., pp. 130–40.

411

Since the result of putting on is to lead "to the cognizance that *Christ* is all and is in all" (cf. v 11), the question arises whether Christ himself is not meant by "new self."[68] Two statements favor this interpretation, namely the one in Rom 13:14, "Put on the Lord Jesus Christ," and the other in Gal 3:27, "For you, who are baptized to Christ, have put on Christ." Both of these declarations are in a context that is related to the declaration in Col 3:5–11. If these are applicable, then we can find the so-called "Adam—Christ—typology in Col 3:9ff. which also occurs in Paul in Rom 5:12–21 and 1 Cor 15:21f. The 'old self' is the Adam as representative of the old order, the sin of degenerate humanity, and the 'new self' is Christ as representative of the new, redeemed order of humanity.[69] To put on Christ and to take off (the old) Adam means then to allow the redeemed humanity to become visible in the deeds of the community (cf. Gal 3:27b/29), whose representative is Christ."[70]

which is constantly renewed in knowledge. The continuation of the preceding passage is expressed by the present participle of the verb *anakainoomai* (to be renewed).[71] Here, also, a compositum is used, *anakainoomai*. Even if we wished to attribute some special significance to the added prefix *ana* (see above to "to take off"), there is certainly not sufficient evidence to conclude that the idea of *restoration* of a lost primitive state is present in the compound verb. The use of *ana* would serve, at most, to underscore the durational aspect of the chosen verb form, the continuing renewal (and in this sense *re*newing).

Does such a declaration then permit the interpretation that Christ is intended by "new self"? O. Merk answers this question in the negative, "because we cannot say of Christ that he is constantly renewed or must be renewed."[72]

---

68. See H. von Soden, p. 60; comp. E. Lohmeyer, p. 142; Dibelius-Greeven, p. 42.—The idea is also represented that the "new human being" was also intended to be the "body of Christ," the church (comp. for example E. Käsemann, *Leib Christi*, op. cit., p. 148). We could cite Eph 2:15 in support of this thesis, but we would not want to introduce new difficulties into the text with the resultant summons, "put on the church!"

69. Comp. C. F. D. Moule, p. 119.—Further literature is cited in M. Barth, AB 34A, p. 824 (Bibliography 18).

70. For this exposition, comp. M. Barth, AB 34A, pp. 537–40.—J. Jervell, *Imago Dei*, op. cit., pp. 241–43, excluded this interpretation. According to him, the old human being was presented as "a living spirit in the present human being" in Eph 4:8–12 and in Col. However, this conceptualization, derived from Adam, was foreign to Paul and made derivation from late-Jewish sources impossible.—But J. Jervell's hesitations concerning Eph 4 and Col 3 are unfounded. The obscuring of reason, as well as the obduracy of the heart, in the activities cited in Col 3:10 can be understood as manifestations belonging to the "old human being." The concept of "gnostic anthropos" (as a heavenly, as well as an inner, greatness), which is fused with the concept of Heilsgeschichte of the "old and new Adam" (p. 242) does not need to be advanced into the explanation of Col 3:9f.

71. Comp. 2 Cor 4:16f., ". . . our inner (person) is renewed day after day."

72. O. Merk, *Handeln*, op. cit., p. 206. F. W. Eltester, "Eikon im Neuen

Perhaps the author of Col suspected some difficulty here, and therefore did not expressly speak of "Adam" and "Christ." We need to consider, however, that this declaration remains within the framework of putting on a garment: Christ, insofar as he is "put on," thus Christ as the garment of the Christian, is constantly renewed. The passive "he is renewed," as also the following "of having created him" (see below), point to God as the one who performs the actions. Based on the declaration in v 8, according to which the Christian life is not automatically "free of vices" but represents rather the battle against these vices, we then have the subsequent declaration: Even in the face of the incompleteness of Christians, God himself constantly sees to it anew that the goal of the new life is achieved, namely the unity and community described in v 11. This goal is summarized in the word "recognition" used in Phil 1:9. The fact that we are thus dealing with a "social concept" was demonstrated in the Notes to 1:6.

according to the image of him who has created him (literally: of having created him). The participle "of having created" can very probably be understood as a designation of the deity here.[73] That is also supported by the statement in 1:15–20. The personal pronoun "him" refers to the "new self." W. G. Kümmel argues that the language usage of *ktizō* (to create) requires that the first creation of mankind is meant, not the "new creation,"[74] but this is not convincing, since the discussion expressly concerns the "new human being or self." In addition, the use of *ktizō* in Eph 2:10, 15 (cf. 2 Cor 2:17; Gal 6:15) counters W. G. Kümmel's thesis.

It is more difficult to decide how the entire declaration "according to the image of him who has created him" is to be connected syntactically. There are three possibilities:

1. It can refer to "recognition" so that the term is elucidated more in detail here: cognizance should be certainly determined by the image of the one who created the new human being, thus by the "image of God." *Eikōn* is then probably best understood as the title for the Messiah, as in 1:15.

2. The reference to *neos* (the new) would state that the "new human being" (or self) is created in the image of God.

Testament," BZNW 23, 1958, 158f. Comp. also Dibelius-Greeven, p. 42, "Because of *ton anakainoumenon ktl.* (who is renewed, etc., H.B.), the *neos* (new, H.B.) is not simply equal in thinking to *Christos*, but should surely also be interpreted as such. . . ."

73. See Rom 1:25; Eph 3:9; comp. 1 Cor 11:9; Eph 2:10; 4:24; 1 Tim 4:3; Matt 19:4; Mark 13:19; 1 Pet 4:19; Rev 4:11; but: Eph 2:15.—See also G. Delling, "Partizipiale Gottesprädikationen," StTh 17 (1963) 1–59. There are certain participles which are designations for God, which appear fixed insofar as they occur as firm attributes. To these belongs, according to G. Delling, also *ho ktisas*, adopted from the OT, as a shortened form for "creator."

74. W. G. Kümmel, *Das Bild des Menschen im Neuen Testament*, AThANT 13 (Zürich: Zwingli Verlag, 1948), pp. 38f.

3. Connected with *anakainoumen* (who is constantly renewed), the resultant declaration would affirm that the continuous renewing of the "new self" occurs according to the image of its creator.

Possibilities 2 and 3 are aimed at the same statement and do not involve any contextual alternatives. With the first interpretation, the stress is transferred from a further description of the "new self" to the sense and purpose of the putting on of this new self; nevertheless, this reading does not exclude the possibility of solutions 2 and 3. Since the specified recognition (of the "new self") toward the creator is a consequence of the putting on of the "new self," the conclusion is at hand that even the "new self" is then created according to the image of its own creator and is constantly renewed. If we are proceeding from the vantage point that Christ is the "new human being" (or "self") who is put on, then this correspondence is very clear. An unequivocal decision between the possibilities of interpretation 1, 2, or 3 is hardly possible, and it is also not necessary for the comprehension of the verse, since the different interpretations do not exclude each other. In favor of 1 is the fact that it results most naturally from the construction of the syntax. In favor of 2 and 3 is the parallel in Eph 4:24, and further, that these two interpretations give a better accounting for the relationship to Gen 1:27 (see below).

As regards the proposed reference to the "Adam—Christ—typology," we do have the resultant problem of whether we should attribute to the author of Col the conception of Christ as "created." The use of the verb *ktizō* seems at first glance to counter the thesis of a comparison of "Adam—Christ." Yet on the other hand, precisely the declaration "according to the image of him who created him" could speak in favor of this thesis. A reference to Gen 1:27 ("according to the image of God he created him"; in the LXX, however, we do not have *ktizō*) and the creation of the "first Adam" can hardly be overlooked. Thus the "new" human being would be described here as the second Adam. The author would thus have directly expressed (interpretation 2) or would have stipulated in his statement (interpretations 1 + 3) that Christ is the "new human being," the representative of humanity as it was intended by God at creation.[75] The "indifferent" usage of the verb *ktizō* in reference to Christ could be "excused" by the fact that the author of Col was unaware of the later false teaching of Arius.

11 *Where we no longer have. Hopou* (where) refers to the entire previous statement. That which is proclaimed here in v 11 is applicable there, where one has put on the "new self." Since "cognizance" (v 10) is not limited to the intellect, but rather refers to social behavior here, we cannot come to the conclusion that the resolution of the contradictions (in regard to one's conduct

---

75. The allusion to Gen 1:27 furthers the idea that the determination of man in accordance with creation reaches its climax when the Messiah is recognized as Lord over all things, even if we do not see this founded in the Adam-Christ typology.

toward fellow human beings, see below) would occur initially only in the Christian consciousness, or even when one views *hopou* in relation to this concept alone. Nonetheless, its realization must still wait until the end of time.[76]

Greek *eni* here is just another form of the preposition *en* (in). It stands for the verb *en-estin* (there is), in which it is contained as a prefix. In the same sense, *para* can also substitute for *par-estin* (to be present, cf. BDR 98).

Greek and Jew, circumcised and uncircumcised, barbarian, Scythian, slave, free person. Comparable listings can be found in Rom 10:12, Gal 3:28, and 1 Cor 12:13. The listing of "Jew and Greek" occurs in all the citations. The phrase "slave and free person" is absent only in Rom 10:12. Only in Gal, however, does the word pair "male–female" occur, and only in Col "circumcised and uncircumcised," as well as the listing "barbarian, Scythian." In this passage, the prior positioning of "Greek" before "Jew" is noteworthy. It is questionable that the order has some deeper meaning. E. Lohse (p. 207, fn. 3) suspects that it is conditioned by the fact that the addressees are gentile Christians. But even in 1 Cor 12, presumably gentile Christians are addressed (cf. 1 Cor 12:2) and the order is the other way. A series of commentators has tried to explain the further peculiarities of this verse by means of the special situations in the Colossian community.[77] But even here, we do not get beyond suppositions: whether the false teachers, against whom the Colossian epistle appeals, demanded circumcision is not certain. This specific demand does not surface in 2:16ff. And there are no indications of a specific function of Scythians in the society there. We can say only with some certainty that listings such as these were variable in part, so that a common basic group could be expanded in different ways. The added examples surely serve to illustrate the purposes, and can be chosen on the basis of the experiences of the author, but which do not necessarily arise out of or relate specifically to the circumstances of the addressees. If we consider that we are dealing with examples, then we can hardly be fair to the text if we come to the conclusion, from the absence of the word pair "male–female" in Col (in contrast to Gal), that the enthusiasm of the early era has waned (J. Gnilka, p. 189).

It is further noticeable that the first four elements of the listing are connected in pairs by the conjunction "and." Since the last two elements can also be understood as a contrasting pair, T. Hermann has tried to discern such a connection in the two asyndetically aligned words "barbarian" and "Scythian."[78]

---

76. Thus the Stoic view of equality of all human beings (comp., for example, Seneca, Ep 31, 11), which is justified in that the "inner human being" alone counts and that the "exterior differences" are without significance, is also not taken up in Col.

77. Thus, for example, J. B. Lightfoot, p. 282; E. Lohmeyer, p. 143; R. P. Martin, NCC, p. 108; P. T. O'Brien, p. 192; A. Lindemann, p. 59. E. Lohse (p. 207, fn. 2), however, emphasizes that the listing has doubtless been taken over from tradition.

78. T. Hermann, "Barbar und Skythe. Ein Erklärungsversuch zu Kol 3:11," ThBl 19 (1930) 106–7.

He interprets "Scythian," as well as "barbarian," as proper names which designate the inhabitants of East Africa who were well known at that time, where the Scythian was the representative of the white race and the barbarian of the black race. For the interpretation of Col 3:11, this would mean, "even the contrast of race is overcome next to the national, religious, and social sense" (cf. ibid., p. 107). The elimination of racial barriers would surely be a legitimate actualization of the verse under discussion, but whether this is explicitly expressed in Col seems improbable. T. Hermann obtains his interpretation of "barbarian and Scythian" from statements of John Philoponus and thus from a source from the sixth century. Whether these words were known to Paul with this specialized meaning is uncertain. The common usage of the two concepts was different then. "Barbarian," accordingly, was a designation which differentiated a foreigner from one's own people in a depreciatory way on the basis of language, culture, and morals, among others.[79] "Scythian" is an intensification of "barbarian": he is considered the most barbaric of all barbarians.[80] This exposition of these words is not to be questioned on the grounds that there must be some fundamental contrast between barbarian and Scythian. The possibility should be considered that only the first four terms were intentionally denoted as contrasting pairs. We should additionally consider that "Greek and Jew" hardly described a simple national contrast, but rather especially a "religious" contrast, since the choice of expression plays a central role when a Jew differentiates his people from other peoples.[81] Then the two contrasts connected by "and" fundamentally express the same thing: the dissolution of the contrast between chosen and nonchosen, and thus the enabling of an all-encompassing community among them. The fact that this thought is doubly expressed demonstrates the center of gravity of this declaration and gives an indication of its logical structure. These are not random examples of objects cited in any kind of order. On the basis of the emphatic ranking of this idea of contrast between chosen and nonchosen, we can infer the following manner of argumentation: because the sole significant contrast is stressed, since it is founded in the action of God, it would be absurd to look for reasons which would disturb or hinder the sense of community. The concepts "barbarian," "Scythian," "slave," "free person" are each examples of such a discordance. Christian love of one's neighbor,

---

79. Comp. St.-B. III, pp. 27f., and H. Windisch, ThWNT II, 544–51.

80. See 2 Macc 4:47; 3 Macc 7:5; Josephus, Ap II, 269 ("The Scythians enjoy killing people, and they hardly differentiate themselves from animals. . . ."); Plutarch, Vit Dec Orat 8 (847f.); Cicero, Verr II, 5, 150.—Further, in O. Michel, ThWNT VII, 448–51.

81. See Rom 1:16; 2:9f.; 3:9; 10:12; 1 Cor 1:22–24; 10:32; 12:13; Gal 3:28. Comp. Acts 14:1; 18:4; 19:10, 17; 20:21. "Greek" is used here probably in the comprehensive meaning of "gentiles" (comp. Rom 1:14/16; 2:9/14). When Paul differentiates Greeks from barbarians in Rom 1:14, he becomes a "Greek to the Greeks" and accommodates their self-consciousness. However, this difference loses its meaning in the face of the question of being chosen by God.

however, does not look to national origin, cultural refinement, or social position of that neighbor (except in the manner that would accord special honor to the presumably inferior person; 1 Cor 12:22f.).[82]

rather all things and in all (things is) the Messiah. Paul uses a similar foundation, but oriented toward God and without the conjunction "and," in 1 Cor 15:28.[83] It is very reminiscent of Hellenistic stoic conceptions, according to which the world is encircled and ruled throughout by God. This conception was also given expression through a ritual formula, a good example of which the following invocation of the goddess Isis: "You Isis, a goddess, you are all things!"[84] This telescoping of deity and world, however, contradicts OT Judaic (and thus also Christian) belief in creation. Still, this formula, "You are all things," or "You are in all things," occurs in the NT, as well as in Jewish literature. In Sir 43:27, God is praised as creator (!) in the expression, "He is the all." That demonstrates that this formula, with its Hellenistic prototype, still only has in common the latter function of praising the great dominion of God. The literal sense has been lost. Even in Col, as in 1 Cor, it can no longer be comprehended in its Hellenistic stoic sense. The connection to the statements of 1:15–20 are proclaimed through this formula, namely that the Messiah is Lord over all things,[85] and accordingly, Jews, Greeks, barbarians, Scythians, slaves, and free persons have become equally worthy of having the Messiah as their Lord (cf. esp. the Notes to 1:21f.). Through this "evaluation" of all things, which is undertaken by God, all human valuations have become meaningless in terms of religious, cultural, national, or other criteria as measures of association with one's fellow human beings.

12 *Now put on.* The imagery of putting on is retained. Just, as in v 8f., the "old self" is characterized by "vices," so now, when reference is made to putting on the "new self," this new person is organized with a "catalog of virtues." The participle *oun* (now, accordingly) serves to draw the conclusions indicated in v 11.

---

82. As we can derive from the elucidations in 3:18, when Paul says, "where it does not exist . . . ," he does not wish to do away with slavery, nationalities, etc.

83. Comp. also Eph 1:23; 4:6.

84. ILS II, p. 4362.

85. Comp. also C. F. D. Moule, p. 121.—*En pasin* can also be masculine in this form, but immediately following the neuter *ta panta*, that is hardly the case.—A possibility, but to be elucidated literally, could be to assume an accusativus graecus: "in reference to all things is Christ" [comp. W. Thüsing, *Per Christum in Deum, Studien zum Verhältnis von Christozentrik und Theozentrik in den paulinischen Hauptbriefen*, NTA.NF 1 (Münster: Aschendorff, 1965), p. 244].—"In all things" has a parallel in Lam 4:20 ("our life's breath is the anointed of the Lord . . ."), which follows its wording, only that the statement in Col is expanded cosmologically. It would state the continuing acts of the creator and render a reason for the fact that there is nothing which does not stand except in relation to the Messiah.

as the chosen ones of God, as holy and beloved ones. According to 1:26f., the message with which Paul is charged is contained in the "revealed secret," namely that the Jewish Messiah is also "Messiah among you," among the non-Jews.[86] On the basis of this declaration, it seems most obvious to interpret this verse in terms of the OT covenant bond, namely that the addressees are designated as the "chosen people of God." E. Lohmeyer's interpretation (p. 145), namely that "chosen" here means angels, and that the Colossians are invited to "become like the angels, with whom you are connected in the 'body of Christ,' " is implausible.[87] The recipients of the letter are rather reminded that they are "solely" invited to an orientation of life which corresponds to their "status." The two substantives, "holy" and "beloved," are synonymous with "chosen."[88] The multiple use of synonymous expressions underscores the importance of this declaration in the paraenesis: the invitation is not one that is imposed authoritatively; rather, it is to remind the Colossians that the gift is to be used, not to be left to lie fallow.

The genitive construction "(chosen) of God" is of decisive significance in this connection. The behavior to which they are urged is to reflect upon the one who is choosing them, to God, which means it is to mirror the Lord of the chosen ones, the Messiah. This thought is also the basis for the subsequent "catalog of virtues."

a heart full of compassion, kindness, humility, meekness, patience. It is remarkable that in this catalog exactly those "virtues" are lacking that serve as the four cardinal virtues among the Greeks: wisdom *(sophia)*, bravery *(andreia)*, sobriety *(sōphrosynē)*, and fairness *(dikaiosynē)*.[89] Instead, all the "virtues" listed in the OT or the NT occur here and are called characteristic attributes, or better, characteristic deeds of God or the Messiah. This reference demonstrates how far removed Paul is from Christifying generally valid norms through

---

86. Comp. 1:12–14, 21; 2:11ff. and Comment II to 1:24–2:5.

87. The particle *hōs* is to be translated here with "as" (as in Rom 1:21; 3:7), and it designates that which the Colossians actually are.

88. For "saints," see Notes to 1:12. For "beloved," comp. esp. the coordination of "love of God" and "select/covenant" undertaken in a fundamental way in Deuteronomy (Deut 4:37; 7:6ff.; 7:13; 10:15; 23:6; comp. also Hos 11:1, 4; 3:1; 14:5; Jer 31:3). "The idea that Jahweh loves his people is a relatively new statement. It first appears within the tradent circle, in which Hosea, Deuteronomy, and Jeremiah stand . . . , namely there where, within the tension of theological unfolding, the choice of faith is put into question according to the foundations of the divine selection of Israel. . . ." (E. Jenni, THAT I, p. 69).—The participle used in Col 3:11, *egapēmenoi* (beloved), to designate the recipients of the epistle, occurs only still in 1 Thess 1:4; 2 Thess 2:13. Otherwise, the use of the verbal adjective *agapētos* predominates.

89. Plato, Resp 428Aff. In addition to *sophia* (wisdom), *phronēsis* (insight) is also named (Plato, Men 88A–89A). The four virtues are enumerated in this form in Wis 8:7.

assimilation to his non-Jewish surroundings.[90] The "virtues" are oriented toward human beings, but the vision is toward God/the Messiah, as also all deeds are aimed toward the idea that the Messiah "is all and in all."

a heart full of compassion (literally: intestines/bowels of compassion). In Phil 2:1, the two Greek words *splanchna* (literally: intestines) and *oiktirmos* (compassion) are also placed together. However, there they are not dependent upon one another through a genitive relationship, as they are here in Col, but are rather connected by "and." We can state that, in Phil 2:1, the two concepts *splanchna* and *oiktirmos* summarize a prior enumeration,[91] but it is not discernible from that how the two words are to be differentiated conceptually.

Oiktirmos occurs more than twenty times in the LXX, and describes primarily an attribute of God.[92] The compassion of God is perceived as an antidote to his anger, which is directed at those who also deserve its consequences. The sinner comprehends the misery of his situation as a consequence of sin, which was experienced in its greatest depth in the exile. He appeals to the mercy of God, he hopes for and praises it, because it alone saves him from his misery. Whenever it is withdrawn, he knows that it is shut out by the anger of God (LXX Ps 76 ⟨77⟩:10).[93] In the NT, the substantive *oiktirmos* occurs only five times. Except in Heb 10:28, we find it only in the epistles that name Paul as author. Rom 12:1, as also 2 Cor 1:3, gives prominence to compassion as the paramount characteristic of God, which becomes especially clear in the latter passage.[94]

If *oiktirmos* becomes an obligation for humankind (Phil 2:1; Col 3:12), then we can think particularly of behavior on the basis of the above which does not encounter the fallen neighbor with anger and hardness, but which rather recognizes that his "fallen" misery signifies that he is worthy of compassion.

Splanchna in extra-biblical Greek originally meant the intestines of the sacrificial animal, then also the intestines of the human being and specifically the womb. Further, the "intestines" were considered the seat of "sexual pas-

90. See, for example, H. D. Betz, *Lukian*, op. cit., pp. 206–11.

91. See E. Lohmeyer, *Der Brief an die Philipper*, KEK 9, 11th ed. (Göttingen: Vandenhoeck & Ruprecht, 1956), p. 82.

92. In the Hellenistic Stoic literature, *oiktirmos* is ambivalent. Insofar as it expresses "lament with," it is preceived as a sign of weakness and thus as a vice, as "sickness of the soul." In the sense of "mildness, goodness," *oiktirmos* is evaluated in a positive sense (references in L. R. Stachowiak, "Chrestotes. Ihre biblisch- theologische Entwicklung und Eigenart," SF.NF 17 [1957] 98–102:99, fns. 2–4.)

93. Comp. esp. LXX Neh 9:19, 27, 28, 31; Ps 68(69):17 and also Ps 78(79):8; Hos 2:21; Lam 3:22.

94. "Praised be the God and Father of our Lord Jesus Christ, the father of mercy. . . ."

sion," whereas the "nobler senses" were associated with the "heart."⁹⁵ But this contextual delineation is not always unequivocal.

In the LXX, *splanchna* occurs more rarely than does *oiktirmos*. In LXX Prov 12:10, *splanchna* is used to translate the Hebrew *rhm*, which is otherwise rendered with *oiktirmos* (compassion). In LXX Prov 26:22, it is chosen for the Hebrew *beten* (intestines), which is there used literally.⁹⁶ In LXX Jer 28:13, a Hebrew equivalent is lacking. Otherwise, the word occurs in the late portions of the LXX, so that there, also, a Hebrew original is lacking. In 2 Macc 9:5; 4 Macc 5:30; 10:8; 11:19 it means the intestines of humans in a literal sense. LXX Wis 10:5; 4 Macc 15:23, 29 are more reminiscent of generative passions in the Classical Greek tradition, where *splanchna* means the natural spontaneous (compassionate) feelings of the father and mother toward their offspring, which are, however, "conquered" by obedience to or awe of God. The concept is used differently in the books of the Twelve Patriarchs. There, the meaning of "compassion" predominates (cf. also LXX Prov 12:10). A relationship of this passage in Col to the books of the Twelve Patriarchs indicates that a similar genitive construction in the TestSeb 7:3; 8:2, 6 could be a precedent for *splancha eleous*.⁹⁷ On the one hand, *eleos oiktirmos* is chosen in Col, but on the other hand, Paul uses the corresponding verbs *eleoō* and *oiktirmō* (to be compassionate) synonymously. It is possible that, in this passage, two synonyms with the meaning of "to be compassionate" were connected with each other through a genitive construction. We find this peculiarity of style also in the writings at Qumran.⁹⁸ We could translate this expression perhaps best by the phrase "sincere compassion." A somewhat different meaning results if we interpret the term *splanchna* from 2 Cor 6:12, where it is used synonymously with *kardia*. Based on the meaning of "heart" in OT thought (cf. Notes to 2:2), Paul would have then wanted especially to emphasize that the entire *persona*, in its thinking, feeling, and wishing, was to be controlled by compassion: a "heart full of compassion" is to be put on.

Kindness. *Chrēstotēs* in common Greek means (1) uprightness, and (2) kindness, tenderness, goodness. It also was valued positively by the Greeks, although it was condemned as pernicious when it concerned false mildness toward vices.⁹⁹

In the LXX, *chrēstotēs* was used almost exclusively in the Psalms, specifically for the kindness of God.¹⁰⁰ The richness of this goodness was pointed out in

95. See for that H. Koester, ThWNT VII, 548–59:548f.
96. "The words of the scandal-monger are delicate, for they penetrate into the innermost viscera."
97. See in the NT also Luke 1:78.
98. See H. Köster, ThWNT VII, 552, fn. 28.
99. See for that K. Weiss, ThWNT IX, 472–81:473, 24ff.; 478, 43ff.
100. Outside the Psalms, only in LXX 1 Esdr 5:58; Esther 8:12c. In reference to people, used only in Esther 8:12 c; Ps 13(14):1, 3; 36(37):3; 52(53):4 v 1.

varying ways, directly or indirectly.[101] This is not simply a mental attribute, but is rather "poured out" in the "kindness" Israel knows. This is demonstrated already in the repeated difficulty of deciding in the translation whether *chrēstotēs* means an attribute of God or the bestowed "kindness" of God. In the LXX, this kindness encompasses the compassion (see above) of God (Ps 24⟨25⟩:7), in general all the acts of salvation of his people, who are convinced that God saves the one in distress (Ps 67⟨68⟩:11; 144⟨145⟩:7. Beyond that, this kindness includes all the blessings of this salvation, such as fruitfulness of the land and animals, a long life, protection from enemies, etc. (Ps 20⟨21⟩:4; 62⟨65⟩:12).

In the NT, the substantive "kindness" occurs only in the epistles which name Paul as the author. Here also, his thinking is based on the OT foundation (Rom 2:4; 11:22).[102]

Humility. tapeinophrosynē in ordinary Greek has a negative connotation and designates a low, slavish demeanor. Its positive usage in the NT is determined by the OT; cf. Notes to 2:18.

Meekness. Meaning "mildness," *praytēs* is highly regarded among the virtues of the Greeks and designates the contrast to a rough, raw nature. This virtue is especially contrasted to uncontrolled eruptive anger and rage.[103] The usage of the word is differentiated in the LXX, where *praytēs* is closely related to *tapeinophrosynē* (humility, see above). There, the substantive is rare, but the word *prays* (mild/the gentle one) occurs more frequently. Both concepts can be used to translate the Hebrew word group ʿānāw, ʿǎnāwāh, ʿŏni, which describes human poverty, distress, oppression. These words occur primarily in post-exilic texts and define an attitude or posture, which was pervasive during the exile: the meek one recognizes that the judgment of God (experienced in the exile) is deserved, and he bends himself willingly under this burden and hopes solely for salvation through God. This hope knows that God points the way for the "meek one" (Ps 24⟨25⟩:9), that the latter will inherit the land (Ps 36⟨37⟩:11), that God will appear at the judgment in order to save the meek one and set him upright (Ps 75⟨76⟩:10). God will allow a meek and humble people to remain (Zeph 3:12), and correspondingly, the king at the end of time will be characterized by meekness (Zech 9:9). This declaration from Zech 9:9 is transferred to Jesus in Matt 21:5, and even Paul knows of meekness as an prominent characteristic of the Messiah Jesus (2 Cor 10:1).

Patience. Makrothymia and related concepts occur relatively seldom in extra-biblical Greek. There, they are used negatively (for resigned, despairing patience) as well as positively (for endurance and steadfastness).[104] In the LXX,

---

101. Comp. Ps 20⟨21⟩:4; 30⟨31⟩:20; 103⟨104⟩:28.

102. In reference to human beings, "goodness" is used only in Rom 3:12 (in a citation); Gal 5:22; Eph 2:7; Col 3:12.

103. References in F. Hauck / S. Schulz, ThWNT VI, 645–51:646f.

104. See for that J. Horst, ThWNT IV, 377–90:377f.

patience is foremost a characteristic of God. The Greek concept usually serves to translate the Hebrew *ʾerek ʾappayim* (long-suffering patient).[105] Even in Paul, the word is used in this sense, which emerges very clearly in the statements in Rom 2:4 and 9:22 (cf. also Notes to 1:11).

13 *It is fitting for you to bear one another* (literally: carrying). As in v 10, the two participial verb forms follow after an imperative here (v 12). It is more unequivocal here than in v 10, through the reference to the forgiveness granted by the "Lord" and the subsequent "so you also!" (see below), that the participles are intended imperatively.[106] The participial construction in v 12, in contrast to the imperative, is an indicator that v 13f. sums up the listing in v 12.

The Greek verb *anechomai* here does not have the connotation of endurance whose end is hoped for.[107] That thought is far removed in this passage where the relationship of the community members to each other is described and whose community was only made possible through the Messiah. The same verb, which describes the behavior toward one's neighbor in the previous verse, is used in LXX Isa 46:4 for the attitude of God toward his people. There it means the devoted care by God resulting from being chosen (God took them unto himself) for the chosen ones (he will save them). The interaction of the chosen ones with each other is to mirror this relationship between God and his people—if we can understand Col 3:13 on the basis of the OT passage.

and to forgive one another if someone has a complaint against someone else (literally: forgiving). As in 2:13 (see Notes there), here also the Greek word *charizomai*, which really means "to render something gratifying, a favor, a benefit," is used with the meaning "to forgive." The personal pronoun *heautois*, does not express the idea that those addressed should forgive themselves for their own sins. Rather, *heautois* is here chosen for stylistic reasons, as often in Classical Greek, and it is used as an alternative (cf. BDR 287) to the immediately preceding *allēlōn* (each other). The word *momphē* (reproach, complaint, burden) is familiar from Classical Greek, but occurs in the NT only here; it is lacking in the LXX, as also in the Apocryphal literature.[108]

As the Lord has also forgiven you, so also you (forgive one another) (literally: as also the Lord). The double *kai* (here translated by "also") in both portions of the comparison (as *also* . . . , so *also* . . .) is a stylistic peculiarity which can be observed frequently also in Classical Greek.[109]

The idea that controls the invitation to take off the "old self" and to put on

---

105. Only rarely, as in 1 Macc 8:4, does it mean "perseverance, steadfastness in battle."

106. Differently, A. Lindemann, p. 61.—For the translation, see Notes to v 10.

107. 1 Cor 4:12; 2 Thess 1:4; comp. 2 Cor 11:4, 19, 20.

108. J. Gnilka (p. 196, fn. 14) attributes *momphē* to an official legal character and refers to the use of the corresponding verb.—For the use of the substantive, comp. Pindar, Isthman Odes 4, 36; Euripides, Orestes 1069.

109. See Kühner-Blass-Gerth, II, p. 799 (and p. 524).

the "new" was already evident in v 11 and is formulated once again here: the interaction of Christians among each other is to be a witness to the behavior of their Lord toward them.[110]

In 2:13, God is named as the subject of forgiving, as also in Eph 4:32. The word *kyrios* (Lord) can mean God in association with its usage in the LXX, but this is improbable in this passage. Against this viewpoint is already the fact that, in v 17, where the preceding admonitions are summarized, the text expressly mentions the Lord Jesus (cf. also 1:3, 10; 2:6; 3:18, 20, 22, 23). We can observe several times in Paul that God, as also Jesus, can be named as subject for one and the same action, and this represents no contradiction.[111]

14 *Beyond all (this), put on love* (literally: above all). The verb "to put on" has to be supplemented from v 12. *Epi pasin* (above all) is not to be understood in a sense of locality, and it does not mean that "above" the "virtues" which are listed in v 12, love should be put on as an "upper garment" or "girdle" in order to hold those together. Such a conception does not agree with the practice of dressing at the time of the composition of Col.[112] Therefore it is analogous to Luke 3:20 and should be translated by "in addition to all / except for all." The following relative clause, however, demonstrates that love is not a virtue among the others that should also still be taken into consideration. As in Rom 13:8–10, 1 Cor 13:1ff., and Gal 5:14, love assumes first place. Thus it would be entirely justified here to interpret *epi pasin* elatively, "above all love . . ."[113]

---

110. N. A. Dahl, *Formgeschichtliche Beobachtungen*, op. cit., pp. 6f., recognizes in the words "as also the Lord . . ." a schema belonging to the paraclesis, which he calls "Konformitatsschema." He wants to avoid the concept "imitatio," since we are dealing with the devotion of Christ to us, with his becoming human and going to his death, which determines salvation. One should rather talk about *conformitas* instead of *imitatio* (comp. also O. Merk, *Handeln*, op. cit., p. 211). We need to observe, however, Eph 5:1f.; where the summons is, "become *imitators* of God" in reference to the sacrificial death of Christ (for that, see M. Barth, AB 34A, pp. 588–92).

111. Thus, for example, in Rom 14:3/15:7. Further, see Notes to 1:16, fn. 24.—To the statement that Jesus forgives sins, see esp. Mark 2:5 par.—T. K. Abbott (p. 287) notes that if Christ is meant here by "Lord," then this is the only passage in Col where it is directly stated that Christ forgives sins. This notation can be misleading, since it conveys the impression of a "rule," according to which God is the subject of forgiveness in Paul. But this is expressly stated only in Eph 4:32 and Col 3:13.

112. This interpretation is improbable already because the undergarment or inner garment did not consist of different components. At the time of Paul, people wore an undergarment and an outer garment. This outer garment was removed during physical labor, and the inner garment was then tucked up with a belt. They did this also when they walked. It is uncertain whether they used a belt also for the outer garment.—Comp. for that Benzinger, RAK X, 514–26; "Die Bibel und ihre Welt II," pp. 903–11; A. Oepke, ThWNT V, 302–8. C. F. D. Moule, p. 124, notes to *syndesmos*, that " 'belt' or 'girdle' is not attested among its meanings."

113. A. Fridrichsen, "Charité et perfection. Observation sur Col 3.14," SO 19 (1939) 41–45, "et surtout (revetez-vous de) la charite, . . ."

that is the band of completeness. In a manner characteristic of Col, an important following remark is attached by means of a brief relative clause.[114] The relative pronoun should have been constructed in the feminine (if it had been grammatically correct) to refer to the feminine *agapē* (love). Yet such divergences are common in Greek. In similar formulations, assimilation of the relative pronoun to the predicate noun is to be noted (compare the text preserved in Codex Sinaiticus at Eph 5:5, among others). In this passage, the neuter form preserved in the original text can be explained on the basis of a formulaic usage of the Greek *ho estin* (that means, that is).[115]

Syndesmos (here translated by "band") designates the means by which two or more things are tied to each other (cf. Col 2:19 and further references in LS Lex), as well as the corresponding result, that which is tied, the bundle. Besides that, the word is used metaphorically to designate that which unity creates. Thus for example, Aristotle (Eth Nic VIII 7, 1162a, 28) calls children the *syndesmos* that keeps the parents together. Simplicius (in Epict 30), who however was not active until the sixth century, calls *philia* (love, friendship) the *syndesmos* of all virtues (cf. Dibelius-Greeven, 43).[116] This declaration, together with comparable elucidations in Paul, according to which love is the "fullness of the law" (Rom 13:10), could give rise to the interpretation that love is the "cardinal virtue" which "binds together" all the other "virtues" listed in v 12 and thus enfolds them within itself. But since the paraenesis has its center in the declaration of unity of the chosen ones (cf. v 11), and since also in the verse (v 15) the calling "in *one* body" is emphasized, we can assume that the object of *syndesmos* is not the "virtues," but rather the chosen ones: they are tied together into a unity through love (where neither Greek nor Jew . . . is). Based on this, the genitive attribute "of completeness" attains an emphatic social significance: completeness exists wherever Christians live together in unity.[117] The possible interpretations of the genitive "of completeness" as *genitivus qualitatis*,[118] as

---

114. Comp. 1:7, 24, 27; 2:10, 17, 22; 4:9.

115. See for that BDR 132.2 and the parallels cited there.

116. Further references in G. Rudberg, "Paralella (2. *syndesmos*)," CNT 3 (1938) 19–21. For the philosophic teaching of *syndesmos*, see W. Jaeger, *Nemesius von Emesa* (Berlin: Weidmann, 1914), pp. 96–137, and critically with this, K. Reinhardt, Art. "Poseidonius," in Pauly-W., 22, 558–826:607, 773–78.

117. A. Fridrichsen, "Charité," op. cit., p. 43, refers to cosmological ideas in Greek philosophy (among the Stoics, and others) as background for Col 3:14: for the teaching of harmony in the cosmos produced by *sympatheia*. But it is questionable that Paul had these Greek ideas in mind in describing the unity of the "body" (see for that J. Horst, ThWNT IV, 565–72).

118. The "complete band" would be "complete" if it encompassed the unity of the chosen.

genitive of content,[119] or as genitive of purpose,[120] are neither mutually exclusive possibilities, nor do they reflect weighty contextual differences (cf. also E. Schweizer, p. 156).

15 *And let the peace of the Messiah rule in your hearts. Eirēnē* (peace) has a more encompassing meaning than simply peace and can also be rendered by welfare, well-being, salvation. This is more precisely elaborated in Notes to Col 1:20, where the verb "to create peace" (eirēnopoieo) is an explanatory description of the work of salvation of the Messiah. It describes life in his domain, which encompasses all things. Insofar as the individually enumerated "virtues" in v 12 describe an action of God or the Messiah, that action is here summarized by the word *eirēnē*. It is to be the standard for measuring human action. This passage is not dealing with a subjective peace of mind or an inner peace but a decisive measure for correct action.

Brabeuō (here translated with "to rule") is a word from the world of sports and designates the activity of the umpire. It is, however, also used in a general sense and it then means, "to judge, to decide, to guide, to rule" (cf. Notes to 2:18). In the NT the verb occurs only once, as also once in the LXX.[121] This verse gives no indication that there is any allusion to an athletic contest, and so we can adopt the general meaning of "to rule" here.

Heart refers here also, as in 2:2 (cf. Notes there), to the whole pattern in his thinking, wishing, feeling, and action: the peace which is created through the Messiah should be a determining factor for all areas of life. Here, where the concern is to make manifest the fact of having been chosen in the association of Christians with each other, it would make little sense to assume that the "isolation of the heart" is the subject (cf. for example LXX 1 Sam 16:7).

for which you also are called in one body. In order to take part in the peace that has come with the beginning of the reign of the Messiah, an action of God is necessitated: he calls (cf. also 1:12). In this connection, it is fundamental that participation in this peace is made possible only *"in* one body," that is, in the unity of the chosen people.[122] It is also not incumbent on "individual called ones" to first create this unity. Rather, it is already an established reality

---

119. Love is the band that is completeness.

120. Love is the band so that they are complete (i.e., a unity).

121. In Wis 10:12, it says of wisdom that it adjudicated the competition (*agōn*, see Notes to 1:19) between Jacob and the angel (comp. Gen 32:25ff.) "as umpire or referee."

122. The concept "body" is used here without the article or the genitive attribute "Christ." It depends on the unit of thought that is expressed with image of the body (comp. 1 Cor 12:12ff.), in which both are not necessary. The supposition that the community is meant in contrast to the universal church arises from a false alternative, for what Paul says about the church (i.e., in 1 Cor 12:12ff.) should be conceptualized for the community (comp. also the Notes to 1:24: "for you"—"for his body, i.e. the church").—Important text evidence, such as Papyrus 46 (ca. 200), Codex Vaticanus (fourth century), and Minuscule 1739, leave the numeral "one" out. This does not

from God through a "collective calling." For the chosen ones, it remains to acknowledge this unity through corresponding action and to give thanks for it (see below).

And become thankful. As in 1:12; 2:7; 3:17; 4:2, special emphasis is placed on giving thanks. Since this invitation is repeated in v 17b, it seems obvious to view the declarations between these two invitations (vv 16, 17a) as one concretization of that which is to be understood by giving thanks. In this sense, giving thanks also becomes a social act that gives expression through its external form in "the calling of the Christians 'in one body.' "[123]

16 *Let the word of the Messiah dwell among you in its (rich-making) richness* (literally: in you richly). The "word" *(logos)* is called "the word of truth" in 1:5, and it is identified with the gospel. In 1:25ff., it is called "the word of God" and it is more closely defined as the secret that was hidden since far-distant times but that is now revealed, which is the Messiah. Correspondingly, "the word of the Messiah"[124] is the word which proclaims the Messiah (the revealed secret) and by which the Messiah himself is received as Lord (cf. Notes to 2:6). In 1:6, this word is discussed as a sovereignly acting person (cf. Notes). And here also, in 3:16, the word itself is the subject, not the Colossians. The relationship of the statement before us to 1:6 is also demonstrated in the contextual parallelism of the statements of the "dwelling of the word of God among you"[125] and of the "word having come and having become at home among the Colossians" (1:6). Accordingly, the invitation in this verse should not be understood as an invitation to the Colossians, but rather as a request of God to continue to allow his word to dwell also among the Colossians.

The expression *en hymin* (in you) may take up the expression "in your heart" again from v 15,[126] and it thus emphasizes that the dwelling of this word among the addressees is to be life-determining in all areas of human existence, especially in one's actions toward one's neighbor (cf. Notes to the previous verse).

If the Colossians had been asked to permit the gospel to be heard among them, then *plousiōs* (richly) could state that this should occur often and fully. However, within the framework of the suggested interpretation (see above), such an elucidation makes little sense (cf. 1:6!). The adverb should rather be

---

change the sense, since it only emphasizes that which is said anyway concerning the image of body.

123. Compare for that J. M. Robinson, *Hodajot-Formel*, op. cit., p. 225.

124. The expression "word of Christ" occurs only here. Comp. for that 1 Thess 1:8; 4:15; 2 Thess 3:1; and also 1 Tim 6:3; Heb 6:1; as well as Acts 8:25; 13:44, 48, 49; 15:35, 36; 16:32; 19:10; 20:35.

125. In Greek, the preposition *en* (in you) is repeated as prefix with the verb *enoikeō*. See for that Notes to 2:13, fn. 95.

126. See also LXX Ps 36(37):31, where it is said of the just, "The law of his God is in his heart" (comp. also Jer 31:33 and in the NT, John 15:7; 1 John 2:24.

understood on the basis of the statements in 1:27 and 2:2. The dwelling of this word is characterized by the fact that it shares its richness (1:27) with those to whom it came (2:2).[127]

For you it is (then only) reasonable to teach each other in all wisdom, and to exhort (literally: teaching and exhorting). Syntactically, it is possible to attach *en passē sophia* (in all wisdom) to the previous statement. But because of the reference to 1:28 (see below) and based on structural parallels to the subsequent invitation, it is probable that "in all wisdom" is a qualification of "teaching and exhorting," just as *en te chariti* (in the *charis*, see below) modifies "singing."

The participles can hardly be translated as modals here ("by . . ."). After the elucidation about sovereignty over the world (see above), it would be difficult to agree on a statement according to which the dwelling of this word is brought about through human action. Thus, the participles are to be understood imperatively, and they provide another answer appropriate to the chosen ones for the effect of the word.[128] This answer is qualified by "exhorting and teaching in all wisdom,"[129] and thus it corresponds to the task that is also given to Paul and his co-workers (cf. 1:28): the addressees are not considered as "lay people," but rather as co-workers of the apostle in the proclamation of the revealed secret (cf. Comment II to 1:1 + 2).

with psalms, hymns, and songs produced by the spirit (literally: spiritual). Through these instrumental references to "teaching and exhorting," three motifs which achieve prominence within the context—(1) giving thanks; (2) calling to one body; (3) annulling of differences among the chosen—are unified in a remarkable way. The psalms, hymns, and songs are sung to God (see below), yet such a praise of God is not simply a matter between the individual and God but is rather a mutual teaching and admonition of the chosen ones with each other [and is thus strictly a God-pleasing thanks]. Where mutual teaching and admonition occur additionally in the form of thanks and praise, it gives expression to an orientation in which all recipients understand each other equally and no one elevates himself as "admonisher" or as "teacher."

An exact specific differentiation and a generic ordering of the terms *psalmos, hymnos, ōdē* are not possible based on their usage in the NT (as well as in the LXX). J. B. Lightfoot (p. 291) suggested the following demarcation based on Gregory of Nyssa (fourth century),[130] ". . . while the leading idea of *psalmos* is a musical accompaniment and that of *hymnos* praise to God, *ōdē* is the general word for a song whether accompanied or unaccompanied, whether a praise or any other subject." This differentiation comes close to the original meaning of

---

127. Comp. for that also statements such as Rom 10:12f.; 2 Cor 8:9.

128. For this usage of the participle and its translation, see Notes to 1:10 (esp. also fn. 32).

129. For the meaning of this expression, see Notes to 1:28 and 1:9.

130. In Psalm III, PG 44, 493B.

psalmos, "the rebounding of the bow upon the string," "the playing of a stringed instrument,"[131] but whether this is applicable to Paul is questionable. Paul uses this term in 1 Cor 14:26 in connection with the corresponding verb *psallō* (1 Cor 14:15). It then means the linguistically comprehensible *song* as opposed to the *song in tongues.* The component of musical accompaniment has fully receded there. Thus we will have to understand the listing in Col 3:16 (as well as in Eph 5:19) as a description of the fullness and the multiplicity of possible responses to the word that dwells in its richness among the faithful. The hymn in 1:15–20 is an example of such singing.

The adjective *pneumatikos* (spiritual) probably refers not only to *ōdē* (song), after which it is positioned in the Greek sentence, but to all three substantives, and it is placed after them for emphasis. E. Schweizer's interpretation, that the "spiritual songs" here mean hardly more than the corresponding English expression, namely songs with a sacred content, not a profane one,[132] hardly applies. The connection of 3:16 with the declaration in 1:25ff., according to which the content of exhorting and teaching is entirely subject to the secret that is subordinated to the will of God, makes it clear that "spiritual" is to be read as a precise definition in exactly this circumstance. The adjective then has the theological content that the word "(Holy) Spirit" has in the undisputed Pauline epistles (cf. also J. Gnilka, p. 200, fn. 41).

(and) to sing to God from the heart (standing) in grace (literally: in your heart). The form of this singing, which is intended for God, encompasses the psalms, hymns, and songs cited above, with which the chosen ones are to teach and exhort each other. From that we can already discern that "in your heart" cannot mean simply a "silent singing" in the "secrecy of the heart" ("to heart," cf. the Notes to 2:2). The singing that is meant here should surely have a central position in the worship service of the Colossian community, but v 16 does not need to be limited to the setting of the worship service.[133]

The term *charis* can have different meanings. The use of the word in Greek permits the following translations: (1) "grace or charm" (cf. for example LXX Ps 44⟨45⟩:3), (2) "thanks," (3) "(divine) grace." A decision among these possibilities depends primarily on whether *charis* is construed with or without an article by the author of Col. The determination of the original text is uncertain here and both readings are well attested.[134] It is not certain that the reading with the

---

131. Classical sources in G. Delling, ThWNT VIII, 492–506:494, 28ff.—In the LXX, see esp. Ps 97(98):5; Job 21:12; 30:31; Lam 5:14 (re string instruments or playing a string instrument); Ps 80(81):3 (to designate string instruments); Ps 94(95):2 (song accompanied by a string instrument; in this sense probably also in the prevailing use in the Psalm headings for translation of the Heb *mismor.* For that, see H. J. Kraus, *Psalmen,* Bd. I, BK XV/1, pp. XVIII–XXX, esp. p. XIX).

132. E. Schweizer, *Christus und Geist,* op. cit., p. 189; ibid., p. 157.

133. Comp., for example, E. Haupt, p. 149; J. Gnilka, p. 199.

134. The article is attested, among others, in Papyrus 46 (200), Codex Vaticanus

article is the more difficult and therefore the more original one (cf. E. Schweizer, p. 158). It is also imaginable that the usage without the article seemed a misunderstanding to the scribes because of the theological meaning of *charis* in Paul, and that they therefore tampered with the text in an effort to "correct" it. If the article is original (in favor of which are the readings of such important mss as Codex Vaticanus and Papyrus 36), then only possibility 3 can be considered as an accurate translation, "as such, who are in grace, sing. . . ."[135] But if the article is not original, then *charis* is probably to be rendered by "thanks" because of the strongly emphatic invitation to thank through *eucharistoi* (those who say thanks, v 15) and *eucharistountes* (saying thanks, v 17).

17 *And concerning everything, whatever you do in word or deed, (do) everything* (literally: and everything, which). The predicate of the main sentence is not explicitly named but arises naturally from the previous relative clause. Analogously to the participially constructed imperative in the previous verse, we have to supplement *poiountes* (do!). It is noteworthy that the object already named in the main sentence, *panta* (all things, everything), is repeated while it is placed ahead of the main sentence, although now in the singular form *pan* (everything), and it is also elucidated by a relative clause. Probably, *pan* is not in the accusative case but is rather a nominative. This is a construction that is favored in an underlying Hebrew usage. It is easily varied in Col in that the precedent object *pan* in the nominative is not taken up again in the main sentence by a pronoun but the corresponding substantive is cited once again.[136]

M. Dibelius (Dibelius-Greeven, p. 45) points out the possibility that *logos kai ergon* (word and deed) can be understood to refer to the worship service and can thus be a reference to "word and sacrament."[137] But here we have an emphatic "everything" at the end of the elucidations that deal with "putting on the new self" and thus with the actions of Christians in all areas of life. Simultaneously, this "everything" is in a declaration that can serve as a superscript to the following *Haustafel* (3:18–4:1), because there the reference is repeatedly back to "Lord" in v 17. Thus any restriction to the worship service is improbable.

in the name of the Lord Jesus. The expression *en onomati* is familiar from the LXX and corresponds to the Hebrew *běšhem*. It also occurs frequently in the NT, but in the Pauline Epistles only at 1 Cor 5:4; 6:11; Eph 5:20; Phil 2:10; Col

---

(fourth century) and Minuscule 1739, the reading without article, among others, in Codex Sinaiticus (fourth century) and Codex Alexandrinus (fifth century).

135. "To be in peace" would be understood from 3:15: called for the peace of the Messiah in one body.

136. Comp. K. Beyer, *Semitische Syntax im Neuen Testament*, Bd. I: *Satzlehre*, Teil 1, StUNT 1 (Göttingen: Vandenhoeck & Ruprecht, 1962), pp. 156, 168f.

137. W. Bousset, *Kyrios Christos*, FRLANT.NF 4 (Göttingen: Vandenhoeck & Ruprecht, 1913), pp. 102f., fn. 5, supposed this.

3:17; 2 Thess 3:6. Its meaning needs to be determined each time from its context. [138]

In the OT, the common expression is "in the name of Yahweh," and perhaps originally it meant "under the intercession of the name of Yahweh." [139] Besides that, a commission is often described by this usage. Deut 18:18f. clarifies what is then intended: God will put his own words into the mouth of his prophet, and he will speak what God commands.

For Col 3:17, W. Heitmüller suggested the translation, "in the naming, appellation of the name of the Lord Jesus," and he suspects that Paul there "simply had in mind the use of the formula 'in the name of Jesus.' " [140] The sense of this naming of a name lies in the fact that Jesus is named as the one who effects the thanks in a prayer of thanksgiving, or that he is the one who is addressed as the one who intercedes for the thanks (p. 262). But in our opinion, W. Heitmüller developed his idea of intercession on the basis of an unacceptable interpretation of the false teaching in Colossae (see below).

A different understanding can be recommended on the basis of v 11. There the goal of "putting on the new self" is the affirmation that Christ is Lord over all things. Here in v 17, the effect of what it means to put on the new self is drawn from the summons that is aimed at the chosen one, and which is then elucidated further, but in different words. What is meant, therefore, by the expression, "the deed in the name of the Lord Jesus," [141] is that it proclaims the name of this lord, or in other words, that Jesus is the Lord. [142] Just as in the OT

---

138. For the significance of the concept "name," see esp. A. S. van der Woude, THAT II, 935–63; H. Bietenhard, ThWNT V, 242–83; E. Lohmeyer, Vater-unser, op. cit., pp. 41–59.

139. See G. von Rad, Theol.d.AT. I, 184f.: "Kara' b·shem yahwe (literally 'call in the name of YHWH,' H.B.) is originally a cultic term and means to call Jahweh by using his name (Gen 12:8; 13:4; 21:33; 1 Kgs 18:24; and others)."—Comp. among others also Lev 19:12; Deut 6:13; 10:8; 1 Sam 20:42; 2 Sam 6:18; Ps 129:8; Jer 12:16.

140. W. Heitmüller, "Im Namen Jesu." Eine sprach- und religions-geschichtliche Untersuchung zum Neuen Testament, speziell zur altchristlichen Taufe (Göttingen: Vandenhoeck & Ruprecht, 1903), pp. 68, 263.

141. This is the best-attested reading, rendered among others by Papyrus 46 and Codex Vaticanus. Other text evidence reads the variant "Jesus Christ," "Lord Jesus Christ," or simply "Lord" instead of "Lord Jesus."

142. E. Lohmeyer, Vater- unser, op. cit., p. 42, refers to the Gospel of John, where "I have come in the name of my father" (5:43) means as much as, "I have proclaimed your name" (17:6, 26).—Comp. also G. Delling, Die Zueignung des Heils in der Taufe. Eine Untersuchung zum neutestamentlichen "taufen auf den Namen" (Berlin: Ev. Verlagsanstalt, o.J.), p. 54, "The expression 'in the name' in Col 3:17 is not relevantly different from l·schem: every act of the Christian occurs in reference to the Lord being Christ (once again, it is demonstrated that the interpretation of the expression 'in the name' comes from its context; thus it can also be used in proximity to a prepositional usage of l·schem.)."

the "name Yahweh" meant Yahweh himself, the God who is close to his people (cf. for example Deut 12:5, 11, 21), so also the phrase "the name of Yahweh" points to the deeds of God with which he demonstrates to and establishes for his people his reputation throughout the whole world.[143] So also does the "name of the Lord Jesus" mean here in Col this Lord himself in his "nearness" to all of creation: it presents him as the Lord and king over all things (cf. v 11 and 1:15–20).

Thank God, the Father, through him (literally: thanking). For the imperatival translation of the participle, cf. Notes to v 16; for the expression "God the Father," cf. the Notes to 1:12 and Comment II to 1:3–8.

The invitation here cannot simply be ranked equally with the preceding one in vv 16 + 17. It frames the preceding one, along with the words "become thankful," (v 15) which are placed prior to vv 16 + 17. Thus it is probable that the differing forms of the inclusive imperatives instructing the hearers to give thanks mean that they should continually give thanks. A technical meaning of *eucharisteō* is barely possible, whether for the designation of the hymn sung in the worship service,[144] or for the designation of the prayer of thanks that constitutes the celebration of the communion meal or the entire communion service.[145]

The recipient of the expression of thanks is God, as is the case in most places in the Pauline writings.[146] For Paul, giving thanks is the appropriate act of the created being toward its creator (cf. Rom 1:21), because it increases the renown of God (cf. 2 Cor 4:15). As in Rome 1:8 (compare also Rom 7:25), so here also the discussion concerns the giving of thanks "through him (Christ)." G. Harder[147] reads these words formulaically, as a description of the new

---

143. Comp. among others, Ps 9:11f.; 18:50f.; 68:5(29ff.). We need to observe in these references how "name of Jahweh" is used as an interchangeable concept of "Jahweh."

144. H. Löwe, "Bekenntnis," op. cit., p. 303.

145. *eucharisteō* (and related concepts) are used in this sense in NT times (references in G. Conzelmann, ThWNT IX, 405).—H. Schlier, *Epheser*, op. cit., p. 248, thinks that the expression "in the name" in Paul refers to the "situation of the cult." The few references in Pauline literature are not sufficient for the thesis that Paul understood "in the name" with this limited meaning, and the other usage of the formula argues against it. Yet the summons "to do *everything* in the name of the Lord Jesus" includes also the "sacraments." In this context, this then means that it is only a God-pleasing thanks if it is used "socially" [comp. for that 1 Cor 11:17ff. and esp. M. Barth, *Das Mahl des Herrn* (Neukirchen-Vluyn: Neukirchener Verlag, 1987)].

146. Only in Rom 16:4 are people recipients of thanks.

147. G. Harder, *Paulus und das Gebet*, op. cit., pp. 175–83, "that Paul wants to say with his formula, that the prayer of thanksgiving occurs through Christ in the condition and in the manner in which a Christ prays, a baptized person who is placed into the community of the dying and rising, to them who know God's will and secret, to

Christian way of praying. G. Conzelmann criticizes this interpretation, since the function of Christ in the act of salvation is misunderstood: only through him do we have access to God, and thus the opportunity for prayer (Rom 5:2).[148] W. Heitmüller interprets the expression differently: it is "doubtless *antithetical* toward the angels worshipped by the false teachers."[149] Thus, the meaning of the words "through him" (cf. previous Notes) becomes clear from the Judaic perspective on angels, where the angels are understood as intermediaries. But it is improbable that angels were worshipped as intermediaries in competition with Christ in Colossae (cf. Comment V to 2:6–23), and thus the idea of intercession with God for mankind through Christ does not intrude itself here in this exposition.

Because the "new self" can be put on through the dying and the rising with him, i.e., that the person can perform a new action only "through him," every such action should occur as a form of giving thanks in the name of Jesus. In other words, "through him" in this passage is to be understood as designating the constant giving of thanks "which was only made possible and effected through him."[150]

2. The Haustafel (3:18–4:1)

18 Wives, be subject to your husbands, as it is fitting in the Lord. 19 Husbands, love your wives and be not harsh against them. 20 Children, be obedient to your parents in all things, for that is well-pleasing in the Lord. 21 Fathers, do not embitter your children, so that they will not lose courage. 22 Slaves, obey your earthly masters in all things, not with eye-service, as someone who wishes to please human beings, but rather fear the Lord with a sincere

---

whom God has given the ability to thank because he has shown them Christ and his divine acts."

148. ThWNT IX, 397–405:403, fn. 72.

149. W. Heitmüller, *Im Namen Jesu*, op. cit., pp. 68f.; 260ff.; Comp. also J. A. Bengel, p. 794.—A. Oepke, ThWNT II, 67f., points out that *dia* with the genitive is used not only instrumentally, but also causally (like *dia* with the accusative): thus of people (or angels) (comp. Mark 14:21 par; Acts 12:9; 24:2; Rom 5:12, 16; 1 Cor 11:12; 15:21; and others), and of God (Rom 11:36; 1 Cor 1:9; Heb 2:10). From there, we can also interpret the peculiar formula in Christian language usage, "through Christ." To thank through Christ does not have the meaning that Christ inserts himself between God and man as facilitator and transmitter of prayer. We should rather observe that the formula "through Christ" occurs nowhere in connection with verbs of petition, as we might expect if the derivative concept is correct.

150. Comp. also W. Thüsing, *Per Christum*, op. cit.: because this living Lord is understood by Paul through and through as the effectual one, the expression demonstrates basically the effect of Christ (p. 233). "The Pauline *dia Christou* means basically 'through the working *of Christ, in whom we are.*' " In the preponderance of cases, it is homogeneous with "through the pneuma" (p. 235).

heart. 23 Whatever you do, do it from the heart for the Lord and not for human beings. 24 For you know that you will receive the reward, the inheritance, from the Lord. (Thus) serve the Lord the Messiah! 25 Because the unrighteous will receive whatever he has done wrong—without regard of person. 4:1 Masters, give your slaves whatever is right and fair. For you know that you also have a master in heaven.

NOTES

Verses 3:18–4:1 contain the so-called *Haustafel* (Table of Household Duties). For this concept and the genre characterized by it, as well as for the significance of its declarations within the framework of the Epistle to the Colossians, see Comment II.

18 *Wives.* Addressed are the members of a household in ancient times.[1] We find such a direct form of address also in the *Haustafel* of the Epistle to the Ephesians and the First Epistle of Peter, in distinction from 1 Tim 2:8–15; 6:1–10 and Titus 2:1–10. In much the same way, they occur in the catalog of obligations in Stoic sources, but there neither "the woman nor the child is exhorted, and Epictetus, at least, never refers to slaves in such contexts, though he himself was a former slave."[2] It is not justified from our modern perspective, however, to set off Christianity in a positive sense from its environment by the fact that women (as well as children and slaves, see below) are addressed as ethically responsible persons. D. L. Balch refers specifically to Platonic and Neo-Pythagorean literature in which we find ethical admonitions addressed to women.[3]

be subject to your husbands (literally: the husbands). The possessive pronoun "your" is deleted here, as also in the remaining instances of address in this *Haustafel*, with the exception of v 21. Only the definite article is used with the substantive ("the husbands") here, as is often the case in Greek when the relationship is self-evident.[4]

Hypotassō in the Greek means "to order accordingly, to join below, to subordinate, to subjugate." In the middle voice, it means "to subject oneself, to subjugate oneself," as well as "to be subservient."[5] In the Letter to Aristeas 257, an intertestamental Jewish work from the second/first century B.C.E., the word

---

1. The substantive *gynaikes* (women) in the nominative with the article is used instead of the vocative. But we do not have a semitism here (comp. J. B. Lightfoot, p. 292) and thus also no indication of a Jewish *Vorlage* of the *Haustafel* (see BDR 147).

2. D. L. Balch, *Let Wives Be Submissive: The Domestic Code in 1 Peter*, SBL.MS 26 (Chico: Scholars Press, 1981), p. 97.

3. Ibid.

4. See for this BauerLex, pp. 1088f.

5. S. G. Delling, ThWNT VIII, 40–47.

is used in a positive sense for a humble, humanly accommodating, and therefore God-pleasing demeanor.[6]

In the NT, the verb occurs thirty-eight times; twenty-three of those are in the Pauline corpus. M. Barth differentiates two varying usages in the Pauline letters (AB 34A, pp. 709f.):

1. When *hypotassō* is used in the active or as a *passivum divinum*, thus as a description of the name of God, "the act of subjugation and the fate of submission reveal the existence of a hierarchy, or establish the proper order of right and might."

2. Through the use of "middle or passive indicatives, participles or imperatives of this verb, however, Paul describes a voluntary attitude of giving in, cooperating, assuming responsibility, and carrying a burden." This kind of subjection is demanded only of Christ, or of persons who are "in Christ."

Outside of the Pauline writings, these observations are not applicable, however, as Luke 10:17 and 20 demonstrate, where in the Greek an indicative form of the middle voice is also used.

E. Kähler[7] also emphasizes that, in the NT, the element of voluntariness is associated with *hypotassesthai*. She differentiates this verb sharply from "to obey," because where the concern is obedience, it is already decided for the subordinate ones why their obedience is necessary. This is not a concern with *hypotassesthai*. Wherever it occurs, any kind of compulsion is excluded. The concern is with the order of God, who desires observance and response, and when this answer is expressed by *hypotassestai*, it is an entirely voluntary decision. She observes for this passage, "Their subjection (that of the wives, H.B.) is valid for the order of God, not really that of the husband as the final goal. Thus their subjection can never be blind obedience which she would have to render to her husband or which he could even demand" (p. 180).

These observations of E. Kähler can be verified basically in Col. The ethical admonitions proceed from the "glorious abundance" of the now-revealed secret, so that the action to which they are summoned can be understood as the joyful affirmation of that which is given, and the idea of compulsion and involuntariness is misplaced here. In addition, especially for Col, we are ultimately dealing with subjection to the Messiah (cf. esp. 3:11). Additionally, v 18 does not contextually deal with "blind obedience" since it is preconditioned that women, insofar as they are married to non-Christian husbands, can refuse

---

6. "To this he agreed also, and asked another how he might find recognition on journeys. And he said: if you show equal justice to everyone, and if you appear lower rather than higher to those with whom you are traveling. For God accepts everything that humbles itself, and even human beings are accustomed to being gracious to those who subordinate themselves."

7. E. Kähler, *Die Frau in den paulinischen Briefen. Unter besonderer Berücksichtigung des Begriffs der Unterordnung* (Zürich/Frankfurt a.M.: Gotthelf, 1960), esp. pp. 176–80; 201f.

this obedience in an essential point, namely in that they do not venerate the gods of their husbands.[8] Then, however, we would hardly do justice to the statements of the *Haustafel* if we viewed E. Kähler's findings as the intent of the declaration in Col 3:18. That would all too easily create the impression that the author wished to remove a "crude patriarchalism" in v 18.[9] Such an interpretation would ignore the sociological background upon which the *Haustafeln* are surely based (cf. Comment II). The statements here which cannot be viewed separately from the accusation made against the Christians, namely that they endanger the social and political order in that they assign to women, children, and slaves their autonomous and independent religious decision-making power, separately from their husbands, parents, and masters.

It is, however, improbable that the author of Col for apologetic reasons simply incorporates and motivates on a Christian basis the socioethical norms from his surroundings in the instruction to women to subject themselves to their husbands. The context in which the *Haustafel* stands (cf. Comment II) rather points to the idea that a reproach against the Christian community can be demonstrated in the form at hand, because the theme of "subjection" expresses a uniquely Judeo-Christian obligation. Statements such as Matt 20:27f. and Phil 2:7f. can serve to illustrate this point.[10] Beyond that, the use of *hypotassesthai* in 1 Pet 5:5 (cf. Jas 4:6f.) demonstrates the background from which this verb was understood in the Christian community. As we find already in the Aristeas epistle (see above), "subjection" is interpreted from OT statements, namely that God accepts the humble one (cf. Job 22:29; Prov 3:34).[11] If we can assume this background also for Col 3:18, then a connection with Col 3:12 becomes evident,

---

8. See for this the elucidations in Comment II.

9. K. Müller, "Die Haustafel des Kolosserbriefes und das antike Frauenthema. Eine kritische Rückschau auf alte Ergebnisse," in *Die Frau im Urchristentum*, eds. G. Dauzenberg, H. Merklein, K. Müller (Freiburg i.B.: Herder, 1983), pp. 263–319: esp. pp. 292–98, points in this connection expressly and by way of correction to a practice frequent among theologians, namely of skewing phenomena in antiquity in an undifferentiated way "onto a unilinear path of crude patriarchalism" and thus to act "as though ancient times exclusively advocated subjection of women and only the NT demanded deference on the part of the husband."—Equally necessary is a differentiating presentation of the role of the woman in the Judaica of its time. B. J. Brooten, "Jüdinnen zur Zeit Jesu. Ein Plädoyer für Differenzierung," ThQ 161 (1981) 281–85 pleads for this. Comp. also F. Dexinger, TRE XI, 424–31.

10. "And whoever among you wants to be first, let him be your servant. Even as the Son of man came not to be served but rather to serve, and to give his life as a ransom for many" (Matt 20:27f.). In Eph, the subordination of man and woman is compared to that of the Messiah and the church. See for that M. Barth, AB 34A, pp. 700ff.

11. Comp. Notes to Col 2:18 and 3:12. See also E. Kamlah, "*hypotassesthai* in den neutestamentlichen Haustafeln," in FS für G. Stählin zum 70. Geburtstag, *Verborum Veritas*, eds. O. Böcher and K. Haacker (Wuppertal: Brockhaus, 1970), pp. 237–43:242.

according to which the "subjecting oneself" as an expression of humility is a mark of the chosen one. Thus, the interpretation that the summons to subjection has only a time-conditioned validity within the framework of societal structures in antiquity is further challenged or negated. In place of a concrete summons, the modern reader could then readily read the fundamental declaration of this verse to the effect that the believer, in order to live within his faith, must acknowledge as given the social structures of those times in which he lives.[12] Yet the offensiveness of this verse lies less in the social structure of antiquity and more in the gospel itself as proclaimed by Paul.[13]

The demands of this verse would be justifiably offensive and problematic if they demanded a subjected demeanor from the wife alone, and not from the husband as well. For that, see the Notes to the next verse.

as it is fitting in the Lord. On the basis of the word order and because of the parallel expression in v 20 ("this is well-pleasing in the Lord"), it is improbable that "in the Lord" is to be attached to the verb "to be subject."

The Greek *anēkō* occurs in the NT only in Eph 5:4, Col 3:18, and Phlm 8 (here in the substantival form: "that which is fitting"). In Col, as also in Eph, it is construed in the imperfect. E. Lohmeyer (p. 156) saw in this an indication that the "past" is viewed here "as the profferred authority of all present action." This tradition is seemingly "Christianized" by the addition of "in the Lord." The use of the imperfect here does not support this thesis, however. As also in Classical Greek, this tense is used to express necessity, obligation, etc., and is not necessarily to be translated in the past tense, but rather in the present (cf. BDR 358). The expression "it is fitting" does not demonstrate, as M. Dibelius (Dibelius-Greeven, pp. 46, 48–50) and K. Weidinger[14] assume, along with many other exegetes in their following, that a generally valid custom has been Christianized. In Col, we are clearly dealing not with the idea that the Christian

---

12. Comp. for that, for example, J. E. Crouch, *The Origin and Intention of the Colossian Haustafel*, FRLANT 109 (Göttingen: Vandenhoeck & Ruprecht, 1972), p. 160, and W. Lillie, "The Pauline Housetables," ET 86 (1974/75) 179–83.

13. L. Goppelt's explanation [*Theologie des Neuen Testaments*, ed. J. Roloff, 3d ed. (Göttingen: Vandenhoeck & Ruprecht, 1978), pp. 487f.] is problematic in some respects also because his emphasis in the verb "subordinate" is less on "sub-" and more on "order." In his view, the concern is to check "emigration" and to assert "the existing institutions."—L. Goppelt's remarks are appropriate also for Col, since this epistle states a clear affirmative to the world and its "institutions" (see 1:12–20). Yet world responsibility and subordination are not contradictory things: this epistle, in its assertion of reconciliation "of all things," counters world flight and emphasizes humility (3:12) at the same time, as characteristic of those who follow the reconciler. Humility and subordination should consequently be understood as a form of active world responsibility—on the basis that "humility" also characterizes the Messiah, who is king over "all things."

14. K. Weidinger, *Die Haustafeln. Ein Stück urchristlicher Paränese*, UNT 14, (Leipzig: Hinrichs, 1928), esp. p. 51.

community sanctioned any extra-Christian behavioral patterns, but rather, on the basis of accusations which were raised against the Christian community, the attitude and practice of subordination were emphasized as the essentially correct behavior of those people who have "put on the new human being (the new self)," who are "in the Lord." For further explication, cf. the preceding Notes and Comment III.

19 *Husbands, love your wives* (literally: the wives). On the absence of the personal pronoun, see the Notes to the previous verse.

If we assume that the *Haustafeln* contain non-Christian traditions, then it would be appropriate to imagine that the term "love" is not intended in the way in which it is praised, for example, in 1 Cor 13. Thus, E. Lohmeyer (p. 156) points out that the same word is used as in 1 Cor 13, but the parallel line in v 19b, in which "love" and "be not harsh" stand on one level, teach us that "love" is here intended in a conventional sense, namely that, "it is clear that the love of the husband for the wife here approximates the friendliness of a master to the servant."[15] W. Schrage's assertion, that the admonition to love *(agape)* the wife was then something unheard of, is misleading and in this blanket statement is hardly fair to "that time."[16] Still, we can agree when he emphasizes, "Yet even if the admonition of the *Haustafel* to the husbands in Col 3:19 could be proven to be proper within its surroundings, it would not be a coincidence that exactly *this* admonition was adopted as binding for the Christians, and to prove a different content for *agapan* (love, H.B.) in 3:19 within this context and understanding of Col than for 2:2 and 3:14 would be difficult to accomplish" (ibid., p. 13, fn. 2). Wherever an injunction to "love"—even when it is traditional—is combined with the admonition "to do everything in the name of the Lord Jesus" (3:17), and when the outstanding feature of such action is described as the love that comes from the Messiah Jesus

---

15. Comp. also J. E. Crouch, *Haustafel*, op. cit., p. 112, "The simple, most natural sense of *agapē* in the *Haustafel* is the normal, human love of a husband for his wife."

16. W. Schrage, "Zur Ethik der neutestamentlichen Haustafeln," NTS 21 (1975) 1–22:12f.; H. Greeven, "Zu den Aussagen des Neuen Testaments über die Ehe," ZEE 1 (1957) 122; H. Greeven, Art. "Ehe (im NT)," RGG II, pp. 318–20.—W. Schrage refers to Plutarch in this connection, as happens again and again, who speaks of *kratein* (control) in reference to the husband in the passage where he praises the *hypotassesthai* of the wife. In this way, however, what *Plutarch* says (Praec Coniug 33 ⟨Mor II, 142E⟩) is turned into its opposite, for concerning "ruling on the part of the husband" he says further, "And control ought to be exercised (*kratein*, H.B.) by the man over the woman, not as the owner has control of a piece of property, but, as the soul controls the body, by entering into her feelings and being knit to her through goodwill *(sympathounta kai sympephykota tē eunoia)*." See for that K. Thraede, "Zum historischen Hintergrund der 'Haustafeln' des NT," in, FS für B. Kötting, *Pietas*, eds. E. Dassmann and K. Suso Frank, JAC Erg. Bd. 8 (Münster: Aschendorff, 1980), pp. 359–68:365 fn. 33; K. Müller, *Haustafel*, op. cit., p. 297.

(3:14), we cannot then accept the argument that such love has a different meaning from its usage elsewhere in the NT and especially the Pauline Epistles. But then this admonition to the husbands also contains a summons to servile self-subjection, which easily arises from the reading of 1 Cor 13. The parallel declaration in Eph also points in this direction, in which all the injunctions of the *Haustafel* there are placed under the same rule: "Subordinate yourselves *to one another!*" (Eph 5:21; cf. also Gal 5:3).[17]

That means, then, that these declarations of the *Haustafel* of Col assign the final word in the relationship between husband and wife not to the patriarchate but also not to the matriarchate. The concern is then not only the abolition of power of the husband in favor of the wife, and thus not about concessions through which the wife "may" participate in the power of the husband, but also the abolition of structures of dominion in the relationship between the sexes. There is no striving for equality in the sense of equal plenitude of power, but rather an equality based on loving and serving one another.

and be not harsh against them. Plutarch also gives a similar admonishment to his male readers (De cohibenda ira 8; Mor VI, 457A, "*pros gynaia diapikrai-nontai*"), and in the rabbinic literature, although in a reference from the third century, we read, "Let the man always be careful, lest he annoy his wife; for since her tear is (soon) found, her retribution is close to her annoyance" (St.-B. III, 631).

The verb *pikrainō* occurs in the NT besides this passage only in Rev (8:11; 10:9, 10). The corrresponding adjective, *pikros*, originally meant "sharp, pointed," and in addition, predominantly "sharp, rough, bitter" (in taste). *Pikrainō* carries the sense "to be/become sharp, rough, bitter" in the extra-biblical references, as well as in Rev. In addition, it is used in traditional texts, where in the oldest attestations its meaning is "to be wrathful."[18] In this

---

17. As however it is problematic to reconcile the statements about the "serving-subjugating" of husband and wife, based on statements in Col 3:11 and Gal 3:28, with statements such as 1 Cor 11:8+9; 14:34f.; and 1 Tim 2:8–15. The polemic which we encounter in 1 Cor 15 and 1 Tim against the wife seems to be of one kind, of which we might say, based on Col 3:11, Gal 3:28, and 1 Cor 11:11f., that it had been overcome.—But we need to observe the following: the disagreement in the manuscripts about the place of 1 Cor 14:34f. in the text is probably an indication for the fact that a later marginal gloss slipped into the text here; and the Pauline authorship of 1 Tim is to be regarded with caution at any rate. As concerns 1 Cor 11:8+9, Paul himself (attributed to him by tradition) seems to have had problems with these statements in the face of the gospel. For he renders an argument in 11:10f. which removes his justification in 11:8+9. He then summons his readers literally to "judge for yourselves" (1 Cor 11:13) and, seemingly consciously, leaves no "instructions" to this question. This becomes evident in 1 Cor 11:17, the next subject with which he deals, which is introduced with the words, "But *this I command.* . . ."

18. Comp. W. Michaelis, ThWNT VI, 122–27:122, fn. 1.

connection, the occurrence of *pikria* (bitterness) at the beginning of a catalog of vices in Eph 4:31 is interesting. M. Barth (AB 34A, p. 521), in his exposition of this passage, points out that the series "bitterness, passion, anger, shouting, cursing" is ordered climactically, and it "moves from a hidden state of the heart to public disgrace caused by words." He supports this exposition, among others, with a reference to Aristotle, who "described 'bitterness' as the attitude that creates a lasting wrath, hard to reconcile, and sustaining anger for a long time." A concern is given expression in this warning about anger that was already emphasized in 3:8, in order to underscore the difference between the "old" and "new self." Thus, in this verse, the concern is hardly with a transference and Christianizing of generally recommended socioethical patterns of behavior, but rather it is in agreement with an ethical concern that can also be found outside the Christian community. On this point, there is no contradiction to the new life "in Christ," and there is no reason here to accuse the Christians of destroying acknowledged customs (cf. also Comment II).

20 *Children.* The Greek term *teknon* means "offspring, child," without having a specific age in mind. The word alone does not give sufficient reason to think of a minor child.[19] It is possible and probable that "grown children" are addressed, who lived in one household with their parents as was customary in the extended family in antiquity, where the father remained head of the household until his death. The Fifth Commandment in the OT ("honor your father and mother. . . .") is also to be interpreted this way. This commandment is to be understood primarily as the summons to children to the appropriate care of their parents in their old age.[20] It is also to be understood as the command to grown-ups in Matt 15:4 and Mark 7:10.[21] In Eph 6:1–4, the parallel passage to our verse, the reference is equally to the Fifth Commandment. But the command to the fathers follows the reminder to the children, "Fathers, *raise* your children. . . ." The verb *ektrephō*, which is used here, could be an indication that minor children are meant. But the usage of this verb alone does not require such an interpretation. In 2 Macc 7:27, it is used in reference to a son who is already mature enough so that official positions in the state government are offered to him (cf. 2 Macc 7:24). Thus the assumption is justified that *ektrephō* points to the obligation of the father as the head of the house for the upbringing of children throughout his whole life, and to command his children and his household to keep the way of the Lord and to do that which

19. See for this G. Delling, "Lexikalisches zu *teknon.* Ein Nachtrag zur Exegese von 1. Kor 7,14," in FS für E. Barnikol, ". . . und fragten nach Jesus," *Beiträge aus Theologie, Kirche und Geschichte* (Berlin: Evangelische Verlagsanstalt, 1964), pp. 35–44.

20. Comp., for example, J. J. Stamm, *Der Dekalog im Lichte der neueren Forschung,* 2d ed. (Bern und Stuttgart: Haupt, 1982), pp. 51–52; F. Crüsemann, *Bewahrung der Freiheit. Das Thema des Dekalogs in religionsgeschichtlicher Perspektive* (München: Kaiser, 1983), pp. 58–65.

21. The same also of the synagogue; see G. Schrenk, ThWNT V, 975.

is right and good (cf. Gen 18:19). However, if *also* minor children are meant, then the contention of E. Schweizer could be somewhat justified, namely that in the group which is addressed, "women—children—slaves," we are dealing with an OT concern in contrast to Greek *Haustafeln:* "the central interest is no longer that perfect inner freedom of the individual who would free himself as much as possible from all ties, but rather the protection of those who are weak, helpless and unfree."[22] But we scarcely do justice to the statement of this verse if we interpret E. Schweizer (cf. esp. *Kol-Kommentar,* pp. 161–64) in the formal sense of this reminder which is essentially significant for this exegesis and is relative in our context only for that which is conditioned by time. For him, the "truly Christian" view is for the weak person. The importance, he says, lies in the fact that the group of persons cited is actually addressed, and further in an "affirmation of creation, marriage, family and work," which manifests itself in the unconcerned acceptance of time-conditioned orders. Even if there is reference here to OT concerns, then still the meaning of the OT tradition is misjudged. For Paul—and even for a follower of Paul, if such a person composed the Colossian epistle—the relationship to the Fifth Commandment was the most immediate element in an order to obey one's parents. In Eph 6:2, this relationship is expressly established. Even if we assume that an adapted formulation from a Greek *Haustafel* is a precedent here (for which there is no attestation, however), we still have to account for the fact that it was adapted exactly because *the association with the Fifth Commandment* could be emphasized. Then, however, the author of Col saw the central issue of the injunction before us in the *content,* since he declared a holy commandment of God here. His central concern is distorted if the encountered "commandment" is explained as a variable means for the affirmation of creation.

be obedient to your parents in all things (literally: the parents). For the absence of the personal pronoun "you," cf. Notes to 3:18.

Unlike the Fifth Commandment, which says "*honor* your father and mother," the call here is to *obey.* J. E. Crouch remarks, "Indeed, the christian

---

22. E. Schweizer, "Traditional Ethical Patterns in the Pauline and Post-Pauline Letters and Their Developments (lists of vices and housetables)," in FS for M. Black, *Text and Interpretation,* ed. E. Best and R. McL. Wilson (Cambridge: University Press, 1979), pp. 195–209:202; comp. also E. Schweizer, *Kol-Kommentar,* p. 162; E. Schweizer, "Die Weltlichkeit des Neuen Testaments: Die Haustafeln," in *Neues Testament,* op. cit., pp. 194–210:201.—E. Lohmeyer (p. 155) already referred to the connection with OT ideas, "They (wives—children—slaves, H.B.) have formed a unit since the Deuteronomium only because they are the less legitimate than men in terms of cult and law, faith and custom; they cannot be included in the fulfillment of the law, nor in cultic obligations to the same extent as the men. Yet nonetheless, they are a part of the nation; and it is therefore also necessary to formulate the easier burden of their obligations on a special tablet, as it was already begun in the Deuteronomium, and was continued into rabbinic times."

[sic] exhortation to children gives the impression of a certain degree of independence from its nonchristian [sic] parallels by demanding 'obedience' rather than 'honor.' "[23] He suspects influence from the express admonishment to the slaves in v 22. It should, however, be observed that in the determination of the relationship between parents and children, the concepts of "honor" and "obedience" can hardly be separated from one another, and that the latter is not at all unusual. In the OT, the command to *obey* on the part of the son toward the parents is very rare, but on the other hand it occurs in an expository passage: in the Torah, in Deut 21:18–21, the death sentence is imposed upon the "disobedient" (in the LXX: *hypakouō*) son.[24] And even *Philo* of Alexandria interprets the obligation of honoring the parents as obedience.[25] But non-Jewish and non-Christian writers equally know the express exhortation to obey parents alongside the command to honor the parents.[26] Still, the OT traditions were surely primary for the author of Col.

It is also noteworthy that the declaration in this passage is strengthened by the addition "in all things." This is all the more surprising when we consider that even "children" are exhorted to obey when their parent (or even both parents) serves other gods.[27] J. Gnilka thinks that this "sternness" is comprehensible from the role of the child in the contemporary society, in which the child was perceived as "immature, inconstant, undecided, hardly capable of a serious occupation." But here the supposition that a child of the young age implied in J. Gnilka's characterization is the central concern is already problematic. And even in that "contemporary society," the problem of "unconditional obedience" is not sufficiently discussed in reference to a child of an age at which no "serious occupation" can be expected.[28]

---

23. J. E. Crouch, *Haustafel*, op. cit., p. 114.

24. As is clearly indicated, the "grown son" is meant also here ("He is a glutton and drunkard," v 20).

25. Spec Leg II, 234.236: "With all these facts before them (i.e., what parents are doing for their children, H.B.), they do not do anything deserving of praise who *honour* their parents. . . . For parents have little thought for their own personal interests and find the consummation of happiness in the high excellence of their children, and to gain this the children will be willing to hearken their commands and to *obey* them in everything that is just and profitable; for the true father will give no instruction to his son that is foreign to virtue" (Herv. H.B.).

26. "Honor," see for example, Hierocles, in *Stobaeus* IV, 640, 8–10; Plutarch, Lib Ed 10 (Mor I, 7 E). "Obey," see, for example, Epictetus, II, 10, 7; Dionysius of Halicarnassus, Ant Rom II, 26, 3ff. (first century B.C.E.).

27. W. M. L. de Wette (p. 69) concluded from this addition that it was written for pious parents.

28. Comp., for example, Musonius, "Must One Obey One's Parents Under All Circumstances?," Or XVI. Musonius, a Stoic from the first century B.C.E., discussed the problem of whether a son must obey the prohibition of his father to study philosophy.

J. E. Crouch defends this thesis, that as opposed to the Stoa, to the popular philosophy as well as in the rabbinic traditions, the "corresponding statements in our Hellenistic Jewish sources, however, show no trace of casuistry"; rather "they intensify the punishment of children who fail to offer absolute obedience to their parents."[29] Thus, the statements in Col 3:20 can best be understood on the basis of Hellenistic-Jewish sources.

These observations are conditionally correct. Even Philo limits the command to obedience to "everything *that is just and profitable*" (see above, fn. 25). On the other hand, the differentiation of Judaic-Hellenistic sources from the popular philosophy, as described by J. E. Crouch, is misleading.[30] For a comprehension of the declaration in Col 3:20, the situation in the society of the time needs to be considered as well. By the fact that "children" in a household became Christians in opposition to their parents, they put the Roman *patria potestas*, the position of the father in the household in antiquity, in a questionable position from a non-Christian viewpoint, which could leave them subject to the reproach that they were undermining the Roman societal order (cf. Comment II). On this basis, we can understand the emphasis "in all things." It is expressed because just this decision of "children" against the religion of their parents and in the Jewish Messiah is excepted from obedience. Obedience to parents is emphasized as a characteristic concern in the faith of the Messiah against all accumulated accusations, as these are formulated not only by Tacitus (Hist V, 5; cf. Comment II), but as they are also transmitted in the NT (cf. Acts 16:20f.). See also Notes to v 22.

for that is well-pleasing in the Lord. Instead of the expected simple dative (well-pleasing to the Lord),[31] the expression is construed with the preposition *en* (*in* the Lord). M. Dibelius (Dibelius-Greeven, p. 46) concluded from this unusual formulation that *euareston* (well-pleasing) evidently serves as a fixed social value that is Christianized by the *formula* "in the Lord." Just so, his student K. Weidinger saw evidence in the words "in the Lord" for the idea that the declarations "as it is fitting" (v 18) and "it is well-pleasing" are not Christian valuations, but are rather social ones, and that "in the Lord" is an attached supplement; "if they had formulated anew, then they would probably have said

---

29. J. E. Crouch, *Haustafel*, op. cit., p. 114. He justifies on the basis of Philo, Spec Leg II, 232; Josephus, Ant IV, 264.

30. D. L. Balch, *Wives*, op. cit., p. 7, refers to Epictetus, Ench 30, and to Perictione, "On the Harmony of a Woman," in *The Pythagoreans: Texts of the Hellenistic Period*, ed. H. Thesleff, Acta Academiae Aboensis, Ser. A., Humaniora, vol. 30 (Abo: Abo Akademie, 1965), 145, 13.

31. Comp. in addition to Eph 5:10: Rom 12:1; 14:18; 2 Cor 5:9; Phil 4:18.—In Rom 12:2: Tit 2:9 and Heb 13:21, *euarestos* is used in the absolute. Except in Titus 2:9, the word always refers to God/Christ.

tō kyriō ("to the Lord," H.B.)."[32] A series of exegetes followed him in this interpretation.[33]

Why should precisely such points that are generally valid norms in the society be Christianized, when the gospel itself, or the Bible of the Christians, the OT, gives clear instructions? It is more likely that the author of Colossians did not wish to adapt and Christianize general standards, but that he rather used OT Christian norms, and that he kept in mind that false accusations against the Christians were thereby unmasked (cf. 4:5 and esp. 1 Pet 2:12). The prepositional phrase, which is unusual in the sense that the words "in the Lord" appear appended, does not need to indicate a subsequent Christianization. We can just as readily have an original formulation, which, in the face of cited accusations, give expression to the obligation of obedience toward parents that is pleasing not only generally (outside the Christian community), but also and specifically "in the Lord," that is, there, where the Messiah is "acknowledged as Lord" (cf. also Comment II).

21 *Fathers.* While in the previous verse "children" are admonished to obey their *parents*, in this verse, the substantive "parents" is not taken up again in the address, but rather "fathers" is chosen in its place. We need to observe, however, that in the Greek, the word *patēr* (father) used in the plural can designate both parents (father and mother).[34]

do not embitter your children. In the NT, the verb *erethizō*, used here, otherwise occurs only in 2 Cor 9:2, where it is used in a positive sense with the meaning "to stimulate." Here in Colossians, on the contrary, it designates something negative. The usage in 2 Macc 14:27 (cf. 1 Macc 15:40) is comparable, where this word occurs together with another verb, "to become angry." Even the parallel admonition in the *Haustafel* of Ephesians to Col 3:21 speaks of anger, "And fathers, do not provoke the wrath of your children. . . ."[35] If in our verse anger also is in the mind of the writer, this anger can be more closely defined on the basis of the attached sentences (see below): what is in mind is impotent rage which then culminates in bitterness and resignation.

The reprimand before us, in comparison to the Roman *patria potestas*, as it is described in detail by Dionysius of Halicarnassus, appears milder and more humane. This Dionysius, a Greek rhetorician, who came to Rome in 30 B.C.E.

---

32. K. Weidinger, *Haustafeln*, op. cit., p. 51.

33. Comp., for example, E. Lohse, p. 226, fn. 7; E. Schweizer, p. 166; J. Gnilka, p. 220; R. P. Martin, NCC, p. 120.

34. See, in the NT, Heb 11:23. Comp. also the references in LSLex, 1348.—J. E. Crouch, *Haustafel*, op. cit., p. 116, on the contrary, refers to Kiddushin 1:7: "All the obligations of a father towards his son enjoined in the Law are incumbent on men but not on women, and all obligations of a son towards his father enjoined in the Law are incumbent both on men and on women."

35. Correspondingly, some texts compared Col 3:21 to Eph 6:4, such as Codex Alexandrinus (fifth century) and Codex Ephraemi Syri Rescriptus (fifth century).

and who lived there under Augustus, writes on this subject in his history, "But the law-givers of the Romans gave virtually full power to the father over his son, even during his whole life, whether he thought proper to imprison him, to scourge him, to put him in chains and keep him at work in the fields, or to put him to death, and this even though the son were already engaged in public affairs, though he were numbered among the highest magistrates, and though he were celebrated for his zeal for the commonwealth. Indeed, in virtue of this consideration, law-men of distinction, while delivering speeches from the rostra hostile to the senate and pleasing to the people, and enjoying great popularity on that account, have been dragged down from thence and carried away by their fathers to undergo such punishment as these thought fit; and while they were being led away through the Forum, none present, neither consul, tribune, nor the very populace, which was flattered by them and thought all power inferior to its own, could rescue them" (Ant Rom II, 26, 4–5). We would, however, not do justice to the Greek and Roman understanding of the relationship between parents and children if we saw in the present more "humane" view of the parent-child relationship a special Christian or (rabbinic or Hellenistic) Jewish[36] concern. Plato's elaborations already give a different impression, "by then punishment must be used to prevent their getting pampered,—not, however, punishment of a degrading kind, but just as we said before (cf. esp. Leg VI, 777D–E; H.B.), in the case of slaves, that one should avoid enraging the persons punished by using degrading punishments, or pampering them by leaving them unpunished, so in the case of the free-born the same rule holds good" (Leg VII, 793E–794A). And Aristotle determines that the behavior of the father to his son as "regal in type" (koinonia basileias echei schēma), because the father is concerned foremost with the "welfare" of his children. There Aristotle differentiates sharply the relationship between master and slave, which he characterizes by the word "tyrannic" (tyrannikē). He criticizes "the Persian paternal rule" in this connection, which is "tyrannical," "for the Persians use their sons as slaves" (Eth Nic VIII, 1160b, 23–1161a, 10). The instructions in Plutarch (Lib Ed 12 [Mor I, 8F]) are especially worthy of notice: "This I also assert, that children ought to be led to honorable practices by means of encouragement and reasoning, and most certainly not by blows or ill-treatment, for it surely is agreed that these are fitting rather for slaves than for the free-borns. . . ."[37]

---

36. Comp. for that J. E. Crouch, Haustafel, pp. 115f.

37. Comp. Lib Ed 18 (Mor I, 13D), "I do not think they (fathers, H.B.) should be utterly harsh and austere in their nature, but they should in many cases concede some shortcomings to the younger person, and remind themselves that they once were young. As physicians, by mixing bitter drugs with sweet syrups, have found that the agreeable taste gains access for what is beneficial, so fathers should combine the abruptness of their rebukes with mildness, and at one time grant some license to the desires of their children, and slacken the reins a little, and then at another time draw them tight again. Most desirable is that they should bear misdeeds with serenity, but if that be impossible, yet, if

This list could be expanded further.

so that they will not lose courage. The verb *athymeō* occurs only here in the NT. Its use in the LXX illustrates this meaning. In LXX Deut 28:66f., in the chapter on the proclamation of blessings and curses, it occurs in connection with the following concrete threats, "Day and Night will you fear and not believe in your life. In the early morning, you will say, 'Oh, would that it were evening!' And in the evening you will say, 'Oh, would that it were morning!'—from the fear in your heart. . . ." The terms in Jdt 7:22 are equally graphic: there *athymeō* designates desperate dejection, a frame of mind that is prepared to give up everything of one's own. In cases where they are tortured by thirst under enemy siege, women and children lose courage *(athymeō)* and they enjoin the superiors of the city to deliver them up as slaves to their besiegers.

22 *Slaves, obey.* Since the *Haustafeln* are aimed at the members of the household of antiquity (cf. Comment II), the house slaves are the ones addressed here, not the slaves on large estates, in mines, or on galleys. For the author of Colossians, this kind of slavery was not a major problem. He proceeds naturally from the point that in the relationship of slave-master/master-slave what it means to have put on the "new self" (cf. esp. 3:11) can be made manifest. The fact that there, where this new self is put on, is neither slave nor free person, does not mean for Paul the abolition of slavery, but it is a summons for him to shape the contact with each other in such a way that it will be revealed that the Messiah takes slaves, as well as masters, into his service in order to proclaim that he, the Messiah, is *the master* over all things.[38]

The exhortation to the slaves may have been extended because Paul wanted to emphasize that he viewed the state of slavery precisely as not reconcilable with the servitude of a Christian. We need to remember Phil 2:7f. in this connection, where it says in a hymn about the Messiah Jesus, "He took the form of a slave . . . he lowered himself, he was obedient unto death, unto the death on the cross."[39] Such an evaluation of the issue of slavery sounds problematic in the face of the challenge to slavery which has continued to the present day and which should not serve to make slavery as palatable as an institution sanctioned by Christianity. In order to understand the declarations of Paul, a precise analysis of the historic situation into which it was inserted is indispensable. For that, cf. M. Barth, *Philemon* (AB 34C).

your earthly masters in all things (literally: the masters according to the flesh). Regarding the absence of the possessive pronoun, cf. Notes to 3:18.

---

they be on occasion angered, they should quickly cool down. For it is better that a father should be quick-tempered than sullen, since a hostile and irreconcilable spirit is no small proof of animosity towards one's children."

38. Comp. also 1 Cor 7:22, "For the called slave is a freedman in the Lord, just as the called freedman is a slave in Christ."

39. See also the Notes after this. For the theme "slavery" see further M. Barth, *Philemon,* AB 34C (fc).

In spite of the phrase *kata panta* (in all things),[40] the call is not to unconditional obedience. These words are to be understood in view of the fact that the community of Christians granted to the slaves a decision in matters of faith that was independent of the religious convictions of their masters. This then implied that the community accepted the accusation that it might be inciting to disobedience and disturbing the order of the households involved.[41] It was therefore careful to emphasize, in the face of one such summary accusation, that it was not in their interest to incite slaves against their masters (cf. previous Notes).

not with eye-service, as someone who wishes to please human beings. The Greek word *ophthalmodoulia* is not attested before Paul and occurs in the NT again only in Eph 6:6. Translated literally, it means "eye-service." According to the explanation that is offered in the text itself, such behavior is characteristic of an *anthrōpareskos* ("one who wishes to please people"). This expression is rare in Greek, and in the NT it occurs elsewhere only in the *Haustafel* in Ephesians. It is used, however, in the LXX (cf. Ps 52 ⟨53⟩:6; PsSol 4:7, 8, 19). In the PsSol, the *anthrōpareskos* is equated with a hypocrite. If we applied this meaning to Col, we could arrive at the interpretation that the generally recognized obligation of obedience on the part of slaves could still be sharpened by requiring not only obedience of slaves in deed, but also in an obedient attitude.[42] But in our opinion, the sense of the admonishment is to be sought elsewhere. The slaves were in fact admonished as Christians, who should act "in the name of the Lord Jesus" (cf. 3:17), and thus declarations such as 1 Thess 2:4 and Gal 1:10 need to be considered for the exegesis of our verse. According to those, "serving Christ" and "wishing to please people" are mutually exclusive opposites. The context of 1 Thess 2 narrates the struggle and suffering associated with such service. We can assume that the idea of suffering is also not present in our verse. Since we can proceed from the assumption that slaves of gentile masters are addressed, an obedience which does not seek to please human beings, and thus one which is without suffering, is hardly imaginable. The expositions of the *Haustafel* of 1 Peter are illuminating here. 1 Pet 2:19ff. alludes to "renown" and to "grace" within the framework of admonitions to the slaves to subject themselves, in order to endure injustice and beatings "for the sake of their conscience." The suffering of Christ is there cited as the model. As in 1 Peter, where the willing endurance of punishment "because of good deeds" is understood as a form of submission, so in Col, the readiness to suffer is required along with the obedience which seeks not to please persons, whenever the slaves, on account

---

40. Papyrus 46, among the important manuscripts, leaves this expression out. Its attestation through other important manuscripts, however, argues in its favor of being original. Besides that, the deletion of these words appears as a correction.

41. Comp. for that D. L. Balch, *Wives*, op. cit., pp. 68f.; 88f.

42. Comp. E. Haupt, p. 157.

of their faith, are caught in a conflict with their obligation to carry out the instructions of their masters.

but rather fear the Lord with a sincere heart (literally: in sincerity of the heart). *Haplotēs* (sincerity) is in opposition to the immediately preceding "eye-service," which is closely aligned with hypocrisy (see above). According to 2 Cor 1:12, "sincerity" is a sign of the service of Paul and his co-workers. It is contrasted with "fleshly wisdom," which, according to 1 Cor 1:17, is opposed to divine wisdom, which does not know anything except Christ, the crucified one.

The summons to fear the Lord (cf. 2 Cor 5:11; 7:1) is comprehensible from OT declarations. It does not mean a kind of fear, as it is called in Rom 8:15 and which does not suit Christians, but it rather describes unconditional obedience and joyful service to God (see, for example, LXX Gen 22:12; Deut 6:13; 10:12, 20; 13:5). As the cited passages demonstrate, this kind of "fear" can be said in the same breath with terms such as "love" and "devotion." The word "Lord" in Col 3:20, however, refers not to God but rather to the Messiah Jesus.[43]

23 *Whatever you do, do it from the heart for the Lord and not for human beings* (literally: from [the] soul). The phrase *ek psychēs* (from [the] soul) picks up the expression "sincerity of the heart" from the previous verse and is synonymous with it.[44] It really only underscores what was said in v 22 and again in v 23. The superscript to the entire *Haustafel* (v 17) is repeated in somewhat different words,[45] whereby it is emphasized that slaves especially are worthy of alluding to the "Lord Jesus" through their conduct (cf. for this the Notes to v 22). E. Schweizer (p. 167) remarks with justification that the sense of the verse is turned around "if the expression 'for the Lord' (cf. BDR 425, p. 4; H.B.) is understood in a way that the earthly master stands in the place where the heavenly one stands, and that every service rendered to the earthly master is a service to Christ."

24 *For you know that you will receive the reward, the inheritance, from the Lord. (Thus) serve the Lord the Messiah!* (literally: knowing that . . . the reward of the inheritance). The participle "knowing" can have an imperative meaning,[46] but it can also introduce a participial phrase. It can thus be subordinated to or modify: (1) the main sentence in v 23, or (2) the attached "you serve/serve (*douleuete* can mean both) the Lord Christ." Possibility 1 should not be given priority, in our opinion.[47] Because the phrase "serve the

43. See for that Notes to 1:15–20, fn. 24.—E. Lohmeyer's (p. 158) viewpoint that this exhortation remains stuck in Pharisaic ideas, for Pauls never says in the NT that the Lord Christ is to be feared by his believers, but only God, is hardly apt here.

44. Comp. for that also E. Lohse, p. 228, fn. 9.

45. A few manuscripts, which however presumably do not transmit the original reading, read, as in 3:17, "*and everything* that you do, ..." This makes the connection between both verses even clearer.

46. Comp. for that Notes to 1:10, fn. 32.

47. A few less important texts that have tried to make the text more uniform have

Lord" is separated from the preceding phrase, the impression is created that v 24 is a warning or even a threat to the slaves. That, however, is improbable (cf. Notes to the next verse). If we interpret the charge "serve the Lord" as the sum of that which was stated previously, it does not matter whether the participle "seeing" is translated as an imperative or not. The sense remains the same.

In Greek, the expression "the reward of the inheritance" is a *genitivus appositivus*. It indicates what the reward consists of (cf. BDR 167, 2). The term *antapodosis*, which is attested back to the fifth century B.C.E., occurs in the NT only once. In the LXX, it occurs more frequently. Usually it carries a negative connotation: "vengeance, retaliation" (cf. LXX Judg 16:28; Ps 68⟨69⟩:23; 90 ⟨91⟩:8; 93⟨94⟩:2; Isa 34:8; etc.), but it is also used in a positive sense (cf. LXX 2 Sam 19:37; Ps 18⟨19⟩:12; 102⟨103⟩:2).[48] Since the discussion simultaneously concerns "inheritance," it is clear that we are not dealing with a reward that the slaves still need to earn. This reward has already been "earned" by the Messiah (cf. 1:12).[49] It is put into the future sense, since the "revelation" of this inheritance "in glory" is still to come (cf. 3:1–4).

What is exciting in the declaration before us is the fact that slaves are designated as inheritors. In other passages, "slave" and "heir" are opposing concepts (cf. Matt 21:35–38; Rom 8:15–17; Gal 4:1, 7). Thus, we have the indication to the slaves that is because of their position as heirs of the Messiah that they should respond positively to the summons to serve the "Lord Christ."

The expression *kyrios christos* ("Lord Christ") occurs very rarely in the Pauline literature: only here and in Rom 16:18.[50] There, as here, it is conditioned by the contrast of the *"Lord* Christ" to another lord. This usage points out that a certain conflict is in mind, in which a decision between one lord and another is demanded. That means, according to v 22, by means of eye-service to act as though there were only one earthly lord or else to suffer the eventual consequences of a decision for the true Lord, the Messiah (cf. Notes to v 22). E. Lohse's (p. 229) interpretation, that the slave is obedient to the one *Kyrios* when he serves his earthly lord in good faith, seems to us to go beyond the intention of this verse.

25 *Because the unrighteous will receive whatever he has done wrong—without*

---

interpreted in this way. They read, "the inheritance of our Lord Jesus Christ, whom we serve." Others, among them also the major texts, prefer "you serve the Lord" by inserting "for."

48. The corresponding Greek verb *antanadidomi* occurs in the NT seven times, with the corresponding positive (comp. Luke 14:14; 1 Thess 3:9), as also the negative (Rom 12:19; 2 Thess 1:6; Heb 10:30) meanings.

49. *ant-apo-dosis* is a double composite. It is doubtful whether, as J. B. Lightfoot (p. 295) thinks, it should be specially emphasized that we are dealing with an "exact requital." See for that BDR 116.

50. This passage is also suspected as being unoriginal. See for that W. Kramer, *Christos, Kyrios, Gottessohn*, op. cit., pp. 213f.

regard of person (literally: and it is no regard of person). The warning expressed here is reminiscent of the well-known so-called *jus talionis* (cf. Gen 9:6; Ex 21:23–25; Lev 24:18ff.; Deut 19:21).[51] It is then underscored by the reference, also from the OT, that before God, no regard of person is valid (cf. Deut 10:17f.; Job 34:19, etc.). The expression *prosōpolēmpsia*, which in our verse means the factor of partiality, is formed from the Hebraism *prosōpon lambanō* (literally: to take the face).[52]

There is dispute among the exegetes as to who is addressed here. Is there (1) a warning here to the slaves, or (2) are the masters who are unjust to their slaves meant, so that the warning is intended as a consolation to the slaves, or (3) are both masters and slaves meant?[53] If we accept meaning 1, then we have to assume that the problem behind the admonition in the *Haustafel* in the early Christian community was that the slaves concluded from their disadvantaged position in society that they could expect mildness in the judgment as a counterbalance and that they consequently did not need to take seriously any "relative" injustice in their own behavior. There is no substantive support for the correctness of such a thesis. On the other hand—and this is in favor of solution 2—the *Haustafel* in 1 Peter expressly indicates that in the exhortations of slaves, the admonishment to suffer willingly the injustice inflicted on them by their masters plays a significant role.[54] We need also to observe that the statement that with God there is no regard of person emphasizes in the OT, as well as in the NT (among others, in Deut 10:17; Job 34:19; 2 Chr 19:7; Acts 10:34; Rom 2:11), that God provides justice for the *weak*.[55] Thus, Col 3:25 probably is intended to encourage slaves, and is also applicable to both slaves and masters.

---

51. For a discussion concerning the significance of such judicial tenets in the early Christian community, see E. Käsemann, "Sätze Heiligen Rechts im Neuen Testament," EVB II, pp. 69–82, and critically to this, K. Berger, "Zu den sogenannten Sätzen Heiligen Rechts, NTS 17 (1970/71) 10–40; K. Berger, "Die sog. Sätze Heiligen Rechts im N.T. Ihre Funktion und ihr Sitz im Leben," ThZ 28 (1972) 305–30.

52. See for that E. Lohse, ThWNT VI, 780f. In addition to unjustified partisanship, this expression also designates consideration in the positive sense. See, for example, Gen 19:21; 32:21; Num 6:26; and others.

53. Interpretation 1 is represented, among others, by: J. A. Bengel (p. 794); A. Schlatter (p. 307); E. Haupt (p. 160); P. Ewald (p. 434)M; E. Lohmeyer (p. 159); E. Lohse (p. 230); P. T. O'Brien (p. 230); F. F. Bruce (p. 169); W. Bieder (p. 269); A. Lindemann (p. 67). Interpretation 2 among others by: Thomas Aquinas (p. 80); J. Calvin (p. 126); T. K. Abbott (pp. 295f.); H. A. W. Meyer (p. 402); comp. E. Schweizer (p. 168); R. P. Martin, NCC, p. 123. Interpretation 3 among others by: J. B. Lightfoot (p. 295); J. Gnilka (pp. 223f.).

54. Comp. also Eph 6:9, where only the *men* are referred to the fact that before God there is no cognizance of person.—In Phlm 18, however, it is the slave Onesimus who has "done wrong."

55. Comp. for that E. Schweizer, p. 168, esp. fn. 3.

4:1 *Masters, give (your) slaves whatever is right and fair. For you know that you also have a master in heaven* (literally: the just thing and the equal thing knowing). The fact that the verb *parechō* (to grant) is construed in the middle voice, instead of in the active, has no contextual significance (cf. BDR 316, 3). The insertion of the possessive pronoun (your) into the translation, which is lacking in the Greek text, has been justified in the Notes to 3:18. For the translation of the participle "knowing" *(eidotes)*, see the Notes to v 24.

Both concepts, *dikaios* (just) and *isotēs* (equality) are closely aligned and define each other mutually. Aristotle (Eth Nic V, 1129a, 34a) defines, " 'The just' therefore is that, which is lawful and equal *(hoti kai ⟨ho⟩ dikaios estai ho te nommikos kai ho isos)*." Accordingly, justice is safeguarded where equal rights are granted to all. "But the development of the meaning of *isos* ("equal," H.B.) itself, which continuously comes closer to the concept of *dikaios* ("just," H.B.) and became assimilated to it, gradually leads to the interpretation (justicial *isotēs* = granting of equal rights for all) that true justice consists in allowing each person to receive not the same reward but rather that which is their due."[56] In our verse, the summons is then to grant the slaves what is theirs, what is their due, what is "just and fair."[57] It remains to explain what, in the opinion of Paul, is "just and fair" for slaves. E. Lohse (p. 231) points out that this question had been considered again and again in popular philosophical discussion, and that therefore everyone knew what was understood by these terms as normal customary action. On the other hand, the statement that *masters* also have a master in heaven is hardly a reminder that they must someday account to a heavenly master for their actions. While it is stated to the masters, within the admonishments to the slaves, that they also have a master, this is undoubtedly to make it clear to them that the masters also are "slaves." Paul expressly writes in 1 Cor 7:22, "whoever is called as a free person, that person is a slave of Christ." However, we then have to account for the fact that the dealings of the *master* Christ with his "slaves" are to be accepted as a definitive model for the dealings of earthly masters with their slaves (cf. Matt 18:21–35).[58] This interpretation hardly differs from the generally rejected exposition of H. A. W. Meyer (p. 405),

---

56. G. Stählin, ThWNT III, 348, 18ff. Comp. also E. Schweizer, p. 168.—Erasmus v. Rotterdam (*Opera omnia*, Tom VI [Hildesheim: Olms, 1962], p. 886E) interpreted according to the Aristotelian principle of equality: all slaves should be treated equally. This explication is probably not applicable.

57. Comp. also T. K. Abbott (p. 296), "*isotēs* differs from *to dikaion* nearly as our 'fair' from 'just,' denoting what cannot be brought under positive rules, but is in accordance with the judgement of a fair mind."

58. The fact that general concepts such as "just" and "fair" do not necessarily need to refer to generally applicable norms, but rather that they needed to be newly applied in the church, is demonstrated by 2 Thess 3:6: the judgment "of living in disorder" does not refer back to a generally valid concept of order, but rather to the norm for "the teaching that you have received."

who translated *isotēs* not as "equity" but as "equality." In his opinion, the masters are summoned to view slaves as their equals and to deal with them accordingly, without having in mind any equality in their exterior condition. However, this concerns only slaves who are also Christians, which H. A. W. Meyer infers from Phlm 16.

3. Concluding Petitions and Exhortations (4:2–6)

2 Be steadfast in prayer: be watchful therein with thanksgiving. 3 Pray also for us, that God may open a door for our word, to proclaim the secret, the Messiah. Because of this (secret) I am also bound, 4 so that I may reveal it, as it is determined for me, to proclaim (it). 5 In wisdom conduct your lives toward those who are on the outside; redeem that which is offered now. 6 Let your word be determined by grace at all times, seasoned with salt; then you will know how you are to answer every one.

NOTES

Verses 4:2–6 conclude the exhortations and thus the main portion of the epistle. The words are rich in imagery, from being watchful, to opening of a door, from buying or redeeming of time, to the word that is seasoned with salt. Because these images were surely easily comprehensible to the readers of the time, they are not more precisely elucidated. Today, on the contrary, we have difficulty in understanding them.

Verses 2–4/5 + 6 have parallel structural elements, which is an indication to the reader that contextual analogies can also be discovered. Each imperative at the beginning ("be steadfast"; "conduct your lives") is followed by two participially constructed verbs ("watching," "praying"/"redeeming," "seasoned"). Each time, at the end of a section, in v 4 and v 6, a declaration is made in which the Greek words *pōs . . . dei* occur ("as ⟨*pōs*⟩ it is determined ⟨*dei*⟩ for me to say"; "as/how ⟨*pōs*⟩ you are to answer ⟨*dei*⟩ every one"). And in both sections, the word *logos* (word, speech) plays an important part. The verses are not entirely symmetrical, however. Thus, in v 4, the second participle of this paragraph is elucidated by a terminal sentence, while the corresponding one in v 6 is joined to an additional imperative.

Verses 2–4 make reference to Paul's commission (and that of his co-workers), while vv 5 + 6 deal with the commission to the Colossians. As the detailed exegesis will attempt to demonstrate, the close of the epistle gives expression to one and the same concern that was already observed at the beginning of the epistle (cf. Comment II to 1:1 + 2): Paul views himself *and* the community as *co-workers* in a common service.

2 *Be steadfast in prayer.* The same summons occurs in Rom 12:12, but there in a participial construction. The verb *proskartereo* occurs ten times in the

NT, and of that total, six times in Acts alone. It designates a steadfastness of action, which probably implies something that occurs without interruption, continuously (cf. Acts 6:4; 8:13; 10:17), as well as something that occurs regularly (cf. esp. Acts 2:46). Whether the antecedent in this verse is a summons to an uninterrupted prayer which accompanies all one's doings cannot be decided from the verb. However, the following admonition to be watchful could point in that direction. Further, cf. Notes to 1:3.

Paul exhorts his readers to do something that he himself practices. Here we can assume, analogously in 1:3, 9, that *proseuche* (prayer) encompasses both prayer and intercession.

be watchful therein with thanksgiving (literally: watching in him). The basic exhortation, to be steadfast in prayer, is elucidated by two participles. That is already demonstrated by the pronoun "in *him*" in the reference back to "prayer." It is unimportant for the meaning whether we translate the participles as modals ("by . . ."), or whether we read them as imperatives,[1] which are preceded by a colon.

"Watch" is used frequently in the NT in an eschatological context in order to call one to an action that is appropriate for the impending arrival of the Lord at the end of time.[2] It is also used, however, in order to admonish to watchfulness against false teachings (cf. Acts 20:31; 1 Pet 5:8). These are not mutually exclusive alternatives, not even in view of Col, because the readers of this epistle are also waiting for the return of their Lord (see 3:1–4 and Comment I to 3:1–4:5). Still, in the face of the possible threat to the Colossian community that Paul dealt with in detail in 2:6–20, it was of special concern to him to refer to it again at the close of the epistle. Once more the central significance of thanksgiving becomes clear (cf. 1:12; 2:7; 3:15, 17). An example of these thanks was given in 1:12–20. Wherever thanks are given for such a Lord as the one who is praised here, any kind of false teaching seems paltry, so that thanksgiving is the recommended kind of watchfulness.[3]

3+4 *Pray also for us, that God may open a door for our word, to proclaim the secret, the Messiah* (literally: us a door of the word). For the translation of the participle, see the Notes to the previous word.

The imagery of "opening a door or a door being open" (cf. also 1 Cor 16:9; 2 Cor 2:12; Acts 14:27) occurs also outside the NT. Thus, Epictetus (for example, Diss II, 1, 19f.) uses it in order to designate the freedom of choice among various possibilities. This meaning probably does not come under consideration in Col. Parallels in rabbinic literature are of interest in order to understand the imagery. The image of the master of the house, who, by opening

---

1. Comp. Notes to 1:10, esp. fn. 32.
2. Matt 24:42f.; 25:13; Mark 13:35, 37; Luke 12:37; 1 Thess 5:6, 10; Rev 3:2f.; 16:15.
3. H. Löwe, "Bekenntnis," op. cit., p. 304, saw also here a summons not to leave the position gained in confession. This is hardly the concern in Col. See Notes to 2:7.

the door, allows entry to the person who knocks, teaches that symbolically God opens a door, and thus he *allows* the act of penance or the offering of intercession.[4] Applied to our verse, that could mean that Paul is exhorting to intercession that he (also) be allowed or be given the opportunity to preach in captivity,[5] or that hindrances be removed from his listeners,[6] or even that he be released from prison, so that he could resume his mission activity.[7] Yet a further possibility should be considered. The fact that he speaks of the "door of the word," in which the substantive *logos* (word) has no attribute, as in 1:5 ("of truth"), 1:25 ("of God"), 3:16 (of the "Messiah"), could be a signal that the word of Paul and his co-workers is to be differentiated from the "mystery," cited subsequently, which in 1:25 is also called "word of God." "Our (that of Paul and his co-workers') word" would then be intended as a contrast to 4:6, where the discussion concerns "your (the Colossians') word."[8] The community is to intercede with God to allow Paul's (and his co-workers') proclamation of the secret, the Messiah; not in the sense that they might have the opportunity to speak, but rather that God might use their speech to make known the revealed secret. That would then emphasize that the proclamation of the secret is not in the power of the proclaimer but that it is constantly dependent on God to reveal the secret through their words (cf. 2:6).[9] The request for intercession by the Colossians thus becomes an impressive witness that community and apostle stand on the same plane as supplicants before God, the so-called laypeople, not as though the professional clerics have a privileged position as the possessors and distributors of the word.

Col 1:26 + 27 argue in favor of such an interpretation, according to which the revelation of the secret stands within God's power of disposition (cf. Notes). The declarations about the sovereign working of the gospel in 1:6 argue in favor of this as well. This interpretation is further supported by the parallel statements in Ephesians, where the concern is not with a removal of hindrances that are caused by the external situation of Paul or that are to be sought in the

4. See the references in St.-B., II, 728; III, 484f.
5. Comp., for example, J. B. Lightfoot (p. 297); E. Lohse (p. 233); P. T. O'Brien (p. 239).
6. P. Ewald (p. 5); H. von Soden (p. 66); K. Staab (p. 102).
7. Comp., for example, H. A. W. Meyer (p. 407); E. Schweizer (p. 172); A. Lindemann (p. 69).—This explication is hardly fitting, since Paul sees the fulfillment of his missionary charge in his suffering (comp. Comment I to 1:24–2:5).
8. In place of the possessive pronoun, the bare determined form was selected. Comp. for that BauerLex 1088f.
9. The explication which says that the image of "opening the door of the word" means "opening the mouth" goes in a similar vein. It is represented by: Thomas Aquinas (p. 184); J. Calvin (p. 128); J. A. Bengel (p. 794). Comp. also E. Lohmeyer (p. 161) and W. Bieder (p. 268). The explication that "door" is a plastic circumscription for "mouth" gives too little credit to the broadly used expression "opening a door."

circumstances of his possible listeners: "(Pray) also for me, that the word may be given to me to open my lips and in high spirits to make the secret known (by proclaiming) the gospel" (Eph 6:19).[10]

For the expression *mystērion tou theou* ("secret of God") and interpretation of the genitive as *genitivus exepegeticus* ("the secret, ⟨which is⟩ the Messiah"), see Notes to 1:26f., as well as Comment II to 1:24–2:5.

Because of this (secret) I am also bound, 4 so that I may reveal it, as it is determined for me, to proclaim (it) (literally: because of which). For the change from the plural "we" (v 3) to the singular "I," see Comment I to 1:3–5.

The significance that Paul attributes to his suffering and thus also to the circumstance under which he writes the Colossian Epistle as prisoner is misunderstood, in our opinion, if we read the relative clause "(literally) because of which I am also bound" as parenthetical. Because Paul views his suffering as the fulfillment of his service, which was imposed on him, and because he elucidates this view in Col (cf. Comment I to 1:24–2:5), it is advisable to subordinate the final sentence, "so that I . . . ," to the relative sentence immediately preceding it ("because of which . . ."). Paul here calls attention to his comments in 1:24ff. and points to the art and manner of revealing the secret which was assigned to him by God. Imprisonment is precisely not a misfortune for him; it does not restrict or hinder his missionary activity; on the contrary, it allows this activity to achieve its aim (cf. 1:14).

It should be noted that Paul uses the verb *phaneroō* (to reveal) to describe his service, rather than one of the otherwise more customary words, such as *kēryssō* or *euangelizomai* or *kataggellō*. *Phaneroō* seemed to be reserved for the activity of God in 1:26. But precisely because of the declarations in 1:26f., as well as because of the request expressed in 4:3 that God may grant that the secret be spoken, the verb form "I (Paul) may reveal" does not express anything different from 2 Cor 2:14 and 4:10, namely that it is God who reveals through (and in) Paul. Paul hardly takes the position of God here (cf. E. Schweizer, p. 171); and it also does not mean that the apostle embodies the revelation in his person (cf. A. Lindemann, p. 70).

5 In wisdom conduct your lives toward those who are on the outside (literally: walk). The kind of wisdom that is intended here and that is to determine and guide the way of life of the Colossians is the equipment granted by God for living in obedience to his will (cf. Notes to 1:9 and 10). Beyond all moralizing, the invitation is to use a gift of God. Just as Paul is called to make the secret known (cf. previous verse), so also do all the members of the community take an active part in this great calling. Their life in obedience toward God is not an end in itself but is rather oriented toward those who are "outside" *(hoi exō).*

---

10. Such self-evident confidence of the proclaimer arises from the tradition of OT declarations such as Deut 18:18; Isa 51:16; Jer 1:9; Ps 40:4; comp. Isa 6:7; Ezek 24:27; 29:21.

Those words are used to designate those who do not serve the Messiah and who therefore do not belong to the church, thus those who have not yet recognized the "revealed secret."[11] The Christians, insofar as they hold firm to the word of life, shine as lights in the world, as Paul illustrates in Phil 2:15, 16. In Matt 5:16 (cf. 1 Pet 2:12), this idea is elucidated still further, "so that they may see your good works and praise your father in heaven."[12]

redeem that which is offered now (literally: buy the time [from]). Here also, as in vv 2 + 3, an imperative is modified by two participles (see Notes there).

We find a similar mode of speech in LXX Dan 2:8, which there means "to win time." But there the verb is not construed in the middle voice as in Col and Eph, but rather in the active, and even the meaning in the passage cited from Daniel does not seem to aid in the interpretation of Col 4:5. Since no further parallels to this expression have been found, the modern reader is dependent on internal evidence in Col in order to understand the image used. Various interpretations have been suggested.

The Greek term *kairos* which is used here often means a fixed time or point in time, in contrast to *chronos*, which means the passage of time. But this differentiation is not valid without qualification either in extra-biblical or in biblical Greek. A comparison between Gal 4:4 and Eph 1:10 shows that both words can be used synonymously, and that *kairos* is used in Eph 1:10, where we would expect *chronos* according to the distinction in meaning cited above.

The verb *ex-agorazō* occurs only in Gal 3:13 and 4:5, besides the present text (Col 4:5) and Eph 5:16. In both verses in Gal it means "to buy from, to redeem." This meaning has been accepted also for the expression in Eph and Col by some exegetes.[13] Accordingly, the instruction would be to take possession of the "time"—whether the time remaining until the return of the Lord or any proffered opportunity—and to use it according to the will of God, not to leave it to those who would use it for bad deeds.

A different exegesis has found more support. It interprets *ex-agorazō* not as "to buy from," but rather attributes at most an intensive meaning to the prefix *ex-*: what is meant is to buy totally out or simply to buy. Then the image, which

---

11. See for that 1 Cor 5:12f.; 1 Thess 4:12; comp. also Mark 4:11; Rev 22:15.—The expression "those outside" also occurs beyond the biblical corpus. Thucydides, for example, describes "exiles" this way. In the rabbinic literature, it is used for those who do not belong to the covenant (St.-B. III, 362) and occasionally also for people who represent heretic viewpoints (see J. Behm, ThWNT II, 572). Comp. also W. C. van Unnik, "Die Rücksicht auf die Reaktion der Nichtchristen als Motiv in der altchristlichen Paränese," in FS für J. Jeremias, *Judentum, Urchristentum, Kirche*, ed. W. Eltester, BZNW 26 (Berlin: Töpelmann, 1960), pp. 221–34:223, fn. 6.

12. Comp. also W. C. van Unnik, op. cit.

13. See among others J. A. Robinson, *St. Paul's Epistle to the Ephesians*, 2d ed. (London: Clark, 1922), in his explication to Eph 5:16 (cited in M. Barth, AB 34A, p. 578).

we should picture as a market stall, is that the objects on display should be purchased until it is entirely empty, or simply that the time of possession should be put to use. Accordingly, whether we conceptualize "time" as a point, as the continually proffered opportunity, or in a spatial sense in space, the resultant meanings are either to use every opportunity, or to take advantage of the remaining time with all its possibilities, to exploit the time to the last, to buy up the time (like a wise merchant) in order to utilize it, etc.[14]

A further suggested meaning can be recommended on the basis of the use of *kairos* in Rom 13:11. There, Paul remarks within the framework of ethical admonitions, "for you recognize the time *(ho kairos)*, that the hour is at hand to arise from sleep, for our salvation is closer now than it was then when we began to believe." Here, *kairos* is the time that requires a certain decision.[15] In extra-biblical Greek, compliance with this request is expressed by "to use the time," "to take time," or even "to rob time." The word *ex-agorazō* suits also verbs such as "to take" and "to rob," so long as we translate it by "to buy" (rather than "to buy from/out,"[16] since it also signifies "to take possession." "To buy time" would then mean to accede to the "requirement" of time, which is characterized, in contrast to all other times, by the revelation of the secret (1:26f.) and by the impending revelation of the Messiah in glory (3:4). This requirement is the invitation to serve the Messiah, the Lord over all things. In this way, the same kind of conduct of life is recommended to all the members of the community, as opposed to those who are outside, just as to the slaves as opposed to their (unbelieving) masters (3:24).

But even this interpretation cannot be more than a supposition.

6 *Let your word be determined by grace at all times* (literally: in grace). It is not possible to decide precisely what is meant by *en chariti* (literally: in grace). It is also possible here, as already in 3:16, that *charis* means the "friendly," "charming" tone of speech. That does not need to mean that an "ingratiating manner of speech" is recommended to the Colossians (cf. E. Haupt, p. 165). We would do more justice to the author of Col in this case if we understood the friendliness of speech requested by him in 3:12 as a manifestation of the positive behavior of the "new self," such as compassion, goodness, humility, mildness,

---

14. Comp. among others E. Haupt (p. 165); E. Lohse (p. 237); E. Schweizer (p. 173); J. Gnilka (p. 231); P. T. O'Brien (p. 241); R. P. Martin (NCC, p. 127); C. F. D. Moule (pp. 134f.).

15. Thus also frequently in extra-biblical Greek. See for that G. Delling, ThWNT III, 456–563:458f.; R. M. Pope, "Studies in Pauline Vocabulary, ET 22 (1910/11) 552–54.

16. It is not unusual in the Koine, the Greek dialect in which the NT was written, to have a composite which is not differentiated in meaning from the simplex (see BDR 116). *Exagorazō* with the meaning "buy" is attested; see Polybius III, 42:2, where he reports of Hannibal, "doing his best to make friends with the inhabitants of the bank, he bought up all their canoes and boats, . . ."

and patience. This friendliness would then be an acknowledgment of the friendliness of God or of the Messiah (cf. Notes to 3:12). The omission of the article before *charis* (in the Greek text) cannot exclude the alternate interpretation that *charis* should be understood as "grace," as Eph 2:5 demonstrates. Although both interpretations are not mutually exclusive, this interpretation is probably perferable, because then there is a contextual parallel in vv 2–4/5 + 6, which corresponds to the structural parallel in these verses. In Col, "grace of God," "gospel," "word of truth," "word of God," and "secret" are synonymous concepts (cf. 1:15/1:6/1:25/1:26), and thus, analogously to the "exhortation" regarding the word of Paul and his co-workers in v 3, so here also regarding the word of the Colossians, the point is that the decisive factor lies in one's own speech, which is to be determined by "grace," thus by "the secret."

seasoned with salt. This imagery occurs in the NT also in Matt 5:13; Mark 9:49f.; and Luke 14:34. According to W. Nauck,[17] "Rabbinic words taken from a certain code of instruction for the disciples of scribes (provide) a parallel enabling us to understand the New Testament metaphor of 'salt.' " In his investigation of Mark 9:49f., he arrives at the conclusion that *echete en autois hala* is a literal translation of the rabbinic form *mmwlh*, "having been salted oneself," and that it means, "be 'sagacious,' 'wise' or 'bright.' "

With respect to Col 4:5, the interpretation of "salt" as "wisdom" signifies the application of the more basic exhortation "conduct your life in wisdom" (cf. Notes to v 5) in the speech to the Colossians.

Since it is supported by the parallel declarations in Eph 4:29 ("no foul talk shall pass your lips"), a further meaning should be considered. The image employed here could be that of salt in its function of preventing decay or rot.[18] Then, analogously again to the thought in v 3, the "secret" would be understood as the salt that makes the speech of the Colossians an *imperishable* word (of God).[19]

then you will know how you are to answer every one (literally: in order to know). If we translate the infinitive as final, that would state that the Colossians are instructed by their own speech about what they are to say to one another. Such an assertion is only sensible, as E. Lohmeyer (p. 163) notes correctly, "if this word is not discovered on its own but is rather fulfilled by the 'word of Christ' and is inspired."

It is also possible, however, to translate the infinitive as a modal ("so that")

---

17. W. Nauck, "Salt as a Metaphor in Instructions for Disciplineship," StTh 6 (1952) 165–78.

18. See for that the examples in St.-B. I, 235.

19. The image of salt does not mean here, as for example in the extra-biblical Greek (see references in J. B. Lightfoot, pp. 298f.), a rhetorical versatility, specifically a jesting play on words. Against this speak statements such as 1 Thess 2:3, to which no contradiction should be construed through forced explication.

or as an *infinitivus exepegeticus* ("then you will know"). These latter translations have much to recommend them, since subsequently we read "how you are to *answer* every one." Apparently, in their present circumstances, an "answer" is expected of the Colossians (cf. 1 Pet 3:15) from various sides.[20] Paul confronts the concern as to how to respond to all the "questions" that could arise even in the form of denial[21] with the declaration that the requisite answer is simply given by retaining in one's own speech nothing but the "secret": the Messiah, who has reconciled all things and who has become their Lord (see Comment II to 1:2–2:5).

COMMENTS I–II TO COL 3:1–4:6

I. Salvation in the Present and in the Future

What has been articulated in other Pauline Epistles as hope, which is to be fulfilled at the end of time, is represented in Col as an already present reality. In NT research, this phenomenon is called "realized eschatology" and it is differentiated from the so-called "futuristic eschatology." This conceptualization has not been an especially happy choice, because both "eschatologies" seemingly and paradoxically do not exclude one another. Next to "realized eschatology," we also find "futuristic eschatology" in Col, especially in 3:4. We encounter this juxtaposition not only in the NT, but also in the literature of Qumran.[1] Futuristic eschatology has an important role in the uncontested Pauline Epistles (cf., for example, Rom 8:18ff.; 1 Cor 15:12ff.; 1 Thess 4:13ff.) to which group, in the opinion of a series of researchers, Col does not belong. E. Grässer, following G. Bornkamm and correcting him, represents the viewpoint that the author of Col has assimilated himself to the world and salvation views of his Hellenistic readers. The futuristic expectation of the early Christians, in its reduced form without resurrection or last judgment, served only to preserve them from the misconception of salvation as an unhistorical mystique.[2] F. J. Steinmetz (PHZ, pp. 30ff.) expresses himself in a similar vein. He says that the expectation was only for the revelation of that which was given. The declaration in Col 3:4 was moving in the direction of a transcendent-immanent schema. In comparison with the language of the older Pauline Epistles, he writes, the expressions and perspectives are so changed in view of

20. That they should know to answer "each and every one" points to this. To judge from the admonitions of the *Haustafel*, they perhaps had in mind unbelieving husbands, masters, and parents. But even the threat from the false teachers in chap. 2 comes under consideration.

21. Comp. for that 1 Pet 3:15, as well as Notes to 3:18, 20, 22 and Comment II to 3:1–4:6.

1. For that, see K. G. Kuhn, *Enderwartung*, op. cit., esp. pp. 181–88.

2. Further, see Comment III to 1:3–8.

the parousia that one could speak at most of "traces" of futuristic eschatology. We find such a trace also in Col 3:24. But if we consider that Col 3:18–4:1 represents a traditional piece at its core, then we cannot attribute too much weight to this fragment of futuristic judgment-expectation in the dominant pattern of the epistle. The resultant research of A. Lindemann[3] is formulated on the same fashion. For him, the basic difference from Pauline theology lies in the fact that in Col "present" and "future" exist *simultaneously* on two planes, while for the real Paul the future is realized in hope, that is, in faith, without denying the historicity and thus the future relationships of human existence. If "future" for Col is an unveiling of already spatial present time—even if also still hidden—then that means that future does not have any real existence.

H. E. Lona proposes corrections of such viewpoints.[4] He works it out that the statements in Col, which represent a concentration on the present, pursue a pragmatic goal. There is no attempt, however, to achieve some general or objective comprehension of time and history. He therefore considers the consequence, namely that the moment in time in Col was almost entirely eliminated, as not to the point.[5] Still, however, a shift in the eschatology of Col as opposed to the undisputed Pauline Epistles has taken place. This is demonstrated by the fact that the author of Col writes of the resurrection of the dead in the traditional sense, which differentiates this letter from those of Paul. The line of demarcation between Paul and the Deutero-Paulines runs through this point (p. 187). According to Col, the resurrection of the believers takes place in baptism. But this does not signify the end of time and the historicity of the faithful, for life "up above" is hidden in God. The temporal tension in the final revelation of life is thus accompanied by a spatial component, the connection between heaven and earth. This spatial schema establishes the reality of the eschatological life in the present, and at the same time also its concealment (p. 171). But Paul was never able to accomplish such a transmutation of the concept of the resurrection, which in the reasoning of the apostle is founded on the significance of corporality. As concerns the resurrection, his language remained unambiguous, for the human being was for him a somatic reality and formed an indivisible unity. But death destroyed this concrete reality. Since for Paul there existed no final shape of the human being without its corporality, no emphasis on the presence of salvation and life could have caused him to lose sight of the hope of resurrection (p. 187). This sense of loss has occurred in Col according to H. E. Lona. He maintains that the author of Col speaks of a resurrection of the

---

3. A. Lindemann, *Aufhebung der Zeit*, op. cit., pp. 40ff.

4. H. E. Lona, *Die Eschatologie im Kolosser- und Epheserbrief*, FoB 48 (Würzburg: Echter, 1984).

5. Ibid., for example p. 234: "The time-frame in Col is not eliminated, but is rather integrated into a Christological concept which forbids a 'neutral' or rather an 'objective' discussion of time."

faithful that has already occurred in baptism, and he consequently uses this concept to emphasize the corporal unity of the human being; for death also smites the baptized one. But that does not mean that the anthropology in Col is different from the Pauline one, for the hope of resurrection as the hope at the end of time has not been abandoned. If 3:4 speaks of glory *(doxa)*, then *doxa* is the splendor of the heavenly world and is connected with the corporality of the resurrected ones in 1 Cor 15:43 and Phil 3:21. The body of the resurrected ones in turn is the model into which the debased human body is metamorphosed. Thus, if in Col there is discussion of a revelation of the faithful with Christ "in glory," then that means that at the end of time not only will the revelation of the hidden life occur, but also beyond that the body of the faithful Christian receives a new, final form or shape that it has not yet received at the resurrection in baptism (p. 183). Thus, what has been carried out in Col—within the framework of the same human image—is a shift in the evaluation of corporality, which now no longer has the conspicuous significance that it possessed for Paul. Because of the fact that the "body" concept is attended to in an ecclesiastic sphere, thus serving as a designation of the church, and in addition, because of the spatial orientation of the author of Col (which, in the opinion of H. E. Lona, is conditioned by the exposition of the false teaching, cf. p. 236), hope has been thrust into the background at the level of changed corporality (p. 188). Despite all this, an important commonality between Paul and Col should not be overlooked: in the fact that Col understands the origin of the eschatological life, its hidden reality, and its revelation at the end of time, only in the sense of a *syn christō* (with Christ; 3:4), the author of Col remains in this point entirely on the level of Paul (p. 181).

H. E. Lona is correct in writing that the declarations of Col, which are designated as "realized eschatology," do not pretend to be a treatise about time or history. They are to be understood from their specific context and especially from their place and function in the epistle. The reason for these statements, however, is not primarily to answer the false teaching, in our opinion, however it may have been construed (cf. Comment V to 2:6–23). Paul rather responds to the distress of the Colossians, who view themselves as being neglected by the apostle. He gives them to understand what has been granted to them, (!) the non-Jews, through the Messiah, and that his charge lies exactly in proclaiming this truth to them, and that it fulfills itself especially in his service to the Colossians (cf. Notes and Comments to 1:24–2:5). On this basis, the concentration on the present is understandable and hardly contradicts the uncontested Pauline Epistles; the conclusion, that the temporal hope has been set aside or transcended, is unfounded here.

H. E. Lona's explanation of the expression "in glory" in 3:4 is also very much to the point. The revelation of the faithful with Christ is more than simply a necessary occurrence. The declarations about the suffering in 1:24–2:5

also point this out, as well as the author's plea for "perseverance and patience in joy" (1:11, cf. Notes).

However, we can hardly speak of a spatial orientation as a peculiarity of Col. "Heaven" and "on high" are not primarily spatial-geographic categories. Their use is determined by the picture of the enthroned Messiah, whose royal throne is described in a well-known speech from the OT as "heaven" or here as "on high," but whose sovereign jurisdiction extends over all creation, to which heaven (!) and earth belong (cf. 1:16). The perspective at its basis cannot be realized from "geographic" conceptualizations (cf. Notes to 3:1 + 2). Finally, however, H. E. Lona's opinion is not convincing that through the elaborations in Col about the resurrection, a shift has occurred in the view of eschatology and anthropology, in contrast with Paul's views. As we tried to demonstrate in Comment II to 2:6–23, baptism is not the event at which the resurrection has already, or at least partially or essentially, occurred. The author of Col relates the concept of resurrection to the granted forgiveness of sins, which is also granted to non-Jews who formerly lay *dead in sin*. The concept of "being dead in sin," together with the meaning of forgiveness as a component of the resurrection of the Messiah, has brought about the concept of "co-resurrection" (or resurrection with Christ). We have associated with this a choice of ideas that do not occur in the uncontested Pauline Epistles, but this does not touch on the problem of the imagery that is used, as H. E. Lona demonstrates. The corporality of person is not abstracted. The fact that a traditional usage of "resurrection" of necessity decreases in the rest of Col the prominent significance of corporality that we have in the letters of Paul is not convincing. After all, Paul can also speak about an already accomplished "having died" before the "corporal" death, in his uncontested letters (for example, Rom 6:8, 11), without diminishing the significance of corporal death (cf. 1 Cor 15:26). Why does such an application of "death," as in Romans 6, not also contradict the evaluation of the human being as a somatic reality and a unity which cannot be sundered.

We ask, moreover, why the corporal resurrection (or even the judgment) is not explicitly mentioned in Col. But why should this occur? We need to observe the location of the declarations about the future "revelation in glory" here as well. These declarations do not occur in basic explanations about the "last things," but they rather fulfill a function within the paraenesis. The call is to a new way of life in 3:11ff., with reference to the "new status" that had been granted. There is then an additional statement simply to the effect that this new, still hidden, "status" will someday be revealed. The demand that also the *how* of the revelation would need to be explained in this connection, namely through the corporal resurrection and judgment, is an arbitrary assertion of the exegetes.

It seems to us that it is not possible to establish a difference between the eschatology of Col and that of the uncontested letters of Paul that would provide a firm basis for a decision as to the Deutero-Pauline authorship of Col.

461

II. *The* Haustafel

Col 3:18–4:1 stands out from its context as a closed unit. These exhortations exhibit a clear arrangement as a parallel structure, unlike the other exhortations. Six different groups of persons are addressed which form three pairs of relationships (women—men; children—parents/fathers; slaves—masters). The pairs are instructed to achieve an appropriate reciprocal conduct. In this series, the word is first aimed each time at the "weaker" member of this combination. The admonishment directed at this group is followed by a justification each time, in which the orientation is to "the Lord." The case is different with the men, fathers, and masters: the admonition to the first group proceeds without elaboration or justification. In the instruction to the fathers, the reference to "the Lord" is missing, but it is present in the admonition to the masters. If we compare the individual exhortations, it becomes noticeable that the one to the slaves is disproportionately detailed.

Even when deviations exist in structure as well as in content, we can find parallels in the NT for the form of exhortation that occurs here in Col, and which is also differentiated from the context through its terseness and disposition. We can list Eph 5:21–6:9; 1 Pet 2:18–3:7; Titus 2:1–10; 1 Tim 2:8–15; 6:1–2.[6] The designation *"Haustafel"* goes back to M. Luther.[7] It gained general acceptance and is widely used to the present day. It is true that some recent exegetes have proposed that it would be better to speak of *"Ständetafeln"* (assembly tablets).[8] It could be argued in favor of such a designation that the addressees do not belong to Christian "houses," i.e., Christian households. Those admonished are not in fact the members of such households, such as the husband, the father, and the master on the one hand and correspondingly the members of his household who are subordinate to him on the other. Against this view, however, we note that women or slaves or children are addressed who belong to the households of which we can assume that the head was not a Christian at all. Beyond that, recent critics say that the *Haustafeln* of Timothy and Titus cross the threshold of and are beyond the household of antiquity. We need to observe, however, that the groups of persons addressed in Col and Eph (as well as 1 Pet) were probably consciously chosen because they belonged to real households in antiquity, and that the exhortations reflected the reality of household life in antiquity (cf. above). Thus, as concerns the ethical exhorta-

---

6. M. Dibelius, *Geschichte der urchristlichen Literatur*, p. 142, cites the following comparative pieces in the post-NT Christian literature: 1 Clem 21:6–9; IgnPol 5:1–2; PoePhil 4:2–6:3; Barn 19:5–7; Did 4:9–11.

7. Comp. WA 30 I, 397.

8. Comp. among others L. Goppelt, "Jesus und die 'Haustafel'-Tradition," in FS für J. Schmid, *Orientierung an Jesus. Zur Theologie der Synoptiker* (Freiburg: Herder, 1973), pp. 93–106:95; J. Gnilka (p. 205).

tions in Col, Eph, and 1 Pet at least, the designation *"Haustafel"* is thoroughly justifiable.

The *Haustafeln* have been investigated thoroughly in NT research. Important stages in the history of research[9] may be sketched as follows:

E. Seeberg[10] made a decisive contribution to the understanding of the *Haustafeln* by questioning the exposition that had been accepted until then, namely that the exhortations of the NT *Haustafeln* referred to *actual* situations in the community. Rather, he asserted, they were concerned with traditional material. His thesis, however, that the *Haustafeln* were a component of the Christian catechism that in turn went back to a Jewish catechism for proselytes and was transmitted to the early church by way of John the Baptist and Jesus could not be sustained, among other reasons because the question has to remain unanswered as to why—if the *Haustafeln* were a firm component of Christian teaching—do they occur only in the *late* Pauline tradition and in the First Petrine Epistle.

A different attempt to clarify the origin of the *Haustafeln* of the NT did gain acceptance and is acknowledged despite intensive criticism up to the present time. It goes back to M. Dibelius, who proposed the thesis in the first edition of his commentary on Col (HNT 3, 2; 1912), namely that early Christianity, forced to accommodate itself to everyday life because of the delay of the parousia, fell back upon paraenetic materials, above all of Jewish instructions with the *Haustafeln*, and that this was only superficially Christianized. Furthermore, M. Dibelius pointed out that even the philosophic propaganda of Hellenism was familiar with such compilations of obligations, and he cited references from Epictetus, Diogenes Laertius, and the Stoic Hierocles. Since then, Epictetus has been considered the classic source, Diss. II, 17, 31, "As a pious man, as philosopher, and as a circumspect human being, I want to know what my obligation is toward the gods, toward my parents, toward my brothers, toward my fatherland, toward strangers."

K. Weidinger, a student of M. Dibelius, carried out this thesis and attempted to substantiate it in detail by citing extensive extra-biblical materials to compare with the NT *Haustafeln*.[11] Like his teacher, he also viewed the *Haustafeln* of the NT as being occasioned by the task of balancing the unfulfilled expectations at the end of time with the mundane everyday expectations. In doing so, they appropriated materials already at hand by resorting to mundane morality, and by utilizing, transforming, and Christianizing it. Three sources were at the disposal of this early Christianity: (1) the Judaica of the Diaspora; (2) the

---

9. See for that esp. J. E. Crouch, *Haustafel*, pp. 13–31; D. L. Balch, *Wives*, op. cit., pp. 2–10.

10. E. Seeberg, *Der Katechismus der Urchristenheit*, ThB 26 (unaltered reprint of the edition of Leipzig: Deichert, 1903) (München: Kaiser, 1966).

11. K. Weidinger, *Haustafeln*, op. cit.

Hellenistic popular philosophy; (3) the words of the Lord, which, however, did not come into consideration in the *Haustafeln*.

K. Weidinger then offered examples, which demonstrate that in Judaism, and then only in Hellenistic Judaism, however, were there tables of obligations which dealt with the relationship between husband and wife, parents and children, friends and relatives, slaves and masters (pp. 23–27). His investigation of the *Haustafel*-schema in the philosophy of Hellenism (pp. 27–50) then led him to the conclusion that the *Haustafeln* comprised a part of Greek folk ethic which was inculcated again and again by Stoic propagandists and which was thus preserved in the society. Since Christianity was expanding on Hellenistic soil, this material would not remain unknown to them. Christianity was even able to take up these instructions without hesitation, since it expressly recognized that, according to Rom 2:14, the gentiles performed works according to the law of nature (p. 48). Thus, the *Haustafeln* would represent a testimonial for the common ethical perceptions of paganism, Judaism, and Christianity (p. 79). Col 3:18–4:1 thus demonstrates how *Haustafeln* were Christianized through the simple formula "in the Lord." If we remove "in the Lord," then nothing remains that a Stoic or Jewish teacher could not have said (p. 51).

The question, which is unimportant for K. Weidinger, remains open, however, whether the *Haustafel*-schema reached Christianity by a circuitous route, namely by way of Judaism (pp. 48–51). Since that schema occurs only in Hellenistic Judaism, and since it was demonstrated there also to be borrowed material, this question can have only subordinate significance.

We have the opposite extreme in the expositions of the *Haustafeln* that attempt to demonstrate that the *Haustafeln* were not appropriated from other sources but rather were original Christian creations.

K. H. Rengstorf[12] perceives in the usage of the Greek verb *hypotassesthai* (to subordinate) in the exhortations in the NT to the wife a specific Christian language use, among others because the verb (in his opinion) plays only a modest role in corresponding extra-NT exhortations and because the verb is used without the nuance of ignominy, which so often clings to the word.[13] Since the admonitions to the wife to subordinate herself to her husband occur in the *Haustafeln* with only one exception (1 Cor 14:34), K. H. Rengstorf needs to arrive at a different historical religious and traditional evaluation of the *Haustafeln* of the NT, than do M. Dibelius and K. Weidinger. The fact that the *Haustafeln* of the NT deal with the same concerns with much the same regularity and even following in the same sequence points to a prearranged schema (and it goes without saying that there were certain parallels to the NT

---

12. K. H. Rengstorf, "Die neutestamentlichen Mahnungen an die Frau, sich dem Manne unterzuordnen," in FS für O. Schmitz, *Verbum dei manet in aeternum*, ed. W. Foerster (Witten: Luther-Verlag, 1953), pp. 131–45.

13. Comp. for that Notes to 3:18f.

Haustafeln in the surrounding world of early Christianity). Still, these were something new and special. K. H. Rengstorf counters the viewpoint, that we are here simply dealing with the Christianized form of a kind of paraenesis usual in the surroundings of the growing church, with his thesis that the NT *Haustafeln* are a "genuinely Christian creation." In addition, we have the tradition that in the church of Alexandria already around 200, the *Haustafeln* of the NT were perceived as deriving from the apostles, and were cited as authoritative. He also bases his thesis on the following differences by which the NT *Haustafeln* were distinguished from their non-Christian surroundings:

1. We are dealing with exhortations in the NT *Haustafeln* that address correct behavior on the part of the members of the *oikos* (the household) or the *familia*, and only this.

2. Nowhere in the *Haustafeln* is a special or even an absolute right conferred on the husband as house father in contrast to women-children-slaves, and their obligation to be subordinate is also not established on the basis of such a privileged position. All the members of the *oikos* (household) are rather obliged to be subordinate for the sake of the order of God.

Thus, for K. H. Rengstorf, the words "in the Lord" are also not a formula of Christianization; rather through them the *oikos* is moved into the operational realm of effectiveness of the gospel in the outward form according to its time. The *Haustafeln* thus document specifically not the emergence of civil thought patterns in the world of the eschatological proclamation of Jesus and the apostles, but they rather confirm the exact opposite. The final motif of the *Haustafeln* rests in the concern of increasing the praise of God as the creator also in one's existence and in the order of the *oikos*.

D. Schröder[14] also considers the NT *Haustafeln* a Christian creation. He demonstrates the inadequacy of the Dibelius-Weidinger hypothesis by pointing out basic differences between the *Haustafeln* of the NT and those of the stoa: the sequence is not the same as that in Stoic sources, nor are groups of persons admonished in the latter concerning their behavior toward one another, nor are the obligations of the subordinate persons as specifically emphasized as they are in the NT. D. Schröder does indicate analogies in Jewish sources, especially in Philo, but he sees no direct dependence. Rather, he claims, Paul created the NT *Haustafel* in the face of false interpretations of his own declarations in Gal 3:28. In this form (imperative and justification), he thus borrowed from the so-called "apodictic law" and it was known from the OT. Even the stoa made a contribution. This was not of the contextual kind but it was rather in the form of inquiry to which the *Haustafel* responded ("How am I, as wife, slave, etc., to conduct myself?"). Now, since the admonitions, especially those to the subordinate persons, demonstrated a more fixed form than their specific substantiations,

---

14. D. Schröder, *Die Haustafeln des Neuen Testaments*, Diss. [Hamburg, 1959 (Sec.)].

they were therefore also older. And since they were Jewish in nature, D. Schröder concluded that they originally went back to Jesus himself, "There is nothing in the way of viewing them as a 'transmission from the Lord' himself. These individual admonitions, as Jesus gave them, were then arranged and justified by Paul in this way by a question of the gentile Christians stemming from stoicism. The admonitions to the superordinated persons then arose from the subsequent disagreement with the Greek folk-ethic which stemmed from a misunderstanding of the admonitions."[15]

We can incorporate E. Lohmeyer's (pp. 153–55) thesis between these two extremes of interpretation. He traces the *Haustafeln* back to "Judaic tradition." He does not agree with M. Dibelius and K. Weidinger's opinions that the concern of the *Haustafeln* consists in equalizing the tension between daily affairs and end-of-time expectations. He maintains that faith is knowledge of the beginning of a new reality, in which God has already contained within himself all his own action in advance and has already set the specific appearance of his own norm, and the more clearly this reality appeared to be completed within the immediate future, the more difficult it could appear to bend the transient existence of world and human beings within the space and time that were still under hitherto existing laws. The obligation toward these laws was, however, never questioned in terms of the oldest early Christianity. For the "arrival" of the Lord was certain for the early Christians only *because* all the rights and obligations of God were confirmed anew through him; "he would not be the 'anointed of God' if the hitherto existing law and the people of God had not been maintained as valid through him until his parousia." The early community therefore followed Jewish law, and even for Paul, who called the law, as the revelation of God, holy, just, and good, the obligation of such action was unshakable for the sake of the unbreakable correlation between Christ and law (!). But this validity seemed also to be tied to the continuance of the Jewish people and its tradition, and this connection seemed to have become impossible for Paul. Thus, the difficult question arose for Paul, as it did in gentile Christian communities, who were not tied to Jewish tradition and were not permitted to be tied to Jewish tradition, how they were to accommodate the "holy obligation," which was to be sufficient for the law as the revelation of God. The law, as the vehicle of the statutes of God up to then, and that which was set "in the name of the Lord Jesus," were indeed tied to one another, but both were related to each other as something "temporary and *final*." Thus Paul was able to resolve the difficulties mentioned by eliminating everything from the superseded tradition that had not addressed the word of Christ. At the same time, however, such a paraenesis could do without Christianizing its commandments because it drew on the tradition of the God-chosen people.

This position of Paul, in which the concern was to choose that which was

---

15. Ibid., p. 152 (cited in J. E. Crouch, *Haustafel*, op. cit., p. 27).

"essential," was not something entirely new but was very closely related to the situation in which the Jewish mission found itself "among the nations." Its choices had to be determined by the missionary purpose, that is, by consideration for the gentiles who were to be won over. That was the way in which ideas of the surrounding world were able to penetrate into their own tradition and in which the sacred inheritance was variously transformed and refined. Paul was not born into this process; he only took part in it as apostle. He did not advance it, let alone begin it. The general prerequisites of the paraenesis of the *Haustafeln* were comprehensible in this connection, not, however, their peculiarity in form and content. The custom in Hellenistic moral philosophy of clothing the obligations of the individual toward religion, state, society, and family in short impressionistic sentences and to put them together in a table or schedule seems to touch upon the admonitions of Paul in the *Haustafeln*. Yet the problem situation was more complicated than can be assumed (by M. Dibelius and K. Weidinger, for example), if we say that secular morality was taken over and merely Christianized by the formula "in the Lord." Paul was not able to catalog obligations toward God and society *alongside others*, as the Hellenists were able to do, because for him, as for the Jews, it was necessary to begin with a first principle or command and then justify all the other obligations, just as the first principle of God/Christ and community then justify every kind of existence. The paraenesis determined by Hellenistic ideas was handed on by Paul in the form in which the Jewish paraenesis had already shaped it. For E. Lohmeyer, that clearly demonstrates the *Haustafel* of Col. He considers the admonitions to the men, fathers, and masters a supplement. Evidence for that view is the fact that religious motivation is almost totally lacking. Women—children—slaves, who are always addressed first, are thought of as a group to which the admonitions were originally applicable. Since Deuteronomic times, they have formed a unity as the less legitimatized in terms of cult, justice, faith, and custom, as opposed to men. It thus becomes clear that the *Haustafel* of Col goes back to Jewish tradition, namely to Jewish catechism tradition. Based on the disproportionately long exhortation to the slaves, E. Lohmeyer then concludes that the question of slavery in Colossae occasioned the *Haustafel* of Col. Owing to the circumstances in Colossae, however, Paul viewed it more appropriate not to present this question as especially selected but rather to combine it with others for which there existed an inherited tradition and which would give form and substance to his speech.

In his dissertation published in 1972, J. E. Crouch[16] once again thoroughly investigated the problem of the NT *Haustafeln* on the basis of the state of research at the time. He presented the various positions up to that time and he subjected them to an intensive critique. He thus demonstrated the shortcomings of the Dibelius-Weidinger hypothesis, but at the same time, he also raised

---

16. J. E. Crouch, *Haustafel*, op. cit.

questions about the alternative suggestions. His questioning alone is of importance: since there is no exact parallel to the *Haustafeln* of Col outside the NT, we cannot pose the question from the perspective of *Religionsgeschichte*, "From what source did the church borrow this code?" Then only two answers are possible: either the *Haustafel* is pre-Christian (M. Dibelius; K. Weidinger; E. Lohmeyer), or it is Christian (K. H. Rengstorf; D. Schröder). "Because the question in terms of *Religionsgeschichte* is incorrectly posed, one is prevented from offering a solution which accounts for both similarities and differences." We need to ask, "1. From whence did the material come which went into the formation of the *Haustafel?* 2. What was the decisive impulse in the creation of the *Haustafel* as a *Christian* topos?" J. E. Crouch checked the source material presented by K. Weidinger and underscored the latter's failure "to note certain unique factors in the Hellenistic Jewish usage of the stoic schema. Discussion of social duties in reciprocal terms and the distinction between subordinate and superior persons are non-Stoic features which characterize Hellenistic Jewish codes. At the same time, his failure to examine the content of the *Haustafel* exhortations caused him to overlook the fact that exhortations to women and slaves conform neither to the concerns of the stoic schema nor to the presuppositions of stoic philosophy. *Weidinger* further ignored the area in Hellenistic Judaism in which the stoic schema played a role. Consequently, he was unable to observe the contribution made to the tradition by Jewish concerns preserved in the Hellenistic Jewish propaganda. Finally, the weakness of *Weidinger's* work lies in his failure to recognize the situation in Hellenistic Christianity which led to the formation of the *Haustafel* as a Christian paranetic form" (pp. 147f.).

J. E. Crouch demonstrated that, of the entire Stoic source material that K. Weidinger itemized, only one document combined the "women—children—slave" group (Seneca, ep. 94). It is clear that, normally, slaves were not mentioned in Stoic materials. We suspect that their mention in Seneca was occasioned by a special and specific concern about slaves. The grouping "women—children—slaves" was not of Stoic origin, but was rather Hellenistic-Jewish. J. E. Crouch refers to Philo, De Hypothetica 7, 14, where the obligations of the husband, the father, the master to instruct his wife or his children or his slaves in the law are cited. Here, Philo most probably used traditional (Jewish) material, as a comparison with similar statements in his writings demonstrates. J. E. Crouch remarks further, "While this one text alone is not sufficient to prove that the Christian *Haustafel* is dependent on Hellenistic-Jewish material, it demonstrates that the schema husband—wife, father—children, master—slaves was known and used in the Hellenistic-Jewish apologetic; and it offers the closest parallel to the pattern of the Colossian *Haustafel* which we have observed." J. E. Crouch cannot explain the other typical characteristic of NT *Haustafeln* from these sources, however, namely that of reciprocity. For this, he refers to the fact that "social duties in Egypt and Israel were often understood in reciprocal terms" (pp. 102f.). Referring to

H. Bolkestein,[17] he points to the obligation of the rich to grant protection and support to all those in need and suffering, while it is the duty of the poor and the weak to conduct themselves in subservience toward the mighty who look to their welfare. Without hesitation he then explains "reciprocity" as "a Jewish-Oriental characteristic" (p. 103).

The historic context of the NT *Haustafeln* was the convergence of enthusiastic and nomistic tendencies in Hellenistic Christianity. "The *Haustafel* itself was formulated in nomistic circles to combat what was regarded as the growing danger posed by enthusiastic excesses" (p. 157). It was this historic situation also that produced the special status of the "master" in the *Haustafel*. Because the "standards of the social order" "in the Lord" were attached, the term "in the Lord" was used in the *Haustafel* in order to characterize the area in which the exhortations of the *Haustafeln* were to be applied. This, however, did not change the content of the ethical exhortations. "The standards of the social order to which the *Haustafel* requires conformity remain unchanged in their essence" (p. 154, cf. p. 157). The significance of the *Haustafel* for the reader of today, according to J. E. Crouch, consists in that it summons one "to give oneself to one's neighbor within the limitations which the social order places on the relationship" (p. 160).

J. E. Crouch convincingly demonstrated the untenable position of the Dibelius-Weidinger hypothesis, for one thing, and he corrected the "religionsgeschichtliche Fragestellung" (questioning) just as much, for another. His solution, however, is not fully satisfying either.

D. Lührmann[18] correctly points out the main weakness of this proposal, to the effect that Crouch cannot easily explain the triple grouping "wives—children—slaves," nor the reciprocity of the exhortations from one uniform tradition, just as this is also not possible from the Hellenistic catalogs of obligations. Rather unconvincing is also the curt dismissal of K. H. Rengstorf's observation that a peculiarity of the NT *Haustafeln* is that the members of the *oikos* (household) in antiquity were addressed. J. E. Crouch rejected this observation with the comment that the heading *Haustafel* is assigned to those other texts from without, but from within themselves or within their immediate context this consideration does not arise (pp. 26, 104). D. Lührmann's investigation takes us further on this point. He makes a connection with the only evidence that J. E. Crouch considers valid concerning the source material that K. Weidinger produced, namely Seneca, ep. 94. This is no isolated document in which the Hellenistic schema of obligations is limited to the household.

---

17. H. Bolkestein, *Wohltätigkeit und Armenpflege im vorchristlichen Altertum. Ein Beitrag zum Problem "Moral und Gesellschaft"* (Utrecht: Oosthoek, 1939).

18. D. Lührmann, "Wo man nicht mehr Sklave oder Freier ist. Überlegungen zur Struktur frühchristlicher Gemeinden," WuD.NF 13 (1975) 53–83; comp. also Lührmann, "Neutestamentliche Haustafeln und Antike Ökonomie," NTS 27 (1981) 83–97.

Rather, this document belongs to the entirely different tradition of writings "concerning the economy." They deal with the art of conducting a household. "Concerning the economy" means simply, as it says in Seneca, ep. 94, 1, the portion of philosophy "for which there are specific prescriptions for every role in life . . . , for advice which is dispensed to the husband regarding his demeanor toward his wife, to the father regarding his rearing of his children, to the master regarding how he should rule his slaves."[19] The writings about the economy of the household, as D. Lührmann points out, extrapolate the social history of "house" as a social and economic concept, of the Greek *oikos/oikia*, the Latin *familia*, the Hebrew *beth*. And specifically, "house," "household" in this sense was not a social form or an economic form among others, but was rather "the elementary social and economic form not simply of antiquity or even of the NT, but presumably also of all pre-industrial settled cultures. . . ."[20] If we place the *Haustafeln* of Col and Eph within the context of this tradition, then we gain the advantage of being able to explain them on the basis not only of the triplicate schema (wives—children—slaves) but also of the reciprocity of the exhortations of a uniform tradition. This classification led to a new evaluation of the NT *Haustafeln*. Inherent in them we should not recognize, as one had to suspect in the succession of M. Dibelius and K. Weidinger, a civilian application of early Christianity. Much rather there is in them a latent political claim, since the economy was a part of the political order.[21]

K. Thraede developed this train of thought further.[22] He argued from J. E. Crouch's results that in the NT *Haustafeln* we are not dealing with a transferred or direct dependence on an antique schema, but with an already rather late-Jewish adaptation of Hellenistic principles and their transference then as Jewish formulaic and perceptual positions. However, he saw, as had D. Lührmann already, the necessity of expanding the extra-biblical comparative material— going beyond J. E. Crouch—and of taking the relationship to "house" and thus the writings "concerning the economy" more seriously. In so doing, he pleaded for a more careful and a more differentiated consideration of Hellenistic ethics than had been previously encountered, for example, in the "almost rooted-out viewpoint . . . that the perception of marriage in antiquity was only called a crude *kratein* ('governing,' H.B.) of the husband, not an *agapan* ('loving,' H.B.; cf. Col 3:19)."[23] Like D. Lührmann, he also discovered that the writings "concerning the economy" exhibited noticeable similarities to the NT *Hausta-*

19. Ibid., "Ökonomie," p. 85. As further important texts, he mentions Aristotle, Pol I; PsAristotle, Oeconomica I: Philodemus of Gadara (ed. E. Jensen, 1906); Hierocles (Hierocles: *Kleine Schriften*, ed. H. Dorrie, Hildesheim, 1973, pp. 311–467).
20. Ibid., p. 87.
21. D. Lührmann, "Sklave," op. cit., pp. 79f.
22. K. Thraede, " 'Haustafeln,' " op. cit.
23. Ibid., p. 362.

feln. We are there also dealing with "a. a triple schema, b. the mutuality of relationships, c. the attempt to mitigate mere 'domination' ('subjugation'), and finally, d. Leitmotifs such as 'fear' or 'fear and love' (i.e. respect)." We would then not necessarily, as J. E. Crouch meant, presuppose borrowings from Hellenistic Judaism for the first two points.

The thrust of the texts "concerning the economy" was to work out and to maintain the basic pattern of domination and servitude within the realm of the house. Thus they related to one another from above and below "in a humanizing way," and with a recognizably different accentuation. It is decisive that K. Thraede was able to determine that "fronts" could be established in reference to "the house" in the Hellenistic-Roman environment of the NT, "which prohibit attributing 'to antiquity' an unquestioning enlightenment in this field. The option for *hypotagē* ('subordination,' H.B.) was not self-evident, its expression had, if one so wishes, a 'critical component' similar to the *Haustafeln*, only precisely an expressly anti-egalitarian one."[24] What was then expressed in the *Haustafeln*, especially of Col and Eph, with the borrowing from the writings "concerning the economy," was a knowingly responsible *participation* "in Christ" "for an idea of domination which was mitigated or humanized by custom, a position which in the following of correspondingly conservative counterdesign mediated between the extremes of the stoic maxim of equality or Greek liberalism and the harsh postulate of unconditional compliance."[25] Thus the early *Haustafeln* were hardly available for the intent of inserting the "dominion of Christ" in a sociocritical way, but the option for a *via media* between power and "equality" is a very creditable contribution on the part of the author of Col (p. 367).

D. L. Balch specifically occupied himself with the *Haustafel* of 1 Pet.[26] He demonstrated that the ethical schema of subordination in the "household" with the pairs also encountered in the NT, and the weight on subordination of the weaker member of each pair, "was developed in classical Greek discussion of the constitution in which the 'city' and the 'house' were hierarchically ordered" (p. 61). He verified this from Plato[27] as well as Aristotle, in which precisely the three pairs which also occur in Col are named and are designated as constituting

---

24. Ibid., p. 365.

25. Ibid. Compare for that also K. Müller, op. cit.

26. D. L. Balch, *Wives*, op. cit.

27. Esp. Plato, Leg III, 690A–D: ". . . : what and how many are the agreed rights or claims in the matter of ruling and being ruled, alike in states, large or small, and in households? Is not the right of father and mother one of them? And in general would not the claim of parents to rule over offspring be a claim universally just? . . . And next to this, the right of the noble to rule over the ignoble; and then following on these as a third claim, the right of older people to rule and of younger people to be ruled. . . . The fourth right is that slaves ought to be ruled and masters ought to rule. . . . And the fifth is, I imagine, that the stronger should rule and the weaker be ruled. . . ."

the "household."[28] He is also successful in proving that these classical *topoi* can be encountered elsewhere in Plato and Aristotle and among their successors on into Roman times. "They were known and discussed by Middle Platonists, Peripatetics, Stoics, Epicureans, Hellenistic Jews, and Neopythagoreans" (p. 62). In a second part, he demonstrated that the Romans reacted to new strange cults in a certain stereotypical way. Even "Judaism and Christianity inherited slanders which Greeks and Romans originally directed against Dionysus and Isis cults. In Roman culture it was inevitable that Judaism and Christianity would be charged with sedition, with murder, and with practicing rites which corrupted the morality of Roman women" (p. 118). According to D. L. Balch, incriminations are recognizable in the reproaches that the cults under consideration were destroying the order of Greco-Roman "households."[29] He clarified the seriousness of such reproaches by citing sources that emphasize the importance of "harmony" in the "household."[30] Responses to such attacks are found on the Jewish side with Josephus in an "apologetic encomium on the

---

28. Aristotle, Pol I, 1253b, 1–13, "And now that it is clear what are the component parts of the state, we have first of all to discuss household management; for every state is composed of households. Household management falls into departments corresponding to the parts of which the household in its turn is composed; and the household in its perfect form consists of slaves and freemen. The investigation of everything should begin with its smallest parts, and the primary and smallest parts of the household are master and slave, husband and wife, father and children; we ought therefore to examine the proper constitution and character of each of these three relationships, I mean that of mastership, that of marriage (there is no exact term denoting the relation uniting wife and husband) and thirdly the progenitive relationship (this too has not been designated by a special name)."

29. See the interesting reference in Tacitus (55–118 C.E.), Hist V, 5 (comp. D. L. Balch, p. 90), ". . . ; again the Jews are extremely loyal towards one another, and always ready to show compassion, but towards every other people they feel only hate and enmity. They sit apart at meals, and they sleep apart, and although as a race, they are prone to lust, they abstain from intercourse with foreign women; yet among themselves nothing is unlawful. . . . Those who are converted to their ways follow the same practice, and the earliest lesson they receive is to despise the gods, to disown their country, and to regard their parents, children, and brothers as of little account."

30. Dio Chrysostomos, Dis 38, 15, "Again, take our households—although their safety depends not only on the like-mindedness of master and mistress but also on the obedience of servants, yet both the bickering of master and mistress and the wickedness of the servants have wrecked many households. Why, what safety remains for the chariot, if the horses refuse to run as a team? For when they begin to separate and to pull one this way and one that, the driver is inevitably in danger. And the good marriage, what else is it save concord between man and wife? And the bad married, what is it save their concord? Moreover, what benefit are children to parents, when through folly they begin to rebel against them? And what is fraternity save concord of brothers? And what is friendship save concord among friends?" (Comp. D. L. Balch, *Wives*, op. cit., p. 88.)

Jewish nation" (Ap II, 199, 206, 216). Indeed, Josephus did not use the three pairs found in the economy writings, but these are found in an "encomium of Rome," which was composed in the first century B.C.E. by Dionysius of Halicarnassus.[31]

D. L. Balch also understands the *Haustafel* of 1 Pet against this background of stereotypical Roman reproaches against strange cults (cf. esp. 1 Pet 2:11–12; 3:8–9, 15–16).

The connection of the *Haustafel* of Col to the writings "concerning the economy" is convincing, in our opinion. D. L. Balch's reference to the apologetic function of the *Haustafel* of 1 Pet gives us insight beyond that as to why, in contrast to the listing of the pairs: husbands—wives, parents—children, masters—slaves in Aristotle (see above), in Col the wives, children, slaves are named in first place: "The NT writers emphasized the subordinate members who were in a difficult social situation."[32] We can presume this difficult situation for the Christians in Colossae. It is reflected in the arrangement of the pairs of the household, as well as in the form of the exhortations especially to the weaker members of the household (cf. Notes). Nonetheless, the *Haustafel* is not used apologetically in the same way as it is

---

31. Dionysius of Halicarnassus, Ant Rom II, 25, 4–5, "This law obliged both the married women, as having no other refuge, to conform themselves entirely to the temper of their husbands, and the husbands to rule their wives as necessary and inseparable possessions. Accordingly, if a wife was virtuous and in all things obedient to her husband, she was mistress of the house to the same degree as her husband was master of it, and after the death of her husband she was heir to his property in the same manner as a daughter was of that of her father; that is, if he died without children and intestate, she was mistress of all that he left, and if he had children, she shared equally with them. . . ."

32. D. L. Balch, op. cit., p. 96. For this also, he can cite an extra-biblical example (Dionysius of Halicarnassus, Ant, II, 25, 4). This interpretation places E. Schweizer's thesis into question, at least that concerning 1 Pet where he determines the beginning of re-paganization here. E. Schweizer sees in this the idea that the *Haustafeln* received a proper place in the canon, an affirmation to the good worldliness which we encounter also in the wisdom literature of the OT. Like E. Lohmeyer, he sees in the grouping "women—children—slaves" an orientation toward the poor and the weak. In the NT (as also already in Hellenistic Judaism), both components, the primary and the subordinate, are addressed, so that the weak are not viewed as objects of the action. He seems to see a difference to the Stoa here. In the *Haustafeln* after Col and Eph, a stronger and stronger hierarchical order stands out, which demonstrates itself already in the absence of admonishments to those in superior places: thus, in 1 Pet 2:18–25, the admonition to the masters next to that to the slaves is absent. Due to the fact that next to marriage, family, and work, the state and communities stand out more in their hierarchical order, the idea of a divinely legitimized cosmic order is introduced, whereby the "good worldliness" and thus the continually inherent relativity of all order is lost. (Comp. in addition to the citations in his Col Commentary: Schweizer, "Ethical Patterns"; op. cit., "Weltlichkeit," op. cit.)

in 1 Pet. In Col, it stands under the superscript of doing *everything* in the name of the Lord Jesus (Col 3:17). It is instructive that the format of a catalog of ethical exhortations was chosen for the elementary and social form of housekeeping for the express purpose of including also the "everyday" life, next to the behavior in the community, and which also addressed the constituent groupings that were pertinent to the meaning of "household." The "household" was *the* daily sphere of existence for the members of the Christian community. The schema of writings "about the economy," which demonstrated the reciprocity of exhortations as a characteristic, approximated the concerns developed in the ethics in Col, which equally emphasize the "social" element (cf. 3:11). Within the framework of Col, however, the explanation does not reach far enough, which implies that the *Haustafel* simply manifests a *partisanship* for *a* model for the department in the household which existed in the extra-Christian realm. Rather, it gave expression to the especially Christian orientation, that the community decided in favor of a moderate and humanizing model in the relationship between superiors and subordinate persons. The context of the *Haustafel* in Col describes an ethic that is totally oriented toward the Messiah, and it gives expression to this through the imagery of putting on the "new self," which is perhaps also intended to be the Messiah (cf. Notes to 3:10). Listed under these characteristics of the new self are, among others, love, humility, gentleness, etc. (3:12), and it is noticeable that the attributes of God or the Messiah are thus cited. If we add to that the fact that Col understands the Messiah and his work as the revelation of a previously entirely hidden secret, it becomes difficult to interpret an ethic that is determined by this secret as partisanship for a generally familiar ethic which regulates the relationship between "weaker and stronger persons." The interpretation also seems dubious because the *Haustafel* exhorts to conduct that is in close relationship to the characteristics of the "new self" (and thus of the Messiah), which was described previously. This matter is elucidated in more detail in the Notes to the concepts "obey" and "subject" (3:18, 20, 22). In addition, the exhortation to love that we find in this connection in the *Haustafel* can hardly be interpreted differently than it is in 3:14. Likewise, the admonition to the fathers not to embitter their children can be seen in connection with the instruction in 3:8 to cast off wrath and anger as characteristics of the "old self." Thus we do not wish to underestimate the *contextual contribution* that the young church made even when it used the form and conceptualization with which it was familiar from its milieu. What was given expression in the *Haustafel* went beyond partisanship for the humanizing ethic of the surrounding world in regard to the relationships in the "household," since Paul only determined from the revealed secret what was "humane." This occurred in thoroughly familiar concepts such as "to obey," "to subordinate oneself," and "to love" and were contextually fulfilled and comprehended from the perspective of the Messiah and his actions.

VI. THE CONCLUSION OF THE EPISTLE
(4:7–18)

7 Tychicus will tell you all the things that concern me; (he is) the beloved brother and steadfast minister and fellow servant in the Lord. 8 I have sent him to you precisely so that you may know how it is with us, and that he may strengthen your hearts. 9 With (him I have sent) Onesimus, the steadfast and beloved brother, who is from your midst. They will tell you everything (that has taken place) here. 10 Aristarchus, my fellow prisoner, greets you, and Marcus, cousin of Barnabas, concerning whom you have received instructions: when he comes to you, receive him; 11 and Jesus, who is called Justus, who are of the circumcision (i.e., Jews). These alone have become co-workers for the kingdom of God. They have become a comfort to me. 12 Epaphras greets you, the servant of the Messiah Jesus, who is from your midst. He always fights for you with prayers so that you may stand complete and fulfilled in the whole will of God. 13 For I testify for him that he has (endured) great hardship for your well-being and for those in Laodicea and in Hierapolis. 14 Luke, the beloved physician, greets you, and Demas. 15 Give (my) greetings to the brothers in Laodicea, and to Nympha and to the community in her house. 16 And when the letter has been read among you, arrange to have it read also in the community of the Laodiceans, and you yourselves also read the letter from Laodicea. 17 And say to Archippus, "Be mindful of your ministry which you have received in the Lord, that you fulfill it." 18 The greeting, with my hand, of Paul. Remember my chains. Grace (be) with you.

NOTES

The epistle is concluded with personal communications (vv 7–9), a list of greetings (vv 10–14), greetings to the neighboring community in Laodicea (v 15), instructions for an exchange of letters (v 16), a word of encouragement to a certain Archippus (v 17), and a greeting from Paul in his own hand (v 18). With the exception of Gal, Eph, 1 & 2 Thess, and 1 Tim, greetings are also transmitted in the other epistles in the Pauline corpus. If we maintain that Col is a pseudonymous epistle, then the author has imitated the Pauline style successfully, although he could have forgone the greetings in view of the epistles mentioned above.

The companions of Paul who send greetings can also be found in the letter to Philemon which was sent to Colossae. The connection to Phlm is made clear by the reference to Onesimus (Col 4:9), but even such small differences were built in by the author. Thus, in place of Epaphras in Phlm 23, Aristarchus is named as the "fellow captive" in Col 4:10. Also, Jesus Justus does not occur in Phlm. The deviations show that the list of greetings in Col was not simply copied from Phlm; yet the information was still so specific and unequivocal that it would depict the situation of the sender which was familiar to the Colossians from Phlm.

Such a procedure at the close of the letter might be the result of deliberate deception. It can be assumed as a serious possibility in regard to the authorship of the Pastoral Epistles (cf. esp. 2 Tim 4:9ff.). But it should be considered only when the other contents of the epistle pose the most serious questions about the authorship of the epistle. For Col, in our opinion, this is not the case.

7 *Tychicus will tell you.* Even though the verb *gnōrizō* is not a technical concept for the promulgation of the gospel in the Pauline writings (cf. 1 Cor 12:3; 15:1; Gal 1:11; Phil 1:22), it is still noteworthy that it occurs only in Col in 1:27 and here in 4:7 + 9. In 1:27, it designates the activity of God in now revealing the previously hidden secret. Even if the verb in our verse (as well as in v 9) had been chosen with 1:27 in mind, the stipulation of J. Gnilka (p. 234) is hardly applicable, namely that the suffering apostle had become an almost venerable prototype for his communities. Rather, the choice of *gnōrizō* would be an indication that Paul understood his suffering as the fulfillment of his commission to proclaim the gospel (cf. Notes below).

Tychicus originated from the province of Asia, according to the information in Acts 20:4, and he was a companion of Paul at the end of his third missionary journey. The question as to whether he also accompanied the apostle to Jerusalem or even to Rome cannot be answered with any certainty from the information in Acts. Tychicus is not named in the uncontested Pauline Epistles; he is named only in Col, Eph, 2 Tim 4:12; and Titus 3:12.

concern me; . . . (literally: that according to me everything). The Greek expression *ta kat eme* (literally: that according to me) is a customary formula.[1] In Phil 1:12, it is used in a context similar to the one in Col. There, Paul introduces with these words the details of *how* his captivity has served the advancement of the gospel. Here in Col, he presumably has something similar in mind. The information will reach the Colossians through Tychicus, the conveyor of the epistle, and they will attest the truth of the statements in 1:24–2:5 on the basis of concrete reports concerning that which has occurred till then because of the captivity of Paul.

the beloved brother and steadfast minister and fellow servant in the Lord.

---

1. See E. Lohse, p. 240, fn. 2.

There is no convincing reason for referring the words "in the Lord" only to "fellow servant." For their significance, cf. Comment II to 1:1 + 2.

The Colossians are addressed as "beloved brothers in the Lord" (1:2); Timotheus (1:1) and Onesimus (4:9) are also designated as "brothers." But Tychicus is differentiated from these by the fact that he is called "steadfast minister and fellow servant" in addition.[2] The same is the case of Epaphras in Col (cf. 1:7). This parallelism is perhaps an indication of the fact that Tychicus is to take the place of Epaphras (cf. Notes to 1:7), as long as he remains with Paul. Then the detailed remarks about Tychicus could be explained as deriving from Paul's desire to recommend Tychicus most warmly to the community. *Diakonos* (minister) will therefore hardly express that Tychicus is an assistant to Paul.[3] Rather, this concept points out that the one sent to the Colossians by Paul is commissioned by God to proclaim the gospel.[4] What was stated by "minister" is underscored by the concept *syndoulos* (fellow servant; cf. Notes to 1:7).

8 *I have sent him to you* . . . (literally: him I . . . have sent). A form of the past tense is used in the Greek, the so-called aorist of the epistolary style. The author writes from the viewpoint of his readers: when they will have received the letter by the hand of Tychicus and have read or heard it, then the past tense "I have sent" will be literally true and entirely correct.[5]

precisely so that you may know how it is with us, and that he may strengthen your hearts. In the report with which Tychicus is charged, Paul includes his co-workers who are with him and who are mentioned in the list of greetings (cf. also Comment I to 1:3–8).

Among the important manuscript readings, Papyrus 46 (circa 200) preserves the following text: "so that he may know how it is with you. . . ." In contrast to this, we have the reading that is rendered in the translation and that is preserved in manuscripts such as Codex Vaticanus (fourth century), Codex Alexandrinus (fifth century), and the important Minuscule 33. The external evidence thus speaks against the text of the papyrus mentioned above. But even internal reasons speak against this text variant, which is under suspicion of being a scribal correction which intended to show that this statement is not simply a familiar

---

2. For the translation of *pistos* as "faithful," see Notes to 1:2, 4.

3. Thus, for example, J. B. Lightfoot (p. 300); W. M. L. de Wette (p. 73); E. Haupt (p. 168); R. P. Martin (NCC, p. 130).

4. See for that esp. W. H. Ollrog, *Mitarbeiter*, op. cit., pp. 73–74: namely that Paul used the word group "servants, service, serve" in "not few and in not significant places" to describe his missionary activity, esp. the missionary work in general (see Rom 11:13; 2 Cor 5:18f.; 6:3f.; 11:8, 23). He says that all these passages describe the word group (formally) of servitude, commission through God on the one hand, and (contextually) the activity in the proclamation of the mission in its ultimate and unlimited sense on the other.

5. See BDR 334, where references are also cited.

repetition from the previous verse. And finally, vv 2:1f. also speak against it. There, Paul stressed how important it was for him that his readers should learn "what a battle" he had on their behalf, "so that all your hearts should be strengthened." The realization of this concern seems to be proclaimed here, at the conclusion of the epistle. The "strengthening of your hearts" is not dependent on a specific situation in the Colossian community which Tychicus must first bring into their experience in order then to be able to help, in contrast to Paul who was tied to the place of his captivity.[6]

9 *With (him I have sent) Onesimus, the steadfast and beloved brother, who is from your midst* (literally: from you). By Onesimus is meant the slave on account of whom Paul wrote the Letter to Philemon. The fact that he is called "steadfast and beloved brother" is less due to differentiating him in rank from Tychicus, the "steadfast minister and fellow servant,"[7] but more in order to make known to the Colossians the joyful news that this slave, the one familiar to them, has become a Christian.[8] Since there are indications in Phlm of the fact that Paul has incurred financial burdens because of Onesimus (Phlm 18), the adjective *pistos* ("steadfast"; for the translation, see fn. 2) is of special significance.

ex hymōn (literally: from you) is a customary expression.[9] Since Onesimus left Colossae as a non-Christian, these words indicate the place of his origin, but it is not specifically intended as a reference to the community there.

They will tell you everything (that has taken place) here. After Onesimus has been introduced to the Colossians as brother, he is then very naturally included in the commission, along with Tychicus, of transmitting news and of strengthening the community.

10 *Aristarchus . . . greets you.* Aristarchus is named in the Pauline corpus besides Col only in the list of greetings in Phlm. According to information in Acts, he came from Thessalonica and accompanied Paul at the end of the so-called third missionary journey. While Tychicus is mentioned only briefly in Acts 20:4 (see above to 4:7), Acts reports that Aristarchus, as a companion of Paul, was seized in Ephesus by the crowd that had been incited by the goldsmith Demetrius, and was dragged to the theater (Acts 19:29). In Acts 27:2, he is then listed as a companion of the captive Paul on his sea voyage to Rome.

my fellow prisoner. Actually, *aichmalotos* means "prisoner of war." But it is not unusual for Paul to borrow terms from the military sphere and to use them

---

6. For the expression "so that he may strengthen your hearts," see Notes to 2:2, as well as Comment I to 1:24–2:5.

7. Comp. T. K. Abbott (p. 299); E. Lohse (p. 241).

8. That is derived from Phlm 16. See further M. Barth, *Philemon* (forthcoming AB vol.).

9. In the NT, comp., for example, Acts 4:16; 21:8; Rom 16:10; 1 Cor 12:16; Phil 4:22.

for his purpose (cf. Eph 6:10ff.; Phil 2:25; 1 Thess 5:8; Phlm 2). For this passage, there are various possibilities of interpretation:

1. Aristarchus, like Paul, had been apprehended and arrested.

2. Aristarchus shared the arrest of Paul of his own volition. This interpretation can be recommended on the basis of Phlm 23, where Epaphras is designated as a "fellow prisoner." Did co-workers of Paul rotate in sharing the imprisonment of the apostle?

3. Since the expression *synaichmalotos* was also used in Rom 16:7, although Paul had not yet been imprisoned when Romans was written, "prisoner" could be understood in a figurative sense, namely as "prisoner in obedience to the Messiah."[10] Reliance on this interpretation of *synaichmalotos* in Rom 16 is problematic, however, because of the serious question whether the list of greetings there originally belonged to Romans.[11]

An exegetical decision is difficult. Against 3 is perhaps the improbability that Paul wished the concept of co-prisoner to be understood figuratively after having spoken of his own factual captivity just previously. But it is possible that Paul wanted to indicate precisely that even a free, not incarcerated man could also be a prisoner (cf. 1 Cor 7:22). But we should expect that it would then mean "prisoner *of the Messiah.*" Thus, in our opinion, a voluntary imprisonment was intended and solution 2 is probable in view of Phlm 23.

and Marcus, cousin of Barnabas. Through the indication of the relationship to Barnabas,[12] it is almost certain that the John Marcus mentioned in Acts 12:12, 25; 15:37, 39 is meant. According to the report in Acts, the Christians in Jerusalem gathered in the house of his mother. He himself was brought by Paul and Barnabas from Jerusalem to Antioch and from there on the so-called first missionary journey. But Marcus left them in Pamphylia. That is why Paul refused to take him along on the so-called second missionary journey. Subsequently, Paul quarreled with Barnabas, which led to their separation. Marcus and Barnabas went to Cyprus and Paul chose Silas as his new companion. This dissension seems to have been resolved by the time of Col, at any rate as it concerned Marcus and Paul.

concerning whom you have received instructions. To assume an "aorist of the epistle-style" (cf. Notes to v 8) here seems forced. Paul alludes to previously received instructions of which he is aware and with which he agrees. But who gave them, when, and where, is not stated and must remain open.

when he comes to you, receive him. The verb *dechomai* often means "to

---

10. Comp. for that 2 Cor 10:5, "and take every thought captive to obey Christ (*aichmalotizontes*)." This interpretation is represented by Dibelius-Greeven (p. 51) and C. F. D. Moule (pp. 136f.), among others.

11. For this problem, comp. for example W. G. Kümmel, *Einl.*, pp. 278f.

12. The Greek word *anepsios* originally meant "cousin" and is used only in later references to denote different relationships. For that, see J. B. Lightfoot, p. 302.

receive someone with hospitality" in the NT.[13] This hospitality usually implies wanting to hear the message of the person received. That is probably what we have here in Col. Marcus is recommended to the community as a proclaimer of the gospel and is to be received *as such a one*. The fact that the community received this instruction may simply mean that he was still unknown to the communities of Lycostales (cf. Acts 18:24–28). In the face of warnings about false teachers, which are contained in Col (2:6–20), this is understandable. The supposition that the instructions are linked directly to the dissension reported in Acts[14] is unlikely because it must be assumed that Paul summarily excommunicated Marcus and that he advised all the communities of this action. The text basis for such a view is very scanty.

11 *And Jesus, who is called Justus.* It was a widespread custom among Hellenistic Jews to take a Latin or Greek surname in addition to the Jewish name. Even Saulus (Heb. *šāʾûl*) Paulus adhered to this custom.

Jesus Justus is not named otherwise in the NT.[15] Noticeably, he is not mentioned in the greeting list in Phlm. The hypothesis that in Phlm 23f. it is not, "Epaphras greets you, my companion in Christ Jesus, Marcus," but rather, "my co-captive in Christ, Jesus, Marcus. . . ." cannot be supported by any textual evidence.[16]

who are of the circumcision. These alone have become co-workers for the kingdom of God (literally: being of the circumcision, these alone co-workers for the kingdom of God). It is clear what is meant, but the construction of the sentence seems cumbersome. There are various possibilities for solving the syntactic problems of this sentence:

1. "(literally:) Those being of the circumcision" could be attached as a relative clause to the previous statement, to which a new sentence is then added (J. B. *Lightfoot*, p. 304). This solution is not likely, because it requires the tacit addition of an explanatory phrase in the main sentence, such as "among the Jewish Christians." Otherwise a factually incorrect statement would result.

2. No such supplement is necessary if we, along with Dibelius-Greeven (p. 51), E. Lohse (p. 243 fn.1), or J. Gnilka (p. 239), read "these alone" parenthetically which is then strongly emphasized in this way.

3. However, it is also possible that we have a borrowing here of a frequent

---

13. Comp. Matt 10:14, 40f.; Mark 6:11; Luke 9:5; 10:8, 10; 16:4, 9; John 4:45; Gal 4:14.

14. Comp. Thomas Aquinas (p. 191); R. P. Martin (NCC, p. 131).—Hardly satisfactory is also the supposition that the early community was not yet familiar with the custom of giving hospitality to the messenger (at community expense) (comp. H. von Soden, p. 69; J. Gnilka, p. 238).

15. In Acts 1:23, one Joseph named Barnabas is named with the co-name Justus, in Acts 18:7, one Titius Justus.

16. See also A. Lindemann (p. 74), who points out that Paul hardly used the name "Jesus" next to "Christ," as if that Jesus had yet another name.

construction, especially in the Semitic, in which the thing, concerning which something is to be said, is placed in the nominative in the previous sentence and is then replaced by a pronoun in the main sentence where it would really have been expected. The pre-positioned nominative in this case would be expanded by a participle (*ontes*, "being"), while the copula *eisin* (they are) would be left out—as is often the case in Greek (cf. BDR 127f.).[17]

By the "co-workers of the circumcision" are meant the three persons named in vv 10 + 11, who are compressed into one group by the common "(so and so) greet (you)." Not convincing are, in our opinion, arguments that Aristarchus could not be of Jewish heritage, since it is to be concluded from his naming in Acts 20:4 that he belonged to the bearers of the entire collection of gifts donated by the gentile Christians (cf. Rom 15:25ff.) for the brothers of Jerusalem.[18] But there is no reason why another Jew, in addition to the Jew Paul, should not belong to this delegation, especially since these two were not the only brothers who traveled to Jerusalem with pooled monetary funds.

The expression "of the circumcision" is surely to proclaim the Jewish heritage of the three named co-workers. It is used in this sense also in Rom 4:12.[19] The subsequent statement also recommends this interpretation in Col (cf. next Notes). The omission of Timothy, when he was also a member "of the circumcision," may be based on the fact that Paul was responsible for his circumcision (cf. Comment I to 1:1 + 2).

E. E. Ellis has suggested an alternative meaning.[20] He joins O. Cullmann and Schmithals in the interpretation of the terms *hebraios* and *hellēnistēs*, by which in Acts 6:1 two groups of Jews in the Jerusalem community are denominated. "Hebrews" means "those Jews with a strict, ritualist, viewpoint" and "Hellenist" those "with a freer attitude towards the Jewish Law and cultus." He builds his hypothesis of a "twofold diaspora mission" on this differentiation in which he supposes that "Hebrews" and "those of the circumcision" are synonymous designations. "The Hebrews would evangelize the ritually strict congregations. The Hellenists would direct their activities towards the less strict Jewish groups and, of course, the gentiles. . . . Col 4:11 would then reveal, to use a modern term, a venture in ecumenical Christianity."

The Greek word *synergos* (co-worker) was translated by M. Luther as "assistant, helpmate" (*"Gehilfe"*). But that can easily give the impression that Paul placed himself above the three named fellow Christians, who would simply render service as underlings. The Greek concept expresses exactly the opposite. This is clearly indicated in 1 Cor 3:5–9. There, *synergos* is used in a context

---

17. Compare also the sentence construction in 3:17.

18. Comp. P. Ewald (p. 440); E. Haupt (p. 171); F. Mussner (p. 99).

19. It occurs in the NT also in Acts 10:45; 11:2; Gal 2:12; Titus 1:10.

20. E. E. Ellis, "The Circumcision Party and the Early Christian Mission," in *Prophecy and Hermeneutics, NT Essays*, WUNT 18 (Tübingen: Mohr, 1978), p. 116–28.

that argues against differentiation of rank. Neither the one who plants, nor the one who waters, is of importance, but only God, who permits growth. Both are "co-workers of God," which can only mean that both are co-workers commissioned by God to the same task without one being greater than the other.[21]

The choice of the phrase *basileia tou theou* (kingdom of God) is conditioned by the elaborations in 1:12ff.[22] We should therefore not entertain the notion of a formulaic expression whose meaning was smoothed over because the eschatological character of this concept no longer stood out.[23]

They have become a comfort to me (literally: which for me). *Parēgoria* occurs only here in the NT, and it occurs in the LXX only in late writings (4 Macc 5:12; 6:1; compare 12:2). There, it means "encouragement/persuasion." J. B. Lightfoot (p. 305) gives three meanings for the corresponding verb *parēgoreō*: (1) to exhort, to encourage; (2) to dissuade; (3) to appease, to quiet. He points out that this word and its derivatives were used especially in medicinal contexts to mean "assuaging, alleviating." He suggests, "perhaps owing to this usage, the idea of consolation, comfort, is on the whole predominant in the word."[24] The fact that Paul spoke of "comfort," and in doing so referred to his co-workers of Jewish origin, seems to us most comprehensible from Rom 9–11. According to the statements of this chapter in Rom, Paul suffered "great *sorrow* and pain without ceasing in his heart" (Rom 9:2) about the fact that his tribal relatives in the flesh did not follow the Messiah Jesus. To the question as to whether God had rejected his people, on the contrary, he responded with a "No!" among other reasons because he could point to himself, an authentic Jew, who had been called by God (Rom 11:1). This was to him proof that God had in no way rejected his people but had kept a remnant for himself—as already earlier in the history of his people. Thus, the promises that God had made to his people had not fallen by the wayside (Rom 11:2ff.). Based on this exposition, it is understandable that there, where Jews were called to be co-workers in the kingdom of God, Paul was comforted in his sorrow about the unfaithfulness of the Jewish community and of his kinsmen.

12 *Epaphras greets you, the servant of the Messiah Jesus, who is from your midst* (literally: from you, servant of the Messiah Jesus). Epaphras, who was probably the missionary of Lycostales, was already named at the beginning of the epistle, in 1:7f., as the transmitter of the news from Colossae to Paul (cf. Notes there). There, he was called *fellow servant (syndoulos)*, and here also it is

---

21. Further, see W. H. Ollrog, *Mitarbeiter*, op. cit., p. 68–72.
22. See the Notes there.—In Col 1:13, the reference is to the "royal dominion of the son," here to the royal dominion of God. For that, compare the Notes to 1:15–20, fn. 24, and 1:9–14, fn. 81.
23. Comp. E. Lohse (p. 242). For eschatology in Col, see Comment I to 3:1–4:6.
24. E. Lohse (p. 243 fn. 2) points to the frequent occurrence of *paregoria* (meaning "comfort") in grave inscriptions, and he gives references. See also MMLex, p. 494.

stressed that he is the *servant (doulos)* of the Messiah Jesus,[25] by means of which he is placed on the same level as Paul, as we attempted to demonstrate in the Notes.

The words "servant of the Messiah Jesus" could also refer to the subsequent statement, so that a somewhat different emphasis results: "The servant . . . who always fights for you. . . ." This emphasis would have the sense of differentiating Epaphras from other "servants" because of his battle for the Christians of Lycostales. Yet Paul himself writes of the battle he also fought for the readers of the epistle (cf. 1:24–2:5); therefore, such a syntactic connection is improbable.

He always fights for you with prayers (literally: in the prayers). The verb *agōnizomai* (to fight, to battle) and the substantive *agōn* (battle) are used in 1:29 and 2:1 for the sufferings that Paul endured for the church (cf. Comment I to 1:24–2:5). Since it was important for Paul in 1:7f., as also in this verse, to emphasize that Epaphras was commissioned and empowered by God in the same way as he, it is important to interpret the verb *agōnizomai* on the basis of its meaning in 1:24–2:5. Epaphras is highly praised to the communities of Lycostales, and recommended as a worthy substitute for Paul himself, because the latter evidently was unable to visit them in person, and they may have felt that they were being slighted by the apostle. Epaphras is not an "inferior" evangelist (or proclaimer of the gospel). Just as Paul himself, so he shares in the same commission, namely that of furthering the complete human being who is engaged in the battle for the church through suffering, which was true especially of the Christians of Lycostales. The words "in the prayers" are then not to be understood instrumentally, as though a "battle prayer" concerning the Colossianswere meant[26]; rather, it is stated that the described service of Epaphras occurs through prayers (cf. also next Notes).[27] The article is placed in the Greek because specific prayers, namely those of Epaphras, are meant.

so that you may stand complete (literally: you stand). The goal of "fighting" is described in words similar to those in 1:28 (cf. Notes there). That also is an indication of the fact that the elucidations in 1:28–2:5 are taken into account (see above). To be complete refers to the *undivided* obedience to God (or the Messiah; cf. Notes to 1:28). Contextually, it is important to relate the words "in the will of God," which stand at the end of the sentence, also to the previous declaration. Col 1:22 + 28 indicate that it is finally the Messiah himself who sets the chosen ones as complete persons, in his presence *(parhistēmi)*. Here, the

---

25. This rendering is inconsistent: in some texts, we find *iesou christou*, in others only *christou*. Best attested is the reading *christou iesou*, which we find in the following important texts: Codices Sinaiticus (fourth century), Alexandrinus (fifth century), Vaticanus (fourth century), and in the important Minuscule 33.

26. Comp. Luke 22:23f.; see also V. C. Pfitzner, *Agon*, pp. 125f.

27. For this use of the preposition *en*, see for example 1 Thess 2:2 ("in the face of great opposition").

discussion concerns only the result of this being placed, of "standing." This is not the result of their own powers but is rather the consequence of the actions of the deity. As 1:22 indicates, what is meant is a standing in the presence of the Messiah, and thus one's life in his service, under his care and for his pleasure (see Notes to 1:22 + 28).[28]

13 *For I testify for him that he has (endured) great hardship for your well-being.* Paul interpreted the difficulties, hardships, and sufferings that his service had brought upon him as a "means" by which the church and especially the Christians in Colossae were strengthened (cf. Comment I to 1:24–2:5). Since Epaphras had his roots in Colossae and was probably the missionary to Lycostales, and thus had a close relationship to the communities there, it is understandable that Paul especially referred to the hardships *(ponos)* of this co-worker. *Ponos* occurs in the NT in addition to this passage only in Rev 16:10, 11; 21:4, but it occurs more than ninety times in the LXX. It means labor, especially arduous labor, but also the fruit of such labor. Beyond that, it is a description of misery and oppression of all kinds, and it also bears the special meaning of "pain."[29] In this passage, it served to define the context for which Paul used the verb *kopiaō* in 1:29 (cf. Notes there): it meant hard labor and the bearing of great hardships, of which suffering was also a part. These hardships do not reflect abuses within the community, but here, as also in 1:24–2:5, to the bearing of hardships as a consequence of the Messiah, which signified for Epaphras, among others, participation in the captivity of Paul (Phlm 23). This was for the welfare of the community, because through the fact that the proclaimers of the gospel suffered hardships joyfully, the strength of God was revealed, and thus the proclaimed gospel was confirmed (further cf. Comment I to 1:24–2:5).

Theories which suppose on the basis of 4:12, 13 (as also 1:7f.) that the orthodox teaching was evangelically legitimized by a *laudatio* (commendation) of Epaphras the representative of orthodoxy, in the face of the false teaching at Colossae, so that the false teaching in Colossae was "simultaneously" refuted by "apostolic succession," which would in sum argue against Pauline authorship,[30] hardly do justice to the meaning of this verse. It is also hardly correct that the position of Epaphras in Colossae was shaken, and that Paul (or a different author of Col) was endeavoring to reestablish the former's position again.[31]

and for those in Laodicea and in Hierapolis. Laodicea was the city of most

---

28. For the preposition *en* (in) in verbs of filling, see BDR 172.

29. Comp. among others LXX Gen 34:25; Ex 2:11; Deut 28:33; 1 Chr 10:3; Ps 127 (128):2, as well as the references in LSLex.

30. Comp. W. Marxen, *Einl.*, pp. 153–61, esp. pp. 154, 156f.

31. W. Bieder (p. 304); A. Lindemann (p. 75); op. cit., "Die Gemeinde von 'Kolossa.' Erwägungen zum 'Sitz im Leben' eines pseudopaulinischen Briefes," WuD.NF 16 (1981) 111–34:127.

significance next to Colossae and Hierapolis (cf. Notes to 2:2, esp. fn. 75 and the Introduction). Hierapolis ("holy city") is mentioned in the NT only here in Col. The city was built around several hot springs, and due to the special quality of the water there, important wool-dyeing operations were located in this city which in turn contributed to the wealth of the other cities of Lycostales.[32] Sib XII, 286 and Eusebius (Chron II, 154) report that Hierapolis was stricken by the same earthquake as Colossae and Laodicea in the year 62 C.E.

14 *Luke, the beloved physician, greets you.* In the NT, we discover very little about Luke. His name is given only in Phlm 24 and 2 Tim 4:11, besides Col 4:14, where we are told that he was a physician. If the church tradition of the second century is applicable, then Luke the physician, a companion of Paul, is the author of the Lukan Gospel and of Acts. We cannot exclude, however, that this assertion is derived *a posteriori*, based on Col 4:14.[33]

and Demas. Little is also transmitted about this companion of Paul. His name occurs in the NT only in Col 4:14, Phlm 24, 2 Tim 4:10, where Luke is also named. 2 Tim relates that Demas left Paul and that he "became enamored of the world."

15 *Give (my) greetings to the brothers in Laodicea, and to Nympha and to the community in her house.* This verse also stirs up questions which cannot be answered with certainty, since reference is made to circumstances which were self-evident to the recipients of the epistle and concerning which nothing is related elsewhere.

1. It is uncertain, whether the Greek form of *Nymphan* indicates a man or a woman. Both are possible from this word. Given the presence of a possessive pronoun in the immediate context, we should be able to make a decision on the basis of the gender of the following pronoun. The text transmission, however, is not unambiguous. Some of the surviving manuscripts, among them Codex Claromontanus from the sixth century, record *autou* (*his* house) and read the form *Nymphan* as a masculine name. However, a more original and superior reading (*autōn*, "their" pl.) is superior to the value of the evidence of this transmission, since it is preserved by early manuscripts such as Codex Sinaiticus (fourth century), Codex Alexandrinus (fifth century), and the Minuscule 33. According to these, either the house of the "brothers" (including that of Nymphus) is meant, or *Nymphan* stands for a married couple of whom only one partner is named. The latter alternative is less likely, however, because if two people were intended, both would have been named, as in the case of Prisca and Aquila (Rom 16:3; 1 Cor 16:19; 2 Tim 4:19; cf. Acts 18:2, 18, 26). And if

---

32. See Strabo, 630.

33. H. J. Cadbury, *The Beginning of Christianity*, II, pp. 250ff., pointed out that the early church tradition arrived at the idea of Luke as author of the Lukan Gospel and of Acts through comparisons of the we-reports in Acts with companions of Paul in his imprisonments.

the use of the term the "brothers" is actually a reference to the "community" (cf. Col. 1:2), then what is the connection between the community and the house of the "brothers"? In the transmission of the text, the reading of the third plural possessive pronoun *autōn* seems to be a correction, perhaps to give grammatical support to the relationship between the "house" and the "brothers" or to offer a compromise between the readings *autou* (his, of Nymphas) and *autēs* (her, the Nympha) that a woman had an important position in the community. Thus, probably the reading of the most important Majuscule, Codex Vaticanus from the fourth century, is original, which has *Nymphan* as the name of a woman along with the possessive pronoun *autēs*.[34]

2. But why was the community in the house of Nympha especially noted? That the community in Hierapolis was meant,[35] because it was next to Laodicea and after the greetings to the latter, one might also expect salutations to the former, is improbable. It is noteworthy that the Colossians are not told in v 16 to see to it that their letter was also to be read in Hierapolis. Hence we must look for "the brothers" in Laodicea. Then either the church in Laodicea consisted of several house communities, as was probably the case in Rome (cf. Rom 16:5, 14, 15), and Paul greeted Nympha and the community in her house in a special way for some reason which is not known to us, or the Greek *kai* is a *kai exepegeticus* with the meaning "and specifically" (cf. BDR 442, 6a). Then, Nympha would be the hostess of the whole community in Laodicea, as Gaius was for the community in Corinth (cf. Rom 16:23).

The communities at the time of Paul met chiefly in private houses in Jerusalem, and thus also in Asia Minor, Greece, and Rome.[36] The early church did not have ecclesial edifices. In a similar sense, the oldest synagogues were house synagogues, especially in the Diaspora. For this purpose, either remodeled private houses were used, or rooms in still inhabited private homes.[37]

16 *And when the letter has been read among you, arrange to have it read also in the community of the Laodiceans.* In the exchange of letters between neighboring communities, the arrangement for the collection of letters can be recognized, which finally also led to the collection of our NT.[38]

---

34. J. B. Lightfoot (pp. 308f.) considers it unlikely that a feminine name is meant. Then a Doric form would be presumed which "here seems in the highest degree improbable" in meaning. J. H. Moulton: "Nympha," ET 5 (1893/94) 66–67, countered, "Why not simply Nymphan, gen. Nymphes, in the ordinary Attic declensions?"

35. Comp. J. Gnilka (pp. 243f.); H. von Soden (p. 70).

36. Comp. Acts 1:13; 2:46; 5:42; 12:12; 18:7; 20:8, 20; Rom 16:5, 14, 15, 23; 1 Cor 16:19; Phlm 2.

37. Further, see J. Gnilka, "Philemon," HThK, X, 4, 1982, pp. 17–33; P. Stuhlmacher, "Philemon," EKK, 1975, pp. 70–75; H.-J. Klauck, *Hausgemeinde und Hauskirche im frühen Christentum*, SBS 103 (Stuttgart: Kath. Bibelwerk, 1981).

38. Comp. E. Schweizer (p. 179) and R. F. Collins, ⟨. . . that this letter be read to all the brethren.⟩ A New Testament Note, LouvStud 9 (1982) 122–27.

For A. Lindemann,[39] this verse is the "kingpin" in his theory that Col is a pseudonymous, post-Pauline epistle to the community in Laodicea. He maintains that the pseudonymous author composed a fictive letter to the community in Colossae in order thus—in the name of Paul—to affect immediately the problems of the other community. He chose the Colossians as addressees, and not the Laodiceans themselves, because in this way he did not have to grant the pseudonymous Pauline epistolary "prophetic" traits and refer to the situation in Laodicea in the form of "divinations." Rather, by describing a situation in Colossae at the time of Paul similar to the later one in Laodicea, he could "immediately influence the actual development." Beyond that, the location of Colossae was strange to the Laodiceans, but not far removed. Colossae was especially suitable as an address for a pseudonymous letter because the city was destroyed by an earthquake in 61/62 and was probably never rebuilt, and therefore the danger of the unmasking of the pseudonymous author was relatively small.

However, the fact that a Laodicean epistle is mentioned in Col 4:16 seems to contradict the thesis of Lindemann (see above). He counters this difficulty, however, by saying that the reference to a Laodicean epistle argues in favor of this thesis. He says that the Christians in Laodicea had come to the conclusion at the end of the reading of Col that the imprisoned Paul was not able to write a letter directly to them. But it is entirely legitimate to take the warnings of "Paul" to the Christians in Colossae seriously also in Laodicea, for "Paul" had also wanted his critique of the situation in Colossae made known in Laodicea in order, in this way, to protect the community there from an analogous threat.

This theory is designed to explain this verse on the hypothesis that the theological ideas of Col, especially the elucidations regarding baptism and resurrection (2:12ff.), and the teaching about the head and the body (1:18; 2:19), rule out actual Pauline authorship. We have attempted to undermine this presumption in our exegesis of the corresponding passages of Col.

For the opinion that Col was not also to be read in Hierapolis, cf. Notes to 2:1.

and you yourselves also read the letter from Laodicea (literally: from Laodicea). In the Greek, the words "that (the letter) from Laodicea" precede the conjunction *hina* (so that), and they are therefore emphasized (cf. BDR 475, 1).

There are several different possibilities in interpreting this portion of the verse:

1. A letter is meant, which was written *from* Laodicea, namely:
   a. by Paul to an unnamed community.
   b. by the Laodiceans to Paul.
   c. by the Laodiceans to the heads of the Colossian community.

---

39. See in addition to his Commentary to Col esp. his essay: "Die Gemeinde von 'Kolossa,' " op. cit.

2. The letter was not written in Laodicea, but was rather to be picked up from Laodicea by the Colossians so that it could be read in their community. It was written:

    a. by Paul.

    b. by one of the people named as co-workers in the list of greetings.

Since the letter to Laodicea that was mentioned and the letter *to* the Colossians were to have been exchanged, it seems to be presupposed that a letter *to* the Laodiceans is meant. Thus, only solution 2 comes under consideration, where solution 2a is more likely, since it mentions both the sender of Col and the letter to the Laodiceans in one breath. Then the question becomes urgent as to why Paul sends greetings to this community through the Colossians, especially when he has written to them. It is possible that the letter to the Laodiceans has already been in their hands for some time but still has relevance for the Colossians. C. P. Anderson suggested a different explanation.[40] He considers Epaphras the author of the letter to the Laodiceans: "By this hypothesis we can understand more readily why Paul in Colossians greets the Laodiceans, why no trace of a Pauline letter to Laodicea has survived, and why Paul refers to two letters in spite of the fact that we are unable to discover a sufficient motive for his writing the second letter" (p. 440). If Paul did not compose that letter, then of the co-workers named in the list of greetings, Epaphras would most likely be the author. But he would surely also have sent greetings from Paul, so that the problem is not thereby resolved. The fact that a letter from Epaphras, who is so highly praised by Paul, would not naturally be preserved—which seems to be the argument according to C. P. Anderson—is not convincing. And the idea that a motive for a second letter in addition to Col is lacking would only apply if we suppose that the two letters were written simultaneously (see above). The question as to who thus wrote the letter to Laodicea is also, according to C. P. Anderson's article, not easier to answer.

The existence of an apocryphal letter to Laodicea has been attested since the fifth/sixth century.[41] Such a letter has been preserved in Latin. It was widely disseminated in the West and it even found entry into pre-Lutheran Bible translations. This letter consists of few verses that contain general statements borrowed from canonical Pauline Epistles, and it certainly is a forgery. The idea of placing it at Laodicea in order to have it read there next to Col would not have been worth the effort. The letter cited in Col was probably lost. In addition

---

40. C. P. Anderson, "Who Wrote 'the Epistle from Laodicea'?" JBL 85 (1966) 436–40.

41. See PsAugustinus, *De divinis scripturis*, L (CSEL XII, 516, 16). He was also retranslated back into Greek, and we also have a transmitted Hebrew version. Further, see J. B. Lightfoot (pp. 340–66); Hennecke-Schneemelcher, II, pp. 81–85; R. Y. Ebied, "A Triglot Volume of the Epistle to the Laodiceans, Psalm 151 and Other Biblical Materials," Bibl 47 (1966) 243–54.

to this opinion, the idea that one of the letters in the NT is the Laodicean epistle also has support. Ephesians has been the primary candidate, concerning which Tertullian already reported (Marc V, 17 [CSEL] 47, p. 632), that it was viewed as the Laodicean epistle by the Marcionites. This thesis is widely discounted today, however.[42]

17 *And say to Archippus, "Be mindful of your ministry which you have received in the Lord, that you fulfill it."* Archippus is mentioned in the address in Phlm (cf. Notes on Phlm in the companion commentary-fc). We do not know why Paul wished to send a message to Archippus. It is not obvious that we are dealing with a form of chastisement.[43] These words could just as easily be intended to give encouragement (cf. 2 Tim 4:5). The Greek word *diakonia* (service) can designate various things. It is uncertain to what kind of "service" of Archippus Paul was referring. Possibly, the special "office of deacon" was meant (Acts 6:11), or also a special service such as the delivery of money to the community in Jerusalem (Acts 12:25), or the service connected with the gift of the Spirit provided by God (Rom 12:7; 1 Cor 12:5), or "service" may even have meant the commission from God of proclaiming the gospel (among others Rom 11:13; 2 Cor 4:1; 5:18; compare 2 Tim 4:5).[44]

Finally, this question must surely also remain unanswered, as to why Archippus was not addressed directly. Did Paul know (from Epaphras) that Archippus had been absent from Colossae for an extended period of time and that he would not be back when the letter arrived there? Or did Paul wish to avoid the appearance of acting as a "grand overseer" (cf. Comment II to 1:1 + 2)? Thus the instructions given to the community are intended to have the members teach and exhort *each other* to perform good deeds, based on his words in 3:16.

18 *The greeting, with my hand, of Paul.* A signature in the hand of the sender himself, written below a dictated letter, is attested even in extra-biblical letters. In 2 Thess 3:17, there is a reference to the effect that this personal signature is the mark of all genuine letters of Paul (cf. 2 Thess 2:2).[45]

---

42. It is represented, among others, by J. B. Lightfoot, T. K. Abbott, P. Ewald, and J. Rutherford, "St. Paul's Epistle to the Laodiceans," ET 19 (1907/08) 311–14. E. Schweizer (p. 179) considers the possibility that Phlm is intended. Even Heb has already been considered for the Epistle to the Laodiceans (see in H. A. W. Meyer, p. 420).

43. A. Lindemann (p. 77) thinks the formulation is less than friendly.

44. See also the Notes to *diakonos* (servant) in 1:7, 23, 25; 4:7.—J. Knox, *Philemon Among the Letters of Paul*, 2d ed. (Nashville: Abingdon, 1959) proffered the idea that Archippus was Onesimus' master, and that Paul was admonishing him in Col to observe the instructions given in Phlm.

45. A. Deissmann, *Licht vom Osten*, op. cit., pp. 137f., cites a letter (50 C.E.), in which the closing greeting was written by a different hand from the rest of the letter without this (as in Col) being expressly stated. See also G. J. Bahr, *Letter Writing*, op. cit.—Also in 1 Cor 16:21 and Phlm 19, Paul expressly refers to the closing greeting in

Remember my chains. Two motives are at the basis of this assertion: 1. By the fact that the readers of Col are called to remember the captivity of Paul, they are also strengthened (cf. to that 2:1 and 4:7f., as well as Comment I to 1:24–2:5). 2. As can be derived from 4:3, it is an important concern for Paul that the community should pray for him (and his co-workers; cf. the Notes).[46]

Grace (be) with you. The blessing at the beginning of the letter was noticeably short (cf. Notes to 1:2). This is equally true of the concluding blessing; for the brevity of which in the Pauline corpus only 1 Tim 6:21 and Titus 3:15 are parallels. For the contextual meaning, see Notes to 1:2. As the address already borrowed from the Jewish-Oriental custom of the opening of letters, so there are certain analogies for the concluding blessing of our letter which are true not of the Hellenistic epistles, but are true of the Aramaic and Hebrew epistles.[47] According to K. Berger, the generic origin of these formulas of the so-called farewell blessing can be found at the conclusion of letters and also in testaments. This points to the fact that, at any rate, we are dealing with an authoritative pronouncement which was legitimized by the deity and which pointed to the future.[48]

---

his own hand. Gal 6:11 will probably not affirm that Paul appended a summary to the epistle written in his own hand, but rather that he wrote out the entire letter.

46. E. Lohmeyer (p. 170, fn. 3) points out that *mnemoneuein* with the genitive can have the meaning "to remember one's obligation in something."—The other explications in Col about Paul's "battle," to which his captivity also belongs, do not support the interpretation that cognizance of the authority of the apostle was demanded (comp. among others E. Lohse, p. 248; R. P. Martin, NCC, p. 141).

47. See for that K. Berger, *Apostelbrief*, op. cit., pp. 204–7.

48. Ibid. This is important for K. Berger's determination of genre for early Christian letters (see Notes to 1:2).

BIBLIOGRAPHY

◆

I. TEXTS

1. Biblical Texts

Biblia Hebraica Stuttgartensia, eds. K. Elliger et W. Rudolph, cooperantibus H. P. Rüger et J. Ziegler (Stuttgart: Deutsche Bibelstiftung, 1967–1977).

Septuanginta, id est Vetus Testamentum graece iuxta LXX interpres, ed. A. Rahlfs (Stuttgart: Deutsche Bibelgesellschaft, 1935).

Novum Testamentum Graece, eds. K. Aland, M. Black, C. M. Martini, B. M. Metzger, A. Wikgren, 26th ed. (Stuttgart: Deutsche Bibelstiftung, 1979).

Synopsis quattuor Evangeliorum, Locis parallelis evangeliorum apocryphorum et patrum adhibitis, ed. K. Aland, 9th ed. (Stuttgart: Deutsche Bibelstiftung, 1976).

2. Apocryphal Texts

Die Apokalypse des Elias, eine unbekannte Apokalypse und Bruchstükke der Sophanias-Apokalypse, TU 17, 3 (Leipzig, 1899).

Die Apokryphen und Preudepigraphen des Alten Testaments, in Verbindung mit Fachgenossen, ed. E. Kautzsch, vols. I + II (Darmstadt: Wiss. Buchgesellschaft, 1975).

Hennecke, E.: *Neutestamentliche Apokryphen in deutscher Übersetzung*, vols. I + II, ed. W. Schneemelcher, 3d ed. (Tübingen: Mohr, 1959 and 1964).

Testamenta XII Patriarcharum, ed. M. de Jonge (Leiden: Brill, 1954).

3. Other Literature

Corpus scriptorum ecclesiasticorum Latinorum (Brunsuiga: Schwetschke, 1895) (repr. New York and London: Johnson; Frankfurt: Minerva, 1964).

Diels, H.: *Fragmente der Vorsokratiker, Greek-Germ.*, ed. W. Kranz, vol. I, 17th ed. (reprint. of the 6th ed. of 1951), (Berlin: Weidmann, 1974).

Orphicorum Fragmenta, collegit O. Kern (Berlin: Weidmann, 1822).

Die Gnosis, vol. I, Zeugnisse der Kirchenväter, ed. C. Andresen (Zürich and Stuttgart: Artemis, 1969).

Flavius Josephus: *De bello Judaico. Der Jüdische Krieg, Greek-Germ.*, vols. I–III, eds. O. Michel and O. Bauernfeind (München: Kösel, 1959ff.).

The Loeb Classical Library, ed. E. H. Warmington (London: Heinemann; Cambridge: Harvard University Press).

Mackail, J. W.: *Select Epigrams from the Greek Anthology* (London, New York, Bombay: Longmans, Green, & Co., 1906).

Philo of Alexandria: *Opera quae supersunt*, eds. L. Cohn, P. Wendland, vols. 1–7 (Berlin: de Gruyter, 1896–1930).

491

————: *Die Werke in deutscher Übersetzung*, eds. L. Cohn, I. Heinemann, M. Adler, W. Theiler, vols. 1–7 (Berlin: de Gruyter, 1909–1964).

Patrologia Graeca, ed. J.-P. Migne (Paris: Migne) (cited: **PG**).

Patrologia Latina, ed. J.-P. Migne (Paris: Migne) (cited: **PL**).

Sylloge Inscriptorum Graecorum, 3d ed. (Leipzig, 1915–1924).

Die Texte aus Qumran, Heb.-Germ., ed. E. Lohse, 3d ed. (Darmstadt: Wiss. Buchgesellschaft, 1981).

II. GENERAL REFERENCES

Aland, K.; Aland, B.: *Der Text des Neuen Testaments* (Stuttgart: Deutsche Bibelgesellschaft, 1982).

Bauer, W.: *Griechisch-Deutsches Wörterbuch zu den Schriften des Neuen Testaments und der übrigen urchristlichen Literatur*, reprint of the 5th ed. (Berlin: de Gruyter, 1971) (cited: **BauerLex**).

Die Bibel und ihre Welt. Eine Enzyklopädie zur Heiligen Schrift. Bilder—Daten—Fakten, eds. G. Cornfeld und G. J. Botterweck (Bergisch-Gladbach: Lübbe, 1969).

Blass, F.; Debrunner, A.: *Grammatik des neutestamentlchen Griechisch*, rev. by F. Rehkopf, 14th ed. (Göttingen: Vandenhoeck & Ruprecht, 1976) (cited: **BDR**).

Beyer, K.: *Semitische Syntax im Neuen Testament*, vol. I: *Satzlehre Teil 1*, StUNT 1 (Göttingen: Vandenhoeck & Ruprecht, 1962).

Gesenius, W.; Kautzsch, E.; Bergsträsser, G.: *Hebräische Grammatik*, reprint of the 28th ed. (Leipzig, 1909, Hildesheim: Olms, 1962) (cited: **GK**).

Hatch, E.; Redpath, H. A.: *A Concordance to the Septuagint and the Other Greek Versions of the Old Testament*, vols. I–III, reprint of the edition of 1897 (Graz: Akademische Druck- und Verlagsanstalt, 1975).

Jenni, E.; Westermann, C., eds.: Theologisches Handwörterbuch zum Alten Testament, vols. I+II, 2d ed. (München: Kaiser, Zürich: Theologischer Verlag, 1975) (cited: **THAT**).

Vollständige Konkordanz zum Griechischen Neuen Testament. Unter Zugrundelegung aller modernen kritischen Textausgaben und des Textus receptus. Newly revised under the direction of K. Aland in assoc. with H. Riesenfeld, H. U. Rosenbaum, C. Hannick, vols. I+II (Berlin: de Gruyter, 1980).

Kühner, R.: *Ausführliche Grammatik der griechischen Sprache*, vol. I.1 (1890), I.2 (1892) rev. by F. Blaß; vol. II.1 (1898), vol. II.2 (1904) rev. by B. Gerth (Hannover and Leipzig: Hahn).

Kuhn, K. G.: *Konkordanz zu den Qumrantexten* (Göttingen: Vandenhoeck & Ruprecht, 1960).

Liddell, H. G.; Scott, R.: *A Greek-English Lexicon*, reprint of the 9th ed. 1940 (Oxford: Clarendon, 1977) (cited: **LSLex**).

Mayer, G.: *Index Philoneus* (Berlin: de Gruyter, 1974).

Metzger, B. M.: *Der Text des Neuen Testaments*, transl. from Engl. by W. Lohse (Stuttgart: Kohlhammer, 1966).

Moulton, J. H.; Milligan, G.: *The Vocabulary of the Greek Testament*, reprint of the edition of 1930 (Grand Rapids, Mich.: Eerdmans, 1980) (cited: **MMLex**).

Moulton, J. H.: *A Grammar of New Testament Greek*, vol. III, Syntax, by N. Turner (Edinburgh: Clark, 1963).

Preisigke, F.; Kießling, E.: *Wörterbuch der griechischen Papyrusurkunden mit Einschluß der griechischen Inschriften, Aufschriften, Ostraka, Mumienschilder usw. aus Ägypten*, vols. I–III (Berlin: Selbstverlag d. Erben, 1925) (cited: **PreisigkeLex**).

Schwyzer, E.: *Griechische Grammatik. Auf der Grundlage von K. Brugmanns Griechischer Grammatik*, vols. I–III (München: Beck, 1934ff.).

Theologisches Wörterbuch zum Neuen Testament, eds. G. Kittel and G. Friedrich, vols. I–X (Stuttgart: Kohlhammer, 1933–1979) (cited: **ThWNT**).

Wigram, G. V.: *The Englishman's Hebrew and Chaldee Concordance of the Old Testament*, 5th ed. (Grand Rapids, Mich.: Zondervan 1970).

III. COMMENTARIES TO COLOSSIANS

(Commentaries are cited under the name of the publisher and the page numbers.)

Abbott, T. K.: *Critical and Exegetical Commentary on the Epistles to the Ephesians and to the Colossians*, ICC [Edinburgh: Clark, 1897 (repr. 1974)].

Bengel, J. A.: *Gnomon Novi Testamenti*, Editio tertia 1773 (Stuttgart: Steinkopf, 1860), pp. 782–95.

Bieder, W.: *Der Kolosserbrief*, Proph. (Zürich: Zwingli Verlag, 1943).

Bruce, F. F.: *The Epistles to the Colossians, to Philemon, and to the Ephesians*, NIC (Grand Rapids, Mich.: Eerdmans, 1984).

Calvin, J., in: *Opera Exegetica et Homiletica*, vol. 30, eds. E. Reuss, A. Erichson, L. Horst, CR 80, Columns 77–132.

———, in: *Auslegung der Heiligen Schrift*, vol. 17, *Die kleinen paulinischen Briefe*, transl. & ed. by O. Weber (Neukirchen: Neukirchener Verlag, 1963).

Conzelmann, G. (Becker, J., Friedrich, G.): *Die Briefe an die Galater, Epheser, Philipper, Kolosser, Thessalonicher und Philemon*, NTD 8, 14th ed. (Göttingen: Vandenhoeck & Ruprecht, 1976).

Dibelius, M.: *An die Kolosser, Epheser, an Philemon*, 3d ed. newly revised by H. Greeven, HNT 12 (Tübingen: Mohr, 1953) (cited: **Dibelius-Greeven**).

Estius, D. G.: *In omnes Divi Pauli Apostoli epistulas commentariorum*, vol. II, Paris, 1652, pp. 680–712.

Ewald, P.: *Die Briefe des Paulus an die Epheser, Kolosser und Philemon*, KNT 10, (Leipzig: Deichert, 1905).

Gnilka, J.: *Der Kolosserbrief*, HThK X/1 (Freiburg i.B.: Herder, 1980).

Grotius, H., in: *Opera omnia theologica*, vol. III (Basel, 1732), pp. 922–35.

Haupt, E.: *Die Gefangenschaftsbriefe*, KEK VIII. u. IX. Abt., 8. bzw 7th ed. (Göttingen: Vandenhoeck & Ruprecht, 1902).

Johannes Chrysostomos, in: PG 62, Columns 299–392.

Lightfoot, J. B.: *St. Paul's Epistles to the Colossians and to Philemon* (London: Macmillan, 1875).

Lindemann, A.: *Der Kolosserbrief*, ZBK 10 (Zürich: Theologischer Verlag, 1983).

Lohmeyer, E.: *Der Brief an die Kolosser*, KEK 9, 9th ed. (Göttingen: Vandenhoeck & Ruprecht, 1953).

Lohse, E.: *Die Briefe an die Kolosser und an Philemon*, KEK IX/2, 14th ed. (Göttingen: Vandenhoeck & Ruprecht, 1968).

Martin, R. P.: *Colossians and Philemon*, NCC (Grand Rapids, Mich.: Eerdmans; London: Morgan & Scott, 1973).

————: *Colossians. The Church's Lord and the Christians' Liberty* (Exeter: Paternoster, 1972).

Meyer, H. A. W.: *Kritisch Exegetisches Handbuch über die Briefe Pauli an die Philipper, Kolosser und an Philemon*. 4th ed. (Göttingen: Vandenhoeck & Ruprecht, 1874).

Moule, C. F. D.: *The Epistles of Paul the Apostle to the Colossians and to Philemon*, CGTC [Cambridge: University Press, 1968 (Repr. of the edition of 1957)].

Mußner, F.: *Der Brief an die Kolosser*, Geistliche Schriftauslegung 12/1 (Düsseldorf: Patmos, 1971).

O'Brien, P.: *Colossians, Philemon*, WBC 44 (Waco, Tex.: Word Books, 1982).

Schlatter, A.: *Der Brief an die Kolosser*, EzNT 7 (Stuttgart: Calwer, 1963).

Schweizer, E.: *Der Brief an die Kolosser*, EKK XII [Zürich/Einsiedeln/Köln: Benziger; Neukirchen: Neukirchener Verlag, 1976 (2d ed., 1980)].

Soden, H. von: *Der Brief an die Kolosser*, HC 3 (Freiburg i.B.: Mohr, 1891).

Staab, K.: *Die Thessalonicherbriefe und die Gefangenschaftsbriefe*, RNT 7, 3d ed. (Regensburg: Pustet 1959).

————, (ed): *Pauluskommentare aus der griechischen Kirche*. Collection of Katenenhandschriften, collected and ed. K. Staab, 2d ed., NTA 15 (Münster: Aschendorff, 1933).

Strack, H., Billerbeck, P.: *Kommentar zum Neuen Testament. Aus Talmud und Midrasch*, vol. 3, 7th unrev. ed., (München: Beck, 1979), pp. 625–31.

Thomas von Aquin, in: *Super Epistolas S. Pauli Lectura, cura P. Raphaelis*, vol. II, 8th ed. (Turin/Rome: Marietti, 1953), pp. 125–61 (citations according to numbering of paragraphs).

Wette, W. M. L. de: *Kurze Erklärung der Briefe an die Colosser, an Philemon, an die Ephesier und Philipper*, KEH II/4 (Leipzig: Weidmann, 1847).

IV. LITERATURE ON THE COLOSSIAN EPISTLE

Anderson, C. P.: "Who Wrote 'The Epistle from Laodicea'?," JBL 85 (1966) 436–40.

Anderson, F.: "A Peculiar Reading of Colossians II,5," ET 51 (1939/40) 394–95.

Anwander, A.: "Zu Kol 2:9," BZ 9 (1965) 278–80.

Bammel, E.: "Versuch Col 1:15–20," ZNW 52 (1961) 88–95.

Bandstra, J.: *The Law and the Elements of the World*, Diss. [Kampen: Kok, 1964 (Sek.)].

————: "Pleroma as Pneuma in Colossians," in: FS für R. Schippers, Ad Interim (Kampen: Kok, 1975), pp. 91–102.

Barth, M.: "Introduction to the Colossian Epistle," AB 34B.

————: Rezension, N. Kehl, "Der Christushymnus im Kolosserbrief," CBQ 30 (1968) 106–10.

————: "Kol 4,2–6," GPM in: WPKG 65 (1976) 225–33.

————: "Die Taufe—Ein Sakrament? Ein exegetischer Beitrag zum Gespräch über die kirchliche Taufe" (Zollikon-Zürich: Evang. Verlag, 1951), pp. 246–61.

Bauckham, R. J.: "Colossians 1:24 Again: The Apocalyptic Motif," EvQ 47 (1975) 168–70.

Beasley-Murray, G. R.: "The Second Chapter of Colossians," RExp 70 (1973) 469–79.

Benoit, P.: "Colossiens 2:2–3," in: *FS für Bo Reicke, The New Testament Age*, vol. I, ed. W. C. Weinrich (Macon, Ga.: Mercer Univ. Press, 1984), pp. 41–51.

———: "*Hagioi* en Colossiens 1.12: Hommes ou Anges?," in: *FS für C. K. Barrett, Paul and Paulinism*, eds. M. D. Hooker and S. G. Wilson (London: SPCK, 1982), pp. 83–101.

———: "L'Hymne Christologique de Col 1:15–20. Jugement critique sur l'état des recherches," in: *FS für M. Smith, Christianity, Judaism and Other Greco-Roman Cults*, ed. S. Neuser, vol. I, New Testament (Leiden: Brill, 1975), pp. 226–63.

———: "Leib, Haupt und Pleroma in den Gefangenschaftsbriefen," in: *Exegese und Theologie*, collected works, transl. by E. S. Reich (Düsseldorf: Patmos, 1965), pp. 246–79 [= *Exégèse et Théologie* (Paris: Cerf, 1964) = RB 63 (1956) 5–44].

Blanchette, O. A.: "Does the Cheirographon of Col 2:14 Represent Christ Himself?," CBQ 23 (1961) 306–12.

Blinzler, J.: "Lexikalisches zu dem Terminus *ta stoicheia tou kosmou* bei Paulus," AnBibl 18 (1963) 429–43.

Bogdasavich, M.: "The Idea of Pleroma in the Epistles to the Colossians and Ephesians," DR 83 (1965) 118–30.

Bornkamm, G.: "Die Häresie des Kolosserbriefes," in: *Das Ende des Gesetzes, Paulusstudien*, collected works, vol. I, BevTh 16 (München: Kaiser, 1952), 139–56 [= ThLZ 73 (1948) 11–20].

———: "Die Hoffnung im Kolosserbrief. Zugleich ein Beitrag zur Frage der Echtheit des Briefes," in: *Geschichte und Glaube II*, collected works, vol. IV, BevTh 53 (München: Kaiser, 1971), pp. 206–13.

Bowers, W. P.: "A Note on Colossians 1:27a," in: *FS für M. C. Tenney, Current Issues in Biblical and Patristic Interpretation*, ed. G. F. Hawthorne (Grand Rapids, Mich.: Eerdmans, 1975), pp. 110–14 (Sek.).

Brooten, B. J.: "Jüdinnen zur Zeit Jesu. Ein Plädoyer für Differenzierung," ThQ 161 (1981) 281–85.

Bujard, W.: *Stilanalytische Untersuchungen zum Kolosserbrief als Beitrag zur Methodik von Sprachvergleichen*, StUNT 11 (Göttingen: Vandenhoeck & Ruprecht, 1973).

Buls, H. H.: "Luther's Translation of Colossians 2:12," CTQ 45 (1981) 13–16.

Burger, C.: *Schöpfung und Versöhnung. Studien zum liturgischen Gut im Kolosser- und Epheserbrief*, WMANT 46 (Neukirchen-Vluyn: Neukirchener Verlag, 1975).

Burney, C. F.: "Christ as the APXH of Creation," JThS 27 (1925) 160–77.

Carr, W.: "Two Notes on Colossians," JThS 24 (1973) 492–500.

Carrez, M.: "Souffrance et gloire dans les épîtres pauliennes (Contribution à l'exégèse de Col 1,24–27)," RHPhR 31 (1951) 343–53.

Clapton, E.: "A Suggested New Reading in Col II,23," ET 36 (1924/25) 382.

Collins, R. F.: " '. . . that this letter be read to all the brethren.' A New Testament Note," LouvSt 9 (1982) 122–27.

Coutts, J.: "The Relationship of Ephesians and Colossians," NTS 4 (1957/58) 201–7.

Craddock, F. B.: " 'All Things in Him': A Critical Note on Col 1:15–20," NTS 12 (1966) 78–80.

Crouch, J. E.: "*The Origin and Intention of the Colossian Haustafel*," FRLANT 109 (Göttingen: Vandenhoeck & Ruprecht, 1972).

Daniélou, J.: *Théologie du judéo-christianisme*, Bibliothèque de Théologie (Paris: Desclée, 1958), esp. pp. 151–63 (Sek.).

Deichgräber, R.: *"Gotteshymnus und Christushymnus in der frühen Christenheit,"* StUNT 5 (Göttingen: Vandenhoeck & Ruprecht, 1967).

Dibelius, M.: "Die Isisweihe bei Apuleius und verwandte Initiations-Riten," in: *Botschaft und Geschichte*, collected works II, ed. G. Bornkamm (Tübingen: Mohr, 1956), pp. 30–79.

Dölger, F. J.: "Die Sonne der Gerechtigkeit und der Schwarze. Eine religionsgeschichtliche Studie zum Taufgelöbnis," LF 2 (Münster: Aschendorff, 1918), pp. 129–41.

Draper, C. M.: " 'Your Life Is Hid with Christ in God' (Colossians III.3)," ET 27 (1915/16) 427.

Ebied, R. Y.: "A Triglot Volume of the Epistle to the Laodiceans, Psalm 151 and Other Biblical Materials," Bibl 47 (1966) 243–54.

Eckart, K. G.: "Exegetische Beoobachtungen zu Kol 1:9–20," ThViat 7 (1959/60) 87–106.

———: "Urchristliche Tauf- und Ordinationsliturgie. (Col 1:9–20; Acts 26:18)" ThViat 8 (1961/62) 23–37.

Egan, R. B.: "Lexical Evidence on Two Pauline Passages," NT 19 (1977) 34–62.

Ernst, J.: *Pleroma und Pleroma Christi. Geschichte und Deutung eines Begriffs der paulinischen Antilegomena*, BU 5 (Regensburg: Pustet, 1970).

Evans, C. A.: "The Colossian Mystics," Bibl 63 (1982) 188–205.

Farmer, G.: "Colossians III.14," ET 32 (1920/21) 427.

Feuillet, A.: "La création de l'univers 'dans le Christ' d'après l'épîtres aux Colossiens (I.16a)," NTS 12 (1966) 1–9.

Findeis, H. J.: "Versöhnung—Apostolat—Kirche. Eine exegetischtheologische und rezeptionsgeschichtliche Studie zu den Versöhnungsaussagen des Neuen Testaments (2 Kor, Röm, Kol, Eph)," FoB 40 (Würzburg: Echter, 1983), pp. 344–445.

Foerster, W.: "Die Irrlehre des Kolosserbriefes," in: *FS für T. C. Vriezen*, Studia biblica et semitica (Wageningen: Veenman & Zonen, 1966), pp. 71–80.

Francis, F. O.; Meeks, W. A. (ed): *Conflict at Colossae. A Problem in the Interpretation of Early Christianity Illustrated by Selected Studies*, Sources of Biblical Study 4 (Missoula, Mont.: Society of Biblical Literature, 1973).

Francis, F. O.: "The Background of Embateuein (Col 2:18) in Legal Papyri and Oracle Inscriptions," in: Meeks, W. A. (ed.), *Conflict*, op. cit., pp. 197–207.

———: "Humility and Angelic Worship in Col 2:18," in: *ders.*, Meeks, W. A., *Conflict*, op. cit., pp. 163–95.

Fridrichsen, A.: "Charité et Perfection. Observation sur Col 3:14," SO 19 (1939) 41–45.

———: "THELŌN Col 2:18," ZNW 21 (1922) 135–37.

Gabathuler, H. J.: *Jesus Christus, Haupt der Kirche—Haupt der Welt*, AThANT 45 (Zürich, Stuttgart: Zwingli Verlag, 1965).

Gardner, P. D.: " 'Circumcised in Baptism—Raised Through Faith': A Note on Col 2:11–12," WThJ 45 (1983) 172–77.

Getty, M. A.: "The Primacy of Christ," BiTod 23 (1985) 18–24.

Gewieß, J.: *Christus und das Heil nach dem Kolosserbrief* [(Teildruck), Breslau, 1932 (Sek.)].

Gibbs, J. G.: "Creation and Redemption. A Study in Pauline Theology," NT.S 26, 1971, pp. 94–114.

Gräßer, E.: "Kol 3:1–4 als Beispiel einer Interpretation secundum homines recipientes," ZThK 64 (1967) 139–68.

Gustafson, H.: "The Afflictions of Christ: What Is Lacking?," BR 8 (1963) 28–42.

Hall, B. G.: "Colossians II,23," ET 36 (1924/25) 285.

Hanssler, B.: "Zu Satzkonstruktion und Aussage in Kol 2,23," in: FS für K. H. Schelke zum 65. Geburtstag, eds. H. Feld and J. Nolte (Düsseldorf: Patmos, 1973), pp. 143–48.

Hatch, W. H. P.: "Ta stoicheia in Paul and Bardaisan," JThS 28 (1927) 181–82.

Hedley, P. L.: "Ad Colossenses 2:20–3:4," ZNW 27 (1928) 211–16.

Hegermann, H.: Die Vorstellung vom Schöpfungsmittler im hellenistischen Judentum und Urchristentum, TU 82 (Berlin: Akademie Verlag, 1961).

Helyer, L. R.: "Colossians 1:15–20: Pre-Pauline or Pauline?," JETS 26 (1983) 167–79.

Hermann, Th.: "Barbar und Skythe. Ein Erklärungsversuch zu Kol 3:11," ThBl 19 (1930) 106–7.

Hiebert, D. E.: "Epaphras, Man of Prayer," BS 136 (1979) 54–64.

Hinson, E. G.: "The Christian Household in Colossians 3:18–4:1," RExp 70 (1973) 495–506.

Hockel, A.: Christus der Erstgeborene. Zur Geschichte der Exegese von Kol 1:15 (Düsseldorf: Patmos, 1965).

Hollenbach, B.: "Col II.23: Which Things Lead to the Fulfilment of the Flesh," NTS 25 (1979) 254–61.

Hooker, M. D.: "Were There False Teachers in Colossae?" in: FS for C. F. D. Moule, Christ and the Spirit in the New Testament, eds. B. Lindars and S. S. Smalley (Cambridge: University Press 1973), pp. 315–31.

Horst, P. W. van der: "Observations on a Pauline Expression," NTS 19 (1972/73) 181–87.

Jeremias, J.: "Beobachtungen zu neutestamentlichen Stellen an Hand des neugefundenen griechischen Henoch-Textes," ZNW 38 (1939) 115–24.

Käsemann, E.: Rezension, J. Kremer, "Was an den Leiden Christi noch mangelt," ThLZ 82 (1957) 694f.

———: "Eine urchristliche Taufliturgie," in: FS für R. Bultmann (Stuttgart und Köln: Kohlhammer, 1949), pp. 133–48 (= EVB I, 34–51).

Kamlah, E.: "Wie beurteilt Paulus sein Leiden? Ein Beitrag zur Untersuchung seiner Denkstruktur," ZNW 54 (1963) 217–32.

Kehl, N.: Der Christushymnus im Kolosserbrief: Eine motivgeschichtliche Untersuchung zu Kol 1:12–20, SBM 1 (Stuttgart: Kath. Bibelwerk, 1967).

———: "Erniedrigung und Erhöhung in Qumran und Kolossä," ZKTh 91 (1969) 364–94.

Kennedy, H. A. A.: "Two Exegetical Notes on St. Paul: II. Colossians II.10–15," ET 28 (1916/17) 363–66.

Kern, W.: "Die antizipierte Entideologisierung oder die 'Weltelemente' des Galater- und Kolosserbriefes heute," ZKTh 96 (1974) 185–216.

Kittel, G.: "Kol 1:14," ZSTh 18 (1941) 186–91.

Kremer, J.: *Was an den Leiden Christi noch mangelt. Eine interpretationsgeschichtliche und exegetische Untersuchung zu Kol 1:24b*, BBB 12 (Bonn: Hanstein, 1956).

Kurze, G.: "Die *stoicheia tou kosmou* Gal 4 und Kol 2," BZ 15 (1927) 335–37.

Ladd, G. E.: "Paul's Friends in Colossians 4:7–16," RExp 70 (1973) 507–14.

Lähnemann, J.: *Der Kolosserbrief. Komposition, Situation und Argumentation* (Gütersloh: Mohn, 1971).

Lane, W. L.: "Creed and Theology: Reflections on Colossians," JETS 21 (1978) 213–20.

Langkammer, H.: "Die Einwohnung der 'absoluten Seinsfülle' in Christus. Bemerkungen zu Kol 1:19," BZ.NF 12 (1968) 258–63.

Larsson, E.: *Christus als Vorbild. Eine Untersuchung zu den paulinischen Tauf- und Eikontexten*, ASNU 23 (Lund: Gleerup; Kopenhagen: Munksgaard, 1962), esp. pp. 188–223.

Leaney, R.: "Colossians II.21–23. (The Use of *pros*)," ET 64 (1952/53) 92.

Lincoln, A. J.: "Paradise Now and Not Yet. Studies in the Role of the Heavenly Dimension in Paul's Thought with Special Reference to His Eschatology" (Cambridge: University Press, 1981), pp. 110–35.

Lindemann, A.: "Die Gemeinde von 'Kolossä.' Erwägungen zum 'Sitz im Leben' eines pseudopaulinischen Briefes," WuD.NF 16 (1981) 111–34.

Löwe, H.: "Bekenntnis, Apostelamt und Kirche im Kolosserbrief," in: *FS für G. Bornkamm*, eds. D. Lührmann and G. Strecker (Tübingen: Mohr, 1980), pp. 299–314.

Lohse, E.: "Bekenntnis, Apostelamt und Kirche im Kolosserbrief," in: *Kirche, FS für G. Bornkamm zum 75 Geb.*, eds. D. Lührmann and G. Strecker (Tübingen: Mohr, 1980), pp. 299–314.

———: "Ein hymnisches Bekenntnis in Kolosser 2,13c–15," in: *Einheit*, op. cit., pp. 276–84.

———: "Christologie und Ethik im Kolosserbrief," NTS 11 (1964) 203–16 (repr. in: *Einheit*, op. cit., pp. 249–61).

———: "Christusherrschaft und Kirche im Kolosserbrief," in: *Einheit*, op. cit., pp. 262–75 [=NTS 11 (1964/65), pp. 203–16].

———: "Imago Dei bei Paulus," in: *FS für F. Delekat, Libertas Christiana*, BevTh 26 (München: Kaiser, 1957), pp. 122–35.

———: "Taufe und Rechtfertigung bei Paulus," in: *Einheit*, op. cit., pp. 228–44 [= KuD 11 (1965) pp. 308–24].

Lona, H. E.: *Die Eschatologie im Kolosser- und Epheserbrief*, FoB 48 (Würzburg: Echter, 1984).

Lyonnet, S.: "Paul's Adversaries in Colossae," in: F. O. Francis, W. A. Meeks, (eds), *Conflict*, op. cit., pp. 147–61.

Martin, R. P.: "Reconciliation and Forgiveness in the Letter to the Colossians," in: *FS for L. L. Morris, Reconciliation and Hope. New Testament Essays on Atonement and Eschatology*, ed. R. Banks (Exeter: Paternoster, 1974), pp. 104–24 (American Edition: Grand Rapids, Mich.: Eerdmans, 1974).

Maurer, C.: "Die Begründung der Herrschaft Christi über die Mächte nach Kolosser 1:15–20," WuD.NF 4 (1955) 79–93.

Megas, G.: "Das *cheirographon* Adams. Ein Beitrag zu Col 2:13–15," ZNW 27 (1928) 305–20.

Michl, J.: "Die 'Versöhnung' (Kol 1:20)," ThQ 128 (1948) 442–62.

Moir, I. A.: "Some Thoughts on Col 2:17–18," ThZ 35 (1979) 363–65.

Moir, W. R. G.: "Colossians 1.24," ET 42 (1930/31) 479–80.

Moule, C. F. D.: " 'The New Life' in Colossians 3:1–17," RExp 70 (1973) 481–93.

Moulton, J. H.: "Nympha," ET 5 (1893/94) 66–67.

Moyo, A. M.: "The Colossian Heresy in the Light of Some Gnostic Documents from Nag Hammadi," JTSA 13 (48/1984) 30–44.

Müller, K.: "Die Haustafeln des Kolosserbriefes und das antike Frauenthema. Eine kritische Rückschau auf alte Ergebnisse," in: *Die Frau im Urchristentum*, eds. G. Dautzenberg, H. Merklein, K. Müller (Freiburg i.B.: Herder, 1983), pp. 263–319.

Münderlein, G.: "Die Erwählung durch das Pleroma," NTS 8 (1961/62) 264–76.

Mullins, T. Y.: "The Thanksgiving of Philemon and Colossians," NTS 30 (1984) 288–93.

Munro, W.: "Col. III.18–IV.1 and Eph V.21–VI.9: Evidences of a Late Literary Stratum?," NTS 18 (1971/72) 434–47.

Nash, H. S.: "*Theiotēs—Theotēs*. Rom I.20; Col II.9," JBL 18 (1899) 1–34.

Nauck, W.: "Freude im Leiden. Zum Problem einer urchristlichen Verfolgungstradition," ZNW 46 (1955) 68–80.

Norden, E.: "Agnostos Theos. Untersuchung zur Formengeschichte religiöser Rede," (Leipzig: Teubner, 1913), pp. 150–54.

Oke, C. C.: "A Hebraistic Construction in Col 1:19–22," ET 63 (1951/52) 155–56.

O'Neil, J. C.: "The Source of the Christology in Colossians," NTS 26 (1980) 87–100.

Percy, E.: "Die Probleme der Kolosser- und Epheserbriefe," SHVL 39 (Lund: Gleerup, 1946) (cited: **PKE**).

————: "Zu den Problemen des Kolosser- und Epheserbriefes," ZNW 43 (1950/51) 178–94.

Pfister, F.: "Die *stoicheia tou kosmou* in den Briefen des Apostels Paulus," Ph 69 (1910) 411–27.

————: "Zur Wendung *apokeitai moi ho tēs dikaiosynēs stephanos*," ZNW 15 (1914) 94–96.

Pöhlmann, W.: "Die hymnischen All-Prädikationen in Kol 1:15–20," ZNW 64 (1973) 53–74.

Pollard, T. E.: "Colossians 1.12–20: A Reconsideration," NTS 27 (1981) 572–75.

Pope, R. M.: "Studies in Pauline Vocabulary," ET 22 (1910/11) 552–54.

Reicke, Bo: "The Historical Setting of Colossians," RExp 70 (1973) 429–38.

————: "Zum sprachlichen Verständnis von Kol 2:23," StTh 6 (1952) 39–53.

Reuman, J.: "OIKONOMIA = "Covenant"; Terms for Heilsgeschichte in Early Christian Usage," NT 3 (1959) 282–92.

————: "OIKONOMIA—Terms in Paul in Comparison with Lucan Heilsgeschichte," NTS 13 (1966/67) 147–67.

Robinson, J. M.: "A Formal Analysis of Colossians 1:15–20," JBL 76 (1957) 270–87.

Rodd, C. S.: "Salvation Proclaimed, XI. Colossians 2:8–15," ET 94 (1982/83) 36–41.

Rowland, C.: "Apocalyptic Visions and the Exaltation of Christ in the Letter to the Colossians," JSNT 19 (1983) 73–83.

Rutherford, J.: "Note on Colossians 2:15," ET 18 (1906/07) 565–66.

————: "St. Paul's Epistle to the Laodiceans," ET 19 (1907/08) 311–14.

Sanders, E. P.: "Literary Dependence in Colossians," JBL 85 (1966) 28–45.

Saunders, E. W.: "The Colossian Heresy and Qumran Theology," in: *FS for K. W. Clark, Studies in the History and Text of the New Testament* (Salt Lake City: University of Utah Press, 1967), pp. 133–45.

Schenk, W.: "Christus, das Geheimnis der Welt, als dogmatisches und ethisches Grundprinzip des Kolosserbriefes," EvTh 43 (1983) 138–55.

Schenke, H.-M.: "Der Widerstreit gnostischer und kirchlicher Christologie im Spiegel des Kolosserbriefes," ZThK 61 (1964) 391–403.

Schierse, F. J.: "Suchet, was droben ist!", GuL 31 (1958) 86–90.

Schille, G.: *Frühchristliche Hymnen* (Berlin: Evang. Verlagsanstalt, 1965).

———: *Rezension*, N. Kehl, "Der Christushymnus im Kolosserbrief," ThLZ 93 (1968) 267–68.

Schleiermacher, F.: "Über Kolosser 1:15–20," ThStKr 5 (1832) 497–537 (Sek.).

Schmid, J.: "Kol 1,24," BZ 21 (1933) 330–44.

Schnackenburg, R.: "Die Aufnahme des Christushymnus durch den Verfasser des Kolosserbriefes," EKK Vorarbeiten Heft 1 (Zürich/Einsiedeln/Köln und Neukirchen: Benziger und Neukirchener Verlag, 1969), pp. 33–50.

———: "Der neue Mensch—Mitte christlichen Weltverständnisses, Kol 3,9–11," in: *Schriften zum Neuen Testament, Exegese in Fortschritt und Wandel* (München: Kösel, 1971), pp. 392–413.

Schweizer, E.: "The Church as the Missionary Body of Christ," NTS 8 (1961/62) 1–11 (repr. in: *Neotestamentica*, op. cit., pp. 317ff.).

———: "Christianity of the Circumcised and Judaism of the Uncircumcised. The Background of Matthew and Colossians," in: *FS for W. D. Davies, Jews, Greeks and Christians: Religious Cultures in Late Antiquity*, eds. R. Hamerton-Kelly and R. Scroggs (Leiden: Brill, 1976), pp. 245–60.

———: "*Christus und Geist* im Kolosserbrief," in: *Neues Testament*, op. cit., pp. 179–93.

———: "Die 'Elemente der Welt'. Gal 4:3.9.; Kol 2:8.20," *G. Stählin zum 70. Geburtstag*, in: *Beiträge*, op. cit., pp. 147–63.

———: "Zur neueren Forschung am Kolosserbrief seit 1970," in: *Neues Testament*, op. cit., pp. 122–49.

———: "Die Kirche als Leib Christi in den paulinischen Antilegomena," in: *Neotestamentica*, op. cit., pp. 293–316.

———: "Versöhnung des Alls," in: *Neues Testament*, op. cit., pp. 164–78.

Sittler, J.: "Zur Einheit berufen," in: *Neu Delhi Dokumente. Berichte und Reden auf der Weltkirchenkonferenz in Neu Delhi 1961* (Witten: Luther Verlag, 1962), pp. 300–11.

Stegemann, E.: "Alt und Neu bei Paulus und in den Deuteropaulinen (Kol-Eph)," *H. Thyen zum 50. Geburtstag*, EvTh 37 (1977) 508–36.

Steinmetz, F.-J.: *Protologische Heilszuversicht. Die Strukturen des soteriologischen und christologischen Denkens im Kolosser- und Epheserbrief*, FTS 2 (Frankfurt: Knecht, 1969) (cited: **PHZ**).

Trudinger, L. P.: "A Further Brief Note on Colossians 1:24," EvQ 45 (1973) 36–38.

Uprichard, R. E. H.: "The Relationship of Circumcision to Baptism with Particular Reference to Colossians 2.11–13," IBS 2 (1980) 203–10.

Vawter, B.: "The Colossians Hymn and the Principle of Redaction," CBQ 33 (1971) 62–81.

Walle, R. van de: "Jesus: Christ of Atonement or Christ the New Man?," IJT 24 (1975) 151–61.

Walter, N.: "Die 'Handschrift in Satzungen' Kol 2,14," ZNW 70 (1979) 115–18.

Wambacq, B. N.: "Adimpleo ea quae desunt passionum Christi in carne mea . . . ," VD 27 (1949) 17–22.

————: "Per eum reconciliare . . . quae in caelis sunt (Col 1,20)," RB 55 (1948) 35–42.

Wegenast, K.: Das Verständnis der Tradition bei Paulus und in den Deuteropaulinen, WMANT 8 (Neukirchen: Neukirchener Verlag, 1962).

Weiss, H.: "The Law in the Epistle to the Colossians," CBQ 34 (1972) 294–314.

Wengst, K.: "Christologische Formeln und Lieder des Urchristentums," StNT 7 (Gütersloh: Mohn, 1972), pp. 170–80.

————: "Versöhnung und Befreiung. Ein Aspekt des Themas 'Schuld und Vergebung' im Lichte des Kolosserbriefes," EvTh 36 (1976) 14–26.

Whitaker, G. H.: "Synarmologoumenon kai symbibazomenon," JThS 31 (1929/30) 48–49.

Williams, A. L.: "The Cult of the Angels at Colossae," JThS 10 (1909) 413–38.

Williamson, L.: "Led in Triumph. Paul's Use of Thriambeuō," Interp. 22 (1968) 317–32.

Windisch, H.: "Paulus und Christus. Ein biblischreligionsgeschichtlicher Vergleich," UNT 24 (Leipzig: Hinrichs, 1934), pp. 236–50.

Wulf, F.: " 'Suchet, was droben ist, wo Christus ist, sitzend zur Rechten Gottes!' (Kol 3,1)," GuL 41 (1968) 161–64.

Yates, R.: "A Note on Colossians 1:24," EvQ 42 (1970) 88–92.

————: " 'The Worship of the Angels' (Col 2:18)," ET 97 (1985/86) 12–15.

Zeilinger, F.: Der Erstgeborene der Schöpfung. Untersuchungen zur Formalstruktur und Theologie des Kolosserbriefes (Wien: Herder, 1974) (cited: ESpg).

V. OTHER LITERARY REFERENCES

Allan, J. A.: "The 'In Christ' Formula in the Pastoral Epistles," NTS 10 (1963) 115–21.

Bahr, G. J.: "Paul and Letter Writing in the Fifth Century," CBQ 28 (1966) 465–77.

Balch, D. L.: Let Wives Be Submissive. The Domestic Code in I Peter, SBL.MS 26 (Chico: Scholars Press, 1981).

Baltensweiler, H.: Die Ehe im Neuen Testament, AThANT 52 (Zürich/Stuttgart: Zwingli, 1967).

Bartchy, S. S.: MALLON XPHΣAI: First Century Slavery and the Interpretation of 1 Corinthians 7:21 (Cambridge, Mass.: Society of Biblical Literature, 1973) (Sek.).

Barth, C.: Die Errettung vom Tode in den individuellen Klage- und Dankliedern des Alten Testamentes (Zollikon: Evang. Verlag, 1947).

Barth, M.: "Christ and All Things," in: FS für C. K. Barrett, Paul and Paulinism, eds. M. D. Hooker and S. G. Wilson (London: SPCK, 1982), 160–72.

————: Ephesians. Introduction, Translation, and Commentary, AB 34 and 34A (Garden City, N.Y.: Doubleday, 1974).

————: "Theologie—ein Gebet (Röm 11:33–36). Abschiedsvorlesung an der Universität Basel, gehalten am 21. Februar 1985," ThZ 41 (1985) 330–48.

Baumert, N.: *Täglich Sterben und Auferstehen. Der Literalsinn von II Kor 4:12–5:10*, StANT 34 (München: Kösel, 1973).

Bedale, S.: "The Meaning of *kephalē* in the Pauline Epistles," JThS 5 (1954) 211–15.

Die Bekenntnisschriften der evangelisch-lutherischen Kirche, ed. Deutschen Evangelischen Kirchenausschuß (Göttingen: Vandenhoeck & Ruprecht, 1930).

Berger, K.: "Apostelbrief und apostolische Rede. Zum Formular frühchristlicher Briefe," ZNW 65 (1974) 190–231.

————: "Die sogenannten 'Sätze heiligen Rechts' im NT. Ihre Funktion und ihr Sitz im Leben," ThZ 28 (1972) 305–30.

————: "Zu den sogenannten Sätzen Heiligen Rechts," NTS 17 (1970/71) 10–40.

Betz, H. D.: *Lukian von Samosata und das Neue Testament. Religionsgeschichtliche und paränetische Parallelen. Ein Beitrag zum Corpus Hellenisticum Novi Testamenti*, TU 76 (Berlin: Akademie Verlag, 1961).

————: "Schöpfung und Erlösung im hermetischen Fragment 'Kore Kosmu,' " ZThK 63 (1966) 180–83.

Betz, O.: "Felsenmann und Felsengemeinde. Eine Parallele zu Mt 16:17–19 in den Qumranpsalmen," ZNW 48 (1957) 49–77.

Beyer, K.: *Semitische Syntax im Neuen Testament*, vol. I: Satzlehre Teil 1, StUNT 1 (Göttingen: Vandenhoeck & Ruprecht, 1962).

Bietenhard, H.: *Die himmlische Welt im Urchristentum und Spätjudentum*, WUNT 2 (Tübingen: Mohr, 1951).

Biser, E.: "Die Idee des Friedens nach den paulinischen Gefangenschaftsbriefen," GuL 27 (1954) 165–70.

Bjerkelund, C. J.: *Parakalō. Form, Funktion und Sinn der parakalō-Sätze in den paulinischen Briefen*, BTN 1 (Oslo, Bergen, Tromsö: Universitetsforlaget, 1967).

Bonhöffer, A.: *Epiktet und das Neue Testament*, RVV 10 (Gießen: Töpelmann, 1911).

Bornkamm, G.: "Das Bekenntnis im Hebräerbrief," in: *Studien z. Antike und Urchristentum*, Collected Works II, BevTh 28 (München: Kaiser, 1959), pp. 188–203.

————: "Glaube und Vernunft bei Paulus," in: Ibid., pp. 119–37.

Bousset, W.: *Kyrios Christos*. FRLANT.NF 4 (Göttingen: Vandenhoeck & Ruprecht, 1913).

————: *Die Religion des Judentums im späthellenistischen Zeitalter*, 3d ed., H. Gressmann, HNT 21 (Tübingen: Mohr, 1926).

Braun, H.: *Qumran und das Neue Testament*, vols. I + II (Tübingen: Mohr, 1966).

Brocke, M., "Art. 'Bestattung, III. Judentum'," TRE 5, 738–43.

Broek, L. van der: "Women and the Church: Approaching Difficult Passages," RefR(H) 38 (1985) 225–31.

Brooten, B. J.: "Jüdinnen zur Zeit Jesu. Ein Plädoyer für Differenzierung," ThQ 161 (1981) 281–85.

Brown, R. E.: "The Semitic Background of the New Testament *Mysterion* (I)," Bibl 39 (1958) 426–48.

————: "The Semitic Background of the New Testament *Mysterion* (II)," Bibl 40 (1959) 70–87.

Brox, N. (ed.): *Pseudepigraphie in der heidnischen und jüdischchristlichen Antike*, WdF 484 (Darmstadt: Wiss., Buchgesellschaft, 1977).

————: "Zum Problemstand der Erforschung der altchristlichen Pseudepigraphie," in: (ed.), *Pseudepigraphie*, op. cit., pp. 311–34.

Bultmann, R.: "Die Bedeutung der neu erschlossenen mandäischen und manichäischen Quellen für das Verständnis des Johannesevangeliums," in: *Exegetica*, op. cit., pp. 55–104.

————: *Exegetica. Aufsätze zur Erforschung des Neuen Testaments*, ed. E. Dinkler (Tübingen: Mohr, 1967).

————: "Das Problem der Ethik bei Paulus," ZNW 23 (1924) 123–40 (repr. in: *Exegetica*, op. cit., pp. 36–54).

————: *Theologie des Neuen Testaments*, 8th ed. (Tübingen: Mohr, 1980).

————: "Theon oudeis eōraken pōpote. (Joh 1:18)," ZNW 29 (1930) pp. 169–93 (repr. in: *Exegetica*, op. cit., pp. 174–97).

Burton, E. de Witt: *The Epistle to the Galatians*, ICC [Edinburgh: Clark, 1921 (Repr. 1950)].

Caird, G. B.: *Principalities and Powers. A Study in Pauline Theology* (Oxford: Clarendon, 1956).

Chadwick, H.: "All Things to All Men," NTS 1 (1954/55) 261–75.

Colpe, C.: *Die religionsgeschichtliche Schule*, FRLANT 78 (Göttingen: Vandenhoeck & Ruprecht, 1961).

Coppens, J.: " 'Mystery' in the Theology of Saint Paul and Its Parallels at Qumran," in: *Paul and Qumran. Studies in New Testament Exegesis*, ed. J. Murphy-O'Connor (London: Chapman, 1968), pp. 132–58.

Crüsemann, F.: *Bewahrung der Freiheit. Das Thema des Dekalogs in sozialgeschichtlicher Perspektive* (München: Kaiser, 1983).

————: *Studien zur Formgeschichte von Hymnus und Danklied in Israel*, WMANT 32 (Neukirchen: Neukirchener Verlag, 1969).

Cullmann, O.: *Die Christologie des Neuen Testaments* (Tübingen: Mohr, 1957).

————: *Christus und die Zeit. Die urchristliche Zeit- und Geschichtsauffassung*, 2d ed. (Zollikon-Zürich: Evang. Verlag, 1948).

————: *Königsherrschaft Christi und Kirche im Neuen Testament*, ThSt 10 (Zollikon-Zürich: Evang. Verlag, 1941).

————: *Die Tradition als exegetisches, historisches und theologisches Problem* (Zürich: Zwingli Verlag, 1954).

————: *Urchristentum und Gottesdienst* (Basel: Majer, 1944).

Cumont, F.: *The Oriental Religions in Roman Paganism* (Chicago: Open House, 1911).

Dahl, N. A.: "Formgeschichtliche Beobachtungen zur Christusverkündigung in der Gemeindepredigt," in: *Neutestamentliche Studien für R. Bultmann*, BZNW 21, 1954, pp. 3–9.

Daniélou, J.: "La Session à la droite du Père," TU 73, Studia Evangelica, *Papers presented to the International Congress on "The Four Gospels in 1957" held at Christ Church, Oxford, 1957*, eds. K. Aland, F. L. Cross, J. Daniélou, H. Riesenfeld, and W. C. van Unnik (Berlin: Akademie Verlag, 1959), pp. 689–98.

Daube, D.: "Participle and Imperative in 1. Peter," in: *E. G. Selwyn: The First Epistle of St. Peter* (London: Macmillan, 1947), pp. 467–88.

Davies, W. D.: *Paul and Rabbinic Judaism. Some Rabbinic Elements in Pauline Theology* (London: SPCK, 1948).

Debrunner, A.: "Grundsätzliches zur Kolometrie im Neuen Testament," ThBl 5 (1926) 120–25; 231–33.

Deichgräber, K.: "Hymnische Elemente in der philosophischen Prosa der Vorsokratiker," Ph 88 (1933) 347–61 (Sek.).

Deissmann, A.: *Bibelstudien. Beiträge zumeist aus den Papyri und Inschriften, zur Geschichte der Sprache, des Schrifttums und der Religion des hellenistischen Judentums und des Urchristentums* (Marburg: Elwert 1985).

———: *Licht vom Osten*, 4th ed. (Tübingen: Mohr, 1923).

———: *Paulus. Eine kultur- und religionsgeschichtliche Skizze* (Tübingen: Mohr, 1911).

Delling, G.: "Eheleben," in: RAC IV, 691–707.

———: "Lexikalisches zu *teknon*. Ein Nachtrag zur Exegese von I Kor 7,14," in: *FS für E. Barnikol, . . . und fragten nach Jesus, Beiträge aus Theologie, Kirche und Geschichte* (Berlin: Ev. Verlagsanstalt, 1964), pp. 35–44.

———: "Partizipiale Gottesprädikationen," StTh 17 (1963) 1–59.

———: *Die Taufe im Neuen Testament* (Berlin: Evang. Verlagsanstalt, o.J.).

———: *Die Zueignung des Heils in der Taufe. Eine Untersuchung zum neutestamentlichen "taufen auf den Namen"* (Berlin: Evang. Verlagsanstalt, o.J.).

Dibelius, M.: "*Epignōsis alētheias*," in: *Botschaft und Geschichte, Collected Essays II,* ed. G. Bornkamm (Tübingen: Mohr, 1956, pp. 1–13).

Dobschütz, E. von: "Wir und Ich bei Paulus," ZSTh 10 (1933) 251–77.

Dunn, J. D. G.: *Baptism in the Holy Spirit. A Re-examination of the New Testament Teaching on the Gift of the Spirit in Relation to Pentecostalism Today* (London: SCM, 1970).

———: *Jesus and the Spirit. A Study of the Religious and Charismatic Experience of Jesus and the First Christians as Reflected in the New Testament* (Philadelphia: Westminster, 1975).

Easton, B. S.: "New Testament Ethical Lists," JBL 51 (1932) 1–12.

Eckert, J.: *Die urchristliche Verkündigung im Streit zwischen Paulus und seinen Gegnern nach dem Galaterbrief,* BU 6 (Regensburg: Pustet, 1971).

Eichrodt, W.: *Theologie des Alten Testaments,* vol. II, 4th ed. (Stuttgart: Klotz; Göttingen: Vandenhoeck & Ruprecht, 1961).

Elert, W.: "Redemptio ab hostibus," ThLZ 72 (1947) 265–70.

Elliott, J. K.: "Paul's Teaching on Marriage in I Corinthians: Some Problems Considered," NTS 19 (1972/73) 219–25.

Ellis, E. E.: "The Circumcision Party and the Early Christian Mission," in: *Prophecy,* op. cit., pp. 116–28.

———: "Paul and His Co-Workers," in: *Prophecy,* op. cit., pp. 3–22.

———: "Spiritual Gifts in the Pauline Community," NTS 20 (1974) 128–44 (repr. in: *Prophecy,* op. cit., pp. 23–44).

———: *Prophecy and Hermeneutics in Early Christianity. New Testament Essays,* WUNT 18 (Tübingen: Mohr, 1978).

Eltester, F.-W.: *Eikon im Neuen Testament,* BZNW 23, 1958.

Ernst, J.: *Pleroma and Pleroma Christi. Geschichte und Deutung eines Begriffs der paulinischen Antilegomena,* BU 5 (Regensburg: Pustet, 1970).

Foster, J.: "St. Paul and Women," ET 62 (1950/51) 376–78.

Frankemölle, H.: *Das Taufverständnis des Paulus. Taufe, Tod und Auferstehung nach Röm 6*, SBS 47 (Stuttgart: Kath. Bibelwerk, 1970).

Friedrich, G.: "Lohmeyers These über das paulinische Briefpräskript kritisch beleuchtet," ThLZ 81 (1956) 343–46.

Gäumann, N.: *Taufe und Ethik. Studien zu Röm 6* (München: Kaiser, 1967).

Gerstenberger, E. J.; Schrage, W.: *Frau und Mann* (Stuttgart: Kohlhammer, 1980).

Gnilka, J.: "II Kor 6:14–7:1 im Lichte der Qumranschriften und der 12-Patriarchen-Testamente," in: *FS für J.Schmid*, eds. J. Blinzler, O. Kuss, F. Mussner (Regensburg: Pustet, 1963), pp. 86–99.

————: *Der Philipperbrief*, HThK X.3 (Freiburg: Herder, 1968).

————: *Die Verstockung Israels. Isaias 6:9–10 in der Theologie der Synoptiker*, StANT 3 (München: Kösel, 1961).

Goppelt, L.: "Jesus und die 'Haustafel'-Tradition," in: *FS für J. Schmid: Orientierung an Jesus. Zur Theologie der Synoptiker* (Freiburg: Herder, 1973), pp. 93–106.

————: *Theologie des Neuen Testaments*, ed. J. Roloff, 3d ed. (Göttingen: Vandenhoeck & Ruprecht, 1978).

————: "Tradition nach Paulus," KuD 4 (1958) 213–33.

Grabner-Haider, A.: *Paraklese und Eschatologie bei Paulus. Mensch und Welt im Anspruch der Zukunft Gottes*, NTA.NF 4 (Münster: Aschendorff, 1968).

Grant, R. M.: "Causation and 'the Ancient World View,' " JBL 83 (1964) 34–40.

Greeven, H.: "Zu den Aussagen des Neuen Testaments über die Ehe," ZEE 1 (1957) 109–25.

————: "Propheten, Lehrer, Vorsteher bei Paulus. Zur Frage der 'Ämter' im Urchristentum," ZNW 44 (1952/53) 1–43.

Güttgemanns, E.: *Der leidende Apostel und sein Herr. Studien zur paulinischen Christologie*, FRLANT 90 (Göttingen: Vandenhoeck & Ruprecht, 1966).

————: *Offene Fragen zur Formgeschichte des Evangeliums. Eine methodische Skizze der Grundlagenproblematik der Form- und Redaktionsgeschichte*, 2d ed., BevTh 54 (München: Kaiser, 1971).

Hahn, F.: *Christologische Hoheitstitel. Ihre Geschichte im frühen Christentum*, 3d ed., FRLANT 83 (Göttingen: Vandenhoeck & Ruprecht, 1966).

————: *Das Verständnis der Mission im Neuen Testament*, WMANT 13 (Neukirchen-Vluyn: Neukirchener Verlag, 1963).

Hall, B.: "Church in the World. Paul and Women." ThTo 31 (1974) 50–55.

Harder, G.: *Paulus und das Gebet* (Gütersloh: Mohn, 1936).

Harnack, A. von: "*Kopos (Kopian, Hoi Kopiōntes)* im frühchristlichen Sprachgebrauch," ZNW 27 (1928) 1–10.

Harrisville, R. A.: "The Concept of Newness in the New Testament," JBL 74 (1955) 69–79.

Haufe, G.: "Das Kind im Neuen Testament," ThLZ 104 (1979) 625–38.

Hay, D. M.: *Glory at the Right Hand. Psalm 110 in Early Christianity*, SBL.MS 18 (Nashville/New York: Abingdon, 1973).

Heitmüller, W.: "*Im Namen Jesu.* Eine sprach- und religionsgeschichtliche Untersuchung zum Neuen Testament, speziell zur altchristlichen Taufe (Göttingen: Vandenhoeck & Ruprecht, 1903).

Hengel, M.: "Hymnus und Christologie," in: *FS für K. H. Rengstorf, Wort in der Zeit*,

Neutestamentliche Studien, eds. W. Haubeck and M. Bachmann (Leiden: Brill, 1980), pp. 1–23.

———: *Der Sohn Gottes. Die Entstehung der Christologie und die jüdisch- hellenistische Religionsgeschichte* (Tübingen: Mohr, 1975).

Hill, D.: *Greek Words and Hebrew Meanings: Studies in the Semantics of Soteriological Terms*, SNTS.MS 5 (Cambridge: University Press, 1967).

Holtz, T.: "Zum Selbstverständnis des Apostels Paulus," ThLZ 91 (1966) 322–30.

Jaeger, W.: *Nemesius von Emesa* (Berlin: Weidmann, 1914).

Jensen, J.: "Does Porneia Mean Fornication? A Critique of Bruce Malina," NT 20 (1978) 161–84.

Jeremias, J.: "Abba," in: *Abba. Studien zur neutestamentlichen Theologie und Zeitgeschichte* (Göttingen: Vandenhoeck & Ruprecht, 1966), pp. 16–67.

———: *Die Abendmahlsworte Jesu*, 3d ed. (Göttingen: Vandenhoeck & Ruprecht, 1960).

———: *Die Kindertaufe in den ersten vier Jahrhunderten* (Göttingen: Vandenhoeck & Ruprecht, 1958).

———: *Neutestamentliche Theologie, Teil I, Die Verkündigung Jesu* (Gütersloh: Mohn, 1971).

Jervell, J.: *Imago Dei. Gen 1:26f im Spätjudentum, in der Gnosis und in den paulinischen Briefen*, FRLANT.NF 58 (Göttingen: Vandenhoeck & Ruprecht, 1960).

Jonas, H.: *Gnosis und spätantiker Geist*, vol. I, FRLANT 51, 3d ed. (Göttingen: Vandenhoeck & Ruprecht, 1964).

———: *The Gnostic Religion. The Message of the Alien God and the Beginning of Christianity* (Beacon Hill/Boston: Beacon Press, 1958).

Jones, A. H. M.: *The Cities of the Eastern Roman Provinces*, 2d ed. (Oxford: Clarendon, 1971).

Kähler, E.: *Die Frau in den paulinischen Briefen. Unter besonderer Berücksichtigung des Begriffes der Unterordnung*, (Zürich/Frankfurt a.M.: Gotthelf, 1960).

Käsemann, E.: "Amt und Gemeinde im Neuen Testament," EVB I, pp. 109–34.

———: "Erwägungen zum Stichwort 'Versöhnungslehre im Neuen Testament,' " in: *FS für R. Bultmann*, ed. E. Dinkler (Tübingen: Mohr, 1964), pp. 47–59.

———: "Gottesgerechtigkeit bei Paulus," EVB II, 181–93.

———: *Leib und Leib Christi. Eine Untersuchung zur paulinischen Begrifflichkeit*, BHTh 9 (Tübingen: Mohr, 1933).

———: *An die Römer*, HNT 8a (Tübingen: Mohr, 1973).

———: "Römer 13:1–7 in unserer Generation," ZThK 56 (1959) 316–76.

———: "Sätze Heiligen Rechts im Neuen Testament," EVB II, pp. 69–82.

———: *Exegetische Versuche und Besinnungen*, vols. I + II, 6th ed. (Göttingen: Vandenhoeck & Ruprecht, 1970) (cited: **EVB**).

Kamlah, E.: *Die Form der katalogischen Paränese im Neuen Testament*, WUNT 7 (Tübingen: Mohr, 1964).

———: "*hypotassesthai* in den neutestamentlichen Haustafeln," in: *FS für G. Stählin zum 70. Geburtstag*, Verborum Veritas, eds. O. Böcher und K. Haacker (Wuppertal: Brockhaus, 1970), pp. 237–43.

Karlsson, G.: "Formelhaftes in Paulusbriefen," Er 54 (1956) 138–41.

Kim, S.: *The Origin of Paul's Gospel*, WUNT 2. R. 4 (Tübingen: Mohr, 1981).

Kirk, J. A.: "Apostleship Since Rengstorf: Towards a Synthesis," NTS 21 (1975) 249–64.

Klauck, H.-J.: *Hausgemeinde und Hauskirche im frühen Christentum*, SBS 103 (Stuttgart: Katholisches Bibelwerk, 1981).

Krämer, H.: "Die Isisformel des Apuleius (Met. XI 23,7)—eine Anmerkung zur Methode der Mysterienforschung," WuD 12 (1973) 91–104.

————: "Zur Wortbedeutung 'Mysteria,' " WuD.NF 6 (1959) 121–25.

Kramer, W.: *Christos, Kyrios, Gottessohn. Untersuchungen zu Gebrauch und Bedeutung der christologischen Bezeichnungen bei Paulus und in den vorpaulinischen Gemeinden*, AThANT 44 (Zürich-Stuttgart: Zwingli Verlag, 1963).

Kümmel, W. G.: *Das Bild des Menschen im Neuen Testament*, AThANT 13 (Zürich: Zwingli Verlag, 1948).

————: *Einleitung in das Neue Testament*, 18th ed. (Heidelberg Quelle und Meyer, 1973).

Kuhn, H.-W.: *Enderwartung und gegenwärtiges Heil. Untersuchungen zu den Gemeindeliedern von Qumran*, StUNT 4 (Göttingen: Vandenhoeck & Reprecht, 1966).

Kuhn, K. G.: "Der Epheserbrief im Lichte der Qumrantexte," NTS 7 (1960/61) 334–46.

————: "*Peirasmos—harmatia—sarx* im Neuen Testament und die damit zusammenhängenden Vorstellungen," ZThK 49 (1952) 200–22 [= in: K. Stendahl (ed.): *The Scrolls and the New Testament* (New York: Harper, 1957), pp. 94–113, with some revisions].

Lampe, P.: "Kleine 'Sklavenflucht' des Onesimus," ZNW 76 (1985) 135–37.

Leivestad, R.: *Christ the Conqueror* (London: SPCK, 1954).

Lidzbarski, M.: *Ginzà. Der Schatz oder das große Buch der Mandäer* (Göttingen/Leipzig: Vandenhoeck & Ruprecht/Hinrichs, 1925).

Lietzmann, H.: *Der Brief des Apostels Paulus an die Römer*, 3d ed., HNT 8 (Tübingen: Mohr, 1928).

Lillie, W.: "The Pauline House-tables," ET 86 (1974/75) 179–83.

Lindemann, A.: *Die Aufhebung der Zeit. Geschichtsverständnis und Eschatologie im Epheserbrief*, StNT 12 (Gütersloh: Mohn, 1975).

Loader, W. R. G.: "Christ at the Right Hand—Ps CX.1 in the New Testament," NTS 24 (1977/78) 199–217.

Lohfink, G.: "Gab es im Gottesdienst der neutestamentlichen Gemeinde eine Anbetung Christi," BZ.NF 18 (1974) 161–79.

Lohmeyer, E.: "Der Begriff der Erlösung im Urchristentum," in: *Deutsche Theologie II. Bericht über den 2. deutschen Theologentag in Frankfurt a.M. (1928)*, ed. E. Pfennigsdorf (Göttingen: Vandenhoeck & Ruprecht, 1929), pp. 22–45.

————: *Der Brief an die Philipper*, KEK 9, 11th ed., 1956.

————: "*Syn Christo*," in: *FS für A. Deissmann zum 60. Geburtstag* (Tübingen: Mohr, 1927), pp. 218–57.

————: "Probleme paulinischer Theologie. I. Briefliche Grußüberschriften," ZNW 26 (1927) 158–73.

————: *Das Vater-unser*, 2d ed. (Göttingen: Vandenhoeck & Ruprecht, 1947).

Lohse, E.: *Die Einheit des Neuen Testaments. Exegetische Studien zur Theologie des Neuen Testaments* (Göttingen: Vandenhoeck & Ruprecht, 1973).

————: *Märtyrer und Gottesknecht. Untersuchungen zur urchristlichen Verkündigung vom Sühnetod Christi* (Göttingen: Vandenhoeck & Ruprecht, 1955).

Lührmann, D.: "Neutestamentliche Haustafeln und antike Ökonomie," NTS 27 (1981) 83–97.

———: *Das Offenbarungsverständnis bei Paulus und in paulinischen Gemeinden*, WMANT 16 (Neukirchen-Vluyn: Neukirchener Verlag, 1965).

———: "Wo man nicht mehr Sklave oder Freier ist. Überlegungen zur Struktur frühchristlicher Gemeinden," WuD.NF 13 (1975) 53–83.

Lumpe, A.: "Artikel 'Elementum,' " RAC I, 1073–1100.

Lyall, F.: "Roman Law in the Writings of Paul—The Slave and the Freedman," NTS 17 (1970/71) 73–79.

Macgregor, G. H. C.: "The Concept of the Wrath of God in the New Testament," NTS 7 (1960/61) 101–9.

———: "Principalities and Powers: The Cosmic Background of Paul's Thoughts," NTS 1 (1954/55) 17–28.

Malina, B.: "Does Porneia Mean Fornication?," NTS 14 (1972) 10–17.

Marshall, H.: "Palestinian and Hellenistic Christianity: Some Critical Comments," NTS 19 (1972/73) 271–87.

Marxsen, W.: *Einleitung in das Neue Testament. Eine Einführung in ihre Probleme* (Gütersloh: Mohn, 1963).

Meecham, H. G.: "The Use of the Participle for the Imperative in the New Testament," ET 58 (1946/47) 207–8.

Meeks, W. A.: *The First Urban Christians. The Social World of the Apostle Paul* (New Haven and London: Yale Univ. Press, 1983).

Merk, O.: *Handeln aus Glauben. Die Motivierungen der paulinischen Ethik*, MThSt 5 (Marburg: Elwert, 1968).

Merklein, H.: *Das kirchliche Amt nach dem Epheserbrief*, StANT 33 (München: Kösel, 1973).

Metzger, B. M.: *The Text of the New Testament. Its Transmission, Corruption, and Restoration* (Oxford: Clarendon, 1964).

Michaelis, W.: *Einleitung in das Neue Testament. Die Entstehung, Sammlung und Überlieferung der Schriften des Neuen Testaments*, 2d ed. (Bern: BEG, 1954).

———: *Versöhnung des Alls. Die frohe Botschaft von der Gnade Gottes* (Grümligen: Siloah, 1950).

Mullins, T. Y.: "Disclosure. A Literary Form in the New Testament," NT 7 (1964/65) 44–50.

Munck, J.: "Die judaistischen Heidenchristen. Studien über den Galaterbrief," in: *Paulus und die Heilsgeschichte*, Acta Jutlandica, Aarsskrift for Aarhus Universitet XXVI,1, Theolisk Serie 6, Aarhus: Universitetsforlaget, Kopenhagen: Munksgaard 1954, 79–126.

Munro, W.: *Authority in Paul and Peter. The Identification of a Pastoral Stratum in the Pauline Corpus and 1 Peter*, SNTS.MS (Cambridge: University Press, 1983).

Mussner, F.: *Christus, das All und die Kirche*, TThSt 5, 2d ed. (Trier: Paulinus, 1968).

———: *Der Galaterbrief*, HThK IX (Freiburg i.B.: Herder, 1974).

Nauck, W.: "Das oun- paräneticum," ZNW 49 (1958) 134–35.

———: "Salt as Metaphor in Instructions for Discipleship," StTh 6 (1952) 165–78.

Neugebauer, F.: *In Christus. EN CHRISTŌ. Eine Untersuchung zum Paulinischen Glaubensverständnis* (Göttingen: Vandenhoeck & Ruprecht, 1961).

Nieder, L.: *Die Motive der religiös- sittlichen Paränese in den paulinischen Gemeinde-briefen. Ein Beitrag zur paulinischen Ethik*, MThS.H 12 (München: Zink, 1956).

Nilsson, M. P.: *Geschichte der griechischen Religion*, II, 3d ed. (München: Beck, 1974).

Norden, E.: *Agnostos Theos. Untersuchungen zur Formengeschichte religiöser Rede* (Leipzig: Teubner, 1913).

Noth, M.: "Die Gesetze im Pentateuch. (Ihre Voraussetzungen und ihr Sinn)," in: *Gesammelte Aufsätze zum AT*, ThB 6 (München: Kaiser, 1957), pp. 9–141.

O'Brien, P. T.: "Thanksgiving and the Gospel in Paul," NTS 21 (1974/75) 144–55.

Ollrog, W. H.: *Paulus und seine Mitarbeiter. Untersuchungen zur Theorie und Praxis der paulinischen Mission*, WMANT 50 (Neukirchen-Vluyn: Neukirchener Verlag, 1979).

Overfield, P. D.: "Pleroma: A Study in Content and Context," NTS 25 (1979) 384–96.

Pardee, D.: "An Overview of Ancient Hebrew Epistolography," JBL 97 (1978) 321–46.

Peterson, E.: "Zur Bedeutungsgeschichte von *Parrēsia*," in: *FS für R. Seeberg 1929*, vol. I (Leipzig: Deichert, 1929), pp. 283–97.

Pfitzner, V. C.: "Paul and the Agon Motif. Traditional Athletic Imagery in the Pauline Literature," NT.S 16, 109–29.

Rad, G. von: "Das theologische Problem des alttestamentlichen Schöpfungsglaubens," BZAW 66, 138–47.

——: *Theologie des Alten Testaments*, vols. I + II (München: Kaiser, 1958 and 1960).

Rader, R.: "Recovering Women's History: Early Christianity," Horizons 11 (1984) 113–24.

Rahner, K.: "Ertraget einander und vergebet einander!," GuL 38 (1965) 310–12.

Reicke, Bo: "The Law and This World According to Paul. Some Thoughts Concerning Gal 4:1–11," JBL 70 (1951) 259–76.

——: *The Disobedient Spirits and Christian Baptism. A Study of 1. Pet. III. 19 and Its Context*, ASNU 13 (Kopenhagen: Munksgaard, 1946).

Reitzenstein, R.: *Das iranische Erlösungsmysterium* (Bonn: Marcus, 1921).

——: "Nachrichten von der Gesellschaft der Wissenschaften zu Göttingen," 1916, pp. 367–411 (Sek.).

——: *Die hellenistischen Mysterienreligionen*, reprogr. reprint of the 3d ed. of 1927 (Darmstadt: Wiss. Buchgesellschaft, 1980).

Rengstorf, K. H.: "Die neutestamentlichen Mahnungen an die Frau, sich dem Manne unterzuordnen," in: *FS für O. Schmitz, Verbum dei manet in aeternum*, ed. W. Foerster (Witten: Luther, 1953), pp. 131–45.

Ritschl, A.: *Die christliche Lehre von der Rechtfertigung und Versöhnung*, vol. II, 4th ed. (Bonn: Marcus & Weber, 1900).

Robinson, H. W.: "The Hebrew Conception of Corporate Personality," BZAW 66, 49–62.

Robinson, J. A. T.: "The One Baptism," in: *Twelve New Testament Studies*, SBT 34 (London: SCM, 1962), pp. 158–75.

——: *The Body. A Study in Pauline Theology*, SBT 5 [London: SCM 1952 (repr. 1957)].

Robinson, J. M.: "Die Hodajot-Formel in Gebet und Hymnus des Frühchristentums," in: *FS für E. Haenchen, Apophoreta*, BZNW 30 (1964) 194–235.

Rogerson, J. W.: "The Hebrew Conception of Corporate Personality: A Re-Examination," JThS 21 (1970) 1–16.

Rudberg, G.: "Parallela," CNT 3 (1938) 17–21.

Rudolph, K.: " 'Gnosis' and 'Gnosticism'—the Problems of Their Definition and Their Relation to the Writings of the New Testament," in: *FS für R. McL. Wilson, The New Testament and Gnosis*, eds. A. H. B. Logan and A. J. M. Wedderburn (Edinburgh: Clark, 1983), pp. 21–32.

Sanders, J. T.: "The Transition from Opening Epistolary Thanksgiving to Body in the Letters of Pauline Corpus," JBL 81 (1962) 348–62.

Satake, A.: "Apostolat und Gnade bei Paulus," NTS 15 (1968/69) 96–107.

Schenke, H.-M.: "Die neutestamentliche Christologie und der gnostische Erlöser," in: K.-W. Tröger (ed.): *Gnosis und Neues Testament* (Berlin: Evang. Verlagsanstalt; Gütersloh: Mohn, 1973), pp. 205–29.

———: *Der Gott "Mensch" in der Gnosis* (Göttingen: Vandenhoeck & Ruprecht, 1962).

———: " 'Denn wie das Weib aus dem Mann ist, so auch der Mann aus dem Weib' (1 Kor 11,12). Zur Gleichberechtigung der Frau im Neuen Testament," Diakonia 15 (1984) 85–90.

Schlier, H.: *Der Brief an die Epheser. Ein Kommentar* (Düsseldorf: Patmos, 1957).

———: "Vom Wesen der apostolischen Ermahnung," in: *Die Zeit der Kirche. Exegetische Aufsätze und Vorträge* (Freiburg: Herder, 1956), pp. 74–89.

———: *Der Brief an die Galater*, 5th ed., KEK 7, 14th ed. (Göttingen: Vandenhoeck & Ruprecht, 1971).

———: "Mächte und Gewalten nach dem Neuen Testament," in: *Besinnung auf das Neue Testament, Exegetische Aufsätze und Vorträge II* (Freiburg: Herder, 1964), pp. 146–59.

Schmidt, K. L.: "Eschatologie und Mystik im Urchristentum," ZNW 21 (1922) 277–91.

Schmithals, W.: *Die Gnosis in Korinth. Eine Untersuchung zu den Korintherbriefen*, 3d ed., FRLANT.NF 48 (Göttingen: Vandenhoeck & Ruprecht, 1969).

———: "Die Häretiker in Galatien," ZNW 47 (1956) 25–67.

Schmitz, O.: "Der Begriff DYNAMIS bei Paulus. Ein Beitrag zum Wesen urchristlicher Begriffsbildung," in: *FS für A. Deissmann zum 60. Geburtstag*, Tübingen: Mohr, 1927), pp. 139–67.

———: *Die Christus-Gemeinschaft des Paulus im Lichte seines Genitivgebrauchs*, NTF I/2 (Gütersloh: Bertelsmann, 1924).

Schnackenburg, R.: *Das Heilsgeschehen bei der Taufe nach dem Apostel Paulus. Eine Studie zur paulinischen Theologie*, MThS.H 1 (München: Zink, 1950) [Engl.: *Baptism in the Thought of St. Paul*. Trans. by G. R. Beasley-Murray (Oxford: Basil Blackwell, 1964)].

Scholem, G. G.: *Jewish Gnosticism, Merkabah Mysticism and Talmudic Tradition* (New York: The Jewish Theological Seminary of America, 1965).

Schrage, W.: *Die konkreten Einzelgebote in der paulinischen Paränese. Ein Beitrag zur neutestamentlichen Ethik* (Gütersloh: Mohn, 1961).

———: "Die Ethik der neutestamentlichen Haustafeln," NTS 21 (1975) 1–22.

Schrenk, W.: "Die Gerechtigkeit Gottes und der Glaube Christi. Versuch einer Verhältnisbestimmung paulinischer Strukturen," ThLZ 97 (1972) 161–74.

Schroeder, D.: *Die Haustafeln des Neuen Testaments*, Diss. Hamburg, 1959 (Sek.).

Schubert, P.: *Form and Function of the Pauline Thanksgivings*, BZNW 20, 1939.

Bibliography

Schürer, E.: *Geschichte des jüdischen Volkes im Zeitalter Jesu Christi*, vol. III (Leipzig: Hinrichs, 1902).

Schütz, J. H.: *Paul and the Anatomy of Apostolic Authority*, SNTS.MS 26, 1957.

Schweizer, E.: "Aufnahme und Korrektur jüdischer Sophiatheologie im Neuen Testament," in: *FS für E. Wolf, Hören und Handeln*, eds. H. Gollwitzer und E. Traub (München: Kaiser, 1962), pp. 330–40 (repr. in: *Neotestamentica*, op. cit., pp. 110ff.).

————: *Beiträge zur Theologie des Neuen Testaments. Neutestamentliche Aufsätze (1955–1970)* (Zürich: Zwingli Verlag, 1970).

————: *Erniedrigung und Erhöhung bei Jesus und seinen Nachfolgern*, AThANT 28 (Zürich: Zwingli Verlag, 1962).

————: *Gemeinde und Gemeindeordnung im Neuen Testament*, AThANT 35 (Zürich: Zwingli Verlag, 1959).

————: "Gottesgerechtigkeit und Lasterkataloge bei Paulus (inkl. Kol und Eph)," in: *FS für E. Käsemann, Rechtfertigung*, eds. J. Friedrich, W. Pöhlmann, P. Stuhlmacher (Tübingen: Mohr/Göttingen: Vandenhoeck & Ruprecht, 1976), pp. 461–77.

————: *Matthäus und seine Gemeinde*, SBS 71 (Stuttgart: Kath. Bibelwerk, 1974).

————: "Die 'Mystik' des Sterbens und Auferstehens mit Christus bei Paulus," in: *Beiträge*, op. cit., pp. 183–203 [Engl. in: NTS 14 (1967/68) 1–14].

————: *Neotestamentica. Deutsche und englische Aufsätze 1951–1963* (Zürich/Stuttgart: Zwingli Verlag, 1963).

————: *Neues Testament und Christologie im Werden. Aufsätze* (Göttingen: Vandenhoeck & Ruprecht, 1982).

————: "Die Sünde in den Gliedern," in: *Abraham unser Vater. Juden und Christen im Gespräch über die Bibel, FS für O. Michel zum 60. Geburtstag*, eds. O. Betz, M. Hengel, P. Schmidt, AGSU 5 (Leiden: Brill, 1963), pp. 437–39.

————: "Traditional Ethical Patterns in the Pauline and Post-Pauline Letters and Their Development (Lists of Vices and Housetables)," in: *FS für M. Black, Text and Interpretation*, eds. E. Best and R. McL. Wilson (Cambridge: University Press, 1979), pp. 195–209.

————: "Das hellenistische Weltbild als Produkt der Weltangst," in: *Neotestamentica*, op. cit., pp. 15–27.

————: "Die Weltlichkeit des Neuen Testamentes: Die Haustafeln," in: *Neues Testament*, op. cit., pp. 194–210.

Scott, R. B. Y.: "Wisdom in Creation: The ʿĀmôn of Proverbs VIII.30," VT 10 (1960) 213–23.

Seeberg, E.: *Der Katechismus der Urchristenheit*, ThB 26 (München: Kaiser, 1966) (reprint: Leipzig: Deichert, 1903).

Sellin, G.: "Lukas als Gleichniserzähler: Die Erzählung vom barmherzigen Samariter (Luk 10:25–37)," ZNW 66 (1975) 19–60.

Siber, P.: *Mit Christus leben. Eine Studie zur paulinischen Auferstehungshoffnung*, AThANT 61 (Zürich: Theologischer Verlag, 1971).

Sölle, D.: "Gottes Selbstentäußerung. Eine Meditation zu Philipper 2:5–11," in: *Atheistisch an Gott glauben. Beiträge zur Theologie* (Olten and Marburg i.B.: Walter, 1968), pp. 9–25.

Speyer, W.: "Religiöse Pseudepigraphie und literarische Fälschung im Altertum," in: N. Brox (ed.), *Pseudepigraphie*, op. cit., pp. 195–263.

Spicq, C.: *Théologie Morale du Nouveau Testament*, vol. I (Paris: Gabalda, 1965).

Spitta, F.: *Der zweite Brief des Petrus und der Brief des Judas. Eine geschichtliche Untersuchung* (Halle a.S.: Verlag der Buchhandlung des Waisenhauses, 1885).

Stachowiak, L. R.: "Chrestotes. Ihre biblisch-theologische Entwicklung und Eigenart," SF.NF 17 (1957) 98–102.

Stamm, J. J.: *Der Dekalog im Lichte der neueren Forschung*, 2d ed. (Bern and Stuttgart: Haupt, 1962).

———: *Erlösen und Vergeben im Alten Testament. Eine begriffsgeschichtliche Untersuchung*, (Bern: Francke, 1940).

Stendahl, K.: *Der Jude Paulus und wir Heiden. Anfragen an das abendländische Christentum* (München: Kaiser, 1978).

Strugnell, J.: "The Angelic Liturgy at Qumran—4Q Serek Širot ʿolat haššabbat, Congress Volume Oxford," VT.S 7 (1960) 318–45.

Stuhlmacher, P.: *Gerechtigkeit Gottes bei Paulus*, FRLANT 87 (Göttingen: Vandenhoeck & Ruprecht, 1965).

———: *Der Brief an Philemon*, EKK 18, 1975 (2d ed., 1981).

———: Rez.: Bartchy, S. S.: "MALLON XPHΣAI," op. cit., ThLZ 101 (1976) 837–39.

Suhl, A.: "Der Davidssohn im Matthäus-Evangelium," ZNW 59 (1968) 57–81.

Tachau, P.: *"Einst" und "Jetzt" im Neuen Testament. Beobachtungen zu einem urchristlichen Predigtschema in der neutestamentlichen Briefliteratur und zu seiner Vorgeschichte*, FRLANT 105 (Göttingen: Vandenhoeck & Ruprecht, 1972).

Tannehill, R. C.: *Dying and Rising with Christ. A Study in Pauline Theology*, BZNW 32, 1967.

Thraede, K.: "Ärger mit der Freiheit. Die Bedeutung von Frauen in Theorie und Praxis der alten Kirche," in: G. Scharffenroth (ed.): *"Freunde in Christus werden . . ." Die Beziehung von Mann und Frau als Frage an Theologie und Kirche* (Berlin: Burckhardthaus, 1977), pp. 31–181 (Sek.).

———: "Zum historischen Hintergrund der 'Haustafeln' des NT," in: *FS für B. Kötting, Pietas*, eds. E. Dassmann and K. Suso Frank, JAC, Erg. vol. 8 (Münster: Aschendorff, 1980, pp. 359–68).

Thüsing, W.: *Per Christum in Deum. Studien zum Verhältnis von Christozentrik und Theozentrik in den paulinischen Hauptbriefen*, NTA.NF 1 (Münster: Aschendorff, 1965).

———: *Erhöhungsvorstellung und Parusieerwartung in der ältesten nachösterlichen Christologie*, SBS 42 (Stuttgart: Kath. Bibelwerk, 1969).

Unnik, W. C. van: "Die Rücksicht auf die Reaktion der Nicht-Christen als Motiv in der altchristlichen Paränese," in: *FS für J. Jeremias, Judentum, Urchristentum, Kirche*, ed. W. Eltester, BZNW 26 (Berlin: Töpelmann, 1960), pp. 221–34.

Vermes, G.: "Baptism and Jewish Exegesis: New Light from Ancient Sources," NTS 4 (1958) 309–19.

Vielhauer, P.: *Oikodome. Das Bild vom Bau in der christlichen Literatur vom Neuen Testament bis Clemens Alexandrinus*, Diss., (Karlsruhe, 1940).

Vögtle, A.: *Das Neue Testament und die Zukunft des Kosmos* (Düsseldorf: Patmos, 1970).

Weidinger, K.: *Die Haustafeln. Ein Stück urchristlicher Paränese*, UNT 14 (Leipzig: Hinrichs, 1928).

Wendland, H.-D.: "Zur sozialethischen Bedeutung der neutestamentlichen Haustafeln," in: *Botschaft an die soziale Welt, Studien zur Evang. Sozialtheologie und Sozialethik,* vol. V (Hamburg: Furche, 1959), pp. 104–14.

White, J. L.: "Introductory Formulae in the Body of the Pauline Letter," JBL 90 (1971) 91–97.

Wibbing, S.: *Die Tugend- und Lasterkataloge im Neuen Testament und ihre Traditionsgeschichte unter besonderer Berücksichtigung der Qumran-Texte,* BZNW 25 (Berlin: Töpelmann, 1959).

Wilckens, U.: *Der Brief an die Römer,* EKK VI/1 (Zürich, Einsiedeln, Köln: Benziger; Neukirchen: Neukirchener Verlag, 1978).

————: *Weisheit und Torheit. Eine exegetisch-religionsgeschichtliche Untersuchung zu 1. Kor 1 und 2,* BHTh 26 (Tübingen: Mohr, 1959).

Wildberger, H.: "Das Abbild Gottes," ThZ 21 (1965) 245–59; 481–501.

Wilson, R. McL.: *Gnosis und Neues Testament,* transl. from Engl. by L. Kaufmann (Stuttgart: Kohlhammer, 1971).

Wink, W.: *Naming the Powers: The Language of Power in the New Testament* (Philadelphia: Fortress, 1984).

————: *Unmasking the Powers. The Invisible Forces That Determine Human Existence,* vol. II (Philadelphia: Fortress, 1986).

Wisse, F.: "Prolegomena to the Study of the New Testament and Gnosis," in: *FS for L. McL. Wilson, The New Testament and Gnosis,* eds. A. H. B. Logan and A. J. M. Wedderburn (Edinburgh: Clark, 1983), pp. 138–45.

Zahn, T.: *Einleitung in das Neue Testament.* 2d ed., vols. I + II (Leipzig: Deichert, 1900).

INDEX OF SCRIPTURAL REFERENCES

♦

515

519

Acts 3:20–21 106n
Acts 3:21 360n
Acts 4:6 273n
Acts 4:10 129
Acts 4:14 350n
Acts 4:16 478n
Acts 5:2 359
Acts 5:3 359
Acts 5:15 339n
Acts 5:17 21n
Acts 5:41 183n
Acts 5:42 486n
Acts 6:1 481
Acts 6:4 452
Acts 6:7 156n
Acts 6:9 209
Acts 6:11 489
Acts 6:14 214n
Acts 7:48 317n
Acts 7:49 200
Acts 8:13 452
Acts 8:21 187n
Acts 8:25 426n
Acts 9:15 170n
Acts 9:22 181n, 277
Acts 10:3 349n
Acts 10:4 394n
Acts 10:10–16 349n
Acts 10:17 452
Acts 10:30 200n
Acts 10:34 449
Acts 10:38 93n
Acts 10:45 481n
Acts 11:2 481n
Acts 11:23 286n
Acts 12:7 200n
Acts 12:9 432n
Acts 12:12 479, 486n
Acts 12:25 479, 489
Acts 13:2 17
Acts 13:22 188n
Acts 13:35–14:19 18
Acts 13:43 18
Acts 13:44 426n
Acts 13:48 426n
Acts 13:49 17, 426n
Acts 14:1 416n
Acts 14:13 204
Acts 14:15–17 65
Acts 14:22 291n
Acts 14:27 452
Acts 15:5 21n
Acts 15:12 170n
Acts 15:20 402
Acts 15:23 135
Acts 15:23–29 142
Acts 15:29 402

Acts 15:35 426n
Acts 15:36 426n
Acts 15:37 479
Acts 15:39 479
Acts 16:1–3 369
Acts 16:5 289n
Acts 16:6 19n
Acts 16:9 349n
Acts 16:10 277
Acts 16:32 426n
Acts 17:3 208n
Acts 17:4 143n
Acts 17:14 142
Acts 17:22–31 48n, 65
Acts 17:23 195
Acts 17:24 317n
Acts 17:31 106n
Acts 17:32 208n
Acts 17:33 331n
Acts 18:2 485
Acts 18:4 416n
Acts 18:5 143
Acts 18:7 480n, 486n
Acts 18:9 349n
Acts 18:17 138n
Acts 18:18 485
Acts 18:23 19n
Acts 18:24–28 480
Acts 18:26 485
Acts 19:1 19n
Acts 19:1–20:1 127
Acts 19:8–10 18
Acts 19:10 416n, 426n
Acts 19:17 416n
Acts 19:19 359
Acts 19:22 142
Acts 19:26 18, 188n
Acts 19:29 129, 478
Acts 19:33 277
Acts 20:4 129, 142, 476, 478, 481
Acts 20:8 486n
Acts 20:19 343
Acts 20:20 486n
Acts 20:21 416n
Acts 20:28 52n
Acts 20:31 18, 127, 266, 267, 452
Acts 20:35 269n, 426n
Acts 20:38 275
Acts 21:8 478n
Acts 21:25 402
Acts 21:27–30 16
Acts 23:6 208n
Acts 23:10 331n
Acts 23:23–26 127
Acts 23:23–26:32 133

Acts 24:2 432n
Acts 24:5 21n
Acts 24:23 133
Acts 25:11 133n
Acts 26:5 21n, 344
Acts 26:18 186, 225
Acts 26:23 208
Acts 27:2 129, 142, 478
Acts 27:4 330n
Acts 27:23 200n
Acts 27:24 222
Acts 28:14–31 127
Acts 28:16 145n
Acts 28:16–31 133
Acts 28:17–24 133
Acts 28:22 395n
Acts 28:28–31 133
Acts 28:30 145n
Acts 28:31 133, 134, 158

Rom 1:1 164, 196n
Rom 1:1–7 232
Rom 1:3 189n, 208n
Rom 1:3–4 70n, 125n
Rom 1:5 158n, 167, 259
Rom 1:7 139n, 301n
Rom 1:8 152, 152n, 155, 158n, 431
Rom 1:9+10 152n
Rom 1:10 172, 173n
Rom 1:10–13 130n
Rom 1:11 275n, 276n
Rom 1:11+12 151n
Rom 1:13 59n, 157, 270
Rom 1:14 416n
Rom 1:16 155n, 161, 186n, 416n
Rom 1:17 153
Rom 1:18 404n, 405, 407n
Rom 1:18–32 24, 48n
Rom 1:20 155, 196n, 312n, 362, 363
Rom 1:21 378, 418n, 431
Rom 1:23 214n, 403, 404n
Rom 1:24 402
Rom 1:24+26 405
Rom 1:25 155, 196, 413n
Rom 1:29 219
Rom 1:29–31 400n
Rom 2:4 182n, 363n, 421, 422
Rom 2:5 404, 407n
Rom 2:5–11 99n
Rom 2:7 180n
Rom 2:8 155, 407n

529

INDEX OF PREMODERN SOURCES

◆

INDEX OF MODERN AUTHORS

INDEX OF FOREIGN WORDS

◆

Unless noted all citations are to Greek

544

INDEX OF SUBJECTS

◆

mysticism 37
other heresies as sources 26–27
pagan elements 32–33
pejorative sense of word 21–23
philosophical systems' influence 35–36
post-biblical sources 27–28
practical wisdom 24
religion vs. philosophy 23
sectarian Judaism 30–31
sources generally 23–28
syncretism 38–39
theology, soteriology, liturgics, ethics
    combined 25
Comfort 275–276, 482
Compassion 418–420
Conclusion (4:7–18)
  Archippus's ministry 489
  Aristarchus as fellow prisoner 478–479
  blessing 490
  comfort 482
  coworkers of circumcision 480–482
  Epaphras's hardships 484–485
  Epaphras who fights with
    prayer 482–483
  Jesus Justus 480
  Laodicea 486–488
  Laodicea's and Hierapolis's
    communities 484–485
  Luke 485
  Marcus 479–480
  Nympha 485–486
  Onesimus 478
  Paul sending report 477–478
  Paul's captivity 490
  Paul's signature 489
  Tychicus as brother 476–477
Condemnation 342
Conduct of congregation 20–21
Conflation, Eph and Col 74, 83–85
Corruption 356–357
Cosmic Christology 45
Coworkers of circumcision 480–482
Created matter as evil 25, 36, 45–46

Date and place of composition 126–135
Deceitful religion (2:6–15)
  baptism 363–365, 368–369
  baptism, buried in 319–320
  betrayal of people 311
  beware of deception 310
  bill of indictment 327–330, 369–372
  circumcision not done by human
    hands 317, 366–368
  dead in sin 324–325
  disarming powers 332–334
  elements of the world 373–378
  exposing forces as they are 334–336

firm in faith 305
forgiveness of sins 326–327
fulfillment in God 315–316
fullness of deity in Messiah 311–315
God's attributes 362–363
human body cast off by Messiah's
    circumcision 318–319
made alive with him 325–326
nailing to cross 330–332
obedience to the Messiah 302–303
philosophy 306–310
receiving the Messiah 299–302
resurrection 320–322, 367–368
rooted and built up in Messiah 303–305
taught faith 305
thanksgiving 306–307
working of faith in God 322–324
Deception 285
Deference 358–362
Demas 129, 130, 131
Dialogue, Colossians as 42–44
Disarming powers 332–334
Doctrinal text 76–79
Doctrine
  date and place of composition 132–135
  Eph and Col 111–112
Dominion of world 355
Doppelgesicht 125
Doublets 108–109

Ecclesiastical elements 64–69
Elements of the world 373–380, 386, 395
Epaphras 17–19, 22, 53, 61n, 115, 129,
    482–485
Ephesians and Colossians compared
  biographical text 73–75
  Christology 87–90
  conflation 83–85
  dependence 101–111
  doctrinal text 76–79
  doctrines in common 87–101
  eschatology 96–98
  ethics 99–101
  Holy Spirit 92–93
  hymnic text 75–76
  love 90–92
  ministry 98–99
  parenetic text 76–79, 82
  power 90–92
  primacy of Colossians 112
  primacy of Ephesians 112–113
  text adapted to Ephesians' wording 55–56
  vocabulary, style, structure 80–87
  world 93–95
Epistolary address (1:1–2)
  authorship 142–144
  blessing formula 140–141